making sense of land law

WITHDRAWN

making sense of land law

APRIL STROUD

BSc (Hons) in Linguistic and International Studies, LLB (Hons)
Principal Lecturer, Southampton Solent University

Fourth edition

palgrave
macmillan

First published 2005 by Oxford University Press, Oxford, UK

This edition published 2013 by PALGRAVE MACMILLAN

Palgrave Macmillan in the UK is an imprint of Macmillan Publishers Limited, registered in England, company number 785998, of Houndmills, Basingstoke, Hampshire, RG21 6XS.

Palgrave Macmillan in the US is a division of St Martin's Press LLC, 175 Fifth Avenue, New York, NY 10010.

PALGRAVE MACMILLAN is the global academic imprint of the above companies and has companies and representatives throughout the world.

Palgrave® and Macmillan® are registered trademarks in the United States, the United Kingdom, Europe and other countries

ISBN 978–0–230–35578–1   paperback

This book is printed on paper suitable for recycling and made from fully managed and sustained forest sources. Logging, pulping and manufacturing processes are expected to conform to the environmental regulations of the country of origin.

A catalogue record for this book is available from the British Library.

Outline contents

Contents

For Susan and Rosemary

Preface

When writing the original *Making Sense of Land Law*, I set out to explain the concepts of land law in plain, straightforward, comprehensible English using a series of boxes in the text to aid analysis and understanding. The feedback from students and academics has been very positive, so I have continued to build on this original concept. Many students have found the book's style and reader-friendly approach useful in unravelling what is often (among students at least) considered an almost impenetrable subject. Various suggestions for improvement have been made by lecturers and students and this fourth edition now includes these welcome and valuable contributions. Changes to the law since 2010 have been incorporated whilst still retaining the ease of understanding and accessibility already found in the book. The date cited in the text refers to the first law report cited in the Table of cases.

Several areas of law have been expanded to ensure that students have a complete understanding of the subject. The important developments in the law relating to constructive and resulting trusts have been discussed in detail.

As in other subject areas, not all academics or judges are agreed on the interpretation of various points of law. There are 'discussion' sections at the ends of several chapters which look at these differing viewpoints. I have done this so that students can grasp the various arguments put forward, easily allowing them to form their own conclusions, and to highlight the areas that are the focal points of much academic research. Such sections include the non-proprietary lease, the interrelationship between constructive trusts, proprietary estoppel and section 2 of the Law of Property (Miscellaneous Provisions) Act 1989, sections 78 and 62 of the Law of Property Act 1925 and a new section looking at the meaning of actual occupation under the Land Registration Act 2002. Each discussion section continues to stand on its own so that it can be read if and when the student wishes.

The book is accompanied by a website at www.palgrave.com/law/Stroud4e. This is used to inform students' understanding of the latest developments in the law. Finally, but most importantly, the book continues to offer the box structure and conversational style of learning, attributes that have been the source of praise from students.

My thanks go to the longsuffering efforts of Tony and Nick Curwen for their unfailing endeavours to improve the understanding of land law by ensuring that what is written is comprehensible, accessible and, most of all, enjoyable. The word 'enjoyable' has been used frequently both by students and academics alike to describe this book, and if I have succeeded in making land law enjoyable then that is some achievement.

AS
April 2013

Although land law is often perceived as being complex, it is actually a very structured subject. This means that it is possible to put the essential rules and conditions for each particular topic into boxes that you can tick. This will enable you to see how the rules apply to a particular situation. By following such a process within each chapter, you can work through problem scenarios systematically and effectively. An example of a problem question and answer showing you how to use the boxes is included at the ends of the majority of the chapters.

If you have any comments about this book or suggestions, please e-mail them to feedback@palgrave.com. Your views and thoughts will be appreciated.

Table of cases

Table of legislation

Chapter 1

The essence of land law

www.palgrave.com/law/Stroud4e

Introduction

This chapter looks at what is meant by the ownership of land, the difference between law and equity, and the nature of legal and equitable rights. The chart on page 2 shows the way the chapter is structured, and will introduce the way boxes are used in the text throughout this book. In later chapters we will use this box structure to understand the nature of land law and the different interests in land.

Let's examine each box in the chart on page 2 in turn.

The ownership of land

> **Box A**
>
> THE OWNERSHIP OF LAND
>
> **1.** Title to land
>
> **2.** Interests in and over land

The first part of this section gives you a very brief history of the ownership of land. While it may be the part of a book you might initially miss out, may I suggest that you don't do so here? The history explains how people own land and gives you an insight into some of the rather archaic but important terms that are still used today.

From the early Middle Ages all land was owned by the Crown. However, the King used to give out parcels of land to his lords in return for services to the Crown. Of course, in those far-off days, owning land did not just mean enjoying lots of space. The landowner would also own the crops, woodland, fish and wildlife, all of which could be exploited for his benefit. Land meant wealth. The King would give Lord Toff a parcel of 1,500 acres of land in Derbyshire, for example, and in return Lord Toff would supply the King with 30 fully equipped mounted soldiers when necessary. The name of the interest the King gave to Lord Toff was 'estate'. Lord Toff held an estate in land. The conditions on which Lord Toff held the land were known as tenure, a word which comes from Latin, meaning 'to hold'. Lord Toff would then give his servant, Joleyn, the use of 250 acres of the land in return for Joleyn working on the land for him and also for saying prayers at least three times a week to absolve Lord Toff of his sins. Joleyn would also hold an estate in the land

THE ESSENCE OF LAND LAW

Box A

THE OWNERSHIP OF LAND

1. Title to land

2. Interests in and over land

Box B

LAW AND EQUITY

1. Legal and equitable estates and interests

2. The creation of legal and equitable estates and interests

Box C

THE PROCESS OF BUYING AND SELLING LAND

Box D

PERSONAL AND PROPRIETARY RIGHTS IN LAND

Box E

THE WHOLE PICTURE

granted to him, again subject to the conditions of tenure that were determined by Lord Toff.

Q: *When did these feudal services end?*

A: Over the years many of the services performed for the Crown were replaced by monetary payments. However, the whole system started to become extremely unwieldy, a situation compounded by social change following the English Civil War. The monetary payments ceased to become worth collecting and the difficulty in obtaining remedies against people who didn't provide services, or the cash equivalent, meant that the system collapsed. One aspect remains, though. All land is still owned by the Crown. If there really is no one to inherit land when a person dies, the land will return to the Crown and be sold in the normal way on the Crown's behalf. Although you think you own the property called Yourland, it is actually still owned by the Crown, and the interest that you own in the land is still called an estate.

Q: *Were there different types of estate that the King could give you?*

A: Yes. The name of the estate you held was determined by how long you had been granted the land for. There were two main estates: the freehold estate, which can be split into three further estates, and the leasehold estate.

A freehold estate is one whose duration is unknown when it is first acquired.

Compare this to a leasehold estate. A leasehold estate is one that goes on for a period of time that is set when you acquire the estate. A more familiar way of putting this is to say that land is leased. A lease for 10 years gives you a leasehold estate for 10 years.

The freehold estate can be split into three further parts.

Look at each of these in turn. First, the *fee simple absolute in possession*.

FREEHOLD ESTATE

| Fee simple absolute in possession | Life estate | Fee tail |

Fee means an estate capable of being inherited. As long as there is someone to inherit, the estate can go on forever.

Simple means there are no restrictions on who can inherit the estate.

Absolute means there are no conditions attached to the holding of the estate. For example, if you own the fee simple in Yourland until you marry, your estate is not absolute because there is a condition attached to it.

In possession means the estate is being enjoyed at the present. The enjoyment of it is not postponed to a future date. You are in possession of this book right now. Your use of it is in the present, not postponed to sometime in the future. You must note, though, that *in possession* does not mean in occupation of the land.

Q: *So when people say that they own their houses, do they actually hold a freehold estate in fee simple absolute in possession?*

A: They hold an estate that doesn't have a predetermined ending (freehold); it is capable of being inherited (fee); it can be inherited by anyone (simple); there are

no conditions attached to the holding of the estate (absolute); and they are actually in possession of their interest in the land (in possession), so yes. This is what the lay term *ownership* means, as in 'Fred owns Greenacres'. Although it can never be absolute ownership, an estate in fee simple absolute in possession is the closest you can have to it. While we will talk about ownership in this book, you must always remember that people don't actually own land, but hold an estate in it.

Q: *Is a* **life estate** *as obvious as it sounds?*

A: Yes. Imagine you have been left Yourland in a will for you to use during your lifetime, after which Yourland is to pass to Fred. You have a life estate. It is classified in the freehold category because, at the start of your life, no one can tell how long you are going to live.

Q: *And the* **fee tail?**

A: *Fee* means it is an estate capable of being inherited. *Tail* means there are restrictions on who can inherit the estate, for example only male heirs. A fee tail falls under the freehold estate because the estate has no predetermined end.

Now look at the leasehold estate.

A leasehold estate is where you hold an estate in the land for a certain period of time. If you lease Greenacres from Fred for 10 years, you own a leasehold estate in Greenacres for 10 years, after which Greenacres returns to Fred. Fred continues to hold the freehold estate in fee simple absolute in possession of Greenacres during the lease. Technically speaking, Fred owns the *freehold reversion* of Greenacres, which comes from the fact that, after 10 years have passed, Greenacres reverts to him, as the leasehold estate has then ended.

Q: *How can Fred still own a fee simple absolute in possession when I am in possession of Greenacres under the lease?*

A: 'In possession' does not mean in occupation. It means that Fred is enjoying his interest in Greenacres at the present time and his interest is not postponed to a future date. Being *in possession* also includes receiving rents and profits. Fred will be receiving rent from you so he still has an estate in possession.

Q: *Why do I need to know about estates in land?*

A: The point is that people who think they own their houses actually own an estate in fee simple absolute in possession. People who lease property actually own a leasehold estate. Furthermore, section 1 of the Law of Property Act 1925 is a very important statutory provision in land law and it uses the terms described above.

Box A1	Title to land

Although we often talk about ownership of land, the correct way of putting it is to say that a person has title to land, for example Fred holds the title to Greenacres. Title here means a claim to ownership of an estate in land.

Q: *How do you show a claim to ownership of an estate in land?*

A: This used to be determined by possession. If you had possession of the land, you were deemed to have title to the land. This is where the phrase 'possession is nine-tenths of the law' comes from. Your possession could be defeated only by someone who could claim a better right to possession of the land. A better right meant a prior right.

Q: *So if someone could prove that he had possessed the land before you, he had a better right to it and you had to leave?*

A: Yes. This was less than helpful when it came to buying land. To remedy this situation a number of Limitation Acts were passed. The current one is the Limitation Act 1980. These Limitation Acts barred any person with prior possession from claiming the land after a certain period of time had passed. This meant that if you were in possession of the land, nobody could challenge your possession after this set period of time. However, if you yourself stopped possessing the land and a stranger started to possess it, you would also be time-barred from reclaiming the land after the set period of time. This area of law is known as adverse possession, with the more familiar term of 'squatter's rights'.

Q: *Is possession of land still relevant today?*

A: Not nearly as much as it used to be. In the United Kingdom land is classified as unregistered land or registered land. The difference between the two is that in unregistered land title to an estate in land is proved by documentation and possession, although it is still possible to acquire land by possession alone. In registered land, a person's title to an estate in land is entered on a register and this title is guaranteed by the state. It is still possible, although difficult, to acquire registered land by possession. Where title to an estate in land is entered on a register that is guaranteed by the state, the owner will have title because of the fact of registration. In unregistered land, where there is no register, title to an estate in land must be proved by documentation, and the owner is said to have documentary title to the land. Acquiring land by possession alone gives a possessory title.

Box A2   Interests in and over land

Even though Fred may hold the estate in fee simple absolute in possession in Greenacres, other people can have lesser interests in and over Greenacres at the same time. Look at some examples of possible interests that other people could have in and over Greenacres.

Greenacres owned by Fred

Mr Black, the next-door neighbour who owns Blackacres, has a right of way over Greenacres.

Bundy's Bank has lent money to Fred using Greenacres as security for the loan.

Sophie, Fred's partner, contributed to the purchase price of Greenacres.

These are just some of the interests in and over land that are discussed in this book.

Law and equity

Box B

LAW AND EQUITY

1. Legal and equitable estates and interests

2. The creation of legal and equitable estates and interests

Throughout the whole of land law you will continually refer to law and equity, and legal and equitable rights. Strict legal rights that came from the common law were often seen as unfair. Over time, rules of equity or fairness were developed to balance the common law, giving people an equitable right as distinct from a legal right. The acquisition and administration of legal and equitable rights differ, as do the remedies, and these differences pervade much of land law. A historical perspective will explain how these jurisdictions have developed and the distinctions between them.

The Norman Kings were responsible for the development of a centralised court system. If your right was recognised at law by the common law courts, you had a legal right which was enforceable against everybody. A legal right was an important right, just as it is these days. However, actions in the common law courts were very difficult to pursue because you had to obtain a writ which matched the type of action you wanted to bring, and that cost money. If there wasn't a writ already in existence for a situation similar to your claim, you then had to persuade the Chancellor to come up with a new one, which was not an easy matter. So instead people petitioned the King for 'justice'. The King was chosen because he was the most powerful person in the kingdom. The King passed the petition to the Chancellor, who took a look and decided whether to intervene. If the Chancellor approved of your petition he would award you a right – a right recognised in the interests of justice and fairness in any given situation. The result was a system of rules and precedents that became known as equity, and the right you were awarded was known as an equitable right, rather than a legal right.

Q: *Is this where the Court of Chancery and the Chancery Division originate from?*
A: Yes. The Chancellor was so inundated with enquiries during the fourteenth and fifteenth centuries that a separate court was established. This was the Court of Chancery, in which the equitable principles and rules were administered. These principles were based on fairness and justice, and, over time, became an established set of rules. It was not until the Judicature Acts (Supreme Court of Judicature Acts of 1873 and 1875) that common law and equity were administered in the same court.

Q: *So did the Court of Chancery just say that the common law decision was wrong and then impose its own solution?*
A: The Court of Chancery didn't just dismiss the common law decision. Instead, in situations where it was unjust or unfair for one party to rely on his strict legal rights, the Court of Chancery would tell that party either to do or refrain from doing something, which would then lead to a just result. The courts administering the principles of equity imposed equitable remedies, such as specific performance

and the injunction, which are remedies directed against a particular person. Specific performance requires a party to carry out an act, for example to transfer land to someone else. An injunction requires a party to stop doing something, for example, to stop building a house. If you didn't do what the court told you to do or stop doing what you weren't supposed to do, you were in contempt of court and liable to find yourself in prison.

Q: *What happens if there is a conflict between law and equity?*

A: Equity will prevail: see section 25(11) of the Supreme Court of Judicature Act 1873, now incorporated into section 49(1) of the Supreme Court Act 1981, and *Walsh v Lonsdale* (1882). If there is a conflict between common law, equity and statute, statute will prevail over both common law and equity.

Q: *Are equitable remedies granted automatically?*

A: No. Equitable remedies are discretionary. Furthermore, given that the rules of equity are based on fairness, rather than on strict legal rights, if you want to claim an equitable remedy then you must have behaved equitably yourself. These rules of etiquette are encapsulated in a series of moral proverbs. Examples include:

> *Delay defeats equity.* If you wait too long before seeking an equitable remedy, you will not be awarded one as it will be seen to be unfair to the other party who has relied on his legal rights for a long time.
> *Equity will not assist a volunteer.* If you haven't given some form of consideration, payment or service for the act of the other party, you will not obtain an equitable remedy.
> *He who comes to equity must come with clean hands.* If you have behaved with bad faith, for example by lying or causing a nuisance to the other party, then again you will not be awarded an equitable remedy.
> *Equality is equity.* Generally, equity will divide property equally in the absence of any other evidence to the contrary.

There are many more examples but these give the general picture.

Box B1   Legal and equitable estates and interests

Before 1926, there were a large number of estates and interests in and over land that could be legal. There were problems with allowing such a large number of legal estates and interests. The problem with legal estates was as follows. When land was sold, everyone with a legal estate in the land had to sign the documents of sale, which made selling land difficult or impossible if you couldn't find them. As far as legal interests were concerned, a purchaser of land was bound by any legal interests that existed over the land, whether or not he knew about them. This meant that buying land was difficult for a purchaser, because he could never be sure who had a legal interest over the land he had purchased.

Q: *So if Lord Toff bought Greenacres centuries ago, he would have been bound by the rights of other people over the land provided that their rights were legal?*

A: Yes, and it wouldn't have mattered whether Lord Toff knew about, or could have found out about, such legal rights. Legal rights were important then, and are still so today. If you have a legal right to drive on the road, you expect to be able to exercise that right. You don't expect Mr Brown, the next-door neighbour, to tell you that you can't drive when you have a legal right to do so. The number of legal estates and interests that existed in land before 1926 made the selling of land difficult because of the number of legal owners there could be, and it made the buying of land precarious because you couldn't be totally sure who would appear to claim a legal right over the land after you'd bought it. The result was the enactment of section 1 of the Law of Property Act 1925, which reduced the number of estates and interests in land that were capable of being legal. Section 1(1) states:

> The only estates in land which are capable of subsisting or of being conveyed or created at law are –
>
> (a) An estate in fee simple absolute in possession
> (b) A term of years absolute.

Section 1(1) talks about estates. The fee simple absolute in possession is ownership as we know it today. A term of years absolute refers to the leasehold estate. Section 1(1) states that these two estates alone are capable of subsisting or of being conveyed or created at law. The section doesn't state that these estates are legal, only that they are capable of being so. Whether the estate is actually legal or not is then determined by how it has been created or transferred. The distinction here is that estates in section 1(1) can be legal, but only if they are created or transferred in an approved manner. If you create or transfer them in the wrong way, they will not be legal.

Q: *What was the effect of this section?*

A: As there were fewer legal estates in land, fewer people were required to sign if the land was sold. The situation was further improved here, because the Trustee Act 1925 also limited the number of people who could appear on the documentation to a legal estate to four.

Q: *What happened to estates that were legal before 1926 and were prevented from continuing as legal estates because they were not in section 1(1) of the Law of Property Act 1925?*

A: Section 1(3) of the Law of Property Act 1925 says that all other estates, interests and charges in or over land take effect as equitable interests. This meant that the estate was recognised in equity, but not at law.

Q: *Did this matter?*

A: A legal estate was enforceable against everyone in the world. An equitable estate was not enforceable against everyone in the world, so in this respect it did matter.

Section 1(2) of the Law of Property Act 1925 is concerned with interests in or over land. Before 1926, a large number of interests in or over land could be legal, and would therefore bind a person who bought the land they were exercised over. Section 1(2) of the Law of Property Act 1925 reduced the number of legal interests that could exist at law. The main ones that will concern you are detailed in sections 1(2)(a) and (c) of the Law of Property Act 1925. Section 1(2)(a) relates to an easement. An easement is a right over someone else's land. An example could be a right of way or a right to lay drains. Section 1(2)(c) relates to a mortgage. When Fred, for example, grants a mortgage over Greenacres to Bundy's Bank, Bundy's Bank lends a capital sum of money to Fred to be repaid with interest. Bundy's Bank will use Greenacres as security for this loan. If Fred defaults on the mortgage repayments, Bundy's Bank has the power to sell Greenacres to recoup any outstanding mortgage money. After 1925 an easement and a mortgage have been the two main interests over the land of another capable of being legal, and therefore binding a person who buys that land. Section 1(2) doesn't state that these interests are legal, only that they are capable of being so. Again, the distinction here is that these interests can be legal, but only if they are created in an approved manner. If you create them in the wrong way, they will not be legal. The exact detail of each of these clauses is discussed in Chapter 17 on easements and Chapter 18 on mortgages.

Q: *What happened to interests that were legal before 1926 and were prevented from continuing as legal interests because they were not in section 1(2) of the Law of Property Act 1925?*

A: Section 1(3) of the Law of Property Act 1925 says that all other estates, interests and charges in or over land take effect as equitable interests. This meant that the interest is recognised in equity, but not at law.

Q: *Did this matter?*

A: A legal interest was enforceable against everyone in the world. An equitable interest was not enforceable against everyone in the world, so in this respect it did matter.

Summary of section 1 of the Law of Property Act 1925
Section 1 of the Law of Property Act 1925 reduced the number of estates and interests in land that were capable of being legal. This section did not state that these estates and interests were legal, only that they were capable of being legal. The effect of this reduction in the number of legal estates and interests in land was to make the selling and buying of land easier and safer.

Box B2   The creation of legal and equitable estates and interests

Q: *If only certain estates and interests are capable of being legal, how do you know whether they are actually legal?*

A: Section 52(1) of the Law of Property Act 1925 states:

> All conveyances of land or of any interest therein are void for the purpose of conveying or creating a legal estate unless made by deed.

A conveyance is any instrument, excluding a will, that transfers property from one person to another. This section means that if you want to create or transfer a legal estate or interest in land you must use a deed.

Q: *What is a deed?*

A: A deed is a document that has legal bearing. A deed is defined in section 1 of the Law of Property (Miscellaneous Provisions) Act 1989.

A deed

▶ must make clear on the face of it that it is a deed, either by describing itself as a deed or by stating that it has been executed or signed as a deed or otherwise

and

▶ it must be signed by the person granting the interest in the deed in the presence of a witness who attests his signature

and

▶ it must be delivered as a deed.

By definition, then, a deed must be in writing. The witnessing of a deed is called attestation and the witness must sign and date the deed.

Q: *How do you make clear on the face of it that it is a deed if you don't actually use the word 'deed'?*

A: Not easily. In *HSBC Trust Company (UK) Ltd v Quinn* (2007) it was held that if the word 'deed' wasn't used, the fact that a document was a deed had to be clear from the face of the document, i.e. from the wording in the document. In the case, the parties hadn't used the word 'deed'. Although they had used formal language and formal signatures and had ensured that the signatures were witnessed, this only showed that they intended the document to be legally binding. It wasn't clear on the face of the document that it was a deed. Something showing that the parties intended it to have the extra status of a deed was needed.

Q: *How do you deliver a deed?*

A: You do not have to deliver a deed physically. It's sufficient that the person granting the interest in the deed makes it clear that he intends to be bound by the deed. This is usually inferred from the fact that he signs it.

Q: *Overall, then, are there two conditions for an estate or interest in land to be legal?*

A: Yes. The estate or interest must be capable of being legal, which means it must be mentioned in section 1(1) or (2) of the Law of Property Act 1925, and the estate or interest must have been created by means of a deed. As always, there are exceptions to every rule, and so there are exceptions to the requirement that you have to use a deed to create a legal right.

Q: *Why are there exceptions?*

A: A deed is rather bureaucratic and, by the time you've consulted a solicitor, expensive. It would be unfair to impose the requirements of a deed on some of the most common short-term transactions in land, and so exceptions are created. One example is where a flat is let out on a short-term lease. It would be impractical to expect people to use a deed every time this happens. Thus, a short-term lease can be created under section 54(2) of the Law of Property Act 1925 either orally, or else in writing which doesn't have to comply with any formality.

Q: *So how do you create an equitable interest in land?*

A: As the system of rules and precedents in equity became established, the conditions in which equitable interests were recognised also became established. Equitable interests can be created both formally and informally, and both intentionally and unintentionally.

One of the most common instances where an equitable interest arises is when there is an agreement, a contract, to create an interest in land or to sell land. Before we look at why this happens, we'll go through the requirements for the contract.

Before 1989 a contract for the creation or sale of an interest in land could be:

either

▶ in writing

or

▶ by an oral agreement if the oral agreement was evidenced in writing

or

▶ by an oral agreement where the party relying on the oral agreement had started to carry out his side of the bargain. If A promised B a right in A's land, and B acted in reliance on that promise, the courts of equity would recognise that B did have a right in A's land. It couldn't be a legal right as it hadn't been created by deed, but, in the interests of justice, equity would grant B an equitable right in A's land. This was called the equitable doctrine of part performance.

After 26 September 1989, all contracts for the creation or sale of an interest in land became governed by section 2 of the Law of Property (Miscellaneous Provisions) Act 1989. Under section 2, the contract must be:

▶ in writing

and

▶ signed by or on behalf of both parties to the contract

and

▶ it must contain all the express terms of the agreement.

Q: *What kind of transaction does section 2 apply to?*

A: It applies to a contract for the creation of a new interest in land and to a contract for the sale, transfer, lease or mortgage of other interests in land. Just about everything you are likely to come across, really.

Q: *So if Fred agrees in a contract to sell Lilac Cottage to me, does that contract have to be in writing, signed by or on behalf of me and Fred, and contain all the express terms of the agreement?*

A: Yes. It is a contract for the sale of Fred's legal fee simple estate in the land, and so it must meet the requirements of section 2. It is known as an estate contract, as it is a contract for the sale of a legal estate in the land.

Q: *What happens if the contract doesn't meet the requirements of section 2?*

A: It is void. It is as though it never existed. This means that the equitable doctrine of part performance can no longer exist. You cannot have part performance of a void contract as you do not have a contract at all to perform.

Q: *Do you have to sign the contract yourself?*

A: No. It can be signed by an authorised agent. In *Re Stealth Construction Ltd* (2011), also known as *Green v Ireland*, there were indications that a contract satisfying section 2 of the Law of Property (Miscellaneous Provisions) Act 1989 could be created in an email together with the reply to that email if the emails formed a string of communication. The names inserted at the end of the emails constituted signatures. In the case, though, the contract did not include all the express terms and so didn't satisfy section 2. If you want to ensure that you don't inadvertently create a contract by email exchange, you should say in the email that the contract will be made only by means of a separate signed and exchanged document.

Q: *Do all the terms have to be in the document?*

A: No. You can incorporate them into the main document by referring to them. It is possible for both parties to sign one document which contains all the expressly agreed terms. Alternatively, and more commonly under section 2, two identical copies of the document containing all the express terms of the contract are made, and the purchaser signs one, while the vendor signs the other. Until the exchange of contracts actually takes place, either party can withdraw from the transaction because there is no valid contract that meets section 2 of the Law of Property (Miscellaneous Provisions) Act 1989. If there is a variation of the contract, the variation must also meet section 2: see *McCausland v Duncan Lawrie Ltd* (1997).

Q: *What happens if you forget to put an expressly agreed term into the contract?*

A: The court has been able to view the term missed out of the written agreement as a collateral contract – a separate contract – provided the missing term is not for the sale or disposition of an interest in land. In *Record v Bell* (1991) the missing term was to do with providing evidence that the seller was the owner of the land. The purchaser, who wanted to get out of buying the property, argued that the contract for sale was void because it did not contain all the express terms of the contract. It was held that the missing term was a second contract. This second contract was collateral to and separate from the first contract which was for the sale of the land. The second contract was not for the sale of land, so did not have to meet the requirements of section 2 and was enforceable. Given that this second contract was separate from the main contract for sale of the land, the main contract therefore contained all the express terms and was held to be enforceable. *Tootal Clothing Ltd v Guinea Properties Management Ltd* (1992) is another case that illustrates this point. In *Grossman v Hooper* (2001) there was criticism of the use of collateral contracts and emphasis was placed on looking at whether the term missed out of the written agreement was vital to the contract going ahead.

The court is able to order rectification and performance of the contract under section 2(4) of the Law of Property (Miscellaneous Provisions) Act 1989 if it is convinced that the term should have been included. In *Wright v Robert Leonard*

(Developments) Ltd (1994) the term missing in the written agreement was held to be an integral part of the contract, so it could not be seen as a separate collateral contract. Even so, because there was evidence that the parties had intended to include the term, the contract was rectified and enforced.

All these ruses rather make nonsense of the fact that a written contract which does not include an express term is void because it does not satisfy the requirements of section 2 and they don't always work. In *Oun v Ahmad* (2008) the claimant asked for rectification of a contract for sale because not all the express terms had been included. However, the parties had specifically agreed not to include these express terms in the contract. As such, there was no mistake in recording the agreement and therefore no place for rectification. The parties had recorded what they intended to record but their mistake (rather a major one) was to fail to appreciate the legal consequences of not including all the express terms. The contract was therefore void. In *Francis v F Berndes Ltd* (2011) there was an oral agreement to buy a property. This was followed by a letter signed by both parties. Whilst confirming the offer of sale, the letter did not contain an obligation on the buyer to purchase the property. This term would not be implied and rectification would not be ordered because there was 'no mistake about the factual or legal nature of the bargain which the parties intended to record'. It was said that whilst this might be a highly technical distinction and could cause injustice where the missing term was obvious, one of the main aims of the 1989 Act was to ensure certainty as regards contracts for the sale of land and avoid the need for extrinsic evidence. An application to raise a claim in restitution was allowed though.

People have arguably tried to avoid the formal requirements of section 2 also in other ways which will be discussed in Chapter 12.

Contracts are important because we use them constantly in buying and selling land. They are also important because they are capable of specific performance. This means that the court can order specific performance of the contract in the event of a breach.

Q: *Why wouldn't you just award damages, for example, if a vendor refused to sell the land after he'd entered into a contract to do so?*

A: Land is considered to be unique. Damages are inadequate if there is a breach of a contract to sell land to you, because you could never find an identical piece of land again, even if you were awarded damages. This means that where there is a breach of a contract for the sale of land, you can claim the remedy of specific performance, and ask the court to order that the contract is carried out according to its terms and that the land is sold to you.

And now we will return to the question of how an equitable interest arises here. Because the contract is capable of specific performance, it will immediately create an equitable interest in favour of the purchaser.

Q: *Why does the contract immediately create an equitable interest in favour of the purchaser?*

A: This is because of two factors. First, a contract relating to land is capable of specific performance. Secondly, there is an equitable maxim that states 'equity looks on that as done which ought to be done'. As the court will enforce the contract, equity views the purchaser as having a right in the land immediately. It can be only an equitable right, as the land has not yet been conveyed by deed to the purchaser.

Take an example and look at a situation that everyone will recognise. Fred owns Lilac Cottage. It is a delightful, charming, thatched cottage with a brook running through the garden, apple trees laden with fruit and birds chirping merrily in the trees. You have fallen in love with it and, in return for a large sum of money, you enter into a written contract with Fred which satisfies section 2 of the Law of Property (Miscellaneous Provisions) Act 1989, in which Fred agrees to sell Lilac Cottage to you. Several days later, Fred changes his mind about selling. You are distraught. You are never going to find another cottage like it, so the common law remedy of damages would never compensate you adequately. Lilac Cottage is unique and the contract for the sale of it is capable of specific performance. This means that you could go to court and demand that Fred sell the legal estate of Lilac Cottage to you. As 'equity looks on that as done which ought to be done', this will immediately give you an equitable right, an equitable estate in Lilac Cottage, because specific performance is available.

Q: *Can you argue that no two houses are the same, even ones on a housing estate?*

A: Yes. Each plot of land is unique because, for example, it doesn't have the same view.

We can now widen this argument to say that all contracts for the creation or sale of interests in or over land are also contracts capable of specific performance. Because land is unique, the rights in and over land are also unique, and so specific performance is the only acceptable remedy.

Q: *So if a contract to create or sell an interest in or over land is breached, equity can order specific performance of it?*

A: That's right. And because these sorts of contracts are capable of specific performance and equity looked on that as done which ought to be done, equity recognised that you had a right in or over the land, an equitable right, before the case ever went to court. You could never have a legal right because you hadn't used a deed.

This means that, within the framework of the law, you can have either legal or equitable interests in land depending on how they have been created.

Q: *If, for example, Fred grants Peter a lease of Lilac Cottage for 10 years by deed, will this be a legal lease or an equitable lease?*

A: Putting Boxes B1 and B2 together, it is capable of being a legal estate in land in accordance with section 1 of the Law of Property Act 1925. It has been created by deed, therefore satisfying section 52(1) of the Law of Property Act 1925, and so it will be a legal lease.

Q: *And if Fred had agreed in a written contract satisfying section 2 of the Law of Property (Miscellaneous Provisions) Act 1989 that he would grant Peter a lease of Lilac Cottage for 10 years, Peter would have an equitable lease?*

A: Yes. The lease in this case could never be legal as it hadn't been created by deed. Provided the agreement satisfied section 2 of the Law of Property (Miscellaneous

Provisions) Act 1989, Peter could go to court and ask for the remedy of specific performance. Lilac Cottage is unique, and a lease of Lilac Cottage is unique, so damages are an inadequate remedy. As 'equity looks on that as done which ought to be done', the agreement or contract would immediately create an equitable interest in favour of Peter, here an equitable lease.

The process of buying and selling land

> **Box C**
>
> THE PROCESS OF BUYING AND SELLING LAND

It is important to know the mechanics involved in buying and selling land, and conveyancing is the process by which this is done. To illustrate the conveyancing process, imagine that Fred owns Greenacres.

Q: *Is that the shorthand way of saying that Fred owns the legal estate in fee simple absolute in possession in Greenacres?*

A: Yes. He owns a freehold estate that has no determinable end. There are no restrictions on who can inherit Greenacres. There are no conditions attached to the holding of Greenacres, and Fred is in possession of his interest in Greenacres right now. Fred decides to sell Greenacres and puts the house on the market. Peter looks round Greenacres and decides he wants to buy it. A 'deal' is negotiated. The first thing Peter will want to check, usually via his solicitor, is whether Fred actually owns Greenacres. How he does this depends on whether or not Greenacres is registered. Two systems exist in parallel in the United Kingdom – unregistered land and registered land – and they are discussed in detail in Chapters 3 and 4. If Greenacres is unregistered land, Fred will have to rely on documentation to prove that he holds the title to Greenacres. These documents are called 'title deeds'. Registered land is what it says it is. The estate of Greenacres will appear on a register, and the name of the owner, Fred in this instance, will also appear on the register.

Q: *Doesn't the purchaser, Peter, have to carry out searches as well?*

A: Yes. In addition to checking the title to Greenacres, Peter's solicitor will also make searches to check that there are no adverse matters affecting the property. Some examples of these searches are:

a. A search of the Local Land Charges Register together with enquiries of the Local Authority. The Local Land Charges Register is held by the Local Authority and shows restrictions or burdens on the land which are binding on any owner. The enquiries reveal information about the property such as its planning history and whether any new roads or traffic calming measures are proposed.

b. An environmental search to check the past use of the land. Is Greenacres built on a landfill site? Is it on contaminated land which will cause risk to the occupiers? Is it in an area prone to flooding?

c. A drainage search to check that the property is connected to the mains drainage and mains water supply. The alternative would be septic tanks or a private water supply from the ground, and this can put a buyer off.

d. A search to check whether other people have an interest in the land. The owner of adjoining Blackacres may have a right of way, for example, over Greenacres. How this information is obtained depends on whether the land is registered or not, and this is discussed in detail in Chapters 3 and 4.

Q: *Does Fred still have to provide a Home Information Pack for Peter?*

A: No. Home Information Packs (HIPs) were suspended from 21 May 2010 following a general election. A Home Information Pack used to give information on, for example, electricity and gas safety, any previous structural damage, flood risk information and it also included an Energy Performance Certificate showing how energy-efficient the house was. Even though HIPs have been suspended, before marketing a residential or commercial property today for sale or rent, an Energy Performance Certificate must still have been commissioned, or be available. There is a financial penalty for not doing so.

Q: *Does the seller have to provide any other information?*

A: The seller also has to fill in a Seller's Property Information Form, also known as 'pre-contract enquiries', which asks general questions about the house, such as about the supply of gas and electricity and disputes with the neighbours. The form used to have the following question 13: 'Is there any other information which you think the buyer might have a right to know?' In *Sykes v Taylor-Rose* (2004), Mr and Mrs Sykes had purchased a house from Mr and Mrs Taylor-Rose and had subsequently discovered, by courtesy of a television documentary and a note pushed under their door, that the house had been the scene of a gruesome murder and dismembered body parts had been hidden around the property. They moved out and had to sell the house at a loss of £25,000 because of its history. They therefore claimed damages from Mr and Mrs Taylor-Rose because the latter had answered 'No' to question 13 on the form, although they had known about the murder. It was held that the words in the question were to be given their normal meaning and an honest, personal and subjective answer did not amount to misrepresentation. There was no legal obligation to give the history of the house, and the words 'right to know' did not include anything which might affect the enjoyment or value of the property. Although Mr and Mrs Taylor-Rose knew about the murder, their answer was honestly given and they were not liable. Question 13 has now been omitted from the form, but if you'd been in the same situation, what answer would you have given?

When everyone is happy with the title and the search results a contract is signed.

Q: *Does this contract have to satisfy section 2 of the Law of Property (Miscellaneous Provisions) Act 1989?*

A: Yes. As discussed in Box B2, the contract must be in writing, it must be signed by or on behalf of both Fred and Peter, and it must contain all the express terms of the agreement. It is known as an estate contract because it is a contract to convey the legal estate in Greenacres to Peter. Normally the seller and the buyer each have an identical contract which they each sign. Their solicitors telephone each other to agree that the contracts are identical, to confirm the amount of the deposit to be paid by the buyer and to agree that they are to enter into an exchange of contracts by telephone. If the contract doesn't satisfy section 2, it will be void, which means it is as though it never existed. This doesn't mean to say that Peter cannot buy Greenacres, only that the contract to sell Greenacres to Peter does not exist.

Q: *Assuming the contract satisfies section 2, is it a specifically enforceable contract?*

A: Yes. Greenacres is land. Land is unique. If Fred backed out of the agreement, damages would be an inadequate remedy for breach of the contract, because Peter would never be able to find a property identical to Greenacres. This means that Peter could ask the court to order specific performance of the contract, and Fred would have to sell Greenacres to him. It also means that equity views Peter as having an equitable interest in Greenacres already because of the maxim 'equity looks on that as done which ought to be done'. After all, he has complied with the statutory requirements for the contract, he has given consideration in the form of a deposit, and he would never be able to find another house like Greenacres. As equity regards that as done which ought to be done, Peter will have an equitable interest in Greenacres. This will be an equitable estate in Greenacres. He cannot own the legal estate in Greenacres yet, as it has not been transferred to him by deed. Remember that section 52(1) of the Law of Property Act 1925 states that a legal estate or interest in land must be created by a deed. Peter must then enter his estate contract on a register. This ensures that his estate contract takes priority over that of anyone else Fred might be tempted to sell Greenacres to if a higher offer were made.

Q: *Why doesn't Fred just transfer Greenacres to Peter by deed immediately Peter tells him that he wants to buy Greenacres?*

A: There is nothing to stop this happening. However, there is no proof at this point that Fred actually owns Greenacres! If Fred conveyed Greenacres to Peter immediately by deed, Peter could be in for an unpleasant surprise. Also, Fred needs to make sure that he has somewhere to move to, so all the people in a chain of transactions agree to the same completion date, which is when the legal estate is transferred to the purchaser by deed.

Q: *What happens if Fred hasn't told the whole truth and the terms of the contract don't reflect the actual situation?*

A: In this case, Peter is allowed to withdraw from the contract and the court will not order specific performance. Assuming everything is in order, a completion date will be written into the contract on exchange. The completion date for a house could be 10 working days from the date of exchange. For a development site, it could be 10 working days from the date the buyer received his planning permission, which could be some six months after the date of exchange. On the completion date the purchase price minus the deposit is paid. Fred then transfers the legal estate in Greenacres to Peter by deed and Peter can take physical possession of the land. Even so, Peter is not recognised as having the legal title until the transaction has been registered at the Land Registry. This is discussed in Chapter 4. When this has happened, in lay terms, Peter will own Greenacres. Tax is payable on residential property as a percentage based on its market value. The scale is 1% of the market value for properties valued at between £125,000 and £250,000. Properties over £250,000 are charged from 3% upwards.

Q: *What happens if I'm buying a house with someone else, like my spouse or partner?*

A: In this case, your solicitor will ask you how you intend the property to be owned. For example, do you want to own it in equal or unequal shares? The deed which transfers the land to you has an option which your solicitor fills in to confirm how the property is to be held. The ways in which you can hold land together are covered in Chapter 8.

Q: *Is the conveyancing process the same for the purchase of a house such as Greenacres as for the purchase of several acres of land for redevelopment?*

A: Yes, except that some terms of the contract may be different. In a development situation, the trigger for completion may be the grant of planning permission, and, of course, value added tax (VAT) will come into it.

Q: *What will Peter actually own when he buys Greenacres?*

A: Section 205(1)(ix) of the Law of Property Act 1925 gives a definition of land.

> 'Land' includes land of any tenure, and mines and minerals, whether or not held apart from the surface, buildings or parts of buildings (whether the division is horizontal, vertical or made in any other way) and other corporeal hereditaments, also a manor, an advowson, and a rent and other incorporeal hereditaments, and an easement, right, privilege, or benefit in, over, or derived from land.

So land includes mines and minerals. In *Coleman v Ibstock Brick Ltd* (2007) the court had to decide whether brick shale, clay and fireclay were minerals because 'minerals' had been excluded from the sale. Only the fireclay was classified as a mineral and the seller was able to claim damages for the fireclay that had already been mined by the purchaser. Coal belongs to the Coal Authority under the Coal Industry Act 1994 and oil, gas and petroleum belong to the Crown under the Petroleum Act 1988. In *Bocardo SA v Star Energy UK Onshore Ltd* (2010) an oil company had drilled from other land some 2800 feet down under Bocardo's land, without Bocardo's permission, to recover petroleum. It was held that the owner of the surface of the land would also own the strata (layers) beneath the surface of his land, including minerals. Although the oil company had a licence to obtain the petroleum, in the absence of permission or statutory authority to actually enter Bocardo's land, the oil company had trespassed and was liable for damages.

As Lord Hope said

> There must obviously be some stopping point, as one reaches the point at which physical features such as pressure and temperature render the concept of the strata belonging to anybody so absurd as to be not worth arguing about. But the wells that are at issue in this case, extending from about 800 feet to 2,800 feet below the surface, are far from being so deep as to reach the point of absurdity. Indeed the fact that the strata can be worked upon at those depths points to the opposite conclusion.

Q: *How can land be divided horizontally?*

A: You could sell the rights to a mine under your land, for example. If you owned a block of flats and sold the top one to Peter, this also would be a horizontal division of land. In this case Peter will own what is called a flying freehold. If Peter allowed the roof to collapse, you wouldn't have any redress against him if the rest of the flats were damaged. Any obligation on him to keep his property in repair is almost impossible to enforce because it is a positive obligation rather than a negative obligation. This is why flats are leased rather than owned outright because in a lease you can impose positive obligations on Peter to keep his roof in repair and these obligations are enforceable. The system of commonhold discussed in Chapter 16 seeks to resolve some of these problems but there are significant difficulties in practice with the system of commonhold to the extent that people try to avoid it.

Q: *How much of the airspace above a house do you own?*

A: There is a Latin phrase, 'cuius est solum eius est usque ad coelum et ad inferos', which means that whoever owns the land owns up to the heavens and down to the bowels of the earth. The claim that you own up to the heavens and down is far from true, not least because if a plane flew over your garden you could not sue for trespass. The Civil Aviation Act 1982 allows an aircraft to fly at a reasonable height given its circumstances over your land and you have the right to the height necessary for the use and enjoyment of your land. You can also sell airspace – think of a walkway suspended over land.

Q: *Can you buy bits of the moon?*

A: Sheer lunarcy! There is no shortage of opportunities on the internet to buy bits of the moon but I suggest that you work out who owns the moon because you cannot buy what someone doesn't own and you cannot sell on something that you don't own.

Q: *In the definition of land, what is meant by a corporeal hereditament?*

A: A corporeal hereditament is a physical attribute of the land, for example, a building. This is in comparison to an incorporeal hereditament, which is an intangible right such as a right of way over the land.

Q: *What happens if I find something on my land? Whom does it belong to?*

A: If something is buried, it is seen as part of the land. Unless the rightful owner claims it, it belongs to you, even if you didn't find it. If something is found lying on the ground, it belongs to the owner of the land provided the owner has made it clear that he has control over the land. The more the public is allowed access, the less likely that is. In *Parker v British Airways Board* (1982) a bracelet found by a passenger on the floor of the airport lounge was held to belong to the finder and not to British Airways because it didn't have sufficient control of the premises. So if you find an envelope with £1 million in it in a bank vault, it belongs to the bank. If you find it in a park, it belongs to you.

Q: *Whom does treasure found on land belong to?*

A: Treasure used to have a limited meaning and belonged to the Crown under the doctrine of treasure trove. This meant that too many items were kept by finders and were lost from the public view so the Treasure Act 1996 has extended the definition of treasure. Under this Act ownership of the treasure rests with the Crown. You must report your find to the local coroner and you may be given a reward from the Crown.

Q: *We've talked about what Peter owns when he buys Greenacres, but what can Fred take with him when he moves out of Greenacres? There are all sorts of stories about people taking the light bulbs and the door knobs.*

A: Under section 62(1) of the Law of Property Act 1925 a conveyance of land includes the following:

> A conveyance of land shall be deemed to include and shall by virtue of this Act operate to convey, with the land, all buildings, erections, fixtures, commons, hedges, ditches, fences, ways, waters, watercourses, liberties, privileges, easements, rights, and advantages whatsoever ...

This means that when land is sold everything described in section 62 will pass to the buyer, so that will include sheds, outhouses and conservatories which come into the definition of a building.

Q: *What's a fixture in section 62?*

A: A fixture is seen as something that is attached to the land and has become part of the land. There is a Latin phrase – 'quicquid plantur solo, solo cedit' – which means that whatever is fixed to the land becomes part of the land. Something that is not attached to the land and does not become part of it is known as a chattel or a fitting.

Q: *Is it important to know the difference between a fixture and a chattel?*

A: Yes, it is, because under section 62 a conveyance of land will include all fixtures with the land. If you are selling a house, after contracts have been exchanged you are not allowed to remove any fixtures from the house because you have then contracted to sell the land which includes the fixtures. You can take any chattels with you as they are not part of the definition of land.

Q: *Can I never remove a fixture from my house?*

A: In your capacity as owner of the freehold you can remove a fixture up to the time you exchange contracts for the sale of the property. You cannot remove fixtures between the time a potential buyer inspects the property and exchange of contracts. In *Taylor v Hamer* (2002), the seller had removed flagstones after the buyer inspected the property but before the exchange of contracts. It wasn't a case of 'buyer beware' because the seller had invited an offer for the property as shown, which would have included the flagstones, and hadn't said anything to the contrary. It was held under simple morality the seller had to tell the buyer if he intended to take something like flagstones that would be classified as fixtures. The seller wasn't stealing the flagstones because they were his, but he did not sell what the buyer was entitled to have conveyed to him. The seller had to replace the flagstones or pay for substitutes.

Q: *Is there an easier way of making sure there is no confusion over what you are going to take with you?*

A: If you sell a house you will be asked to fill in a Fixtures, Fittings & Contents Form. This is a list of just about every item imaginable, asking whether you are taking it or leaving it. This list then becomes part of the contract, and so there is no dispute.

Q: *How do you tell the difference between a fixture and a chattel if you haven't filled in the form or an object doesn't appear on the Fixtures, Fittings & Contents Form?*

A: There are two tests to apply. The first is the degree of annexation. If an object is attached to the land then it is deemed to be a fixture. If it is not attached to the land, it is deemed to be a chattel. So, in *Holland v Hodgson* (1872) spinning looms bolted to the floor of a mill were seen as fixtures, and in *Aircool Installations v British Telecommunications* (1995) an air-conditioning unit fitted onto a building was a fixture. Conversely, printing machines resting on their own weight on the floor were seen as chattels in *Hulme v Brigham* (1943). In *Dean v Andrews* (1985) a large prefabricated greenhouse was bolted to a concrete plinth which stood on the ground but was not fixed to the ground. The greenhouse was a chattel.

Q: *Does it matter how an object is fixed?*

A: No, although the more securely an object is fixed, the more it will be seen as a fixture. The degree of annexation is the first test, but it does not necessarily determine whether the item is a fixture or a chattel because of the second test. This second test looks at the purpose of annexation. It has long since been held that this is the more important test. In *Hamp v Bygrave* (1982) it was stated that the purpose of annexation is now of first importance. The purpose of annexation test looks at why the object was fixed. Was it to improve the land or was it simply fixed so that the owner could enjoy or use the item? If the object was attached to make a permanent improvement to the land or the object was an integral part of the property, it would be a fixture. If the object was attached to the land simply so that it could be enjoyed or because that was the only way it could be used, it could still be a chattel even though it was firmly attached to the land. One of the best illustrations concerns the tapestry cases. In *Re Whaley* (1908) the house was a 'complete specimen of an Elizabethan dwelling house' and the tapestries that had been attached to the walls were held to be an integral part of the property, and therefore fixtures. In *Leigh v Taylor* (1902), though, tapestries had been tacked on to canvas which was nailed to strips of wood which were nailed to the wall. They were held to be chattels because you couldn't enjoy the tapestries other than by hanging them up and they were never intended to become an integral part of the house. It was also said in *Leigh v Taylor* that just because it's far easier to attach things these days (think of Blu-Tack) it doesn't mean to say they become fixtures.

Q: *Does the amount of damage caused by removing an item make a difference?*

A: The view is that the more damage done on removal, the more likely it is to be a fixture. In *Leigh v Taylor* the tapestries had been removed without causing any damage and the very nature of their slight attachment also meant they were chattels.

In *Berkley v Poulett* (1977) there was a dispute over whether pictures which had been fixed into the recesses of a panelled wall in the Queen's Dining Room and the Queen's Ante-Room were fixtures or chattels. Lord Scarman asked whether the design of the room was either panelled walls with recesses for pictures which could be enjoyed as pictures, or a room with walls comprising both panelling and pictures where the pictures were part of the 'composite mural' i.e. were part of the whole effect. He decided that the former had been intended because, although the panelling was Victorian, the pictures were a mixed collection. The rooms were not along the same lines as the Elizabethan rooms in *Re Whaley*. Despite the 'painstaking and attractive arguments of Mr Millett for the plaintiff', which had lasted for five and a half days, Lord Scarman found that the pictures were chattels put on the wall to be enjoyed as pictures.

Q: *Does this second test mean that each case is decided on its facts depending on the circumstances?*

A: Yes. There are examples of cases where the item has been held to be a chattel in one case and a fixture in another, such as the tapestry cases. In *D'Eyncourt v Gregory* (1866) carved figures and marble vases in the hall which rested on their own weight were part of the architectural design of the hall and staircase rather than ornaments which had been added afterwards. They were therefore fixtures. Stone lions at the top of the steps in the garden and stone garden seats were also fixtures on the same basis. *Berkley v Poulett* also concerned a white marble statue weighing half a ton standing on a plinth which itself was fixed in position. The plinth that the statue was on was a fixture because it was an integral part of the architectural design of the west side of the house. The statue was a chattel because the object on top of the plinth could be changed depending on the owner's taste and was not part of the architectural design. A sundial resting on a pedestal was held to be a chattel as it was detachable.

Q: *Does the seller's intention matter?*

A: The court will not take into account the subjective intention of the seller because the answer will inevitably be 'it's a fitting and I can take it with me', but it can look at the objective factors if they throw light on the situation: see *Elitestone Ltd v Morris* (1997). In *Hamp v Bygrave* the garden urns, statues and ornaments could have been chattels because they rested only on their own weight, or they could have been fixtures because they were intended to be part of the garden. Mr Justice Boreham looked at the objective intention of the parties. The fact that the particulars of sale mentioned the items as being included in the sale indicated they were fixtures. The sellers had talked about reducing the price of the property by excluding the items from the sale, again leading to the inference that they were fixtures. The sellers' solicitor had said that the items were included in the sale. On this basis they were fixtures.

Q: *How do you classify the house itself?*

A: The definition of land includes buildings, and a conveyance of land includes buildings. This did not stop the court being asked to adjudicate on this in *Elitestone Ltd v Morris*, where the parties had disagreed about the status of a chalet bungalow which rested on concrete foundation blocks in the ground. It was argued that it was a chattel on the basis that it wasn't attached to the land. The House of Lords held that when considering a house the answer 'was as much a matter of common sense as precise analysis'. Whereas a house that could be moved in sections could arguably be a chattel, the bungalow couldn't be removed without destroying it. Lord Lloyd of Berwick drew an analogy with an example given in *Holland v Hodgson*, where stones placed on top of one another to form a drystone wall would become part of the land, but the same stones piled up in a builder's yard for convenience in the form of a wall would remain a chattel. When the timber was assembled into wall frames for the bungalow, it became part of the structure which was part and parcel of the land. The reason the timber was brought onto the land was so obvious that the fact the bungalow wasn't attached was irrelevant. Lord Lloyd went to cite, per curiam, a threefold classification from Woodfall on Landlord and Tenant, release 36 (1994):

> ... an object brought on to land is either (i) a chattel, (ii) a fixture, or (iii) part and parcel of the land itself, with objects in categories (ii) and (iii) being treated as being part of the land.

This classification seems eminently sensible and deals with cases like *Elitestone Ltd v Morris*, where the chalet bungalow was seen as part and parcel of the land.

Q: *What about a houseboat then?*

A: In *Chelsea Yacht and Boat Co Ltd v Pope* (2000) it was held that it was a chattel because the mooring ropes could be undone, the boat could be moved without damaging it or the land and it had not become part of the land, not least because it was unclear what land it might have become part of. As Lord Justice Tuckey said:

> I support this conclusion on the grounds of common sense. It is common sense that a house built on land is part of the land. (See Lord Lloyd in *Elitestone Ltd v Morris* at page 692 H.) So too it is common sense that a boat on a river is not part of the land. A boat, albeit one used as a home, is not of the same genus as real property.

Hurrah for common sense.

Cinderella Rockerfellas Ltd v Rudd (2003) also confirmed the status of a boat as a chattel, although the case was to do with rateable values.

The latest boat case is *Mew v Tristmire* (2011) which concerned two residential houseboats that rested on a platform supported on wooden piles set into the sea bed. The case was to do with whether there was a tenancy but the court had to decide whether the houseboats were fixtures or chattels. Unlike the bungalow in *Elitestone Ltd v Morris* which was a permanent feature and could be moved only by demolishing it, the houseboats were designed to be moveable like caravans. Notwithstanding their condition today (they had deteriorated and moving them would result in damage or destruction), when they were first put on the platform they could have been moved off it in one piece and floated elsewhere without dismantling or destroying them. The Court of Appeal came to the conclusion that they were chattels.

Q: *Apart from boats, most of the cases relate to grand houses with grand schemes. What happens in a mock Elizabethan, Tudor style, Renaissance inspired suburban house today with all mod cons?*

A: *Botham v TSB Bank plc* (1996) is a good example here. Mr Botham's house had been repossessed by the Bank. The Bank wanted to sell the house to recover the money that Mr Botham still owed on the mortgage. When there is a mortgage, any fixtures belong to the lender whether the objects became fixtures before or after the creation of the mortgage.

Q: *Presumably it was in the Bank's interests to argue that everything was a fixture?*

A: Yes, because if items were classified as fixtures, they would be included in the sale. The price the Bank could ask for the house would be higher, and so the Bank would stand more chance of getting back the money it had lent to Mr Botham. Conversely, it was in Mr Botham's interest to argue that everything was a chattel so that he could take it with him. Starting off in the soft furnishings department, it was held that carpets could be easily removed from gripper rods and could be used elsewhere. They were not intended to make a permanent improvement to the building. The curtains were only attached to enable them to be used as curtains. Removal of either the carpets or the curtains would not cause damage. Both were chattels.

Q: *What would happen if there were carpet squares stuck down with glue?*

A: According to *Botham v TSB Bank plc*, they would be fixtures.

Q: *And in the lighting department?*

A: The light fittings were chattels, as would be lampshades and chandeliers. The judge adopted the test in *British Economical Lamp Co Ltd v Empire, Mile End, Ltd* (1913), where the light fittings were not shown to be part of the electrical installation in the flat and so were not fixtures. And, once and for all, in any exam question, under the same authority the light bulbs are chattels. In *Botham v TSB Bank plc*, the gas fires, which were attached by a gas pipe with a gas tap to turn the gas on and off at the mains, were the same as electric fires plugged in. They rested on their own weight and were attached to the gas pipe only so as to be usable, and so were also chattels.

Q: *And in the kitchen area?*

A: As far as the gas hob, the extractor fan unit, the integrated dishwasher and the fitted oven were concerned, the degree of annexation was slight and simply enabled the item to be used. They could be disconnected without damage and were not a permanent improvement to the building. They were also items that would need replacing after a relatively short period of time. The kitchen units, including the sink, would cause damage if removed and were surrounded by wall tiling, which meant that they would be seen as a permanent improvement and therefore a fixture.

Q: *And I don't suppose the facilities for ablution were left out of the discussion?*

A: No. The taps, plugs, soap dish, towel rail and lavatory roll holders were fixtures because they were items necessary for a room used as a bathroom and were intended to be a lasting improvement to the property. Had there been a freestanding Victorian bath, this could have been a chattel and, if so, any Victorian taps would also have been chattels.

Q: *What happens if the land is leased to a tenant and the tenant installs fixtures? Who is entitled to these fixtures when the lease comes to an end?*

A: All fixtures become part of the land, but the tenant is entitled to remove fixtures that have been attached for trade, ornamental or domestic purposes at the end of the lease or within a reasonable time afterwards. In *Spyer v Phillipson* (1929) the tenant was allowed to remove antique panelling that he had put up because it was an ornamental fixture. An agricultural tenant has the right to remove any fixtures under the Agricultural Holdings Act 1986. This must be done either before the end of the lease or within two months thereafter, provided the tenant has given one month's notice to the landlord and has paid all the rent. Any tenant must repair damage caused by the removal of fixtures. In *Mancetter Developments Ltd v Garmanson* (1986) the tenant was liable for the repair of holes in the walls left by the removal of extractor fans.

Q: *Fred is clearly going to be concerned about things like fixtures and chattels when he sells Greenacres. What sorts of issues can arise when there is more of a business element in the sale?*

A: Consider the following examples. You want to buy a small area of land from the Local Authority to extend your garden and have agreed a purchase price of £5,000. This price reflects the land value as garden land. If the land was large enough to construct a house on though, you could make a profit by developing the land, and so the £5,000 paid would not reflect the true value of the land. A Local Authority is under an obligation to achieve the best possible price for land and so wouldn't want to miss out on the profit it could have made had it sold the land for redevelopment instead. The Local Authority could therefore extract a negative promise from you restricting the use of the land to a garden only. This is known as a negative or restrictive covenant and is discussed in Chapter 14. Alternatively, it could impose a positive promise, a positive covenant, on you, where you would have to pay a percentage of any profit you made from any later development of the land. The Local Authority will need to know whether and how these promises can be enforced against anyone you sell the house to.

Now consider a different example. A developer is negotiating to buy a plot of land for several million pounds which he intends to develop as a housing estate. The land is accessed by crossing over adjoining land that the seller wants to keep. The developer needs to secure a right of way over that adjoining land and he needs to ensure that the right of way can be used forever by the individual owners of the houses that are going to be built on the housing estate. This right of way is known as an easement and is discussed in Chapter 17. Other property issues will need to be resolved here as well. The seller might make it a condition that the developer constructs a road (a positive covenant) and also maintains it (a positive covenant). The developer will want to pass on this liability to individual house buyers (again a positive covenant) until the road is adopted by the local authority.

Q: *Does the law in this book apply to both residential and commercial situations?*

A: Yes.

Personal and proprietary rights in land

<table>
<tr><td>

Box D

PERSONAL AND PROPRIETARY RIGHTS IN LAND

</td></tr>
</table>

You must now distinguish between rights that are personal in nature and rights that are proprietary in nature. A personal right can be enforced only against a specific individual. For example, if you enter into a contract with Fred to buy a book and Fred sells the book to Jemima instead, your right to the book is enforceable only against Fred. You have only a right to claim damages for breach of contract. However, if you had paid for the book and ownership had passed to you, but Fred had given it to Jemima, you would have a right to claim the book itself. This is a proprietary right, a right in the property itself. Interests in land are either personal or proprietary. If a right is personal, it can be enforced only against the person who granted it, not against anyone else. If a right is proprietary in nature, it can be enforced against other people. Personal rights are called rights *in personam*, rights against the person. Proprietary rights are called rights *in rem*. 'Rem' means 'object' in Latin so you have a right in the object itself, here in the land. Look at the example of Fred and the range of possible interests over Greenacres.

Greenacres owned by Fred

Mr Black, the next-door neighbour who owns Blackacres, has a right of way over Greenacres.

Bundy's Bank has lent money to Fred using Greenacres as security for the loan.

Sophie, Fred's partner, contributed to the purchase price of Greenacres.

Now imagine that Fred has decided to move house. He has put Greenacres on the market and Peter is interested in buying it. If the rights of Mr Black, Bundy's Bank and Sophie are personal rights, they will be enforceable only against Fred. If their rights are proprietary in nature, they could be binding on Peter.

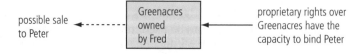

possible sale to Peter   Greenacres owned by Fred   proprietary rights over Greenacres have the capacity to bind Peter

Q: *How do you know which rights in land are personal and which are proprietary?*

A: There is a recognised category of proprietary rights in land. The main ones are discussed in this book and include leases, easements, restrictive covenants, equities acquired by estoppel, mortgages and interests acquired under a trust.

Q: *Who decides whether rights are proprietary or not?*

A: The courts or Parliament.

Q: *Does the list of proprietary rights in land increase all the time?*

A: No. An increase in the list would make the buying and selling of land more uncertain. Peter would have no wish to buy Greenacres if more and more people could claim a proprietary right over Greenacres which could be binding on him. Even if he did buy Greenacres, his own use of the land might be hampered by other people's rights over Greenacres, and so owning Greenacres would become less and less attractive.

Q: *Is there a unifying link between all the proprietary rights you can have in and over land?*

A: There is no clear unifying link. However, a proprietary right in land must be capable of clear definition, not least so that the parties are fully aware of the individual rights and duties of each of them: see *National Provincial Bank Ltd v Ainsworth* (1965).

Q: *Can both legal and equitable rights be proprietary in nature?*

A: Yes.

Q: *So if Mr Black, Bundy's Bank and Sophie had either legal or equitable proprietary rights over Greenacres, their rights could bind Peter?*

A: Yes.

 The whole picture

Box E
THE WHOLE PICTURE

You can now start to bring strands of this chapter together. Imagine the following situation. Fred owns Greenacres. This means he owns the legal estate in fee simple absolute in possession in Greenacres. He has given Mr Black, the next-door neighbour who owns Blackacres, the right to walk over his land as a short cut. The right could have been given in either a deed or a contract.

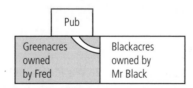

Mr Black has an interest over Greenacres.

If Fred refuses to let Mr Black walk over Greenacres, Mr Black can sue for breach of Fred's promise in the deed or contract and ask for specific performance. This is not a problem.

Imagine that Fred then sells Greenacres to Peter.

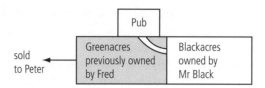

The question is whether Peter has to let Mr Black continue to use the right of way he was granted by Fred over Greenacres. You now have several questions to answer.

What sort of right does Mr Black have over Greenacres? How has it been created? Is it legal or equitable, or is it not recognised in either jurisdiction? Is it proprietary in nature and therefore capable of binding Peter when he buys Greenacres? Under what circumstances should it be binding on Peter?

If it is binding on Peter, it means that he must let Mr Black continue to use the right of way over Greenacres even though he, Peter, is now the new owner of Greenacres.

The answers to these questions are the essence of land law. The next three chapters look at the circumstances in which Peter will be bound by any interest that Mr Black has over Greenacres, the answer to which will be of paramount importance to both Peter and Mr Black.

Chapter 2 looks at what their position would have been before 1926, some aspects of which are still relevant today. Chapters 3 and 4 look at their position following the major reform that took place in land law in 1925. The remaining chapters in this book look at the nature and the creation of the individual estates and interests in land.

Reform

The Law Commission proposed a project to reform feudal land law because the several remaining but significant elements of feudal law dating from 1066 cause uncertainty for the public, practitioners and the courts, and there is conflict with modern case law and statute. After nearly 950 years, clearly there is no urgency to complete this project not least because the review was proposed in the ninth Programme, deferred to the tenth and then the eleventh Programme and now the Commissioners have again taken the view that other proposed law reform projects offer the potential for greater public benefit than work on feudal land law.

The situation will be reviewed in the future.

Further reading

S. Bridge, 'Part and Parcel: Fixtures in the House of Lords', 56 *CLJ* (1997) 498
M. Haley, 'The Law of Fixtures: An Unprincipled Metamorphosis?' *Conv and Prop Law*, Mar/Apr (1998) 137
Law Commission (1987), Formalities for Contracts for Sale etc. of Land (Law Com No 164)

Rights in land before 1926

www.palgrave.com/law/Stroud4e

▶ Introduction
▶ The rule governing legal rights in land before 1926
▶ The rule governing equitable rights in land before 1926

Introduction

There was a major reform of land law in 1925 which affected the position of purchasers of land. The aim of this chapter is to set the scene before 1926. If you understand what the problems were before 1926, you will be able to understand why the 1925 reform was so important. Even more importantly, some of the pre-1926 law is still relevant today.

Let's start off with the basic problem. Imagine Fred owns Greenacres. His next-door neighbour is Mr Black, who owns Blackacres. If Fred and Mr Black make an agreement between themselves about the use of Greenacres, the agreement will be enforced according to the rules of contract. Fred may agree, for a suitable sum of money, that Mr Black can walk over Greenacres as a short cut to get to the pub, for example.

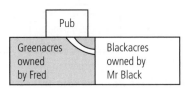

This is a right of way. The right of way that Fred has granted to Mr Black is called an easement, an easement of a right of way over Greenacres. If Fred subsequently refuses to let Mr Black walk over Greenacres, Mr Black will go to court and sue for breach of contract. He will ask for the remedy of specific performance, and Fred will be told by the court to allow Mr Black to use the easement of a right of way over Greenacres, as agreed in the contract.

Imagine that Fred then sells Greenacres to Peter.

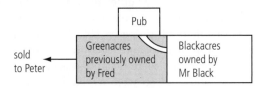

The question is whether Peter has to let Mr Black continue to use his easement of a right of way over Greenacres. If Mr Black's easement of a right of way is binding on Peter, Mr Black can continue to walk over Greenacres even though Peter is now the owner.

An easement is a proprietary right in land, which means that it is capable of binding third parties (here Peter). For the purposes of this chapter you need to know that an easement can be either a legal or an equitable proprietary right. You do not need to know how, or why, an easement of a right of way can be legal or equitable. All you need to know for now is that it is one or the other. The answer to whether Peter is bound by Mr Black's easement of a right of way now depends on whether Mr Black's easement is a legal or equitable proprietary right in the land.

The rule governing legal rights in land before 1926

The rule governing legal rights in land before 1926 was very clear.

> Legal rights bind the world

Legal rights were recognised in the common law courts and were binding on everyone in the world. Before 1926, if Mr Black had a legal right over Greenacres, Mr Black's legal right would bind everyone in the world. Therefore, if Mr Black had a legal easement of a right of way over Greenacres as shown, his right would be binding on Peter when he bought Greenacres and Peter would have to let Mr Black continue to walk across the land.

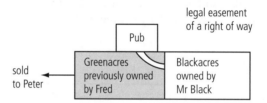

Q: *Would it matter if Peter didn't know about Mr Black's legal easement of a right of way?*

A: Not in the slightest. Legal rights bound the world regardless. Peter would be bound by Mr Black's legal easement of a right of way if he bought Greenacres.

Q: *Wasn't this rather unfair on Peter?*

A: There are several responses to this. First, a purchaser of land would be expected to make his own enquiries into what was happening on the land. Secondly, it would be a solicitor's duty to enquire whether there were any interests over Greenacres and then to have informed Peter, so Peter could well have a claim in negligence if his solicitors hadn't done their job properly. Thirdly, legal rights were usually created by a deed, which is a formal document requiring a witness. Deeds relating to the creation of interests over land were usually attached to the rest of the paperwork connected with the land, and so were available for inspection by any potential purchaser. Finally, legal rights were likely to have been visible on an inspection of the land. When Peter bought Greenacres, it's highly likely he'd have spotted a track or path over Greenacres. Even if he hadn't spotted it, and didn't know about it from any other source, Peter would still be bound by the legal easement of the right of way because legal rights bound the world. He would therefore have to allow Mr Black to continue to use the right of way over Greenacres.

The rule governing equitable rights in land before 1926

As we said, easements of a right of way can be either legal or equitable. Using the same example, but this time using an equitable easement as an illustration of an equitable right, we will now consider the position before 1926 where Mr Black has an equitable easement of a right of way over Greenacres.

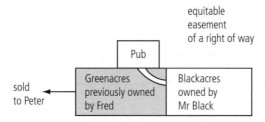

The rule governing equitable rights in land before 1926 was the following:

> Equitable rights bind everyone *except* a *bona fide* purchaser of a legal estate for value without notice of the equitable interest.

In this case Mr Black's equitable easement of a right of way would bind everyone *except* a *bona fide* purchaser of a legal estate for value without notice of his equitable interest, here his equitable easement of a right of way. It would therefore bind Peter unless Peter could show that he was a bona fide purchaser of a legal estate for value without notice of Mr Black's equitable easement of a right of way.

Q: *How would Peter show that?*

A: *Bona fide* means in good faith. Peter must have acted in good faith. This part of the definition refers not only to Peter's genuine and honest absence of notice of the equitable interest when he buys Greenacres, but also his position as a genuine purchaser of a legal estate for value: see *Midland Bank Trust Co Ltd v Green* (1981).

   Purchaser for value means that the purchaser of the land that the right is over gave some form of consideration, usually money, for his purchase. As Fred sold Greenacres to Peter, this implied that Peter paid good money for Greenacres.

Q: *Why do you need the 'for value' part? If Peter is a purchaser, then he must have given value.*

A: The word 'purchaser' is not used in its everyday sense in land law. In land law a purchaser of land means someone who takes land, whether or not he has given value. If you inherit land you will be deemed to be a purchaser. You will not be a purchaser for value, however, as you have not given any consideration or value for your inheritance. Within the context of equitable rights, you have to be a purchaser for value and to have given consideration for the land to be in the exception.

Q: *Did the consideration have to be the true value of the land?*

A: No. Even if Peter had paid £1 for Greenacres and it had been valued at £100,000, that would still count as consideration or value. You also need to be aware that there is something called marriage consideration. This occurs when land is transferred to a party in return for marriage. Imagine that, instead of selling Greenacres to Peter, Fred had promised to transfer Greenacres to Peter if he married Belinda, Fred's beautiful daughter. If Peter had married Belinda and Fred had transferred Greenacres to Peter, Peter would have given marriage consideration for Greenacres. His consideration for Greenacres was the act of marrying Belinda. Marriage consideration is included in the word value here. The whole idea dates from the time when women were 'married off' and the promise of property acted as an incentive to the suitor. The marriage had to take place otherwise it would not be seen as value.

Of a legal estate means that the purchaser bought a legal estate in the land. It didn't matter what estate, as long as it was legal. Remember that before 1926 a large number of estates could be legal. When Greenacres was sold to Peter, he purchased the freehold legal estate of Greenacres.

Without notice of the equitable interest. This is a quaint way of saying 'and doesn't know about the equitable interest'. There are three types of notice or knowledge in land law: *actual notice, constructive notice* and *imputed notice*. Actual notice is when you actually know about something. Constructive notice is notice you would have had if you had inspected the documentation to the land or the land itself. The courts assume that you have knowledge from such inspections, whether or not you made the inspections in practice. From your inspection of the land you were also deemed to have knowledge of the rights of anyone in actual possession of it. This is known as the rule in *Hunt v Luck* (1902). Imputed notice is what your solicitor or agent knew, or ought to have known, and which you are deemed to know as well. If your solicitor didn't pass the knowledge on, you could sue him for negligence. Peter would have notice of Mr Black's equitable easement of a right of way if he knew about it, or could have found out about it, or ought to have known about it through his solicitor.

Q: *So if Peter acted in good faith, gave consideration for the purchase of the legal estate of Greenacres, and had no actual, constructive or imputed notice of Mr Black's equitable easement of a right of way, then he would not be bound by the equitable easement and could tell Mr Black to stop using the right of way?*

A: Yes. If Peter didn't know about the right of way and couldn't have found out about it, this would be quite fair and just. If this was the case, Peter would be known as equity's darling.

Q: *Why equity's darling?*

A: The chances of Peter not knowing about Mr Black's equitable easement would be pretty slim by the time actual, constructive and imputed notice had been taken into account. If he really had no knowledge of Mr Black's easement, he would be one in a million as far as equity was concerned, otherwise known as equity's darling: see *Pilcher v Rawlins* (1872).

Q: *Say that Peter happened to be equity's darling and was therefore not bound by Mr Black's equitable easement of a right of way. If Peter then sold Greenacres on to Sahib, and Sahib did know about Mr Black's right of way, would Sahib then be bound by it?*

A: No. If the equitable easement of a right of way wasn't binding on Peter, then it wouldn't be resurrected again, even if a later purchaser of Greenacres knew about it: see *Wilkes v Spooner* (1911).

Q: *Is it fair to say that whether Peter was bound by Mr Black's equitable easement of a right of way was mainly determined by whether he knew about it?*

A: Yes. That's why the rule was known as the doctrine of notice, because that's really what it came down to: whether or not a purchaser for value had notice of the equitable right. It's important that you remember this phrase, 'the doctrine of notice', because the rule relating to equitable interests and the phrase 'the doctrine of notice' are still used today.

Q: *Is it fair on anybody that whether Peter was bound by an equitable interest depended on whether he knew or should have known about it?*

A: No. If Peter had bought Greenacres and had no idea that Mr Black had an equitable easement of a right of way over Greenacres, and could not have found out, then it was fair that the interest was not binding on him. Peter should be able to stop Mr Black using the right of way. Mr Black, however, would never be able to use the right of way again. This is unfair, as Mr Black wouldn't necessarily have known that Fred was selling Greenacres and couldn't have ensured that any purchaser of Greenacres knew about his right. Mr Black had no control over the situation, and yet could find that Peter was equity's darling and could stop him using his right of way. Now look at another situation from Peter's point of view. He bought Greenacres and moved in on the Saturday. On the Sunday morning he opened the curtains to find Mr Black walking across Greenacres along his right of way. He was furious because he thought he knew everything about the land. It transpired that his solicitor had known about Mr Black's equitable easement of a right of way, but had forgotten to tell Peter about it. Peter would be deemed to have the knowledge that his solicitor had through imputed notice. While it would give Peter another reason to sue his solicitor in negligence, he couldn't get out of the fact that he was not equity's darling. Mr Black's right of way would therefore be binding on him. He would have to let Mr Black continue to walk over Greenacres, whether he liked it or not.

Q: *So you can say that the rule relating to equitable interests, known as the doctrine of notice, was unsatisfactory from both Mr Black's and Peter's points of view?*

A: Yes, particularly as the courts of equity were supposed to work on fairness and justice. In 1925 there was a wholesale re-evaluation of this area. It was acknowledged that the rule relating to equitable interests and the doctrine of notice was unsatisfactory. The only really effective solution was to have a register of all rights in land. Such a system was enacted by the Land Registration Act

1925 and registration of rights in land under this Act started in 1926. Land that had been transferred onto this system was thereafter known as registered land. As registration was not going to be achieved overnight, the Land Charges Act was also enacted in 1925 as a temporary measure to ease the problems associated with equitable interests and the doctrine of notice. This was obviously a use of the word 'temporary' of which we were previously unaware, as the registration of all rights in land on a Register is still incomplete over three quarters of a century later. It does mean, though, that we still have to worry about unregistered as well as registered land. Chapter 3 looks at the rules we've been talking about in this chapter as amended by the Land Charges Act 1925, now the Land Charges Act 1972. This land is still called unregistered land. Chapter 4 looks at the new system that was introduced under the Land Registration Act 1925, now the Land Registration Act 2002, where the land is called registered land.

Summary of legal and equitable rights before 1926

Before 1926 two rules existed for determining whether the right of another person over land was binding on a purchaser of that land. The first related to legal rights and the second to equitable rights. The latter involved the doctrine of notice, which led to an unsatisfactory situation for both the person claiming the right and the purchaser of the land. As a result, the Land Charges Act 1925, now the Land Charges Act 1972, was introduced to resolve the problems relating to equitable interests in unregistered land. At the same time the Land Registration Act 1925 was passed to introduce a different system for the registration of rights in land. Land transferred into this different system was called registered land. The Land Registration Act 1925 has now been replaced by the Land Registration Act 2002.

www.palgrave.com/law/Stroud4e

Chapter 3

Rights after 1925 in unregistered land

▶ Introduction
▶ The Land Charges Acts of 1925 and 1972
▶ The unregistered land system in operation
▶ Summary of the land charges system
▶ Using the Land Charges Act 1972
▶ The advantages and disadvantages of the Land Charges Act 1972
▶ Summary of the advantages and disadvantages of the Land Charges Act 1972
▶ Buying and selling unregistered land
▶ Further reading

Introduction

Before 1926 unregistered land was governed by two rules: (1) legal rights bind the world; (2) equitable rights bind everyone except a bona fide purchaser of a legal estate for value without notice of the equitable interest (known as the doctrine of notice). The rule relating to equitable rights was not ideal, because whether an equitable interest bound a purchaser depended largely on whether he or she had knowledge or notice of the equitable interest. In 1925 there was a reform of this area. It was decided to retain the rule that legal rights would bind the world. The more immediate problem was with equitable interests and the doctrine of notice. The Land Charges Act 1925, now the Land Charges Act 1972, came onto the statute books and dealt almost exclusively with this problem of equitable interests. It is important to understand that these Land Charges Acts relate only to unregistered land. Unregistered land is land that has yet to be transferred to the different system created under the Land Registration Acts 1925 and 2002 discussed in Chapter 4. You must not confuse the two. Land is either unregistered or registered, and the two systems are completely separate. This chapter covers unregistered land as governed by the Land Charges Act 1925 (now 1972).

Q: *How do I know whether land is unregistered?*

A: Phrases like 'Fred holds the unregistered fee simple in Greenacres', or 'title to Greenacres is unregistered', or 'Greenacres has not yet been registered at the Land Registry' all refer to unregistered land.

The Land Charges Acts of 1925 and 1972

The Land Charges Act 1925 was the main originating Act. The Land Charges Act 1972 replaced the 1925 Act. These Acts were almost exclusively concerned with equitable interests.

Q: *So the Land Charges Act 1925, now the Land Charges Act 1972, dealt with equitable interests in unregistered land and the problems associated with the doctrine of notice?*

A: Yes. The rule relating to legal rights – legal rights bind the world – wasn't too much of a problem. Legal rights were generally discoverable either by looking at the documentation relating to the land, called the title deeds, or by a physical inspection of the land. With one exception, legal rights were not affected by the Land Charges Act 1925 or the 1972 Act. Equitable interests suffered from the problems discussed in Chapter 2. The aim was to remove these problems by requiring people with equitable interests over another's land to enter them on a register. The register could be inspected, or searched, by anyone who was thinking of buying the land, and he would know what equitable interests there were over the land. If a purchaser knew what equitable interests there were over the land before he bought it, the equitable interest would be binding on him. Look at the example which we used in Chapter 2, where Fred had granted Mr Black an equitable easement of a right of way over Greenacres.

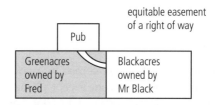

Fred then sold Greenacres to Peter.

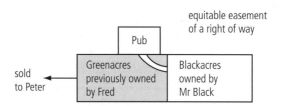

If Mr Black's equitable easement of a right of way is entered on a register, and Peter can search this register, then Peter can find out about Mr Black's interest. If Peter has the opportunity to find out about Mr Black's interest, it's fair to say that he should be bound by it, as it is his choice to buy Greenacres with Mr Black's interest included. Peter must then let Mr Black continue to use his right of way. If Peter doesn't like the idea of Mr Black's right of way over Greenacres, he can find somewhere else to buy. This system for the protection of equitable interests was originally governed by the Land Charges Act 1925 and is now governed by the Land Charges Act 1972.

When Mr Black originally acquired the equitable easement of a right of way over Greenacres, you could say that a burden or a charge was imposed on the land Greenacres. The aim was to ensure that all the different charges, or land charges as they're called, were entered on a register called, not unsurprisingly, the Land Charges Register. The interests that had to be entered on the Land Charges Register were virtually all equitable interests, and each interest or charge was given a class of its own. These classes are denoted alphabetically and are listed below. The ones you are most likely to come across are in bold.

Class A   – financial charges on land created by statute
Class B   – charges imposed automatically by statute
Class C(i)   – **a puisne mortgage**
Class C(ii)   – a limited owner's charge
Class C(iii) – a general equitable charge
Class C(iv) – **an estate contract**
Class D(i)   – an Inland Revenue charge
Class D(ii) – **a restrictive covenant**
Class D(iii) – **an equitable easement**
Class E   – a charge concerning annuities
Class F   – **a spouse's statutory right of occupation**

The detail of where each individual interest in land fits into the unregistered land system is given in the chapter on that interest.

The Land Charges Act of 1972 allows for the entry of an equitable easement of a right of way as a land charge on the Land Charges Register. If it is entered as a land charge, it will be binding on anyone who buys Greenacres from Fred (Peter in our example). First, you must decide in whose interest it is to enter the equitable easement on the Land Charges Register. Here, it's in Mr Black's interest to enter it on the Land Charges Register.

Q: *Why is it in Mr Black's interest to do so and not Fred's?*

A: Because Mr Black has the benefit of the right of way over Greenacres. He needs to protect himself against anyone who buys Greenacres who may wish to stop him using his right of way, and he does so by entering his interest as a land charge. It will then be binding on anyone who buys Greenacres from Fred. It is not in Fred's interest to announce to the world via a register that Mr Black has a right of way over his land, because all he does is to reduce the selling price of Greenacres.

Q: *How should Mr Black enter his equitable easement as a land charge?*

A: Look at the classification list to find out where equitable easements fit into the system. They are in class D(iii), and so Mr Black's equitable easement must be entered as a class D(iii) land charge. The Land Charges Register is a name-based system. Interests are entered against the name of the estate owner of the land over which the right is exercised. As a shorthand here we will use the lay phrase 'owner of the land' to denote the estate owner. This means Mr Black has to enter his equitable easement of a right of way as a class D(iii) land charge against Fred's name on the Register. Note the use of the word 'enter'. In reality you register your interest. However, there are several uses of the word 'register' around now, and, by the time we've covered registered land, there are even more. It's therefore easier to use the word 'enter' here; otherwise it just gets more and more confusing.

Q: *Presumably, then, whatever interest Mr Black has over Fred's land, he has to find the correct class for it and then enter it under that class against Fred's name?*

A: Yes. Remember, though, that you're entering only equitable interests here, with just the one exception. The one exception is in Class C(i). It's called a puisne (pronounced 'puny') mortgage and it's covered in Chapter 18.

UNREGISTERED LAND—THE LAND CHARGES ACTS 1925 AND 1972

The registration of an equitable interest as a land charge

THE RULES BEFORE 1926

UNREGISTERED LAND—THE LAND CHARGES ACTS 1925 AND 1972

Box A

1. Legal rights bind the world.

2. Equitable rights bind everyone except a *bona fide* purchaser of a legal estate for value without notice of the equitable interest – the doctrine of notice.

Box B

Non-registrable legal rights bind the world.

Box C

Non-registrable equitable interests are subject to the pre-1926 equitable rule – Equitable rights bind everyone except a *bona fide* purchaser of a legal estate for value without notice of the equitable interest – the doctrine of notice.

Box D

Registrable land charges entered on the Land Charges Register bind all

Section 198 of the Law of Property Act 1925

Box E

If an equitable interest is in class C(iv), D(i), D(ii) or D(iii) and has not been entered on the Land Charges Register, it is not binding on a purchaser of a legal estate for money or money's worth. Money or money's worth does not include marriage consideration.

Section 4(6) of the Land Charges Act 1972

Box F

If an equitable interest is in class A, B, C(i), C(ii), C(iii) or F and has not been entered on the Land Charges Register, it is not binding on a purchaser of a legal or equitable estate for valuable consideration. Valuable consideration does include marriage consideration.

Sections 4(2), (5), (8) and 17(1) of the Land Charges Act 1972

The unregistered land system in operation

It's now possible to look at how the unregistered land system works overall. You need to look at the chart on page 38 which describes this process. We will continue to use Fred, Greenacres, Mr Black's equitable easement of a right of way, and Peter as an example.

The rules before 1926

> **Box A**
>
> **1.** Legal rights bind the world.
>
> **2.** Equitable rights bind everyone except a *bona fide* purchaser of a legal estate for value without notice of the equitable interest—the doctrine of notice.

Box A1 Legal rights bind the world

Box A2 Equitable rights bind everyone except a *bona fide* purchaser of a legal estate for value without notice of the equitable interest – the doctrine of notice.

This was the position before 1926, as discussed in Chapter 2.

The rules after 1925 – The Land Charges Act 1925, now the Land Charges Act 1972

> **Box B**
>
> Non-registrable legal rights bind the world.

Apart from the exception in Class C(i), the Land Charges Acts of 1925 and 1972 did not make any provision for legal rights. So legal rights bound the world before 1926 (Box A1), and legal rights still bind the world even after the Land Charges Acts of 1925 and 1972 (Box B).

Q: *Why wasn't anything done about legal rights?*

A: Because they weren't the problem. They were rights created formally and it was quite difficult to miss them. Look at the example where Mr Black has a legal easement of a right of way over Greenacres.

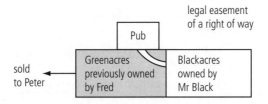

Mr Black's legal easement would bind Peter both before (Box A1), and after (Box B) 1926. There is no provision in the Land Charges Act for entering legal rights on the Land Charges Register, and this was intentional.

> **Box C**
>
> Non-registrable equitable interests are subject to the
> pre-1926 equitable rule – Equitable rights bind everyone
> except a *bona fide* purchaser of a legal estate for value
> without notice of the equitable interest – the doctrine of
> notice.

The Land Charges Act 1972 lists a number of commercial interests in land which can be protected by entering a land charge. Here, 'commercial' means interests associated with the value and exploitation of land. Those equitable interests not on the list are protected by other mechanisms. The most important equitable interests you will come across here are family-type equitable interests, which are protected by a mechanism called overreaching, discussed in Chapter 11. The mechanism of overreaching was designed to protect not only people holding these family-type interests in land but also a purchaser of the land. Imagine a young couple, Darren and Sally. Darren bought a house for himself and Sally to live in. The house was conveyed to Darren alone, so only his name appeared on the legal title. If Sally had contributed to the purchase price of the house, she would have an interest in the house. She couldn't have a legal interest because she wasn't on the legal title, but she would have an equitable interest, an interest recognised in equity. The mechanism of overreaching was designed to protect Sally's interest in the house, and it also enabled a purchaser, Peter in our example, to avoid her interest altogether. However, if Peter didn't use this mechanism to avoid her interest altogether, whether he was bound by it still depended on the doctrine of notice. It is sufficient to realise for now that there is an important category of equitable family interests that cannot be entered on the Land Charges Register, but that Peter is given a way of avoiding them binding him. If he chooses not to use this way, his position will be governed by the doctrine of notice.

Equitable easements created before 1926 and restrictive covenants created before 1926 are interests you may come across. They are also excluded from being entered as land charges and are still covered by the doctrine of notice. A restrictive covenant is a promise not to do something on land. Imagine that Mr Black had purchased Blackacres from Fred and had promised not to build more than one house on Blackacres. This would be a restrictive covenant, a promise not to do something on Blackacres. Both equitable easements and restrictive covenants created before 1926 are examples of other equitable interests that cannot be entered on the Land Charges Register, and are therefore subject to the doctrine of notice.

> **Box D**
>
> Registrable land charges entered on the Land Charges
> Register bind all
>
> Section 198 of the Law of Property Act 1925

The Land Charges Act 1972 lists those equitable interests that should be entered on the Land Charges Register. If an equitable interest has been entered as a land charge on the Land Charges Register, it constitutes actual notice to everyone in the world under section 198 of the Law of Property Act 1925. Actual notice means that everyone is deemed to have notice of the land charge and will therefore be bound by it.

In our example, Fred had granted an equitable easement of a right of way to Mr Black.

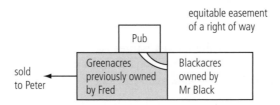

If Mr Black enters his equitable easement of a right of way as a class D(iii) land charge against Fred's name on the Land Charges Register, it constitutes actual notice to the whole of the world and will bind anyone who buys Greenacres, Peter in our example.

Q: *And the rationale is that before Peter decides to buy Greenacres he can go and search the Land Charges Register and see whether there are any entries against Fred's name? If he doesn't like what he sees, he needn't buy Greenacres.*

A: That's the whole idea behind having a central Land Charges Register. People can enter their equitable interests over someone else's land, and other people can find out about their equitable interests. You can inspect the Land Charges Register yourself under section 9 of the Land Charges Act 1972, but usually a search will be carried out by the Land Charges Department, which will issue a search certificate detailing the land charges affecting the land. Of course, Mr Black must enter his equitable easement of a right of way on the Land Charges Register the moment it's created, or at least before Fred sells Greenacres to Peter. This is because Mr Black won't know whether, or when, Fred may sell Greenacres to Peter. If Mr Black's interest is not entered on the Register before Peter buys Greenacres, then Peter will not be deemed to have actual notice under section 198 and it won't be binding on him.

Q: *So the whole aim of the exercise is to protect an interest over someone else's land in case the land over which the right is exercised is sold?*

A: Exactly.

Q: *What happens if Mr Black enters another land charge against Fred's name after Peter has searched the Land Charges Register but before Greenacres has been sold to him?*

A: There is a priority period in favour of Peter under sections 11(5) and (6) of the Land Charges Act 1972. If Peter completes the purchase of Greenacres within 15 working days of the date of an official search certificate, he will not be affected by a land charge entered on the Land Charges Register in that 15-day period.

Now look at what happens if an equitable interest is not protected as a land charge.

> **Box E**
>
> If an equitable interest is in class C(iv), D(i), D(ii) or D(iii) and has not been entered on the Land Charges Register, it is not binding on a purchaser of a legal estate for money or money's worth. Money or money's worth does not include marriage consideration.
>
> Section 4(6) of the Land Charges Act 1972

Under section 4(6) of the Land Charges Act 1972 equitable interests within these particular classes will not be binding on a certain type of purchaser if they have not been entered on the Land Charges Register.

Q: *In our example, then, you're saying that if Mr Black has the opportunity to enter his equitable easement of a right of way as a class D(iii) land charge, but does not do so, his equitable easement of a right of way will not be binding on a purchaser of a legal estate for money or money's worth?*

A: Correct. In our example, Peter purchased the legal estate of Greenacres for money. Money is implicit in the word 'sold'. If Mr Black had not entered a class D(iii) land charge against Fred's name, Peter would not be bound by the equitable easement and could stop Mr Black using his right of way.

Q: *That seems quite harsh, doesn't it?*

A: Not really. Mr Black is given the opportunity to enter his equitable interest on the Land Charges Register and he's chosen not to do so. That means other people can't find out about it, so it seems quite fair that the interest is not binding on them. After all, what's the point of a register if it's only voluntary?

Q: *Why wouldn't Mr Black enter his interest on the Register?*

A: Ignorance. Error. Inadequate solicitor. Any or all of these.

Q: *What's the effect of marriage consideration not being included in the definition of money or money's worth?*

A: Imagine that, instead of selling Greenacres to Peter, Fred had transferred Greenacres to him on the basis that he married Fred's beautiful daughter, Belinda. Peter had agreed and married Belinda. Peter would have given marriage consideration for Greenacres. If Mr Black had not entered his equitable easement of a right of way as a class D(iii) land charge against Fred's name, it would still be binding on Peter, as he had given marriage consideration which does not count as money or money's worth because you can't put a monetary value on marriage.

Q: *What happens if Mr Black has not entered his equitable easement as a class D(iii) land charge and Peter inherits Greenacres from Fred, or Fred has given Greenacres to him as a gift?*

A: In this case, Peter is not a purchaser for money or money's worth because he has given no consideration for Greenacres. Again, Mr Black's equitable easement will be binding on him.

Q: *Doesn't that seem a bit unfair on Peter though?*

A: No. Remember that Peter has given no consideration at all for Greenacres here and has therefore gained much from the transaction, even though Mr Black's interest is binding on him.

Box F

If an equitable interest is in class A, B, C(i), C(ii), C(iii) or F and has not been entered on the Land Charges Register, it is not binding on a purchaser of a legal or equitable estate for valuable consideration. Valuable consideration does include marriage consideration.

Sections 4(2), (5), (8) and 17(1) of the Land Charges Act 1972

If an equitable interest is in class A, B, C(i), C(ii), C(iii) or F, and has not been entered on the Land Charges Register, it is not binding on a purchaser of a legal or equitable estate for valuable consideration: see sections 4(2), (5), (8), and 17(1) of the Land Charges Act 1972. This definition is wider than the one in Box E because it includes the purchaser of a legal or equitable estate and it includes marriage consideration. If Mr Black had an equitable interest that came into one of these classes but had not entered it on the Land Charges Register, Peter would be deemed to have given valuable consideration whether he had given hard cash for Greenacres or married Belinda. He would therefore not be bound by the equitable interest. Again, as in Box E, if Mr Black had not entered a land charge in any of these classes and Peter had inherited Greenacres or received the land as a gift from Fred, he wouldn't be a purchaser for valuable consideration, and so whatever right Mr Black had failed to protect would still be binding on him. Peter should think himself fortunate that he owns Greenacres at all.

Summary of the land charges system

Land that was not transferred to the registered land system after 1925 remained unregistered land. The original Land Charges Act 1925 was implemented to resolve the problem of equitable interests and the doctrine of notice in unregistered land. It enabled certain equitable interests in unregistered land to be entered on the Land Charges Register using a name-based system. The Land Charges Act 1972 replaced the 1925 Act.

Using the Land Charges Act 1972

Most problem scenarios look at one or both of the following. First, you are asked to examine how an interest between two parties has been created. Is it a valid interest? Has it been created in a way that is recognised at law or in equity? Does the creation of the interest have to satisfy any statutory formalities? Secondly, you are asked to look at what happens when the land which the interest is over is sold on to a third party. Look at the example of Fred, Mr Black and Peter again. Fred, the owner of Greenacres, has given Mr Black, who owns Blackacres, a right over Greenacres. Part of the question could well be to look at how any particular right is created, and whether Fred and Mr Black have satisfied any requirements for its valid creation. The other part of the question could be to look at what happens when Greenacres is sold to Peter. Does Peter have to let Mr Black continue to use his right over Greenacres?

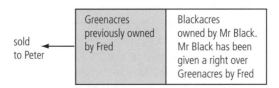

You can establish a procedure to check whether an interest in unregistered land is binding on a purchaser of the land that the right is over.

Step 1. Establish whether it is a legal or equitable interest that is being claimed. If it is a legal interest, legal rights bind the world both before 1926 (Box A1), and, excluding a puisne mortgage, after then (Box B). If it is an equitable interest, you must see whether the equitable interest is capable of entry as a land charge under the Land Charges Act 1972.

Step 2. If the equitable interest is not capable of entry as a land charge, use Box C and the rule that governed equitable interests before 1926, known as the doctrine of notice. If the equitable interest is capable of entry as a land charge, work out in whose interest it is to enter it as a land charge. This will be the person who benefits from the equitable interest.

Step 3. Check to see whether that person has entered his equitable interest as a land charge in the correct class on the Land Charges Register against the name of the owner of the land that the right is over.

▶ An equitable interest that has been entered as a land charge binds everyone who takes the land under section 198 of the Law of Property Act 1925 (Box D).
▶ If the equitable interest has not been entered as a land charge, it will not be binding on some classes of purchaser (Boxes E and F).

You can apply this to the example we've been using of Fred, Peter and Mr Black's right of way. Imagine that Fred had granted an equitable easement of a right of way over Greenacres to Mr Black six years ago and that Peter has just purchased Greenacres.

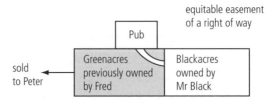

Step 1. Mr Black is claiming an equitable easement. An equitable easement is an equitable interest. An equitable easement created after 1925 is capable of entry as a land charge under the Land Charges Act 1972.

Step 2. It was in Mr Black's interest to enter the equitable easement as a land charge as he receives the benefit from it.

Step 3. Mr Black should have entered his equitable easement as a class D(iii) land charge against Fred's name on the Land Charges Register as Fred owns the land that Mr Black's right is over.

- ▶ If the equitable easement has been entered as a class D(iii) land charge, it will bind Peter under section 198 of the Law of Property Act 1925 and he must let Mr Black continue to use the right of way.
- ▶ If the equitable easement has not been entered as a class D(iii) land charge, it will not be binding on a purchaser of a legal estate for money or money's worth. Peter paid money and purchased the legal estate of Greenacres. If Mr Black has not entered his equitable easement as a land charge, Peter will not be bound by it and can stop Mr Black using the right of way.

And, at the risk of repetition here, Mr Black must enter his equitable easement of a right of way on the Land Charges Register the moment it's created, or at least before Fred sells Greenacres to Peter. This is because Mr Black won't know whether, or when, Fred may sell Greenacres to Peter. If Mr Black's interest is not entered on the Register before Peter buys Greenacres, then Peter will not be deemed to have actual notice under section 198 and the interest won't be binding on him.

Q: *Now that we have the Land Charges Register and anyone can see what's on the Register, is it fair to say that the doctrine of notice is no longer applicable to equitable interests that must be entered as a land charge?*

A: Yes. This was confirmed in *Midland Bank Trust Co Ltd v Green* (1981), a case in which the House of Lords was looking at the definition of money or money's worth. A son had an equitable interest in land owned by his father which he should have entered as a class C(iv) land charge against his father's name. He did not do so. Some six years later, his father discovered that the land charge had not been entered. The father then immediately sold the land to his wife, the son's mother, for a mere pittance. The wife was also aware that the land charge had never been entered. Box E states that an equitable interest that is in class C(iv) and not entered on the Land Charges Register is not binding on a purchaser of a legal estate for money or money's worth, the wife here. The Court of Appeal, through Lord Denning MR, argued that money or money's worth did not include a mere pittance or an undervaluation of the property. However, the House of Lords held that the mere pittance was still money or money's worth. As the son had not entered his equitable interest as a class C(iv) land charge on the Land Charges Register before his mother bought the land, his right was not binding on his mother, as her pittance still counted as money. It was also not binding on her despite the fact that she actually knew about his interest. This is quite fair really, but do you think the parents were trying to tell their son something? This case should warn you of the dangers of not complying with the Land Charges Act 1972.

The advantages and disadvantages of the Land Charges Act 1972

Q: *Did the Land Charges Register improve the situation relating to equitable interests?*

A: It is better than everyone having to rely on the doctrine of notice. However, it is flawed in several respects. The main flaw comes from the fact that it is a name-based system. People call themselves by nicknames or sometimes use their middle names so it's possible to search quite innocently against the wrong name. A classic example is found in *Oak Co-operative Building Society v Blackburn* (1968). Mr Blackburn's real name was Francis David Blackburn. He traded under the name Frank David Blackburn. The land charge was entered against the name Frank David Blackburn. The Building Society requisitioned a search against the name Francis Davis Blackburn. It was held that if you enter a land charge against a reasonable guess at the correct name, it will take priority over the interests of someone who does not search at all or who searches against the wrong name. It will not take priority over the interests of someone who requisitions a search against the correct name and who receives a certificate stating that there are no land charges entered against that name. In the case itself the Building Society had searched against the wrong name, and so the land charge took priority and was binding on it. Just to confuse matters further, one of the solicitors who had been involved was called Davis – so a recipe for disaster from the start. Another case that illustrates the difficulty in using a name-based system is *Diligent Finance Co Ltd v Alleyne* (1972).

Q: *What name are you supposed to use?*

A: The correct name you should enter a land charge against is the name that appears on the title deeds of the land. Title deeds are the documents showing the historical and current ownership of land. The correct name is the name of the owner of the land as it appears on these documents when the land was sold to him: see *Standard Property Investment plc v British Plastics Federation* (1985). You must also use the name on the title deeds to search against on the Land Charges Register. If you're buying land from Fred, for example, Fred should be only too pleased to help you in this process and show you his name on the title deeds to the house because he wants you to buy his property.

Q: *What happens if there's a mistake by the Land Charges Department, and the results from a search against the correct name give the all-clear when there are actually land charges against the name?*

A: Under section 10(4) of the Land Charges Act 1972 the search is deemed to be conclusive. The land charge that has been missed by officials will not bind the purchaser who has received the all-clear.

Q: *Is there a remedy for the person whose land charge is now no longer binding because of an official mistake?*

A: He must sue for negligence and claim damages.

Q: *Are there any more disadvantages?*

A: Yes. Cast your mind back to when Mr Black was exercising his equitable easement of a right of way over Greenacres, land that was owned by Fred. Peter then came along with a view to buying Greenacres from Fred. After Peter had looked round Greenacres and decided he wanted to buy it, Fred and Peter would have entered into an agreement, a contract, that Fred would sell Greenacres to Peter. This contract is called an estate contract. It is a contract to sell a legal estate in land and should be entered by Peter as a class C(iv) land charge.

Q: *Why should Peter enter his estate contract as a land charge?*

A: An estate contract is an equitable interest. If it's entered as a class C(iv) land charge it binds everyone under section 198 of the Law of Property Act 1925 (Box D). It says to the rest of the world 'I have an agreement, a contract to buy Greenacres, and my right in that contract is now binding on everyone'. It's in Peter's interest to enter his contract as a land charge against the name of the owner over whose land he has the right – here Fred. Peter enters his contract as a class C(iv) land charge against Fred's name. Imagine that Peter then bumps into Albert, who has always wanted to buy Greenacres. Albert offers Peter such a large sum of money to sell Greenacres to him that Peter can't refuse his offer. Peter and Albert themselves then enter into a contract whereby Peter agrees to sell Greenacres to Albert. This contract should be entered as a class C(iv) land charge by Albert on the Land Charges Register against the name of the owner over whose land his right is over. Albert thinks Peter is the owner.

Q: *But is there a problem here because Fred hasn't sold the legal estate by deed to Peter yet? Fred is still the owner of Greenacres.*

A: Yes. If Albert enters his estate contract as a class C(iv) land charge against Peter's name he hasn't protected his interest at all because he's got the wrong owner and therefore the wrong name. If Peter bought Greenacres and then decided to sell it to Matilda, Albert would have no redress against Matilda because his land charge was not entered against the name of the true owner of the land, who was Fred. Albert could only sue Peter for damages for breach of contract.

Q: *Why was the Land Charges Register introduced when there are so many potential problems with it?*

A: The original 1925 Land Charges Act, whatever its defects, was seen as a temporary measure. It would deal immediately with the problem of equitable interests while the new superior system of land registration under the Land Registration Act 1925 was being imposed on the country during the following decades. Any problems with the Land Charges Register would go away as more and more land came under the new system. As at mid 2013 approximately 23 million titles, representing just over 80% of the land area in England and Wales, have been registered. A number of large ancient estates remain to be registered. This remaining unregistered land still comes under the Land Charges Act 1972 and its defects.

Summary of the advantages and disadvantages of the Land Charges Act 1972

The problems of the doctrine of notice were addressed by introducing a system for protecting certain equitable interests in unregistered land on the Land Charges

Register. However, not all equitable interests are capable of being entered as a land charge. There are also defects within the system, mainly stemming from the fact that it is a name-based system.

Buying and selling unregistered land

This section looks at how the Land Charges Register fits into the scheme of buying and selling unregistered land. Take, again, the example of Fred, who wishes to sell Greenacres to Peter.

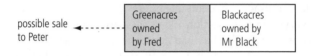

possible sale to Peter ◄-------- | Greenacres owned by Fred | Blackacres owned by Mr Black |

Before Peter purchases Greenacres he will want to know:

- that Fred actually owns Greenacres;
- whether Greenacres can claim the benefit of rights over other land, for example over Blackacres; and
- what right others have over Greenacres: for example, what rights Mr Black may have.

Let's take each of these points in turn.

The first piece of information Peter will want to find out about is whether Fred actually owns Greenacres. In unregistered land, proof of ownership of land, or proof of title as it's called, is found in the documents relating to the previous purchases and sales of the land in question. Put together, these documents are known as title deeds: the deeds that give evidence of ownership. You must not confuse 'title deeds' with 'a deed'. Title deeds are the documents showing the historical and current ownership of land. A deed is a formal document, and need not have anything to do with houses or land at all. The title deeds to land will show who owned the land and at what time. If you ask any older member of your family they will certainly remember title deeds. This title deed documentation will show any sale or transfer of the land, any legal mortgages which have been taken out over the land, and all the paperwork relating to the property if any previous owner has died, including the subsequent transfer of the land.

Q: *How many documents does the owner have to produce to prove ownership?*

A: Under section 23 of the Law of Property Act 1969, the owner has to produce a good root of title which is at least 15 years old, that is a document that is at least 15 years old that gives a description of the land, deals with the entire estate, both legal and equitable, and shows previous ownership. A document showing the previous sale of the land is a good example, as this sort of information should be there. Note that you must go back at least 15 years to the first good root of title before the 15-year minimum period. Take the following example:

    1980 – Greenacres sold by Claudia to Syed
    1992 – Greenacres sold by Syed to Tom
    1999 – Greenacres sold by Tom to Jim

2002 – Greenacres sold by Jim to Tara
2008 – Greenacres sold by Tara to Fred
2013 – Peter is thinking of buying Greenacres

Peter must search back to the first good root of title that is at least 15 years old. This means that in 2013 he must go back to 1998 as a minimum. The first good root of title before this 15-year minimum period is in the document of sale from Syed to Tom in 1992. Peter must then be able to see an unbroken chain of ownership right up to Fred.

Q: *What's the significance of going back 15 years?*

A: You may well have heard of squatter's rights, which is known as adverse possession in legal terms. If a squatter uses someone else's unregistered land as his own for 12 years, the original owner will be time-barred from reclaiming possession of the land. You can also add together the periods of time spent by different squatters to make up the 12 years. If Fred can prove ownership for at least 15 years, it at least shows that he has acquired the land by squatter's rights, as you can add the periods of time of any different owners together. Anyone trying to claim ownership before the 15-year period will now be time-barred from doing so. You can assume that there were no squatters during the 15-year period of time if the previous purchasers of Greenacres paid money for the land, because, having paid good money, they would have evicted any squatters.

Q: *Can you rely completely on the documentation to show that a vendor owns the land he is selling?*

A: Not quite. There is still an outside chance that a squatter has managed to squat on Greenacres in the 15-year period, perhaps because Greenacres was inherited by Fred and he hadn't taken much interest in the land. Therefore, although Peter can rely to a large extent on the documentary proof of ownership of Greenacres, he must still inspect the land in person before he buys for any evidence of the outside chance of a squatter.

Q: *What happens if Fred can't produce documentation that satisfies the minimum 15-year period?*

A: Peter is allowed to withdraw from the sale on the basis that Fred cannot show good title to, and therefore ownership of, Greenacres.

The next piece of information Peter will want to know is what rights Greenacres has over other land, for example over Blackacres.

Generally, the details of these rights will be found with the documentation of Greenacres. It's in the interest of the owner of Greenacres to keep a record of these rights with the title deeds because they will be a selling point of the house.

And, last but not least, Peter will want to find out what rights others may have over Greenacres; for example, what rights Mr Black may have.

You know from the previous discussion in this chapter that Peter will be bound by any legal rights that other people have over Greenacres (Box B), as legal rights bind the world. Some of these may be discoverable, but, even if they aren't, Peter will still be bound by them. Peter will also be bound by any equitable family interests that are not capable of being entered on the Land Charges Register if he

HOW INTERESTS IN UNREGISTERED LAND ARE PROTECTED

The type of interest	A legal right that binds the world	An equitable interest that must be entered as a land charge	An equitable interest governed by the pre-1926 equitable rule—the doctrine of notice
A contract to sell land or create an interest in land		Class C(iv)	
An option to purchase land		Class C(iv)	
A legal lease created by deed	✓		
A legal lease created under s.54(2) of the Law of Property Act 1925	✓		
An equitable lease		Class C(iv)	
An equitable interest under a trust of land or under a strict settlement that has not been overreached			✓
An equity by estoppel			✓
The rights of an adverse possessor (squatter's rights)	✓		
A legal easement	✓		
An equitable easement created before 1926			✓
An equitable easement created after 1925		Class D(iii)	
A restrictive covenant created before 1926			✓
A restrictive covenant created after 1925		Class D(ii)	
A legal mortgage	✓		
A puisne mortgage		Class C(i)—the only legal right capable of entry as a land charge	
A spouse's statutory right of occupation		Class F	

has notice of them (Box C), unless he has availed himself of the way of avoiding them altogether. He will also be bound by any other equitable interests not capable of entry on the Land Charges Register, again if he has notice of them (Box C). Peter will also be bound by any entries appearing on the Land Charges Register (Box D), which means he must search against the names of previous owners of Greenacres to find out whether there are any land charges entered against their names. If there are, he will be bound by these land charges if he buys Greenacres. If Peter doesn't like what he sees, he may decide to look elsewhere for somewhere to live.

Q: *When Peter searches against the names of previous owners of Greenacres to see whether there are any land charges entered against them, how many names does he have to look against?*

A: He has to look against the name of every person who has owned Greenacres since 1925. There is a problem here, as the vendor, Fred, has to produce only documentation showing a good root of title which is at least 15 years old. The names of any people who owned Greenacres before the minimum 15-year period do not have to be divulged. If Peter doesn't know these names, he cannot search against them, and so he may be bound by land charges that he couldn't possibly have discovered. In 1925 this wasn't so much of a problem because a purchaser had to look back for a minimum of 30 years to the first good root of title. When the minimum period of time was reduced in 1969 to 15 years by section 23 of the Law of Property Act 1969, the potential problems were rather ignored because people were hoping to rely on the superior system introduced by the Land Registration Act 1925. As all land was transferred to the superior system, this particular problem would disappear. However, at the same time as the minimum period of time was reduced, section 25(1) of the Law of Property Act 1969 set up a system of compensation for people who found themselves bound by land charges that they couldn't have found out about. Surprisingly, there have been very few claims. Any previous search certificates relating to the time before the 15-year minimum period tend to be kept with the title deeds of the land so a purchaser can look at them and see what entries were made before then. Also, not all interests in land are created for ever, or even for a long period of time.

You can now summarise the interests that will bind Peter when he buys Greenacres from Fred. These are any legal rights that other people have over Greenacres. Peter will be bound by any entries on the Land Charges Register and by any equitable family interests that are not capable of being entered on the Land Charges Register if he has notice of them, unless he has availed himself of the way of avoiding them. He will also be bound by any other equitable interests that are not capable of being entered on the Land Charges Register, again if he has notice of them.

The table on page 50 is for reference for you to look back at during your studies. It shows the overall picture of how the main interests are protected in unregistered land. The different interests are discussed in detail in the relevant chapter.

Further reading

J. Howell, 'The Doctrine of Notice: an Historical Perspective', *Conv and Prop Law*, Nov/Dec (1997) 431

Chapter 4

Registered land

www.palgrave.com/law/Stroud4e

Introduction

Three major Acts were passed in 1925. The first was the Law of Property Act 1925. The second was the Land Charges Act 1925, now the Land Charges Act 1972, which related to unregistered land. The third was the Land Registration Act 1925, which introduced a system of land registration that aimed to enable a purchaser to be able to see accurately

▶ who actually owned the land he wished to purchase;
▶ whether the land he wished to purchase could claim the benefit of rights over other land; and, most importantly,
▶ what rights other people held over the land he wished to purchase.

Look at the diagram below.

Before Peter purchases Greenacres he will want to know

▶ that Fred actually owns Greenacres;
▶ whether Greenacres can claim the benefit of rights over other land, for example over Blackacres; and
▶ what right others have over Greenacres, for example, what rights Mr Black may have.

The Land Registration Act 1925, which has now been replaced by the Land Registration Act 2002, to a large extent made it possible to find out this sort of information. Land that is governed by any Land Registration Act is known as registered land. The Land Registration Act 2002 mainly came into force at the end of 2003, so this chapter concentrates on the 2002 Act. Some textbooks will give you all the information about registered land at the beginning, whereas others will put the chapter on registered land at the end of the book. Neither way is satisfactory. If the chapter is at the beginning, you won't understand the actual interest in land at that point. If the chapter is at the end, you'll be wondering all the way through the book how you protect any interest you have in the land against other people. So we'll adopt the middle way. This tells you about the reasons for the registered land system and the principles of how it works, but looks at each of the different interests in land in the registered system in detail in the relevant chapter on that interest.

Q: *How do I know whether land is registered?*

A: Phrases like 'Fred holds the registered fee simple in Greenacres', or 'title to Greenacres is registered', or 'Fred is the registered proprietor of Greenacres' all refer to registered land.

The Registers of the Land Registration Act 2002

Q: *I imagine that if you want to make it possible to find out whether someone really owns the land, or whether someone else has rights over it, this kind of information should be written down somewhere, shouldn't it?*

A: It is. The country is divided into areas, each with its own District Land Registry, where this information is kept. The person responsible overall for the system is called the Chief Land Registrar. An individual register of a property will be held at the appropriate District Land Registry. This individual register is divided into three sections: the first called the Property Register, the second called the Proprietorship Register and the third called the Charges Register. These three sections contain the following information.

The Property Register

This describes the property, usually its postal address, and any rights the owner of the property has over other land. There will be reference to a filed plan of the property, which will also show the general boundaries. The case of *Milsum v Gorman (Easements)* (2011) confirmed that boundaries on a filed title plan are not definitive but general only. If people want their boundaries to be precise they must apply to the Land Registry to have the exact line of the boundary determined under Part 10 of the Land Registration Rules 2002. A fee is payable and the exact line of the boundary is recorded on the registered title.

The Proprietorship Register

This gives the name and address of the registered owner, known as the registered proprietor. This Register also lists restrictions that should be complied with before any dealing with the land takes place, and also any restrictions imposed on the power of the registered proprietor to deal with the land. For example, if the registered proprietor has been declared bankrupt, his affairs will be dealt with by a trustee in bankruptcy. The registered proprietor will be prevented from dealing with the property himself in case he sells the land and disappears with the proceeds. This restriction on the registered proprietor's powers to deal with the property will be put on the Proprietorship Register.

The Charges Register

This Register contains details of other people's rights over the property. These are technically called encumbrances on the land.

From now on we will use the word Register to cover all three Registers for each property.

Q: *Before you buy a house, can you inspect the Register?*

A: Before 1988 you could search the Register only if you were actually buying the property. After the 1988 Land Registration Act the Register was opened to the public, with the idea of making dealings with land more transparent. If you want to look at the entry of a property in the Register, you have to pay a fee. Although it is possible for people to make searches personally, it is far more common for a search to be requested and then to be undertaken by Land Registry staff.

Q: *Does the actual owner of the land, the registered proprietor, receive a copy of the information in the file?*

A: He receives a title information document which is a copy of the Register. However, the Register itself constitutes actual proof if there is any dispute, for the following reason. Imagine you purchased Greenacres, which was registered land, and you obtained a title information document. Some years later you granted a right over Greenacres to Mr Black. Although that newly created right would be entered on the relevant Register at the District Land Registry, the title information document you held would be out of date because it wouldn't contain information about the newly created right. This is why a purchaser of land always has to consult the Register, because the registered proprietor's document could be out of date. In the not-so-distant future dealings will be carried out electronically, and so paper copies will become redundant.

The basic principles behind the Land Registration Acts 1925 and 2002

Now that you understand what information is held at the District Land Registry, it's possible to look at the basic principles behind these Acts. The Land Registration Act 2002 repealed the 1925 Act, but is still based on many of the same principles and ideas. It also deals with some of its shortcomings.

Title (ownership) to land is registered

Although we refer to registered land, it is actually title to a registrable estate that is registered.

Q: *What is meant by title to a registrable estate?*

A: If you remember from Chapter 1, Box A, you do not actually own land, but you own an estate in it. You can own a freehold estate, which is one that has no foreseeable end to it. The lay term for this is ownership, as in 'Fred owns Greenacres'. Or you can own a leasehold estate, where the amount of time you hold the land for is set. The Land Registration Act 2002 allows for the actual substantive registration of the freehold estate and certain leasehold estates. Each of these estates is registered with its own number, called a title number, and is shown in the Property Register, where it will appear as something like:

Title number 31222
The freehold property of Greenacres, 99 Green Road, Greentown.

Or alternatively it could say:

Title number 12344
The leasehold property of Blackacres, 22 Black Road, Greentown.

The title to land is a person's claim to ownership of the land. When you register your title, you are registering your claim to ownership of a freehold estate or your claim to ownership of certain leasehold estates. So although it looks as though you're registering the land, you are actually registering your claim to ownership of a registrable estate in land.

Title is guaranteed by the state

The basic principle here is that once title or ownership is registered, it is guaranteed by the state. If you have been registered as proprietor of a registrable estate, the state will guarantee that you have effective ownership of the estate. This makes the position of a purchaser far more secure, as he no longer has to rely on title deeds to prove that the vendor owns the land.

Section 58(1) of the Land Registration Act 2002 states:

> If, on the entry of a person in the register as the proprietor of a legal estate, the legal estate would not otherwise be vested in him, it shall be deemed to be vested in him as a result of the registration.

This means that even if a person wasn't entitled to the legal estate, but was still registered as proprietor, section 58(1) of the Land Registration Act 2002 would deem that he was now so entitled because the Register guarantees title or ownership. He would remain registered as proprietor unless the Register was amended.

If a defect in the title is found after a purchaser has acquired land, there are provisions for amendment of the Register and the award of compensation. Although there were fears that amendment of the Register would detract from the state guarantee of title, this has not been a problem in practice.

The Register should reflect the state of the title as far as possible

The aim was to show as many rights as possible that other people held over the land on the Register. This would enable purchasers to see exactly what they were buying. It would also allow people to protect their interests in the land on the basis that if an interest was on the Register it would bind a purchaser. This aim has largely been achieved, although there is one class of interest that does not appear on the Register and which is discussed in full on page 63.

E-conveyancing

The Land Registration Act 2002 is important because it allowed for the introduction of a computerised system for buying and selling land, a system known as e-conveyancing. The idea is that all dealings and transactions with land must be registered online, thereby saving time, paper and money. There has been some development here but, following a third consultation paper in March 2010, the Land Registry has come to the conclusion that the development of an e-transfer system should be put on hold until there is a healthier financial climate and more movement in the property and mortgage market. Work will concentrate on a simpler e-delivery service whereby applications for most transactions, together with scanned documents, would be lodged and confirmed electronically. As with e-commerce and e-learning, adding 'e-' to something will make everything so much better.

Distinguishing between 'first registration of title' and 'dispositions of registered land'

It is now important to distinguish between 'first registration of title' and what are called 'dispositions of registered land'. First registration of title occurs when land which was previously unregistered becomes registered land. A disposition of registered land occurs when land is already registered and then something happens to it. It could be sold, transferred or some other interest created over it, for example.

The next part of this chapter deals with first registration of title. Once we've done this we'll move on to look at the position when some transaction takes place concerning land that has already been registered.

Events which trigger the first registration of land that was previously unregistered land

We will talk about registering the land because it's easier but, in reality, it is actually title to a registrable estate that is registered.

Q: *Why isn't all land registered already?*

A: There were a few attempts to produce a working system for the registration of land during the nineteenth century, but they didn't come to much. The Land Registration Act 1925 was the first major concerted effort. When the system for registering land was introduced under that Act, you couldn't expect all land in this country to be catalogued overnight onto pieces of paper held at the District Land Registries. It had to be a gradual process. So, in 1925, there were some areas in England where it was compulsory to register dealings with land on the occasion of specified trigger events. The main example of a trigger event was the sale of land. In 1990 the whole of the country was made subject to the compulsory registration of dealings with land on the occasion of these trigger events. The main trigger events now given in section 4 of the Land Registration Act 2002 are as follows. We'll use Gladys and Fred as an example to show how they work in practice. Greenacres is unregistered land owned by Gladys.

MAIN TRIGGER EVENTS UNDER SECTION 4 OF THE LAND REGISTRATION ACT 2002	

TRIGGER EVENT	ACTION TO BE TAKEN
If Gladys sells or gives Greenacres to Fred	Fred must register any of these dealings at the District Land Registry
If Fred inherits Greenacres from Gladys	
If Gladys grants a legal lease of more than seven years to Fred	
If Gladys grants a legal lease to Fred but the lease doesn't take effect in possession (start) for a period of at least three months	
If Gladys creates a first legal mortgage over Greenacres with Bundy's Bank	Bundy's Bank must register this mortgage at the District Land Registry

Q: *Following one of these trigger events, whose responsibility is it to register the transaction?*

A: The person who buys the land or who receives the land by gift or inheritance or the person who takes the lease. This is Fred in our example. In the case of a mortgage, the lender of the money must register the mortgage. This is Bundy's Bank here.

Q: *What happens when Fred makes an application for first registration?*

A: Take each of the trigger events individually.

If Gladys sells or gives Greenacres to Fred

or

If Fred inherits Greenacres from Gladys

The procedures of conveyancing in unregistered land will govern the sale or transfer. These procedures are discussed in Chapter 3, at page 48. Once Greenacres has been either sold or transferred to Fred, an application must be made by Fred for registration. The Registrar will check through all the documents relating to the history of the land, and, if he's satisfied that everything is in order, he will register Fred as proprietor. The Registrar will also transfer all the interests that previously existed over Greenacres onto the Register at the District Land Registry. Fred will take Greenacres subject to these interests that are now on the Register. Fred will also take Greenacres subject to a category of interests that are called interests that override. These interests do not appear on the Register and are found in Schedule 1 to the Land Registration Act 2002. Although it may appear rather self-defeating that some interests don't appear on the Register, an explanation of why they exist is given later in this chapter on page 63. And there you have it. Greenacres is now registered land. The only difficulty of course is that the registered land system has its own language. This is different from that used in unregistered land, so you'll now be in registered land 'speak'.

If Gladys grants a legal lease of more than seven years to Fred

or

If Gladys grants a legal lease to Fred but the lease doesn't take effect in possession (start) for a period of at least three months

In either of these cases Fred will apply to be registered as proprietor of the legal lease which will receive its own title number.

Q: *Is Greenacres itself, the freehold estate, registered at the same time, or is it just the legal lease, the leasehold estate, that is registered?*

A: Just the legal lease. This means that Gladys will still own the unregistered freehold estate of Greenacres while Fred will be registered as proprietor of a registered leasehold estate over Greenacres.

Q: *When will Greenacres itself be registered?*

A: When it is sold in its entirety. This means that if you are buying unregistered land, you must also check to see whether any legal leases over the land have been registered with their own title numbers at the District Land Registry.

If Gladys creates a first legal mortgage over Greenacres with Bundy's Bank

In this case Bundy's Bank must protect its mortgage by what is called a registered charge. This registered charge must be put on the Charges Register of Greenacres. By definition, this means that the freehold estate of Greenacres must also be registered if Gladys creates a first legal mortgage over Greenacres; otherwise there won't be a Charges Register for Greenacres.

Q: *If Fred buys Greenacres, is there a time limit for registering this transaction?*

A: Fred should do so within two months.

Q: *Can Fred apply for registration late?*

A: Yes. The Registrar has the discretion to extend the two-month period under section 6 of the Land Registration Act 2002.

Q: *What happens if Fred doesn't register his purchase of Greenacres?*

A: Under section 7 of the Act, the transaction will not be recognised at law. Fred, who should have completed the dealing by registration, will have only an equitable estate and not a legal estate.

Q: *Does that matter?*

A: Yes. If Fred does not complete his purchase of Greenacres by registration within two months, the legal estate of Greenacres will be transferred back to Gladys, who will be said to be holding the land on trust for or on behalf of Fred, even though it is highly unlikely that Gladys has any idea that this has happened or that she has this responsibility. If Fred were then to try and sell Greenacres to Zeus, he would not have a legal estate to sell and he wouldn't be registered as proprietor of Greenacres. Zeus's solicitor would discover that Greenacres should have been registered when it was sold to Fred and will insist that Fred register the property late. If Fred does so, the legal status of the estate will be restored, so that Zeus can buy the legal estate of Greenacres. If any of the other transactions is not registered within the two months, the transaction will not retain its legal status and will instead only be equitable.

Q: *Why can the fact of not registering a trigger event take away the legal status of an interest in land?*

A: The reason is that for a system of land registration to work effectively everyone must co-operate. The statute acts as a stick here. It won't matter how many documents you've used, or how many expensive solicitors you've consulted, if you haven't registered your estate or interest it will not be recognised at law, and will therefore not be legal.

Q: *Can new trigger events be introduced?*

A: Yes. The Land Registration Act 2002 (Amendment) Order 2008 added two new triggers from April 2009. The first is when a new trustee is appointed of unregistered land held in trust and where the land vests in the trustee by deed or by vesting order. Trusts are discussed in Chapter 6. The second is when unregistered land held in trust is partitioned. Partitioning is explained on page 223. The Land Registry intends that these measures will add more than 7% to the area of land registered by April 2014. The purpose of highlighting these two new trigger events is to show you that the Land Registry is continuing to take measures to bring as much land as possible onto the Register.

Summary of events which trigger first registration

When land is unregistered, there are a number of trigger events which necessitate the registration of the dealing at the District Land Registry. If registration of the dealing does not occur within two months of a trigger event, the transaction will not retain its legal status.

Dealing with land when it is already registered

Let's now assume that Fred purchased Greenacres and has been successfully registered as proprietor. He has been living in Greenacres in contented bliss for several years but has now decided to move. Greenacres is on the market and Peter is the potential purchaser. You now need to look at the chart on page 60. The boxes in the chart show you how transactions are dealt with in registered land, that's to say, land that has already been registered.

DEALINGS WITH LAND WHEN IT IS ALREADY REGISTERED

Box A

DEALINGS WHICH MUST BE COMPLETED BY REGISTRATION

SECTION 27 OF THE LAND REGISTRATION ACT 2002

1. A transfer or sale of the land.

2. A legal lease granted for more than seven years over the land.

3. A legal lease which is granted over the land but which does not take effect in possession (start) until three months after the date of the grant.

4. An express grant or reservation of a legal easement over the land.

5. A grant of a legal charge over the land.

A purchaser for valuable consideration will take subject to the dealings above that have been completed by registration.

Box B

INTERESTS WHICH OVERRIDE A REGISTERED DISPOSITION

SCHEDULE 3 TO THE LAND REGISTRATION ACT 2002

1. A legal lease granted for seven years or less (paragraph 1).

2. The interests of a person in actual occupation (paragraph 2).

3. Legal easements that are not granted or reserved expressly (paragraph 3).

Interests that override will bind a purchaser for valuable consideration automatically whether or not they have been put on the Register or could have been put on the Register.

Box C

INTERESTS ENTERED AS A NOTICE OR PROTECTED BY A RESTRICTION

SECTIONS 34 AND 43 OF THE LAND REGISTRATION ACT 2002

1. A notice entered on the Charges Register (Section 34)

OR

2. A restriction entered on the Proprietorship Register (Section 43)

An interest that has been entered as a notice will be binding on a purchaser for valuable consideration. A restriction regulates dealing with the land.

Dealings which must be completed by registration

Box A

DEALINGS WHICH MUST BE COMPLETED BY
REGISTRATION

SECTION 27 OF THE LAND REGISTRATION ACT 2002

1. A transfer or sale of the land.

2. A legal lease granted for more than seven years over
the land.

3. A legal lease which is granted over the land but which
does not take effect in possession (start) until three
months after the date of the grant.

4. An express grant or reservation of a legal easement
over the land.

5. A grant of a legal charge over the land.

A purchaser for valuable consideration will take subject to
the dealings above that have been completed by
registration.

Box A contains a list of dealings with Greenacres, land that is already registered,
which must be completed by registration.

Box A1 **A transfer or sale of the land**

Any transfer or sale of Greenacres would be a dealing that had to be completed
by registration. If Peter, the potential purchaser here, were to buy Greenacres
from Fred, this sale would have to be completed by registration. The same would
apply if Fred gave Greenacres to Peter as a gift or Peter inherited Greenacres
from Fred. Peter would have to apply for registration of the dealing, which
would receive its own title number, and he would be registered as proprietor of
the land.

Box A2 **A legal lease granted for more than seven years over the land**

This is the grant by Fred of a legal lease for more than seven years over Greenacres.
Fred, for example, may have granted Syed a legal lease of the small cottage at the
bottom of his garden for a period of 10 years. This dealing must be completed by
registration. The person who took the lease, Syed, has to apply for registration
of his legal lease, which receives its own title number on the Register. He is
then registered as proprietor of that lease. Notification of the lease, by means of
something called a notice, must also be put on the Charges Register of Greenacres,
so that anyone buying Greenacres, Peter here, knows that there is a separate
registration of a lease when he inspects the Charges Register of Greenacres before
purchase.

Box A3   A legal lease which is granted over the land but which does not take effect in possession (start) until three months after the date of the grant

This type of lease occurs when a legal lease is granted, but possession of the property does not take place for at least three months. Typical examples here are students. Students take out a lease in the June of a given year, but are not allowed to move in until three months later in October. Fred may have granted a lease of this type to two university students, Sophie and Sarah. Again, Sophie and Sarah have to apply for registration of the legal lease. However unrealistic this may be, the legal lease must be registered with its own title number and, again, notification of the lease by means of a notice must be put on the Charges Register of Greenacres. This is so that a potential purchaser, Peter, is aware of the separate registration of a lease when he inspects the Charges Register before he buys Greenacres.

Box A4   An express grant or reservation of a legal easement over the land

An easement is a right over someone else's land. A right of way is a classic example. An easement is not an estate in land, in that it does not constitute ownership of land, but it is an interest over someone else's land. An easement can be made expressly between two parties. So, for example, Fred may have expressly granted Mr Black, the owner of Blackacres, the neighbouring property, the right to walk over Greenacres as a short cut to the pub. Providing it has been granted in a recognised way, Mr Black has an easement of a right of way. As the easement has been created expressly between Fred and Mr Black, it is then the responsibility of Mr Black to complete the dealing by registration, providing it is a legal easement. Don't worry about the 'legal' part because we look at it in detail in the chapter on easements. All we're doing here is pointing out that the easement has to be legal rather than equitable. The registration of an express grant or reservation of a legal easement is carried out as follows. The person who has the benefit of the legal easement is entered as its owner on the Property Register of his own land. A notification of the legal easement is put on the Charges Register of the land over which the right is exercised, again by means of a notice. So Mr Black has to be registered as owner of the legal easement on the Property Register of Blackacres, and a notice of the legal easement has to be put on the Charges Register of Greenacres. Peter will then know about the grant of the legal easement by inspecting this Register.

Box A5   A grant of a legal charge over the land

A charge is a way of creating a legal mortgage. This means that if Fred creates a legal mortgage over Greenacres with Bundy's Bank, this mortgage must be entered on the Charges Register of Greenacres. Bundy's Bank will be registered as proprietor of the charge, and again Peter will know by inspecting the Charges Register that a legal mortgage exists over Greenacres.

Summary of dealings that must be completed by registration

Some dealings with Greenacres must be completed by registration. In terms of our example, when Peter searches the Register he will be able to see that Fred is registered as proprietor on the Proprietorship Register, which means Fred owns

Greenacres. The Property Register will describe Greenacres, and will show what rights an owner of Greenacres has over other land. When he searches the Charges Register, Peter will find a notification of any legal lease for more than seven years granted over Greenacres (Box A2), and a notification of any legal lease that does not take effect in possession until three months after the date of the grant (Box A3), both of which will have been registered separately with their own title numbers. There will also be a notification of any express grant or reservation of a legal easement (Box A4), and of any legal charge over Greenacres (Box A5), again on the Charges Register. All these interests will be binding on him if he purchases Greenacres.

Interests which override a registered disposition

Box B

INTERESTS WHICH OVERRIDE A REGISTERED DISPOSITION

SCHEDULE 3 TO THE LAND REGISTRATION ACT 2002

1. A legal lease granted for seven years or less (paragraph 1).

2. The interests of a person in actual occupation (paragraph 2).

3. Legal easements that are not granted or reserved expressly (paragraph 3).

Interests that override will bind a purchaser for valuable consideration automatically whether or not they have been put on the Register or could have been put on the Register.

Box B deals with Schedule 3 to the Land Registration Act 2002 and will make you wonder why we bother writing anything down at all on any Register anywhere. This is because there is a category of interests that will take priority over Peter's interests and be binding on him, and indeed on any other purchaser, whether they have been entered on the Register or not. In fact there are some interests in Box B that will bind anyone who takes the land, including Peter here, even though it is expressly forbidden to put them on the Register!

Q: *I thought the rationale behind land registration was to ensure that any interest that a person held over another person's land was entered on the Register. This would mean that a purchaser of land couldn't say that he didn't know about other people's interests over the land because they were in writing for all to see. If you didn't search the Register, that was your lookout. And now you're telling me that there's a whole category of interests that you needn't, or can't, put on the Register?*

A: Yes. There is a category of interests where it would be unfair or impractical for people to have to put their interests on the Register. However illogical it seems, this is what happens. The list of interests that will be binding on everyone, even though they're not on the Register, has been reduced considerably by the Land Registration Act 2002.

This doesn't alter the fact that they are an important feature (or an important failing) of the system. Under the Land Registration Act 1925, these interests were called overriding interests. Under the Land Registration Act 2002, they are called 'interests that override'. Not very helpful language for anyone. However, the word 'overriding' has the same effect in both cases. It means that when a person has an interest that overrides, that interest will override (take priority over) and be binding on anyone who takes the land. The interest will bind a purchaser, despite the fact that the purchaser has complied with all the registration requirements, without the person who owns the interest having to put notification of his interest on the Register.

Q: *But surely the whole reason behind a Register is to ensure people enter their interests on the Register so that everyone else can find out about them?*

A: This is the basic premise of a registered land system. However, taking each of the points in Box B in turn, we'll look at the general reasons each of these interests will be binding on anyone who takes the land, including Peter in our example, even though they haven't been entered on the Register. This is not a detailed explanation of each of the points in the context of the different interests in land. This sort of detail will be covered in later chapters when you look at the actual interest itself. The aim is to give you a general appreciation of why these interests that override exist.

Q: *In the title of Box B, what's meant by the words 'registered disposition'?*

A: A disposition is a disposal of the land or part of the land. This can be by sale, transfer or gift. A registered disposition is a sale, transfer or gift of land where the dealing has been completed by registration of the dealing at the District Land Registry.

Q: *How do interests override a registered disposition?*

A: Look at this in an example: Fred sells Greenacres to Peter.

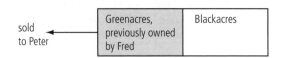

Fred has *disposed of* (sold) Greenacres to Peter. This is a disposition. Peter must then apply for *registration* of the sale, after which he will be registered as proprietor. This is the *registered disposition* part of the sentence. *Interests that override* are those *interests* in Box B which *override* (take priority over) Peter's rights acquired through the purchase of Greenacres. These interests will be binding on Peter, even though he's now the registered proprietor of Greenacres and has complied with all the registration requirements. Now let's look at the category of interests themselves.

Box B1   A legal lease granted for seven years or less

Let's say that Fred had granted Timothy a four-year legal lease of the substantially built summer house nestling in the woods at the end of his garden.

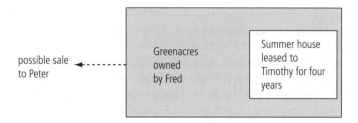

The legal lease granted to Timothy was for less than seven years. It comes into the category of interests that override a registered disposition in paragraph 1 of Schedule 3. Although paragraph 1 doesn't actually use the words *legal* lease, it talks about a lease being granted for a term not exceeding seven years from the date of the grant. As the word 'grant' is a technical term and refers only to a legal lease, this means that only legal leases for seven years or less can be interests that override: see *City Permanent Building Society v Miller* (1952). If Peter bought Greenacres, he would have to register the sale and he would be registered as proprietor. This would be a registered disposition. A legal lease for seven years or less would override (take priority over) this registered disposition and would be binding on Peter. This is despite the fact that Timothy has not had to put notification of his legal lease on any Register. Quite simply, Timothy's legal lease for four years would be an interest that overrode a registered disposition. It would therefore override and take priority over Peter's registered disposition and would be binding on Peter, who would have to give effect to the terms of Timothy's legal lease.

Q: *Why should we allow this?*

A: Practicality. There are thousands of short legal leases of seven years or less in this country, not least those taken out by students. The Register would be overwhelmed with entries if all these people had to put an entry on it. And, let's face it, how many of them would actually know they had to do so in the first place? Furthermore, before Peter bought Greenacres, he would be expected to look round the property. The fact that Timothy was there should be fairly obvious, so Peter should start asking a few questions about Timothy's rights in the land before he decided to buy Greenacres. Purchasers of land do have some responsibility to find out what's going on before they decide to purchase. Therefore, Timothy's legal lease for less than seven years would override a registered disposition, here a sale to Peter.

Box B2 The interests of a person in actual occupation

This is a quotation from a report entitled Land Registration for the Twenty-First Century (1998, Law Commission Report number 254).

> … when people occupy land they are often unlikely to appreciate the need to … register rights in it. They … regard their occupation as the only necessary protection …

Now imagine a past history of Greenacres.

When Fred originally bought Greenacres he paid £70,000 of the purchase price of £100,000 and Sophie, his partner, contributed the remaining £30,000. Fred did all the paperwork, and he alone was registered as proprietor on the Proprietorship

Register of Greenacres. Fred has decided to emigrate, which is why Greenacres is on the market. He has decided to do so without Sophie, who has no idea that he has put Greenacres on the market, let alone that Peter is interested in buying it.

First, do you think Sophie has any interest in the house? You will probably answer yes because she contributed to the purchase price. Secondly, what sort of interest do you think Sophie has in the house? Remember, she is not on the legal title and she is not on the Proprietorship Register. Silence? You'll know the answer when you've read Chapter 9 and, in actual fact, Sophie has an equitable interest in the house. Think about it though. If you don't know what interest Sophie has in the house, and you're studying law, why should Sophie know? And how can she put on the Register something she can't put a name to and probably doesn't even know she's got? The fact is, as far as she's concerned, she's living in the house. She would stand on the doorstep and say to anyone who disputed it, 'I've got rights in this house'. It would be unfair on Sophie, or indeed anyone else in her position, to expect her to know about land registration. So, in order to protect Sophie, her interest in Greenacres and the rights that come from that interest bind anyone who buys the land as an interest that overrides. This includes Peter. However, she must be in actual occupation, that is, living there, when Peter buys Greenacres, and she must meet the requirements given in paragraph 2 of Schedule 3 to the Land Registration Act 2002.

Schedule 3, paragraph 2(b) and (c) gives the requirements for an interest in this category to override a registered disposition as follows.

> 2. An interest belonging at the time of the disposition to a person in actual occupation, so far as relating to land of which he is in actual occupation except for –
>
> ...
>
> (b) An interest of a person of whom inquiry was made before the disposition and who failed to disclose the right when he could reasonably have been expected to do so;
> (c) An interest –
>   (i) which belongs to a person whose occupation would not have been obvious on a reasonably careful inspection of the land at the time of the disposition, and
>   (ii) of which the person to whom the disposition is made does not have actual knowledge at that time.

In plain English, paragraph 2 of Schedule 3 states that an interest in this category will override (take priority over) a registered disposition if

1. The person claiming the right has a proprietary interest in the land

and

2. That person is in actual occupation at the time of the disposition.

However, the interest will not be an overriding interest if

1. When the land was purchased, the fact that the person was in actual occupation was not obvious on a reasonably careful inspection of the land and the purchaser didn't know about the interest

or

2. The person in actual occupation claiming the interest did not tell the purchaser about his interest in the land if asked, and it would have been reasonable for him to have done so.

Paragraph 2 of Schedule 3 is essentially saying that a person who is relying on the fact that he or she is living in the property to claim priority over a purchaser must make it obvious that he or she lives in the property. If asked, he or she should tell any purchaser about his or her interest whether it would be reasonable to do so. If the purchaser still chooses to buy the property, he deserves to be bound by the rights of anybody who lives there.

Q: *How does this apply to the example between Sophie and Peter?*

A: This means that Sophie must have an interest in Greenacres and she must have been in actual occupation at the time of the disposition (sale) to Peter. If Sophie's occupation was not obvious on a reasonably careful inspection of the land at the time of the sale and Peter does not have any actual knowledge of her interest at the time of the sale, then her interest will not be one that overrides. Her interest will not take priority over Peter's and it will not be binding on him. If she had been asked by Peter about her interest before he bought Greenacres, and it would have been reasonable for her to have told him but she hadn't done so, again her interest will not be one that overrides. Her interest will not take priority over Peter's interests and it will not be binding on him.

Q: *Could you argue that if Sophie didn't even know she had an interest, it would be reasonable for her to have said nothing when asked?*

A: Quite possibly.

Q: *So, under Box B2, Sophie must have an interest in Greenacres and she must be in actual occupation?*

A: That's right. She must have a proprietary interest in Greenacres though. A proprietary interest is an interest in the land itself rather than just a personal interest. An invitation to your neighbour's house to supper is not a right in his land. It is a right given to you personally. It does not bind other people. Any interest can override as long as it's a proprietary interest in land: see National Provincial Bank Ltd v Hastings Car Mart Ltd (1964) and Strand Securities v Caswell (1965). Although these cases were decided under the Land Registration Act 1925, the decision would be the same today – there must be a proprietary interest in the land. In the example between Fred and Sophie, we're looking at a recognised proprietary interest arising from a contribution to the purchase price of Greenacres.

Q: *Can you give me another example of a proprietary interest in land?*

A: A lease is a proprietary interest in land. Imagine you had an equitable lease for four years of the cottage at the bottom of the garden of Greenacres. You would not fit in Box A2 because only legal leases of more than seven years must be completed by registration. Your equitable lease would not be an interest that overrode in Box B1 because only a legal lease for seven years or less overrides here. However, an equitable lease is a proprietary right in land; so, provided you were in actual occupation of the cottage when Greenacres was sold to Peter, you would have an interest that overrode in Box B2. Peter would be bound by the terms of your equitable lease.

Q: *Is there a list of proprietary interests in land?*

A: Excluding some licences, the chapter headings at the front of this book are a good place to start.

Q: *Why does Sophie have to be in actual occupation of Greenacres?*

A: So that when Peter goes and looks round Greenacres, he is alerted to the fact that there are other people living there who may well have an interest in the land. This gives him the opportunity to make some inquiries, after which he can decide whether he still wants to buy Greenacres.

Q: *What is meant by actual occupation? Can you go away for the weekend?*

A: Yes. Sophie is not a prisoner in her own home. There are several cases on what is understood by actual occupation, and these are looked at in detail at the end of Chapter 11.

Q: *Is it Sophie's occupation that overrides Peter's rights, even though he's bought Greenacres and completed the transaction by registration, or is it her interest that does so?*

A: It's the interest that Sophie has that overrides and is binding on Peter. Whatever rights her interest gives her will override or take priority over any rights of Peter. You must be clear about that. Her occupation is simply to alert Peter that she is living there and may have an interest in the house which Peter is unaware of. She could have an interest that had nothing to do with the house or the occupation of the house, but Peter would still be bound by the rights that arose from that interest.

Q: *What can Peter do if he finds out that Sophie has an interest that overrides and that would therefore bind him if he bought Greenacres?*

A: This depends on what type of interest Sophie has. There is a process called overreaching, which is looked at in detail in Chapter 11. Overreaching covers certain types of interest and would solve Peter's problems if this were the case. However, there are some interests that, when coupled with occupation, Peter can do nothing about. They are simply interests in land that will bind anyone who takes the land, even purchasers who have complied with all the requirements of registration. They do so, first, because you can't expect everyone to know about interests in land and, secondly, because purchasers are still expected to make inquiries about the land, particularly inquiries about the rights of anyone living there.

In essence therefore:

A proprietary interest in land + actual occupation ⟶ the rights arising from the proprietary interest in land bind anyone who takes the land, including a purchaser who has given valuable consideration for the land.

Q: *Were there overriding interests to do with actual occupation in the Land Registration Act 1925?*

A: Yes. Paragraph 2 of Schedule 3 to the Land Registration Act 2002 replaced section 70(1)(g) of the Land Registration Act 1925. Section 70(1)(g) stated that 'the rights of every person in actual occupation of the land or in receipt of the rent and profits thereof, save where enquiry is made of such person and the rights are not disclosed' were overriding interests. As you can see, the two provisions are very similar, although there are differences. Cases like *Williams & Glynn's Bank Ltd v Boland* (1981) and *Abbey National Building Society v Cann* (1991) are important cases that were decided under section 70(1)(g) of the Land Registration Act 1925. These cases still remain useful for determining what is meant by actual occupation.

Box B3 Legal easements that are not granted or reserved expressly

An easement is a right over someone else's land. A right of way is a classic example of an easement. A right of way over land can be created expressly between two parties or it can be implied from the circumstances. A right of way can also arise simply because a person has used a right of way for a period of at least 20 years. Easements acquired by this long use are called presumed easements. They are presumed from the fact of long use of the right of way. These implied and presumed easements are legal and are also given overriding status under paragraph 3 of Schedule 3 to the Land Registration Act 2002, even though it may be quite difficult for a purchaser to see that they exist over the land. In the example below, Mr Black has an implied legal easement of a right of way over Greenacres.

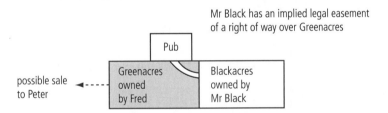

Mr Black's implied legal easement of a right of way is an interest that overrides a registered disposition. If Peter bought Greenacres he would have to complete the dealing by registration. This would be a registered disposition. Mr Black's implied legal easement would override this registered disposition. Peter would have to continue to let Mr Black use the right of way over Greenacres. There are additional qualifying factors before this can happen.

The implied legal easement of a right of way will be an interest that overrides only if:

▶ the person who bought the land that had the right over it, Peter, knew about the right; or
▶ the right would have been obvious to the person who bought the land, Peter, on a reasonably careful inspection of the land; or
▶ the right had been used in the last year before the land was sold, here to Peter.

Q: *So safeguards have been built into this category of interest that overrides?*

A: Yes. Most of them depend on the fact that it is up to Peter to find out about Greenacres and about what goes on there.

Q: *Doesn't this sound worryingly like the doctrine of notice?*

A: Yes.

The discussion around Box B is to show you that there is some rationale behind having interests that will take priority over those of someone who buys the land even though they do not have to be put on the Register. It simply means the buyer must beware. As always. Some of these interests that override will also override the first registration of land. This means that if you purchase unregistered land, interests that override will be binding on you after first registration, even though they were not put on the Register by the Registrar. A list of the interests that override first registration is found in Schedule 1 to the Land Registration Act 2002.

Summary of interests that override a registered disposition

There are some interests which will bind anyone who takes the land including a purchaser for valuable consideration. These interests will take priority whether or not they have been or could have been put on the Register. They are known as interests that override a registered disposition. If Peter were to buy Greenacres, he would be bound by the category of interests that override.

Interests entered as a notice or protected by a restriction

Box C

INTERESTS ENTERED AS A NOTICE OR PROTECTED BY A RESTRICTION

SECTIONS 34 AND 43 OF THE LAND REGISTRATION ACT 2002

1. A notice entered on the Charges Register (Section 34)

OR

2. A restriction entered on the Proprietorship Register (Section 43)

An interest that has been entered as a notice will be binding on a purchaser for valuable consideration. A restriction regulates dealing with the land.

These are interests which do not fall into Box A, and which do not attract the overriding status in Box B. They must be entered on the relevant Register of the land over which they are exercised in order to bind a purchaser, Peter in our example.

Q: *How do these interests appear on the Register? Do the owners of such interests write, 'I have the following interest ... Beware'?*

A: Not far off. There are two ways of dealing with these interests that are technically called encumbrances on the land:

Either

an entry by means of a notice under section 34 of the Land Registration Act 2002

or

an entry by means of a restriction under section 43 of the Land Registration Act 2002.

The notice or restriction must be entered on the relevant Register against the title of the land over which the interest is exercised. You must note that simply putting a notice or restriction on the relevant Register will not guarantee the validity of the interest. That depends on whether it's been created in the correct way.

Q: *Whose responsibility is it to put the notice or the restriction on the Register?*

A: The person who receives the benefit of the interest and in whose interest it would be to protect it against anyone else. In the case of a restriction, the Registrar is also given both a duty and a power to enter a restriction depending on the circumstances.

Given the frequent use of the word 'registered', we suggest that you use the words 'entered on the Charges Register as a notice' or 'entered on the Proprietorship Register as a restriction' when you're talking about these interests, to avoid further confusion.

Box C1 A notice entered on the Charges Register (section 34)

Q: *What's a notice?*

A: A notice is where Mr Black records a 'notice' of the fact that he has an interest over Greenacres. The actual content and detail of the interest will be stated in the notice. The interest is entered on the Charges Register for Greenacres, so that if Peter is thinking of buying Greenacres he can look in the Charges Register for Greenacres and see Mr Black's notification of his interest over Greenacres.

Look at an example again. Fred gave Mr Black a right over Greenacres. It's a right of way which is called an easement, and this time we'll say that it's an equitable easement. Peter is thinking of buying Greenacres.

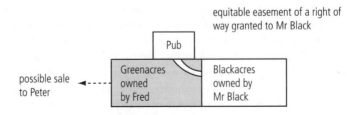

In this case the equitable easement of a right of way doesn't fall into Box A or Box B because these boxes cover only legal, not equitable easements. It must therefore fall into Box C. An equitable easement must be entered as a notice on the Charges Register of Greenacres in order to bind a purchaser of Greenacres, here Peter. It's entered on the Charges Register of Greenacres because that's the land over which the right is exercised. First of all, you must decide in whose interest it is to enter the interest on the Charges Register. Here, it's in Mr Black's interest to enter his equitable easement of a right of way by means of a notice.

Q: *Why is it in Mr Black's interest to do so and not Fred's?*

A: Because Mr Black has the benefit of the right of way over Greenacres. He needs to protect it against anyone who buys Greenacres who may wish to stop him using his right of way, and he does so by means of a notice. It is not in Fred's interest to announce to the world via a Register that Mr Black has a right of way over his land, because all he does is reduce the selling price of Greenacres.

Q: *When must Mr Black enter the notice?*

A: Mr Black must enter his equitable easement of a right of way on the Charges Register the moment it's created, or at least before Fred sells Greenacres to Peter. This is because Mr Black won't know whether, or when, Fred may sell Greenacres to Peter. If Mr Black's interest is not entered on the Register before Peter buys Greenacres, then Peter will not be bound by it.

Q: *What happens if someone enters a notice of an interest on the Charges Register after Peter has searched the Register but before he actually buys Greenacres?*

A: Under section 72 of the Land Registration Act 2002, there is a priority period in favour of Peter. Once a search of the Register has been completed, the Register will be frozen as far as Peter is concerned for 30 working days. Peter must complete and register his purchase of Greenacres within this priority period. Any request by another party to put an interest on the Register during this time will be postponed in Peter's favour until after the 30-day period and will not bind him.
  A notice can be

agreed

or

unilateral.

An agreed notice is when the registered proprietor of Greenacres, Fred, agrees that Mr Black can enter a notice on the Charges Register of Greenacres. A unilateral notice is used when Fred doesn't agree to this, possibly because he doesn't think that he ever granted a right over Greenacres to Mr Black in the first place. This is when the Registrar enters the notice without Fred's agreement. The Registrar has to notify Fred that he's done so, and, if Fred wants to apply for cancellation of the notice, he can do. Mr Black is then given 15 days to prove that the right he is claiming is valid. If Fred chooses not to object, the right claimed will have the same standing as an agreed notice.

Q: *What happens if someone maliciously enters a unilateral notice on another person's land?*

A: The Registrar will obviously notify the registered proprietor, who should object. The person who entered the notice maliciously will be liable for damages if the registered proprietor suffers any loss. The same is true if a registered proprietor objects without any reasonable cause to a unilateral notice.

Q: *What interests have to be entered by means of a notice?*

A: Generally, it's any interest that doesn't have to be registered with its own title (Box A) and is not classified as an interest that overrides (Box B). Usually that means it's an equitable interest. Most of the interests entered here are commercial and arise in business transactions, as compared to family interests which arise in the context of home ownership. Many of the interests that came under classes A to F in unregistered land will be in Box C1. These interests will be discussed in detail later in the book. The point of discussing them now in general terms is to give you an idea of how the system works overall, not how it works in technical detail, which you won't understand until you've looked at the individual interests in land.

Box C2   A restriction entered on the Proprietorship Register (section 43)

Q: *What's a restriction?*

A: Restrictions are entered onto the Proprietorship Register against the name of the registered proprietor of the land. The restriction sets out any conditions that should be met before dealing with the land takes place. The restriction does not prevent the actual dealing taking place but, if the conditions of the restriction are not met, the transaction will not be registered or entered afterwards on the Register by the Land Registrar. This means the purchaser will not be able to obtain a legal interest in the land. An example of a restriction is when land should not be sold unless a third party consents to the sale. The requirement for consent will be entered as a restriction on the Proprietorship Register and must be complied with before the Registrar will register any sale. Restrictions can be entered without the registered proprietor's consent, although, again, the registered proprietor must be notified if this happens so that he can object if necessary. Restrictions are important in the context of family-type interests in land.

Summary of interests entered as a notice or protected by a restriction

Some interests must be protected by a notice on the Charges Register or by a restriction on the Proprietorship Register of the land over which the right is exercised. A notice will protect an interest. A restriction will regulate the circumstances in which dealing can take place.

The interaction between interests that override and interests entered as a notice or protected by a restriction

Some interests in land can fall into both Box B point 2 and Box C. If your interest has been entered as a notice (Box C point 1), it can no longer be an interest that overrides (Box B point 2). However, if you have forgotten to enter an interest by means of a notice (Box C point 1), you may be saved by discovering that your interest also falls into Box B point 2. This is because if it is a proprietary interest in the land and you are in actual occupation, it can be an interest that overrides. This means the interest is automatically binding on a purchaser of the land. This overlap can be very convenient for the forgetful. The same will happen if an interest is not protected by a restriction (Box C point 2). If it is also an interest that overrides, it will bind a purchaser.

The effect of complying with the requirements of the Land Registration Act 2002

Under section 29 of the Act a purchaser of land for valuable consideration will take subject **only** to:

▶ dealings that have been completed by registration (Box A);
▶ interests that override (Box B); and
▶ interests that have been entered as a notice on the Charges Register (Box C1).

He should also comply with any conditions given in a restriction (Box C2).

Q: *What happens if you are not a purchaser for valuable consideration but have inherited the land or have been given it as a gift?*

A: You will take subject to any valid proprietary interests over the land even if they have not been entered on the Register. The rationale behind this is based on the fact that you didn't pay anything for the land. You gave no consideration, so nobody owes you anything. You should just be extremely grateful that you've had such a windfall.

In *Halifax plc v Curry Popeck* (2008) a transfer was deemed not to be for valuable consideration because of its fraudulent nature. The case is a complicated one looking at competing equitable interests and is not for the faint hearted.

The effect of not complying with the requirements of the Land Registration Act 2002

Look at Box A first. These are dealings that must be completed by registration. If registration doesn't happen, the dealing will not be recognised at law under section 27 of the Land Registration Act 2002. There is no time limit for registering a dealing here, but it means the purchaser will have only an equitable estate or interest until he registers: see *Sainsbury's Supermarkets Ltd v Olympia Homes Ltd* (2005). This equitable estate or interest can lose its priority to other interests created subsequently, and must fall into the category of an interest of a person in actual occupation that overrides in Box B2 in order to bind a subsequent purchaser of the land.

The interests in Box B are automatically binding without any need for registration.

Now look at Box C. If an interest is not protected by a notice, it is not binding on a purchaser for valuable consideration under section 29 of the Land Registration Act 2002. It may still be protected, however, if it is an interest that overrides in Box B2 where the owner of the interest is in actual occupation of the land. A restriction does not mean that the transaction cannot be carried out. It does mean, though, that the transaction will not be registered by the Land Registrar afterwards, so the purchaser will not be able to obtain a legal interest in the land.

Q: *What would happen if Peter purchased Greenacres, for example, and knew that Mr Black had a right over Greenacres that should have been entered as a notice on the Charges Register, but he also knew that Mr Black had forgotten to enter it and it wasn't an interest that overrode?*

A: In any system of land registration, it is what is on the Register that counts. It wasn't the intention to return to the old system that was governed by notice and what you knew or should have known. If the interest has not been entered as required on the Register, it will not bind a purchaser. It has to be this way otherwise there wouldn't be much point in having a Register. There have been a few cases where, although a right has not been protected on the Register, it has been recognised on the basis that the purchaser bought the land expressly subject to the right. This recognition is by means of something called a constructive trust, which means the purchaser has to hold the land subject to the rights of another. An example is *Lyus v Prowsa Developments Ltd* (1982) where a contract over land should have been protected by registration, but wasn't. A purchaser of the land promised that he would honour the contract. When he went back on this promise, it was held that he still had to give effect to the contract. This was a personal obligation. If the burdened land had been sold on again, the unprotected interest would not have been binding unless it had been registered or unless the new purchaser had put himself in a similar position. In *Lloyd v Dugdale* (2001) it was said that the conscience of the purchaser must be affected. Another way of showing this could be by the purchaser paying less for the land. In *Lloyd v Dugdale*, the purchaser had not taken on a new obligation and there was no constructive trust.

Q: *Surely allowing an unprotected interest to be recognised in this way detracts from the principles behind land registration?*

A: Yes, but what you are trying to do is to prevent obvious fraud. What the cases are saying is that the purchaser will be bound where he has expressly undertaken a new obligation and then gone back on his word. This was reaffirmed in *Chaudhary v Yavuz* (2011). In *Chaudhary v Yavuz* the claim for a right to be recognised under a constructive trust failed because the purchaser had not taken on a new obligation. The following passage was quoted from *Lloyd v Dugdale*:

> There is no general principle which renders it unconscionable for a purchaser of land to rely on a want of registration of a claim against registered land, even though he took with express notice of it. A decision to the contrary would defeat the purpose of the legislature in introducing the system of registration embodied in the 1925 Act.

The court said that approach was even more justified under the Land Registration Act 2002 and cases such as *Lyus v Prowsa Developments* were very unusual and exceptional and would be rare.

Alteration and rectification of the register

If an interest is incorrectly entered onto the register or missed out by mistake, the register can be changed. Overall, this is called an alteration of the register.

Q: *Who can alter the Register and on what grounds?*

A: Paragraphs 2 and 5 of Schedule 4 to the Land Registration Act 2002 respectively state that an alteration may be made either by a court order or by the Registrar for the following purposes:

- To correct a mistake; for example if an entry was made fraudulently.
- To bring the Register up to date; for example, a landlord could bring a tenant's lease to an end if the tenant hadn't paid the rent. Notice of the lease would be removed from the Register.
- To give effect to any interest excepted from the effect of registration.

In addition, under paragraph 5 of Schedule 4 the Registrar can remove a superfluous entry. For example, the Registrar could remove a restriction if it was no longer applicable.

Under paragraph 1 of Schedule 4 when an alteration involves the correction of a mistake and the alteration prejudicially affects the title of the registered proprietor the alteration is called a rectification. Under paragraph 3 of Schedule 4 if the registered proprietor is in possession of his land, rectification can take place only if the registered proprietor in possession consents.

If the registered proprietor in possession doesn't consent, the Register can still be rectified if:

▶ the registered proprietor in possession has caused or substantially contributed to the mistake through fraud or lack of care; or
▶ it would be unjust if the Register wasn't altered.

Q: *What is meant by the registered proprietor in possession?*

A: This means that the registered proprietor is in physical possession of his land. The definition of a registered proprietor in possession is extended under section 131 to people who are occupying the land in other relationships. For example, if the registered proprietor was a landlord and the tenant was in possession, the landlord would still be treated as being in possession. Similarly, if the land was subject to a mortgage and the lender had taken possession because the registered proprietor had not kept up with the mortgage repayments, the registered proprietor would still be treated as being in possession.

Look at the conditions for rectification. Rectification can take place only when the registered proprietor is in possession and he consents. This is because it would be unfair to alter the Register in a manner which prejudicially affects the registered proprietor's title when he is in possession of his land, having almost certainly paid good money for it and having relied on a state-guaranteed Register to give him information about the land. It is easier and fairer here to compensate a third party who has lost an interest in or over the land. On the other hand, if the registered proprietor doesn't consent but he has caused or contributed to the mistake, there is no reason to take much notice of what he feels about such a rectification. An example of where it was held unjust not to rectify the Register can be found in *Rees v Peters* (2011). There was a mistake because the burden of a restrictive covenant had been missed off the Charges Register of the title to Court Barn, property purchased by Mr Peters from the Reeses. The Register was rectified (so the burden of the restrictive covenant was put on the Charges Register) because, although compensation would have been ordered if the Register hadn't been rectified, this would be of little value compared with the enforcement of the Rees' rights under the covenant. Also, Mr Peters had known about the covenant at all times. It would be unjust not to order rectification.

Rectification is not limited to procedural errors made by the Land Registry. *Baxter v Mannion* (2011) held that where a person had been registered as proprietor, but it transpired subsequently that he had no legal right to be registered as such, this was a mistake. The mistake on the Register could be rectified under Schedule 4 and it would be unjust not to do so.

If the registered proprietor is not in possession the Register must be rectified unless there are exceptional circumstances not to do so: see paragraphs 3 and 6 of Schedule 4.

Q: *Does the Land Registry have to pay compensation if the Register is incorrect?*

A: Yes. Title is guaranteed by the State, so if the Register is incorrect compensation can be claimed from the State. Paragraph 1 of Schedule 8 states when a person may receive compensation (i.e. be indemnified for his loss). The main situations are where there is:

- rectification of the Register;
- a mistake where correction of that mistake would involve rectification of the Register but rectification has not been ordered;
- a mistake in an official search;
- a mistake in an official copy;
- a mistake in a document kept by the Registrar which is not an original and is referred to in the Register;
- loss or destruction of a document lodged at the registry for inspection or custody;
- failure by the Registrar to perform his duty under section 50. This is where the Registrar has a duty to notify people of certain entries.

Q: *How much money can a person claim?*

A: If rectification is not ordered, the person who has suffered loss can claim an amount up to the value of the claimed estate or interest at the time when the mistake, omission or error occurred. If the mistake was made some time in the past and the value of land has gone up in the interim period, the person claiming will lose out, although interest can be paid on the sum claimed under paragraph 9 of Schedule 8. If rectification is ordered, the person who has suffered loss can claim an amount up to the value of the claimed estate or interest at the time immediately before rectification took place. In both cases if the person claiming the loss caused it because of his own fraud, he will not obtain compensation. If he suffered loss through his own lack of care, again he will not obtain compensation. If he contributed in part to the loss through his own lack of care, his compensation will be reduced proportionately under paragraph 5 of Schedule 8. The person claiming compensation has six years in which to do so under the Limitation Act 1980.

You must be careful here if you purchase land and then discover that you are bound by an interest that overrides (Box B). You will automatically be bound by the interest whether you knew about it or not. You will not be allowed to claim compensation as you are deemed to take the land subject to interests that override in the first place: see *Re Chowood's Registered Land* (1933). As such, there's no mistake and no compensation.

Barclays Bank Plc v Guy (2008) provides an excellent illustration of the workings of the Land Registration Act 2002 in this area. Guy claimed that a transfer of land, worth some £30 million, from him to the company Ten Acre Ltd had been obtained by fraud. Ten Acre had itself created a legal mortgage (technically called a charge when you read the case) in favour of Barclays Bank. Having received the mortgage money Ten Acre defaulted on the repayments. Barclays Bank wanted to sell the land to recoup its mortgage money. Guy wanted to have the land transferred back to him and he wanted it transferred back free from the mortgage.

Under Schedule 4 of the Land Registration Act 2002 when an alteration involves the correction of a mistake and the alteration prejudicially affects the title of the registered proprietor, the alteration is called a rectification. If the registered proprietor doesn't consent to the rectification, the Register can still be rectified if the registered proprietor in possession has caused or contributed to the mistake through fraud. The Register could be rectified against Ten Acre even though it didn't consent because it had obtained the transfer by fraud and Guy could claim compensation from the Land Registry. No problem. The next concern was Guy's request that the land was transferred back without the mortgage. The question here was whether the registration of the mortgage was a mistake. It was held that the registration of the mortgage was not a mistake because the Register showed that Ten Acre was the registered proprietor of the land. This is the effect of section 58 of the Land Registration Act 2002 (page 55) which states that even if a person isn't entitled to be registered as the proprietor of the legal estate, the legal estate becomes vested in him as a result of registration and third parties are entitled to rely on the Register as shown. When the mortgage had been created, Ten Acre was registered as proprietor of the land and Barclays had every right to rely on the register which showed Ten Acre as the proprietor. The registration of the mortgage was not a mistake. Only if Barclays Bank had actual notice of the fraud and knew that the title of Ten Acre was defective, or had turned a blind eye to it, would the court consider that registration of the mortgage had been a mistake and could therefore rectify the Register.

Q: *Why does any knowledge that Barclays might have come into it? I thought the purpose of section 58 was to enable third parties to rely on the Register and any notice or knowledge they had was irrelevant?*

A: This is a worrying aspect of the case. In the event Guy could not prove that Barclays had such knowledge. Barclays could therefore keep its mortgage and sell the land to recoup its outstanding mortgage money. The purchaser who bought the land would take it free from any claim by Guy.

Q: *Could Guy have protected himself in any other way?*

A: He could have entered a unilateral notice on the Register (Box C1) warning of the dispute. In actual fact he had asked his solicitor to do this but unfortunately (!) his solicitor only did so the day AFTER Barclays had registered its mortgage, so Barclays' mortgage came first in line. And, just to wrap things up, Guy did not have an overriding interest under Schedule 3 paragraph 2 of the Land Registration Act 2002 (Box B2) which might have been binding on Barclays because he was not in actual occupation at the time the mortgage was created. In *Guy v Barclays Bank plc* (2010) an application to reopen a refusal of permission to appeal failed. Lord Neuberger MR said, though, that the case could have been argued on the following grounds. Mr Guy's argument was based on the mistake being the registration of the mortgage in the Charges Register. A different argument would be to say that removing Mr Guy's name on the Proprietorship Register was a mistake, and, to correct that mistake, the charge would have to be removed from the Charges Register. Alternatively, the registration of the transfer was a mistake and the registration of the mortgage was part and parcel of that mistake and could be removed. However, the decision would not be reopened to allow Mr Guy another go at putting his arguments better than before. Just because points had been argued ineptly or not at all were not grounds for reopening a case and there would be no corruption of the judicial process in refusing the appeal. In *Knights Construction (March) Limited v Roberto Mac Ltd* (2011) Knights Construction was the registered proprietor. The Salvation Army had been registered as proprietor by mistake, but not fraudulently. The Salvation Army had then sold the land to Roberto Mac, which had created a mortgage over the land in favour of Barclays Bank. The two arguments suggested by Lord Neuberger MR in *Guy v Barclays Bank* formed part of the basis on which rectification was ordered in favour of Knights Construction. This meant Roberto Mac no longer owned the land and Barclays Bank no longer had a mortgage over it. Compensation was recommended given there would be a breach of human rights legislation otherwise. There is a comprehensive explanation given of the development of the law in this case.

Further tightening up of proof of identity to prevent fraudsters becoming registered was incorporated into the Land Registration (Amendment) Rules 2008. To prevent these types of situations happening, you could also consider putting a restriction (Box C2) on the Proprietorship Register of your property. This would say that the Land Registrar could not register any dealings with your land, for example, a lease or a mortgage, unless a solicitor had certified that you were the registered proprietor of that land and therefore had the authority to dispose of the interest.

The mirror, curtain and insurance principles

These three principles are often quoted in the context of the Land Registration Acts. The mirror principle refers to the fact that the register is a mirror of the interests found in and over the land.

Q: *But surely overriding interests detract from this principle?*

A: Yes, they do. Interests protected by substantive registration or by a notice or restriction, for example, mean that the register mirrors these interests. This is not true for interests that override but there are policy reasons for their existence and they should be discoverable. When electronic conveyancing is in full force, the creation of rights will have to be carried out electronically and simultaneously with their registration. Rights not created electronically will not exist. This will reduce the number of interests not on the register, including interests that override, although some interests, particularly those arising in the context of the family home, will almost certainly continue to arise informally. The curtain principle refers to the fact that interests that arise under a trust, the main one being interests in the family home, do not have to be investigated by the purchaser. They can remain behind a theoretical curtain. This is because the purchaser is given the mechanism of overreaching to protect himself. This is discussed in Chapter 11. The insurance principle relates to the fact that title to registered land is guaranteed by the State but that compensation is available where there are errors or defects in the register. The availability of compensation backs up the presumed accuracy of the register. These principles are often jumped on by land law lecturers to form the basis of an essay question.

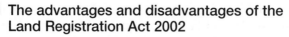

The advantages and disadvantages of the Land Registration Act 2002

There are clearly advantages to this type of system of registration. The Register gives a far more accurate representation of interests in and over land. Registering title to land which is then guaranteed by the state gives security to purchasers and avoids the problems associated with bundles of documents. The Land Registration Act 2002 also allows for the implementation of e-conveyancing, whereby all creation of interests in land and transactions concerning land will have to be carried out online. This will cut down on duplication, paper and time, and will mean that transactions and registration of those transactions can be carried out simultaneously. The category of interests that override (Box B) clearly detracts from the objective of ensuring that all interests over land can be inspected on the Register. However, it is a way of protecting those people who do not understand land law, as well as confirming that purchasers have some responsibility to take their own precautions, noted in the old adage 'buyer beware'.

Buying and selling in registered land

There are explanations and worked examples at the end of each chapter which deal with an individual interest over land. The following is a brief summary of what buying and selling in registered land entails, still using Fred as an example:

▶ Fred bought the previously unregistered land Greenacres. He is bound by the Land Registration Act 2002 to register his title to Greenacres.
▶ Following this registration Greenacres is now registered land.
▶ Fred may grant interests over Greenacres to other people. In these cases:

- Certain dealings must be completed by registration (Box A).
- An interest granted to another person may be protected by virtue of the fact that the interest falls into Box B, and will therefore be an interest that overrides.
- If the interest is not one that overrides, it should be entered by means of a notice on the Charges Register of Greenacres or by a restriction on the Proprietorship Register of Greenacres (Box C).

If Peter decides to buy Greenacres, he will be bound by any entries relating to Greenacres on the Register (Boxes A and C). The Register is open to inspection and Peter is expected to avail himself of this opportunity to search the Register and discover what is happening on Greenacres. Peter will also be bound by any interests that are classified as interests that override (Box B). The interests that override in Box B should be reasonably obvious on an inspection of Greenacres. Peter is expected to carry out this kind of inspection before he purchases Greenacres, and his solicitor should also make inquiries on his behalf. Peter's position can be summarised as follows:

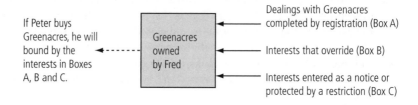

If Peter decides to buy Greenacres, Fred will convey the land to him. Peter will then have to register this dealing and will himself be registered as proprietor of Greenacres (Box A1). The whole process of buying and selling registered land is far simpler than that for unregistered land. It's just a pity that it's taken so long to transfer land out of the unregistered land system into the registered land system.

How does this translate in an examination question? Most questions look at one or both of the following. First, you are asked to examine how an interest between two parties has been created. Is it a valid interest? Has it been created in a way that is recognised at law or in equity? Does the creation of the interest have to satisfy any statutory formalities? Secondly, you are asked to look at what happens when the land is sold on to a third party. Putting this diagrammatically:

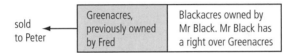

| sold to Peter ← | Greenacres, previously owned by Fred | Blackacres owned by Mr Black. Mr Black has a right over Greenacres |

Fred, the owner of Greenacres, has given Mr Black a right over it. It doesn't matter what right. Part of any question could well be to look at how the right has been created and whether Fred and Mr Black have satisfied any requirements for its creation, statutory or otherwise. The other part of the question could be to look at what happens when Greenacres is sold to Peter. Does Peter have to let Mr Black use his right over Greenacres? The Land Registration Act 2002 deals with the registration of rights over another's land, and so will deal with this situation. Assuming a valid right has been created, you will be advising Mr Black how, if at all, he should have protected his right under the Land Registration Act 2002.

On this basis the procedure for the protection of interests in registered land can be summarised as follows:

1. Identify the interest under discussion.
2. Check whether the dealing should have been completed by registration (Box A).
3. If not, check whether it is an interest that overrides a registered disposition (Box B).
4. If not, it should be entered by means of a notice or a restriction (Box C).

You then need to consider the effects of any non-compliance with the Land Registration Act 2002.

The table below is not something you will understand right now. It sets out the most common proprietary interests in land and gives the method of protection under the Land Registration Act 2002. It is designed to be used as a quick reference guide when you have studied the individual interests in the rest of the book. Some interests appear in more than one Box as they are interests that can be entered by means of a notice or a restriction and they also fall into the category of interests that override.

THE PROTECTION OF INTERESTS IN REGISTERED LAND UNDER THE LAND REGISTRATION ACT 2002

The type of interest	Dealings which must be completed by registration Box A	Interests which override a registered disposition Box B	Interests entered as a notice or protected by a restriction Box C
Conveyance (sale or transfer) of land by deed	A1		
A contract to sell or transfer land or to create an interest in land		B2	C1
An option to purchase land or a right of pre-emption (a right of first refusal to buy the land)		B2	C1
A legal lease by deed for more than seven years taking effect in possession immediately	A2		
A legal lease by deed for seven years or less taking effect in possession immediately		B1	
A legal lease created under section 54(2) of the Law of Property Act 1925		B1	
A legal lease for any period but which does not take effect in possession until three months after the date of the grant	A3		
An equitable lease		B2	C1
Legal co-ownership			C2
An equitable interest under a trust of land or under a strict settlement that has not been overreached		B2	
An equity by estoppel		B2	C1
Adverse possessor's rights (squatter's rights)		B2	
A legal easement granted or reserved expressly	A4		
An implied or presumed legal easement		B3	
An equitable easement			C1
A restrictive covenant			C1
A legal mortgage	A5		
An equitable mortgage			C1
A spouse's statutory right of occupation			C1

Further reading

D. Capps, 'Conveyancing in the 21st Century: An Outline of Electronic Conveyancing and Electronic Signatures', *Conv and Prop Law*, Sep/Oct (2002) 443

M. Dixon, 'The Reform of Property Law and the Land Registration Act 2002: A Risk Assessment', *Conv and Prop Law*, Mar/Apr (2003) 136

M. Dixon, 'Proprietary Rights and Rectifying the Effect of Non-registration', *Conv and Prop Law*, Sep/Oct (2005) 447

J. Howell, 'Land Law in an e-conveyancing World', *Conv and Prop Law*, Nov/Dec (2006) 553

Law Commission, *Land Registration for the Twenty-first Century: A Conveyancing Revolution* (Law Com No 271, 2001)

Chapter 5

Adverse possession

www.palgrave.com/law/Stroud4e

Introduction

This chapter is about adverse possession, something that you probably recognise more as squatter's rights. Squatter's rights occur when someone takes over a piece of land that belongs to someone else and uses it for his or her own benefit. After a set period of time the squatter can claim the land as his or her own. This probably sounds unfair. After all, if you own land, the mere fact that you don't use it shouldn't necessarily give someone else the right to it, even if he or she has used it for a long time. However, in order for adverse possession to be claimed, several conditions must be met, and they are considered in this chapter. The phrase 'paper owner' is used to describe the person who actually owns the land before the squatter makes a claim. Some textbooks use the term 'legal owner', which means the same. The word 'squatter' is used, although some textbooks use the words 'adverse possessor'.

The rationale for adverse possession

Ownership of land in this country is not absolute ownership. It has always been based on a better right to possession of land. This is where the well-worn phrase 'possession is nine-tenths of the law' comes from. If there was a dispute over who owned a piece of land, the party with the prior possession would have the better entitlement to the land. A result of this was that possession was relative. You were entitled to possess the land unless another party proved a prior, and therefore a better, right to possession. This was not without problems. However long a party had been in possession of land, he or she could never be sure that someone else wouldn't come along and claim prior, and better, possession. Consequently a statutory time limit was imposed after which the party with the prior possession could not claim the land back. The current statute is the Limitation Act 1980. However, a person did not become time-barred from claiming his land simply by not using it. His claim became time-barred only when another party took possession of his land and satisfied the conditions for adverse possession. These are the conditions that you will look at in this chapter. If the squatter can't satisfy these conditions, the paper owner is not time-barred from claiming his land back and the time will not start to run in favour of the squatter.

While you may not immediately agree with the concept of adverse possession, there are some sound reasons for its existence.

First, if you are buying land, you need to ensure that the person you are buying the land from actually owns it. In unregistered land this means going back through the documentation relating to previous sales of the land. These documents are called title deeds. The purchaser must look back over a period of at least 15 years and satisfy himself that there is an unbroken chain of ownership to the current vendor. The problem is that old documentation is not always available. If there is a period of time after which previous owners cannot come forward and claim the land, this gives a purchaser some security.

Secondly, it is an ideal way of solving minor boundary disputes. Imagine neighbours arguing about the exact position of their shared boundary fence. Rather than arguing about exactly where the fence was, and where it is now, it is far easier simply to bar the paper owner's claim to the disputed part of the land if the conditions for adverse possession have been met by the neighbour.

Thirdly, there is the argument that if the paper owner neglects his land to such an extent that someone else can use it unchallenged for his own benefit, the squatter's possession should be recognised. Land is an extremely valuable commodity and should not be allowed to be withdrawn from circulation because it is impossible to prove who owns it.

Fourthly, allowing a claim based on adverse possession gives security to a squatter who has possessed and probably considerably improved the disputed land for a long period of time without challenge.

There is a useful discussion justifying the existence of adverse possession in the European Court of Human Rights case of *J A Pye (Oxford) Ltd v UK* (2007) (application number 44302/02). On the other hand, there are those who believe that squatter's rights are nothing but legalised theft. As Neuberger J said in *J A Pye (Oxford) Ltd v Graham* (2002):

> It is hard to see what principle of justice entitles the trespasser to acquire the land for nothing from the owner simply because he has been permitted to remain there for 12 years.

You now need to look at the chart on page 85, which gives the requirements to prove a claim in adverse possession.

ADVERSE POSSESSION

Box A

THE ESSENTIALS OF ADVERSE POSSESSION

You must tick all boxes

☐ **1.** There must be discontinuance of possession by the paper owner followed by possession of the squatter or dispossession of the paper owner by the squatter

2. Possession

☐ **(i)** There must be factual possession

☐ **(ii)** There must be open possession

☐ **(iii)** There must be an intention to possess

☐ **(iv)** The possession must be adverse

☐ **3.** The squatter has not acknowledged the paper owner's title in writing.

Box B

PERIOD OF TIME REQUIREMENTS FOR ADVERSE POSSESSION

Either:

Unregistered Land

1. At least 12 years required under the Limitation Act 1980

2. Occupancy conditions must be met

3. No disability of the paper owner

4. There are no future interests in succession or in reversion

Or

Registered Land

5. At least 10 years required under the Land Registration Act 2002

6. Occupancy conditions must be met

7. No disability of the registered proprietor

8. There are no future interests in succession or in reversion

Further conditions to be met in registered land. Either:

9. An equity by estoppel has arisen or

10. The applicant is entitled to be registered as proprietor for some other reason or

11. The application relates to a boundary dispute or

12. The squatter's application was rejected but he has remained in possession for a further two years.

Box C

POSSIBLE RESULTS OF A CLAIM TO ADVERSE POSSESSION

Look at either

Unregistered Land

1. The effect of a successful claim.

2. The effect of an unsuccessful claim.

Or look at

Registered Land

3. The effect of a successful claim.

4. The effect of an unsuccessful claim.

The essentials of adverse possession

Box A

THE ESSENTIALS OF ADVERSE POSSESSION

You must tick all boxes

☐ **1.** There must be discontinuance of possession by the paper owner followed by possession of the squatter or dispossession of the paper owner by the squatter

2. Possession

☐ **(i)** There must be factual possession

☐ **(ii)** There must be open possession

☐ **(iii)** There must be an intention to possess

☐ **(iv)** The possession must be adverse

☐ **3.** The squatter has not acknowledged the paper owner's title in writing.

You must meet all the conditions here in order to prove the existence of adverse possession.

Box A1 There must be discontinuance of possession by the paper owner followed by possession of the squatter or dispossession of the paper owner by the squatter

There are two elements in a successful claim for adverse possession. The paper owner must cease to possess the land and the squatter must meet the conditions for possession. Only then can the period of time start to run in favour of the squatter: see paragraphs 1 and 8 of Schedule 1 of the Limitation Act 1980.

Q: *What's the difference between discontinuance of possession by the paper owner followed by possession of the squatter and dispossession of the paper owner by the squatter?*

A: Discontinuance of possession means that the paper owner simply ceases to possess the land. The squatter then takes possession. To understand the concept of possession, let's first examine the difference between ownership and possession. If I own something or possess it, there should be some evidence of this. Consider something simple like a television. I have evidence of ownership in the form of a receipt for payment. To demonstrate that I possess the television, I must do something like use it, protect it by keeping it in my house and look after it. If the television was left alone in the street for a period of time without any of these things happening, it would be difficult to determine who had possession, but ownership is still demonstrated by the receipt. If a stranger came across the television and started using it and looking after it, he would possess the television even though I still owned it. I had discontinued possession by ceasing to do the things that denoted possession and the stranger took possession.

In the case of land, ownership is demonstrated by the holding of title deeds and possession in unregistered land or by the entry of the owner's name on the Proprietorship Register in registered land. Possession of the land is demonstrated by living there, carrying out activities on the land, cultivating it and exploiting its amenity. You would also expect that someone who possessed land would inspect it, maintain it and check the boundaries for the security and the safety of the land. Even if a possessor allowed the land to become derelict because he wished to redevelop it, you would still expect him to inspect the land and the buildings, not least to check that unauthorised people, namely squatters, had not moved in.

If an owner of land ceases to do these activities that demonstrate possession, there is a 'discontinuance of possession'. He still owns the land but is no longer demonstrating that he possesses it, so his possession is in question.

If a stranger moves onto the land and starts to behave as though he is in possession, securing the boundary to exclude others, adding a lock to the gate, planting cabbages in an open fashion with an intent to possess the land, then an observer may well conclude that he is in possession of the land. As only one person can possess land, possession is with the squatter.

On the other hand, dispossession of the paper owner by the squatter happens where possession is taken from the paper owner and the paper owner does not object or reclaim possession. This is unlikely to happen and mostly occurs during minor boundary disputes where boundary fences are moved accidentally or deliberately.

Where a person has been occupying land with permission from the owner, and that permission is then withdrawn but the occupier remains on the land, this is seen as dispossession: see *J A Pye (Oxford) Ltd v Graham*. In this case, Michael Graham had remained on and farmed the disputed land following the expiry of a grazing agreement between himself and J A Pye.

Thus the distinction between 'discontinuance of possession' and 'dispossession' is an identifiable one. Whether it makes much difference is a moot point. Any owner demonstrating possession is likely to spot any act of dispossession very quickly and do something about it unless he is very careless, which apparently a good number are.

Q: *Where is the 'adverse' part of adverse possession then?*

A: Adverse simply means that the possession must occur without the consent of the paper owner.

Q: *What happens if the paper owner has discontinued possession or has been dispossessed and then returns to take possession again? How does he show that he's back in possession?*

A: The paper owner doesn't have to do much to show this. Even quite small acts on the land will allow him to claim his right to possession. Allowing others to occupy the property on his behalf, friends and relatives, for example, will also count as resuming possession.

In *J A Pye (Oxford) Ltd v Graham* the paper owner of the land, J A Pye, had done nothing to show possession of the disputed land. As Lord Browne-Wilkinson stated:

> As to the activities of Pye on the disputed land between 1984 and 1999, there were none. In 1993 a representative of Pye visited the disputed land to inspect it but even then he

only viewed it from the road and from the drive; he did not actually go on to the land. Pye showed no interest in the agricultural management of the land. Pye carried out certain paper transactions during this period relating to the disputed land. But it is not suggested that they were sufficient to constitute possession. Indeed nothing was done by or on behalf of Pye to the land itself from 1 January 1984 onwards.

In other words, J A Pye had done nothing to claim its right to possession.

In *J Alston & Sons Ltd v BOCM Pauls Ltd* (2008) the paper owner had walked over the land and had discharged water onto it. This was not enough to show that the paper owner was in possession rather than the squatter. Walking over the land was for access and was not a use of the land. The discharge of water had been minor, and was on a small part of the land; the activity was not known to the squatter and it had not interfered with the squatter's activities.

Box A2   Possession

There are two elements of possession: factual possession and the intention to possess. Factual possession requires physical possession of the land, and the intention to possess requires the mental intention to possess the land.

Box A2i   There must be factual possession

This means that the squatter must show that he is in factual possession of the land.
In *Powell v McFarlane* (1979), Mr Justice Slade said:

> Factual possession signifies an appropriate degree of physical control.

Whether the factual possession is sufficient is an objective test and very much depends on the nature of the land that is being possessed. This was summarised by Mr Justice Slade again in *Powell v McFarlane*:

> The question what acts constitute a sufficient degree of exclusive physical control must depend on the circumstances, in particular the nature of the land and the manner in which land of that nature is commonly used or enjoyed … Everything must depend on the particular circumstances, but broadly, I think what must be shown as constituting factual possession is that the alleged possessor has been dealing with the land in question as an occupying owner might have been expected to deal with it and that no-one else has done so.

Enclosure by fencing is one of the strongest forms of evidence of factual possession, as stated by Chief Justice Cockburn in *Seddon v Smith* (1877).

Q: *What happens if you put a fence up to keep something in rather than to show factual possession? Does that still count?*

A: It depends. In *Basildon DC v Charge* (1996) a fence to keep the geese in was not evidence of fencing that showed factual possession of the land. The fencing had been put up on a short-term basis for practical reasons and had been abandoned once the geese were no longer there. In *Inglewood Investments Co Ltd v Baker* (2002), there was a similar result but this time it was fencing sheep in. In *Hounslow London Borough Council v Minchinton* (1997) it was decided that it didn't matter that the fence was to keep the dogs in. What did matter was the fact that the use of the enclosure was inconsistent with any continuance of possession by the owner. *Chambers v Havering*

(2011) summed the situation up by saying each case would turn on its facts and the significance of fencing could point either way. As Lord Justice Etherton said:

> In some cases, it will be cogent evidence, perhaps the most cogent evidence, of adverse possession where its effect is wholly to exclude the paper owner, even if it was erected to keep animals inside rather than to exclude people, including the paper owner. In other cases, when considered in the context of the evidence as a whole, fencing may be not be inconsistent with the absence of actual possession and of an intention to possess on the defendant's part, even where the fencing physically excludes the paper owner.

Fencing can back-fire though. In *Generay Ltd v The Containerised Storage Co Ltd* (2005) the squatter company had actually fenced off and excluded itself for a period of about four months from part of the land it claimed it was adversely possessing. It was held that the company couldn't say it had factual possession of the land when it had deliberately excluded itself, particularly as it had used actual fencing to do so.

Q: *Why ever would you want to fence yourself out of land if you were trying adversely to possess it?*

A: Because of litigation going on elsewhere.

Building on land clearly constitutes factual possession but you need to beware of so-called trivial acts that do not show true factual possession. In *Tecbild Ltd v Chamberlain* (1969), allowing children to play on the land and tethering and grazing ponies there were seen as trivial acts, and therefore not factual possession. You can compare the trivial acts in *Tecbild Ltd v Chamberlain* with the serious acts of possession undertaken in *Buckinghamshire CC v Moran* (1990), where Lord Justice Slade stated:

> On the evidence it would appear clear that by 28 October 1973 the defendant had acquired complete and exclusive physical control of the plot. He had secured a complete enclosure of the plot and its annexation to Dolphin Place … The defendant had put a new lock and chain on the gate and had fastened it … They had incorporated it into the garden of Dolphin Place. They had planted bulbs and daffodils in the grass. They had maintained it as part of that garden and had trimmed the hedges. I cannot accept Mr Douglas's submission that the defendant's acts of possession were trivial. It is hard to see what more he could have done to acquire complete physical control of the plot by October 1983. In my judgment, he had plainly acquired factual possession of the plot by that time.

In *Purbrick v Hackney London BC* (2003) the defendant stored his equipment in a building with no roof and no door, but with a sheet of corrugated iron across the doorway secured with a chain and two padlocks. This possession counted towards his time for adverse possession on the basis that, as Mr Justice Neuberger said:

> if he was not in possession, who was? To say that the Council was in possession of the building, when someone else had installed his equipment, had locked it so that nobody could obtain access, other than by putting a ladder up against the wall and climbing over the top of a 4 metre wall, appears to me, at least on the face of it, and subject to any special rule or principle to the contrary, to flout common sense and reality.

Q: *What happens with land where you can't do much with it because of the nature of the land?*

A: The answer here is to do what you can with the land.

In *Hounslow London BC v Minchinton* there was rough land at the end of the garden. The activities that had gone on included hedge trimming, weeding and the building of a compost heap. This constituted factual possession on the basis that it was the only sensible use of the land.

In *Red House Farms (Thorndon) Ltd v Catchpole* (1976) the land in question was very marshy. It was held that shooting over it constituted factual possession because, again, that was all you could do with it.

In *J A Pye (Oxford) Ltd v Graham* the activities undertaken included grazing, rolling, harrowing, fertilising and liming the land. Dung was spread and the hedges and ditches were looked after. The Grahams had done all that was possible when cultivating the land. Lord Browne-Wilkinson stated:

> When asked in cross-examination what an occupying owner of the disputed land might have done, over and above what had been done by the Grahams between 1984 and 1997, Mr Evans, an experienced chartered surveyor, was unable to think of anything.

Furthermore, in this case, the land under dispute was fully enclosed and Mrs Graham held the key to the padlocked road gate.

Palfrey v Wilson (2007) is a singular case that concerned a claim to adverse possession of a wall. The Wilsons' predecessor, Mr Heelas, had done all that was needed to maintain the wall by repairing it, putting in a damp proof course and raising the height by three feet, having applied for planning permission to do so in 1979. Taken together, these were seen as unequivocal acts of possession dispossessing the paper owner. The claim in adverse possession succeeded and Mr Palfrey was left to pick up the costs bill of over £260,000, which makes Humpty Dumpty's problems pale into insignificance. It was held that a holistic approach could be taken when looking at all the requirements for adverse possession and a judge was 'not required to fine-slice each and every event and assess its individual merit'.

Q: *Does this mean you don't have to tick all the boxes?*

A: No. It means that you look at all the evidence as a whole to decide whether the conditions in Box A have been met. An example given in the case was that merely repairing someone else's wall which you've damaged cannot amount to possession or dispossession if such an act is looked at in isolation. In *Palfrey v Wilson* this same act did amount to adverse possession.

The time period in adverse possession can be interrupted by the paper owner taking back possession. If this happens, the clock is set back to zero and the squatter must start the time period again, so knowing what constitutes an interruption in possession is important. In *Zarb v Parry* (2011) there had been disputes over a strip of registered land called the Strip by the Parrys' predecessors and the Zarbs' predecessors. The Parrys were now claiming adverse possession of the Strip. The Zarbs said that they had taken back possession based on the following events. On 29 July 2007, whilst the Parrys were taking photographs around their house and garden, in an attempt to regain possession the Zarbs had banged fence posts into the Strip, removed some of the original fencing and cut down an elderflower tree, and Mr Zarb had enclosed the Strip with a surveyor's tape. Twenty minutes later, when the Parrys came to see what was going on, the Zarbs refused to leave but did so when the Parrys went to call the police. The question was whether there had been an interruption in the Parrys' adverse possession. The court said that to interrupt possession, the paper owner must take possession in the ordinary sense of the word and exclude the squatter. The paper owner's acts must be open and not symbolic such as putting up a notice or saying that he was the true owner. It was the quality of the acts that counted, not oral declarations.

Q: *Had the Zarbs done enough to interrupt the Parrys' possession?*

A: The court held that although the Zarbs intended to take possession, they had to withdraw half way through and so did not take possession 'in any meaningful sense'. For example, the tree chopping was seen as 'little more than rather a spiteful act'. The Parrys had not lost exclusive physical control and there was no interruption of time.

Q: *Can you lose adverse possession simply by going out shopping then if the true owner returns and takes possession?*

A: In *Randall v Stevens* (1853) it was held that whether possession was retained for an hour or a week was immaterial. In *Zarb v Parry* it was said that the squatter could be at risk of losing possession whilst he was out shopping but this reinforced the view that any interruption must bring the squatter's exclusive possession to an end. Symbolic acts wouldn't suffice. Although a claim wouldn't necessarily fail if events took place over a limited period, the fact the Zarbs were relying on actions that had happened over a very short period was still a relevant factor.

Box A2ii   ### There must be open possession

Under section 32 of the Limitation Act 1980 possession must not be fraudulent or deliberately concealed. This means that possession must be open. It would be unfair to allow a claim to succeed if the paper owner hadn't been given the opportunity to find out what was happening on the land, and so to have been given the opportunity to remove the squatter.

Q: *Does the paper owner actually need to know that the land is being adversely possessed?*

A: No. He only needs to be given the opportunity to be able to find out on a reasonably careful inspection of the land.

Q: *Does the squatter have to tell the paper owner that he's squatting on the land, or at least bring it to his attention?*

A: No. In *Topplan Estates Ltd v Townley* (2004) it was held that the squatter is under no obligation to tell the paper owner that time is running against him.

Q: *What happens if the factual possession is deliberately concealed or fraudulent?*

A: Time does not start to run in favour of the squatter until the paper owner could have found out about the factual possession with reasonable diligence. If the possession is always concealed, there can never be a successful claim.

There must be an intention to possess

The intention to possess is also called the 'animus possessendi' or the mind to possess. A definition of the intention to possess was given by Mr Justice Slade in *Powell v McFarlane*. It is:

> The intention, in one's own name and on one's own behalf, to exclude the world at large, including the owner with the paper title ... so far as is reasonably practicable and so far as the processes of laws will allow.

Q: *Does a squatter need to prove an intention to own the land?*

A: No. It was decided definitively in *J A Pye (Oxford) Ltd v Graham* that there is no need to prove an intention actually to own the land. The squatter just has to show an intention to possess the land. An example was given of a person, A, who occupied a locked house. He could be there as a squatter, or as an overnight trespasser, or as a friend looking after the house during the owner's absence on holiday. If A was there as a squatter for his own benefit then he would have the intention to possess. If he was only an occasional trespasser or just looking after the house while the owner was on holiday, he would not have the intention to possess. The nature of A's acts determines whether there is factual possession, while the intention with which he does the acts determines whether or not there is an intention to possess. Clearly, factual possession and the intention to possess overlap. Trivial acts on land are unlikely to show an intention to possess, whereas making the place into Fort Knox will clearly show this intention to possess. This overlap was shown clearly in *SS Global Ltd v Sava* (2008). Mr Sava was claiming adverse possession. He had not fenced across the garden gate which meant that the owner of the land and his family could continue to come and go as they had always done and, indeed, they had used the land for car parking, picnicking and quad biking. This failure to fence made his claim of factual possession and his claim that he was excluding the world at large, including the paper owner, hopeless. Advice for would-be possessors – bar every gate there is.

In *Powell v McFarlane* a 14-year-old boy was using the disputed land for grazing his cow. Mr Justice Slade held that the intention to dispossess the paper owner and possess the land couldn't be inferred from the behaviour of a boy aged 14. He was simply grazing the land for the benefit of the family's cows when the owner was absent, and he had no intention to possess the land as his own.

The intention to possess was examined in *J A Pye (Oxford) Ltd v Graham*, where the House of Lords held that the following showed an intention to possess the land once the grazing agreement between Mr Graham and J A Pye had expired:

- The Grahams had carried out activities other than grazing. They would not have been allowed to carry out these activities under the grazing agreement.
- The Grahams had not left the land at the end of the grazing agreement and had remained there without the permission of Pye. In not leaving they had acted directly against the known wishes of Pye, who wanted the land vacant for planning purposes.
- The fact that the Grahams had farmed the disputed land on the same basis as the rest of their farm demonstrated further that there was an intention to possess the land.

The House of Lords also looked at Graham's admission that he would have paid for the occupation of the land if requested. The question was whether this negated the intention to possess. Lord Browne-Wilkinson stated that once you had accepted that it was the intention to possess that was important, rather than the intention to own, and that the intention was to exclude the paper owner only so far as was reasonably possible, then an admission that the squatter would pay if asked was not inconsistent with his being in possession.

In *Ocean Estates Ltd v Pinder* (1969) it had also been held that evidence that the squatter would have paid for the use of the land, or taken a lease, did not show that the intention to possess was lacking.

Provided the acts of the squatter show a clear intention to possess, it doesn't matter that he knows the land belongs to someone else. In *J Alston & Sons Ltd v BOCM Pauls Ltd* (2008) Mr Alston knew the land didn't belong to him but he intended to possess the land. He also accepted that if he was asked to go, he would have to do so. This did not negate his intention to possess. It also doesn't matter that the squatter is using the land in the mistaken belief that it belongs to him or that he is leasing it: see *Lodge v Wakefield Metropolitan City Council* (1995). In registered land, one of the possible grounds for a claim is the fact that the squatter reasonably believes that the land is his.

Q: *Does what the squatter himself has to say on his own intention to possess have any influence on the court?*

A: Definitely not. The squatter is just going to say what the court wants to hear, so he's going to say he intended to possess the land. Unfortunately, you can't prove what someone thought!

Box A2iv ## The possession must be adverse

Q: *This sounds really hostile. Is it?*

A: No. It just means that the squatter must not have permission to be there, because otherwise his presence is not 'adverse': see *BP Properties Ltd v Buckler* (1987). There cannot be shared possession: see *Powell v McFarlane*. Either the paper owner is in possession or the squatter is in possession. Permission which defeats a squatter's claim can be express or implied. In *Batsford Estates (1983) Co Ltd v Taylor* (2005) the claim centred round the blue land – the farmhouse – the adjoining farmyard and buildings – the green land – and the land across the road – the red land. It was held that as there had been implied permission to occupy the blue land this negated adverse possession. The occupation of the green and the red land had been inextricably bound up with the blue land, and so there was implied permission to use those pieces of land as well, so that adverse possession could not be claimed. In *Colin Dawson Windows Ltd v BC of King's Lynn and West Norfolk* (2005) the claimant company had been using the disputed part of the land as a car park whilst negotiations went on for it to buy the land from the paper owner. Although the negotiations subsequently broke down, it was held that whilst they were going on, permission to be there could be inferred for two reasons. The correspondence between the parties was an open act by the paper owner from which you could infer that the claimant company had been allowed to remain on the land during the negotiations. Secondly, a reasonable person would take the view that the use of the land was with the permission of the owner. The claim in adverse possession failed.

Q: *Why couldn't Dawson claim adverse possession when the negotiations broke down?*

A: Because it didn't have the required time period.

Implied permission was looked at again in *Chaplin v Hicks Developments Ltd* (2007). If permission is to be implied, the paper owner has to behave in a way that proves he is content with the use of the land by the squatter, rather than merely indifferent to it. The fact that Hicks had erected a fence well inside the boundary, rather than at the edge of his land, didn't prove that he'd given implied permission to the Chaplins to use the strip between the edge of his land and the fence, thereby defeating their claim to adverse possession. The siting of the fence was consistent with his having given implied permission but didn't actually prove that he had done so, which was the important factor. The Chaplins' claim succeeded.

The intentions of the paper owner as regards any future use of the land can also be discussed here. The development of the law can be traced back by looking at *Leigh v Jack* (1879), the Limitation Act 1980 and *Buckinghamshire CC v Moran*. *Leigh v Jack* stated that a claim for adverse possession could be successful only if the acts of the squatter hindered, and were inconsistent with, the intended future use of the land by the paper owner. Imagine I own Myland. You are squatting on it. I intend to build a hotel on Myland in the future. You have put up a couple of sheds and fenced the land in. You haven't hindered my plans to build a hotel because I could just take down the sheds and remove the fence. Under *Leigh v Jack* you would not be able to claim adverse possession because you had not hindered my future plans. Now imagine you had used Myland and excavated a two-mile deep quarry on it. I would have severe difficulties in building a hotel when faced with a hole in the ground. Under *Leigh v Jack* you would be able to claim adverse possession assuming all other requirements were met.

Q: *Was the effect of this case to make it quite difficult to claim adverse possession? I mean, not all squatters excavate quarries.*

A: Yes. The words used in *Leigh v Jack* were interpreted in *Wallis's Cayton Bay Holiday Camp Ltd v Shell-Mex and BP Ltd* (1975) by Lord Denning to mean that a licence to be on the land could be implied where the squatter had not hindered the intended future use by the paper owner. A licence is permission. Permission to be on the land meant the permission was not adverse. This meant that it became difficult to succeed in a claim for adverse possession. However, Schedule 1, paragraph 8(4), to the Limitation Act 1980 changed the situation. A licence or permission would not be implied simply because the acts of the squatter did not hinder the future plans of the paper owner. This was upheld in *Buckinghamshire CC v Moran*, where it was held that any intended future use of the land of the paper owner was irrelevant. What really mattered was the intention of the squatter. And, if you think about it, if the squatter carried out only trivial acts that didn't interfere very much with the land, it's unlikely he'd prove the intention to possess anyway.

In *J A Pye (Oxford) Ltd v Graham*, Lord Browne-Wilkinson stated:

> The suggestion that the sufficiency of the possession can depend on the intention not of the squatter but of the true owner is heretical and wrong.

There was a brief interlude following *Beaulane Properties Ltd v Palmer* (2005) when the idea that the squatter had to carry out acts that were inconsistent with the future plans of the paper owner was re-introduced. This was because the law was reinterpreted to ensure that adverse possession was consistent with human rights. However, this re-interpretation affected only certain claims in registered land and *J A Pye (Oxford) Ltd v UK* (2007) (application number 44302/02) has now rendered the *Beaulane* case redundant. Adverse possession in the context of human rights is discussed in the section at the end of this chapter. Overall, then, it continues to be safe to say that the squatter's acts do not have to interfere with the future plans of the paper owner.

Box A3 | ### The squatter has not acknowledged the paper owner's title in writing

Under sections 29 and 30 of the Limitation Act 1980, a written acknowledgement of the paper owner's title by the squatter will stop the time running in favour of the squatter. The time will have to start at the beginning again. Any acknowledgement counts on the day it is given or served only. It does not continue after that day and so time can run again in favour of the squatter from that date: see *Ofulue v Bossert* (2009).

Q: *Does it have to be a clear and actual acknowledgment of the paper owner's title?*

A: It can be, but acknowledgement can also be implied from the circumstances.

In *Edgington v Clark* (1964) the squatter had offered in writing to purchase the property. It was held that this was an implied acknowledgement of the paper owner's title. In *Ofulue v Bossert* (2009), though, a previous letter in which the Bosserts had offered to buy the Ofulues' property, thereby acknowledging their title to the property, had been written 'without prejudice'. The acknowledgement could not be used as a defence by the Ofulues to a claim for adverse possession. This would defeat the public policy behind 'without prejudice' letters which allowed disputes to be settled by negotiation without the party making the offer having to worry about such correspondence being used against them at a later date. This case was taken to the European Court of Human Rights on the basis that the 'without prejudice' rule was a breach of human rights. The European Court disagreed.

An oral (spoken) acknowledgement of the paper owner's title will not stop the time running in favour of the squatter, because there'd be too many arguments about who said what, to whom, and when and where they said it.

Q: *How does the paper owner stop time running in favour of the squatter?*

A: A possession order from the courts will stop time running. You must note that a letter telling the squatter to leave the property will not stop the time running: see *Mount Carmel Investments Ltd v Peter Thurlow Ltd* (1988). The paper owner must be prepared actually to remove the squatter through the court process if he doesn't go willingly.

Q: *What happens if you can't tick all the boxes in Box A?*

A: The squatter does not meet the essential requirements for a claim in adverse possession. The paper owner will not be time-barred from bringing an action for possession. He can bring an action for possession at any time in the future, as an adverse possession claim doesn't exist until all the conditions in Box A are met at the same point in time.

Summary of the essentials of adverse possession

Adverse possession has both a factual and a mental element, and the possession must be adverse to that of the paper owner. Unless all the conditions in Box A are met at the same time, there can be no claim.

Period of time requirements for adverse possession

Box B

PERIOD OF TIME REQUIREMENTS FOR ADVERSE POSSESSION

Either:

Unregistered Land

1. At least 12 years required under the Limitation Act 1980

2. Occupancy conditions must be met

3. No disability of the paper owner

4. There are no future interests in succession or in reversion

Or

Registered Land

5. At least 10 years required under the Land Registration Act 2002

6. Occupancy conditions must be met

7. No disability of the registered proprietor

8. There are no future interests in succession or in reversion

Further conditions to be met in registered land. Either:

9. An equity by estoppel has arisen or

10. The applicant is entitled to be registered as proprietor for some other reason or

11. The application relates to a boundary dispute or

12. The squatter's application was rejected but he has remained in possession for a further two years.

In addition to ticking all the boxes in Box A, you must satisfy the statutory period of time requirements in Box B for a claim in adverse possession to succeed. Decide whether the land in dispute is unregistered or registered land.

Unregistered land

Box B1   At least 12 years required under the Limitation Act 1980

Remember that the squatter must satisfy the conditions in Box A before time can run in his favour. The running of time in unregistered land is governed by the Limitation Act 1980. This Act put a limit of 12 years on the time the paper owner had in which to evict the squatter. Section 15(1) of the Limitation Act 1980 states:

> No action shall be brought by any person to recover any land after the expiration of twelve years from the date on which the right of action accrued to him.

This means that the moment the paper owner discontinues his use of the land and the squatter possesses it and satisfies all the conditions in Box A, or the paper owner is dispossessed from the land by the squatter, who again satisfies all the conditions in Box A, the paper owner has 12 years in which to recover his land. After the 12-year period is up, he is barred from doing so by section 15(1).

Q: *What sort of interest does the squatter hold while he is in adverse possession of the land?*

A: All title to land is relative and is based on possession. Title is liable to be defeated by prior, and therefore better, possession. If the squatter has possession of the land it is assumed that he has the title from the moment he possesses it. This is so, even though his title is liable to be defeated by the prior, and therefore better, right to possession of the paper owner if claimed within the 12-year period. It is assumed that the squatter's possession entitles him to the fee simple, which is ownership as we know it: see *Leach v Jay* (1878). The squatter's title co-exists with that of the paper owner. It is good against the whole of the world, but will be defeated by a claim for recovery from the paper owner within the 12-year period.

Q: *Does that mean that the squatter can sell the land?*

A: Yes. It also means that he can leave it in his will.

Q: *How would you know if you were buying unregistered land from a squatter?*

A: He would be unable to produce the title deeds to the land which showed the previous chain of ownership, so it would be an extremely foolish move to continue with the purchase at this point.

Q: *What happens then?*

A: The squatter must give evidence of his claim, and must provide a statutory declaration of his entitlement to the land in court. You could also pay a reduced price for the land or take out indemnity insurance.

Q: *What happens if a squatter adversely possesses against a tenant who is leasing the land?*

A: As the tenant is in possession of the land, time can run in favour of the squatter against the tenant. After 12 years, the tenant will be time-barred from claiming his lease. However, until the land reverts to the landlord at the end of the lease, the landlord is not in possession of it, and so time cannot run against him. Time can start to run against the landlord only when the lease comes to an end and he is entitled to take possession of the land again. At that point, under section 15(2) of the Limitation Act 1980 he must evict the squatter either within six years from this point or within 12 years from when the squatter evicted the tenant, whichever is the longer.

Q: *Who should pay the rent if the squatter is adversely possessing the land against a tenant?*

A: The original tenant should, because he entered into a contract with the landlord to do so.

Q: *Is the tenant likely to continue paying the rent?*

A: No, but this helps the landlord. If the squatter has not squatted for the full 12 years, the landlord can evict him at this point for the following reason. If the tenant has stopped paying the rent, the landlord can forfeit the lease. This means he can bring the lease to a premature end on the basis that the tenant is in breach of contract for refusing to pay the rent. The landlord can take possession of his land again and evict the squatter either within a six-year period or within 12 years from when the squatter evicted the tenant.

Q: *Is there anything the landlord can do if the squatter has time-barred the original tenant from claiming the lease?*

A: The tenant will have undoubtedly stopped paying rent again. There is one argument here to say that the landlord cannot forfeit the lease. When the squatter acquired 12 years' adverse possession, the tenant's leasehold title was extinguished, and there is consequently no title to forfeit. However, in *Fairweather v St Marylebone Property Co Ltd* (1963) it was held that the landlord could still forfeit the lease even though the tenant's title had been extinguished.

Q: *On what basis was this decision made?*

A: Creative thinking. It was held that the title was extinguished between the tenant and the squatter, but not between the tenant and the landlord. A leasehold title still existed between the landlord and the tenant, and that title could still be forfeited by the landlord. If there wasn't a title, there would be no lease and the landlord could take immediate possession, which wasn't so. The decision in *Fairweather v St Marylebone Property Co Ltd* has been criticised.

Box B2   Occupancy conditions must be met

There must be 12 years' continuous possession. If a person squats for five years and then leaves, he cannot count the five years if he moves back in again two years later, for example.

Q: *Can different squatters add their periods of time together to make up the full 12 years?*

A: Yes. Look at an example to show how it all adds up. First, just consider the position of P, the paper owner, in relation to the squatters, S and T.

Paper Owner	Squatter	Squatter
P	S	T
	4 years + 8 years = 12 years.	

P's claim to his land is time-barred because 12 years have elapsed. Now look at the position of S and T in the same situation after P's claim has been time-barred.

Paper Owner	Squatter	Squatter
P	S	T
P's claim		
time-barred	4 years	8 years

P's claim has been barred. The argument will now be between S and T. If you remember, ownership of land is based on possession. The party who can prove prior possession can claim a better right to possession, and therefore ownership, unless he or she has been time-barred under section 15(1) of the Limitation Act 1980. Squatter S was there first in time, so he has a better right to possession than T. Although T is in possession at the moment, and has his own title, he has not possessed the land for 12 years. This means that S is not time-barred from bringing an action to evict him. Squatter S must bring an action to evict T within four years, because after four years S will be time-barred from doing so. On the assumption that S does evict T within four years, S will have a title that cannot be challenged unless another squatter moves in and the whole process starts again. Until then S's title cannot be challenged, because P is already time-barred and T had not possessed the land for 12 years. If S does not evict T and T continues to occupy the land, T will have to stay there another four years. He will then have 12 years' adverse possession. Any claim by S based on prior possession, and therefore better possession, will be time-barred by section 15(1) of the Limitation Act 1980. You see, squatting is not as simple as it could be. You have to be quite good at sums too.

Box B3

No disability of the paper owner

'Disability' here means that the paper owner is either a minor under the age of 18 or suffering mental impairment and a patient under the Mental Health Act 1983.

Q: *Is a longer period of time allowed if the paper owner is suffering from a disability?*

A: Yes. Under section 28 of the Limitation Act 1980, if the paper owner is already suffering from the disability when the squatter takes possession, the paper owner has (a) 12 years from the date when the squatter first took possession or (b) six years from the ending of the disability, whichever is the longer period. This is subject to a maximum of 30 years from the time when the adverse possession started. If the paper owner suffering from the disability dies without regaining his faculties, his estate has either (a) 12 years from the date when the squatter first took possession or (b) six years from the paper owner's death, whichever is the longer period. Again, this is subject to a maximum of 30 years from the time when the adverse possession started.

Q: *What happens if the disability happened after the squatter took possession?*

A: The period stays at 12 years because the paper owner will have been over 18 or of full mental capacity when the squatter moved in, and could, and indeed should, have done something about the situation at that time.

Box B4 There are no future interests in succession or in reversion

First, look at future interests in succession. Imagine a situation where Greenacres is left to Bert for his lifetime and then to Claudia.

Bert will be in possession of his interest in Greenacres during his lifetime. If a squatter takes possession of Greenacres during his lifetime interest, Bert's claim to possession will be barred after 12 years by the Limitation Act 1980 as usual. The squatter will be able to claim the land, but only for the length of time that Bert is alive. After this the squatter will have to start a new claim in adverse possession against Claudia, and so will have to acquire another 12 years.

Q: *Why must the squatter start a new period of time against Claudia?*

A: Claudia will take possession of her interest in Greenacres only when Bert dies, and it is only then that the possession of a squatter can be adverse against her own possession. Under section 15(2) of the Limitation Act 1980, Claudia has two alternatives when she takes possession of her interest after Bert's death. (a) She has six years from the date of Bert's death to claim possession of Greenacres, after which she will be time-barred from doing so. Alternatively, (b) she has 12 years to claim possession from the date when the squatter first took possession of Greenacres during Bert's life interest.

Q: *Which period should she choose?*

A: The longer one. Look at the example that follows.

Squatter S took possession five years ago ⟶ Bert has just died ⟶ Claudia has either (a) six years from the date of Bert's death or (b) the remaining seven years counting from the date when S first took possession.

Claudia can rely on the longer seven-year period.

Now look at future interests in reversion.

Imagine that Arthur owns Greenacres. He has given Jane the use of it during her lifetime. When Jane dies, the property of Greenacres will revert to Arthur if he is still alive, or to his relatives under his will if he has died. The interest that reverts to Arthur or his relatives is known as an interest in reversion. Arthur and his relatives will not be in possession of the interest in reversion until Jane dies. This means that there can be no claim in adverse possession against Arthur or his relatives until Jane has died. In this case, the two alternative periods of time discussed above will be relevant. Arthur or his relatives will have six years from Jane's death or a total of 12 years from when the squatter first took possession, whichever is the longer.

Registered land

Box B5 At least 10 years required under the Land Registration Act 2002

Remember that the squatter must satisfy the conditions in Box A before time can run in his favour. The running of time in registered land is governed by the Land Registration Act 2002 and not by the Limitation Act 1980.

Q: *Why not?*

A: In registered land, title or ownership to land is registered at the District Land Registry. The registered proprietor (owner) on the Proprietorship Register is guaranteed by the State to be the legal owner of a registered freehold or certain leasehold estates. Registration of title also gives security to a purchaser by reason of this guarantee. It would be unfair on the registered proprietor and on any purchaser to say that a state-guaranteed title could be lost because a squatter had adversely possessed the land. The Register would be worthless. Therefore, section 96 of the Land Registration Act 2002 states that the 12-year period under the Limitation Act 1980, after which the paper owner is barred from claiming his land, will not apply to registered land. This prevents a squatter automatically claiming the land simply because a certain period of time has passed. As the squatter will not automatically acquire the land simply by adversely possessing it for a set period of time, he now has to claim the title to the registered estate by applying to the Land Registrar to be registered as proprietor (owner) of the land. The Land Registration Act 2002 also imposed further statutory conditions that have to be met to claim adverse possession of a registered estate.

Q: *Why does the squatter have to claim the title to a registered estate?*

A: Because land itself is not registered at the District Land Registry. It is the estate in land that is registered: the freehold estate and certain leasehold estates. A person registers his or her title or ownership to the estate. Registered land was discussed in Chapter 4.

Q: *Is there a different period of time in registered land?*

A: The period is 10 years under Schedule 6, paragraph 1, to the Land Registration Act 2002, not 12 years as in unregistered land. There must be a minimum of 10 years' adverse possession, and there must be no gap in time between the actual adverse possession and the date of an application to the Land Registrar.

Q: *So, overall, does this mean that whether you've adversely possessed land for 10, 20 or 50 years, you do not automatically acquire the land simply because you have been there for over the 10-year period?*

A: Yes. The registered proprietor is never time-barred from bringing an action for possession. However, if the squatter has a minimum of 10 years' adverse possession, he can make an application to the Land Registrar to be registered as the proprietor on the Proprietorship Register of the land. Only then will the Land Registrar determine whether he has met all the conditions in Box A and the further conditions now imposed by the Land Registration Act 2002.

Q: *When the squatter is adversely possessing the land, does he still have his own title at common law?*

A: Yes. This is the same as the position in unregistered land.

A squatter can also apply to be registered as proprietor if he has adversely possessed the land for 10 years but has then been evicted. In this case there are three further requirements under Schedule 6, paragraph 1, to the Land Registration Act 2002.

▶ The squatter must have had at least 10 years' adverse possession behind him and was entitled to make an application the day before he was evicted, and
▶ His eviction must not have been because of a judgment for possession of the land against him, and
▶ He must have brought the application within six months of his eviction.

Q: *Why can a squatter still apply if he's been evicted?*

A: Because it would be unfair to deny a squatter's application simply because the registered proprietor had evicted him after he had met all the other requirements.

Q: *What happens if a squatter adversely possesses against a tenant who is leasing the registered land?*

A: Providing the squatter has met all the conditions required, he will be registered as the proprietor of the leasehold estate. As the squatter has now been registered as the proprietor of the lease, he will be bound by all the conditions in it, including the condition to pay the rent. At the end of the lease, the land will revert to the landlord again. As the squatter becomes the registered proprietor of the lease, it means conclusively, as far as registered land is concerned, that there is no further relationship between the landlord and the original tenant, as claimed in *Fairweather v St Marylebone Property Co Ltd*, a case which was discussed in Box B1.

| Box B6 | **Occupancy conditions must be met** |

There must be at least 10 years' continuous use by the squatter.

Q: *Can you add successive periods of time together here?*

A: Not in the same way as for unregistered land. Schedule 6, paragraph 11, to the Land Registration Act 2002 states that if you are a successor in title to a squatter, you can add your periods of time together. This means that if you purchase land or receive it as a gift or inherit it under a will or through intestacy as a successor in title, and the person you inherited it or purchased it or received it from was a squatter, you can carry on squatting and add his previous period of time to yours until you have 10 years' adverse possession. (Intestacy is where the deceased person has not left a will.) However, if you are adversely possessing land but are yourself dispossessed by another squatter, providing you then dispossess the other squatter and complete the 10-year period, you can claim adverse possession. In this case you must be there at the beginning and there at the end of the period for it to count in your favour and the whole period must be 10 years.

Q: *So if I squat for four years and then Fred squats for six years, no one can claim adverse possession?*

A: Correct. Fred must squat for another four years. But if you squat for four years, are then dispossessed by Fred who squats for four years, and then you dispossess Fred and resume squatting for another two years, you can claim adverse possession. You must finish what you start.

Box B7   ## No disability of the registered proprietor

Q: *Does this still concern mental incapacity?*

A: Yes, and the incapacity has been extended to physical incapability under Schedule 6, paragraph 8, to the Land Registration Act 2002. A squatter is not allowed to make an application to the Land Registrar to be registered as the new proprietor where the registered proprietor's mental disability would prevent him from making decisions on the kinds of issues that would be raised if the application concerning adverse possession went ahead. The same applies where the registered proprietor is unable to communicate such a decision because of his mental disability or physical impairment. Unlike the position in unregistered land, the disability does not have to have started before the adverse possession began. It has to exist only at the date of the application.

Box B8   ## There are no future interests in succession or in reversion

The position in registered land is now different from that in unregistered land. Under Schedule 6, paragraph 12, to the Land Registration Act 2002 a squatter is not able to claim that he is in adverse possession of registered land if there are successive interests in the land or interests in reversion. The nature of these types of interest has already been discussed in Box B4. Imagine a situation where Greenacres is left to Bert for life and then to Claudia. In registered land a squatter will be unable to claim that he is in adverse possession until Bert has died, and the 10-year period will run only from Bert's death. Similarly, if Arthur owned Greenacres and gave the property to Jane for her lifetime, a squatter could claim that he was in adverse possession only after Jane's death, and the 10-year period would run only from Jane's death.

Further conditions to be met in registered land

Q: *If the squatter has at least 10 years' adverse possession, what does he have to do next?*

A: The squatter must make an application to the Land Registrar to become the registered proprietor (owner) of the land. When the squatter makes this application, under paragraph 2 of Schedule 6 to the Land Registration Act 2002, the Registrar must notify the following people that an application has been made:

1. The registered proprietor (owner) of the land.
2. If the land is leased, the landlord who is registered as proprietor of the lease.
3. The owner of any registered charge (mortgage) on the land. If Bundy's Bank, for example, had lent £50,000 on a mortgage to the registered proprietor, for example, it would have to be notified.

Q: *Why should Bundy's Bank be notified?*

A: Because Bundy's Bank will hold the registered proprietor's land as security in case the registered proprietor doesn't keep up with the mortgage repayments. That land is just about to be claimed by someone else who has nothing to do with the mortgage agreement. Bundy's Bank should start to worry because it is just about to lose its security!

The Registrar must also tell these people that, unless they serve a counter notice under Schedule 6 paragraph 3(1) and section 189 of the Land Registration Rules 2003 within 65 business days, the squatter will be registered on the Proprietorship Register as the proprietor of the land. This is one good reason why the registered proprietor who uses a different address for correspondence from the actual land should make sure his correspondence address is known to the Land Registry.

Q: *What action has to be taken by the people who have been notified?*

A: If they do nothing, the squatter will be registered as proprietor of the land under Schedule 6, paragraph 4, to the Land Registration Act 2002.

This is what happened in *Baxter v Mannion* (2011) where Mr Mannion had failed to serve a counter notice and Mr Baxter, the squatter, had been registered as proprietor. Fortunately for Mr Mannion it then transpired that Mr Baxter had not satisfied the requirements for adverse possession in the first place. His registration was a mistake which would be rectified under Schedule 4 of the Land Registration Act 2002 (discussed in Chapter 4 page 75). If it were otherwise, someone could make a fraudulent application knowing the registered proprietor was away or unable to reply within the 65 days and so could not serve a counter notice. It was highly improbable that this was what Parliament would have intended.

If any of the people notified object within 65 business days, they can ask for the squatter's application to be considered under Schedule 6, paragraph 5, to the Land Registration Act 2002. Under this paragraph, the squatter must satisfy one of the following three conditions.

Box B9 Either an equity by estoppel has arisen …

The basis of estoppel is when person A allows person B to do something on A's land either by expressly encouraging B or by simply allowing B to do something without A saying anything. Person B acts in reliance either on the express encouragement or on the basis that nothing is said. Person A then turns round and denies B the interest he had expected in the land. An equity, or right, arises in favour of B. Estoppel is a cause of action in its own right, and is discussed in Chapter 12. There is an additional requirement under the Land Registration Act 2002 that the squatter ought to be registered as proprietor of the land if this condition is to be satisfied.

Q: *In what circumstances could a squatter meet this condition?*

A: Estoppel could arise in the context of adverse possession where the squatter has built on the land in the mistaken belief that it was his, but the registered proprietor knew about his mistaken belief and did nothing to stop him. It is difficult to see how a squatter will be able to make a claim under estoppel if the registered proprietor has encouraged the squatter to use his land. The squatter's possession will not be adverse because it will be with the permission, and indeed the encouragement, of the registered proprietor. This means that you are not able to meet the basic essentials for adverse possession in Box A2(iv).

Q: *Why is an equity by estoppel mixed up with adverse possession?*

A: Because applying to the Land Registrar under the Land Registration Act 2002 to be registered as proprietor may be quicker and cheaper than going to court to pursue a claim in estoppel. However, as well as meeting the requirements for estoppel here, the claimant must also meet all the requirements in Box A and the period of time and the occupancy conditions in Box B, which he wouldn't have to do under a straightforward claim of estoppel in court.

When there is an estoppel-based claim in court, the court has a wide discretion in terms of the remedy it can grant. This can vary from transferring the land to the claimant to compensation, depending on the circumstances of the case. If a squatter makes an application to be registered as proprietor but the circumstances are such that the squatter ought not to be so registered, then, under section 110 of the Land Registration Act 2002, these same remedies can be granted instead.

Box B10 ... or the applicant is entitled to be registered as proprietor for some other reason

This is where the squatter is entitled to be registered as proprietor for some other reason. *Bridges v Mees* (1957) is an example of a case where this condition could have been used. The purchaser had paid for the land and had moved in. The legal title had never been conveyed to him. The purchaser would have been entitled to be registered as proprietor. Another example is where the squatter is entitled to the land under the will or intestacy of the deceased registered proprietor. Again, the usefulness of this condition is in question because of the word 'entitlement'. If the squatter is entitled to be registered as proprietor anyway, he will not need to claim adverse possession. It may be quicker and cheaper to apply to the Land Registrar under the Land Registration Act 2002 rather than go to court, but remember that the claimant still has to prove he has met all the conditions in Box A and the period of time and the occupancy conditions in Box B.

Box B11   … or the application relates to a boundary dispute

If there has been a boundary dispute, the squatter can claim title to the disputed part of the land he's been using if:

▶ the land in dispute is next to land owned by the squatter; and
▶ the exact boundary line between the two has not been determined; and
▶ the squatter or his predecessor must have reasonably believed for at least 10 years of the period of adverse possession ending on the application date that the land belonged to him; and
▶ the land under dispute must have been registered for at least one year before the date of the application.

Providing all of these conditions are met, an application will be successful. Look at each of the conditions separately.

▶ The land in dispute is next to land owned by the squatter.

This is straightforward.

▶ The exact boundary line between the two has not been determined.

Q: *Are boundary lines not marked exactly on the filed plan of each property registered at the District Land Registry?*
A: No. Although boundaries are shown, they may not be totally accurate to the nearest centimetre and they are not conclusive. It is possible to apply for a boundary to be fixed under Part 10 of the Land Registration Rules 2003. This will be expensive. On the other hand, a fixed boundary means that an application to be registered as a proprietor under this heading will never be successful because the boundary line will have been determined previously. If a landowner is worried about squatters, it would be advisable for him to ensure that his boundary lines are determined.

▶ The squatter or his predecessor must have reasonably believed for at least 10 years of the period of adverse possession ending on the application date that the land belonged to him.

Q: *Isn't 'reasonably believed' a rather vague phrase to use?*
A: Yes.
In *Zarb v Parry* it was asked whether the Parrys, who were adversely possessing land known as the Strip, reasonably believed that they owned it. Given the Parrys knew nothing about the dispute that had gone on between their predecessors and the predecessors of the current owners, plus the fact that they had relied on a surveyor's report that said the land was theirs, they had a reasonable belief that they owned the Strip. In *Iam Group v Chowdrey* (2012) it was held that it was the belief of the adverse possessor that was in question when looking at an application under boundary dispute, not what his solicitor knew or should have known about the disputed land. This could raise the question as to whether the adverse possessor should have been put on notice to consult his solicitor about his use of the land but that wasn't the case in *Iam v Chowdrey*. Also, just because the adverse possessor's ownership is challenged does not make his belief unreasonable. Whether his belief

is reasonable depends on the circumstances. In the case Mr Chowdrey had 18 years' unchallenged use, and letters from the registered proprietor challenging this possession did not make his belief unreasonable.

Q: *Do you have to be careful if you have a dispute over a piece of registered land you are adversely possessing because, if there's a dispute, it might mean that you can't say that you have a reasonable belief any more?*

A: Yes, particularly because in *Zarb v Parry* it was made clear that the reasonable belief must extend up to the date of an application to be registered as proprietor. If you are a squatter and have the required 10 years' use, you should make an application as soon as you can so the registered proprietor can't start making your belief unreasonable. If you are the registered proprietor here, though, it might be a good idea to start destroying the reasonable belief of the squatter so that the condition can't be met, for example, by providing a boundary plan. What you shouldn't do is take possession immediately because the squatter then has six months after his eviction to claim adverse possession under Schedule 6, paragraph 1 to the Land Registration Act 2002 and will still be able to argue boundary dispute regardless of his belief.

▶ The land under dispute must have been registered for at least one year before the date of the application.

Q: *Why must the land under dispute have been registered for at least one year before the date of the application?*

A: Imagine that a squatter had been in possession of a plot of unregistered land called Squatland for 11 years. In this case the paper owner's claim to the land is not yet time-barred by the Limitation Act 1980. However, 11 years is more that the 10 years required under the Land Registration Act 2002. If Squatland were sold to Peter, the sale would have to be registered at the District Land Registry. Squatland would become registered land, and the squatter could immediately claim adverse possession as he had the required 10 years. This would be unfair on Peter. If the squatter in this situation is prevented from making an application for at least a year, Peter has a chance to obtain a possession order and remove the squatter from the land.

Q: *What happens if the registered proprietor brings a claim for possession, rather than the squatter making an application to be registered as proprietor?*

A: First, it is important to realise that the registered proprietor is not time-barred from bringing a claim for possession. This is because the Limitation Act of 1980, which bars a paper owner's claim after 12 years, no longer applies to registered land. To be successfully registered as proprietor in defence, the squatter must prove all the conditions in Box A for 10 years immediately before the registered proprietor's claim and he must prove either estoppel, entitlement or a boundary dispute.

Q: *Is it now much more difficult for a squatter to claim adverse possession as far as registered land is concerned?*

A: Yes, simply because the squatter must prove all the conditions in Box A, the period of time and the occupancy conditions in Box B, and either estoppel, entitlement or boundary dispute, conditions which are themselves limited in scope.

This means that it will be virtually impossible for a squatter to claim vast tracts of land or entire houses, claims which have been successful in the past. The idea of making life more difficult for the squatter ties in with the basic idea of registration of land where all interests in land should be shown on a Register as far as possible.

Box B12 **… or the squatter's application was rejected but he has remained in adverse possession for a further two years**

Q: *What happens if the Land Registrar rules that the squatter's application is unsuccessful and he is not entitled to be registered as proprietor, but the squatter stays on the land or leaves a boundary fence where it is?*

A: The answer to this is determined under Schedule 6, paragraphs 6 and 7, to the Land Registration Act 2002. This gives the squatter one last chance to make a successful application, and it is up to the registered proprietor to be very careful here. If the squatter's application has been rejected, the registered proprietor needs to obtain a possession order from the courts and remove the squatter from his land or else he must formalise the squatter's use of the land by the granting of a lease, for example.

If the registered proprietor doesn't take either of these steps, and the squatter continues his adverse possession of the land, the squatter can put in another application to be registered as proprietor after a further two years. This time the registered proprietor can do nothing about it and the squatter is entitled to be registered as proprietor. The squatter cannot apply at the end of a further two years if the registered proprietor has already started possession proceedings against him at that time though.

The Adjudicator to HM Land Registry is an independent position which has been created by the Land Registration Act 2002. The Adjudicator determines disputes in registered land in England and Wales. A transcript of these disputes and their outcome, including those relating to adverse possession, can be found at www.ahmlr.gov.uk/Public/Search30May.aspx.

Summary of the period of time requirements for adverse possession

The Land Registration Act 2002 has significantly changed the position of squatters in registered land. Although there is still a time requirement, the ability of a squatter to obtain adverse possession of registered land has been severely curtailed.

Possible results of a claim to adverse possession

Box C

POSSIBLE RESULTS OF A CLAIM TO ADVERSE POSSESSION

Look at either

Unregistered Land

1. The effect of a successful claim.

2. The effect of an unsuccessful claim.

Or look at

Registered Land

3. The effect of a successful claim.

4. The effect of an unsuccessful claim.

Unregistered land

The effect of a successful claim

If you can tick all the boxes in Box A and all the boxes for unregistered land in Box B, a claim for adverse possession will be successful. Section 17 of the Limitation Act 1980 states that after the minimum period of 12 years' adverse possession, the paper owner's title is extinguished. The squatter continues to hold his own fee simple title in the land that he held from the moment he started his adverse possession of the land, only now it cannot be challenged by the paper owner.

Q: *If the squatter, Sidney for example, has successfully claimed adverse possession, is he bound by any rights that anyone else has over the land?*

A: Let's consider an example, say, where Mohammed, the owner of the next-door land, came along and claimed he had a right over Sidney's land. Remember this is unregistered land we're talking about, so the situation will be as follows. In unregistered land:

- Legal rights are binding on everyone.
- Equitable right are governed by the Land Charges Act 1972 or the doctrine of notice.

If Mohammed had a legal right over Sidney's land, Mohammed's legal right would be binding on Sidney.

If Mohammed had an equitable right capable of protection under the Land Charges Act 1972, then it should have been entered as a land charge on the Land Charges Register. If this had been done, under section 198 of the Law of Property Act 1925 his equitable right is binding on everyone. It is therefore binding on Sidney. If Mohammed's equitable right has not been entered on the Land Charges Register then, depending on which class of land charge it falls under, it is not binding on either a purchaser for money or money's worth or a purchaser for valuable consideration (sections 4(2), (6), (5), (8) and 17(1) of the Land Charges Act 1972). Sidney does not fit into either of these definitions because he gave no value for the land, and so the equitable right will be binding on him. If the equitable right is governed by the doctrine of notice, Sidney will also be bound by it, as he is not a purchaser for value in this definition either.

Q: *So whatever legal or equitable rights Mohammed has over the land, Sidney will be bound by them?*

A: Yes. Sidney *took* the land, remember.

Q: *What would happen in the following situation? I buy the unregistered land of Greenacres from Fred without inspecting the land. After I have moved in, Sidney turns up claiming that he has been squatting on Greenacres for over 12 years.*

A: Provided Sidney can satisfy all the conditions for adverse possession, he will have extinguished Fred's title and will be holding his own title at common law to the land. Legal rights bind the world in unregistered land. As Sidney has a legal right, this will be binding on you and you will have to leave. This may seem unfair on you, but look at the pretty severe conditions of Box A. It should have been obvious to you that someone other than Fred was in possession of the land had you inspected it. You could, however, claim damages from Fred for breach of the contract to sell Greenacres to you with vacant possession.

Box C2   The effect of an unsuccessful claim

Until the paper owner's title is extinguished, the squatter is always a trespasser on the paper owner's land. If the claim in adverse possession is unsuccessful, the squatter continues to be a trespasser. The paper owner must now obtain a possession order to remove him from the land. If the paper owner doesn't do so, he runs the risk of a further – and possibly successful – claim for adverse possession.

Registered land

Box C3   The effect of a successful claim

Assuming you can tick all the boxes in Box A and all the boxes for registered land in Box B, an application to be registered as proprietor based on adverse possession will be successful.

Q: *Is the situation here different from the position in unregistered land?*

A: Yes. Title is transferred to the squatter and the squatter's name is inserted as proprietor on the Proprietorship Register instead of the existing registered proprietor's name.

Q: *Is the registered proprietor's title extinguished?*

A: No. The position here is fundamentally different from that in unregistered land. It doesn't matter how long the squatter has been in possession; he will never extinguish the title to a registered estate. Instead, he takes the title of the previous registered proprietor and becomes the registered proprietor of the land by virtue of this transfer. This transfer is known as a parliamentary conveyance of the title. When this happens, the squatter's title in fee simple that he held at common law from the moment he started squatting is extinguished.

Q: *Is the squatter bound by the rights other people have over the land?*

A: Under paragraph 9 of Schedule 6 to the Land Registration Act 2002 the squatter will take the land subject to the same interests that bound the previous proprietor.

Note that there is one exception here. If you look back at page 104, you will see that when a squatter makes an application, several people must be notified by the Registrar. One of those people is any chargee, a party who has a charge over the land. This includes anyone lending money on a mortgage. If Bundy's Bank, for example, has a mortgage over the land, it should have been notified of the application for adverse possession. It should object to this application. If it doesn't do so, the squatter will not be bound by the mortgage as Bundy's Bank has had the opportunity to object and has chosen not to do so. If Bundy's Bank does object to the application, even if its objection is unsuccessful and the squatter is registered as proprietor, it can demand the mortgage repayments from the squatter who is now the registered proprietor. If the squatter has been registered as proprietor over only part of the land that is mortgaged, the mortgage repayments will be apportioned accordingly.

Q: *What happens in the following situation? I buy Greenacres, which is registered land, from Fred, the registered proprietor. After I have moved in, a squatter, Sidney, turns up claiming that he has been squatting on the land and that he is entitled to a claim in adverse possession.*

A: You know that Sidney has not yet made a successful claim in adverse possession through the Land Registrar because he is not the registered proprietor of Greenacres. Remember that simply squatting for 10 years on registered land does not automatically give Sidney the title to the land. He must make an application to the Land Registrar and prove he has met all further conditions. However, any interest that Sidney has acquired through adverse possession will be binding on you as an interest that overrides a registered disposition under paragraph 2 of Schedule 3 to the Land Registration Act 2002. The registered disposition here is your purchase of Greenacres that you should have registered at the District Land Registry.

Paragraph 2 of Schedule 3 states that an interest in this category will override (take priority over) a registered disposition if:

1. The person claiming the right has a proprietary interest in the land

and

2. That person is in actual occupation at the time of the disposition.

However, the interest will not be an overriding interest if:

1. When the land was purchased, the fact that the person was in actual occupation was not obvious on a reasonably careful inspection of the land and the purchaser didn't know about the interest

or

2. The person in actual occupation claiming the interest did not tell the purchaser about his interest in the land if asked, and it would have been reasonable for him to have done so.

Paragraph 2 of Schedule 3 is essentially saying that a person who is relying on the fact that he is living in the property to claim priority over a purchaser must make it obvious that he lives in the property. If asked, he should tell any purchaser about his interest if it would be reasonable to do so. If the purchaser still chooses to buy the property, he deserves to be bound by the rights of anybody who lives there.

You can now apply this to Sidney.

1. Sidney holds his own fee simple at common law. This is a proprietary interest in land.
2. If Sidney was in actual occupation of the land when it was sold to you, his interest will bind you.

However, Sidney's interest will not bind you if:

1. When you bought the land Sidney's actual occupation would not have been obvious to you if you had made a reasonably careful inspection of the land and you didn't know about his interest

or

2. Sidney didn't disclose his interest if you asked him when it would have been reasonable for him to have done so.

If Sidney has 10 years' adverse possession, meets the conditions in the Land Registration Act 2002, and his interest is one that overrides, you will be bound by it. Remember that you have had the opportunity to inspect the land and ask anyone living there about the exact nature of their rights. Sidney can apply to the Land Registrar to be registered as proprietor, as his interest takes priority over yours. You could, however, claim damages from Fred for breach of the contract to sell Greenacres to you with vacant possession. If Sidney does not have 10 years' adverse possession, you must obtain a possession order from the courts to evict him. You must do this to ensure that he does not squat for the full 10-year period.

<table>
<tr><td>Box C4</td></tr>
</table>

The effect of an unsuccessful claim

Until the registered proprietor's title is transferred to the squatter, the squatter is always a trespasser on the registered proprietor's land. If the claim is unsuccessful, the squatter continues to be a trespasser. The registered proprietor must now obtain a possession order to remove him from the land. This is particularly important in registered land, as a further two years' adverse possession by the squatter means that if he makes another application he will be automatically entitled to be registered as proprietor, as discussed in Box B12.

Summary of the possible results of a claim to adverse possession

When all the conditions for adverse possession have been met, and the land is unregistered, the paper owner's title is extinguished. In registered land, title is transferred to the squatter. If a claim in adverse possession is unsuccessful, the owner of the land must obtain a possession order to evict the squatter in both unregistered and registered land.

Reform

Section 144 of the Legal Aid, Sentencing and Punishment of Offenders Act 2012 came into force in September 2012 introducing the criminal offence of squatting in residential buildings. This will be committed where a person is in the building as a trespasser having entered as such, knew or ought to have known he or she was a trespasser, and is living or intending to live in the building. Criticism has been voiced because it is thought that the existing civil and criminal law is sufficient. Charities are concerned about the criminalisation of homelessness.

A question on adverse possession

This example is intended to illustrate how to use the Boxes in this chapter to analyse the legal position. If you are using this method in undergraduate law exam questions, you will need to include statutory and case authority and detailed discussion of the various points of law. This information is found both in the text and from other sources.

Fred owns Greenacres, a large property with several acres of woodland. Robert, his next-door neighbour, has been using a small strip of this woodland, called Firtrees, which is adjacent to his property, under the mistaken belief that it was conveyed to him when he bought his own property, Redacres.

Robert ran a company on Redacres called 'War Games', which he set up for the purpose of organising training courses for business executives. Fifteen years ago he constructed an underground tunnel running from his own property across the strip of woodland called Firtrees. Thirteen years ago he erected a barbed wire fence across Firtrees in order to practise army manœuvres. Twelve years ago he secured a wooden fence around Firtrees and padlocked the entrance gate.

Fred had always intended to incorporate Firtrees into his development plans for Greenacres. In January of this year Fred went to view the land with the aim of starting development. He discovered the barbed wire fence, which was broken in several places, the wooden fence and the padlocked entrance gate, but continued with his development plans.

Fred has now received a letter from Robert claiming that the land belongs to him, Robert, and that Fred is to move his bulldozer forthwith.

Advise the parties.

In order to advise the parties, you will need to establish whether Robert can claim adverse possession and therefore title to Firtrees.

Box A The essentials of adverse possession
You must tick all the boxes here.

A1 There must be discontinuance of possession by the paper owner followed by possession of the squatter or dispossession of the paper owner by the squatter
Fred has discontinued his use of Firtrees. Robert has taken over possession of Firtrees. You can tick this box.

A2 Possession

A2i There must be factual possession
You now need to look at the different acts that Robert has carried out on Firtrees.

The underground tunnel
You could argue that the underground tunnel is evidence of factual possession using *Rains v Buxton* (1880), where there was adverse possession of an underground cellar with a clearly visible door. You can tick this box.

The barbed wire fencing
While *Seddon v Smith* held that enclosing land is one of the strongest forms of factual possession, it is debatable here whether the barbed wire fencing is indicative of possession. It sounds as though the fence is across the land, rather than enclosing it. The fence is also broken in several places. This would indicate that even if there had been factual possession, it had not been maintained. This box cannot be ticked.

The wooden fencing and the padlocked entrance gate
There is clear evidence of factual possession from this act, particularly as the entrance gate is padlocked: see *J A Pye (Oxford) Ltd v Graham*. You can tick this box.

A2ii There must be open possession

If possession is fraudulent or deliberately concealed, under section 32 of the Limitation Act 1980 the period of time will not start to run in favour of the squatter.

The underground tunnel

This is a discussion point. Given the circumstances, it is arguable that the tunnel is deliberately concealed. However, it has not been deliberately concealed to prevent Fred from finding out about Robert's use of the land, but rather to ensure that Robert's escape plans aren't rumbled. By its very nature it would not be obvious on a reasonably careful inspection of the land, and you know from the facts given that Fred did not find it when he inspected the land. We will assume that the underground tunnel is concealed, and so does not satisfy the requirement of open possession. This box cannot be ticked.

The barbed wire fencing

This would be obvious on an inspection of Firtrees. You can tick this box.

The wooden fencing and the padlocked entrance gate

These would be obvious on an inspection of Firtrees. You can tick this box.

A2iii There must be an intention to possess

Robert does not need to show an intention to own Firtrees: see *J A Pye (Oxford) Ltd v Graham*. An intention to possess will suffice. It does not matter that he was using the disputed land in the mistaken belief that it was his own. It is arguable that the erection of the barbed wire fence does not show an intention to possess Firtrees because it was put up to enable Robert to practise army manœuvres, not to show an intention to possess. However, Robert's intention to possess is shown by the construction of the underground tunnel and the wooden fence, neither of which is a trivial act. The wooden fence in particular would show evidence of an intention to possess, particularly as the entrance gate is padlocked: see *J A Pye (Oxford) Ltd v Graham*. You can tick this box.

A2iv The possession must be adverse

There is no indication that Fred has given Robert permission to use Firtrees or that the use of Firtrees was shared. Fred's development plans for Firtrees are not taken into account: see *Buckinghamshire CC v Moran*. You can tick this box.

A3 The squatter has not acknowledged the paper owner's title in writing

There is no evidence to suggest that Robert has acknowledged Fred's title in writing, and therefore sections 29 and 30 of the Limitation Act 1980 will not be relevant. You can tick this box.

Summary of Box A

The only time that you can tick all the boxes in Box A is when Robert puts up the wooden fence and padlocks the entrance gate. At this point there has been discontinuance of possession by Fred followed by Robert's possession, A1; factual open possession, A2i and A2ii; an intention to possess, A2iii; possession which is adverse, A2iv; and no acknowledgment of Fred's title in writing, A3. At this point, time can run in favour of Robert. While the underground tunnel is evidence of factual possession, you cannot tick open possession, A2ii. The barbed wire fence was not erected to show factual possession, A2i. Even if it was, it is broken in several places, and so would no longer constitute factual possession, nor does it support an intention to possess Firtrees, A2iii. The only time you are able to tick *all* the boxes in Box A at the same time is when the wooden fencing is put up and the entrance gate padlocked. This is the point at which it is possible for time to run in favour of Robert.

Box B   Period of time requirements for adverse possession

In addition to ticking all the boxes in Box A, you need to satisfy the statutory period of time requirements. You are not told whether the land is unregistered or registered, so you must discuss both.

If Firtrees is unregistered land

B1 At least 12 years required under the Limitation Act 1980
Twelve years have elapsed since Robert put up the wooden fence and padlocked the entrance gate. Under section 15(1) of the Limitation Act 1980, Fred is time-barred from recovering Firtrees. This condition is satisfied.

B2 Occupancy conditions must be met
Robert has used Firtrees continuously for 12 years. There are no successive squatters. This condition is satisfied.

B3 No disability of the paper owner
There is no indication that Fred is suffering from any mental disability, therefore section 28 of the Limitation Act 1980 is not relevant.

B4 There are no future interests in succession or in reversion
There are no future interests in succession or in reversion, therefore section 15(2) of the Limitation Act 1980 is not applicable.

If Firtrees is registered land

B5 At least 10 years required under the Land Registration Act 2002
Providing Robert is in adverse possession of Firtrees immediately before any claim to the Land Registrar, he has the 10-year period required under Schedule 6, paragraph 1, to the Land Registration Act 2002. This condition is satisfied.

B6 Occupancy conditions must be met
Robert's adverse possession is continuous. There are no successive squatters, therefore Schedule 6, paragraph 11, to the Land Registration Act 2002 is not applicable.

B7 No disability of the registered proprietor
There is no indication that Fred is suffering from mental impairment or physical disability, therefore Schedule 6, paragraph 8, to the Land Registration Act 2002 is not applicable.

B8 There are no future interests in succession or in reversion
Schedule 6, paragraph 12, to the Land Registration Act 2002 is not applicable here as there are no future interests in succession or in reversion.

Further conditions to be met

Robert must make an application to the Land Registrar to be registered as proprietor of Firtrees. He must have been in adverse possession immediately before his application. Under paragraph 2 of Schedule 6 to the Land Registration Act 2002, the Registrar must notify Fred. If Fred does not object, which is most unlikely, Robert is entitled to be registered as proprietor of Firtrees under paragraph 4 of Schedule 6 to the Land Registration Act 2002. Assuming Fred does object, Robert's application will be considered under paragraph 5 of Schedule 6, and he must prove either that an equity by estoppel has arisen or that he is entitled to be registered as proprietor for some other reason or that the application relates to a boundary dispute.

B9 Either an equity by estoppel has arisen

You would have to argue that Fred had stood by without saying anything and watched Robert carry out acts which constituted possession, in which case an equity by estoppel could have arisen. This is unlikely, as you are told that Fred 'discovered' Robert's use of the land.

B10 Or the applicant is entitled to be registered as proprietor for some other reason

There is no indication that Robert is entitled to be registered as proprietor for any other reason.

B11 Or the application relates to a boundary dispute

It is possible that Robert could claim that the application relates to a boundary dispute. Firtrees is next to Redacres. Robert reasonably believed that Firtrees belonged to him. Assuming the exact boundary line has not been determined under the Land Registration Rules 2003 and Firtrees was registered for at least one year before the date of Robert's application, he will be able to plead boundary dispute.

B12 Or the squatter's application was rejected but he has remained in adverse possession for a further two years

Paragraphs 6 and 7 of Schedule 6 to the Land Registration Act 2002 will be relevant only if Robert's application is rejected.

Box C Possible results of a claim to adverse possession

Unregistered land

C1 The effect of a successful claim

Fred's title will have been extinguished under section 17 of the Limitation Act 1980 and Robert will continue to hold his own fee simple title to the land.

C2 The effect of an unsuccessful claim

Robert continues to be a trespasser. Fred should be advised to obtain a possession order to remove Robert from Firtrees if he does not go willingly.

Registered land

C3 The effect of a successful claim

Fred's title to Firtrees will be transferred to Robert, who will be registered as proprietor of Firtrees instead of Fred.

C4 The effect of an unsuccessful claim

Robert continues to be a trespasser. Fred should be advised to obtain a possession order to remove Robert from Firtrees if he does not go willingly. If Fred does not evict Robert from the land, Robert can apply to be automatically registered as proprietor under paragraphs 6 and 7 of Schedule 6 to the Land Registration Act 2002 if he continues adversely to possess Firtrees for a further two years.

Conclusion

Robert appears to have satisfied the conditions required for a claim in adverse possession from the time he erected the wooden fencing and padlocked the entrance gate. He has possessed Firtrees for the requisite period in both unregistered and registered land. If Firtrees is unregistered land, Fred's title will be extinguished. If Firtrees is registered land, Robert must make an application to the Land Registrar to be registered as proprietor of Firtrees. If the application is successful, Fred's title to Firtrees will be transferred to Robert.

Adverse possession and human rights

The Annex at the end of this book contains a brief description of human rights legislation and how it works. It is designed for those of you who have not studied human rights before so you can see how human rights law fits into the cases in this section.

There have been a number of recent cases in which owners of land have claimed that losing their land to a squatter has been in breach of their human rights. Much hot air has been expended on these cases and the law has been shown to be compatible with human rights. Even so, it is important to understand and be familiar with the arguments put forward in this area. The following is a brief summary for those of you who only need to know the outline. The detailed version of events follows after that.

When land is unregistered, there can be no claim that adverse possession is in breach of human rights legislation. In unregistered land there is no state guaranteed register of title. Ownership is proved by possession and documentation. Imposing a time limit after which the owner cannot claim back his land prevents the uncertainty and injustice that can arise if the paper owner is allowed to reclaim land at any time from a squatter. Adverse possession in unregistered land regulates the use and ownership of the land. When land is registered, adverse possession has been subject to challenge. The challenge was made in cases where the period of limitation ended after the Human Rights Act 1998 came into force in October 2000 but before the Land Registration Act 2002 came into force.

Q: *What do you mean by the end of the period of limitation?*

A: The end of the period during which the owner could claim his land back from the squatter. In other words, the squatter had reached the end of the period without being removed by the owner and the owner was now barred from doing so.

The Land Registration Act 2002 came into force in October 2003, and this Act is deemed to be compatible with both human rights and adverse possession. This is because it is far more difficult to claim adverse possession, the registered proprietor is notified of any claim and he has a right to be heard.

The first challenge where the period of limitation ended between October 2000 and October 2003 was in *Beaulane Properties Ltd v Palmer*. It was held that as Beaulane had lost its property without compensation, this violated the owner's human rights. To avoid this, the court reinterpreted the law relating to adverse possession to be consistent with human rights legislation. This meant that in order to make a successful claim, the squatter now had to prove that his use of the land was inconsistent with the registered proprietor's intended future use of it. The next case after *Beaulane Properties Ltd v Palmer* was *J A Pye (Oxford) Ltd v UK* (2005), heard in the Chamber of the European Court of Human Rights. It was held that the substantive law on adverse possession breached Pye's rights to peaceful enjoyment of its property under Article 1, Protocol 1 to the European Convention on Human Rights. The result was that compensation could be claimed from the UK, i.e. the government, by a registered proprietor who had lost his land to a squatter. The UK government appealed against this decision to the Grand Chamber of the European Court of Human Rights in *J A Pye (Oxford) Ltd v UK* (2007). It was held that the law relating to adverse possession was not a violation of the Convention. This is the final result, which means that there is no need to reinterpret the law and no need for the government to pay compensation to a registered proprietor where the limitation period ended between October 2000 and October 2003. The Land Registration Act 2002 is deemed to be compatible with human rights where the limitation period ends after October 2003.

Q: *That's the short version?*

A: Yes. The resolution of this area of law has been a long-drawn-out process. The next part of this section is the long and detailed version of the chain of events. We'll start off with unregistered land. The legislation relating to adverse possession of unregistered land is compatible with human rights.

Q: *Why is adverse possession of unregistered land compatible with human rights?*

A: Because adverse possession here regulates the use of the land. There is no register which gives a guaranteed state title. The limitation period in unregistered land creates certainty, in that after a person has possessed the land for 12 years he is the legal owner. This prevents the uncertainty and the injustice that can arise if the paper owner is allowed at any time to reclaim land from a squatter. This is the position of unregistered land in table format.

	Statute(s) governing adverse possession	Is the Human Rights Act 1998 in issue?
UNREGISTERED LAND	Limitation Act 1980	Unregistered land system compatible with HRA 1998

This leads on to registered land, which is where the problems with compatibility have been. Before we start, you need to know the following five points of law.

1. The Human Rights Act 1998 brings into domestic law the First Protocol to the Convention for the Protection of Human Rights and Fundamental Freedoms. Article 1 of the Protocol states:

> Every natural person is entitled to the peaceful enjoyment of his possessions. No one shall be deprived of his possessions except in the public interest and subject to the conditions provided for by law and by the general principles of international law. The preceding provisions shall not, however, in any way impair the right of a State to enforce such laws as it deems necessary to control the use of property in accordance with the general interest or to secure the payment of taxes or other contributions or penalties.

Note the use of the word 'State'. This is the UK, as represented by the government.

2. The Human Rights Act 1998 does not apply retrospectively. The 1998 Act does not apply if the limitation period ended before 2 October 2000, whereas the Convention applies to all claims after 1953. The Convention has largely been ignored by property lawyers.

3. If a UK statute is incompatible with human rights, under sections 2, 3 and 4 of the Human Rights Act 1998 the courts must interpret the law so that it is compatible as far as this is possible, or a superior court can declare incompatibility.

4. If there is a breach of Article 1, the claimant is entitled to just satisfaction or some other order, for example compensation, under Article 41 of the Convention.

5. The Land Registration Act 2002, which came into force on 13 October 2003, changed the rules relating to adverse possession in registered land.

6. Before the Land Registration Act 2002 came into force, adverse possession in registered land was governed by the Limitation Act 1980 and the Land Registration Act 1925. We'll call this the LA1980/LRA1925 combination. You had to meet the common rules in Box A and the conditions B1, B2, B3 and B4 in Box B, just as you did for unregistered land. The difference for registered land under the LA1980/LRA1925 combination occurred only when you reached Box C. The effect of a successful claim in registered land under the LA 1980/LRA1925 combination meant that, under section 75 of the Land Registration Act 1925, the registered proprietor held the legal title for or on behalf of the successful squatter until the title was officially transferred to the squatter by the Land Registrar. In technical terms, the registered proprietor held the land that had been adversely possessed on trust for the squatter. Unlike with unregistered land, the title of the registered proprietor was not extinguished because you can't go around extinguishing titles on a register guaranteed by the state.

Q: *So before the Land Registration Act 2002 came into force, the only difference when making a claim for adverse possession of registered land was how the squatter formally obtained the title to the land?*

A: Yes. The registered proprietor held the land on trust for the squatter until the squatter's name was entered onto the Register instead of that of the registered proprietor.

Q: *Why do I need to know the law for adverse possession in registered land before 2002?*

A: Because *Beaulane Properties Ltd v Palmer* and *J A Pye (Oxford) Ltd v UK* (2007) were cases to do with human rights under the European Convention on Human Rights and were cases decided on the basis of this LA 1980/LRA 1925 combination.

Now we can look at the human rights issues in registered land in detail. Start off with claims made under the Land Registration Act 2002, which is uncontroversial.

The Act came into force in October 2003. The provisions relating to adverse possession in the Act are deemed to be compatible with the European Convention on Human Rights.

Q: *Why is the Land Registration Act 2002 deemed to be compatible with the law relating to human rights?*

A: This is because the conditions the squatter has to meet under the Act have made it more difficult to claim adverse possession, and the registered proprietor will now be warned that a claim is being made so he can defend himself. This takes into account the human rights aspect. When adverse possession in registered land was governed by the LA 1980/LRA 1925 combination, the registered proprietor simply lost his right to the land after 12 years of successful adverse possession without any notification or warning, and he couldn't do anything about it. Under the Land Registration Act 2002, you can argue that at least the registered proprietor now gets a right to a fair trial, even though he will lose the land if the squatter has met all the conditions prescribed in the Act. The following table shows the effect of a claim when the 10-year period claimed by the squatter comes to an end after 13 October 2003 (the date the Act came into force). Remember a squatter only needs 10 years if he is claiming under the Land Registration Act 2002. Look at the row in italics.

	Statute(s) governing adverse possession	Is the Human Rights Act 1998 in issue?
REGISTERED LAND **Limitation period ends**		
After 13 Oct 2003	*Land Registration Act 2002*	*Yes but LRA 2002 is human rights compatible.*
UNREGISTERED LAND	Limitation Act 1980	Unregistered land system compatible with HRA 1998

Q: *So what happens when a claim is made for adverse possession of registered land and the limitation period ends before 13 October 2003?*

A: The Land Registration Act 2002 was not in force so the claim for adverse possession will be governed by the LA 1980/LRA 1925 combination and a 12-year time period. Before 2 October 2000, the Human Rights Act wasn't in force and the European Convention on Human Rights was little used by lawyers. This was the case in *J A Pye (Oxford) Ltd v Graham*, heard in the House of Lords.

Q: *What had been decided in the UK courts between the Grahams and the company?*

A: In essence this is what happened. In the High Court the Grahams were awarded adverse possession of 25 hectares of Pye's land. In the Court of Appeal they were not awarded the adverse possession because the fact that they would have been willing to pay for their usage of the land negated the intention to possess. In the

House of Lords the Grahams were again awarded adverse possession because a willingness to pay for the use of it did not negate the intention to possess. When the case went to the House of Lords in July 2002, the Human Rights Act didn't apply because the 12-year period of adverse possession had been completed before the Human Rights Act came into force on 2 October 2000.

Q: *Even so, was nothing said about the human rights issue?*

A: There had been some grumblings in the House of Lords by Lord Bingham of Cornhill who said

> But where land is registered it is difficult to see any justification for a legal rule which compels such an apparently unjust result, and even harder to see why the party gaining title should not be required to pay some compensation at least to the party losing it.

Even so, Pye lost his land worth £2 million to the Grahams.

So, to summarise the position where the 12-year limitation period ends before 2 October 2000. Look at the row in italics.

	Statute(s) governing adverse possession	Is the Human Rights Act 1998 in issue?
REGISTERED LAND **Limitation period ends**		
Before 2 Oct 2000	*LA1980/LRA 1925*	*No. HRA 1998 not in force*
After 13 Oct 2003	Land Registration Act 2002	Yes but LRA 2002 is human rights compatible.
UNREGISTERED LAND	Limitation Act 1980	Unregistered land system compatible with HRA 1998

Now look at *Beaulane Properties Ltd v Palmer*, heard in March 2005. Mr Palmer had adversely possessed registered land owned by Beaulane Properties Ltd. The 12-year limitation period ended in June 2003 and this meant two things. First, the claim would be dealt with under the LA 1980/LRA 1925 combination, not the Land Registration Act 2002, because the Land Registration Act 2002 wasn't in force. Secondly, the Human Rights Act 1998 was relevant because it was in force. It was held that, as Beaulane had lost its property without compensation, this would be a disproportionate interference with its rights not justified in the public interest under Article 1 of the Convention. To avoid declaring incompatibility, the judge reinterpreted the law in such a way that adverse possession of registered land was compatible with the Convention rights.

Q: *By what means?*

A: By requiring that the squatter had to interfere with the future plans of the registered proprietor, thus returning to *Leigh v Jack*. This aspect of adverse possession was discussed in Box A2(iv). If this was the case, there would be no issue over human rights.

Q: *Did Beaulane Properties win the case?*

A: Given the new interpretation of the law, yes. As developers, Beaulane Properties had plans for the land but Mr Palmer hadn't done anything on the land other than graze horses. As Mr Palmer couldn't show that his use interfered with the future plans of Beaulane Properties, his claim failed.

Q: *Did this mean that where the 12-year limitation period in registered land ended between 2 October 2000 and 13 October 2003, the squatter now had to prove that he had hindered the future plans of the registered proprietor?*

A: Yes, and the Land Registry issued a practice note to this effect that you could see on its website. The following table shows the position after March 2005 following *Beaulane Properties Ltd v Palmer* where the 12-year period of adverse possession ended between 2 October 2000 and 13 October 2003. Look at the row in italics.

	Statute(s) governing adverse possession	Is the Human Rights Act 1998 in issue?
REGISTERED LAND **Limitation period ends**		
Before 2 Oct 2000	LA1980/LRA 1925	No. HRA 1998 not in force
2 Oct 2000–13 Oct 2003	*LA1980/LRA 1925*	*Yes, so the acts of the squatter have to interfere with future plans of the registered proprietor* (Beaulane)
After 13 Oct 2003	Land Registration Act 2002	Yes but the LRA 2002 is human rights compatible.
UNREGISTERED LAND	Limitation Act 1980	Unregistered land system compatible with HRA 1998

This was not the end of the story. In November 2005, Pye, the company that had lost some £2 million worth of land to the Grahams in *J A Pye (Oxford) Ltd v Graham*, took the UK, i.e. the government, to the European Court of Human Rights in *J A Pye (Oxford) Ltd v UK* (2005). The case was heard in the Chamber.

Q: *I thought you said that the Human Rights Act wasn't in force when the limitation period ended in* **J A Pye (Oxford) Ltd v Graham** *and so human rights weren't an issue?*

A: The Human Rights Act was not in force so Pye claimed under the European Convention on Human Rights which has been in force since 1953. The Convention allows a claimant to petition the European Court once he has exhausted all domestic remedies.

Q: *On what basis did Pye make its application to the European Court in the 2005 case?*

A: On the basis that the law on adverse possession had breached its rights to peaceful enjoyment of its property in a way which was not in the public interest and which was not proportionate under Article 1 of the First Protocol.

Q: *Why was the UK involved?*

A: Because the UK is responsible for securing the rights under Article 1 of everyone in its jurisdiction, so the case was brought against the State, not the squatter. It is then the UK government that is responsible for arguing the case of behalf of the UK.

Q: *Could you argue that it wasn't exactly the State's fault, i.e. the government's fault, that Pye had sat on its rights and could very easily have evicted the Grahams long before the 12 years was up?*

A: But it was the legislation that caused Pye to lose its land. If there hadn't been a Limitation Act 1980 and a Land Registration Act 1925, the Grahams could have been evicted as trespassers however long they had been there. It was the effect of the legislation that caused Pye to lose its land, and legislation is passed by the state.

The European Court held that depriving Pye of its title to the land imposed an individual and excessive burden on it and upset the balance between the public interest and its right to peaceful enjoyment of its property. This was highlighted by the fact that the law relating to adverse possession in registered land had already been changed under the Land Registration Act 2002, which meant that the law had been in need of amendment. The new provisions of the Land Registration Act 2002 also meant that the registered proprietor would be notified when a squatter put in a claim, which would allow a fair trial, neither of which had happened for Pye. Under Article 41 of the Convention the court ordered the UK, i.e. the government, to pay compensation to Pye to give just satisfaction for violation of Pye's rights.

Q: *Did the decision in the European Court change the decision in the House of Lords?*

A: No. All the European Court said was that Pye should be compensated for its loss by the UK because there had been a violation of Pye's rights. The Grahams kept the land.

Q: *So who exactly was to pay this compensation?*

A: The UK government, and so ultimately you and me. Now you know why you pay taxes. It was left that the parties would try and sort out the amount of compensation between themselves. If they couldn't do so, the matter would go back to court.

Q: *Who would be affected by this decision?*

A: Cases where the limitation period ended after 2 October 2000, i.e. after the Human Rights Act 1998 came `into force, and before 13 October 2003, i.e. before the Land Registration Act 2002 came into force. The following table shows the position after November 2005 following *J A Pye (Oxford) Ltd v UK* (2005). Look at the row in italics.

	Statute(s) governing adverse possession	Is the Human Rights Act 1998 in issue?
REGISTERED LAND **Limitation period ends**		
Before 2 Oct 2000	LA1980/LRA 1925	No. HRA 1998 not in force
2 Oct 2000–13 Oct 2003	*LA1980/LRA 1925*	*Yes so the acts of the squatter have to interfere with future plans of the registered proprietor* (Beaulane) *and compensation is payable by the UK government to the registered proprietor under* J A Pye v UK (2005)
After 13 Oct 2003	Land Registration Act 2002	Yes but the LRA 2002 is human rights compatible
UNREGISTERED LAND	Limitation Act 1980	Unregistered land system compatible with HRA 1998

The overall effect of *Beaulane Properties Ltd v Palmer* and *J A Pye (Oxford) Ltd v UK* (2005) was as follows for claims where the limitation period ended between October 2000 and October 2003. A squatter would have to prove interference with the future plans of the owner if he was to be successful (the *Beaulane* case). The registered proprietor would be able to claim compensation from the State if his land were adversely possessed (the *J A Pye (Oxford) Ltd v UK* (2005) case). Fortunately for you and me, the UK government decided that it wasn't going to pay up without a challenge.

Q: *Presumably the thought of paying out lots of money to registered proprietors who'd sat around and watched their land being adversely possessed was too much to bear?*

A: Well, I'd be really cross if I thought my taxes were going that way and I expect the government would rather any taxes went into their coffers rather than those of J A Pye. The UK asked for the case to be heard in the Grand Chamber, which is the highest Court as far as the Convention is concerned. There is no right of appeal against a decision from the Grand Chamber. In *J A Pye (Oxford) Ltd v UK* (2007) (application no 44302/02) the Grand Chamber held by 10 votes to seven that there had been no violation of Article 1 of the Convention when Pye lost ownership of its land through adverse possession.

Q: *What? After all that?*

A: Yes. The results of the deliberations of the Grand Chamber were as follows.

▶ Pye had lost 25 hectares of land as a result of the LA 1980/LRA1925 combination. Article 1 was applicable. The effect of this legislation was not to deprive Pye of its land. Its effect was to regulate title to land in the context of use and ownership of land. Pye was affected not by 'a deprivation of its possessions' but by a 'control of use' of land. The words 'control of use' are found in sentence three of Article 1.

▶ The existence of a 12-year limitation period pursued a legitimate aim in the general interest. This legitimate aim was still valid because the Land Registration Act 2002 had not abolished adverse possession altogether. It was open to the government to give more weight to long possession that had gone unchallenged than to consider the formal fact of registration. If the squatter had made a successful claim, extinguishing the owner's title was reasonable. There was a general interest in the limitation period itself and in the extinguishment of title at the end of that period.

▶ The European Court of Human Rights granted a wide margin of appreciation to the state and held that there was a fair balance between the general interest and the interests of Pye. The legislation on adverse possession had been in force for many years. Pye couldn't say that it didn't know the law or that it came as a surprise to it.

▶ The limitation period was quite long, and in any event it wouldn't have taken much for Pye to have stopped the time running, by either asking for rent or obtaining a possession order.

▶ Asking for compensation would not sit easily with the idea of limitation periods. The idea of a limitation period was to stop Pye pursuing any action after a certain date, not to start a cause of action in asking for compensation. Furthermore, the provisions of the Land Registration Act 2002 did not require a squatter who had been registered as proprietor to pay compensation to the previous registered proprietor.

▶ Pye was not without procedural protection because it could have taken action in the courts for possession of its land. It also had the opportunity of arguing that the requirements of adverse possession – such as factual possession and the intention to possess – hadn't been met in the first place.

▶ Although the Land Registration Act 2002 meant that the registered proprietor was notified of any claim by a squatter, the court had to consider the law as it was when the limitation period came to an end for Pye. Just because judges in previous cases had criticised the law relating to adverse possession it didn't mean that the parties weren't bound by it.

▶ Pye's claim that the fair balance was upset because its loss was so great and the windfall to the Grahams was so substantial was unfounded. Where one party gains, another must lose. Providing the legislation was not in breach of human rights, this moral argument had no ground.

▶ Finally, the limitation period would apply regardless of the value of the land lost.

As an aside, it is interesting to note that when the provisions of the Land Registration Act 2002 relating to adverse possession were discussed, the Grand Chamber misinterpreted them in one way in the judgment and in another way in the press release. This inspires confidence.

Q: *What is the overall result?*

A: The decision in *Beaulane Properties Ltd v Palmer* is incompatible with the decision in the Grand Chamber, but it still stands because the Grand Chamber cannot change a decision made in a UK court. The decision in the Grand Chamber must, however, be taken into account in any future cases under section 2 of the Human

Rights Act 1998. In effect this means that the decision in *Beaulane Properties Ltd v Palmer* can be safely ignored because any attempt to invoke it is likely to result in an application to the European Court of Human Rights. This means that there is no need to prove that the acts of the squatter are inconsistent with the future plans of the registered proprietor. The decision of the Chamber in *J A Pye (Oxford) Ltd v UK* (2005) was reversed by the Grand Chamber and there is no need for the UK to pay compensation to registered proprietors who have lost their land. All this did not stop another try in *Ofulue v Bossert* (2008). The Bosserts had completed the period of adverse possession by 1999 so the case was determined under the Land Registration Act 1925. Mr Ofulue, the registered proprietor of the land in dispute, argued breach of his human rights by trying to distinguish *J A Pye (Oxford) Ltd v UK* (2007) on its facts. He failed. The Court in *J A Pye (Oxford) Ltd v UK* (2007) had held that the legislation relating to adverse possession came within the margin of appreciation accorded to each State. It was not possible to challenge that determination because a case was distinguishable on its facts. The UK legislation satisfied the requirements of legitimate aim and proportionality and this applied to all decisions. This meant the Court would not look at legitimate aim and proportionality in the context of Mr Ofulue's specific case. A good try, though, Mr Ofulue. The Court of Appeal did not overrule *Beaulane Properties Ltd v Palmer* in *Ofulue v Bossert* because an application for permission to appeal out of time had been made for *Beaulane Properties Ltd v Palmer*. Regardless of this, the effect of *J A Pye (Oxford) Ltd v UK* (2007) and *Ofulue v Bossert* makes it impossible to claim breach of human rights when land is adversely possessed. The eventual outcome looks like this. Look at the row in italics.

	Statute(s) governing adverse possession	Is the Human Rights Act 1998 in issue?
REGISTERED LAND **Limitation period ends**		
Before 2 Oct 2000	LA1980/LRA 1925	No. HRA 1998 not in force
2 Oct 2000–13 Oct 2003	*LA1980/LRA 1925*	*Yes but no violation of human rights* – J A Pye (Oxford) Ltd v UK (2007)
After 13 Oct 2003	Land Registration Act 2002	Yes but the LRA 2002 is human rights compatible.
UNREGISTERED LAND	Limitation Act 1980	Unregistered land system compatible with HRA 1998

So, overall, human rights are not a problem at all in the law relating to adverse possession in any claim now, whatever the date.

PS: A note to property developers. Watch out because you cannot rely on human rights to claim your land back if it has been adversely possessed. You must protect your land from squatters.

Further reading

M. Dockray, 'Why Do We Need Adverse Possession?' *Conv and Prop Law*, Jul/Aug (1985) 272

C. Harpum, 'Adverse Possession and Future Intentions', 49 *CLJ* (1990) 23

S. Nield, 'Adverse Possession and Estoppel', *Conv and Prop Law*, Mar/Apr (2004) 123

L. Tee, 'Adverse Possession and the Intention to Possess', *Conv and Prop Law*, Mar/Apr (2000) 113. In reply: C. Harpum and O. Radley-Gardner, 'Adverse Possession and the Intention to Possess – A Reply', *Conv and Prop Law*, Mar/Apr (2001) 155. In reply: L. Tee, 'Adverse Possession and the Intention to Possess', *Conv and Prop Law*, Jan/Feb (2002) 50

www.palgrave.com/law/Stroud4e

Chapter 6

The use of trusts in land

▶ Introduction
▶ The origins of the trust
▶ An overview of the use of trusts in land

Introduction

This chapter and the five that follow look at the role of the trust in land. The trust is an extremely important feature in the context of ownership of the family home. It is important to know why trusts exist in land, how they come into being and whether interests under a trust can bind a third party. The first part of this chapter looks at what a trust is and how it works. The second part gives you a brief overview of how the trust fits into land law. Subsequent chapters look at each of the areas identified in the overview in detail. Successive interests are covered in Chapter 7, express co-ownership in Chapter 8, implied co-ownership and the use of the trust when there is express co-ownership but the beneficial interests have not been recorded in Chapter 9, the Trusts of Land and Appointment of Trustees Act 1996 in Chapter 10, and, finally, the mechanism of overreaching and the protection of interests in a trust of land in Chapter 11. It is important to understand each of the different areas in its own right. It is equally important to view the area as a whole, made up of component parts – a jigsaw if you like – so that you can see the final picture of how everything fits together at the end.

The origins of the trust

The concept of the trust began in feudal times with the idea of the 'use'. Imagine Fred as a soldier in the King's service. He owns Greenacres, a large estate that supports him, his wife and family. Fred is called away to go and fight for the King. He wants to ensure that Greenacres will still be there when he returns, and that someone has the power to deal with it in his absence. As he is likely to be away for some years, he asks Marmaduke, his longstanding friend, to run Greenacres when he is away. To ensure that Marmaduke can deal with the land in his absence, Fred conveys (transfers) Greenacres to him on the understanding that Marmaduke will convey (transfer) it back to him at the end of the war. In an ideal world, when Fred returns triumphant from the war, Marmaduke will convey (transfer) Greenacres back to Fred. In a more normal sort of world, Marmaduke will use some of the profit from Greenacres for himself and he will refuse to transfer Greenacres back to Fred when he returns. If Fred were to go to court over this, the common law courts would just point out that Marmaduke had the legal title to Greenacres; he was the legal owner and could therefore do exactly what he wanted with the land, which is absolutely true.

Q: *Did Fred have any remedy?*

A: Yes. In order to ensure justice, the courts of equity stepped in. The rules of equity are based on fairness and justice. Fred clearly didn't hold the legal title because that was held by Marmaduke. However, the courts of equity recognised that Fred did have rights in the land, regardless of the transfer to Marmaduke. These rights were known as equitable rights, rights recognised and enforced by the courts of equity but not by the common law courts. As Fred had conveyed (transferred) Greenacres to Marmaduke purely so that he could manage the land for the benefit of Fred, Marmaduke held Greenacres for the 'use' of Fred. The courts of equity held that Marmaduke could take no benefit at all from Greenacres. He held the legal title in the capacity of a trustee of Greenacres so that he could manage the estate and deal with the paperwork when necessary. Everything that Marmaduke did with the land had to be in the best interests of Fred, which usually meant his best financial interests. As Marmaduke could take no benefit from Greenacres, it followed that all the enjoyment rights in it, for example the right to receive the income and profits from the land, should still belong to Fred. These rights were attached to the equitable interest. This is why the 'equitable' interest is often referred to as the 'beneficial' interest. The two words are synonymous. While the legal title to Greenacres, which enabled Marmaduke to deal with it, was recognised by the common law courts, Fred's equitable, or beneficial, rights were enforced in the courts of equity. After the Judicature Acts 1873 and 1875, common law and equity were administered in the same court, which made life much easier because both legal and equitable rights were recognised in the one place.

Q: *What happened if Marmaduke started using Greenacres for his own benefit?*

A: Marmaduke would have to restore any loss caused to Greenacres and would be liable to imprisonment.

Q: *Were there other situations involving the mechanism of the 'use'?*

A: Yes. The 'use' was also applied by orders of monks who couldn't hold land because their creed forbade it. To avoid this restriction, any land left to the order was held 'to the use of' the monks. A person outside the order would be appointed to hold the legal title and would be able to sign the paperwork. The equitable or beneficial interest of the monks gave them the enjoyment rights in the property, which would include any profits from the land or probably, in the case of the monks, any produce grown on the land. Because they didn't actually own the legal title, the monks could safely say that they didn't own land.

The 'use' was even more significant in the avoidance of feudal dues. In feudal times tax was payable by the heirs of a tenant on his death. To avoid this payment, land would be conveyed to a group of people who would hold the legal title to the land in the capacity of trustees to the 'use' of the tenant and his heirs. The interest of the tenant was recognised in equity as an equitable interest, and the courts of equity would intervene to enforce the tenant's beneficial rights if necessary. As any members of the group acting as trustees died, they were replaced. This meant that the legal title would always remain with the group and would never be passed to an heir at common law, with the result that no feudal dues were owed. This way of holding land deprived the King of revenue, so in 1535 he attempted to stop the process by implementing the Statute of Uses. Although this was unsuccessful, the collection of feudal dues as a source of revenue became less important.

The word 'use' was subsequently replaced by the word 'trust', and over the centuries trusts continued to be used in a number of situations. The trust still plays a very important part in modern society, and can still be used to minimise tax. The person who holds the legal title is called the trustee and holds the property for the benefit of those with an equitable or beneficial interest, who are called beneficiaries. The trustee holds the trust property on behalf of any beneficiary and can take no profit or gain from the land in his capacity as trustee. He has onerous duties and responsibilities, and must manage the trust property in the best interests of the beneficiary. The beneficial ownership provides the enjoyment rights and any income or profit from the trust property.

Q: *Can any kind of property be held on trust?*

A: Yes. Other than land, the main type of property held on trust is money. An example is where £100,000 is held on trust by Marmaduke for Jemima until she reaches 18. In this case Marmaduke will have to invest the money, as he has to act in the best interests of Jemima. This will usually be her best financial interests. Marmaduke will then transfer the money to Jemima, together with the income from the investments, when she reaches 18.

Q: *How many trustees can you have?*

A: In a trust containing land, under section 34(1) of the Trustee Act 1925 the maximum number of trustees allowed to be on the legal title is four. For a trust containing property other than land, there isn't a limit. You need to think carefully, though, about how many you would appoint. Trustees have to exercise their powers unanimously, so if you appoint too many then they'll never agree on anything. On the other hand, if you appoint just one, there is always the temptation for that one trustee to abscond with the trust property. So at least two is probably a good idea, especially as two trustees are needed in some transactions relating to land.

Q: *Why do trustees have to act unanimously?*

A: Trustees have to act in the best interests of the beneficiaries. To ensure that one trustee doesn't come up with some wayward idea and carry it out without discussion, all trustees have to agree on any action they take.

Q: *Are there any formalities for declaring a trust?*

A: There is a difference between a trust containing land and a trust that does not contain land. Section 53(1)(b) of the Law of Property Act 1925 states:

> A declaration of a trust respecting any land or any interest therein must be manifested and proved by some writing signed by some person who is able to declare such a trust or by his will.

This means that any express declaration of a trust of land must be evidenced in writing and signed by its creator. Writing is not required when there is no land in the trust. A trust of £50,000 set up by Marmaduke for David and Goliath does not need to be in writing because the trust does not contain land.

There is also another exception. There are some situations concerning land where a trust is implied from the actions of the parties. These types of trusts, which we cover in Chapter 9, are exempt from being in writing by section 53(2) of the Law of Property Act 1925.

Q: *Why are trusts important in land law?*

A: You can set up an express trust of land. The owner of land can expressly declare himself trustee of the land for the benefit of others, or he can transfer the land to trustees to hold for the benefit of beneficiaries named by him. However, trusts also feature prominently in land law because whenever two or more people have an interest in the same piece of land a trust is imposed. The most common situation where this arises is when Greenacres is conveyed (sold) to Thomas and Lucy, a happily married or happily unmarried couple. Thomas and Lucy both have an interest in the same piece of land, Greenacres, and a trust will be imposed. The different ways in which people can hold an interest in land together are discussed in Chapters 7, 8 and 9. The one feature that is common to all of them is that they involve a trust.

Q: *If a trust is imposed when two or more people have an interest in the same piece of land, does that mean that these people will wear the labels of trustee or beneficiary?*

A: Yes. Whenever a trust arises, there is a split in ownership. The legal title will be held by people in the capacity of trustees and the equitable title will be held by people in the capacity of beneficiaries. People can also wear the labels of trustee and beneficiary at the same time.

Q: *Do Mr and Mrs Brown down the road, who own their house together, actually have the labels of trustee and beneficiary attached to them?*

A: Almost certainly. It may be rather strange, but you must familiarise yourself with this concept because trusts are a very important part of land law. Just think along the lines of 'Mrs Brown – beneficiary', or Mr Brown – 'trustee and beneficiary'.

An overview of the use of trusts in land

The next chapters look at the different aspects of trusts shown on the chart 'The Use of Trusts in Land' on page 132.

Chapters 7, 8 and 9 explain the ways in which two or more people can have an interest in land together.

Chapter 7 looks at successive interests in land where two or more people have an interest in the same piece of land, and the individual interests follow one after the other. An example is when George leaves Greenacres to Bert for life and then to Claudia. The interests of Bert and Claudia are successive. They come in succession, not at the same time. A trust is imposed to simplify the procedure if Greenacres is sold.

Chapter 8 examines express co-ownership where two or more people expressly set out to own land together at the same time. This is also called concurrent ownership, as the parties have interests in the land at the same time, rather than successively. An example is when Greenacres is sold to Thomas and Lucy. A trust is imposed to simplify conveyancing.

Chapter 9 discusses implied co-ownership, where one person is the legal owner of the land but another person has acted in such a way that he will acquire an interest in the land by implication. Such an action could include contributing to the cost of the property, for example. His interest arises under a trust. This chapter also discusses the use of the trust when there is express co-ownership but there is no declaration of the beneficial interest or when the parties claim that the beneficial interests have changed over time. In either case the percentage share of each party in the property is not known.

You will have noticed that these three ways in which two or more people have an interest in the same piece of land give rise to a trust. With one exception, all trusts containing land, however created, are now governed by the Trusts of Land and Appointment of Trustees Act 1996. This Act, which is discussed in Chapter 10, defines a trust of land and also governs the rights and duties of the parties with the labels of trustee and/or beneficiary in a trust containing land.

Chapter 11 looks at the position of a purchaser when there are interests under a trust of land. The purchaser will clearly want to take the land free from these interests. Conversely, anyone who holds an interest in land under a trust will want to make sure that his interest is protected when the land is sold.

You should try and see this whole area as separate pieces of a jigsaw puzzle that ultimately fit together. Chapters 7, 8 and 9 explain the ways in which two or more people can have an interest in land together. These chapters stand on their own, although they all involve a trust of land. Chapters 10 and 11 apply to all situations where there is a trust of land. The 'Use of Trusts in Land' chart below summarises the overall picture.

USE OF TRUSTS IN LAND

WHAT IS A TRUST?	USING TRUSTS WHERE TWO OR MORE PEOPLE HAVE AN INTEREST IN THE SAME PIECE OF LAND	HOW TRUSTS WORK	BUYING AND SELLING WHERE THERE IS A TRUST OF LAND
CHAPTER 6 THE USE OF TRUSTS IN LAND	CHAPTER 7 SUCCESSIVE INTERESTS IN LAND CHAPTER 8 EXPRESS CO-OWNERSHIP IN LAND CHAPTER 9 IMPLIED CO-OWNERSHIP IN LAND – CONSTRUCTIVE AND RESULTING TRUSTS	CHAPTER 10 THE TRUSTS OF LAND AND APPOINTMENT OF TRUSTEES ACT 1996	CHAPTER 11 OVERREACHING AND THE PROTECTION OF INTERESTS UNDER A TRUST OF LAND

Chapter 7

Successive interests in land

www.palgrave.com/law/Stroud4e

Introduction

In the chart 'The Use of Trusts in Land' in Chapter 6 on page 132, you will see that successive interests in land are one of the ways in which two or more people can hold an interest in the same piece of land and where a trust will be imposed. Successive interests in land are discussed in this chapter.

The nature of successive interests in land

Q: *What are successive interests in land?*

A: When land is given or left to people in succession or in turn, they have successive interests in the land. One interest follows another. These types of interests are also known as consecutive interests in land. An example would be if George left Greenacres in his will to Bert for life and then to Claudia absolutely.

Q: *When George died, would Bert enjoy the land during his own lifetime and then would Claudia own the land when Bert died?*

A: Yes. Bert is said to have a life interest, an interest for his lifetime, and Claudia has what is known as an interest in remainder. A remainder interest is the interest remaining to go to Claudia after Bert's lifetime interest. You could have more successive interests if you wanted, so Greenacres could be left to Bert for life, then to Harriet for life, and then to Claudia absolutely.

Q: *Could this list go on forever?*

A: No. The length of time you could tie up land like this was limited, on the basis that you could not impose your will on countless generations. The length of time was subject to the rules on perpetuities. These rules are outside the scope of this book.

Q: *What does 'absolutely' mean when the example says 'to Claudia absolutely'?*

A: It means that there are no conditions attached to Claudia's interest. Claudia's interest is absolute, therefore she will have absolute ownership of Greenacres when Bert dies. On the other hand, Bert's interest in Greenacres has a condition attached because his interest is only for his lifetime.

Q: *Why were successive interests like this set up?*

A: Basically to keep land in the family. Old George was probably very proud of his country pile, Greenacres, and envisaged countless generations of Georgelets running along the dusty old corridors, reminiscing about 'good old Gramps'. He therefore left the land to successive generations in the family.

A trust was imposed when successive interests in land were created because of the effect of section 1 of the Law of Property Act 1925, which limited the number of estates in land that could be legal. The only estates in land which were capable of subsisting or of being conveyed or created at law after 1925 were:

▶ An estate in fee simple absolute in possession and
▶ A term of years absolute.

The *fee simple absolute in possession* is ownership as we know it. A *fee* is an interest capable of being inherited, *simple* means there are no restrictions on who can inherit, *absolute* means that there are no conditions attached to the interest, and *in possession* means that the interest is in immediate possession and not postponed to a future date. This is what you have when you own a house. You can leave your house in your will to anyone you like; there are no conditions attached to your interest and you are actually in possession of your interest. Note that possession does not mean occupation in this context. It is actual possession of the interest that we're talking about.

The *term of years absolute* is the leasehold estate where you are granted the use of land for a set period of time, otherwise known as a lease.

In the example of Bert and Claudia, when George dies neither Bert nor Claudia has an interest that can be legal. Bert's life interest is not capable of being legal under section 1 of the Law of Property Act 1925. This is because his interest is not absolute, as there is a condition that he can only use Greenacres for his lifetime. Also, because his interest is only for his lifetime, it cannot be inherited. Claudia's interest is not capable of being legal either. She does not have an interest in possession while Bert is alive because she is not in immediate possession of her interest. As their interests are not capable of being legal, section 1(3) of the Law of Property Act 1925 states that they are equitable instead. You therefore have to find a legal owner for Greenacres. Whoever is appointed as legal owner is a trustee of Greenacres holding it on behalf of Bert and Claudia. Hence a trust is created. The trustee holds the legal title and Bert and Claudia hold the equitable title as beneficiaries under the trust.

Q: *What form did the trust take?*

A: The trust could take one of two forms. The first was the settlement governed after 1925 by the Settled Land Act 1925. The second was the trust for sale governed after 1925 by the Law of Property Act 1925. The settlement and the trust for sale governed successive interests in land until 1997.

Q: *Why only until 1997?*

A: Because from then on there was a new regime under the Trusts of Land and Appointment of Trustees Act 1996 which came into force on 1 January 1997. However, settlements which were created before 1997 continue to be governed by the Settled Land Act 1925. This is one reason for knowing something about this area even though there may not be many of these settlements still in existence today. The second reason for understanding the pre-1997 legislation is that the post-1996 regime is explicable only by reference to what went on before. Although this chapter is brief, it will be enough to give you an idea of the problems arising from the creation of successive interests in land before 1997.

Successive interests held under a settlement before 1997

Q: *Who held the legal title as trustee in a settlement before 1997?*

A: In a settlement the person with the first life interest was given the legal title so that someone could deal with and manage the land. This would be Bert in our example, so he would deal with the legal title to Greenacres. He was known as the tenant for life, which was nothing to do with a tenant under a lease. Because he was looking after the land for Claudia as well, Bert became a trustee holding Greenacres on trust for himself and for Claudia, as both he and Claudia held equitable interests in the land. As a beneficiary Bert could enjoy the benefits of Greenacres during his lifetime, after which Claudia became the absolute owner. However, supervisory trustees were also appointed to make sure that Bert dealt properly with the land because he had to bear Claudia's best interests in mind as well. Bert was certainly not allowed to let Greenacres run to ruin. The Settled Land Act 1925 stipulated what Bert could do with the land. It was possible for him to live in Greenacres or to lease or sell Greenacres. Some dealings had to be notified to the supervising trustees and, in the case of certain dealings, he would need their consent. If he sold Greenacres, the supervisory trustees would receive the money from the sale, just in case Bert decided to ignore Claudia's interests altogether and start a new life in Rio with the money. The money from the sale of Greenacres also had to be paid to the trustees to ensure that the process of overreaching took place. Overreaching is discussed in Chapter 11 and means that a purchaser can take Greenacres free from the interests of Bert and Claudia. The supervising trustees would then have either to invest the money from the sale or to purchase further land, and Bert hold these investments or the land on trust for himself and Claudia. The structure of the settlement before 1997 can be summarised as follows.

Legal title vested in Bert. The Settled Land Act 1925 gave Bert his powers	GREENACRES left by George
	$\downarrow$
<u>Documents required</u> Document to vest the legal title in Bert Document showing the line of succession	to Bert for life
	$\downarrow$
	Bert holds Greenacres on trust for himself and Claudia
	$\downarrow$
	then to Claudia absolutely

Q: *What were the problems with this arrangement?*

A: It was a lot of paperwork because you had to vest the legal title in Bert. When Bert died you had to vest the legal title in the next person, Claudia. You also needed two documents. One would show the vesting of the legal title and the other the line of succession. The document showing the line of succession was technically called the trust instrument. In George's case, this was his will. A settlement could also be created accidentally. Imagine old George making a homemade will and thinking along the following lines.

> I'll leave Greenacres to Bert while he's alive and then because I like young Claudia I'll leave it to her after that. That's nice and straightforward. Bert will always have Claudia's best interests at heart and I'm sure he'll look after the place. I'll write that down as to Bert for life and then to Claudia absolutely.

This kind of thinking, apart from being very optimistic, created a settlement because the Settled Land Act 1925 imposed a settlement on successive interests in land. Supervisory trustees would have to be found, the legal title would have to be vested in Bert, and, when he died, the legal title had to be vested in Claudia. This was complicated and expensive. Furthermore, as Bert was given the power to sell Greenacres under the Settled Land Act 1925, he could defeat old George's wish that generations of Georgelets could enjoy it by selling the property and investing the money elsewhere.

Q: *What is a strict settlement?*

A: You could have different forms of settled land and a strict settlement is one such form.

Q: *What was the alternative to holding successive interests in land by way of a settlement?*

A: The trust for sale.

Successive interests held under a trust for sale before 1997

If interests in land were left successively but the words 'trust for sale' were used, a trust for sale would be created. An example is where George left Greenacres on trust for sale to Bert for life and then to Claudia absolutely. The interests of Bert and Claudia are still successive, but the wording indicated that George wished Greenacres to be held on a trust for sale.

Q: *How did a trust for sale work?*

A: You still had the same problem, in that neither Bert nor Claudia could legally own Greenacres. You therefore had to find trustees who would hold the legal title on their behalf. Unlike in a settlement, this was not the person with the first life interest. Trustees were appointed either expressly by George or, if he did not do so, by the court. The structure imposed was as follows.

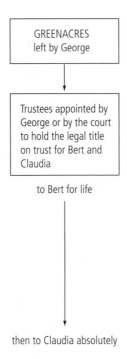

GREENACRES
left by George

Trustees appointed by
George or by the court
to hold the legal title
on trust for Bert and
Claudia

to Bert for life

then to Claudia absolutely

Q: *How many trustees did you have to appoint?*

A: There was no law that stated that you had to have more than one trustee. However, if you had more than one trustee there was less chance of fraud. Two trustees were also required for overreaching, which is discussed in Chapter 11.

Q: *What did the words 'trust for sale' imply?*

A: That there was an imperative duty to sell Greenacres.

In the 1920s land tended to be either the huge, crumbling mansion that old George wanted to keep in the family or land used for commercial and business purposes. Ordinary people didn't own their own houses in those days, but rented instead. If Greenacres was commercial land, it would be viewed as an investment opportunity. The aim would be to sell Greenacres when the property market was favourable, and then invest the money elsewhere. When George left Greenacres to Bert and then to Claudia, it made more sense to create a trust for sale if Greenacres was commercial property, as it would be treated as an investment. This was reflected in the fact that there was no right to live in the property if a trust for sale was created unless it was expressly allowed in the terms of the trust document, and the chances were that Greenacres had a factory belching fire and brimstone on it anyway.

Q: *If there was a trust for sale in this situation, what benefit did Bert receive in his lifetime?*

A: He received the income from Greenacres, the rent from the owners of the factory for example.

Q: *Was it compulsory to sell Greenacres?*

A: There was an imperative duty to sell. This reflected the fact that, as Greenacres was seen as an investment opportunity, the ability to sell was extremely important. You didn't want one trustee holding up an investment opportunity by objecting to a proposed sale. There was also a power to postpone sale. However, in order to postpone sale, all the trustees had to agree to postpone. If any one of them disagreed with postponement, then Greenacres had to be sold. The problem with the duty to sell was that, under the doctrine of conversion, the interests of the beneficiaries were seen from the very beginning as interests in money. This was because of the imperative duty to sell. If you had to sell Greenacres, then you might as well save time and just say that Bert's and Claudia's interests were in the money from the start. This didn't represent the situation in reality, especially when the sale of Greenacres was postponed.

In a trust for sale, the trustees had no obligation to consult the beneficiaries over the running of the trust unless it was expressly stated in the trust document that they had to do so. Even then, they didn't necessarily have to act on these views. Any unresolved disputes over Greenacres were taken to court under the Law of Property Act 1925, where the court decided the outcome.

Q: *How did the trust for sale compare with the settlement?*

A: It was easier in terms of paperwork. It was less complicated and less expensive. If the property was commercial property it made sense to create a trust for sale, so that the property was looked after by professional trustees rather than by a beneficiary who might not have had any interest or experience in running a business.

Successive interests in land after 1996

Q: *What happened after 1996?*

A: It was no longer possible to create a settlement. Settlements created before 1997 continue to be governed by the Settled Land Act 1925. Successive interests in land created after 1996 are now governed by the Trusts of Land and Appointment of Trustees Act 1996, which is discussed in Chapter 10. Existing trusts for sale have been converted into trusts of land which, again, are governed by the 1996 Act.

Summary of successive interests

Before 1997 successive interests in land were held under either a settlement or a trust for sale, depending on the wording used in their creation. Settlements could be created accidentally and were complicated and unwieldy. The trust for sale was more flexible, but the land had to be sold unless all the trustees agreed to postpone sale. In a trust for sale the interests of the beneficiaries were seen from the very start as being in money, because the land had to be sold. This was confusing for everyone. After 1996 successive interests created in land were governed by the Trusts of Land and Appointment of Trustees Act 1996.

A sample question on successive interests in land is included at the end of Chapter 10.

Chapter 8

Express co-ownership in land

www.palgrave.com/law/Stroud4e

Introduction

In the chart 'The Use of Trusts in Land' in Chapter 6 on page 132, you will see that express co-ownership is one of the ways in which two or more people can hold an interest in the same piece of land and where a trust will be imposed. Express co-ownership is discussed in this chapter.

The nature of express co-ownership

Q: *What is express co-ownership?*

A: *Co-ownership* is where two or more people hold an interest in land at the same time. The interests of the parties are said to be concurrent. The parties hold interests concurrently, at the same time, rather than successively, which is when interests are held one after the other, as discussed in Chapter 7. *Express* co-ownership occurs when land is conveyed (sold or transferred) to two or more people by an *express* act. An example of express co-ownership is where Greenacres is expressly sold or transferred to Thomas and Lucy, where both Thomas and Lucy will own an interest in it at the same time. Another example is where Abigail, Luke and Selina finish university and buy Greenacres together. All three will own an interest in it at the same time. These are examples of express co-ownership where the land has been expressly conveyed to two or more people. Implied co-ownership, where co-ownership is implied from the behaviour of the parties, is discussed in Chapter 9.

Q: *How do co-owners hold land?*

A: There are two main types of co-ownership.

1. The joint tenancy and
2. The tenancy in common.

The joint tenancy

Q: *How do co-owners hold land in a joint tenancy?*

A: In a joint tenancy the co-owners, who are called tenants, hold as joint tenants. This means that they hold the land as one unity, and do not have separate

139

individual shares in the land. Each 'owns the whole'. The main feature of the joint tenancy is the presence of the four unities. These are four requirements that show that the land is held jointly, and they must all be met for a joint tenancy to exist.

Q: *What are the four unities?*

A: You can remember them by remembering the acronym PITT.

P = Possession
I = Interest
T = Time
T = Title

Q: *What do they all mean?*

A: The *unity of possession* means that each tenant (party) has an equal right to possession of all of the land. The land is not split up into a separate part for each tenant, as this would show separate ownership rather than a joint ownership of the whole.

The *unity of interest* means that each tenant has the same interest in the land as the other tenants and for the same length of time. So if one tenant has a different interest in the land from the others, there will be no unity of interest. An example is where Albert has a life interest in, and Charles has a lease over, the same piece of land. There is no unity of interest because their interests in the land are not the same, nor do they go on for the same length of time.

The *unity of time* means that all the tenants receive their interests in the land at the same time.

The *unity of title* means that the tenants must receive their interest in the land in the same way from the same document. If land is sold to the tenants, the conveyance, the deed of sale, must be to all of them to satisfy the unity of title.

Q: *Do you have to satisfy all the four unities in order to have a joint tenancy?*

A: Yes. It is essential to do so. If you cannot meet the four unities, you do not have a joint tenancy.

Q: *What's the effect of parties holding as joint tenants in a joint tenancy relationship?*

A: The main effect is something called the 'right of survivorship'. This is known as the *ius accrescendi* in Latin. The right of survivorship rule states that if any one of the joint tenants dies, his interest will automatically vest in (pass to) the other joint tenants. In a joint tenancy the parties do not have individual interests. They hold 'the whole' together. As they do not have an individual interest to call their own, if any one of them dies, their interest in the land simply devolves to the other joint tenants. Look at this in an example where Albert (A), Belinda (B), Charles (C) and David (D) hold their interests together in Greenacres as joint tenants. If Albert dies, his interest devolves to the other three tenants, who simply carry on holding Greenacres as joint tenants. A good way of showing the relationship of joint tenants is to put the parties holding in the joint tenant relationship as a whole in brackets.

(A B C D) ———————→ A dies ———————→ the right of survivorship applies ———————→ (B C D)
joint tenants   joint tenants

Q: *When A dies, can't he leave his interest in Greenacres to his family in his will?*

A: No. He can't leave his interest in his will, nor can it pass under the rules of intestacy. Intestacy is where someone dies without a will and there is a distribution of the deceased's property according to a statutory list. People holding as joint tenants own the whole together. They do not hold individual interests in the land and, as such, have nothing to leave either in their wills or on their intestacies. The right of survivorship also takes effect on the moment of death and takes precedence over any will.

Q: *Isn't the right of survivorship unfair, as the person who survives the longest ends up owning the land?*

A: Taking the previous example above, the following may happen.

(A B C D) ———————→ A dies ———————→ the rule of survivorship applies ———————→ (B C D)
(B C D) ———————→ D dies ———————→ the rule of survivorship applies ———————→ (B C)
(B C) ———————→ B dies ———————→ the rule of survivorship applies ———————→ C

C is the sole owner of the land. So, yes, it's a lottery system and it is unfair.

Q: *Why would anyone want to be a joint tenant when so much depends on chance?*

A: There are several very good reasons which we'll look at later, but first, look at the opposite form of land holding, the tenancy in common.

The tenancy in common

A tenancy in common requires only the unity of possession, that is, all the tenants have a right to possess all of the land. This means the other three unities do not have to be satisfied, so a tenant in common can obtain his interest at a different time from everyone else. He can also have a different interest from everyone else, for example a larger interest, and he does not have to receive his interest in the same way, from the same document for example.

Q: *Why does a tenancy in common require the unity of possession?*

A: As all the parties have the right to possess the whole of the land, it shows that the land is co-owned. No one person has his or her own individual part of the land which would imply sole ownership rather than co-ownership.

Unlike in a joint tenancy, however, in a tenancy in common each tenant holds an individual share in the land.

Q: *Does this mean that the land is physically divided up?*

A: No. It just means that each tenant is recognised as having his own share in the land although it has not yet been divided up. This explains the term 'undivided shares in land'.

There is an important advantage of holding as a tenant in common. As a tenant in common holds his own individual share in the land, he can leave his interest in the land in his will, or it can pass under the rules of intestacy. In any example it's convenient to depict tenants in common without the brackets. This shows that they stand on their own with their own individual interest. So, if A, B, C and D hold as tenants in common, it would look like this.

A	B	C	D
tenant in common	tenant in common	tenant in common	tenant in common

If A died, his interest in the land would pass under his will or under the rules of intestacy.

Q: *How do the joint tenancy and the tenancy in common fit into express co-ownership?*

A: To answer this you need to look at the chart on page 143.

Express co-ownership

The legal title

Box A

THE LEGAL TITLE

After 1925 the legal title must be held as a joint tenancy

In order to sell land, everyone on the legal title must sign the conveyance, the deed of sale. Before 1926 it was possible for people to hold the legal title to land as tenants in common. Remember that tenants in common have their own individual shares which they can do with as they wish. If Greenacres were sold to A, B, C and D in 1920 as tenants in common, they would all hold a separate interest in the legal title. Now imagine that the following events have taken place since 1920:

A – has died and left his interest in the legal title to Y and Z;
B – has given his interest in the legal title to his grandchildren, S, T and U;
C – has sold his interest in the legal title in Greenacres to F and G;
D – has done nothing.

If Greenacres were sold after these events, effecting a sale would require the signature of every person who held an interest in the legal title.

Q: *Does that mean you'd need eight signatures in all, Y, Z, S, T, U, F, G and D to sell Greenacres?*

A: Yes. That starts to get very complicated and it becomes virtually impossible to sell the land. In 1925 the Law of Property Act changed the way in which the legal title could be held.

After 1925 the legal title must be held as a joint tenancy: see sections 1(6), 34(1) and 36(2) of the Law of Property Act 1925. A consequence of this is that the right

EXPRESS CO-OWNERSHIP AND SEVERANCE

EXPRESS CO-OWNERSHIP

Box A

THE LEGAL TITLE

After 1925 the legal title must be held as a joint tenancy

Box B

THE EQUITABLE TITLE

1. Unity of possession met but any or all of the other three unities missing = Tenancy in common

2. Four unities met and an express declaration of a tenancy in common = Tenancy in common

3. Four unities met and an express declaration of a joint tenancy = Joint tenancy

4. Four unities met, no express declaration but words of severance = Tenancy in common

5. Four unities met, no express declaration, no words of severance but equal contribution to the purchase price = Joint tenancy

6. Four unities met, no express declaration, no words of severance but purchase price paid in unequal shares = Tenancy in common

7. Four unities met in a business partnership = Tenancy in common, even if purchase price paid in equal shares

8. Four unities met when two or more people lend money on a mortgage = Tenancy in common, even if the mortgage money is lent in equal shares

SEVERANCE

Box C

THE LEGAL TITLE

The legal title cannot be severed

Box D

THE EQUITABLE TITLE

The equitable title can be severed by:

1. Section 36(2) of the Law of Property Act 1925 or

2. *Williams v Hensman* (1861) – A person acting on his own share or

3. *Williams v Hensman* (1861) – Mutual agreement or

4. *Williams v Hensman* (1861) – Mutual conduct or

5. Homicide.

of survivorship now applies to the legal title. If Greenacres had been conveyed (sold) to A, B, C and D today, and the same events had happened, the picture would look very different. First, the legal title of Greenacres could be held by A, B, C and D only as a joint tenancy. Secondly, when A died, his interest in the legal title would simply vest in B, C and D under the right of survivorship. Thirdly, in a joint tenancy, the parties own the whole of the whole and do not have a separate interest. This means B and C do not have individual shares in the legal title to give or sell to anyone, so their interest in the legal title could not pass to S, T, U, F or G. Parties B, C and D would therefore remain on the legal title until either the right of survivorship operated or they removed themselves from the legal title.

Furthermore, section 34 of the Trustee Act 1925 states that the maximum number of people who can be on the legal title is four. There do not have to be four, but there can be no more than four. If land is sold to more than four people, those on the legal title will be the first four people named on the conveyance, the deed of sale, who are 18 or over and willing to be on the legal title. This means that the maximum number of signatures ever required to sell land is four. The overall effect of these provisions in the Law of Property Act 1925 and the Trustee Act 1925 made it much more practical to sell Greenacres.

Q: *How do you remove yourself from the legal title while you're alive?*

A: The way to remove yourself is by retirement following the formal statutory requirements of the Trustee Act 1925.

The equitable title

Box B

THE EQUITABLE TITLE

1. Unity of possession met but any or all of the other three unities missing = Tenancy in common

2. Four unities met and an express declaration of a tenancy in common = Tenancy in common

3. Four unities met and an express declaration of a joint tenancy = Joint tenancy

4. Four unities met, no express declaration but words of severance = Tenancy in common

5. Four unities met, no express declaration, no words of severance but equal contribution to the purchase price = Joint tenancy

6. Four unities met, no express declaration, no words of severance but purchase price paid in unequal shares = Tenancy in common

7. Four unities met in a business partnership = Tenancy in common, even if purchase price paid in equal shares

8. Four unities met when two or more people lend money on a mortgage = Tenancy in common, even if the mortgage money is lent in equal shares

---

Q: *What happens if more than four people want to buy Greenacres together, if section 34 of the Trustee Act 1925 states that there's a maximum of four people allowed on the legal title?*

A: You would have a problem. Take the example of five friends, Adrian (A), Bob (B), Clare (C), David (D) and Emilio (E), buying a house together. You couldn't just ignore the interests of E simply because he wasn't allowed to be on the legal title. To deal with this situation, a trust was imposed by sections 34(2) and 36(1) of the Law of Property Act 1925 where there was express beneficial co-ownership.

Q: *What's express beneficial co-ownership?*

A: Co-ownership exists where two or more people have an interest in the land at the same time. 'Express' means that land was sold or transferred to the parties expressly. 'Beneficial' means rights of enjoyment in the land. 'Express beneficial co-ownership' means that two or more people have rights of enjoyment at the same time in land which was sold or transferred to them expressly. In the example of A, B, C, D and E, Greenacres would be expressly sold to them all and they would all have the right to enjoy the benefits of it and to live there.

Q: *Is there an example where the co-owners have no beneficial enjoyment?*

A: Look at this example. Tick and Tock hold Redacres on trust for Jemima. Tick and Tock are trustees. They hold the legal title and Jemima holds the equitable title. Tick and Tock cannot take any benefit from Redacres because they are holding Redacres on trust for Jemima, for her benefit. They have no right to live there or to take any profit from the land or to benefit in any way from Redacres. There is co-ownership because both Tick and Tock have a legal interest in Redacres together at the same time, but it is not beneficial co-ownership because they have no enjoyment rights in Redacres.

The imposition of a trust where there was express beneficial co-ownership meant that the ownership of the land was split into a legal title and an equitable title. If A, B, C, D and E bought a house together, there was express beneficial co-ownership. They all had the right to the beneficial enjoyment of Greenacres. A trust was imposed, and the title of Greenacres was split into the legal title and the equitable title. The first four people named on the conveyance, A, B, C and D, held the legal title as joint tenants, as discussed in Box A, and were given the label of trustees. The legal title gave A, B, C and D the ability to manage Greenacres and sign the paperwork in any dealings, for example if Greenacres was sold. They also each had an equitable title, an equitable interest in Greenacres, and so A, B, C, and D wore the label of beneficiaries as well. The equitable title recognised their enjoyment or beneficial rights in the land. Emilio, of course, also had an enjoyment or beneficial right in Greenacres. The imposition of a trust allowed his beneficial enjoyment to be recognised on the equitable title, even though he couldn't be on the legal title. Emilio held an equitable interest in Greenacres and also wore the label of beneficiary. Adrian, B, C and D held Greenacres on trust for themselves and E. Don't worry whether the equitable title is held as a joint tenancy or a tenancy in common. This is discussed later.

Legal title	Equitable title
(A B C D) Joint tenants	A B C D E

Q: *Why do A, B, C and D hold on trust for themselves in equity as well as E?*

A: Because if they weren't on the equitable title, the position would look like this:

Legal title	Equitable title
(A B C D)	E
Joint tenants	

As you know, the equitable title is the beneficial title or the enjoyment title. If only E were on the equitable title, only E could enjoy the property and live there. However, A, B, C and D also have beneficial rights in Greenacres. So, peculiar as it may sound, A, B, C and D hold Greenacres on trust for themselves and E in equity. That way, they all enjoy the benefits of Greenacres and can live there. This is what everyone would expect to happen anyway.

Q: *As E is not on the legal title, who is going to look after his interests?*

A: A trustee has to work in the best interests of the beneficiaries who hold an equitable interest in the property. Adrian, B, C and D will work in their own best interests anyway but, because they wear the label of trustees, they will also have to look after the interests of E. When you look at the duties of A, B, C and D in their capacity as trustees, you will find that they have a duty to consult E before they can consider selling Greenacres, for instance.

Q: *How many people can you have on the equitable title?*

A: There is no limit.

There is another very common example of express beneficial co-ownership. Imagine Thomas and Lucy buy Greenacres together. It is conveyed (sold) to them both. Where two or more people, here Thomas and Lucy, have an interest in the land at the same time, there is co-ownership. Greenacres has been expressly conveyed (sold) to them, so there is express co-ownership. Both Thomas and Lucy have enjoyment or beneficial rights in Greenacres, so there is express beneficial co-ownership. A trust is imposed, and because Thomas and Lucy are on the legal title they now wear the label of trustees and must hold the legal title as joint tenants. Because they both have an enjoyment right in Greenacres, they are both on the equitable title and both are beneficiaries. They hold Greenacres on trust for themselves.

Legal title	Equitable title
(T L)	T L
Joint Tenants	

Q: *Isn't that a rather strange situation?*

A: Yes. And I imagine if you told the millions of people in this country that they were in the same position as Thomas and Lucy, they probably wouldn't believe you. However, this is what happens. And, of course, you could easily find yourself in the same situation as either Thomas or Lucy, wearing these labels of trustee and beneficiary.

There are other reasons why a trust is imposed when there is express beneficial co-ownership. Imagine that A, B, C, D and E have bought Greenacres together and don't want to hold as joint tenants. They want their individual shares recognised, and certainly don't want the lottery of the right of survivorship to apply, so that one of them ends up with Greenacres completely by chance.

Q: *I'm sure some people would feel like this. How do you avoid the right of survivorship?*

A: You cannot do anything about the legal title which gives the authority to manage Greenacres and sign the paperwork. The legal title must be held as a joint tenancy under the Law of Property Act 1925 for the reasons already given in Box A. It's on the equitable title that you find the rights of enjoyment in Greenacres. So, given that the equitable title is the enjoyment part of Greenacres, A, B, C, D and E are allowed to have either a joint tenancy or a tenancy in common on the equitable title.

Legal title	Equitable title
(A B C D) Joint Tenants	either (A B C D E) as joint tenants or A B C D E as tenants in common

If a person holds his equitable interest as a tenant in common, rather than relying on the right of survivorship, he can leave that equitable interest in his will or it can pass on his intestacy. This is another advantage of imposing a trust. It allows the parties to hold their equitable, or enjoyment, interests in Greenacres either as joint tenants or as tenants in common.

Q: *How does this work in practice?*

A: Take A, B, C, D and E again. They buy Greenacres together. The property is specifically conveyed (sold) to them as 'equitable joint tenants'. There is express beneficial co-ownership, so a trust is imposed. Under the Law of Property Act 1925 the legal title must always be held as a joint tenancy. The equitable title will also be held as a joint tenancy because the property was specifically conveyed to them as 'equitable joint tenants'.

Legal title	Equitable title
(A B C D) Joint tenants	(A B C D E) Joint tenants

Adrian has left his interest in Greenacres in his will to his son, Xanadu. If A dies, his interest in the legal title vests in B, C and D under the right of survivorship. Similarly, A's equitable interest in the equitable title simply vests in B, C, D and E, again under the right of survivorship.

Legal title	Equitable title
(B C D) Joint tenants	(B C D E) Joint tenants

As the right of survivorship has operated on the equitable title, Xanadu will receive nothing under A's will.

Q: *Absolutely nothing?*

A: Nothing. Adrian's equitable interest in Greenacres has now vested in B, C, D and E, and with it all the beneficial enjoyment of Greenacres. Even if Greenacres were sold the day after A's death, Xanadu would not receive A's share of the proceeds as A's equitable interest in Greenacres vested in the others on his death.

Q: *Is this so even though A specifically left his interest in Greenacres in his will to Xanadu?*

A: Yes. If A holds as a joint tenant, the right of survivorship applies and takes precedence over any will he may have made.

Now let's say that Greenacres was conveyed to A, B, C, D and E as equitable tenants in common instead.

Legal title	Equitable title
(A B C D)	A B C D E
Joint tenants	Tenants in common

When A dies, his interest in the legal title vests in B, C and D under the right of survivorship again. As A holds his equitable interest as a tenant in common, he has an interest to leave, and so can leave his equitable interest in Greenacres to his son, Xanadu, in his will. This is extremely convenient for him. While A is alive, he can live in Greenacres along with B, C, D and E. If Greenacres is sold, A will receive his share of the money in proportion to how much he put in when the land was bought, or whatever share the parties agreed each were to have. If A dies, his equitable interest in Greenacres passes in his will to Xanadu who then has the equitable or beneficial interest in the land and can live there. If Greenacres is sold after A has died, Xanadu will receive A's monetary share in it, as the equitable interest will have now been turned into money.

Q: *Does this idea of choosing whether you hold the equitable title as joint tenants or as tenants in common apply to every situation where there is express beneficial co-ownership?*

A: Yes. You could have the situation where A and B hold property for X, Y and Z,

Legal title	Equitable title
(A B)	either (X Y Z) as Joint tenants or
Joint tenants	X Y Z as Tenants in common

or the very common situation indeed, where Greenacres is sold to Thomas and Lucy. Thomas and Lucy can be a happily married couple or they can be a happily cohabiting couple. Either way, there is express beneficial co-ownership.

Imagine that Thomas and Lucy have chosen to hold Greenacres as joint tenants in equity.

Legal title	Equitable title
(T L)	(T L)
Joint tenants	Joint tenants

The legal title must always be held as a joint tenancy. If Thomas dies, the right of survivorship applies to the legal title, which vests in Lucy. Lucy then continues to deal with the legal title of Greenacres. As they hold as joint tenants on the equitable title, Thomas's equitable interest will also devolve to Lucy on his death under the right of survivorship.

Legal title	Equitable title
L	L

Q: *Is there still a trust?*

A: No. There is no longer beneficial co-ownership. Lucy no longer co-owns Greenacres with anyone. You cannot be a 'co-' or 'together with' owner if there is nobody to be 'co-' with. She owns Greenacres absolutely.

This way of holding Greenacres is very convenient. When either party dies, the other party will own it and can do what he or she wants with it. In any happy relationship, this is the outcome most people would desire, and so it makes sense for many people to choose to hold the equitable title as joint tenants.

Q: *What happens if Thomas and Lucy hold the equitable title as tenants in common?*

A: The situation will be different.

Legal title	Equitable title
(T L)	T L
Joint tenants	Tenants in common

The legal title will still be held as a joint tenancy. When Thomas dies, the right of survivorship applies on the legal title, which vests in Lucy. Because Thomas and Lucy each had an individual share in Greenacres as tenants in common, the right of survivorship does not apply. Thomas's interest will pass under his will or under the intestacy rules, let's say to Z. Lucy will still keep her own individual share as a tenant in common.

Legal title	Equitable title
L	T's interest passes under his will or intestacy to Z
	L remains a tenant in common

Q: *Is there still a trust here?*

A: Yes. There is still beneficial co-ownership on the equitable title. Lucy will be a trustee holding the legal title on behalf of herself and Z. Party Z will now have an equitable interest in Greenacres and enjoyment rights. If Greenacres is sold, Z will receive what would have been T's share of the proceeds.

Q: *Why would Thomas and Lucy choose to hold as tenants in common?*

A: When they don't want the right of survivorship to apply, but prefer to leave their interest in Greenacres to someone else in a will.

Q: *When do they first choose which way to hold the equitable title?*

A: When they buy the house, their solicitor should explain to them the consequences of both the joint tenancy and the tenancy in common. They can then decide whether to have the house conveyed to them as equitable joint tenants or equitable tenants in common. If they decide to hold as equitable tenants in common, they will also decide on the size of their respective shares.

Many couples buying a house will probably choose to hold the equitable title as joint tenants. Friends buying a property together would probably choose to hold the equitable title as tenants in common. In this case the right of survivorship will not apply, and each tenant will be able to leave his equitable interest in the property to whom he wants in his will.

Q: *How do I know whether people are holding as joint tenants or as tenants in common if there is no express declaration?*

A: The legal title always has to be held as a joint tenancy. If Greenacres is simply conveyed to Thomas and Lucy with no express declaration as to how they hold the equitable title, they satisfy the four unities of possession, interest, time and title. They both have a right to possession of Greenacres; they both have the same interest; and the land was conveyed to them at the same time by the same document. This would lead to the presumption of a joint tenancy on the equitable title as well. However, equity favours the tenancy in common because the unfairness of the lottery effect of the right of survivorship does not operate in a tenancy in common. This means that there are some situations where, even though the four unities are met on the equitable title, equity will presume a tenancy in common instead. The situations where a joint tenancy and a tenancy in common arise on the equitable title are looked at in Boxes B1 to B8. The only unity required for a tenancy in common is the unity of possession.

Q: *Why is the unity of possession required for a tenancy in common?*

A: If all the tenants could not possess the whole of the land, it would imply that they each had their separate share. This would mean there was no co-ownership.

Box B1 Unity of possession met but any or all of the other three unities missing = tenancy in common

This reflects the fact that a joint tenancy cannot exist unless the four unities are met. Providing the unity of possession exists, there will be a tenancy in common.

Box B2 Four unities met and an express declaration of a tenancy in common = tenancy in common

Even though the four unities have been met, the declaration of a tenancy in common will be conclusive and the parties will hold the equitable title as tenants in common.

Box B3   Four unities met and an express declaration of a joint tenancy
= joint tenancy

If the four unities are satisfied and there is an express declaration that the parties are
to hold as joint tenants, this express declaration will be conclusive: see *Goodman v
Gallant* (1986). This is so unless there is fraud or proprietary estoppel can be argued
as in *Clarke v Meadus* (2010). Proprietary estoppel is discussed in Chapter 12.

Box B4   Four unities met, no express declaration but words of severance
= tenancy in common

Q: *What are words of severance?*

A: Words of severance are words that indicate that the parties are intended to have
their own individual and separate shares. The following words in the conveyance,
the deed of sale, all indicate this: 'equally': see *Lewen v Dodd* (1599), 'between':
see *Lashbrook v Cock* (1816), and 'share and share alike': see *Heathe v Heathe* (1741).
If Greenacres is conveyed to Thomas and Lucy 'to share and share alike', in the
absence of an express declaration they will hold as tenants in common even though
the four unities are met.

Box B5   Four unities met, no express declaration, no words of severance but equal
contribution to the purchase price = joint tenancy

If the four unities are satisfied and there is no express declaration or words of
severance but the parties contribute equally to the purchase price, they will hold as
joint tenants. If land is conveyed to A, B, C, D and E and they contribute equally to
the purchase price, in the absence of an express declaration or words of severance,
they will hold as joint tenants.

Box B6   Four unities met, no express declaration, no words of severance but
purchase price paid in unequal shares = tenancy in common

Q: *Why does an unequal contribution to the purchase price result in a tenancy in
common?*

A: If parties contribute unequally to the purchase price, it's not as easy to decide
that all the parties hold 'the whole' together. If they did hold as joint tenants,
the party who had paid the least might end up as the sole owner if the right of
survivorship went in his favour. Equity saw this as unfair, so a tenancy in common
is presumed where there is unequal contribution to the purchase price even though
the four unities are met. The size of each party's share will be in proportion to his
respective contribution: see *Lake v Gibson* (1729) and *Bull v Bull* (1955).

Box B7   Four unities met in a business partnership = tenancy in common,
even if purchase price paid in equal shares

If two or more people buy land together as a commercial venture, it is presumed
that they would not want the right of survivorship to operate. If David and Goliath
buy land together as a business partnership, either David or Goliath would expect
to be able to leave his interest in the business to anyone he wanted in his will when
he died. Therefore a tenancy in common is presumed in this business situation,
even though the four unities are met and there is equal contribution to the purchase
price. In *Malayan Credit Ltd v Jack Chia-MPH Ltd* (1986) the parties had taken a

joint lease. The fact that they had used the premises for their separate businesses indicated that they held as tenants in common.

Four unities met when two or more people lend money on a mortgage = tenancy in common, even if the mortgage money is lent in equal shares

If David and Goliath together lend you £50,000 on a mortgage to buy Greenacres, they will hold the land as security if you don't pay the mortgage repayments. If necessary, they will repossess and sell Greenacres to recoup their outstanding mortgage money. It is presumed that David and Goliath will hold their security for the money in Greenacres as tenants in common: see *Petty v Styward* (1632). If you don't pay the mortgage repayments and Greenacres is sold, David and Goliath will receive £25,000 each. If David has died, his £25,000 will pass under his will or intestacy because it is presumed that he was holding as a tenant in common.

Summary of legal and equitable express co-ownership

There are two types of co-ownership: the joint tenancy and the tenancy in common. The right of survivorship operates in a joint tenancy. The legal title to land must be held as a joint tenancy. A maximum of four people can be on the legal title. The equitable title is held as either a joint tenancy or a tenancy in common.

Severance

Q: *What's severance?*

A: Severance is the act of converting a joint tenancy into a tenancy in common.

Q: *Why would you want to do this?*

A: First, because of the lottery effect of the right of survivorship. People who start off by holding as joint tenants may subsequently decide that they want to hold their own individual interests in the property as a tenant in common. They may want to be able to leave their interests in a will, for example. The way of achieving this is through severance, the severing of an individual interest from the whole.

Look at one of the examples we've used. Greenacres is conveyed to A, B, C, D and E as 'equitable (or beneficial) joint tenants'. The parties A, B, C and D will hold the legal title as joint tenants, and they will hold the equitable title as joint tenants for themselves and E as the four unities are met and an express declaration is conclusive (Box B3). If any of them wishes to hold his equitable interest as a tenant in common, he may sever it from the whole by recognised means.

Q: *Why would they want to do this?*

A: Imagine that B decides to emigrate. He no longer wishes to live in Greenacres and would rather use his share of the money he contributed to it to buy a property abroad. The others refuse to sell just so that he can realise his share. One option is for B to sell his equitable interest to Raj. The act of selling severs B's equitable interest from the joint tenancy. Raj will have the equitable or beneficial rights in Greenacres and will be able to live there. B is happy as he has his money and Raj has somewhere to live. If Greenacres is sold, Raj will receive the proportionate share of money that would have been due to B.

Look at one of the other examples we've used. Greenacres was conveyed to Thomas and Lucy as 'equitable joint tenants' 20 years ago. The legal title must be held as a joint tenancy and they are holding the equitable title as joint tenants, as the four unities are met and the express declaration is conclusive (Box B3). Last year the relationship broke down and Lucy moved out. If they continue to hold the equitable title as joint tenants and Lucy dies, her equitable or beneficial interest will devolve automatically to Thomas under the right of survivorship. Even if Greenacres were sold the day after Lucy's death, whoever inherited under Lucy's would not receive any of her interest in Greenacres. Lucy's equitable interest, including her right of occupation and her monetary share in the property, would have vested in Thomas. As she is no longer talking to him after the breakdown of their relationship, she may not wish this to happen if she dies. She would far rather leave her equitable interest in Greenacres in her will to their daughter, Jane. The means by which she can convert her equitable joint tenancy into a tenancy in common is the process called severance. When she has converted her equitable interest into a tenancy in common, Lucy will be seen to have her own individual share that she can leave to whomever she wants in her will. She must of course sever her interest in her lifetime.

Q: *Why?*

A: Because in a joint tenancy she does not have an interest to leave in a will until she has severed it. She must sever it before she dies. By definition she must sever in her lifetime! If she hasn't severed her interest prior to her death, the right of survivorship will apply and will take precedence over any will she may have made.

Q: *Does it matter whether Thomas and Lucy are married or cohabiting in the example above?*

A: No. It will be exactly the same situation whether they are married or not.

We can now look in detail at how severance is achieved.

The legal title

> **Box C**
>
> THE LEGAL TITLE
>
> The legal title cannot be severed

It is important to note that under section 36(2) of the Law of Property Act 1925 you cannot sever the legal joint tenancy.

Q: *Why not?*

A: Because if you do, you will convert it into a tenancy in common. Sections 1(6) and 34(1) of the Law of Property Act 1925 state that you cannot have a legal tenancy in common. If you have a legal tenancy in common, people on the legal title will have their own individual interests in it, which makes selling property virtually impossible, as discussed in Box A. This is why you can no longer have a legal tenancy in common, still less try to create one.

The equitable title

> **Box D**
>
> THE EQUITABLE TITLE
>
> The equitable title can be severed by:
>
> **1.** Section 36(2) of the Law of Property Act 1925 or
>
> **2.** *Williams v Hensman* (1861) – A person acting on his own share or
>
> **3.** *Williams v Hensman* (1861) – Mutual agreement or
>
> **4.** *Williams v Hensman* (1861) – Mutual conduct or
>
> **5.** Homicide.

Only the equitable title can be severed, and the act of severance must be by one of the following ways.

Box D1

Section 36(2) of the Law of Property Act 1925

This is a statutory method of severance. It involves a notice in writing sent by one joint tenant to all the other joint tenants stating that he wishes to hold his interest as a tenant in common. Although the notice doesn't have to be signed, it must be sent to all the other joint tenants and delivered to their last known home or business addresses.

Q: *What happens if the others don't receive it?*

A: If it's registered or sent by recorded delivery to the person/people upon whom it's being served, and not returned by the Post Office, it is deemed under section 196(4) of the Law of Property Act 1925 to have been delivered. In *Re 88 Berkeley Rd NW9* (1971) Miss Goodwin and Miss Eldridge owned the house as beneficial joint tenants. Miss Goodwin served notice of severance by recorded delivery. Miss Goodwin herself signed the receipt for the recorded delivery because Miss Eldridge was away at the time. Although Miss Eldridge never actually saw the notice and died soon after, the notice was held to be effective for severance to have occurred.

Q: *That seems very unfair, doesn't it?*

A: Although section 36(2) states that 'any tenant ... shall give to the other joint tenants a notice in writing ...', section 196(4) states that a notice will be 'sufficiently served if it is sent by post in a registered letter' and not returned through the Post Office undelivered. The claimant argued that although section 196(4) requires the notice to be served, section 36(2) requires the notice to be given. Mr Justice Plowman held that there was no distinction between serving notice and giving notice. The notice was sufficiently served for the purposes of section 36(2) and severance had taken place.

In cases where the notice has not been registered or sent by recorded delivery, provided it can be proved that the notice was left at the last known home or business address of the joint tenant or tenants, it will still be effective under section 196(3) of the Law of Property Act 1925, even if it hasn't been received by the intended joint tenant. In *Kinch v Bullard* (1999) the wife was terminally ill and sent a statutory notice of severance under section 36(2) of the Law of Property Act 1925 by first class post to her husband. Before he read it, he was admitted to hospital with a heart attack. The wife realised that if the husband died first, she would receive his interest under the right of survivorship. Given her husband's condition, she destroyed the notice. The husband died a week later. The court held that notice had still been effectively served because it had been delivered to the address of the husband. The court also found time to discuss what would have happened if the dog had eaten the notice instead. In *Quigley v Masterson* (2011) Mrs Masterson was arguing that Mr Pilkington's two attempts to sever the joint tenancy by written notice had failed. The court agreed. The first notice failed because it had been served on solicitors that Mrs Masterson no longer retained and they had no authority to accept the notice on her behalf. The second notice failed because the notice, and there was doubt as to whether it had been served at all, had been sent to Mrs Masterson's place of work and had also been addressed to a misspelling of her name. The court held that sending a notice to a workplace is not sending it to a last known business address under section 196(3) of the Law of Property Act 1925.

Q: *Does a notice have to be sent to each of the other joint tenants individually to be an effective means of severance?*

A: Yes.

Q: *What does the notice actually have to say?*

A: The notice doesn't have to be in any particular form, but has to show an unequivocal intention to sever immediately and not at some time in the future. In *Harris v Goddard* (1983) a divorce petition that requested the court to distribute the property in a just way was held not to effect severance because it did not have immediate effect. It asked the court only to consider the request at some time in the future. *Harris v Goddard* does show, however, that a notice can include a writ or a summons.

These points were illustrated in *Quigley v Masterson*. Whilst Mr Pilkington had failed to serve notice on Mrs Masterson, in previous dealings she had made an application to the Court of Protection where she had acknowledged in her application to that court and in her witness statement that Mr Pilkington had a 50% share in the house. The court saw this as an immediate and unconditional notice of severance.

Q: *Does a notice need the consent of the other joint tenants for it to be effective?*

A: No. Statutory notice is a totally unilateral act of severance.

It's easier to see how this works by looking at an example. Take the example where Greenacres is conveyed to A, B, C, D and E as 'equitable joint tenants'. Only the first four people named on the conveyance, the deed of sale, who are able and willing can be on the legal title. This will be A, B, C and D, who will be trustees holding Greenacres on trust for themselves and E as joint tenants in equity (Box B, point 3).

Legal title	Equitable title
(A B C D)	(A B C D E)
Joint tenants	Joint tenants

If joint tenant A serves a statutory notice of severance on B, C, D and E, this will sever his equitable interest, and he will now hold his equitable interest as a tenant in common. This means his interest will pass under his will or on his intestacy. (Remember that A cannot sever his legal joint tenancy.)

Legal title	Equitable title	
(A B C D)	(B C D E)	A
Joint tenants	Joint tenants	Tenant in common

Section 36(2) of the Law of Property Act 1925 also allowed for the methods of severance prior to the Law of Property Act 1925 to remain valid. These prior methods were found in a case called *Williams v Hensman* (1861) and included:

▶ a person acting on his own share (Box D2);
▶ mutual agreement (Box D3); or
▶ mutual conduct (Box D4).

Box D2   *Williams v Hensman* (1861) – a person acting on his own share

When a joint tenant acts on his potential share he converts it into a tenancy in common. If he sells his equitable interest, gives it away or mortgages it, that equitable interest will be converted into a tenancy in common.

Q: *Do the other joint tenants have to know about the event, whether it's a sale, gift or mortgage?*

A: No, it doesn't matter.

Q: *Why would a joint tenant mortgage his equitable interest to, for example, Bundy's Bank?*

A: He would do this in return for a mortgage loan where Bundy's Bank would use the value in his equitable interest as security for the mortgage loan.

Q: *Are there any formalities for selling your equitable interest?*

A: Yes. You must satisfy section 53(1)(c) of the Law of Property Act 1925. This states that the sale or disposition of an equitable interest must be in writing and signed by the person selling or disposing of the equitable interest or by his agent. The same section must be satisfied if the equitable interest is mortgaged.

Q: *Why does the sale of an equitable interest have to be in writing?*

A: This is to prevent fraud, because an equitable interest is not exactly obvious. Whereas anyone can find out whether a person is on the legal title, it's more difficult to keep track of who is holding an equitable interest, especially when such interest is sold.

Q: *What happens if there is an agreement, a contract, to sell an equitable interest rather than an actual sale?*

A: In this case you have to meet section 2 of the Law of Property (Miscellaneous Provisions) Act 1989. This means that the agreement must be in writing, contain all the express terms of the agreement and be signed by or on behalf of both parties. Section 2 of the Law of Property (Miscellaneous Provisions) Act 1989 was discussed in Chapter 1.

Q: *Does severance occur whenever an equitable interest is sold, transferred or mortgaged?*

A: Yes. These are voluntary acts which constitute severance of an equitable joint tenancy. It is also possible for an involuntary act of severance to occur. If a joint tenant becomes bankrupt, the issue of a bankruptcy order will sever his equitable interest, and it will automatically pass to his trustee in bankruptcy on his appointment: see *Re Dennis (A Bankrupt)* (1996). The trustee in bankruptcy can then realise the value of the equitable interest to satisfy any debts.

Look at these further examples of severance in practice by continuing the example from pages 155 to 156, where A severed his interest by statutory notice.

Legal title	Equitable title	
(A B C D)	(B C D E)	A
Joint tenants	Joint tenants	Tenant in common
		having served written notice
		under section 36(2) of the Law
		of Property Act 1925

Joint tenant C then decides to move away from the locality. He no longer wants anything to do with Greenacres, but would like his share of its value in money. The others refuse to sell Greenacres so that he can realise his interest. He cannot sever his legal joint tenancy and so will remain on the legal title even after he has moved away. One option is for him to sell his equitable interest to Mohammed (M) by satisfying section 53(1)(c) of the Law of Property Act 1925. The sale is an act of severance on his interest which converts it into a tenancy in common.

Legal title	Equitable title		
(A B C D)	(B D E)	A	M
Joint tenants	Joint tenants	Tenant	Tenant in
		in common	common

Q: *Why has C been removed from the equitable title and why is M a tenant in common?*

A: C has been removed from the equitable title because he sold his equitable interest to M. He no longer has an equitable interest in Greenacres. He has the money from M instead. M now replaces him on the equitable title. For a joint tenancy to exist, the four unities must be satisfied. M does not satisfy the unity of time because he did not receive his interest at the same time as A, B, D and E. He does not satisfy the unity of title either, as he did not receive his interest in the same way, in the same document, as A, B, D and E. He cannot be a joint tenant as he does not satisfy the four unities, so he is a tenant in common.

Imagine that D then becomes bankrupt and a bankruptcy order is issued. This is an involuntary act of severance on his equitable interest. As D will no longer be allowed to deal with his own affairs, his equitable interest will pass to his trustee in bankruptcy.

Legal title	Equitable title			
(A B C D) Joint tenants	(B E)	A	M	D's trustee in bankruptcy
	Joint tenants	Tenant in common	Tenant in common	Tenant in common

The trustee in bankruptcy will be a tenant in common because he has not received D's interest at the same time (unity of time) or in the same way as the others (unity of title), and so cannot be a joint tenant.

Finally, E dies.

Legal title	Equitable title			
(A B C D) Joint tenants	B	A	M	D's trustee in bankruptcy
	Tenant in common	Tenant in common	Tenant in common	Tenant in common

Q: *Why is B now a tenant in common?*

A: The right of survivorship has operated between B and E because they held as joint tenants together. The others are already tenants in common. B no longer has anyone to be a joint tenant with. 'Joint' implies more than one in the relationship. He must therefore be a tenant in common!

Q: *Can you sever your interest just by leaving it in a will?*

A: No. If you hold as an equitable joint tenant you do not have an interest to leave in a will until you have severed it. You must always sever your interest while you are alive. And remember that you can never sever a legal joint tenancy.

Box D3   *Williams v Hensman* (1861) – mutual agreement

Q: *Presumably, mutual agreement means that there must be mutual agreement between the parties that one or more of them will hold their equitable interest as a tenant in common rather than as a joint tenant?*

A: Yes, and it is mutual agreement between all the joint tenants. They must all agree – not just some of them – that one or more of their number will hold as a tenant in common from then on. Look at this in an example where property is conveyed to A, B, C, D and E as equitable joint tenants.

Legal title	Equitable title
(A B C D)	(A B C D E)
Joint tenants	Joint tenants

C decides that he does not want to be bound by the rules of survivorship. Although he can't sever his legal joint tenancy, he agrees with A, B, D and E that he will hold his equitable interest as a tenant in common from then on. The situation then looks like this:

Legal title	Equitable title	
(A B C D)	(A B D E)	C
Joint tenants	Joint tenants	Tenant in common

This kind of mutual agreement can also be found in the example where Greenacres was conveyed to Thomas and Lucy as 'equitable joint tenants':

Legal title	Equitable title
(T L)	(T L)
Joint tenants	Joint tenants

Although they have lived happily in Greenacres for several years, the relationship then breaks down and Lucy moves out. If she dies, she certainly doesn't want her equitable interest with all the associated beneficial rights to devolve to Thomas under the right of survivorship. She and Thomas mutually agree that she will hold her interest as a tenant in common. This, of course, makes Thomas a tenant in common, as he no longer has anyone to be joint with.

Legal title	Equitable title	
(T L)	T	L
Joint tenants	Tenant in common	Tenant in commor

If Thomas won't agree to this, you do not have mutual agreement. Lucy could use the method of written notice under section 36(2) of the Law of Property Act 1925, as discussed in Box D1. If Lucy is going to use mutual agreement though, she must be careful to ensure that it is actually mutual agreement. Statements that are called 'unilateral declarations', which means one party says to the other 'I'm going to hold my share as a tenant in common from now on', do not count as severance: see *Burgess v Rawnsley* (1975), because only Thomas and Lucy are involved. If Lucy made a unilateral declaration to Thomas that she was holding her interest as a tenant in common and then died, Thomas could conveniently forget about Lucy's statement and claim the whole of the property for himself under the right of survivorship.

Q: *If anyone disagrees does it count as severance?*

A: No. It has to be mutual agreement and everyone has to agree.

Q: *Does the agreement between the parties need to be in writing?*

A: No.

Q: *Why not? Everything else seems to have to be in writing in land law.*

A: The mutual agreement serves the purpose of showing an intention to sever, which is the important part. *Burgess v Rawnsley* is frequently cited in any discussion of severance by mutual agreement. Lord Denning gave the facts as follows:

> In 1966 there was a scripture rally in Trafalgar Square. A widower, Mr Honick, went to it. He was about 63. A widow, Mrs Rawnsley, the defendant, also went. She was about 60. He went up to her and introduced himself. He was not much to look at. 'He looks like a tramp', she said. 'He had been picking up fag-ends.' They got on well enough, however, to exchange addresses.

And things became even more romantic because:

> Next day he went to her house with a gift for her. It was a rose wrapped in a newspaper. Afterwards their friendship grew apace.

They obviously got on very well, because Lord Denning then talks about them writing to each other in terms of endearment, and counsel even mentioned love letters. In fact they got on so well they decided to buy a house together. Mrs Rawnsley contributed half the cost and occupied the upper flat, while Mr Honick paid the other half of the purchase price and occupied the lower flat. So, despite the romance, they clearly didn't get on that well. In effect they bought the house as joint tenants of the legal title and as joint tenants of the equitable title.

Reality intervened, and Mrs Rawnsley orally agreed to sell her interest to Mr Honick for £750. She then changed her mind and asked for a higher price. Unfortunately, Mr Honick died before anything further was decided. The court had to decide whether the initial agreement that Mrs Rawnsley would sell her interest to Mr Honick, which he had agreed to, was sufficient to constitute severance of the equitable title even though the price hadn't been agreed. All the agreement had to do was to show an intention to sever. This intention to sever had been clearly agreed to by the parties. Mrs Rawnsley and Mr Honick had agreed that they would no longer hold the equitable title as joint tenants but as tenants in common, even though the price hadn't been decided.

Wallbank v Price (2007) is a good recent example here. Susan Wallbank (known as Mrs Price in the case because she had remarried) held the house as a beneficial joint tenant with Mr Wallbank. The court had to decide whether the following words in a handwritten homemade document signed by Susan Wallbank amounted to severance of the joint tenancy or a conditional release or surrender of her beneficial interest.

> "I Susan Joan Wallbank

> Have voluntarily agreed to vacate the above premises and also to forfeit any monies or profit in any way connected with this property, and by signing this declaration I revoke any rights in the disposal of the above property.

> The only exception to this is that my Daughters Jaime and Lynsey Wallbank should receive my half share of the property on its disposal or at the discretion of my husband Martin Harry Wallbank".

The words 'have voluntarily agreed to vacate the above premises' meant that she had agreed to leave and was giving up her right to live in the property. The words 'to forfeit any monies or profit in any way connected with this property' meant she was giving up all her financial interest in the property. The words 'I revoke any rights in the disposal of the above property' meant that she intended to give up her beneficial interest in the property.

The second part of the declaration in which Susan Wallbank talked about a 'half share' was inconsistent with a continuing joint tenancy in equity. The creation of a half share could come about only through severance of the joint tenancy of the two parties. Mr Wallbank could exercise his discretion in favour of his daughters immediately so that dealt with the requirement that severance must have immediate effect. Mr Wallbank had signed the document so there was agreement between them (mutual agreement). Therefore severance had occurred.

In *Gore and Snell v Carpenter* (1990), though, the parties had been holding the equitable title as joint tenants. They had agreed in principle that they would hold as tenants in common, but were waiting for other financial affairs in their divorce to be settled before they came to a final agreement. The husband died before this could happen. The court held that there had been no mutual agreement because the wife had not committed herself fully to the agreement.

Box D4   *Williams v Hensman* (1861) – mutual conduct

Q: *What amounts to mutual conduct between the joint tenants so that a tenancy in common is created?*

A: There's no hard and fast rule, and it very much depends on the circumstances. Overall, though, the behaviour of the joint tenants must indicate that they saw themselves holding as tenants in common and not as joint tenants and they must have communicated this intention to each other. Some of the ways are by:

▶ A course of dealing.

This is where the joint tenants have behaved as though they were tenants in common, each with his own individual interest. This is not easy to prove. In *Barton v Morris* (1985) the parties, who were joint tenants, put the proceeds from their business into their separate names. This was done for business reasons, and did not give rise to a tenancy in common through mutual conduct. In *Carr v Isard* (2006) Grace and Thomas had owned their house as beneficial joint tenants. They had both died. Whilst severance cannot take place simply by one party leaving their interest in a will, it was argued that the way in which Grace and Thomas had made their wills showed a course of dealing inconsistent with the continuation of the joint tenancy. If so, severance would have occurred in their lifetime. For this to have happened, there had to be a course of dealing inconsistent with the continuation of the joint tenancy and both parties had to know enough about the contents of each others' wills to be aware that the other party was leaving his/her interest in a manner inconsistent with the joint tenancy. On the facts of the case this was not so. Thomas's will was equivocal over the continuation or otherwise of the joint tenancy. Furthermore, there was no evidence that Grace and Thomas knew the contents of each others' wills. Severance by a course of dealing had not occurred and the right of survivorship operated instead. This case reinforces yet again the fact that you cannot sever a joint tenancy by simply making a will.

▶ Mutual wills.

A mutual will occurs when Thomas leaves all his property to Lucy in his will for her to use during her lifetime, after which the property is to pass to their daughter, Jane. Lucy makes her will leaving all her property to Thomas to use during his lifetime, after which the property is to pass to their daughter, Jane. The effect of the mutual will is to deny the right of survivorship and is severance both by mutual agreement and mutual conduct: see *Re Wilford's Estate* (1879). In the case of *Carr v Isard* there was no evidence from which to infer mutual wills.

The following have not amounted to severance by mutual conduct:

▶ Physical division of the property.

In *Greenfield v Greenfield* (1979) the two joint tenants physically divided the house, and each occupied a separate part. This was not enough for severance by mutual conduct because it was done only for convenience.

▶ Inconclusive negotiations between the joint tenants do not usually amount to a course of conduct leading to severance.

This is because of the danger of one party making unilateral statements to the other(s), statements which can be conveniently forgotten if it suits.

Box D5 | ### Homicide

The question here is what happens if one joint tenant kills another joint tenant. On the one hand, the right of survivorship should apply. On the other hand, you are not allowed to profit from a crime, and under the forfeiture rules you would have to forfeit any gain you had made from the crime. The effect of one joint tenant killing another is that the wrongdoer is seen to have severed the joint tenancy, and so the right of survivorship will not operate. Under the Forfeiture Act 1982, the court has the discretion to grant relief against forfeiture in cases of homicide except in the case of murder: see *Re K* (1986).

Summary of severance

Severance is the act of converting a joint tenancy into a tenancy in common, thus avoiding the right of survivorship. The legal title cannot be severed. Severance of the equitable title must be carried out during the lifetime of a joint tenant, either by written notice under section 36(2) of the Law of Property Act 1925 or by one of the ways given in *Williams v Hensman*.

Q: *How does a joint tenancy end when there is no severance by the parties?*

A: A joint tenancy ends when the right of survivorship has operated and there is only one tenant left. If A and B hold the land as joint tenants and A dies, B becomes the sole owner.

Legal title	Equitable title
(A B) Joint tenants	(A B) Joint tenants
A dies	
B	B

In this case B owns the land absolutely. There is no other co-owner on either the legal or the equitable title, and you can just say B owns Greenacres. There is no need to talk about the legal and equitable interest if there is just one owner of Greenacres. The discussion of legal and equitable interests arises only if there is a trust. A trust arises if there is beneficial co-ownership. In the example above there is no co-ownership, beneficial or otherwise, after A dies.

Co-ownership also ends when the co-owned property is sold.

The type of trust in express co-ownership before 1997

Before 1997 the type of trust that was imposed in an express beneficial co-ownership situation was the trust for sale, which was discussed in Chapter 7. A trust for sale imposed a binding duty on the parties who were the trustees to sell the property. Sale could be postponed only if all the trustees were unanimous in the decision to postpone, otherwise the property had to be sold. In 1925, when the Law of Property Act imposed a trust for sale in express beneficial co-ownership situations, there was very little express beneficial co-ownership in the sense that we know it today. Most people rented their homes and did not own them. As people did start to own, rather than rent, the family home, though, the most common example of express beneficial co-ownership occurred when Thomas and Lucy, for example, bought Greenacres together. There was express beneficial co-ownership, so there was a trust. The Law of Property Act 1925 imposed a trust for sale. This meant that Thomas and Lucy, in their capacity as trustees, were under an imperative duty to sell Greenacres unless they both agreed to postpone sale. This concept was far removed from the reality of the situation, as Thomas and Lucy clearly bought Greenacres to live in, not with any notion of being under a duty to sell the property. They probably had no idea of how they held Greenacres anyway, and to some extent it didn't matter when the decisions made about the house were joint. If the relationship broke down, though, Greenacres would have to be sold even if one party wanted to keep the property, because Thomas and Lucy would not be unanimous in their decision to postpone sale. Reform of this area took place in 1996.

The type of trust in express co-ownership after 1996

There is still a trust where there is express beneficial co-ownership because the trust concept works very well in practice, even if not in land law examinations. However, the trust for sale has been replaced by the trust of land, which is governed by the Trusts of Land and Appointment of Trustees Act 1996, discussed in Chapter 10.

A question on express co-ownership and severance

This example is intended to illustrate how to use the Boxes in this chapter to analyse the legal position. If you are using this method in undergraduate law exam questions, you will need to include statutory and case authority and detailed discussion of the various points of law. This information is found both in the text and from other sources.

Two years ago, four workmates, Donatello, Leonardo, Michelangelo and Raphael decided to purchase a house called Greenacres. They all contributed equally to the purchase price of the property and intended to live there together.

Things soon started to go wrong when Donatello was killed in a skiing accident. He left nothing in his will for his estranged wife and three children. Then Leonardo, who had fallen out with the others, verbally agreed to sell his interest in the property to Frankie. Leonardo did not tell his fellow co-owners of his intention. Leonardo then changed his mind about the sale, but shortly afterwards served written notice on Michelangelo and Raphael that he was holding his interest in Greenacres as a tenant in common. Finally, Michelangelo and Raphael were involved in a serious road accident.

Michelangelo died immediately, having left his property in his will to his sister, Cassandra. Raphael died several days later in hospital, having left his property in his will to his sister, Eugenie.

Advise on the devolution of the legal and equitable title.

Start off with the 'Use of Trusts in Land' chart in Chapter 6 on page 132 and look at the different ways of holding interests in land. The parties in the question do not hold their interests in the property successively, one after the other, but concurrently. Greenacres was expressly conveyed to the parties, so this is express beneficial co-ownership. A trust is imposed by the Law of Property Act 1925, which means that the parties will wear the labels of trustees and beneficiaries. There are only four co-owners, so all four can be on the legal title, as permitted by section 34 of the Trustee Act 1925. They will all be trustees holding for themselves in equity. As Greenacres was bought after 1996, this will be a trust of land under the Trusts of Land and Appointment of Trustees Act 1996.

Now that you've established this, turn to the chart relating to express co-ownership in this chapter on page 143.

Express co-ownership

Box A The legal title
The legal title must be held as a joint tenancy: see sections 1(6), 34(1) and 36(2) of the Law of Property Act 1925. Donatello (D), Leonardo (L), Michelangelo (M) and Raphael (R) will hold as legal joint tenants. This can be represented by:

Legal title

(D L M R)
Joint tenants

The use of the brackets indicates that the parties hold as joint tenants.

The effect of a joint tenancy is that the right of survivorship will operate. If any joint tenant dies, his interest in the legal title will simply devolve on the remaining joint tenants.

Box B The equitable title
You now need to establish whether there is a joint tenancy or a tenancy in common on the equitable title by looking at boxes B1 to B8.

All the parties have a right to possess Greenacres and all have the same interest in the land. Greenacres was conveyed to the parties at the same time and by the same document. Thus the four unities of possession, interest, time and title are satisfied. The parties also all contributed equally to the purchase price.

B5 Four unities met, no express declaration, no words of severance but equal contribution to the purchase price = Joint tenancy.
These conditions are met so the parties will hold as joint tenants in equity.

Legal title	Equitable title
(D L M R)	(D L M R)
Joint tenants	Joint tenants

Summary of the legal and equitable title

There is a joint tenancy on both the legal and equitable title.

You can also put notional shares in on the equitable title. Although the joint tenants own the whole together, if the property is sold, any remaining tenants will share in the proceeds. Their share will depend on the devolution of the equitable title. At this point there are four joint tenants. As they own the whole together, the total notional share on the equitable title must be 4/4.

Legal title	Equitable title
(D L M R)	(D L M R) 4/4
Joint tenants	Joint tenants

Severance

The question is whether any of the parties have severed their interest.

Box C The legal title

Section 36(2) of the Law of Property Act 1925 states that a legal joint tenancy can never be severed. If a legal joint tenant dies, his interest in the legal title devolves to the other joint tenants under the right of survivorship. Should a legal joint tenant wish to retire or remove himself from the legal title, this must be done in accordance with the formal requirements of the Trustee Act 1925. Removal cannot be achieved through severance.

Summary of the legal title

If any of the parties dies, the right of survivorship will operate on the legal title. Any attempt at severance by D, L, M or R must relate to the equitable title only.

Box D The equitable title

There can be severance of the equitable title only by means of section 36(2) of the Law of Property Act 1925 or by the methods given in *Williams v Hensman*. The question is whether any of the parties has carried out an act which might constitute severance. Look at each of the events in the question in turn.

> *Donatello was killed in a skiing accident. He left nothing in his will for his estranged wife and three children.*

The right of survivorship will operate on the legal title.

Legal title

(L M R)
Joint tenants

The question is whether there was severance on the equitable title.

D1 to D5
Donatello did nothing in his lifetime which amounted to an act of severance, so he remained a joint tenant on the equitable title. The right of survivorship applies, and his equitable interest devolves to L, M and R. Even if Donatello had left his interest in Greenacres to his estranged wife and three children in his will, this would have had no effect as he had not severed his equitable interest to hold it as a tenant in common during his lifetime. As L, M and R now own the whole together, the total notional share on the equitable title must be 3/3.

Legal title	Equitable title
(L M R)	(L M R) 3/3
Joint tenants	Joint tenants

Then Leonardo, who had fallen out with the others, verbally agreed to sell his interest in the property to Frankie.

It is not possible to sever the legal joint tenancy, so you must establish whether L has severed his equitable interest. Leonardo did not give notice of severance in writing to the other joint tenants under section 36(2) of the Law of Property Act 1925 (Box D1), nor was there any mutual agreement (Box D3) or mutual conduct (Box D4). Homicide (Box D5) is not relevant to the question. However, Leonardo may have acted on his own share so you must discuss Box D2.

D2 Williams v Hensman (1861): A person acting on his own share
Leonardo made a verbal agreement for the sale of his equitable interest in the land. The actual sale of an equitable interest must satisfy section 53(1)(c) of the Law of Property Act 1925, which states that the sale of an equitable interest must be in writing and signed by the party disposing of the interest, which is L here, or by his agent. A verbal agreement does not satisfy this section. Alternatively, if this was an agreement by Leonardo to sell his equitable interest at some time in the future, it would not satisfy the requirements of section 2 of the Law of Property (Miscellaneous Provisions) Act 1989, which states that a contract for the sale of an interest in land must be in writing, signed by or on behalf of both parties, Leonardo and Frankie here, and contain all the express terms of the agreement. The verbal agreement has no effect on L's equitable interest as it does not satisfy statutory formality in either case.

Leonardo has not severed his equitable interest. The equitable title remains the same as before.

Legal title	Equitable title
(L M R) Joint tenants	(L M R) 3/3 Joint tenants

Leonardo did not tell his fellow co-owners of his intention.

Leonardo did not give notice of severance in writing to the other joint tenants under section 36(2) of the Law of Property Act 1925 (Box D1), nor was there any mutual agreement (Box D3) or mutual conduct (Box D4). Homicide (Box D5) is not relevant to the question.

Leonardo has not severed his equitable interest. The equitable title remains the same as before.

Legal title	Equitable title
(L M R) Joint tenants	(L M R) 3/3 Joint tenants

Leonardo then changed his mind about the sale, but shortly afterwards served written notice on Michelangelo and Raphael that he was holding his interest in Greenacres as a tenant in common.

It is not possible to sever the legal joint tenancy, so you must establish whether L has severed his equitable interest.

D1 Section 36(2) of the Law of Property Act 1925
This appears to be written notice to the other joint tenants which satisfies section 36(2) of the Law of Property Act 1925. If this is so, Leonardo will now hold a one-third share as an equitable tenant in common.

D2 to D5
Leonardo has not effected severance of his equitable interest by any other means. He has not acted on his own interest. There is no mutual agreement and no mutual conduct. Homicide is not relevant to the question.

We will assume that severance has taken place under section 36(2) of the Law of Property Act 1925. Leonardo now holds a one third share as a tenant in common.

Legal title	Equitable title	
(L M R) Joint tenants	(M R) 2/3 Joint tenants	L 1/3 Tenant in common

Finally, Michelangelo and Raphael were involved in a serious road accident. Michelangelo died immediately, having left his property in his will to his sister, Cassandra.

When Michelangelo dies, the right of survivorship operates on the legal title, so the legal title vests in L and R.

There was no act by Michelangelo which severed his equitable interest before he died. The right of survivorship will therefore apply on the equitable title as well, and his equitable interest will devolve on R. Cassandra will not inherit because M had not severed his equitable interest to become a tenant in common in his lifetime, and so had no interest to leave in his will. Raphael now becomes a tenant in common (as he has nobody with whom to be a joint tenant) holding a two-thirds share in the property.

Raphael died several days later in hospital having left his property in his will to his sister, Eugenie.

Legal title	Equitable title	
(L R) Joint tenants	R 2/3 Tenant in common	L 1/3 Tenant in common

The right of survivorship operates on the legal title.

Raphael was holding his equitable interest as a tenant in common. The right of survivorship does not apply to a tenancy in common, and a tenant in common has an individual interest that can be left by will. Raphael's sister, Eugenie, will inherit his equitable interest and will hold a two-thirds share in the property.

Legal title	Equitable title	
L Sole owner at law	R 2/3 Tenant in common	L 1/3 Tenant commo

Conclusion

When the four workmates purchased Greenacres, there was express beneficial co-ownership and a trust of land was created. The legal title had to be held as a joint tenancy. The four workmates also held the equitable title as a joint tenancy. Severance of the legal title is never possible. The right of survivorship operated on the legal title, leaving Leonardo as the sole legal owner. The right of survivorship and severance operated on the equitable title, with the result that Eugenie and Leonardo hold equitable interests in Greenacres as tenants in common. If Greenacres were to be sold, Eugenie would receive a 2/3 share of the proceeds and Leonardo a 1/3 share.

This is bad luck for Leonardo. If he hadn't severed his interest, he would have owned Greenacres outright.

Chapter 10 looks at the duties and the rights of the parties when there is express beneficial co-ownership in land. Chapter 11 looks at what happens when property subject to express beneficial co-ownership is sold. The question relating to Donatello, Leonardo, Michelangelo and Raphael is continued at the end of Chapter 10 and at the end of Chapter 11 to show you how these further aspects work in practice.

Further reading

B. Crown, 'Severance of Joint Tenancy of Land by Partial Alienation', 117 *LQR* (2001) 477

D. Hayton, 'Joint Tenancies – Severance', 35 *CLJ* (1976) 20

M. Percival, 'Severance by Written Notice – A Matter of Delivery?' *Conv and Prop Law*, Jan/Feb (1999) 60

L. Tee, 'Severance Revisited', *Conv and Prop Law*, Mar/Apr (1995) 105

M. Thompson, 'Beneficial Joint Tenancies: A Case for Abolition?' *Conv and Prop Law*, Jan/Feb (1987) 29. In reply: A. Pritchard, 'Beneficial Joint Tenancies: A Riposte', *Conv and Prop Law*, Jul/Aug (1987) 273. In reply: M. Thompson, 'Beneficial Joint Tenancies: A Reply to Professor Pritchard', *Conv and Prop Law*, Jul/Aug (1987) 275

www.palgrave.com/law/Stroud4e

Chapter 9

Constructive and resulting trusts

www.palgrave.com/law/Stroud4e

Introduction

In the chart 'The Use of Trusts in Land' in Chapter 6 on page 132, you will see that implied co-ownership under a constructive or resulting trust is one of the ways in which two or more people can hold an interest in the same piece of land and where a trust arises. The law relating to constructive and resulting trusts is also used in express co-ownership when the percentage share of each party in the property is unknown or when the parties think that their percentage shares have changed over time. The law continues to evolve in this area and its application is not always straightforward. Onwards and upwards!

Constructive and resulting trusts

A constructive trust can arise when the family home, Greenacres, is bought by one person, for example, the man, whom we will call Darren. He is the only person on the legal title and so is the sole legal owner. Sally, his partner, may well have contributed to the purchase price of the house. She may also have contributed to the mortgage repayments from her part-time job and spent her time bringing up the children, doing the garden and painting the odd radiator. When the relationship breaks down, the question is whether Sally has acquired any proprietary rights in the house that are recognised by the courts. She will have no rights recognised at law because she is not on the legal title. However, equity may recognise her contributions in the form of an equitable interest in the property based on the shared common intentions of Darren and herself. This equitable interest arises under a trust and will give her rights in the property. Today, following *Stack v Dowden* (2007) and *Jones v Kernott* (2011), in a domestic situation like this, the constructive trust will almost certainly be pleaded. Take another situation. Darren and Sally have purchased Greenacres as part of a business venture. Darren is the only person on the legal title but Sally has contributed to the purchase price. Again, Sally has no rights recognised at law but, based on her contributions to the purchase price, equity may recognise these contributions in the form of an equitable interest under a trust. Nowadays, it will be the resulting trust that is almost certainly pleaded in this business venture situation. The next few pages show you how constructive and resulting trusts work in general. We'll continue to use the example of Darren and Sally because the points being made are relevant to both types of trust, whether it's a constructive trust in the domestic situation or a resulting trust in the business venture situation.

A constructive trust is 'constructed' by the courts when there has been behaviour by Darren and Sally showing a common intention that Sally is to have an interest in the house, so the behaviour merits the award of an interest in equity. Constructive trusts are often referred to as common intention constructive trusts because the trust is based on the parties' common intentions. As you will see, this common intention can be express or implied by the courts. A resulting trust 'results by implication'. This is where Darren and Sally have behaved in such a way that you can imply what they meant to happen from their actions. A constructive trust is imposed when someone has behaved unconscionably to the other party and a resulting trust is based on presumed intention. Section 53(2) of the Law of Property Act 1925 states that constructive and resulting trusts are exempt from the requirement that trusts must be created in writing.

Whether it's a constructive or a resulting trust that arises, the land is now co-owned by Darren and Sally in equity and this is known as implied co-ownership. The fact that two or more people have an interest in the land at the same time is implied from the circumstances.

If Darren is the only person on the legal title and the land is registered, Darren would be the sole registered proprietor on the Proprietorship Register. In unregistered land the deed conveying the house to him would be made out in his name only. If Darren holds the legal title to Greenacres and Sally acquires an interest recognised in equity under a trust, Darren would now be holding Greenacres not only on his own behalf but also on Sally's. A trust is then created. Darren will wear the labels of 'trustee and beneficiary' and Sally will wear the label 'beneficiary'.

Q: *Why is Darren a beneficiary as well?*

A: Look at it this way. If Darren purchased Greenacres and Sally didn't exist, Darren would just own Greenacres. Anything he did with the land would be because he was the legal owner and, provided he kept within the laws of the land, he could do as he pleased. When a trust is created, ownership is split into two parts. The legal title held by the trustee is one part. The equitable title, held by the beneficiary, is the other. The legal title gives the ability to manage the property, whereas the equitable title recognises the enjoyment or beneficial factor, hence beneficial interest. Once you establish that a trust has arisen, whether it's a constructive or a resulting trust, the ownership splits into two parts: the legal title and the equitable title. Darren holds the legal title and he will now be a trustee with the ability to manage Greenacres and deal with the legal title. As he purchased Greenacres for his own use, this is recognised in his equitable or beneficial interest. Sally is not on the legal title so she will have no capacity to manage Greenacres or deal with the legal title. However, she does have an equitable or beneficial interest acquired under a constructive or resulting trust. This is represented as:

Legal title
Darren – trustee

Equitable title
Darren – beneficiary

Equitable title
Sally – beneficiary

If Darren had not purchased Greenacres for his own enjoyment, but was simply holding Greenacres on trust for Sally, the situation would look like this:

Legal title
Darren – trustee

Equitable title
Sally – beneficiary

In this case Sally would be the only person with an equitable interest in the land, and so would have all the enjoyment of Greenacres. In his capacity as trustee, Darren would manage Greenacres with regard to Sally's rights and according to the terms of any trust instrument and would take no benefit for himself.

Of course, Darren could always make an express declaration that he was holding Greenacres on trust for himself and for Sally, in which case Sally would then have an equitable interest in it. The formal way of doing this is to comply with section 53(1)(b) of the Law of Property Act 1925, which states that such a declaration of trust must be evidenced in writing and signed by Darren. It is advisable to state the terms of the trust, for example, the extent of Sally's interest in the property. This declaration is binding on Darren and is conclusive of ownership: see *Goodman v Gallant* (1986). When Darren and Sally are in the domestic situation, in reality such formality is unlikely to happen. There will be nothing in writing and signed. Sally will just presume she has an interest in Greenacres because Darren loves her very much. When she discovers that he doesn't love her quite that much, she will have to prove that she has acquired an equitable interest in Greenacres under, almost certainly, a constructive trust. If Darren and Sally had purchased Greenacres as part of a business venture, it is far more likely that the terms of the trust will have been formally recorded. If they hadn't been, Sally would have to prove that she had acquired an equitable interest in Greenacres under a resulting trust.

Note that there is no male/female divide in the context of acquiring an interest under a trust. Although Darren holds the legal title to Greenacres, the situations would be exactly the same if Sally held the legal title and Darren was trying to claim an interest under a trust.

Q: *What rights does Sally have if she can claim an interest under a trust?*

A: Sally's rights are discussed in Chapter 10, but her main ones are a right to live in the property and a right to go to court if there's a dispute as to who lives there or whether the house should be sold or not. Of course, if Greenacres is sold, her equitable interest in the property will be translated into money, and she will receive a share of the proceeds from the sale depending on the quantification of her equitable interest.

Excluding one statutory provision under the Matrimonial Proceedings and Property Act 1970, it doesn't matter whether Darren and Sally are married or cohabiting in terms of acquiring an interest in the house by means of a trust. If Darren and Sally are married and the marriage breaks down, the courts have a wide discretion to allocate property as they see fit under divorce law. The allocation of property to Sally in a divorce situation would not depend on whether she had acquired an equitable interest under a trust. In cohabitation, though, the party not on the legal title, Sally in this case, will have to rely solely on an equitable interest acquired under a trust. The situation could also arise where Darren had purchased Greenacres and had sometime later taken out a mortgage with Bundy's Bank. If Darren failed to pay the mortgage repayments, Bundy's Bank would want to repossess and sell Greenacres to recoup the outstanding mortgage money. It is at this point that Sally, whether she is married or not, will have to rely on having acquired an equitable interest under a constructive trust in order to try and stop the Bank repossessing and selling the house. Divorce law won't help her here because it's not a divorce situation.

The domestic situation – the two-stage process

So far we have talked generally about whether Sally can acquire an equitable interest in Greenacres under a trust. The part of the chapter that covers the business venture situation starts on page 207 but, from now on, we are going to focus on how Sally goes about proving an interest under a constructive trust in a domestic situation. We'll also look at another situation where the law relating to constructive trusts is used. First, though, let's consider the domestic situation where Darren alone is on the legal title and Sally wishes to claim an interest under a constructive trust. There are two stages to the process. Sally, the non legal owner, must prove that she has met the requirements for acquiring such an interest in the first place. This is the first stage of the two-stage process. She must prove a common intention that she was to have a share in the property along with Darren, whatever that share might be. The factors that the court takes into account to determine whether she qualifies for such an equitable interest are the subject of a large part of this chapter.

Representing this diagrammatically,

	Person not on the legal title (Sally)
Stage 1 Qualification	Needs to meet the requirements for acquiring an equitable interest in the first place

Assuming Sally is able to prove she has met the requirements for acquiring an equitable interest under a trust in the first place, the second stage is for the court to quantify the extent of that interest. That's to say, the court will determine Sally's actual percentage share in the house and therefore the amount of money she will receive if the house is sold. This is the quantification of her share, totally separate from the qualification issue, and it is looked at only when it's proven that Sally deserves an equitable interest in the first place.

Look at the line in bold.

	Person not on the legal title (Sally)
Stage 1 Qualification	Needs to meet the requirements for acquiring an equitable interest in the first place
Stage 2 Quantification	**The court will decide the extent of the equitable interest in percentage terms**

Q: *Why are you so insistent about the two-stage process?*

A: Because the law here is also used in certain situations when two people are on the legal title. The stage at which you start is different.

Q: *If two people are on the legal title, isn't this express co-ownership which we looked at in Chapter 8?*

A: Yes. This leads us neatly on to the next part.

When there are two people on the legal title, this is express co-ownership. An example is when Greenacres is conveyed to Thomas and Lucy who are cohabiting. A trust of land arises under the Law of Property Act 1925 giving both a legal and equitable title. Both Thomas and Lucy are on the legal title as trustees holding Greenacres on trust for themselves in equity.

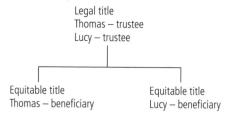

In this situation Thomas and Lucy do not have to go through the stage 1 qualification process of proving that they deserve an equitable interest in the first place because it is presumed that they both have an equitable interest in the property which can be shown as follows.

	When there are two people on the legal title (Thomas and Lucy)
Stage 1 Qualification	Both have an equitable interest – no need to meet any requirements for proving an equitable interest

Because the house was conveyed to them both, they are both registered on the legal title at the Land Registry holding as joint tenants under sections 34 and 36 of the Law of Property Act 1925. It is at this point that they should fill in the TR1 Form at the Land Registry to confirm how they hold their interests in equity, i.e. whether they hold as joint tenants or as tenants in common. There are three boxes on the TR1 Form, one of which should be ticked. The boxes state either

▶ The transferees are to hold the Property on trust for themselves as joint tenants
 or
▶ The transferees are to hold the Property on trust for themselves as tenants in
 common in equal shares *or*
▶ The Transferees are to hold the Property – complete as necessary.

If Thomas and Lucy tick the first box, they hold the equitable title as joint tenants. The right of survivorship will apply if either were to die. Should the relationship break down and the house is sold, they will each have a 50% share in the value of the house. If they tick the tenants in common in equal shares box, they each hold their separate share of 50% and the right of survivorship does not apply. Should the relationship break down, they will each have a 50% share. If they tick the third box and complete it, they might say that they are holding as tenants in common with the shares being 70/30 or 40/60 or whatever else they have decided. If Thomas and Lucy do not tick either of the first two boxes and do not complete the details of the third box, the situation is as follows. From 1998 the Land Registrar has presumed on their behalf that they are holding as tenants in common. This will give them individual separate shares but it doesn't say anything about how much that share is. The Land Registrar will write to Thomas and Lucy and tell them this is what he has presumed. If they object, they can write back stating how they do want to hold the beneficial interest. If they don't reply, although we know they are holding as tenants in common, we don't know in what proportions so it becomes a problem that has to be decided in court if Thomas and Lucy can't agree. This becomes relevant if, for example, the relationship breaks down and the house is sold. There is also the continuing problem where the TR1 Form wasn't filled in properly before 1998 and the Land Registrar didn't write and tell the parties they hadn't completed the form correctly so, again, the quantification of shares becomes an issue at the end of the day for the court. These problems exist despite the warning from Lord Justice Ward in *Carlton v Goodman* (2002). Having speculated sarcastically that conveyancers might not read the law reports he stated in the strongest terms:

> I will try one more time: ALWAYS TRY TO AGREE ON AND THEN RECORD HOW THE BENEFICIAL INTEREST IS TO BE HELD. It is not very difficult to do.

The parties in the two cases of *Stack v Dowden* and *Jones v Kernott* had purchased their properties in 1993 and 1985 respectively but the beneficial interest wasn't recorded at the time. The question as to who owned what percentage share only arose relatively recently when the house was sold.

Q: *How do you work out the percentage share if the beneficial interest isn't recorded because clearly people like Thomas and Lucy will need to know what share they each have in the house, not least if it's sold?*

A: The starting point is as follows. The land lawyers would say that because there is a joint tenancy at law, equity presumes a joint tenancy in equity because equity follows the law. This means it's presumed that Thomas and Lucy hold the equitable title also as joint tenants. In *Jones v Kernott* it was said that the starting point was a joint tenancy in equity because buying a house together was a joint enterprise and also because of the difficulties, if you try and work out the individual shares of a tenancy in common years after the relationship began, of determining who paid for what, where and when. Either way, the starting point is a joint tenancy.

Q: *If they're presumed to hold as joint tenants in equity, what share would each get if the relationship broke down and the house was sold and the proceeds had to be divided between them?*

A: Following on from the presumption of the joint tenancy in equity, the split would be 50/50. This equal split probably sounds fine at the start of the relationship when Thomas and Lucy are deeply in love but when Thomas and Lucy's relationship breaks down several years later, a bitter and enraged Thomas might want to argue that as he brought more money into the household when Lucy changed from full-time to part-time work in order to bring up their children, he should have more than a 50% share. An equally bitter and enraged Lucy might want to argue that she lost money when she went to part-time work in order to be able to look after their children and so she deserves at least 50%. She might also add that she used some inheritance money to put up a new conservatory which added value to the house and so she deserves even more than 50%. Thomas would argue back that he paid for the holidays they took. You can begin to see how easily things turn nasty. When they turn really nasty, the courts can use the law relating to trusts to rebut the presumption of 50/50 shares and to decide what percentage share they each have. The emphasis in a domestic situation will, again, almost certainly be on using the constructive trust to do this. This quantification is shown as follows.

	When there are two people on the legal title (Thomas and Lucy) and no record of their beneficial interests
Stage 1 **Qualification**	Both have an equitable interest – no need to meet any requirements for proving an equitable interest
Stage 2 **Quantification**	**Presumption of 50/50 share. If presumption rebutted, the court will decide the extent of the equitable interests in percentage terms**

Q: *In effect then, if there's one person on the legal title, Darren, for example, Sally must first prove that she meets the requirements for acquiring an equitable interest (qualification) and when she has done this, the court will quantify her interest in percentage terms (quantification). When two people are on the legal title and there's no record of the beneficial interest or they claim that the beneficial interest has changed, you start off with the presumption that they both have an equitable interest in the property so you only have to look at the quantification of their interests, whether that's the presumed 50/50 or something different if the presumption is rebutted?*

A: Yes. In actual fact it always has been like this. The difference today is that the law relating to quantification was stated in cases where one person was on the legal title and now it is stated in cases where two people are on the legal title which is why cases where two people are on the legal title figure so prominently in this chapter. The whole picture is shown below.

	One person on the legal title (Darren). Person not on the legal title (Sally) must	When there are two people on the legal title (Thomas and Lucy) and no record of their beneficial interests
Stage 1 Qualification	Meet the requirements for acquiring an equitable interest in the first place	Both have an equitable interest – no need to meet any requirements for proving an equitable interest
Stage 2 Quantification	The court will decide the extent of the equitable interests in percentage terms	Presumption of 50/50 share. If presumption rebutted, the court will decide the extent of the equitable interests in percentage terms

You should note that regardless of who was on the legal title, if the parties were married and the marriage were to break down, the courts have a wide discretion to allocate property as they see fit under divorce law. The percentage shares awarded would not depend on the law relating to constructive and resulting trusts.

In the past, often the resulting and constructive trust were pleaded in the alternative in a domestic situation for the following reason. Whilst the resulting trust gave certainty because the share awarded was based on financial contribution to the purchase price, the court could take other factors into account in a constructive trust which could lead to a greater share in the property being awarded. Today, the constructive trust should be pleaded in the domestic situation. This move has come from the cases of *Stack v Dowden* and *Jones v Kernott* which have changed the emphasis away from actual contributions to the purchase price, which is the focus of the resulting trust, to the broader approach of looking at a range of factors (such as contribution to the mortgage repayments, payment of household bills and the overall relationship), which is the focus of the constructive trust. The restriction of the use of the resulting trust in this way has meant that its role has been significantly diminished. Box A that follows sets this move in its historical context by looking at the history of the resulting trust when it was usual to plead such a trust.

Q: *Why is it important to go through the history if it's the constructive trust that's important in the domestic situation today?*

A: For two reasons. It shows you why the resulting trust became less and less suitable to modern day living and why the constructive trust has assumed the importance it has in recent years. The resulting trust is also pleaded in a business venture situation so you will need to know the principles that arise from these cases that you can then apply to any situation where property has been purchased as part of a business venture. Although the resulting trust cases are largely domestic based, the principles apply to both situations.

CONSTRUCTIVE AND RESULTING TRUSTS

	THE HISTORY OF THE RESULTING TRUST AND HOW IT WORKS	THE CONSTRUCTIVE TRUST IN A DOMESTIC SITUATION		THE RESULTING TRUST IN A BUSINESS VENTURE SITUATION		OTHER MEANS BY WHICH TO CLAIM AN INTEREST IN THE FAMILY HOME
	BOX A **IMPLIED CO-OWNERSHIP ONE PERSON ON THE LEGAL TITLE**	**Box B** **IMPLIED CO-OWNERSHIP ONE PERSON ON THE LEGAL TITLE** **You must prove either an express agreement constructive trust or an implied agreement constructive trust**		**BOX D** **IMPLIED CO-OWNERSHIP ONE PERSON ON THE LEGAL TITLE**	**BOX E** **EXPRESS CO-OWNERSHIP TWO PEOPLE ON THE LEGAL TITLE BUT NO DECLARATION OF THEIR BENEFICIAL INTERESTS**	**BOX F** **OTHER MEANS BY WHICH TO CLAIM AN INTEREST IN THE FAMILY HOME** **1.** The Matrimonial Proceedings and Property Act 1970 **2.** Proprietary estoppel **3.** The Matrimonial Causes Act 1973 **4.** The Civil Partnership Act 2004 **5.** The Family Law Act 1996
		1. Express agreement constructive trust	**2. Implied agreement constructive trust**			
					Box C **EXPRESS CO-OWNERSHIP TWO PEOPLE ON THE LEGAL TITLE BUT NO DECLARATION OF THEIR BENEFICIAL INTERESTS OR THEY CLAIM THE BENEFICIAL INTEREST HAS CHANGED OVER TIME**	

	BOX A	Box B — 1. Express agreement constructive trust	Box B — 2. Implied agreement constructive trust	Box C	BOX D	BOX E
STAGE 1 **QUALIFICATION** **Proving that the person not on the legal title qualifies for an equitable interest**	**1.** Contribution to the purchase price **2.** Contribution to the initial deposit or legal expenses But exclude (a) A gift or a loan and (b) Advancement **3.** The situation over contributions to the mortgage repayments and other contributions	(a) Express agreement regarding the beneficial interest AND (b) Detrimental reliance AND (c) Express agreement not honoured	(a) Implied agreement regarding the beneficial interest AND (b) Detrimental reliance AND (c) Implied agreement not honoured	**1.** Presumed both have equitable interests of equal shares	**1.** Contribution to the purchase price **2.** Contribution to the initial deposit or legal expenses But exclude (a) A gift or a loan and (b) Advancement **3.** The situation over contributions to the mortgage repayments	Presumption of a tenancy in common **1.** Contribution to the purchase price **2.** Contribution to the initial deposit or legal expenses But exclude (a) A gift or a loan and (b) Advancement **3.** The situation over contributions to the mortgage repayments
STAGE 2 **QUANTIFICATION** **Quantifying the equitable interest**	**4.** Proportionate shares	(d) Express agreement as to the beneficial interest (e) No express agreement as to the beneficial interest. Today use *Jones v Kernott* which builds on *Oxley v Hiscock* and *Stack v Dowden*	(d) A brief history of quantification (e) Today use *Jones v Kernott* which builds on *Oxley v Hiscock* and *Stack v Dowden*	**2.** Shares of 50/50 unless the presumption of equal equitable interests is rebutted **3.** If the 50/50 presumption has been rebutted, today use *Jones v Kernott* which builds on *Oxley v Hiscock* and *Stack v Dowden*	**4.** Proportionate shares	**4.** Proportionate shares

The history of the resulting trust and how it works

	BOX A IMPLIED CO-OWNERSHIP ONE PERSON ON THE LEGAL TITLE
STAGE 1 QUALIFICATION **Proving that the person not on the legal title qualifies for an equitable interest**	**1.** Contribution to the purchase price **2.** Contribution to the initial deposit or legal expenses But exclude (a) A gift or a loan and (b) Advancement **3.** The situation over contributions to the mortgage repayments and other contributions
STAGE 2 QUANTIFICATION **Quantifying the equitable interest**	**4.** Proportionate shares

To show you how the resulting trust works, we'll use the example of Darren's Dad and Darren's Mum rather than Darren and Sally to give more of a historical feel. Darren's Dad was the sole legal owner of the family home Greenacres and this section looks at how Darren's Mum could have qualified for an interest by means of a resulting trust when 'she were a lass'. Today, she would have to plead a constructive trust.

Box A1 Contribution to the purchase price

The basis for a resulting trust is presumed intention. If person A buys property and the property is conveyed (transferred) to person Z, where person Z gives no consideration for the transfer, then it is presumed that person Z holds the property on behalf of, or on trust for, person A.

Q: *So you're saying that if Darren's Mum paid for Greenacres but it was conveyed to Darren's Dad alone, then Darren's Dad held the property on trust for Darren's Mum?*

A: Yes. This meant that Darren's Dad held the legal title as a trustee and Darren's Mum held the equitable or beneficial interest in Greenacres. This was a classic example of a resulting trust, the principles of which were stated very clearly in *Dyer v Dyer* (1788). The word 'resulting' comes from the Latin *resultare*, which means to spring back. What it means is that the equitable interest springs back to the person who paid for the property. There is a presumption that, having paid for Greenacres, Darren's Mum intended to retain the beneficial enjoyment of it even though it had been conveyed to Darren's Dad. You must note, though, that there was only a presumption that a resulting trust arose in this kind of situation.

From the position just described it's not a great leap of the imagination to go one stage further. If Greenacres was purchased by Darren's Dad alone and Darren's

Mum contributed to the purchase price of the house, it was presumed that both she and Darren's Dad intended that she would have an interest in the house in proportion to her financial contribution.

Q: *Was this presumption made because, unless Darren's Mum thought she was to have an interest in the house even if she wasn't on the legal title, she wouldn't have contributed to the purchase price?*

A: Exactly. You don't actually need to look any more at what was intended because it was presumed that this is what she wanted.

Q: *And, by definition, did her interest have to be an equitable interest because she was not on the legal title and so could not have a legal interest?*

A: That's right. These contributions were recognised in equity because that's what would be seen as fair, and so an equitable interest was awarded. If you had contributed to the purchase price of a house, I expect you would see it as fair that you had an interest in the house, even if you weren't on the legal title. Again, you must note, though, that it was only a presumption that this was what the parties intended. This presumption could be rebutted by evidence to the contrary.

Q: *Taking Darren's Mum as an example, if she had an interest in proportion to her financial contribution, presumably the logical consequence was that if Darren's Dad contributed £70,000 to the cost of a £100,000 house and Darren's Mum contributed £30,000, then Darren's Dad would have a 70% share in the house and Darren's Mum would have the other 30%? Whenever the house was sold, the proceeds would be split 70/30.*

A: Yes and this is discussed further in Box A point 4.

You need to note that the contribution had to be to the initial purchase price at the time the house was bought. If Darren's Mum contributed £30,000 after the property was purchased, there was no saying on the face of it why the money was given. It could have been for any reason. If there was a contribution to the initial purchase price then it was presumed that she intended to have an interest in the property. If the contribution of £30,000 was made after the property had been purchased, this contribution would not count as giving an equitable interest under a resulting trust. An equitable interest might be claimed by pleading a constructive trust through this, but it wouldn't arise under a resulting trust in Box A.

Q: *That doesn't sound very fair, does it?*

A: No, but it is a recognised principle.

Box A2   Contribution to the initial deposit or legal expenses

If Darren's Mum had instead or as well as paid the deposit or the legal fees for the purchase of Greenacres, this also would have been seen as a contribution to the initial purchase price.

In *Re Rogers' Question* (1948) the wife had paid an initial payment of £100 while the husband had paid the remaining £900 through a mortgage. It was held that the wife had a 1/10 share in the house.

These contributions had to be paid before the house was purchased. In *Curley v Parkes* (2004) Mr Curley had paid £9,213 to Miss Parkes after the house was bought in her name only, although the reason he did so was in dispute. Mr Curley had also paid the legal fees. It was held that a resulting trust arises once and for all at the date on which the property is acquired. On this basis, as the £9,213 was paid a month after the completion of the purchase, it was not a contribution to the initial purchase price. Had Mr Curley agreed to pay Miss Parkes this sum before the property was purchased, he might have been able to count this as a contribution. However, on the facts there was no date when the agreement was entered into and Mr Curley had not incurred any liability to pay the sum when the house was bought. The legal fees would also have been paid after the purchase of the property, after the date on which any resulting trust would have come into existence, and so were not relevant. The removal costs that he also paid were not relevant to a resulting trust either as they were not a contribution to the purchase price.

Box A2(a)   But exclude a gift or a loan

A resulting trust arose from a presumption of what the parties intended. It was only a presumption, and could be rebutted by evidence of a gift or a loan: see *Re Sharpe* (1980).

Box A2(b)   and exclude advancement

Advancement is an old-fashioned concept. In bygone days, when men were men and women were the fairer sex, the man, in his capacity as husband and father, was seen as provider for the wife and children. Consequently, if the husband bought property and arranged for it to be transferred into his wife's name, it would be presumed that it was a gift to her because he was fulfilling his moral duty of providing for her. The same applied if property was bought by a father and transferred into the name(s) of his child(ren). In both cases, it would be presumed that it was a gift, and the presumption of the resulting trust in favour of the man would be rebutted. Although the presumption of advancement is still with us today, it does not take much to rebut it and when the relevant provisions of the Equality Act 2010 come into force , the presumption will be abolished.

Q: *So you're saying that if Darren's Mum had been the only person on the legal title and Darren's Dad had contributed £30,000 to the purchase price, then, assuming they were husband and wife, there would have been a presumption that the £30,000 was a gift to Darren's Mum?*

A: Yes. Darren's Dad wouldn't have had any interest under a resulting trust because the presumption of advancement would apply. Don't forget that the position of women was very different in days gone by and that such provision for her made sense.

Q: *Does it work the opposite way round if a wife conveys property into the name of her husband or a mother conveys property into the name of her children?*

A: No. it is not presumed to be a gift to the husband/children.

Q: *That's sexist, isn't it?*

A: It is today as recognised in the Equality Act 2010. The presumption of advancement also applies only if the parties are married. Remember, though, that it is only a presumption, and, because it is so outdated, it is a presumption that can be very easily rebutted but it is a reason why there has been a move to the constructive trust in a domestic situation.

Box A3   The situation over contributions to the mortgage repayments and other contributions

Q: *Is it difficult to say that contributing to a mortgage was a contribution to the initial purchase price of the property when a mortgage is paid back over a long period, say 25 years or so?*

A: If Darren's Dad arranged a mortgage with Bundy's Bank to pay for Greenacres, it gave him a lump sum of money, which he then used to pay for Greenacres. The fact that Darren's Dad promised Bundy's Bank that he would repay the money plus interest over a set period didn't alter the fact that Darren's Dad used this lump sum to buy Greenacres initially. So if Darren's Mum also contributed to the payment of the mortgage instalments, she was contributing to the initial purchase price of the house by helping to pay off the lump sum which was used in the initial purchase: see *Gissing v Gissing* (1971). This reasoning was put in doubt in the perplexing case of *Curley v Parkes*. Lord Justice Peter Gibson said that even if the person not on the legal title pays or helps to pay the mortgage instalments either from the outset or later, these payments would not count under a resulting trust. He said that such payments were simply paying off the mortgage debt and did not count as part of the initial purchase price. Only the person who borrowed the money on the mortgage was seen as the person who could claim an interest under a resulting trust because that person had assumed responsibility for repaying the money. So if Darren's Dad was on the legal title and the bank lent him money by means of a mortgage to purchase Greenacres, Darren's Dad could count the amount he'd borrowed on the mortgage as his contribution under a resulting trust. Even if Darren's Mum paid the mortgage instalments from day one, she wouldn't be allowed to count these payments under a resulting trust. Lord Justice Gibson said that a constructive trust should be pleaded where there had been a contribution to the mortgage payments where the contribution to the mortgage payments would show the required common intention.

Q: *So was a constructive trust pleaded in* **Curley v Parkes***?*

A: Although Mr Curley had contributed to the mortgage instalments, inexplicably the County Court could not find grounds to award a constructive trust and, equally inexplicably, permission to appeal on this ground was refused. So a bad day all round for Mr Curley. The decision in *Curley* has been questioned by many who think it was wrongly decided. This is so particularly following *Laskar v Laskar* (2008), a case which concerned a property that had been bought to let out, with the mortgage repayments being met from the rental income. Whilst this was a case where both parties were on the legal title, Lord Justice Neuberger said that helping to pay off the mortgage was seen as a contribution to the purchase price because it had the advantages of simplicity, appeared to be initially correct and on the facts of the case would be the right thing to do.

Q: *What happened if Darren's Mum contributed later to the mortgage?*

A: Because a resulting trust was presumed from the parties' intentions when they initially purchased the house, you could have argued that if Darren's Mum started to contribute later to the mortgage, this was not a contribution at the time the house was purchased. You wouldn't know why Darren's Mum was contributing at this later date. It could have been for any reason and nothing to do with acquiring an interest in the house. On the other hand, it shouldn't have made any difference whether Darren's Mum contributed to the mortgage from the outset or from part way through the mortgage. Either way she was contributing to the initial purchase price of the property.

Q: *Were these difficulties part of the reason why there was a move toward the constructive trust in a domestic situation when the person not on the legal title had contributed to the mortgage repayments?*

A: Yes. You had the problem with *Curley v Parkes* that appeared to reject the idea that a contribution to the mortgage repayments could ever be considered as a contribution to the purchase price under a resulting trust. You then had to have the discussion about whether contributing later to the mortgage repayments could be considered as a contribution to the purchase price of the property. Dicta from the majority in *Stack v Dowden* also made it clear that the route for cohabiting couples here should be the constructive trust and not the resulting trust.

Q: *What advantages does the constructive trust have?*

A: A constructive trust looks at the common intention of the parties at the time the trust was created. Payment of the mortgage either from when the house is purchased or later will allow the courts to find or 'construct' a trust based on this contribution. There are also advantages in pleading a constructive trust because the share awarded to the person not on the legal title is likely to be greater under a constructive trust at the end of the day than under a resulting trust. The reasons for pleading a constructive trust are elaborated on in *Crossco No 4 Unlimited v Jolan Ltd* (2011) at paragraph 85.

There is considerable case law looking at whether contributions other than to the purchase price or mortgage repayments could be taken into account in the context of the resulting trust. The following is a discussion of the cases that have led to the conclusion that such contributions should be argued now under a constructive trust. They show you how the law has developed and why it did so and make for fascinating reading. The example of Darren's Dad and Darren's Mum is continued in this section to illustrate the difficulties.

Q: *What contributions could you have looked at here other than to the purchase price or mortgage repayments?*

A: Contributions to the household expenses such as the bills which would allow the other party to pay the mortgage repayments, for example. In 1971 in *Gissing* *v Gissing* the idea that where one party paid the household expenses enabling the other party to pay the mortgage repayments would confer an interest under a resulting trust was expressed clearly. It was held that the exact mechanics of who paid for what didn't have to be examined literally. So if the use of Darren's Mum's income towards the household expenses allowed Darren's Dad to pay the mortgage repayments and he couldn't have done so without her income, this would have been just as much a contribution as if Darren's Mum had actually contributed to the mortgage repayments.

It had to be clear that the property owner could not have paid the mortgage repayments without the income of the other party to pay the household expenses. Cases here included *Bernard v Josephs* (1982) and *Le Foe v Le Foe* (2001). Contributions to the food and household expenses wouldn't count though where the other party could afford the mortgage repayments without that contribution as in *Gissing v Gissing*. In *Richards v Dove* (1974) a man was cohabiting with his mistress. The house had been purchased by the man. He had paid a small amount in cash towards the purchase price, and the remainder came from a mortgage. The man paid the mortgage repayments and the household bills and the mistress paid for the food and the gas. It was held that the contributions of the mistress to the household expenses would not give her an interest in the house because they were not contributions to the purchase price of the house.

Q: *Wasn't that seen as outrageous? She still contributed to the household expenses.*

A: It certainly made life very difficult for a woman. In the 1970s women didn't go out to work full time as they do today, and so they would not have been able to contribute themselves to the mortgage from their own earnings. After cases like *Gissing v Gissing* and *Pettitt v Pettitt* (1970) and, when we come to it, *Lloyds Bank plc v Rosset* (1991), the woman's lot was not a happy one. Look at the opposite argument, though. If a resulting trust is based on contribution to the initial purchase price of the property, then paying for other expenses afterwards was quite simply not contributing directly to that initial purchase price.

Making improvements to a property was not the same as contributing to the initial purchase price either. It was the contribution to the initial purchase price that mattered for a resulting trust, not what happened afterwards. As Lord Diplock indicated in *Pettitt v Pettitt*:

> If the husband likes to occupy his leisure by laying a new lawn in the garden or building a fitted wardrobe in the bedroom while the wife does the shopping, cooks the family dinner or bathes the children, I, for my part, find it quite impossible to impute to them as reasonable husband and wife any common intention that these domestic activities or any of them are to have any effect upon the existing proprietary rights in the family home on which they are undertaken. It is only in the bitterness engendered by the break-up of the marriage that so bizarre a notion would enter their heads.

While it was possible by other means to acquire an interest by making improvements to a property, it was not under a resulting trust.

This unsatisfactory state of affairs led to the enactment of the Matrimonial Causes Act 1973. This Act gave the courts wide powers on divorce to distribute property according to the financial resources of the parties, their ages, how long they had been married and what each party contributed, or would contribute, to the bringing up of the children. However, these statutory provisions apply only to married couples who are divorcing and cannot be used either by cohabiting couples or married couples who are not divorcing. Similar rights apply to civil partners under the Civil Partnership Act 2004.

In *Burns v Burns* (1984), where the parties were not married, it was held by Lord Justice Fox that:

> But the mere fact that parties live together and do the ordinary domestic tasks is, in my view, no indication at all that they thereby intended to alter the existing property rights of either of them.

In this case Mrs Burns had lived with Mr Burns for 19 years and they had two children together. It was held that she was not entitled to a share in the house because she had made no contribution, either direct or indirect, to its acquisition.

Q: *So, even though she'd looked after Mr Burns and the children for 19 years, run the household, acted as housekeeper, nanny, cook, chauffeur, gardener and decorator, she got nothing?*

A: Yes.

Q: *So in a non-divorce situation, the courts didn't recognise the woman's contribution of bringing up a family or running the household as giving her an interest in the house under a resulting trust?*

A: No.

Q: *Was there an alternative for all these hard-done-by women who had run the household and brought up the children?*

A: If there had been a contribution to the mortgage repayments, the alternative was to argue a constructive trust but in those days women like Darren's Mum did not usually go out to work to be able to make these contributions, and contributions to the expenditure on food must have enabled the man to pay for the mortgage repayments. Not a good place for women to be.

Summary of the requirements for acquiring an interest under a resulting trust

Contributions to the initial purchase price are taken into account under a resulting trust. Contributions to the mortgage repayments have been recognised in the past and, despite *Curley v Parkes*, may be recognised today. Contributions where one party paid the household expenses enabling the other party to pay the mortgage have also been argued under a resulting trust. Today, all these contributions should be argued under the constructive trust in a domestic situation. The party not on the legal title should plead a resulting trust using the principles described only when the property has been purchased as part of a business venture.

| Box A4 | Proportionate shares |

Quantifying shares in a resulting trust is determined on a proportionate basis: *Pettitt v Pettitt*. Imagine that Greencares cost £100,000. Darren's Dad contributed £70,000 to the purchase price and Darren's Mum contributed £30,000. Darren's

Mum would have a 30% equitable interest in the house and a 30% share of the proceeds when Greenacres was sold. It is the initial contribution to the purchase price of the property that matters. It's as simple as that.

Q: *How did you quantify the shares if a contribution to the mortgage repayments was recognised?*

A: This was problematic. The problem came from *Gissing v Gissing* where it was held that if both parties contributed to the mortgage repayments, then the equitable interest of the party not on the legal title would be in direct proportion to the amount contributed to the mortgage repayments.

Q: *Did it matter that mortgage repayments consisted of payment of both capital and interest?*

A: This would be the case when a mortgage was taken out over a long period. The early payments on a repayment mortgage would be mainly interest, with only a small amount of capital being paid off. In later years the mortgage repayments would start to pay off more and more capital, and the interest paid would be less and less. The lump sum of money from the mortgage was a capital sum, so until you started paying off capital rather than interest, you wouldn't be actually contributing to the repayment of the purchase price. If mortgage repayments had been argued under a resulting trust as they were in the past in domestic situations and the relationship between Darren's Dad and Darren's Mum had broken down after eight years, for example, then Darren's Mum's contribution to actually paying off the lump sum would have been minimal because she'd have been mainly been paying off interest. Her proportionate share would have been therefore minimal.

Q: *That didn't sound very fair, did it?*

A: It wasn't, and so what the courts did was to count her total payment, whether it was interest or capital, as a contribution to the purchase price.

Q: *It still didn't sound very fair though. When Darren's Dad had a substantial mortgage and Darren's Mum had contributed half of the mortgage repayments for a long time, for example, wouldn't she just have seen herself as having a half share in the house, not just a proportionate share?*

A: The share awarded under a resulting trust was based on strict mathematical calculations and, if Darren's Mum was arguing her case under a resulting trust, that's all she would have received. This is yet another reason why mortgage repayments are now considered under a constructive trust in a domestic situation.

By now, you should have grasped the principles behind a resulting trust. You will need to revisit these principles when you look at a business venture situation. You should also have understood the disadvantages of the resulting trust, so we can now look at the constructive trust itself which parties today in a domestic situation will almost certainly plead. Some historical perspective is built into the text to give you an idea of why we are where we are today.

The constructive trust in a domestic situation

	BOX B **IMPLIED CO-OWNERSHIP** **ONE PERSON ON THE LEGAL TITLE** **You must prove either an express agreement constructive trust or an implied agreement constructive trust**	
STAGE 1 **QUALIFICATION** **Proving that the person not on the legal title qualifies for an equitable interest**	**1. Express agreement constructive trust** (a) Express agreement regarding the beneficial interest AND (b) Detrimental reliance AND (c) Express agreement not honoured	**2. Implied agreement constructive trust** (a) Implied agreement regarding the beneficial interest AND (b) Detrimental reliance AND (c) Implied agreement not honoured
STAGE 2 **QUANTIFICATION** **Quantifying the equitable interest**	(d) Express agreement as to the beneficial interest (e) No express agreement as to the beneficial interest. Today use *Jones v Kernott* which builds on *Oxley v Hiscock* and *Stack v Dowden*	(d) A brief history of quantification (e) Today use *Jones v Kernott* which builds on *Oxley v Hiscock* and *Stack v Dowden*

This section looks at when a constructive trust arises in a domestic situation when there is one person on the legal title. It looks at whether the person not on the legal title meets the requirements for acquiring an equitable interest in the first place. If so, there is implied co-ownership. Once this has been proved, the court will then look at quantification of that interest.

You must prove either an express agreement constructive trust or an implied agreement constructive trust

A constructive trust tends to be called a common intention constructive trust. This is quite sensible because the trust is constructed based on what the parties intended to happen.

When only one person is on the legal title, there is no trust. Equity follows the law and there is no equitable interest. The person not on the legal title wishing to claim an equitable interest in the property under a constructive trust must prove a common intention that he/she was to have an equitable interest in the property. This is the stage 1 qualification of the two-stage process. This is proved by either an express or an implied agreement between the parties that the person not on the legal title is to have an interest in the property. The person not on the legal title must have acted to his or her detriment in reliance on this agreement but is then denied an interest in the land by the other party. The courts construct a trust based on the agreement, the reliance and the subsequent denial of the interest. The agreement does not have to meet the requirements of section 53(1)(b) of the Law of Property Act 1925, i.e. be in writing, as constructive and resulting trusts are exempt from doing so by section 53(2) of the same Act.

We'll use the example of Darren and Sally. Darren has been brought up by his parents, Darren's Dad and Darren's Mum, and he is cohabiting with Sally. Darren purchased Greenacres from his parents and he alone is on the legal title. Sally has had nothing to do with the paperwork and does not appear as a registered proprietor on the Proprietorship register at the Land Registry. She wishes to claim an equitable interest in the property by means of a constructive trust. What you're doing here is looking at Darren and Sally's shared intentions to establish whether Sally qualifies under constructive trust principles to give her an equitable interest. This is stage 1 of the process. Sally must prove she has met EITHER conditions B1(a) and B1(b) and B1(c) for an express agreement constructive trust OR conditions B2(a) and B2(b) and B2(c) for an implied agreement constructive trust in Box B in order to claim that she has a beneficial interest under a constructive trust. Only after she has done this can the courts quantify the interest.

Box B1 — ## Express agreement constructive trust

Box B1(a) — Express agreement regarding the beneficial interest

Q: *What's the beneficial interest?*

A: The equitable interest is also called the beneficial interest or the beneficial share. Although Sally cannot claim a legal interest in Greenacres because she is not on the legal title, she can claim an equitable interest, which gives her beneficial or enjoyment rights in the land. This equitable interest will be translated into money if Greenacres is sold.

Q: *Does the express agreement have to specifically relate to the property?*

A: Yes. It must be an agreement about the beneficial ownership of the property. Vague phrases such as 'I'll make sure you are alright in the future' are not enough, because they do not sufficiently define a beneficial share in the property. In *Layton v Martin* (1986) a promise of financial security was too imprecise to form an express agreement. The parties do not have to agree on the exact size of their beneficial interest in the property at the time as long as there is an agreement that they are both to have one.

This may sound very much like proprietary estoppel which is looked at in Chapter 12. One of the differences is that proprietary estoppel does not require a shared common intention. Another difference is that when a constructive trust is found, the remedy is the share in the property that was intended. In proprietary estoppel, the court exercises its discretion when deciding what remedy is appropriate, whether that is compensation, a share in the property or any other remedy.

Q: *So, returning to the constructive trust, you're saying that even though the legal title is in Darren's name, Darren and Sally can make an express agreement about the beneficial ownership of the house?*

A: Yes. An express agreement can include a promise or an understanding showing a shared common intention. The agreement doesn't even have to be remembered very precisely provided that it happened.

Q: *Doesn't it have to be remembered in full then?*

A: Well, first of all, you're up against the fact that Darren and Sally, living together, are hardly likely to sit down in front of Eastenders and discuss the beneficial ownership in the house. This is neatly encapsulated in *Pettitt v Pettitt* where Lord Hodson said that the idea of:

> a normal married couple spending the long winter evenings hammering out agreements about their possessions appears grotesque …

In *Lloyds Bank plc v Rosset* Lord Bridge talked about express discussions, 'however imperfectly remembered and however imprecise their terms may have been'.

The following two cases are given as examples of express agreements, although, having read them, you may consider that they are examples of express excuses instead.

In *Eves v Eves* (1975) the parties were cohabiting. Stuart told Janet that she couldn't be on the legal title to the house as she hadn't reached the age of majority, which was 21 at the time. On this reasoning, had she been over 21, she would undoubtedly have been on the legal title. Stuart's words were seen as an express agreement that she was to have an interest in the house. If Stuart hadn't wanted her to have an interest in the house, he wouldn't have bothered with an excuse. He would have just stayed silent or refused her such an interest.

Q: *But couldn't you argue the opposite way? He told her she couldn't be on the legal title, and by definition she would not have an interest in the house.*

A: Of course. That was the reasoning argued by Stuart, but to no avail.

A similar situation happened in *Grant v Edwards* (1986), where the man told the woman that she would not be put on the legal title to the house because it would prejudice her divorce proceedings. The court held that this was again an express agreement because the woman would clearly have been on the legal title had it not been for the divorce proceedings.

Q: *These excuses are hardly express agreements, are they?*

A: They showed a shared common understanding. On the face of it, there was a clear understanding between the parties in both these cases. Based on what they had been told, Janet Eves understood that she was to have an interest in the house in *Eves v Eves* and Linda Grant likewise expected an interest in *Grant v Edwards*.

Hammond v Mitchell (1991) was a case concerning a former bunny girl and a bungalow. The man told the woman that she couldn't be on the legal title because of tax reasons and his impending divorce. He also assured the woman that when they were married they would share ownership of the bungalow equally. Again, the woman successfully claimed an equitable interest based on the shared common intention found from the discussions and because the man's statements about the legal title inferred that she would have had a share otherwise. A happy bunny indeed.

In *Oxley v Hiscock* Mr Hiscock had insisted that the house was conveyed into his sole name in order to defeat any claim that Mrs Oxley's former husband might have against the property. Lord Justice Chadwick held that whatever the reasons for putting the house in Mr Hiscock's name alone, the discussions over whose name the house should be in showed that they both intended to have a beneficial share in the property and had expressed that intention to each other. If Mrs Oxley hadn't intended to have a beneficial interest in the house, the discussion would not have been needed.

Look at *Lloyds Bank plc v Rosset* for an example where it was held that there was not enough evidence for an express agreement. In this case Mr Rosset bought a derelict farmhouse using his own money, which came from a Swiss trust fund. The trustees of the Swiss trust fund insisted that the legal title of the house was put into Mr Rosset's name only. Mrs Rosset tried to claim an interest based on conversations she had held with her husband. However, no decision whether she should have an interest in the house had been reached in these conversations, and so there was no express agreement. Any such agreement would have to be very clear, given that it would have defeated the intention of the Swiss trustees that the house should belong to Mr Rosset alone.

In *Thomas v Fuller-Brown* (1988) the parties were unmarried and, although Mr Thomas virtually rebuilt the entire house and constructed an extension, he acquired no interest in the house because there was no express agreement between the parties.

In *Walsh v Singh* (2009) the court also held that there was no express agreement constructive trust. Whilst there had been a 'joint venture' in that Miss Walsh had helped Mr Singh construct an equine centre, aided him in his dealings with purchasing other land and had given up her career at the Bar to do so, a joint venture was insufficient to found the basis of a trust when the relationship broke down. Mr Singh had never said anything that could be taken as a promise that she would have a share in the property. Promises that her financial future was secure were an expression of love and commitment and couldn't be taken as a promise of an interest in his property.

Q: *Are you serious?*

A: Yes.

Box B1(b)   Detrimental reliance

The idea of *detrimental reliance* is based on the fact that there can't just be an agreement between the parties. There has to be a *detriment* to the person *relying* on the agreement. Equity will not allow a person to claim an equitable interest on the basis of justice and fairness unless that person has also acted to his or her detriment in reliance on that agreement. In an express agreement constructive trust, detriment does not have to be demonstrated so vigorously because you are already starting off with a clear common intention that set the trust terms at the start.

Q: *How does a person act to his or her detriment?*

A: We have already looked at *Eves v Eves* as far as a common express agreement was concerned. The detriment that Janet Eves undertook in reliance on this express agreement included painting the brickwork of the front of the house, breaking up the concrete in the front garden with a 14lb (just over 6kg) sledgehammer, putting the concrete from this destruction in the skip, demolishing a shed and putting another one up and preparing the front garden for turfing. Of course the *Eves* case was in 1975. Women were seen as the fairer and weaker sex and were not expected to do such things.

In *Grant v Edwards* the fact that Linda Grant contributed significantly to the housekeeping expenses and raised the children was held to constitute detrimental reliance following an express oral agreement.

In this case, Lord Browne-Wilkinson VC stated:

> Once it has been shown that there was a common intention that the claimant should have an interest in the house, any act done by her to her detriment relating to the joint lives of the parties is, in my judgment, sufficient detriment to qualify. The acts do not have to be referable to the house.

In *Lloyds Bank plc v Rosset* Lord Bridge said that the person relying on the agreement or promise must show that he or she has acted to his or her detriment or significantly altered his or her position in reliance on the agreement. The agreement doesn't have to stipulate how the person relying on the promise or agreement will actually act to his or her detriment so long as some form of detriment occurs in reliance on the agreement: see *Parris v Williams* (2008) confirming *Rosset*. It wasn't like a bargain where the claimant had to prove he had carried out his part of the bargain.

Today, it is more likely that when property is purchased by cohabitees, it will be transferred into joint names so both parties will be on the legal title. We know that there is a trust here and the only question is one of quantification of the beneficial shares. In these older cases, where there was one person only on the legal title, the person not on the legal title had to show that there was a trust in the first place – the qualification stage – before any issue of quantification could be discussed and so detriment was more important. As stated, though, detrimental reliance today is seen to be quite broad and can be understood from the domestic living arrangements.

Box B1(c)   Express agreement not honoured

It would be unfair or inequitable for the person with the legal title to deny the other person an interest in the house once detrimental reliance had occurred. The withdrawal of the promise allows for the award of an equitable interest under a constructive trust.

Summary of the requirements for an express agreement constructive trust

An express agreement about the beneficial ownership of the property, followed by detrimental reliance of the person relying on the express agreement, followed by the withdrawal of the agreement can give rise to an equitable interest under a constructive trust.

Having established that the person not on the legal title has qualified for an equitable interest in the property under an express agreement constructive trust (stage 1 of the two-stage process), we can now look at how the interest is quantified (stage 2).

Box B1(d)   Express agreement as to the beneficial interest

In determining the shares in an express agreement constructive trust, the courts will try to give effect to the actual oral agreement. If Sally was promised an equal interest, the court will award her a 50% beneficial share in the property.

Box B1(e)   No express agreement as to the beneficial interest

Today use *Jones v Kernott* which builds on *Oxley v Hiscock* and *Stack v Dowden* From the 1970s when there was no indication of the shares intended, the court looked at the circumstances, taking into account all the contributions to the household, which was the broad-brush approach: see *Eves v Eves*. Dividing the property equally, where 'equality is equity', was the backstop position.

The situation today is as follows but, first, if you look along the bottom line of the table on page 178, you will see that the method of quantification is the same (today use *Jones v Kernott*, which builds on *Oxley v Hiscock* and *Stack v Dowden*) whether there is an express agreement constructive trust but no express agreement as to the beneficial interest (Box B1(e)), an implied agreement constructive trust (Box B2(e)) or the situation where two people are on the legal title, so we know there is a trust, but the 50/50 presumption has been rebutted so we need to know what shares the parties have (Box C3). So, getting to the point of finding a trust is different when there is one person rather than two on the legal title, but the means of quantification is the same.

In *Oxley v Hiscock* there was one person on the legal title. In *Stack v Dowden* and *Jones v Kernott*, there were two. This does not matter because, as we've just seen, the second stage of the process, how the share is quantified, is the same whether one person is on the legal title or two. It just so happens that the two most recent cases that you must follow here are cases where two people are on the legal title. Let's work through the cases.

In *Oxley v Hiscock* at paragraph 69 it was held by Lord Justice Chadwick that the shares were decided on the following basis where there was no express agreement between the parties. The italicised words are important.

> *Each [party] is entitled to that share which the court considers fair having regard to the whole course of dealing between them in relation to the property.* And, in that context, the whole course of dealing between them in relation to the property includes the arrangements which they make from time to time in order to meet the outgoings (for example, mortgage contributions, council tax and utilities, repairs, insurance and housekeeping) which have to be met if they are to live in the property as their home.

Q: *Isn't there a problem with a decision based on 'fairness' though?*

A: Yes, because such decisions do not lead to consistency in the courts.

The next view came from the case of *Stack v Dowden* where it was held by Baroness Hale that when working out who should get what share.

> The search is to ascertain the parties' shared intentions, actual, inferred or imputed, with respect to the property in the light of their whole course of conduct in relation to it.

She emphasised that the intention of the parties should be found from their conduct, not by the court stating what it thought was fair. Baroness Hale also quoted from the Law Commission report 'Sharing Homes, A Discussion Paper' (2002, Law Commission No 278) saying that the Law Commission's view was similar to that of the court. The Law Commission had said:

> if the question really is one of the parties' 'common intention' we believe that there is much to be said for adopting what has been called a 'holistic approach' to quantification, undertaking a survey of the whole course of dealing between the parties and taking account of all conduct which throws light on the question what shares were intended.

Q: *What is the difference between the* Oxley *view and the* Stack *view?*

A: The *Oxley* view is the share the court considered fair in the circumstances. This is imputing an intention to the parties. It wasn't what the parties themselves intended but what the court thought they ought to intend. In the *Stack* view and the Law Commission's view you're searching for the shares which the parties themselves must have intended. This is found by looking at their whole course of dealing and conduct. It's the difference between imputing an intention and inferring an intention. Although Baroness Hale does actually still include the word 'imputed' in her judgment, her emphasis is on inference. Imputing means the court decides what it thinks is fair looking at the circumstances, which you can argue shouldn't be the remit of the court. Inferring means you look at what shares the parties intended judged on their conduct. *Stack*, therefore, appeared to be a rejection of the *Oxley* 'imputing an intention to the parties "fairness" approach' and more of an approach focusing on the parties' actual intentions.

The case of *Jones v Kernott* in the Supreme Court is the latest pronouncement on the quantification of shares in a constructive trust and clarifies (according to some) *Stack*. It was said that where there is evidence of an express agreement as to who gets what share, this should be given effect. If the intentions of the parties as regards their shares weren't actually expressly stated or communicated to the other party, the court should look for a common intention as to what shares the parties intended. This is found by looking objectively at their conduct through their words and actions. This is inferring what shares the parties intended by looking at their actual conduct. Where it is clear that the court can't infer what shares they intended from their conduct, Lord Walker and Lady Hale said that the answer is as follows:

> … each is entitled to that share which the court considers fair having regard to "the whole course of dealing between them in relation to the property": Chadwick LJ in *Oxley v Hiscock* [2005] Fam 211, para 69. In our judgment, "the whole course of dealing in relation to the property" should be given a broad meaning, enabling a similar range of factors to be taken into account as may be relevant to ascertaining the parties' actual intentions.

So, to summarise, if there was no express agreement and you couldn't infer what shares the parties had intended by looking at their conduct, the court had to impute an intention to them and decide their shares based on what was fair. This idea of fairness coming into play when there is no other way of deciding the shares has moved the law on again from *Stack*.

Q: *What's the difference again between 'inferring' and 'imputing'?*

A: Inferring is trying to work out what the parties wanted the shares to be by looking at what they did and said. Imputing is the court deeming the parties to have such an intention even though no such intention could be found from their conduct and even though they had no such intention. The intention the court would deem them to have would be based on fairness, i.e. on what was fair as viewed by reasonable and just people.

Q: *Is the basis of fairness acceptable?*

A: It at least acknowledges that the courts are working on fairness if there's no other way of quantifying the shares. As was said in *Jones* by Lord Walker and Lady Hale:

> But if it [the court] cannot deduce exactly what shares were intended, it may have no alternative but to ask what their intentions as reasonable and just people would have been had they thought about it at the time. This is a fallback position which some courts may not welcome, but the court has a duty to come to a conclusion on the dispute put before it.

Q: *What conduct can the court take into account if you can't infer what shares the parties intended and the court has to impute such an intention based on what's fair?*

A: The factors (that were non-exhaustive) that can be taken into account include the factors that were given in *Stack v Dowden* at paragraph 69 which are: any advice given or discussion that took place when the parties bought the house; reasons the house was bought in single or joint names; reasons the house was bought; the nature of the parties' relationship; whether the parties had responsibility to provide a house for any children; how the purchase was financed, both initially and subsequently; how the parties arranged their money – separately or together or both; how the bills were paid, although it could be that each contributed as much as he could, in which case equality could be presumed; the parties' individual characters and personalities and significant improvements to the house. All these factors could be taken into account when deciding what was fair.

Q: *If you can't infer what shares the parties intended from how the parties behaved and what they did, why don't you jump straight to fairness rather than trying to impute intentions to the parties, even if such imputation is based around fairness? The current approach seems a very longwinded way of going about things.*

A: This is what Lord Kerr asked in *Jones*. He distinguished between inferring an intention and imputing an intention. Inferring an intention could be from the parties' words or conduct. He wasn't happy with imputing an intention because at the end of the day the court decides what is fair in light of the whole course of dealing with the property. This has nothing to do with imputing intentions to the parties. In this sense it should either be 'Yes, we can infer what the parties intended' and 'We'll go with that', or 'No, we can't infer what the parties intended' so 'We'll go with what's fair'. This misses out the part where the court imputes an intention to the parties (probably that they never had) and just decides the issue based on fairness. As he pointed out though, the language of imputed intention had entered the vocabulary of the courts. Whilst he found it difficult to infer the shares intended, he allowed the appeal based on imputation and the shares awarded were fair.

Lord Collins said that if it wasn't possible to infer what shares were intended, each person would have a share that was fair given the dealings that had gone on between them. As he said

> ... in the present context the difference between inference and imputation will hardly ever matter (as Lord Walker and Lady Hale recognise at para 34), and that what is one person's inference will be another person's imputation.

Lord Wilson said that he found it difficult to infer what the parties intended but would impute an intention to them based on fairness.

In *Jones* the court found that it could infer the shares from the parties' conduct and so it didn't have to impute the shares. The statements made about imputing shares are therefore obiter so we will have to wait for more cases to see how the law develops here.

In *Gallarotti v Sebastianelli* (2012), which was an 'inference' case, Lady Justice Arden said:

> Accordingly, in my judgment, the inference to be made from the parties' course of conduct was that they intended that their financial contributions should be taken into account but not that there should be any precise accounting.

The decision reflected their respective financial contributions.

In *Aspden v Elvy* (2012), an 'imputing' case, the court imputed an intention by reference to what was fair taking into account the whole course of dealing between the parties. Having determined the shares on this basis, Judge Behrens concluded by saying that

> The figure is somewhat arbitrary but it is the best I can do with the available material.

This shows you why you should record your share in any property formally.

Box B2 ## Implied agreement constructive trust

This section works through the history of the implied agreement constructive trust ending with the present day position. The example of Darren and Sally will be continued to illustrate the law.

In this situation an agreement is implied that the person not on the legal title is to have an interest in the house. This is the first stage, the qualification stage. The person not on the legal title must prove that they qualify for an interest in the property by means of an implied agreement constructive trust. This implied agreement is inferred from the conduct and behaviour of the parties.

Box B2(a) ### Implied agreement regarding the beneficial interest

The implied agreement works on the basis that the person who is not on the legal title would not have undertaken certain activities unless he or she understood or expected that he would have a beneficial interest in the house. When this intention has to be inferred, anything the parties do which they want to rely on later as the basis for an implied agreement constructive trust has to have been communicated to, or known by, the other party. In *Lightfoot v Lightfoot-Brown* (2005) Mrs Lightfoot-Brown didn't know that Mr Lightfoot had paid £41,000 off the mortgage, the payment on which he was basing his claim, so there could be no implied agreement at all that he was to have a beneficial interest in the house, as the conduct must be known to the other party.

Q: *So in our example you're looking for conduct by Sally implying an unstated understanding between her and Darren that she would have an interest in Greenacres and that she wouldn't have undertaken such conduct otherwise?*

A: Yes. We'll work through the cases historically, though you should note that they are not consistent which reflects the evolution of the law over time in the context of changing attitudes. In 1971 in *Gissing v Gissing* it was stated that the parties would not necessarily have made an express agreement, but that a common intention to share the beneficial interest in the house could be inferred from their conduct. The type of conduct that led to an implied agreement included direct contributions to the purchase price or to the deposit on the house, to the mortgage or to the household expenses, but if, and only if, the other party couldn't pay the mortgage without them. Also, the conduct relied on for an implied agreement constructive trust must be undertaken because the person claiming an interest specifically thought that by carrying out that type of conduct he would obtain an interest in the house.

In *Pettitt v Pettitt* Mrs Pettitt had bought a cottage in her own name and she had paid the purchase price. Mr Pettitt spent a total of £275 decorating the property. He could not claim under a resulting trust because improvements to property did not count as a contribution to the initial purchase price: there was no express agreement (Box B1), and no agreement could be implied because the decorating work he had done was not referable to gaining an interest in the house. It could have been done out of love and devotion or simply the fact that Mr Pettitt didn't like the colour of the wallpaper.

In *Burns v Burns*, where the parties were not married, the conduct Mrs Burns tried to rely on to prove an interest in the house under an implied agreement constructive trust was as follows:

- She paid the housekeeping expenses, but as Mr Burns gave her a generous allowance for the housekeeping money, she could not rely on this expenditure as conduct.
- She paid the rates, but the money for the rates was included in the housekeeping money, so she could not rely on this either.
- She paid the telephone bill because she spent a lot of time on the phone, but that was an agreement reached between her and Mr Burns.
- She bought some household items, a dishwasher, washing machine, bed and chairs, but she had taken some of those with her when she left, so she could not rely on this expenditure as conduct.
- She had purchased some doorknobs.

Her conduct was not seen as referable to the acquisition of an interest in the house. The payment of the telephone bill didn't count as it was subject to a separate agreement and nothing to do with the house. Purchasing a few items of furniture did not give evidence of an intention to obtain an interest in the house. And, according to Lord Justice Fox:

the provision of the door knobs, etc, is of very small consequence.

Lord Justice Fox continued the saga of the Burns:

> In 1977 or 1978 the plaintiff (Mrs Burns) decorated the house throughout internally because she wished the house to be wallpapered and not painted. I do not think that carries her case any further.

Again, her work in decorating the house was not related to the expectation of a beneficial interest in the house.

Q: *Wasn't that unfair? Mrs Burns spent 19 years with Mr Burns and they raised a family together.*

A: According to the court, none of her actions was referable to the idea that she would have an interest in the house.

Q: *So it was quite strict then. It was basically still financial contribution to the house, and this financial contribution had to relate to the expectation of an interest in the house. Presumably, just paying the food and household bills wouldn't count either?*

A: No. You paid the food and household bills because you would starve or freeze otherwise, not because you expected an interest in the house. The courts deviated from a strict interpretation of the conduct required during the 1970s when Lord Denning intervened in these family cases. You need to be careful here. There were several cases in the 1970s including *Heseltine v Heseltine* (1971), *Cooke v Head* (1972), *Hussey v Palmer* (1972) and *Hall v Hall* (1982) where Lord Denning interpreted what had been said about conduct in *Gissing v Gissing* very widely. These new model constructive trusts, as they were called, were trusts which involved Lord Denning using an extremely broad-brush approach when establishing an interest under a constructive trust. 'Broad-brush' translates as 'anything goes'. The factors he took into account when establishing an interest included the background of the parties, the physical work on the property, the part played in planning and designing the property and monetary contributions: see *Cooke v Head*; buying furnishings, buying a car, contributing to housekeeping expenses and keeping house: see *Hall v Hall*; and building an extension: see *Hussey v Palmer*; none of which would have counted as conduct from which to imply an agreement as determined in *Gissing v Gissing*. The courts changed their approach in the middle of the 1980s because of the uncertainty of predicting the likely outcome of a case but it means that you do have to be careful if you come across cases around this time, particularly the ones highlighted above, because they did not follow the traditional approach for the creation of a constructive or resulting trust.

Q: *What happened after the mid-1980s?*

A: Lord Denning's input was rather too much for the English courts, so they returned to the traditional approach stated in *Gissing v Gissing*. The decision in *Burns v Burns* simply reflected the law before Lord Denning intervened.

In 1984 in *Burns v Burns* it was held that if Mrs Burns had paid the housekeeping expenses so that Mr Burns could pay the mortgage, a common intention under an implied agreement constructive trust could have been inferred. But she hadn't done so, as Mr Burns provided all the housekeeping money. When Mrs Burns had money to spare which she had earned, she was free to do what she liked with it. It was also held quite forcefully that domestic duties and bringing up children did not lead to the inference that Mrs Burns had an interest in the house (but presumably rather that she liked cleaning and bringing up children). And just in case there was any doubt here about the male viewpoint, Lord Justice May said:

> Finally, when the house is taken in the man's name alone, if the woman makes no 'real' or 'substantial' financial contribution towards either the purchase price, deposit or mortgage instalments by the means of which the family home was acquired, then she is not entitled to any share in the beneficial interest in that home even though over a very substantial number of years she may have worked just as hard as the man in maintaining the family in the sense of keeping the house, giving birth to and looking after and helping to bring up the children of the union.

Q: *That's even more outrageous, isn't it?*

A: Yes.

Moreover, in *Lloyds Bank plc v Rosset* the wife's contribution to the decorating and supervision of the builders was seen as being because she wanted the house to be ready in time for Christmas, not because she specifically thought she would acquire an interest in the property if she did so.

In *Lloyds Bank plc v Rosset* Lord Bridge gave the following requirements for the conduct required in an implied agreement constructive trust:

> In this situation direct contributions to the purchase price by the partner who is not the legal owner, whether initially or by payment of mortgage instalments, will readily justify the inference necessary to the creation of a constructive trust. But, as I read the authorities, it is at least extremely doubtful whether anything less will do.

Q: *So Lord Bridge was saying that only a contribution to the initial purchase price of the house or to the mortgage payments would count as conduct from which you could infer a common agreement?*

A: Yes. According to Lord Bridge in this case, even breaking up concrete, as in *Eves v Eves*, would not count as conduct from which an implied agreement could be inferred.

Q: *But you wouldn't do that sort of work on a house unless you believed you had some sort of interest in it, would you?*

A: Apparently you would, as far as Lord Bridge is concerned.

Q: *So it really went back to financial contribution to the initial purchase price of the house, either directly or through the mortgage repayments?*

A: Yes. Lord Bridge also appeared to reject the idea that indirect payments of the mortgage by paying the household expenses so the other party could afford to pay the mortgage would count as conduct from which to find an implied agreement constructive trust.

Some 20 years later, this narrow interpretation may be changing in light of recent judicial observations notably from *Stack v Dowden* and *Jones v Kernott*. *Stack v Dowden* is a case where both parties were on the legal title and the issue was quantifying the share in the house each party could claim (the quantification stage 2 process) so it was **not** a case that looked at whether the claimant had done enough to be awarded an equitable interest in the first place (the qualification stage 1 process that we're discussing here). This means that the problem with *Stack* is that any views on the qualification issue must be obiter. This is because where both parties are on the legal title, it is presumed that both parties have an equitable interest in the first place so you don't need to look at the qualification issue. However, in *Stack* the obiter words on the qualification issue were as follows. Lord Walker of Gestingthorpe 'respectfully doubted' Lord Bridge's words in *Lloyd's Bank plc v Rosset* where Lord Bridge had said that nothing less than direct contributions to the purchase price, whether initially or by payment of mortgage instalments, would do. Lord Walker also said:

> in my opinion the law has moved on, and your Lordships should move it a little more in the same direction, while bearing in mind that the Law Commission may soon come forward with proposals which, if enacted by Parliament, may recast the law in this area.

He also talked about all significant contributions, direct or indirect, in cash or in kind reflecting the parties' common intention.

Q: *So a party might be able to claim an interest under an implied agreement constructive trust through paying the household expenses, thereby enabling the other party to pay the mortgage?*

A: Possibly, yes, or even just paying the household expenses might be sufficient to support a common intention that the party not on the legal title was to have an interest in the house. A common intention could also extend to non-financial contributions which would have helped Mrs Burns in *Burns v Burns*. *Abbott v Abbott* (2007) was a case heard by the Privy Council. The husband was the sole legal owner and the wife was claiming an equitable interest in the house amongst other things, so this was a 'qualification' case as well as a 'quantification' case. Baroness Hale referred to Lord Walker's words in *Stack*. She said that the law had moved on from *Rosset* and then gave her own opinion:

> The parties' whole course of conduct in relation to the property must be taken into account in determining their shared intentions as to its ownership.

Again, it is clear that she sees Lord Bridge's words as outdated, and that wider contributions should give rise to a common intention for an implied agreement constructive trust. The problem here is that a decision of the Privy Council is only persuasive but given that the same people sit in both the Privy Council and the House of Lords, you could argue that it is very persuasive.

The case of *Jones v Kernott* looked at the use of the constructive trust but it looked only at the stage 2 process of quantification. *Jones*, though, did approve the obiter comments in *Stack* about wider conduct being taken into account when determining the qualification issue, but you must remember that the comments in *Jones* approving *Stack* were also obiter. In essence, when looking at what conduct you can take into account when inferring the intention that the non legal owner was to have a share in the property, you are still technically reliant on *Lloyds Bank v Rosset* but you can quote the obiter words in *Stack* as approved obiter in *Jones*. The courts today do, however, appear to be adopting the wider conduct approach as advocated in *Stack* and *Jones* although the use is inconsistent.

The following is a summary of the cases showing you over time what's been said or done when looking at what conduct you can take into account when deciding whether the person not on the legal title qualifies for an equitable interest. The most recent of these cases reflect a move towards taking into account the wider conduct of the parties. The figure in brackets is the number of people on the legal title so the comments are obiter where there are two people because the only issue to be determined in 'a two people on the legal title case' is quantification, not qualification.

- *Lloyd's Bank v Rosset* (1991) (1) – contribution to purchase price or mortgage repayments only taken into account
- *Stack v Dowden* (2007) (2) – obiter – wider conduct can be taken into account
- *Abbott v Abbott* (2007) (1) – obiter – wider conduct can be taken into account but persuasive authority only
- *Thomson v Humphrey* (2009) (1) – wider conduct can be taken into account but Mr Justice Warren said:

  each case is to be viewed on its facts, but one can obtain a flavour of the correct approach from the reported cases, as in *Burns v Burns* [1984] Ch 317, where performance of domestic duties and staying home to look after the children, contribution to rates and certain utility bills and purchase of some fittings and fixtures and domestic chattels were insufficient to give rise to any interest.

Q: *So that's a restrictive approach then for* **Thomson v Humphrey** *?*

A: Yes.

- *Hapeshi v Allnatt* (2010) (effectively 1) – whole course of conduct can be looked at
- *Jones v Kernott* (2011) (2) – obiter, approved dicta in *Stack*
- *Crown Prosecution Service v Piper* (2011) (1) – whole course of conduct looked at
- *Geary v Rankine* (2012) (1) – whole course of conduct looked at

The summaries above show a move towards wider conduct although there is still uncertainty in the law which serves to emphasise the need to sort things out before you ever cohabit.

Q: *What kind of wider conduct do the courts see as being taken into account?*

A: The non-exhaustive factors given at paragraph 69 in *Stack* are being quoted. The problem is that there were two people on the legal title in *Stack* so it wasn't a question of deciding whether the person not on the legal title qualified for an interest. The factors were used in the quantification context of deciding whether the 50/50 presumption of a joint tenancy had been rebutted which is a different context. On the other hand, if you're taking the parties' overall conduct into account when quantifying the interest, you could argue the same conduct should be taken into account when asking whether someone deserves an interest in the first place, the qualification stage.

Q: *Have the courts tried to impute an intention that the person not on the legal title qualifies for an interest, rather than infer an intention from the parties' conduct?*

A: In *Jones* it was said obiter that you couldn't impute an intention if you weren't able to infer one from the parties' conduct and the same was repeated in *Geary v Rankine*. If you start imputing an intention then you can hardly call it a common intention constructive trust because it's based on the common intention of the court and not of the parties. This is outside the remit of equity and it starts to look as though the courts are simply deciding the issue on fairness and social justice rather than on established principles. However, it will be for later cases to decide whether imputing intent, once out of the box, can be limited like this, particularly given the fairness emphasis of the Supreme Court.

Box B2(b) Detrimental reliance

Detrimental reliance then has to be shown in an implied agreement constructive trust, just as in an express agreement constructive trust. It is likely that the conduct that forms the basis of the implied agreement is the same conduct which forms the detrimental reliance that enables a constructive trust to be recognised by the court.

Box B2(c) Implied agreement not honoured

As for an express agreement constructive trust, the court can impose a constructive trust because it would be unconscionable for the party on the legal title to go back on an implied agreement regarding the beneficial interest that the other party has relied on to his or her detriment.

Summary of the requirements for an implied agreement constructive trust

A constructive trust can be imposed if the conduct of the parties shows an implied common agreement about the beneficial ownership of the house. *Lloyds Bank plc v Rosset* said that contributions to the initial purchase price or to the mortgage repayments only would satisfy the type of conduct required to claim an implied agreement constructive trust. Obiter dicta in *Stack v Dowden* suggest that wider contributions than this could be taken into account. The approval of *Stack* in *Jones v Kernott* was itself obiter although it would now seem that the courts are following what was said in these two cases. Detrimental reliance needs to exist. The implied agreement is then not honoured.

Box B2(d) A brief history of quantification

Assuming the party not on the legal title has met the qualification stage, the next question is to decide what exact share each party has.

In the 1970s the courts started off by trying to work out what share the parties intended they should have by looking at the conduct which formed the basis of the implied agreement and other conduct which was referable to the acquisition of an interest in the house.

Q: *So the courts didn't just look at the actual money paid in an implied agreement constructive trust?*
A: No. Under a constructive trust it was the inferred common intention that was given effect to.

Q: *Wasn't an obvious solution to divide the property 50/50?*
A: The 50/50 split, 'equality is equity', was usually the backstop position. The courts would first try to determine the shares based on the conduct of the parties.

Midland Bank plc v Cooke was decided in 1995 and caused consternation. In an implied agreement constructive trust, once an agreement has been inferred, the court can look at other conduct referable to the acquisition of an interest in the house which might throw light on the shares that the parties had intended. The subsequent conduct Lord Justice Waite took into account to arrive at the 50% share included looking after the children, contributing to the household bills, improving the house and sharing the rewards of Mrs Cooke's career as a teacher. This was not conduct which was necessarily referable to acquiring an interest in the house, as there were many other reasons why Mrs Cooke could have carried out such activities. Furthermore, as it was not conduct which would give rise to an implied agreement constructive trust under *Rosset* in the first place, there was no reason why it should have been relevant in quantifying her share.

Q: *What was the effect of this decision?*

A: The quantification of an interest claimed under a constructive trust became uncertain. What was a solicitor to advise a client? While the decision in *Midland Bank v Cooke* may have been fair in the circumstances, it was not based on recognised property principles.

Q: *Why didn't Mrs Cooke use divorce law?*

A: Because the parties were not divorcing. The dispute arose in the context of a mortgage from the Midland Bank that had not been repaid.

Midland Bank v Cooke (1995) was followed by *Drake v Whipp* (1996) where again the parties' entire course of conduct was looked at and a wide discretion was exercised in determining the extent of Mrs Drake's equitable interest in the house.

Box B2(e) Today use *Jones v Kernott* which builds on *Oxley v Hiscock* and *Stack v Dowden*

Again, you'll notice that how the shares are quantified today is now the same whether there is an implied agreement constructive trust, as here, or an express agreement constructive trust but no express agreement as to the beneficial interest (Box B1(e)). To save the rainforests Box B1(e) has not been repeated here. You need to refer back to page 192 and start reading from the words:

In Oxley v Hiscock at paragraph 69 it was held by Lord Justice Chadwick ...

If you just need a summary of the current position, it is this. The latest pronouncement from the Supreme Court in *Jones v Kernott* is that if the shares the parties intended can't be inferred from the parties' conduct, the court will impute an intention to the parties (decide the shares for them) based on what is fair as viewed by a reasonable person given the whole course of dealing in relation to the property. The non-exhaustive factors that the court can take into account will be based on the factors given in *Stack* at para 69 and include both financial and non-financial contributions.

This discussion serves as a timely reminder to all those of you who are married or thinking of living with your partner. If you marry but are not on the legal title to the family home, the court has a wide discretion to allocate property if the marriage breaks down and you obtain a divorce. Even if you are married, you may still have to rely on a constructive trust in the following situation. Imagine that your husband or wife either remortgages the house or takes out a first mortgage with Bundy's Bank after you have started living in the property. If he or she defaults on the mortgage repayments, Bundy's Bank will want to possess and sell the house in order to recoup its outstanding loan money. There are some circumstances where you will have to rely on having acquired an interest under almost certainly a constructive trust to protect your interest. It's not a divorce situation here, not yet anyway, so matrimonial law will not be relevant. This means that even though you are married, you would well be advised to ensure that there is an express agreement about the beneficial interest in the house when you buy the property if you are not on the legal title.

If you are cohabiting, you must ensure that you are on the legal title to the house or have an agreement in writing and signed, such as a properly drawn-up trust deed, stating the beneficial ownership in the house.

	BOX C **EXPRESS CO-OWNERSHIP** **TWO PEOPLE ON THE LEGAL TITLE BUT NO DECLARATION OF THEIR BENEFICIAL INTERESTS OR THEY CLAIM THE BENEFICIAL INTEREST HAS CHANGED OVER TIME**
STAGE 1 **QUALIFICATION** **Proving that the person not on the legal title qualifies for an equitable interest**	**1.** Presumed both have equitable interests of equal shares
STAGE 2 **QUANTIFICATION** **Quantifying the equitable interest**	**2.** Shares of 50/50 unless the presumption of equal equitable interests is rebutted **3.** If the 50/50 presumption has been rebutted, today use *Jones v Kernott* which builds on *Oxley v Hiscock* and *Stack v Dowden*

So far we have looked at cases where one person is on the legal title and the other person is claiming an equitable interest in the property under a constructive trust. There are other cases where two people have been on the legal title but there is no declaration as to how their actual beneficial share in the property should be split or the beneficial interest has changed since the parties purchased the property. The law relating to constructive trusts is used here.

Box C1 Presumed both have equitable interests of equal shares

As described in the first part of this chapter it is presumed that both parties have an equitable interest of equal shares. This is so regardless of unequal contributions to the purchase price or unequal contributions to anything else. There is no need to go through the stage 1 process of the parties proving that they qualify for an interest. The only question is one of quantification when there is no record of the beneficial interest or the beneficial interest has changed since the parties purchased the property. In these cases in a domestic situation, the law relating to constructive trusts is used to quantify the interests.

Shares of 50/50 unless the presumption of equal equitable interests is rebutted

When one party wishes to rebut the 50/50 split, he/she will have to provide the evidence needed to do so. In this case, the court will try to find a common intention between the parties that the parties are not holding as joint tenants with shares of 50/50 but are instead holding as tenants in common with different shares. The court will then quantify that share having constructed a different trust round that common intention. If the parties can't prove a common intention that the share of 50/50 should be rebutted, the shares will stay at 50/50.

Q: *How do you find a common intention to argue a rebuttal of the joint tenancy and equal shares?*

A: The cases of *Stack v Dowden* and *Jones v Kernott* are the most recent cases where both parties were on the legal title and wanted to rebut the presumption of a 50/50 share. This section traces those developments. In *Stack* Mr Stack and Ms Dowden were cohabiting and held the legal title of the house in their joint names. Whilst the fact that it was in their joint names showed that they each intended to have a beneficial interest in the property, the problem was that there was no declaration as to how they held the beneficial interest, whether as joint tenants or as tenants in common, and, if they held as tenants in common, in what shares.

Q: *Why wasn't this known? I would have thought this would have been very useful for the parties to have worked out before they actually bought the house.*

A: Because in 1993, which was when the house was bought, the parties didn't have to put this information on the Land Registry form.

So the presumption of equal shares on the equitable title was the starting point. If a party wanted to show that there wasn't a beneficial joint tenancy and equal shares, then he/she had to show a common intention that the parties intended otherwise and in what way. Baroness Hale said that cases where the parties intended that the beneficial interest would be different from the legal title would arise only in unusual circumstances. Simply because the parties had contributed unequally to the purchase price didn't mean the court would award unequal shares. She warned against an avalanche of claims of people thinking otherwise, particularly highlighting the extortionate cost of pursuing such claims.

Q: *And were the facts in Stack v Dowden unusual? I would imagine that everyone in this situation would see that they were an unusual case if they thought that they could claim more than a 50% share on the equitable title.*

A: The difficulty is how you define unusual. In *Stack* the facts showed that the parties did have a different common intention from that for a joint tenancy and 50/50 split. First, Ms Dowden had contributed far more to the purchase price of the house. As a point of interest she was the most highly qualified woman electrical engineer in the London area. Secondly, although Mr Stack had paid the interest on the mortgage and the premium on the joint policy, they planned to reduce the mortgage loan as quickly as possible, from which an intention to share unequally could be inferred. Thirdly, they kept their savings and investments 'rigidly separate' as their own property and the house was the only asset in joint names. Fourthly, the only regular expenditure that it was clear that Mr Stack committed himself to was paying the mortgage interest and premiums. Ms Dowden, though, had undertaken all the other regular commitments, both in the present house and the previous one. Overall, the facts of the case were very unusual. The fact that the couple had been together for so long and kept everything separate showed that they didn't intend equal shares even though the property had been put in joint names.

Q: *Couldn't you have argued that, as the house had been put in joint names, it was indicative of the fact that they did intend an equal share in it?*

A: It was held that all this showed was that Mr Stack was to have an interest, not necessarily an equal interest.

Q: *There must be lots of people though who keep their financial affairs separate, particularly those older people who are cohabiting and simply can't be bothered to change all the bank accounts to joint names?*

A: I agree. Simply because the parties keep their finances in separate accounts doesn't mean that they don't intend to share equally. One can speculate how much this is imputing intentions rather than inferring intentions.

Q: *Have unusual circumstances been found in any other cases?*

A: In *Adekunle v Ritchie* (2007) in Leeds County Court it was decided that the approach in *Stack v Dowden* applied to relationships other than cohabiting couples. On the facts the court found unusual circumstances. The situation was not the same as with a normal cohabiting couple. The house had been purchased in the names of mother and son and the mother had obtained a discount as a tenant purchasing from a local authority, meaning that she had contributed more to the purchase price albeit by means of the discount. The house had been bought in joint names because the mother could not obtain a mortgage on her own and she needed a home. It was intended that the son should have an interest in the house on the basis that he contributed to the mortgage and lived there. However, in the unusual circumstances there was no intention to hold as beneficial joint tenants with the right of survivorship applying. The mother and son kept their finances separate and the mother also had nine other children to consider. It was held that the parties had intended that the son should have a 33% share in the house.

Q: *Presumably this made it very difficult for people to know where they stood because you can't know in advance what constitutes an unusual circumstance? The only way to resolve the issue is to go to court.*

A: Yes, which is exactly what Baroness Hale was trying to avoid in *Stack* when she warned against an avalanche of claims. The moral here is that if you buy a house in joint names, make sure that you fill in the Land Registry TR1 Form properly so the beneficial interest in the house is recorded.

Q: *Is there an example of a case where unusual circumstances were not found?*

A: In *Fowler v Barron* (2008) Mr Barron could not rebut the presumption of equal beneficial ownership even though he had paid the deposit on the property, the mortgage repayments, the balance of the purchase price not covered by the mortgage and the utility bills, and he had looked after the children whilst Ms Fowler worked. Ms Fowler had spent her income on herself and the children. Emphasis was put on the couple's pooled assets, unlike the separate finances found in *Stack*.

Jones v Kernott was heard in the Supreme Court. The parties were unmarried and the property was bought in joint names in 1985 although there was no declaration of the beneficial shares. Ms Jones paid the deposit. The interest repayments on the mortgage were paid for by both, as were the bills. Mr Kernott paid for an extension which increased the value of the property by 50%. Mr Kernott moved out in 1993. Ms Jones carried on paying the mortgage and bills and a life insurance policy was cashed in and split equally between the parties enabling Mr Kernott to buy a house of his own elsewhere. Until the couple separated in 1993 there was no evidence to rebut the presumption that the shares were equal. The question in 2009 was 'had the beneficial shares changed following the separation'? Ms Jones thought so, and in her favour.

Q: *Were there unusual circumstances here?*

A: The court didn't talk about unusual circumstances but said that where the parties didn't share their financial resources, this rebutted the presumption of the joint tenancy and unequal shares could be more readily shown.

Q: *Does this mean that there doesn't need to be unusual circumstances?*

A: This is unclear. You can still argue, though, that the circumstances in *Jones* were pretty unusual where the parties had left it 16 years before sorting out who had what share in the house.

Q: *What did* **Jones** *say about how you prove a common intention that the shares were to be other than equal?*

A: You have to look objectively at the words and conduct of each person in the context of what the other person might have understood by those words or that conduct. It's what person A thinks person B meant by B's words or actions even if B didn't intend that or even acted from an entirely different motive but didn't communicate this to A.

Q: *What factors can be taken into account when you're trying to work out the common intention?*

A: Baroness Hale cited the list of factors that were given in Stack at para 69 as examples. These factors are listed on page 194.

Q: *What happened in Jones?*

A: In the event it was the cashing in of the life insurance policy allowing Mr Kernot to buy his own property that allowed the court to infer that his interest crystallised at that point in time and that Ms Jones would have the benefit of any capital gain on the house she had stayed in after then so they no longer held as beneficial joint tenants with equal shares.

Q: *So this wasn't imputing a common intention then?*

A: No, there was sufficient dealings between the parties for the court to infer an intention that the shares had changed. The question as to whether you could impute an intention at this stage was left unanswered.

Q: *Can you argue that if you are trying to prove that the parties intended something other than a 50/50 split, you would need actual evidence to prove this?*

A: This is one of the difficulties of the case. As you say, if the presumption of 50/50 can't be rebutted by actual evidence, you can argue that the presumption of 50/50 should stay. It shouldn't be up to the court to infer the evidence to move away from the 50/50 split.

So, having decided that there is enough evidence to rebut the intention of a 50/50 split, the question is 'what are the shares going to be then?'.

Box C3 If the 50/50 presumption has been rebutted, today use *Jones v Kernott* which builds on *Oxley v Hiscock* and *Stack v Dowden*

Once again, you'll notice that how shares are quantified is now the same whether there is express co-ownership and no record of the beneficial interests or the beneficial interests have changed over time, as here, and an express agreement constructive trust but no express agreement as to the beneficial interest (Box B1(e)). To save the rainforests Box B1(e) has not been repeated here. As before, you need to refer back to page 192 and start reading from the words.

> In Oxley v Hiscock at paragraph 69 it was held by Lord Justice Chadwick...

If you just want a summary, it is this. The latest pronouncement from the Supreme Court in *Jones v Kernott* is that if the shares the parties intended can't be inferred from the parties' conduct, the court will impute an intention to the parties (decide the shares for them) based on what is fair as viewed by a reasonable person given the whole course of dealing in relation to the property. The non-exhaustive factors that the court can take into account will be based on the factors given in *Stack* at para 69 and include both financial and non-financial contributions.

The resulting trust in a business venture situation

So far, we have been talking about constructive and resulting trusts in the context of the family home. What happens when people buy property together in a commercial situation? This section looks at the use of the resulting trust when property has been bought as part of a business venture.

	BOX D **IMPLIED CO-OWNERSHIP** **ONE PERSON ON THE LEGAL TITLE**
STAGE 1 **QUALIFICATION** **Proving that the person not on the legal title qualifies for an equitable interest**	**1.** Contribution to the purchase price **2.** Contribution to the initial deposit or legal expenses But exclude (a) A gift or a loan and (b) Advancement **3.** The situation over contributions to the mortgage repayments
STAGE 2 **QUANTIFICATION** **Quantifying the equitable interest**	**4.** Proportionate shares

We'll use the example of Mr Investment and Miss Décor. Mr Investment and Miss Décor purchased Greenacre Ruin as a business venture five years ago. Mr Investment alone is on the legal title. Their working relationship has broken down and Miss Décor wishes to claim an equitable interest in the house. In this situation, it is the resulting trust that is argued, **not** the constructive trust. This has been reinforced by the Court of Appeal in *Crossco No 4 Unlimited v Jolan*.

Q: *Why is it different in a business venture?*

A: Because investment and business are financial ventures, not personal ventures, and so the shares are worked out on a strict mathematical approach. There are also many other factors that come into play in the domestic scenario.

Q: *Do commercial situations necessarily involve strangers?*

A: No. You could have a situation when family members buy property together, for example, as a buy to let project.

You need to read through Box A again which looked at the principles which established from the cases of resulting trusts in detail, but Boxes D and E provide a summary of the law.

Box D1 Contribution to the purchase price

Miss Décor can claim that she qualifies for an equitable interest in Greenacre Ruin based on any contribution to the initial purchase price.

Box D2 Contribution to the initial deposit or legal expenses

She can also claim an interest if she has contributed to the initial deposit or legal expenses but note that these must be paid before the purchase of the property: see *Curley v Parkes*.

`Box D2(a)` But exclude a gift or a loan and

`Box D2(b)` Advancement

If Miss Décor's contribution is deemed to be a gift then she won't be able to claim that she qualifies for an interest, likewise if her contribution is deemed to be a loan: see *Re Sharpe*. The presumption of advancement won't apply if the parties aren't married and, even if they are, the presumption is outdated and likely to be ignored.

`Box D3` The situation over contributions to the mortgage repayments

In a business venture, payment of the mortgage by the person not on the legal title may be counted under a resulting trust although *Curley v Parkes* cast doubt on this. The reliability of *Curley* has been questioned particularly following *Laskar v Laskar* which stated that contributions to mortgage repayments do count. If this is correct and Mr Investment purchased Greenacre Ruin by means of a mortgage and he alone is on the legal title but Miss Décor contributes to the mortgage repayments, she may be able to claim an interest under a resulting trust based on these payments.

`Box D4` Proportionate shares

If Miss Décor has contributed to the purchase price only, the share awarded by the court will be proportionate to her contribution. If she has contributed to the mortgage repayments, the courts may count her total payment, whether it was interest or capital, as a contribution to the purchase price. Her share is worked out to strict mathematical proportions.

	BOX E **EXPRESS CO-OWNERSHIP** **TWO PEOPLE ON THE LEGAL TITLE BUT NO** **DECLARATION OF THEIR BENEFICIAL INTERESTS**
STAGE 1 **QUALIFICATION** **Proving that the person not on the legal title qualifies for an equitable interest**	Presumption of a tenancy in common **1.** Contribution to the purchase price **2.** Contribution to the initial deposit or legal expenses But exclude (a) A gift or a loan and (b) Advancement **3.** The situation over contributions to the mortgage repayments
STAGE 2 **QUANTIFICATION** **Quantifying the equitable interest**	**4.** Proportionate shares

Presumption of a tenancy in common

When there are two people on the legal title in a business venture situation, there is no need to go through the stage 1 qualification process. It is presumed that both parties have an equitable interest. It is also presumed that they would not want the right of survivorship to apply. Therefore, a tenancy in common is presumed in this business situation, not a joint tenancy. The presumption of a tenancy in common was discussed in Chapter 8 on page 151.

Q: *Does this cover shares changing over time?*

A: No, because unlike in a domestic situation, you are not starting off with a presumption of equal beneficial shares of 50/50. You are simply starting off with a tenancy in common which has yet to be quantified.

Box E1 Contribution to the purchase price

Box E2 Contribution to the initial deposit or legal expenses

Box E2(a) But exclude a gift or a loan and

Box E2(b) Advancement

Box E3 The situation over contributions to the mortgage repayments

When working out what factors can be taken into account, the same factors that were taken into account in Box D will be relevant. That is who contributed what to the purchase price or to the initial deposit or legal expenses or to the mortgage repayments. Evidence of a gift of loan will rebut the presumption of a resulting trust as will advancement.

Box E4 Proportionate shares

When looking at quantification the courts do not use the approach determined in *Jones v Kernott*. They will use the resulting trust proportionate approach as described in Box D4. That's to say, however much money each one put in, either as a contribution to the initial purchase price or to mortgage repayments, that's how much each will receive proportionally.

The Box entitled 'Summary of Constructive and Resulting Trusts' on page 211 gives you an overall summary of Boxes B to E from this chapter, showing you the picture as it is today.

Other means by which to claim an interest in the family home

> **Box F**
>
> **1.** The Matrimonial Proceedings and Property Act 1970
>
> **2.** Proprietary estoppel
>
> **3.** The Matrimonial Causes Act 1973
>
> **4.** The Civil Partnership Act 2004
>
> **5.** The Family Law Act 1996

Box F1 The Matrimonial Proceedings and Property Act 1970

The Matrimonial Proceedings and Property Act 1970 allows a husband or wife to claim a share or an increased share in property if he or she has contributed in a

SUMMARY OF CONSTRUCTIVE AND RESULTING TRUSTS

THE DOMESTIC SITUATION			THE BUSINESS VENTURE SITUATION	
BOX B ONE PERSON ON THE LEGAL TITLE IN A DOMESTIC SITUATION		**BOX C** EXPRESS CO-OWNERSHIP TWO PEOPLE ON THE LEGAL TITLE BUT NO DECLARATION OF THEIR BENEFICIAL INTERESTS OR THEY CLAIM THE BENEFICIAL INTEREST HAS CHANGED OVER TIME	**BOX D** ONE PERSON ON THE LEGAL TITLE	**BOX E** EXPRESS CO-OWNERSHIP TWO PEOPLE ON THE LEGAL TITLE BUT NO DECLARATION OF THEIR BENEFICIAL INTERESTS
CONSTRUCTIVE TRUST You must prove either an express agreement constructive trust or an implied agreement constructive trust		CONSTRUCTIVE TRUST	RESULTING TRUST	RESULTING TRUST
An express agreement constructive trust needs an express agreement, detrimental reliance and the express agreement not honoured	An implied agreement constructive trust needs an implied agreement, detrimental reliance and the implied agreement not honoured. The agreement will be inferred from contributions to the purchase price and mortgage repayments: *Rosset*. Obiter in *Stack* and obiter in *Jones* approving *Stack* would allow wider conduct from which to infer an agreement based on factors in para 69 in *Stack*. Courts are moving to this approach	It is presumed that both parties have equitable interests of equal shares	Contributions taken into account include a contribution to the purchase price, a contribution to the initial deposit or legal expenses, possibly a contribution to the mortgage repayments but exclude a gift or a loan and exclude advancement	In a business venture it is presumed there is a tenancy in common. Contributions taken into account include a contribution to the purchase price, a contribution to the initial deposit or legal expenses, possibly a contribution to the mortgage repayments but exclude a gift or a loan and exclude advancement
QUANTIFICATION If there is an express agreement as to the actual share, this will be used. If not, use *Jones v Kernott* to quantify	**QUANTIFICATION** Use *Jones v Kernott* to quantify	**QUANTIFICATION** If the presumption of equal equitable interests is rebutted using the factors in *Stack* at para 69 to infer a rebuttal, then use *Jones v Kernott* to quantify	**QUANTIFICATION** Proportionate shares	**QUANTIFICATION** Proportionate shares
Jones v Kernott states that if the shares the parties intended can't be inferred from the parties' conduct, the court will impute an intention to the parties (decide the shares for them) based on what is fair as viewed by a reasonable person given the whole course of dealing in relation to the property. The non-exhaustive factors that the court can take into account will be based on the factors given in *Stack* at para 69 and include both financial and non-financial contributions.				

substantial way in money or money's worth to the improvement of the property unless there is an agreement to the contrary.

Q: *Why was this Act passed?*

A: Because people didn't like the effect of *Pettitt v Pettitt* where it was held that DIY didn't count at all.

Q: *How is the money spent on improvements taken into account at the end of the day?*

A: You have to work out the value of the house immediately before the improvement and then work out how much value has been added to the property by the improvement. The share of the person who made the improvement is increased by a proportional amount corresponding to the increase in value. Similar rights are given to civil partners under section 65 of the Civil Partnership Act 2004.

Box F2   Proprietary estoppel

Proprietary estoppel is covered in detail in Chapter 12 and provides another avenue for the hard-done-by woman trying to claim an interest in a property. Proprietary estoppel arises when person A has either actively encouraged person B to believe that he has present or future rights in person A's land or when person A has stood by knowing that person B is mistaken as to his present or future rights in A's land. Even though the formalities for the creation of an interest in land have not been followed, it is possible for person B to claim an interest in the land. This is because person A is estopped, or stopped, from relying on the lack of formalities if he tries to deny person B an interest, because it would be unfair or unconscionable for him to do so. These requirements are very similar to those necessary to prove a constructive trust. While the element of fairness appears to be common to both claims, there are still differences between a constructive trust-based claim and a claim in proprietary estoppel, particularly as far as the remedies available to the court are concerned. These differences are looked at in Chapter 12.

Box F3   The Matrimonial Causes Act 1973

If a couple is married and then divorced, the divorce court has wide jurisdiction under the Matrimonial Causes Act 1973 to divide up the property as it thinks fit. The court will take into account factors such as the length of the marriage, the age of the parties and who will be looking after the children. The outcome is not based on who contributed to the property or who agreed what, where, when or with whom. At the discretion of the divorce court a wife can be awarded the house in its entirety, even though she may not have contributed in any way at all to its purchase.

Box F4   The Civil Partnership Act 2004

Section 1 of the Civil Partnership Act 2004 allows two people of the same sex who are not related to each other to register a civil partnership at a licensed venue. The procedure is purely civil and the Act forbids a religious service. Formal notice must be given to the local authority and there is a minimum of 15 days before the civil partnership can be registered under section 2 unless there are exceptional circumstances.

Q: *What rights does the couple have?*

A: They have the same rights as married couples as far as the rules of intestacy, the rights of next of kin, tax benefits, workplace benefits and pensions are concerned. The partnership ends either on the death of one of the partners or on an application to the court for dissolution following irretrievable breakdown of the partnership. Section 72 and Schedule 5 allow civil partners to be treated in a way similar to divorced couples under the Matrimonial Causes Act 1973 when allocating property on dissolution.

Box F5   The Family Law Act 1996

A statutory right of occupation, previously acquired under the Matrimonial Homes Act 1967, now exists under section 30 of the Family Law Act 1996. Subject to meeting the requirements in the Act, this right means that a spouse or civil partner cannot be evicted or excluded from the matrimonial or civil partnership home without a court order. A spouse or civil partner is also given a right to occupy the matrimonial or civil partnership home, with leave of the court if not already in occupation. Where an application is brought under this Act to resolve a dispute over occupation, the court has a wide discretion. It can take factors such as the welfare of children and the housing requirements of the parties into consideration.

If a spouse or civil partner registers his or her right of occupation as a class F land charge in unregistered land or by a notice on the Charges Register of the land affected in registered land, their right of occupation will be binding both on purchasers and on a trustee in bankruptcy if the other spouse or civil partner is bankrupt.

Q: *If the spouses or civil partners were living happily together, though, would they think of protecting this statutory right of occupation, even if they knew they had one in the first place?*

A: No. It's not the sort of thing you do when you're happily married or civil partnering.

There is also limited protection available to people who are cohabiting and living together as husband and wife under section 36 of this Act. Unlike the protection available to a spouse though, the maximum amount of time a cohabiting party will be allowed to stay in the home for will be one year.

Summary of other means by which to claim an interest in the family home

The Matrimonial Proceedings and Property Act 1970 recognises improvements to a property provided the parties are married. Similar rights apply to civil partners under the Civil Partnership Act 2004. Proprietary estoppel provides another avenue for claiming an interest in the family home. The Matrimonial Causes Act 1973 allows the court to redistribute property on divorce, and similar provisions apply on the breakdown of a civil partnership under the Civil Partnership Act 2004. A spouse or civil partner can claim a statutory right of occupation under the Family Law Act 1996. There is also a limited statutory right of occupation for cohabitees under this Act.

The structure of constructive and resulting trusts before 1997

An interest awarded under a constructive or resulting trust is an instance of implied co-ownership. The party on the legal title holds the property on his or her own behalf and on behalf of those parties who have acquired an interest in equity. Until the 1950s, it was not clear what type of trust this was. If land was expressly conveyed (sold or transferred) to two or more people, it was held on a trust for sale. However, the Law of Property Act 1925 had made no express provision for implied co-ownership, where interests arose under a constructive or resulting trust. This was because they were uncommon in 1925. The problem in implied co-ownership was resolved by *Bull v Bull* (1955). In this case it was held that a trust for sale would also be imposed when interests were held under a constructive or resulting trust. There is an explanation in Chapter 8 on page 163 of why a trust for sale was no longer appropriate for the majority of people who bought houses in the context of express co-ownership. This explanation is equally relevant in the context of implied co-ownership under a constructive or resulting trust.

The structure of constructive and resulting trusts after 1996

After 1996 constructive and resulting trusts came under the Trusts of Land and Appointment of Trustees Act 1996. This Act is discussed in detail in Chapter 10.

Reform

In July 2007 the Law Commission produced Report Number 307 entitled 'Cohabitation: The Financial Consequences of Relationship Breakdown'. The proposals are recommendations only and will apply when cohabiting couples separate or one of them dies. There is no draft Bill. It is acknowledged that the current law is complex, uncertain, expensive to use and leads to unjust outcomes, and children are also detrimentally affected. The proposed scheme would cover cohabitees who had had a child together or who had lived together for a minimum number of years, suggested at between two and five in the report. It would apply to all cohabiting couples, but couples could opt out. The aim of the scheme would be to ensure that the pluses and minuses of the relationship were fairly shared between the couple. The court would look at qualifying contributions which could include care of the children, providing financial support for the family, paying the mortgage and giving up secure accommodation to cohabit with the other party. These qualifying contributions would give rise to relief only where they'd resulted in one party either retaining a benefit or suffering an economic disadvantage when the couple separated. The form which a retained benefit could take is defined in paragraph 4.35 as 'capital, income or earning capacity that has been acquired, retained or enhanced'. An economic disadvantage is defined in paragraph 4.36 as 'a present or future loss. It may include a diminution in current savings as a result of expenditure or of earnings lost during the relationship, lost future earnings, or the future cost of paid childcare'.

There is also discussion on whether a very expensive gift given to Darren by Sally counts against Darren as a retained benefit if he doesn't return it, and whether Sally can argue economic disadvantage, again if he doesn't return it. The answer is in paragraph 4.58 of the report.

Q: *What orders could the court make?*

A: Lump sum payments, property transfers, orders for sale and pension sharing, but not maintenance payments. The court's first consideration here would be the welfare of any child of both parties.

Q: *Would the position of women be improved?*

A: It is clear that the welfare of any children is at the forefront of the proposals and that a woman who had given up work to have children would be better protected financially because she could claim for failure to secure future pension provision, failure to make savings, the loss that giving up work would have on future earning capacity and the effect of future child care responsibility. She would not be able to claim for lost earnings though.

The Government responded by stating that it wished to carry out research on the Family Law (Scotland) Act 2006 which contains provisions similar to those recommended by the Law Commission. This has now been done but it has been announced that the law relating to cohabitation will not be reformed. You should note also that the project on Marital Property Agreements being undertaken by the Law Commission is looking at agreements concerning property and finances between spouses and civil partners. It is not looking at cohabitation agreements. So, all of a sudden, nothing happened. This inactivity continues to mean that anyone thinking of cohabiting who ignores the contents of this chapter does so at his or her own peril.

A question on interests arising under a constructive or resulting trust

This example is intended to illustrate how to use the Boxes in this chapter to analyse the legal position. If you are using this method in undergraduate law exam questions, you will need to include statutory and case authority and detailed discussion of the various points of law. This information is found both in the text and from other sources.

> Six years ago, John and Claire purchased Greenacres together for £200,000. The legal title to the house was put in John's name. John paid £70,000 of the purchase price in cash and Claire contributed £30,000 in cash. John raised the remainder of the purchase price by means of a mortgage in his name. Claire has contributed to the mortgage repayments. Six months after the couple moved in, John's mother, Lily, who had recently become infirm, came to live with them. She paid for the conversion of two rooms downstairs into rooms specially adapted for her needs at a cost of £10,000. Shortly afterwards John agreed with her that she would always have a 10% share in the house. Since they have been there, Claire has done the accounts of John's business in the evenings without payment and has decorated the house throughout. Both John and Claire suffered pay cuts at work six months ago and Lily has helped out with the household expenses since. The parties have now fallen out, and John has just told both Claire and Lily that they have no interest in the house at all.
>
> Advise Claire and Lily what interest, if any, they have in Greenacres.

This is not a question on express co-ownership, as Greenacres was not conveyed to two or more people expressly. John alone is on the legal title. There is no indication of an express trust for either Claire or Lily, as this would have to be declared in writing and signed by John to meet the requirement of section 53(1)(b) of the Law of Property Act 1925. Claire and Lily may have an interest in Greenacres by proving they have an interest under an implied trust.

The history of the resulting trust and how it works

Box A

Following cases such as *Ledger-Beadell v Peach* (2006), *Stack v Dowden* and *Jones v Kernott* (2011), the constructive trust should be pleaded in a domestic situation.

This applies to both Claire and Lily so you should not be discussing the resulting trust here.

The constructive trust in a domestic situation

Box B

Claire and Lily must try to claim an interest in Greenacres under either an express agreement or an implied agreement constructive trust.

B1 Express agreement constructive trust

B1(a) Express agreement regarding the beneficial interest
There is no express agreement or understanding between John and Claire regarding the beneficial ownership of Greenacres: see *Eves v Eves* and *Grant v Edwards*.

Lily was told she would have a 10% share in the house. This is an express agreement regarding the beneficial ownership of Greenacres: see *Eves v Eves* and *Grant v Edwards*.

B1(b) Detrimental reliance
Lily cannot claim the £10,000 she used for the conversion as proof of detrimental reliance. She paid for the conversion costs before John promised her an interest in the house and did not spend the money in reliance on this agreement. However, she has helped out with the household expenses for the past six months and can rely on this payment as detrimental reliance based on the express agreement: see *Grant v Edwards*.

B1(c) Express agreement not honoured
John has not honoured his agreement that Lily should have a 10% share in the house.

B1(d) Express agreement as to the beneficial interest
As there was an express agreement regarding the exact beneficial interest, the court is likely to give effect to it and award Lily a 10% share in Greenacres if her claim is successful: *Jones v Kernott*.

OR

B2 Implied agreement constructive trust

B2(a) Implied agreement regarding the beneficial interest
In *Lloyds Bank plc v Rosset* it was held that only contributions to the initial purchase price of the property or contributions to the mortgage would give rise to an implied agreement constructive trust although dicta in *Stack v Dowden* approved in *Jones v Kernott* indicated that a wider view of contributions might be taken. This is the way the courts have been moving. In any event, Claire contributed to the initial purchase price of Greenacres and to the mortgage repayments. This conduct can be used to infer an agreement that she was to have a beneficial interest in the house.

As regards Lily, the express agreement with Lily will override any implied agreement.

B2(b) Detrimental reliance
Claire can count her contribution to the initial purchase price of Greenacres and her contribution to the mortgage repayments as conduct from which to satisfy detrimental reliance.

B2(c) Implied agreement not honoured

John has told Claire that she has no interest in Greenacres indicating that the implied agreement will not be honoured.

Quantification

B2(e) Today use *Jones v Kernott* which builds on *Oxley v Hiscock* and *Stack v Dowden*

The quantification of Claire's share will be determined using the principles in *Jones v Kernott*. Whilst Claire contributed less to the purchase price, she has contributed to the mortgage repayments and has helped out with John's accounts without payment. Whilst improvements of a significant nature were highlighted in *Stack* as being capable of entering the equation, it is debatable whether decorating will count. The court may infer from the conduct of John and Claire that they intended Claire to have a 50% share in the house. If it is not possible to infer from their conduct what shares Claire and John intended, the court will impute an intention to them and decide the quantification based on fairness taking into account the factors given in *Stack* (at para 69). Based on fairness, Claire may receive 50%. Or, she may not.

(It's interesting to note that if, in the olden days, Claire had claimed under a resulting trust, her share would have been limited to 15% as a result of her contribution to the purchase price plus her proportionate share of the mortgage repayments for the six years they were together. Assuming a long period for repayment, her share under a resulting trust would be unlikely to be the 50% that she could potentially be awarded under a constructive trust. This shows you why pleading a constructive trust is much better.)

Box C

This is not relevant because John alone was on the legal title.

Boxes D and E

These are not relevant because this is a domestic situation

Other means by which to claim an interest in the family home

Box F

F1 The Matrimonial Proceedings and Property Act 1970

We are not told whether the parties are married. In any event it is unlikely that Claire's decorating would be seen as a substantial improvement.

Lily is not a husband or a wife, and so cannot claim under this Act.

F2 Proprietary estoppel

Proprietary estoppel is discussed in Chapter 12. Claire and Lily could also have a successful claim in proprietary estoppel.

F3 The Matrimonial Causes Act 1973

If John and Claire were cohabiting, Claire could not use this Act. If they were married and were to divorce, the court could use its wide discretion under this Act to distribute property according to their individual circumstances. Such distribution would not be dependent on the acquisition by Claire of an interest under a constructive or a resulting trust.

F4 The Civil Partnership Act 2004
This is not relevant.

F5 The Family Law Act 1996
If Claire is married to John, she can claim a statutory right of occupation in the house. Provided she has protected her right under this Act by a class F land charge in unregistered land or by a notice on the Charges Register of Greenacres in registered land, it will be binding on a purchaser of Greenacres. If she is cohabiting with John, she will still have a statutory right of occupation, but any right to stay in Greenacres will be limited to one year.

Lily cannot use this Act as she is not a spouse, nor is she living with John as though they were husband and wife.

Conclusion

Claire and Lily are not on the legal title to the house. There is no express declaration of trust in their favour, so they must try to claim an equitable interest in the house under a constructive or resulting trust. This is a domestic situation so a constructive trust will almost certainly be pleaded. Claire has contributed to the purchase price and also to the mortgage repayments. There was no express agreement between her and John so she must claim under an implied agreement constructive trust where her contributions will form the basis of the implied agreement. The court will infer what shares were intended between herself and John by looking at their whole course of conduct. If the shares they intended cannot be inferred, the court will impute an intention to them and the allocation of shares will be decided on the basis of fairness. Lily must rely on the express agreement made to her by John and her contribution to the housekeeping expenses as the basis for an express agreement constructive trust. If her claim were successful, the court would award her the promised 10% share.

Chapter 10 looks at the duties and the rights of the parties when a constructive or resulting trust has arisen. Chapter 11 looks at what happens when the property subject to the constructive or resulting trust is sold. The question relating to John, Claire and Lily is continued at the end of Chapter 10 and at the end of Chapter 11 to show you how these further aspects work in practice.

Here are some variations on the question to give you an idea of how the other Boxes work.

Let's say both John and Claire were on the legal title in this scenario but with no declaration of the beneficial interest and Lily hadn't been around. In this case it would be presumed that they held as beneficial joint tenants in equal shares. If either party wanted to argue otherwise, they would have to prove a common intention that this was the case using the factors in *Stack* at para 69. It is highly unlikely that the court would see any unusual reason as to why the shares should be other than 50%. If, for example, Claire had inherited a large sum of money and had paid off the mortgage, she could have argued that the beneficial interests had changed over time and that she deserved more than John. The courts would then quantify their interests based on their common intention as inferred from their conduct or, failing that, imputed an intention to them based on fairness.

Q: *And if Lily had still been around and been promised her share?*
A: The presumption of John and Claire's 50/50 share would have been rebutted by the express agreement given to Lily. It would then be a matter of quantification

of John and Claire's share once Lily had her 10% share and that would depend on whether it was John and Claire's common intention that Lily's share would be apportioned equally between them or whether, as John's mother, Lily's share should come totally from John's interest in the house. There's a debate to be had.

Q: What would have happened if Claire had been a business partner with John and they were renovating Greenacre Ruin and Lily had not been around?

A: Claire would have pleaded her case under a resulting trust in which case her contribution to the purchase price and to the mortgage repayments would have taken into account and she would have received her proportionate share. Doing the accounts and decorating the house would not have been taken into account.

Further reading

G. Battersby, 'How Not to Judge the Quantum (and Priority) of a Share in the Family Home', 8 *CFLQ* (1996) 261

B. Bogusz, 'Defining the Scope of Actual Occupation Under LRA 2002: Some Recent Judicial Clarification', *Conv and Prop Law* (2011) 268

M. Davis, D. Hughes and L. Jacklin, ' "Come live with me and be my love" – A Consideration of the 2007 Law Commission Proposals on Cohabitation Breakdown', *Conv and Prop Law*, (2008) 3 197

M. Dixon, 'Constructive and Resulting Trusts of Land: The Mist Descends and Rises', *Conv and Prop Law*, Jan/Feb (2005) 79

M. Dixon, 'The Never-ending Story – Co-ownership after *Stack v Dowden'*, *Conv and Prop Law*, Sep/Oct (2007) 456

G. Douglas, J. Pearce and H. Woodward, 'Cohabitation and Conveyancing Practice: Problems and Solutions', 5 *Conv and Prop Law* (2008) 365

G. Douglas, J. Pearce and H. Woodward, 'Cohabitants, Property and the Law: A Study of Injustice', 72 *MLR* (2009) 24

S. Gardner, 'Quantum in *Gissing v Gissing* Constructive Trusts', 120 *LQR* (2004) 541

S. Gardner, 'Family Property Today', 124 *LQR* (2008) 422

S. Gardner and K. Davidson, 'The Supreme Court on Family Homes', 128 *LQR* (2012) 78

M. Harding, '*Stack v Dowden'*, *Conv and Prop Law*, 4 (2009) 309

N. Hopkins, 'Regulation Trusts of the Home: Private Law and Social Policy', 125 *LQR* (2009) 310

Law Commission, The Financial Consequences of Relationship Breakdown (Law Com No 307, 2007)

J. Miles, F Wasoff and E. Mordaunt, 'Cohabitation: Lessons from Research North of the Border?', 23 *CFLQ* (2011) 302

P. O'Hagan, 'Quantifying Interests under Resulting Trusts', 60 *MLR* (1997) 420

M. Pawlowski, 'Beneficial Entitlement – No Longer doing Justice?', *Conv and Prop Law*, Jul/Aug (2007) 354

C. Rotherham, 'The Property Rights of Unmarried Cohabitees: The Case for Reform', *Conv and Prop Law*, Jul/Aug (2004) 268

M. Thompson, 'Constructive Trusts, Estoppel and the Family Home', *Conv and Prop Law*, Nov/Dec (2004) 496

The Trusts of Land and Appointment of Trustees Act 1996

www.palgrave.com/law/Stroud4e

Introduction

In the chart 'The Use of Trusts in Land' in Chapter 6 on page 132, you will see that how a trust of land works is determined by the Trusts of Land and Appointment of Trustees Act 1996, which is discussed in this chapter. This Act reformed the way in which a trust containing land was held. All trusts containing land, with one exception, would now come under a newly defined statutory trust of land. The Act also clearly defined the duties of the trustees and the rights of the beneficiaries. The first part of this chapter summarises the position before the introduction of the Trusts of Land and Appointment of Trustees Act 1996. The remainder of the chapter concentrates on the Act itself.

A summary of trusts in land so far

Chapter 7 looked at successive interests in land, where two or more people hold an interest in the same piece of land and the individual interests follow one after the other. A trust is imposed to simplify the procedure if the land subject to the successive interests is sold.

Chapter 8 covered express co-ownership, where two or more people expressly set out to own land together at the same time. This is also called concurrent ownership, as the parties have interests in the land at the same time rather than successively. A trust is imposed to simplify conveyancing.

Chapter 9 discussed implied co-ownership where a person not on the legal title to the land has acted in such a way that he or she will acquire an equitable interest in the land under a constructive or resulting trust. This equitable interest is held on trust for them by those on the legal title.

There were major problems with the type of trust imposed in these situations.

Before 1997 successive interests in land were held either under a settlement or under a trust for sale. A trust for sale was also imposed where there was express co-ownership and where there was implied co-ownership under a constructive or resulting trust.

There were problems with both the settlement and the trust for sale. The settlement was complicated, expensive to administer, and could arise accidentally. The trust for sale had as its basis the notion of a duty to sell the land. This was sensible if land was seen as an investment opportunity. However, as the number of people buying a house to live in together increased from 1925 onwards, the concept of holding the land under the imperative duty to sell found in the trust for sale became more and more removed from reality. A couple who bought Greenacres together clearly bought the property to live in, not with the notion of immediately selling it. This problem became more acute as women entered the workplace and contributed to the purchase price of property, thereby acquiring an interest under a constructive or resulting trust. The type of trust imposed here was again a trust for sale and was subject to the same criticism.

Reform occurred with the enactment of the Trusts of Land and Appointment of Trustees Act 1996, which simplified the holding of land when a trust had arisen.

In the situations above where a trust is imposed, perfectly normal people find that they have the label 'trustee' and/or 'beneficiary' attached to them. Most of them probably have no idea of this, and when things go well it doesn't matter. When things go wrong, it does matter, because you have to determine what duties and rights they have in their respective capacities as trustees and beneficiaries. The duties of trustees and the rights of beneficiaries were clarified in the 1996 Act.

The Trusts of Land and Appointment of Trustees Act 1996

The sections of this Act are discussed in their numerical order. There was only this one Act to cover successive interests in land, express co-ownership and implied co-ownership arising under a constructive or resulting trust. These are very different circumstances. Where there are successive interests in land, it is likely that professional advice will be sought before formal documentation is drawn up. Compare this to a constructive trust, where the parties may not even know about the trust, let alone any consequences. Then consider the position of express co-ownership, where Greenacres is sold to Thomas and Lucy, who are told that they are trustees and beneficiaries, something they don't understand and don't believe. The Trusts of Land and Appointment of Trustees Act 1996 governs the duties and rights of the parties arising under the trust of land in each of these situations. This Act has to be sufficiently comprehensive to deal with any situation where a trust of land arises. This necessarily means that not all sections are relevant to all situations. To help explain this, there are examples in the text and at the end of the chapter. The examples at the end of the chapter build on the examples that were used at the end of Chapters 8 and 9. This will allow you to start to see the whole picture of land ownership in these situations. The next few pages cover the theory, but when you reach a few examples you will start to understand how the Act works in practice and in exam questions. You must also remember that, whether they know it or not, the majority of people in England and Wales are governed by this Act.

The general effect of the Act was as follows.

A trust containing land would be known as a trust of land. Existing settlements would continue to be governed by the Settled Land Act 1925. Successive interests in land created after 1996 would exist under a trust of land. Existing trusts for sale, whenever created, whether arising expressly or imposed by statute, would be converted into trusts of land. Any new trusts containing land created after 1996 would take effect as trusts of land.

This means that all trusts containing land, excluding settlements created before 1997, are now trusts of land. Successive interests created after 1996, express beneficial co-ownership whenever created, and interests under a constructive or resulting trust whenever created all exist under a trust of land. There will be people wearing the label of trustee and people wearing the label of beneficiary in each of these situations.

Section 1 – Definition of a trust of land

The reference to a trust of land in the Act includes express, implied, resulting and constructive trusts and trusts for sale. Trusts for sale created before 1997 are now converted into trusts of land. From 1 January 1997 onwards, any trust containing land will be known as a trust of land. A trust of land does not have to be composed entirely of land. So Greenacres and £1 million could be left on trust for beneficiaries Jemima, Albert and Harriett. This will still be a trust of land even though it includes money as well.

Q: *How do Jemima, Albert and Harriet benefit from the £1 million?*

A: The £1 million will be invested on their behalf until the trust comes to an end, when the capital will be divided between them, either in accordance with the trust instrument or else equally. The terms of the trust and statute law determine whether they are entitled to the income in the interim.

Section 2 – Settlements can no longer be created

Section 2 prevents the creation after 1996 of any new settlements when successive interests in land are created. After 1996, successive interests will exist under a trust of land. Any settlements created before 1997 will continue to be governed by the Settled Land Act 1925 and not by the Trusts of Land and Appointment of Trustees Act 1996.

Section 3 – The doctrine of conversion no longer operates

You can still create an express trust for sale, although it will be governed by the 1996 Act because a trust for sale comes within the definition of a trust of land in section 1. Section 3 prevents the doctrine of conversion operating in an express trust for sale. In a pre-1997 trust for sale, the interest of the beneficiary was seen as an interest in money, not in the land. This was because the land had to be sold and converted into money unless the trustees unanimously agreed to postpone sale. There is no longer a duty to sell the land under the Act and any beneficiary will have an interest in the land rather than the money. This section applies to trusts for sale created before and after the Act, excluding those created by will where the testator died before 1997.

Section 4 – There is no longer a duty to sell the land in a trust for sale

In a trust for sale the trustees were under a duty to sell the land. This section allows the trustees to postpone sale in any trust for sale, whenever created, regardless of any other instructions to the contrary. This power cannot be excluded.

Section 5 – A trust for sale implied by statute is now a trust of land

Any trust for sale implied by statute is now a trust of land.

Section 6 – Powers given to trustees

This is an important section. Section 6(1) states that the trustees of land have all the powers of an absolute owner, so trustees can sell, lease or mortgage the land, for example. Section 6(3), as amended by the Trustee Act 2000, also gives the trustees power to purchase land as an investment or for occupation by any beneficiary or for any other reason. The trustees can purchase land only in the United Kingdom.

Section 6(2) gives the trustees the power to transfer the land to the beneficiaries if they are of full age (18 or over) and full capacity and have an absolute right to the land. This means that there must be no conditions attached to their interest. The effect is simply to transfer the land to the beneficiaries. If the land is transferred to two or more beneficiaries, there will still be express beneficial co-ownership and there will be a trust of land again.

Section 6(5) states that when exercising the powers under section 6, the trustees must have regard to the rights of the beneficiaries, which they would have to do anyway in a trust. Section 6(6) states that the powers under section 6 must not be exercised contrary to any rule of law or equity. This means that the trustees are subject not only to this Act, but also to the general law relating to trusts. Under the general law, for instance, trustees cannot profit from their position and must balance the interests of the beneficiaries. If they fail to do this, the beneficiaries can take them to court for breach of trust, and claim for any loss.

Section 6 is important because it gives the trustees freedom to deal with the land without restriction, provided, of course, they act within the usual law of the realm.

Section 7 – Partition

This section allows trustees to partition (divide up) the land with the consent of the beneficiaries if they are of full age and absolutely entitled to an interest in the land. Such action means that the land will no longer be co-owned. Partition is viable only when the land can actually be divided up sensibly and would be applicable only in the division of large estates.

Section 8 – The exclusion of powers under sections 6 and 7

The powers under sections 6 and 7 can be excluded from any trust of land by the settlor, the person who created the trust.

Section 9 – Delegation of the trustees' functions

This section allows trustees of land to delegate any of their tasks in relation to the land to any beneficiary(ies) who is of full age and beneficially entitled to an interest in possession in the land. The trustees must delegate any tasks as a body here. Delegation by individual trustees is covered by section 25 of the Trustee Act 1925 as substituted by the Trustee Delegation Act 1999.

Q: *What does beneficially entitled to an interest in possession in the land mean?*

A: To explain beneficially entitled to an interest in possession in the land, look at an example of Greenacres, land which has been left to Claudia for life and then to David absolutely. During Claudia's lifetime she actually has her interest. She's enjoying it and she doesn't have to wait for it to come to her. Claudia's interest is said to be vested in possession. David's interest, on the other hand, is not vested in possession. He has to wait for Claudia to die before he takes his interest. Note here that possession does not mean occupation.

Section 9(7) states that if trustees have delegated their tasks, the beneficiaries will be in the same position as the trustees, with the same duties and liabilities.

Q: *Are there any tasks the trustees cannot delegate?*

A: Yes. Tasks which do not relate to the land. Nor can trustees delegate the function of receiving capital money. This means that if the land is sold, the trustees themselves must receive the purchase money because this is capital money. Any investment of the capital money could not be delegated to a beneficiary either, as this is not a function relating to the land.

Q: *Does this section mean that a trustee who delegates his tasks can walk away from his responsibilities?*

A: No, it doesn't. Under the original section 9(8), trustees were liable for the default of a beneficiary only if they didn't take reasonable care in their decision to delegate. Paragraph 45 of Schedule 2 to the Trustee Act 2000 has now inserted a new section 9A. Trustees are now under the general duty of care given in section 1 of the Trustee Act 2000, which is to exercise such care and skill as is reasonable in the circumstances when delegating. They must also review the delegation and intervene if necessary. If trustees fail to do this, they will be liable for any loss caused by the beneficiary as a result.

Section 10 – Requirements for consent

It is possible for the creator of a trust to stipulate that specified dealings with the land should not take place unless consent from named parties has been obtained. Section 10 states that if the creator of the trust requires the consent of more than two named people before any dealing with the land can take place, for example a sale, then the trustees must obtain consent from all of the named people. The named people who have to give consent could be the beneficiaries themselves. However, any person buying the land needs to know only that at least two of these named people have given consent.

Q: *What happens if the trustees don't obtain consent?*

A: They will be in breach of trust, which means they could be personally liable for any loss that the trust has suffered.

Section 11 – Consultation with the beneficiaries

Section 11 imposes a duty on the trustees to consult with the beneficiaries. This consultation exercise is likely to take place mainly in the context of whether or not the land should be sold or over rights of occupation.

Q: *Do the trustees have to consult all the beneficiaries?*

A: Only those who are of full age and beneficially entitled to an interest in possession in the land, a phrase explained already under section 9.

Q: *Any other requirements?*

A: The trustees have to consult 'so far as practicable'. If you're a beneficiary expecting to be contacted while you are conquering the North Pole, it's probably an unrealistic expectation. The trustees must give effect to the wishes of the majority of the beneficiaries as long as their wishes are consistent with the general interest of the trust. If the beneficiaries can't agree amongst themselves what they want to do, then the trustees must give effect to the wishes of the majority of the beneficiaries by value.

Q: *What's majority by value?*

A: If Felicity held a 1/8 interest in the land, James held a 2/8 interest and Syed held the remaining 5/8 interest, then the trustees would have to give effect to Syed's wishes because his share by value is the largest. Provided, of course, his wishes accord with the general interest of the trust.

Q: *Do the trustees have to do as the beneficiaries say?*

A: Not necessarily. There is a duty to consult, but to give effect to the wishes of the beneficiaries only in so far as they are consistent with the general interest of the trust.

Q: *What is the point of section 11 then?*

A: The point is found in section 14 of the Trusts of Land and Appointment of Trustees Act 1996. If there's a dispute between the beneficiaries and the trustees as to who wants to do what, the dispute can be taken to court. If the trustees don't follow the beneficiaries' wishes, even though they accord with the general interest of the trust, they may find themselves having to answer for why they won't co-operate with the beneficiaries in front of a court instead. So it's probably a good idea to take notice of their views in the first place.

There are two exceptions to the duty to consult. If a trust was created before 1997 by deed, there is no duty to consult unless the creator of the trust has stated subsequently in a deed that the duty to consult is to apply. If a trust was created in a will made before 1997, then, again, the duty to consult will not apply. It would be unfair to expect people to start rewriting their wills because of this Act, even if you thought they knew about it.

Section 12 – Beneficiary's(ies') right to occupy the land

This section is extremely important. It gives the beneficiaries a right to occupy the land and live there.

Q: *Are there any conditions imposed on the right of a beneficiary to occupy?*

A: Several. The beneficiary must be beneficially entitled to an interest in possession in the land, a phrase explained in section 9.

Section 12 also states that:

▸ the purposes of the trust must include making the land available for occupation by the beneficiaries; or
▸ the land is held by the trustees so as to be available.

The land must also be suitable for occupation.

Q: *How do you find out the purposes of the trust? Can you say that if Thomas and Lucy buy a house to live in, the purpose of the trust must be to provide accommodation for them?*

A: This is a badly worded section in the Trusts of Land and Appointment of Trustees Act 1996. Clearly the purpose of the trust is easy to see in the example of Thomas and Lucy. You can compare this situation with one where the purpose of the trust could not possibly be for the beneficiaries to occupy the land, simply because the land housed a factory. Determining the purpose of a trust can be difficult, and this sort of wording should never have been put in the Act. Unless it is specifically stated otherwise, the purpose of the trust is determined at the time when the trustees are deciding whether the beneficiaries can occupy the land, not when the trust was originally created.

Q: *Can purposes change?*

A: Yes. While Thomas and Lucy are young the purpose of the trust will be to house them. When they grow old and need care in a residential home, the purpose will no longer be to house them. The purpose will be to sell the house to raise the finance necessary for residential care.

Q: *Section 12 states that land must be available and suitable. Why would land be unavailable?*

A: If land was already leased out to a third party, it wouldn't be available for the beneficiaries.

Q: *And unsuitable?*

A: Again this is a very loosely worded section of the Trusts of Land and Appointment of Trustees Act 1996. Whether an older generation trustee would consider a vast country mansion full of antique marble flagstones and intricately carved woodwork suitable for a younger generation beneficiary is debateable. If the land housed a factory or a quarry or was a swamp, it would clearly not be suitable for occupation by any beneficiary.

Q: *What happens if there is more than one beneficiary and there aren't enough bedrooms for them all?*

A: The answer is found in section 13.

Section 13 – Two or more beneficiaries entitled to occupy

If two or more beneficiaries are entitled to occupy, the trustees may exclude or restrict the entitlement of any one or more of them, but not all of them. When deciding who can occupy, the trustees must act reasonably.

Q: *What does 'reasonably' mean?*

A: Apparently whatever you choose it to mean. For example, it would be reasonable for the trustees to take the beneficiaries' existing circumstances into account before making a decision.

When exercising this power, the trustees have to look at the intentions of the person who created the trust (if any), the purposes for which the land is held, and the circumstances and wishes of each of the beneficiaries entitled to occupy the land. If a person is already in occupation, either before the trust commenced or as a result of section 12, the trustees cannot exercise their powers to prevent him from continuing to occupy the land unless either he consents, or the court has given approval.

Q: *Isn't it rather unfair if one beneficiary is excluded and the others are allowed to live in the property?*

A: Yes, though under section 13(6) an occupying beneficiary may be required to pay compensation to the excluded beneficiary(ies).

Q: *Are there any conditions imposed on living in the property?*

A: Under section 13(3) the trustees can impose reasonable conditions on any occupying beneficiary, in particular to pay outgoings on the land.

Q: *What happens if trustees can't agree who is to occupy?*

A: If there's a dispute it will probably end up in court under the next section of the Trusts of Land and Appointment of Trustees Act 1996.

Section 14 – Application to the court in the event of dispute

Section 14 is an important section of the Trusts of Land and Appointment of Trustees Act 1996 because it deals with disputes.

Q: *When is a dispute likely to occur?*

A: The most obvious example is when the parties cannot agree whether or not to sell the land. Other examples could be disputes over occupation or repair. Section 14 of the Trusts of Land and Appointment of Trustees Act 1996 deals with these sorts of problems and allows the parties to apply to the court to determine the outcome. The court can determine whether the property should be sold or not, or who is to occupy and under what conditions.

You must note that in a divorce situation the court will be governed by the Matrimonial Causes Act 1973, in which there is power to transfer and redistribute property according to the parties' circumstances. In a non-divorce situation, the court will be governed by the Trusts of Land and Appointment of Trustees Act 1996 in which, although the court can determine the outcome of the dispute, it cannot alter entitlement to the property.

Q: Who can apply to the court under section 14?

A: Any person who is a trustee or any person who has an interest in property subject to a trust of land. This could be a beneficiary, a creditor or a trustee in bankruptcy. A trustee in bankruptcy will be appointed to take control over a beneficiary's finances if the beneficiary is bankrupt. The position of a trustee in bankruptcy is a professional one and he will not be appointed to the legal title. The equitable interest of a bankrupt beneficiary will vest in the trustee in bankruptcy.

Under section 14, the court has the jurisdiction to decide the outcome of the dispute and direct the trustees accordingly.

Q: On what basis does the court make a decision under section 14?

A: Section 15 deals with this.

Under section 14 the court can also declare the nature or extent of a person's interest in the property.

Q: Why would the court have to declare the nature or extent of a person's interest in the property?

A: For example, if a party who is not on the legal title to the land is claiming an equitable interest under a constructive or resulting trust, the court can determine whether or not he or she has such an interest and the extent of any such interest. This decision is reached using the principles and case law discussed in Chapter 9.

Section 15 – Matters relevant in determining applications under section 14

Under section 15(1) the factors the court must have regard to when deciding what to do in a dispute include:

- section 15(1)(a) – the intentions of the person or persons (if any) who created the trust;
- section 15(1)(b) – the purposes for which the property subject to the trust is held;
- section 15(1)(c) – the welfare of any minor who occupies or 'might' [sic] reasonably be expected to occupy any land subject to the trust as his home; and
- section 15(1)(d) – the interests of any secured creditor of any beneficiary.

You must note that these are not the only factors the court can take into account, as section 15(1) uses the word 'include'. Furthermore, there is no order of importance attached to the factors.

Section 15(2) states that the court should also take into account the circumstances and wishes of those beneficiaries entitled to occupy the land if there is a dispute over occupation arising from the exercise of powers under section 13. Section 15(3) states that the wishes of beneficiaries who are of full age and entitled to an interest in possession should also be taken into account in other disputes.

Look at each of the factors in section 15(1) in turn:

▶ The intentions of the person or persons (if any) who created the trust. This factor will cause problems if nothing was said at the time the trust was created.

▶ The purposes for which the property subject to the trust is held. One purpose is to provide a family home, and the courts will generally not order sale of the house when there are still children living there. If the children have left home, a sale is more likely. A different example is found in *Stott v Ratcliffe* (1982), a case decided under the previous law. Here, the purpose of the co-ownership was to provide a home for an unmarried couple, Mr Stott and Mrs Ratcliffe, who were living together, and also for the survivor when one of them died. When Mr Stott died, his interest in the house vested in Mrs Stott, his wife from whom he was separated. She asked for sale of the house. This was turned down by the court on the basis that the purpose of the co-ownership was to provide a home not only for Mr Stott and Mrs Ratcliffe while they were alive, but also for the survivor.

▶ The welfare of any minor who occupies or may reasonably be expected to occupy any land subject to the trust as his home.

Q: *When does a child stop being a minor?*

A: At the age of 18.

This factor is clearly illustrated in *Re Evers' Trust* (1980), a case which was again decided under the previous law. A cohabiting couple were living in a house with two children from the woman's previous relationship and one child from the current relationship. The man moved out and asked for sale of the house. This was refused on the basis that the underlying purpose of buying the house had been to provide a family home in which to bring up the children. This purpose could still be achieved and so a request for sale was refused.

Q: *This seems rather unfair on a man in a* **Re Evers' Trust** *type situation who has his money tied up in the house. It's all very well saying that while there are children the court can refuse to order a sale, but, if the relationship breaks up, where does the man live if he hasn't got any money to buy another house or pay for alternative accommodation?*

A: The court can determine reasonable conditions. It can require the party remaining in the house to pay compensation under section 13 in the form of an occupation rent to the party who has moved out. This would allow the non-occupying party to use any such money to pay for other accommodation. *Stack v Dowden* (2007) was a House of Lords case that considered section 15 of the Trusts of Land and Appointment of Trustees Act 1996 in the context of a dispute over occupation of the family home. Mr Stack had been excluded from the property without his consent. There had been an order in the Family Proceedings Court requiring Ms Dowden, his partner, who had remained in the house with the children, to pay him £900 per month. When this order came to an end Mr Stack agreed to the exclusion and the payments were discontinued. Mr Stack was now claiming that he should be paid an occupation rent by Ms Dowden until such time as the house was sold. Baroness Hale stated that the statutory criteria in section 15 must be used to decide whether an occupying beneficiary might be asked to pay an occupation rent, not the principles of equitable accounting which were used before the Trusts of Land and Appointment of Trustees Act 1996. She held that whilst the court could make a case for compensating Mr Stack under the statutory criteria in section 15, it would not do so because Mr Stack had agreed to be excluded from the house and the house was going to be sold quickly. Mr Stack would get his money from the sale of the house sooner rather than later.

Q: *If you look at the statutory criteria you can see that the welfare of the Stack-Dowden children could come into the discussion under section 15(1)(c). Where does the fact that Mr Stack agreed to be excluded or that the house was going to be sold quickly come into the statutory criteria?*

A: They don't. The argument that the house was going to be sold quickly didn't alter the fact that Mr Stack was still not living there. He had a beneficial interest in the house and should have been enjoying that beneficial interest by living in it. Lord Neuberger dissented from the majority here and said that the factors in section 15 either favoured compensation or were neutral or were irrelevant. In going through each of the factors in section 15 he held that the following applied. The purpose for which the house was bought and for which it was held was relevant as the purpose was to house everyone – Ms Dowden, Mr Stack and the children. That favoured compensation for Mr Stack because he was not living there. The welfare of the children was a neutral factor to the question of compensation as they would not be affected either way. The issue of creditors was irrelevant to the case. Mr Stack could argue other factors in his defence as well. He had to pay the outgoings on his own accommodation. His own beneficial interest in the house meant he could say that he was helping to house the children. He had been awarded compensation for his exclusion under one previous court order and nothing had changed since then. The fact that he agreed to be excluded shouldn't come into the equation. Lord Neuberger thought that Mr Stack should have been awarded compensation.

Q: *Presumably people will resist exclusion now because it means that it will be difficult to claim compensation?*

A: Quite. Whatever else, this case confirms that you must say that you are using the statutory criteria in section 15 on which to base any decision concerning occupation rent, whether you are doing so or not. In *Murphy v Gooch* (2007), a case relating to occupation rent again, the principles in section 15 were applied, not the principles of equitable accounting which had been used before the Trusts of Land and Appointment of Trustees Act 1996. If the person claiming an occupation rent does not have a statutory right of occupation under section 12, an example being the trustee in bankruptcy in *French v Barcham* (2008), he is not entitled to compensation under section 13(6). In this case under *French v Barcham* the court can still use equitable accounting to charge an occupation rent.

Having dealt with all these 'welfare' factors in section 15(1)(a) to (c), we can now look at the further important factor in section 15(1)(d):

▶ The interests of any secured creditor of any beneficiary.

Q: *Who's a secured creditor?*

A: Creditors are people to whom you owe money. Secured creditors are people who have lent you money based on the fact that they are given an interest in property that you own. This property will be sold if you don't keep up with the repayments on the loan. A bank that lends you money on a mortgage is a secured creditor because it holds the house as security. If you don't pay the mortgage repayments, the bank can apply for sale of the house in order to recoup the outstanding mortgage money. This does not mean that you are bankrupt, only that a secured creditor is calling in its security. In the cases that were decided before the Trusts of Land and Appointment of Trustees Act 1996 under section 30 of the Law of Property Act 1925, secured creditors were treated in the same way as when a trustee in bankruptcy applied, in that sale would be ordered: see *Re Citro* (1991) and *Lloyds Bank plc v Byrne* (1993). However, under section 15 of the 1996 Act, the interests of the secured creditor are not given any particular priority, and are only one of the factors to be taken into account.

Q: *Did the way the courts dealt with secured creditors change under the Trusts of Land and Appointment of Trustees Act 1996?*

A: In *Mortgage Corporation v Shaire* (2001) it was held that the approach had changed. Under section 15 of the Trusts of Land and Appointment of Trustees Act 1996 the interests of the secured creditor were not given any particular priority and were only one of the factors to be taken into account. Discretion could therefore be exercised more in favour of families and against banks and other secured creditors. Before the 1996 Act, the very words 'trust for sale' suggested sale, but there was nothing in the wording of the 1996 Act to suggest that sale should be ordered. Although throwing out past decisions would be arrogant and possibly rash, these decisions had to be treated with caution because of the change in the law. Had Parliament wished to keep the law as it was, it would not have included the four factors in section 15.

Q: *Have the banks lost out in favour of families then?*

A: Seemingly not. In *Bank of Ireland Home Mortgages Ltd v Bell* (2001) the judge considered the factors in section 15. As Mr Bell had left the family home section 15(1)(a) and (b) were not relevant. The son was virtually 18 and very close to being of full age so section 15(1)(c) was only a slight consideration. Mrs Bell's ill health was a reason for postponement of sale, not for refusal of sale. However, the debt owed to the Bank stood at £300,000 and was increasing daily with no chance of it being paid off. This was a 'powerful consideration'. The court ordered the sale of the house because it would be very unfair to make the Bank wait any longer for its money, particularly as the proceeds of sale wouldn't cover the debt owed to the Bank anyway.

Q: *Surely that's an important factor though, because if house prices are falling in a case like this the Bank will recoup less and less of the money it lent to the borrower?*

A: It is a very important factor. A mortgage is a commercial transaction, after all.

When a beneficiary is bankrupt, though, a trustee in bankruptcy is appointed to deal with his affairs just in case he decides to sell up quickly and start a new life elsewhere. Under section 14, as a person with an interest in the property, a trustee in bankruptcy has the right to apply to the court for sale of the property in order to pay the debts of a beneficiary who has become bankrupt. In this case, section 15(4) expressly states that the factors in section 15 will not apply as the application is one now governed by section 335A of the Insolvency Act 1986, which gives a different set of factors to be taken into account in the event of the bankruptcy of one of the beneficiaries under the trust of land.

It states that the interests of the bankrupt's creditors must be examined, that is to say, the interests of the people to whom the beneficiary owes money. The section then continues to say that, if the application concerns land which includes a dwelling house which is or has been the home of the bankrupt or of his spouse or civil partner or former spouse or former civil partner, the courts are to look at:

▷ the conduct of the spouse or civil partner or former spouse or former civil partner in so far as it contributed to the bankruptcy;
▷ the needs and financial resources of the spouse or civil partner or former spouse or civil partner; and
▷ the needs of any children; and
▷ all the circumstances of the case other than the needs of the bankrupt.

Q: *How does section 335A work in practice?*

A: The courts have interpreted this section quite strictly. In general they will order a sale of the house so that debts can be paid. This is particularly so as section 335A(3) goes on to state that if the trustee in bankruptcy makes an application for sale of the property more than a year after the bankruptcy happened, the interests of the creditors will be paramount unless there are exceptional circumstances: see *Re Citro.*

Q: *What counts as exceptional circumstances?*

A: Until *Barca v Mears* (2004) it was really only serious illness. For example, in *Claughton v Charalambous* (1999) the chronic illness and disability of the bankrupt's wife meant that sale was postponed indefinitely. In comparison, postponement of a sale because a teenager was studying for his 'A' levels was refused in *Re Bailey (A Bankrupt)* (1977). In *Barca v Mears* Mr Barca was bankrupt. His trustee in bankruptcy was seeking possession and sale of Mr Barca's house in order to pay off his debts. Mr Barca claimed exceptional circumstances under section 335A(3) of the Insolvency Act 1986 on the basis that his son had special education needs. The court held that the circumstances were not exceptional because they were not extreme and Mr Barca's son would not have to change schools if the house was sold. Mr Barca's next challenge was on the basis that a possession order would be in breach of his son's right to family life, home and privacy under Article 8 of the European Convention on Human Rights. In *Re Citro* the courts had given a narrow interpretation to the words 'exceptional circumstances' in the Insolvency Act. The words were interpreted as meaning 'unusual circumstances', and 'unusual circumstances' had been restricted to cases of very serious illness. The normal consequences of bankruptcy had not been seen as exceptional, however severe they were. The interests of creditors had prevailed over those of the rest of the bankrupt's family, even though the family owed the creditors nothing. The court held that the narrow interpretation of preferring the bankrupt's creditors to his family might need to be reviewed to be compatible with the European Convention on Human Rights. Although the interests of the creditors would normally prevail, the court should be able to find exceptional circumstances within the normal consequences of bankruptcy. Despite this interpretation, the circumstances of Mr Barca's son were not exceptional and the order for sale was upheld.

Q: *So although the interests of the creditors will generally prevail, the court can find exceptional circumstances within the normal range of events that you would expect to happen when someone is bankrupt and his house is sold?*

A: Yes. This takes account of the human rights aspect. It was also held that under this interpretation sale could be postponed when the loss to creditors would be small and would be outweighed by the disruption to the bankrupt and his family. In *Donohoe v Ingram* (2006) the claimant claimed that her circumstances were similar to those in *Re Holliday (A Bankrupt)* (1981) where sale had been postponed because the creditors were guaranteed their money even after postponement of sale. In *Donohoe v Ingram* it was argued that the creditors would be paid off in full even if the sale of the house was postponed until 2017 and this was an exceptional circumstance. It was held that *Re Holliday (A Bankrupt)* should be treated with caution as it had been held in *Harman v Glencross* (1986) that it went against the flow of other authorities. The circumstances of the claimant were not as clear cut as in *Re Holliday (A Bankrupt)* and, taking all her circumstances into consideration, they were not exceptional. The claimant also argued that under *Barca v Mears* greater consideration should be given to her and her family. It was held that even if a wider interpretation of section 335A were to be adopted, the circumstances overall were still not exceptional. The court did allow the claimant an extra three months in the house on the grounds of common humanity though.

Q: *What happens if a trustee becomes bankrupt?*

A: There is no rule of law that states that a trustee who is bankrupt must be removed from his position, particularly if there is no moral blame attached to him. If there were moral blame, it might be more desirable to remove him.

Sections 19 and 20 of the Trusts of Land and Appointment of Trustees Act 1996 give powers to beneficiaries to appoint or remove trustees.

In order to understand the full relevance of the 1996 Act and where it fits into today's society, you need to look at the areas where a trust of land is imposed, namely successive interests in land, express co-ownership in land and implied co-ownership where interests arise under a constructive or resulting trust. At the risk of repetition, these are very different circumstances. In the context of a constructive trust, the parties may not even know about the trust. Compare this to successive interests in land, where it is likely that professional advice will have been sought before formal documentation is drawn up. Then consider the position of express co-ownership where Greenacres is sold to Thomas and Lucy, who are told that they are trustees and beneficiaries, something they don't understand and certainly don't believe. The 1996 Act governs the duties and rights of the parties arising under the trust of land in each of these situations. The following examples put the Act into context in these different types of trusts of land.

The Trusts of Land and Appointment of Trustees Act 1996 applied to successive interests in land

Here is the example we will work from to look at the duties of a trustee and the rights of a beneficiary as determined by the Trusts of Land and Appointment of Trustees Act 1996 when there are successive interests in land.

> Last month George died. In his will, which was written two years ago, he left Greenacres to Bert for life, then to Claudia absolutely. Bert is alive today and is aged 25.

As Bert and Claudia's interests in Greenacres are held one after the other, these are successive interests in land. 'Absolutely' means there are no conditions attached to Claudia's interest. She will own Greenacres absolutely when Bert dies.

Before 1997 this would have created a settlement under the Settled Land Act 1925. The Trusts of Land and Appointment of Trustees Act 1996 now applies, and there will be a trust of land. Both Bert and Claudia are beneficiaries under this trust of land. This is a formal situation and the fact that the duties and rights of the parties are clearly defined by statute makes good sense because it will leave little room for argument.

Section 1 – Definition of trust of land

Successive interests in land now exist under a trust of land.

Section 2 – Settlements can no longer be created

Successive interests in land can no longer create a settlement.

Section 3 – The doctrine of conversion no longer operates

Section 4 – There is no longer a duty to sell the land in a trust for sale

Section 5 – A trust for sale implied by statute is now a trust of land
These sections relate to trusts for sale and are not relevant here.

Section 6 – Powers given to trustees

Trustees have the powers of an absolute owner so they can sell, lease or mortgage Greenacres, for example.

Q: *Who are the trustees?*

A: Under section 1 of the Law of Property Act 1925, life interests can only be equitable. As Bert has a life interest, his interest can only be equitable, not legal. Claudia's interest is not vested in possession, so, under section 1 of the Law of Property Act 1925, her interest cannot be legal either. This was discussed in detail in Chapter 7. You must therefore find someone to act as a trustee holding Greenacres on behalf of, and for the benefit of, both Bert and Claudia. When Bert dies the property will be transferred to Claudia absolutely with no conditions attached. She will then own Greenacres. George may have appointed trustees in his will, in which case they will be known. However, a trust will never fail for want of a trustee, so if nobody is appointed in the will, a trustee will be appointed by the court. This is what will happen here, so let's say Tick and Tock are appointed as trustees of the legal title of Greenacres. Bert and Claudia have equitable interests in Greenacres and are beneficiaries under a trust of land.

Legal title
Tick and Tock

to Bert for life –
equitable title

then to Claudia absolutely –
equitable title during Bert's lifetime

Q: *Why would two trustees be appointed?*

A: If two are appointed there is less chance of fraud because they can supervise each other. Two trustees are also needed for overreaching, which is discussed in Chapter 11.

Q: *Why would the trustees want the power under section 6 to sell Greenacres?*

A: If Greenacres were situated in an area of falling property prices it might be a sensible move to sell up and to purchase land in an area where property prices are rising.

Q: *Do the trustees have to buy land again?*

A: No, although under this section they can do so if they wish, either immediately after any sale or in the future. If they don't buy land again, the trustees must invest the money from the sale of Greenacres. Bert will then receive the income from the investment during his lifetime. On his death, Claudia will receive the capital sum.

Section 7 – Partition

As Bert's interest has a condition attached, in that it is for his lifetime only and Claudia's interest is not absolute, partition is not available.

Section 8 – The exclusion of powers under sections 6 and 7

There is no indication that George has excluded the powers under sections 6 and 7 in his will.

Section 9 – Delegation of the trustees' functions

Delegation is permitted only if a beneficiary is of full age and entitled to an interest in possession in the land. Bert is over 18 and has an interest in possession. Claudia does not have an interest in possession because she doesn't yet have possession of her interest in Greenacres. Tick and Tock together can delegate all or any of their tasks that relate to the land to Bert.

Q: *Why would the trustees delegate their tasks?*

A: Bert is the person who probably cares most about the land, so perhaps he would be the best one to take decisions about it. The trustees must exercise reasonable care and skill when delegating and review such delegation. If they don't do so, they will be liable for Bert's actions.

Q: *When would delegation be unreasonable?*

A: It might be unreasonable if Bert had no experience of managing property or had shown himself incapable of managing his own financial affairs. In this case the trustees would be liable for Bert's actions.

Section 10 – Requirements for consent

If George had said that consent was needed from Aunty Flora, Aunty Doris and Aunty Rose before Greenacres could be sold, for instance, then Tick and Tock would have to obtain all three consents before they could sell the land. Any purchaser of Greenacres would need only to ensure that at least two consents were obtained. In registered land such a restriction would be entered on the Proprietorship Register of Greenacres.

Section 11 – Consultation with the beneficiaries

Tick and Tock would have to consult Bert, as he is over 18 and has an interest in possession in the land. Claudia doesn't have an interest in possession because she is not yet in possession of her interest in Greenacres, and so doesn't have to be consulted. Tick and Tock would have a duty to consider Bert's wishes and would have to put them into effect if they accorded with the general interest of the trust. If they don't do this, Tick and Tock risk Bert complaining about them to the court under section 14. So it's probably a good idea to take notice of his views in the first place.

Section 12 – Beneficiary's(ies') right to occupy the land

Bert has an interest in possession, so can live in Greenacres if the property is available and suitable.

Section 13 – Two or more beneficiaries entitled to occupy

As Bert is the only beneficiary entitled to occupy, section 13 will not apply.

Section 14 – Application to the court in the event of dispute

Either Bert or Claudia can apply to complain about Tick or Tock, or Tick and Tock can apply to complain about Bert or Claudia or each other. Disputes are likely to arise over sale or occupation. The court will look at the factors given in section 15.

Section 15 – Matters relevant in determining applications under section 14

The court will take into account the factors given in section 15(1) to determine the outcome. These factors include the purposes for which Greenacres is held as trust property and the wishes of Bert. If Bert is bankrupt, his trustee in bankruptcy could apply to the court and ask for the sale of Bert's equitable interest to use the proceeds to pay off Bert's debts.

Q: *What would a purchaser buy if this happened?*

A: A purchaser, Peter, would buy Bert's equitable interest under the trust of land. This would give Peter the same rights as Bert under the Trusts of Land and Appointment of Trustees Act 1996. Peter would have bought Bert's equitable life interest. On Bert's death, Claudia would own Greenacres and Peter's interest in it would end.

Q: *Why wouldn't Greenacres just be sold automatically if Bert was bankrupt?*

A: Because when Bert dies, Claudia is entitled to Greenacres or its capital value. Bert was entitled only to the enjoyment of it, or, if it were sold, the income from the resulting capital, for his lifetime. Bert was never given Greenacres, or any part of it, absolutely, and so is not entitled to any of its capital value.

The Trusts of Land and Appointment of Trustees Act 1996 applied to express co-ownership interests in land

Now look at a situation of express co-ownership where Greenacres is sold to two or more people concurrently. We'll use the following example to look at the duties of the parties in their capacity as trustees and the rights of the parties in their capacity as beneficiaries when this occurs. Remember that you could find yourself in a very similar situation.

> Two years ago Adrian, Bob, Clare, David and Emilio purchased Greenacres together. They are all over 18.

This is an example of express beneficial co-ownership, so a trust is imposed. The first four people named on the conveyance are entitled to be on the legal title provided they are able and willing, so these are Adrian (A), Bob (B), Clare (C) and David (D). These four will wear the label of trustees. They hold Greenacres on trust for themselves and Emilio (E), so A, B, C, D and E will all wear the label of beneficiaries. This type of situation was discussed in Chapter 8.

Legal title	Equitable title
(A B C D)	either (A B C D E) as joint tenants
Joint tenants	or A B C D E as tenants in common

Before 1997 there would have been a trust for sale. Because Greenacres was purchased after 1996, the situation is governed by the Trusts of Land and Appointment of Trustees Act 1996 and there will be a trust of land. When you work your way through this example you will probably think, 'well, they would have done this anyway'. This is the statutory authority for 'anyway'.

Section 1 – Definition of a trust of land

This is a trust of land as the trust contains land.

Section 2 – Settlements can no longer be created

The interests of the parties are held concurrently; that is to say they are held at the same time, not one after the other, so this situation would never have created a settlement.

Section 3 – The doctrine of conversion no longer operates

Section 4 – There is no longer a duty to sell the land in a trust for sale

Section 5 – A trust for sale implied by statute is now a trust of land

These sections relate to trusts for sale and are not relevant here.

Section 6 – Powers given to trustees

Trustees have the powers of an absolute owner. Adrian, B, C and D have the power to sell, lease or mortgage Greenacres, for example. As joint tenants they own the 'whole' legal title together, so if there are any dealings with the legal title of Greenacres, they must all sign the required documents. Any sale of Greenacres would therefore require the four of them to sign the conveyance, the deed of sale.

Section 7 – Partition

It is unlikely that Greenacres is a sufficiently large house to divide between the parties, nor would partition appear to be relevant to the circumstances.

Section 8 – The exclusion of powers under sections 6 and 7

This section would be used by a person creating an express trust who wished to restrict the powers of appointed trustees. It is not relevant here.

Section 9 – Delegation of the trustees' functions

With the exception of E, the trustees and the beneficiaries are the same people, so this section is not relevant.

Section 10 – Requirements for consent

This section would be used by a person creating an express trust. It is not relevant here.

Section 11 – Consultation with the beneficiaries

This would happen as a matter of course for A, B, C and D as they are trustees and beneficiaries. However, in their capacity as trustees, they have the duty to consult E, who is also a beneficiary, if they propose to deal with Greenacres in any way. The wishes of the majority by value should prevail.

Section 12 – Beneficiary's(ies') right to occupy the land

All the parties have a right to live in Greenacres.

Section 13 – Two or more beneficiaries entitled to occupy

This section allows trustees to determine which beneficiaries should live in the property and the conditions under which they do so. This means that any dispute over the occupation of Greenacres would be unlikely to be resolved under this section as, apart from E, the trustees and the beneficiaries are the same people. If no mutual decision can be reached between A, B, C, D and E, an application can be made by any party to the court under section 14.

Section 14 – Application to the court in the event of dispute

In the event of a dispute, any of the parties, including E in his capacity as beneficiary, can apply to the court. Disputes could arise over whether Greenacres should be sold, or who should or shouldn't live there, or over repairs. Disputes are likely to occur if the parties fall out or their circumstances change. The court will take the factors given in section 15 into account when determining the outcome.

Section 15 – Matters relevant in determining applications under section 14

If the dispute is over sale, the court will take into account reasons why the house was initially purchased. This would almost inevitably have been to provide a home for A, B, C, D and E. If there are children, their welfare will be taken into account. The wishes of all the parties would also be taken into account. If one of the parties, B for example, was bankrupt, section 15 would not apply, and the court would look instead at the factors in the Insolvency Act 1986. This means that if a year had passed since the bankruptcy happened, Greenacres would be sold so that Bert could realise his share to pay his debts unless there were exceptional circumstances.

Q: *Wouldn't that be unfair on the others who may not want to sell?*

A: Paying B's creditors is of paramount importance in a bankruptcy. Whether the other parties have their share of the money in a house or in their pocket is irrelevant. The value of their money is the same, just in different forms. An alternative could be for A, C, D and E to buy out B's share and pay the money over to his trustee in bankruptcy.

Now to return to the situation that nobody can quite comprehend. Again, you will probably work your way through thinking, 'well, they would do this anyway'. Now you know why they can do it 'anyway'. Remember also that the chances are that you will find yourself in this kind of situation sometime in your life.

> Thomas and Lucy purchased Greenacres together two years ago. They are both on the legal title.

There is express beneficial co-ownership here, and this means that a trust is imposed. Therefore the parties will have the labels of trustee and of beneficiary attached to them, whether they know it or not. Thomas and Lucy will be trustees holding Greenacres on trust for themselves as beneficiaries.

Legal title	Equitable title	
(T L)	either	(T L) as Joint tenants
Joint tenants	or	T L as Tenants in common

Before 1997 this situation would have created a trust for sale. It now creates a trust of land governed by the Trusts of Land and Appointment of Trustees Act 1996.

Section 1 – Definition of a trust of land

This is a trust of land as the trust contains land.

Section 2 – Settlements can no longer be created

This is not relevant. Thomas and Lucy hold their interests in Greenacres concurrently, not successively, so this would never have created a settlement.

Section 3 – The doctrine of conversion no longer operates

Section 4 – There is no longer a duty to sell the land in a trust for sale

Section 5 – A trust for sale implied by statute is now a trust of land

These sections relate to trusts for sale and are not relevant here.

Section 6 – Powers given to trustees

As trustees, Thomas and Lucy have the powers of an absolute owner. If they want to sell Greenacres they must both sign the deed of sale conveying it to a purchaser, as they are both on the legal title. Usually this won't be a problem, because if Lucy doesn't want to move from Greenacres, she'll say so. Thomas will retire to watch football on television and the subject won't be talked about again for years.

Section 7 – Partition

It is unlikely that Greenacres is a sufficiently large house to divide between the parties, nor would partition appear to be relevant to the circumstances.

Section 8 – The exclusion of powers under sections 6 and 7

This section would be used by a person creating an express trust who wished to restrict the powers of appointed trustees. It is not relevant here.

Section 9 – Delegation of the trustees' functions

As the trustees and the beneficiaries are the same people, this section is not relevant.

Section 10 – Requirements for consent

This section would be used by a person creating an express trust. It is not relevant here.

Section 11 – Consultation with the beneficiaries

This will happen as a matter of course as the trustees and beneficiaries are the same people.

Section 12 – Beneficiary's(ies') right to occupy the land

As beneficiaries under a trust of land, both Thomas and Lucy have a right to live in Greenacres.

Section 13 – Two or more beneficiaries entitled to occupy

This section allows trustees to determine which beneficiaries should live in the property and the conditions under which they do so. This means that any dispute over the occupation of Greenacres is unlikely to be resolved under this section as the trustees and the beneficiaries are the same people. Disputes are likely to occur if there is a breakdown in the relationship between Thomas and Lucy. If they can't reach a mutual decision over occupation, an application can be made to the court by either of them under section 14.

Section 14 – Application to the court in the event of dispute

In the event of a dispute, over sale or occupation for example, either Thomas or Lucy can apply to the court. Hitherto it hasn't mattered whether Thomas and Lucy are cohabiting or married. At this point it does. In a divorce situation the courts will be governed by the Matrimonial Causes Act 1973, in which there is greater power to redistribute property according to the parties' circumstances and needs. For cohabiting couples or couples who are not divorcing, though, section 14 of the Trusts of Land and Appointment of Trustees Act 1996 remains the only avenue for dealing with a dispute over Greenacres.

Section 15 – Matters relevant in determining applications under section 14

We are now talking about Thomas and Lucy only if they are cohabiting or not divorcing. The court will take into account reasons why the house was purchased in the first place. This will almost inevitably have been to provide a home for Thomas and Lucy. If there are children, their welfare will be taken into account. The wishes of Thomas and Lucy will also be considered. The court can determine whether Greenacres should be sold or who should live there and under what conditions.

If either Thomas or Lucy was bankrupt, whether they were married or not, the court would look at the factors given in the Insolvency Act 1986. This means that if a year had passed since the bankruptcy happened, the house would be sold to pay off the bankrupt's debts unless there were exceptional circumstances.

The Trusts of Land and Appointment of Trustees Act 1996 applied to implied co-ownership interests

This is the example we will work from to look at the duties of a trustee and the rights of a beneficiary as determined by the Trusts of Land and Appointment of Trustees Act 1996 when an interest has arisen under a constructive or a resulting trust.

> Darren purchased Greenacres last year. He is the sole legal owner. Sally, his partner, contributed to the purchase price.

This is an example of implied co-ownership under a constructive trust. Darren is a trustee holding Greenacres on trust for Sally and himself as beneficiaries. This type of situation was discussed in Chapter 9.

Before 1997 this situation would have given rise to a trust for sale. As the purchase was after 1996, the situation is governed by the Trusts of Land and Appointment of Trustees Act 1996 and a trust of land is created. If the relationship between Darren and Sally had broken down and Sally had consulted you as her solicitor, you would be reaching for the statute book to find out what Sally's rights were. Now you know where to find them.

Section 1 – Definition of a trust of land

This is a trust of land as the trust contains land.

Section 2 – Settlements can no longer be created

This is not relevant. Darren and Sally hold their interests in Greenacres at the same time, concurrently, not successively, so this would never have created a settlement.

Section 3 – The doctrine of conversion no longer operates

Section 4 – There is no longer a duty to sell the land in a trust for sale

Section 5 – A trust for sale implied by statute is now a trust of land

These sections relate to trusts for sale and are not relevant here.

Section 6 – Powers given to trustees

This section gives Darren, as a trustee, the powers of an absolute owner. If Greenacres were sold, Darren would have to sign the conveyance, the deed of sale.

Q: *Wouldn't Darren sell Greenacres anyway if he wanted to, regardless of the Trusts of Land and Appointment of Trustees Act 1996?*

A: Yes, he would. Darren probably isn't even aware that he is a trustee of land for himself and for Sally, because it's not the sort of thing that he knows or thinks about. However, because Darren has the label of trustee, his rights have to be defined. The place for doing this is in the Trusts of Land and Appointment of Trustees Act 1996. If Sally consulted you because she didn't want the house to be sold, you would need to know whether Darren had the power to sell. The Trusts of Land and Appointment of Trustees Act 1996 gives you the answer.

Section 7 – Partition

It is unlikely that Greenacres is a sufficiently large house to divide between the parties, nor would partition appear to be relevant to the circumstances.

Section 8 – The exclusion of powers under sections 6 and 7

This section would be used by a person creating an express trust who wished to restrict the powers of appointed trustees. It is not relevant here.

Section 9 – Delegation of the trustees' functions

In this family situation delegation is not relevant.

Section 10 – Requirements for consent

This section would be used by a person creating an express trust. It is not relevant here.

Section 11 – Consultation with the beneficiaries

Darren has a duty to consult Sally before dealing with Greenacres.

Q: *Wouldn't the two of them take decisions jointly anyway?*

A: When everyone is happily married or happily cohabiting, usually yes. When Darren falls out with Sally though, he may just decide to sell Greenacres without saying anything to her and move to the Bahamas. In that case he's in breach of section 11.

Q: *Can Sally stop him selling Greenacres?*

A: If she hears of the possible sale she can ask for an injunction to stop it because she hasn't been consulted. She can then go to court under section 14, and the court will determine whether Greenacres is sold. If she doesn't hear about the proposed sale, there's not much she can do about it.

Section 12 – Beneficiary's(ies') right to occupy the land

Both Darren and Sally have a right to live in Greenacres.

Section 13 – Two or more beneficiaries entitled to occupy

Darren is a trustee. Under section 13 he is not allowed to exercise his powers to prevent Sally from continuing to live in Greenacres unless she consents or unless the court has given approval. As this section is unlikely to resolve disputes over occupation, either Sally or Darren can apply to the court under section 14 to ask for the sale of Greenacres or to ask the court to determine who should live there.

Section 14 – Application to the court in the event of dispute

Hitherto it hasn't mattered whether Darren and Sally are cohabiting or married. At this point it does. If they divorce, the courts will be governed by the Matrimonial Causes Act 1973 in which there is wider discretion to redistribute property according to the parties' circumstances. The fact that Sally had acquired an interest in Greenacres through her contribution to the purchase price will no longer be the determining factor in the final distribution of the assets unless it has been a very short marriage.

For cohabiting or non-divorcing couples, section 14 of the Trusts of Land and Appointment of Trustees Act 1996 remains the only avenue for dealing with a dispute over Greenacres. If this is the case Sally can apply to the court under this section to have the nature of her interest declared. She can ask the court to declare that she does actually have an interest under a constructive trust. She can also ask for the extent of her interest to be declared, her share in other words, which will be translated into money if Greenacres is sold. The court can then determine the dispute taking into account the factors given in section 15.

Section 15 – Matters relevant in determining applications under section 14

We're talking about Darren and Sally only if they are cohabiting or not divorcing here. The court will take into account reasons why the house was initially purchased, which will almost inevitably have been to provide a home for Darren and Sally. If there are children, their welfare will be taken into account. The wishes of Darren and Sally will also be considered.

If either Darren or Sally was bankrupt, whether they were married or not, the court would look at the factors given in the Insolvency Act 1986. This means that if a year had passed since the bankruptcy happened, the house would be sold to pay off the bankrupt's debts unless there were exceptional circumstances.

Summary of the Trusts of Land and Appointment of Trustees Act 1996

As a summary, consider the way in which a trust has been used to provide a framework when two or more people have an interest in land, whether successively, or concurrently through express or implied co-ownership. Within this framework, the Trusts of Land and Appointment of Trustees Act 1996 lays down the duties of the parties who find the label of trustee attached to them, and the rights of those who find the label of beneficiary attached to them.

The concept of people holding land on trust for themselves is a difficult one to grasp. In the most common situation when a couple buy a house together, it won't occur to them that they have duties as trustees and rights as beneficiaries. If there's a dispute, the man or the woman will go to a solicitor and ask what their position is. The answer is found in the Trusts of Land and Appointment of Trustees Act 1996.

A question on the application of the Trusts of Land and Appointment of Trustees Act 1996 when there are successive interests in land

This example is intended to illustrate how to use the Boxes in this chapter to analyse the legal position. If you are using this method in undergraduate law exam questions, you will need to include statutory and case authority and detailed discussion of the various points of law. This information is found both in the text and from other sources.

> A year ago Den made a will in which he left Greenacres to his trustees, Tick and Tock, on trust for his nephew Samuel and his niece Edwina for their joint lifetimes, and then to Clarissa absolutely. Den has just died. Tick and Tock have decided that it is in the financial interests of the trust to sell Greenacres. Samuel and Clarissa do not wish Greenacres to be sold as they are emotionally attached to it. Samuel, Edwina and Clarissa are all over 18.

> Advise whether Tick and Tock are able to sell the property, whether they can delegate their powers to Samuel and Edwina, and whether Samuel and Clarissa have the right to live there.

The interests of Samuel and Edwina and then Clarissa are held successively, so a trust is imposed. As Greenacres has been left to Samuel and Edwina for their joint lives, Clarissa will own Greenacres absolutely only when both Samuel and Edwina have died. Before 1997, this situation would have created a settlement. These successive interests now exist under a trust of land governed by the Trusts of Land and Appointment of Trustees Act 1996. This Act determines the duties of trustees and the rights of beneficiaries under a trust of land and will enable you to advise the parties.

Section 1 – Definition of trust of land

Successive interests in land now exist under a trust of land.

Section 2 – Settlements can no longer be created

Successive interests in land can no longer create a settlement.

Section 6 – Powers given to trustees

The trustees have been named here as Tick and Tock. Under section 6(1) of the Trusts of Land and Appointment of Trustees Act 1996 they are given the powers of an absolute owner, so they can sell Greenacres if they wish. Tick and Tock do not have to buy land again, although power to do so is given under this section. If they do sell, but do not reinvest the money from the sale in land, they must put it into financial investments. Samuel and Edwina will each receive half the income from any financial investment they make. Should Tick and Tock wish to purchase land again in the future, section 6 gives them the power to do so if the purchase is for investment, occupation by a beneficiary, or for any other reason.

Section 9 – Delegation of the trustees' functions

Tick and Tock can delegate their tasks relating to the land, but only if the beneficiary(ies) is/are of full age and entitled to an interest in possession in the land. As Samuel and Edwina are over 18 and both have an interest in possession, Tick and Tock could delegate their functions as trustees relating to the land to either or both of them. They might wish to do this on the basis that Samuel and Edwina were closely associated with the land. If they did so, Tick and Tock would have to exercise reasonable care and skill when deciding to delegate and to review the situation after they had done so.

Section 11 – Consultation with the beneficiaries

Tick and Tock would have to consult Samuel and Edwina over the proposed sale of the property, as they are both over 18 and they both have an interest in possession in the land. As Clarissa does not have an interest in possession, she does not have to be consulted, and her views and emotional attachment can be safely ignored.

Tick and Tock would have a duty to give effect to Samuel's and Edwina's wishes if they accorded with the general interests of the trust. This appeared to be to sell Greenacres, because you are told it was in the financial interests of the trust to do so. If this were the case, Tick and Tock could ignore Samuel's emotional attachment and any wishes of Edwina. If it were not the case, they risked Samuel, or Edwina, depending on her views, taking any dispute to court under section 14 of the Act.

Section 12 – Beneficiary's(ies') right to occupy the land

Samuel and Edwina can live in Greenacres as they both have an interest in possession in the land. Greenacres must be available and suitable for this purpose. Clarissa does not have an interest in possession and so cannot live there.

Section 13 – Two or more beneficiaries entitled to occupy

The trustees can exclude either Samuel or Edwina, but not both, from occupying Greenacres. If Samuel and Edwina are already living in Greenacres, they cannot be excluded unless they consent or the court gives approval. Reasonable conditions can be imposed on any occupying party, such as the payment of outgoings and/or compensation to the non-occupying party.

Section 14 – Application to the court in the event of dispute

If there is a dispute, any person with an interest in the trust can apply to the court. This includes the trustees, Samuel, Edwina and Clarissa. The dispute here is likely to be over the proposed sale of Greenacres. The court will consider the factors given in section 15.

Section 15 – Matters relevant in determining applications under section 14

In the event of a dispute over sale, the court will take into account factors which include reasons why Greenacres was left on trust. The wishes of Samuel and Edwina will also be taken into account. It is possible that a sale will be ordered, especially as it is in the financial interests of the trust to do so.

Conclusion

Greenacres will be held under a trust of land governed by the Trusts of Land and Appointment of Trustees Act 1996. Tick and Tock, as trustees, have the powers of an absolute owner and so are able to sell Greenacres. Only Samuel and Edwina need to be consulted over this decision but, if it is in the general interest of the trust to sell Greenacres, their wishes may be ignored. Any dispute over sale can be taken to court, where the judge will look at the purposes of the trust and the wishes of Samuel and Edwina. Tick and Tock can delegate to Samuel and Edwina their tasks as trustees in relation to the land. They must exercise reasonable care and review the delegation. Only Samuel and Edwina can occupy Greenacres if the property is available and suitable, not Clarissa. Compensation may be payable to the non-occupying party if only one of them occupies Greenacres.

A question on the application of the Trusts of Land and Appointment of Trustees Act 1996 when there is express co-ownership in land

This example is intended to illustrate how to use the Boxes in this chapter to analyse the legal position. If you are using this method in undergraduate law exam questions, you will need to include statutory and case authority and detailed discussion of the various points of law. This information is found both in the text and from other sources.

A question on express co-ownership was given at the end of Chapter 8 and is repeated below. It has now been extended to include the duties of the trustees and the rights of the beneficiaries under the Trusts of Land and Appointment of Trustees Act 1996.

> Two years ago, four workmates, Donatello, Leonardo, Michelangelo and Raphael, decided to purchase a house called Greenacres. They all contributed equally to the purchase price of the property and intended to live there together.
>
> Things soon started to go wrong when Donatello was killed in a skiing accident. He left nothing in his will for his estranged wife and three children. Then Leonardo, who had fallen out with the others, verbally agreed to sell his interest in the property to Frankie. Leonardo did not tell his fellow co-owners of his intention. Leonardo then changed his mind about the sale, but shortly afterwards served written notice on Michelangelo and Raphael that he was holding his interest in Greenacres as a tenant in common. Finally, Michelangelo and Raphael were involved in a serious road accident.
>
> Michelangelo died immediately, having left his property in his will to his sister, Cassandra. Raphael died several days later in hospital, having left his property in his will to his sister, Eugenie.
>
> Advise on the devolution of the legal and equitable title.

This is the conclusion to the question from Chapter 8, page 168.

When the four workmates purchased Greenacres, there was express beneficial co-ownership and a trust of land was created. The legal title had to be held as a joint tenancy. The four workmates also held the equitable title as a joint tenancy. Severance of the legal title is never possible. The right of survivorship operated on the legal title leaving Leonardo as the sole legal owner. The right of survivorship and severance operated on the equitable title, with the result that Eugenie and Leonardo held equitable interests in Greenacres as tenants in common. If Greenacres were to be sold, Eugenie would receive a 2/3 share of the proceeds and Leonardo a 1/3 share.

Now add on the next part of the question.

> Advise on the duties of the trustees and the rights of the beneficiaries from the time of purchase to the present.

This is a trust of land governed by the Trusts of Land and Appointment of Trustees Act 1996.

Section 1 – Definition of a trust of land

This is a trust of land as the trust contains land.

Section 6 – Powers given to trustees

Trustees have the powers of an absolute owner. If D, L, M and R had wanted to sell, lease or mortgage Greenacres at any time, for example, they could have done so. Leonardo, as the sole remaining trustee, now has the power to do this.

Section 11 – Consultation with the beneficiaries

This would have happened as a matter of course for D, L, M and R as they were all trustees and beneficiaries. However, Leonardo is now the sole surviving tenant on the legal title and he must consult with Eugenie as she has an interest in possession in the land. Her wishes must be taken into account if they accord with the general interest of the trust, as she has the majority share by value. Her wish would probably be for the sale of Greenacres as she only inherited her interest in the property, and this would also appear to be in the general interest of the trust, as the house is no longer required for the four workmates to live in. If this is the case Leonardo must accede to her wishes or risk an application to court by Eugenie under section 14.

Section 12 – Beneficiary's(ies') right to occupy the land

Donatello, L, M and R would all have had a right to live in Greenacres. Both Leonardo and Eugenie now have a right to live there, although it is unlikely that Eugenie would wish to do so as she inherited her interest in the property.

Section 13 – Two or more beneficiaries entitled to occupy

This section allows trustees to determine which beneficiaries should live in the property and the conditions under which they do so. This means that any dispute between D, L, M and R over who lived in Greenacres would probably not have been resolved under this section, as the trustees and the beneficiaries were the same people. If there had been a dispute and D, L, M and R hadn't been able to reach an amicable agreement, an application to court by any party could have been made under section 14.

Eugenie now has an interest in possession in the land, and therefore could live in Greenacres with Leonardo if the accommodation were suitable. This is an unlikely scenario, given that Leonardo and Eugenie probably don't know one another and would have no wish to live together. Unless they can reach an agreement over the occupation of Greenacres and compensation for the non-occupying party, it's likely that Eugenie will have to apply to the court under section 14 to resolve the dispute.

Section 14 – Application to the court in the event of dispute

The original parties, D, L, M and R, could have applied to the court in the event of any dispute. Such disputes could well have arisen over sale, occupation or repair. In the event of a dispute now, either Leonardo or Eugenie can ask the court for directions.

Section 15 – Matters relevant in determining applications under section 14

If any of the original four parties had applied to court in the event of a dispute, the court would have looked at the original purpose of the trust and the wishes of the parties. The original purpose was to provide a home for the four workmates. If this purpose were no longer achievable, the court could have either determined who lived there or ordered sale.

If either Leonardo or Eugenie applied to the court now, the court would examine why the house was initially purchased, whether the situation had changed and what were the wishes of Leonardo and Eugenie. The original purpose of buying Greenacres as a house for D, M, L and R to live in would no longer be applicable. The court could either order sale or require Leonardo to pay compensation in the form of occupation rent to Eugenie if he continued to live there: see *Stack v Dowden*.

Conclusion

As the trust contained land, this would be a trust of land governed by the Trusts of Land and Appointment of Trustees Act 1996. The main rights of D, L, M and R were a right to sell Greenacres, a right of occupation and a right to apply to the court in the event of dispute. Leonardo is the sole surviving owner on the legal title, holding Greenacres on trust for himself and Eugenie. He must consult Eugenie and give effect to her wishes if they accord with the general interests of the trust. Both parties could live in Greenacres, although this is unlikely as Eugenie inherited her interest in the property. If Leonardo and Eugenie can't agree on what is to happen to Greenacres, an application could be made to the court. In view of the circumstances, the court would be likely to order sale or else compensation to the non-occupying party.

A question on the application of the Trusts of Land and Appointment of Trustees Act 1996 when there is implied co-ownership under a constructive or resulting trust

This example is intended to illustrate how to use the Boxes in this chapter to analyse the legal position. If you are using this method in undergraduate law exam questions, you will need to include statutory and case authority and detailed discussion of the various points of law. This information is found both in the text and from other sources.

A question on constructive and resulting trusts was given at the end of Chapter 9 and is repeated below. It has now been extended to include the duties of the trustees and the rights of the beneficiaries under the Trusts of Land and Appointment of Trustees Act 1996.

> Six years ago, John and Claire purchased Greenacres together for £200,000. The legal title to the house was put in John's name. John paid £70,000 of the purchase price in cash and Claire contributed £30,000 in cash. John raised the remainder of the purchase price by means of a mortgage in his name. Claire has contributed to the mortgage repayments. Six months after the couple moved in, John's mother, Lily, who had recently become infirm, came to live with them. She paid for the conversion of two rooms downstairs into rooms specially adapted for her needs at a cost of £10,000. Shortly afterwards John agreed with her that she would always have a 10% share in the house. Since they have been there, Claire has done the accounts of John's business in the evenings without payment and has decorated the house throughout. Both John and Claire suffered pay cuts at work six months ago and Lily has helped out with the household expenses since. The parties have now fallen out, and John has just told both Claire and Lily that they have no interest in the house at all.
>
> Advise Claire and Lily what interest, if any, they have in Greenacres.

This is the conclusion to the question from Chapter 9, page 218.

Claire and Lily are not on the legal title to the house. There is no express declaration of trust in their favour, so they must try to claim an equitable interest in the house under a constructive or resulting trust. This is a domestic situation so a constructive trust will almost certainly be pleaded. Claire has contributed to the purchase price and also to the mortgage repayments. There was no express agreement between her and John so she must claim under an implied agreement constructive trust where her contributions will form the basis of the implied agreement. The court will infer what shares were intended between herself and John by looking at their whole course of conduct. If the shares they intended cannot be inferred, the court will impute an intention to them and the allocation of shares will be decided on the basis of fairness. Lily must rely on the express agreement made to her by John and her contribution to the housekeeping expenses as the basis for an express agreement constructive trust. If her claim were successful, the court would award her the promised 10% share.

This is the next part of the question.

> Advise the parties of their duties and rights.

Assuming that Claire and Lily have interests under a constructive trust, Greenacres is held under a trust of land governed by the Trusts of Land and Appointment of Trustees Act 1996. John is a trustee on the legal title and John, Claire and Lily are beneficiaries on the equitable title.

Section 1 – Definition of a trust of land

This is a trust of land as the trust contains land.

Section 6 – Powers given to trustees

Trustees have the powers of an absolute owner. This section gives John, as the only trustee, the power to sell, lease or mortgage Greenacres, for example. If Greenacres were sold, John would have to sign the conveyance, the deed of sale.

Q: *Wouldn't John sell Greenacres anyway, regardless of the Trusts of Land and Appointment of Trustees Act 1996?*

A: Yes, he would. John probably doesn't even know that he is holding as a trustee for Claire and Lily. It's not the sort of thing that he knows about or something that even crosses his mind. However, because John is a trustee of land his rights and duties have to be defined somewhere, and the place for doing this is in the Trusts of Land and Appointment of Trustees Act 1996.

Section 11 – Consultation with the beneficiaries

John would have a duty to consult Claire and Lily over any proposed sale or over occupation rights, for example.

Q: *Again, wouldn't he do that anyway?*

A: When everyone is happy, then yes. When John falls out with Claire and Lily, he may just decide to sell Greenacres and move to the Bahamas without consulting them.

Q: *Can Claire and Lily stop him?*

A: If they hear of the possible sale they can ask for an injunction stopping the sale on the basis that they haven't been consulted. They can then go to court under section 14 where the judge determines what happens in a dispute.

Section 12 – Beneficiary's(ies') right to occupy the land

John, Claire and Lily have a right to live in Greenacres.

Section 13 – Two or more beneficiaries entitled to occupy

John is a trustee. Under section 13, in his capacity as trustee he is not allowed to prevent Claire or Lily from continuing to live in Greenacres unless they consent or unless the court has given approval. Any disputes over occupation would be unlikely to be resolved under this section, so either John, Claire or Lily could make an application to the court under section 14 to resolve any such arguments.

Section 14 – Application to the court in the event of dispute

Lily could apply to the court under this section to have the nature and extent of her interest in Greenacres, her share in other words, declared which would be translated into money if Greenacres was sold.

As far as Claire is concerned, hitherto it hasn't mattered whether she and John were cohabiting or married. At this point it does. If their relationship broke down and they divorced, the courts would be governed by the Matrimonial Causes Act 1973 in which there is a wide discretion to redistribute property according to the parties' circumstances. The fact that Claire had acquired an interest in Greenacres through her contributions to the property would no longer be the determining factor in the final distribution of the assets once Lily had received her share. For cohabiting or non-divorcing couples though, section 14 of the Trusts of Land and Appointment of Trustees Act 1996 remains the only avenue for dealing with a dispute over Greenacres.

If she were cohabiting with John, Claire could also apply to the court under this section to have the nature and extent of her interest in Greenacres declared. In effect, this would determine her share in Greenacres which would be translated into money if it were sold.

Section 15 – Matters relevant in determining applications under section 14

Again, the previous statements about divorce would apply here, so section 15 would apply to Claire and John only if they were separating but not divorcing or their cohabiting relationship had ceased. Section 15 would apply to Lily. In any application the court would take into account reasons why the house was initially purchased, whether that purpose was still capable of being carried out and what were the wishes of the parties.

Conclusion

A trust of land has been created and will be governed by the Trusts of Land and Appointment of Trustees Act 1996. John has the powers of an absolute owner in his capacity as trustee, and could sell Greenacres. However, he should consult Claire and Lily. An application could be made to the court to determine any disputes.

All the example questions that we have looked at in this chapter are continued in Chapter 11 to show you what happens when property subject to a trust of land is sold.

Further reading

A. Baker, 'The Judicial Approach to "Exceptional Circumstances" in Bankruptcy: The Impact of the Human Rights Act 1998', *Conv and Prop Law* (2010) 352

D. Barnsley, 'Co-owners' Rights to Occupy Trust Land', 57 *CLJ* (1998) 123

M. Dixon, 'Trusts of Land, Bankruptcy and Human Rights', *Conv and Prop Law*, Mar/Apr (2005) 161

N. Hopkins, 'Trusts of Land and Appointment of Trustees Act 1996', *Conv and Prop Law*, Nov/Dec (1996) 411

N. Hopkins and A. Sydenham, 'Trusts of Land and Appointment of Trustees Act 1996', *Conv and Prop Law*, May/Jun (1997) 242

P. Omar, 'Security over Co-owned Property and the Creditor's Paramount Status in Recovery Proceedings', *Conv and Prop Law*, Mar/Apr (2006) 157

S. Pascoe, 'Section 15 of the Trusts of Land and Appointment of Trustees Act 1996 – A Change in the Law?' *Conv and Prop Law*, Jul/Aug (2000) 315

R. Probert, 'Creditors and section 15 of the Trusts of Land and Appointment of Trustees Act 1996: First Among Equals?' *Conv and Prop Law*, Jan/Feb (2002) 61

Chapter 11

Overreaching and the protection of interests under a trust of land

www.palgrave.com/law/Stroud4e

Introduction

You now need to look at what happens when property that is held under a trust of land is sold. This is the last stage of the chart 'The Use of Trusts in Land' in Chapter 6 on page 132. This first part of this chapter looks at the mechanism of overreaching. The second part shows you what happens when overreaching has not taken place. Overreaching is the mechanism which allows a purchaser to buy land free from the rights of any person who is not on the legal title to the land, but who has an equitable interest under a trust of land. Overreaching applies to both unregistered and registered land, and it applies both before and after the Trusts of Land and Appointment of Trustees Act 1996. Throughout this chapter we will be referring to trustees and beneficiaries of a trust of land. Remember that even though Darren, Sally, Bert and Samantha are normal people, when there is a trust of land they will wear the labels of trustee and/or beneficiary and will have to act in these capacities. You now need to look at the chart on page 254.

Interests that can be overreached

Box A
INTERESTS THAT CAN BE OVERREACHED
Successive interests in land
Express co-ownership interests in land
Implied co-ownership interests in land

OVERREACHING AND THE PROTECTION OF INTERESTS UNDER A TRUST OF LAND

Box A

INTERESTS THAT CAN BE OVERREACHED

Successive interests in land

Express co-ownership interests in land

Implied co-ownership interests in land

Box B

ACTION WHICH MUST BE TAKEN IN ORDER TO OVERREACH AN EQUITABLE INTEREST UNDER A TRUST OF LAND

The payment of purchase money or money lent on a post-acquisition mortgage must be paid to two trustees on the legal title of the property and a valid receipt obtained

Box C

THE EFFECT OF NOT OVERREACHING AN EQUITABLE INTEREST UNDER A TRUST OF LAND

Look at either

1. Unregistered land

Or look at

2. Registered land

i) Dealings which must be completed by registration

ii) Interests which override a registered disposition

iii) Interests entered as a notice or protected by a restriction

When land is sold, the legal owner must convey (transfer) the legal title to the land to the purchaser by means of a deed. He will also be required to convey any equitable interest he has in the land. This means that all the legal owner's rights in the land, both legal and equitable, have been conveyed to the purchaser. This conveyance (transfer) must be made by a deed, which must be signed by the legal owner. If there is more than one legal owner, they must all convey their entire legal and equitable interests in the land to the purchaser and they must all sign the deed of conveyance. However, it is possible for other people to hold only an equitable interest in the property under a trust of land, which means they are not on the legal title.

Q: *Who are the people who will hold only an equitable interest in the land?*

A: We are talking about any person who has a successive interest in land. The land is held on trust for them by trustees holding the legal title, and they will have only an equitable interest in the land. We are also talking about a trust in express beneficial co-ownership. In this case, only four people can be on the legal title. Any person not able to be on the legal title will have only an equitable interest in the land. We are also talking about implied co-ownership where an equitable interest in land arises under a constructive or resulting trust. Here, the person not on the legal title acquires an equitable interest only in the land based on financial contribution or informal agreement. These are the situations covered in Chapters 7, 8 and 9. These are people who have only an equitable interest under a trust of land and so do not appear on the legal title. The problem when the land is sold is that they have not transferred their equitable interest under the trust of land to the purchaser. This means that the purchaser may buy the land still subject to their equitable interest and he may be bound by the rights arising from that equitable interest.

Q: *What does this mean in practice?*

A: If you have an equitable interest under a trust of land, you will wear the label of beneficiary. The person who holds the legal title to the land will wear the label of trustee. Your rights as a beneficiary under a trust of land are determined by the Trusts of Land and Appointment of Trustees Act 1996, in particular section 12 of the Act which gives you a right of occupation. This is the right to live in the property. If you haven't transferred your equitable interest to the purchaser, you will continue to hold this equitable interest in the land. If this equitable interest is binding on the purchaser, it gives you the continuing right to live in the property by virtue of section 12. This means you don't have to move out when the purchaser turns up ready to move in.

Look at an example where an equitable interest has arisen under a constructive trust. Let's say that Darren recently purchased Greenacres. Greenacres was conveyed to Darren alone and he is the only person on the legal title. However, Sally contributed 30% of the purchase price of Greenacres and has therefore acquired an equitable interest in Greenacres under a constructive trust. Constructive trusts were discussed in detail in Chapter 9. Darren now wears the label of trustee, and both Darren and Sally have the label of beneficiary, as Darren is now holding Greenacres on trust for himself and Sally.

This is a trust of land governed by the Trusts of Land and Appointment of Trustees Act 1996. Now, imagine that Darren decides to emigrate but has no wish to take Sally with him, or even tell her about his decision to go. In his capacity as trustee on the legal title, Darren has the powers of an absolute owner under section 6 of the Trusts of Land and Appointment of Trustees Act 1996. This means that he has the power to sell Greenacres. He puts the house on the market secretly without telling Sally. Greenacres is sold to Peter and the conveyance (transfer) is by deed. Only Darren, as the legal owner of Greenacres, has to sign the deed in which he must transfer his entire legal and equitable interest in Greenacres to Peter. Peter pays the money for Greenacres to Darren, who promptly uses it to emigrate to Rio and is never seen or heard of again.

Q: *What about Sally's interest though? If she contributed 30% of the purchase price of Greenacres, surely she should receive a 30% share of the proceeds when the house is sold?*

A: She should. But there are difficulties here. The first is that Peter may not even know about Sally, let alone work out how much her proportionate share is under the constructive trust. Even if he did, he cannot be expected to divide the money he's paid for Greenacres into two piles, one of 70% for Darren, and the other of 30% for Sally. The second difficulty is that Sally does not have to be involved in the sale because only Darren, as legal owner, has to sign the paperwork. Sally is not on the legal title and has only an equitable interest in Greenacres. This means she may not even know that Darren has sold Greenacres until Peter turns up on the doorstep. In any event, Sally has probably got no idea that she has an interest under something called a constructive trust anyway. She just thinks that because she and Darren love each other very much, she will get her money back when the house is sold. Whatever the reason though, she has not transferred her equitable interest under the constructive trust in Greenacres to Peter. If Sally's equitable interest is binding on Peter, she will claim her rights as a beneficiary under a trust of land. These rights are found in the Trusts of Land and Appointment of Trustees Act 1996. Section 12 of the Act gives her a right of occupation in Greenacres, which means the right to live there. As she hasn't transferred her equitable interest to Peter, she continues to have the right to live there, which means she doesn't have to move out even though Peter has bought the house. This is completely unacceptable from Peter's point of view.

Q: *How do you protect Peter?*

A: The solution lies in the mechanism of overreaching. Overreaching is a statutory mechanism by which a purchaser can take the land free from the rights of any beneficiary who is not on the legal title to the property, but who has only an equitable interest under a trust of land.

Action which must be taken in order to overreach an equitable interest under a trust of land

> **Box B**
>
> ACTION WHICH MUST BE TAKEN IN ORDER TO OVERREACH AN EQUITABLE INTEREST UNDER A TRUST OF LAND
>
> The payment of purchase money or money lent on a post-acquisition mortgage must be paid to two trustees on the legal title of the property and a valid receipt obtained

Overreaching is governed by sections 2 and 27(2) of the Law of Property Act 1925 as amended by the Trusts of Land and Appointment of Trustees Act 1996. For overreaching to take place, Peter must pay the purchase money for Greenacres to a minimum of two trustees on the legal title of the land he is buying, who must then give him a valid receipt for this money. If he does this, he will overreach any equitable interest under a trust of land from the land into the money from the sale. Instead of the word 'overreach' try the word 'deflect'. It makes more sense than overreach, which is hardly a well-worn word and is also used in the context of horses' hooves. By paying the purchase money for Greenacres to a minimum of two trustees on the legal title and obtaining a receipt, Peter will automatically deflect the equitable interest under a trust of land of any beneficiary who is not on the legal title from the land into the money from the sale.

Q: *What happens if there aren't two trustees on the legal title of Greenacres?*

A: Peter must insist that another person is appointed.

By following this statutory procedure Peter ensures that he takes Greenacres free from the equitable interest. The equitable interest in the land is overreached or deflected from the land into the money from the sale.

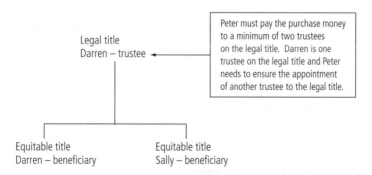

Q: *So Sally's equitable interest is now in the money from the sale of Greenacres and not the land?*

A: Yes. She will now have an equitable interest in the money, which will be held on trust for her instead of the land. As she no longer has an equitable interest in the land, she will no longer have any rights as a beneficiary under the Trusts of Land and Appointment of Trustees Act 1996, so she will no longer have a right of occupation in Greenacres under section 12 and can no longer live there.

Q: *Why must Peter pay to a minimum of two trustees on the legal title?*

A: Section 2(2) of the Law of Property Act 1925 states that there must be two or more. The alternative to paying to a minimum of two trustees is for Peter to pay the money for the purchase to a trust corporation. These are professional organisations that run trusts and, because they are professional, they are expensive. They are also the equivalent to two trustees on the legal title.

Q: *Who would be the second trustee appointed to the legal title in our example?*

A: Darren is one trustee. He wears the label of trustee of the legal title of Greenacres. Peter would have to insist that somebody else be appointed as a second trustee. Darren could choose a solicitor, for example. They are allegedly honest and trustworthy.

Q: *Does that mean that the solicitor would become a co-owner of Greenacres?*

A: Yes, but remember that the solicitor is a trustee of the legal title only to enable overreaching to occur. In his capacity as trustee, the solicitor couldn't take any benefit from Greenacres. When Greenacres is sold, the solicitor becomes a trustee of the money from the sale along with Darren, because Sally's equitable interest in Greenacres has now been deflected to the proceeds of sale through overreaching.

The reason behind appointing a minimum of two trustees is that trustees in the plural are less likely to abscond with the money from the sale of the house. Sally's 30% share should be much safer if Darren and the solicitor can keep an eye on each other. Both Darren and the solicitor in their capacity as trustees should receive the money and give a receipt to Peter. They would have to pay the money from the sale into a separate bank account, which means Darren couldn't pay it into his own bank account and then emigrate with it. They must then ensure that Sally receives her share.

Q: *What would happen if Darren appointed his mate Shady Sid instead of a solicitor?*

A: As far as Peter is concerned, all he has to do is to pay the purchase money to a minimum of two trustees on the legal title of the land he's purchasing to ensure that he meets the statutory requirements of overreaching. As far as Sally is concerned, there's not much you can do here. Sid would have to be formally appointed as a trustee of the legal title of Greenacres by means of a deed. In this case he might decide being appointed as a trustee was too much outside his normal line of work.

Q: *How does Sally obtain her share of the money?*

A: She must contact Darren and the second trustee, the solicitor, as they are holding her share of the money on trust for her. In their capacity as trustees, Darren and the solicitor have a duty to pay Sally her share of the money, and they will be in breach of their trustee position if they don't do so.

Q: *Can Sally find out who has been appointed as the second trustee on the legal title of Greenacres?*

A: As the second appointed trustee will co-own the legal title with Darren, he will have been entered as co-proprietor along with Darren on the Proprietorship Register of Greenacres if Greenacres is registered land. Sally will be able to inspect the Proprietorship Register and find out the name of the second trustee. If Greenacres is unregistered land, there is no way of knowing who was appointed as second trustee, as there is no Register that contains this information. This is a defect of unregistered land which is particularly unhelpful to Sally. Remember, though, that the main objective of overreaching is to ensure that Peter can buy land free from equitable interests under a trust of land, and that this has been achieved.

Q: *What happens if Peter actually knows that Sally has an interest under a constructive trust? Is he still protected if he pays to a minimum of two trustees on the legal title and obtains a receipt?*

A: Yes. The effect of paying to a minimum of two trustees on the legal title is automatically to overreach (deflect) the rights of the beneficiaries into the sale money regardless of what Peter knew, if indeed he knew anything at all.

Q: *What happens if more than one person has only an equitable interest in the land?*

A: Peter is still protected. Paying to a minimum of two trustees on the legal title of the land he is buying means that the interest of any beneficiary under a trust of land who is not on the legal title is overreached (deflected) into the money from sale.

Q: *What happens to Darren's equitable rights in Greenacres though, because although he wears the label of trustee, he is also holding his equitable or beneficial interest on trust for himself?*

A: When Darren sells Greenacres, he has to convey both his legal and equitable interest in the property to Peter. Darren's equitable rights as a beneficiary disappear then. His rights do not need to be overreached (deflected). The only rights that need to be overreached (deflected) are the rights of those beneficiaries who have an equitable interest under a trust of land and who are not on the legal title.

Q: *So, if you're buying a house, should you always ensure that there are a minimum of two trustees on the legal title to whom you must pay the purchase money?*

A: In practice you can protect yourself without having to appoint a second person to the legal title, which is time-consuming and expensive. You or your solicitor must make enquiries to find out whether other people have an interest in the house, and you must also look round the property to see whether there is any evidence of people living there who may have an interest. The seller also has to fill in a Seller's Property Information Form which, if completed inaccurately, can give you an action in misrepresentation against him. If there are other people living in the house, you must ensure that they sign any equitable rights they have over to you at the time of sale. If they refuse to do so, you must then ensure that you overreach their rights. Usually Darren and Sally, or indeed any cohabiting or married couple in a similar situation, have made a joint decision to sell the house. They will both move out and use the money from the sale to go and buy another house and live happily ever after. The problem arises only when Darren sells the house behind Sally's back. If Peter pays the purchase money to only one trustee, Darren, he will not overreach (deflect) Sally's equitable interest from the land into the money from the sale. Sally's equitable interest will remain in the land and, if it is binding on Peter, she will no doubt choose to exercise her right of occupation under the Trusts of Land and Appointment of Trustees Act 1996, given that Darren has long since emigrated, leaving her penniless.

Q: What's the overall effect of overreaching?

A: Peter must pay the purchase money to a minimum of two trustees on the legal title and obtain a receipt. If he does so, he overreaches (deflects) the rights of any person not on the legal title but with an equitable interest under a trust of land, Sally in our example, into the money from the sale. This has two consequences:

▷ Peter is protected, as Sally's equitable interest is no longer in the land. She is no longer a beneficiary under a trust of land. Her rights under the Trusts of Land and Appointment of Trustees Act 1996 cease and she will no longer have the right to live in Greenacres under section 12. This means that Peter can move into an empty house. Sally now has an equitable interest in the money which Peter has paid and which is now held on trust for her by Darren and the solicitor.

▷ As Peter has paid the purchase money to a minimum of two trustees on the legal title, Darren and the solicitor, he has to some extent protected Sally's interest, as fraud is less likely than if he had paid the money for Greenacres to Darren alone.

Q: Can you overreach all types of equitable interests?

A: No. Section 2(3) of the Law of Property Act 1925 states that certain categories of equitable interests cannot be overreached. These are generally equitable commercial interests. For instance, leases are commercial interests so will not be affected by the overreaching mechanism. The overall effect is that you can overreach only these family type equitable interests which arise under a trust of land.

Here's an example of overreaching successive interests in land.

> George has just died. In his will, made four years ago, he left Greenacres to Bert for life then to Claudia absolutely. He has appointed Tick and Tock as his trustees. Both Bert and Claudia are over 18.

The interests of Bert and Claudia are successive as they happen one after the other. This will be a trust of land governed by the Trusts of Land and Appointment of Trustees Act 1996. Trustees of a trust of land have the powers of an absolute owner under section 6 of this Act. This means that Tick and Tock can sell the land if they want to, although they do have a duty to consult Bert under section 11. Bert has a right of occupation under section 12. Tick and Tock decide to sell Greenacres to Peter. Peter must pay the purchase money for Greenacres to a minimum of two trustees on the legal title who must give him a receipt. If he does so, he will overreach (deflect) the equitable interests of any beneficiaries under the trust of land who are not on the legal title from the land into the money from the sale. Bert and Claudia are not on the legal title but they have equitable interests under a trust of land in Greenacres.

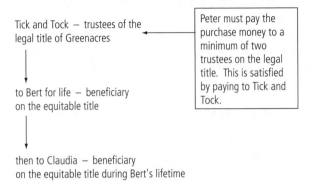

Tick and Tock – trustees of the legal title of Greenacres

to Bert for life – beneficiary on the equitable title

then to Claudia – beneficiary on the equitable title during Bert's lifetime

Peter must pay the purchase money to a minimum of two trustees on the legal title. This is satisfied by paying to Tick and Tock.

Assuming Peter has paid the purchase money to the two trustees on the legal title, Tick and Tock, and has obtained a receipt from them, Bert's and Claudia's equitable interests, and therefore any rights of occupation under the Trusts of Land and Appointment of Trustees Act 1996, cease to be in the land and are of no further concern to him. Bert's and Claudia's equitable interests are now in the money from the sale.

Q: *What do Tick and Tock do with the money from the sale?*

A: Tick and Tock can either use the money from the sale to purchase more land, or they must invest it. If they invest the money, they will pay the income from any investment to Bert for his lifetime as Bert has a life interest. When Bert dies, Claudia will receive the land, if that is what the money has been invested in, or the lump sum that has been invested, or a combination of both.

The following is an example of overreaching equitable interests arising under express beneficial co-ownership.

Last month Adrian (A), Bob (B), Clare (C), David (D) and Emilio (E) bought Greenacres together.

This is an example of express beneficial co-ownership. As you can have only four people on the legal title, A, B, C and D will hold the legal title as joint tenants. They will hold for themselves and Emilio in equity, either as joint tenants or as tenants in common.

Legal title	Equitable title
(A B C D) Joint tenants	(A B C D E) Joint tenants or A B C D E Tenants in common

If Greenacres is then sold to Peter, A, B, C and D must all sign the conveyance transferring Greenacres, and they must convey their entire legal and equitable interests to him. As Peter has paid the money for Greenacres to a minimum of two trustees on the legal title, A, B, C and D therefore making four trustees, he will have overreached (deflected) the equitable interest of any beneficiary who is not on the legal title from the land into the money from the sale. This is Emilio here who was unable to be on the legal title because the maximum number allowed was four. The money from the sale of Greenacres will then be held by A, B, C and D on trust for themselves and Emilio until they decide what to do with it. They could either buy more property or simply share out the proceeds. Whatever happens, Peter will be able to move into an empty house because he has overreached (deflected) Emilio's equitable interest under the trust of land, together with any right of occupation, from Greenacres into the money from the sale.

The situations in which overreaching applies

Q: *Where does overreaching apply?*

A: Section 2 of the Law of Property Act 1925 talks about overreaching applying when capital money is paid. Capital money is the money paid to the vendor when a house is sold. Capital money is also paid when money is paid out in the form of a mortgage, for example from a bank or building society.

The previous part of this chapter looked at overreaching in the context of sale. The next part looks at overreaching in the context of a mortgage when capital money is paid out on a mortgage. The problems usually arise here in the context of constructive and resulting trusts, so we'll look at an example where a constructive trust has arisen to illustrate overreaching in this type of situation. Let's say that Darren recently purchased Greenacres. He is the only person on the legal title. However, Sally contributed 30% of the purchase price of Greenacres and therefore has acquired an equitable interest in it under a constructive trust. Constructive trusts were discussed in detail in Chapter 9. Darren now wears the label of trustee and both Darren and Sally have the label of beneficiary, as Darren is now holding Greenacres on trust for himself and Sally.

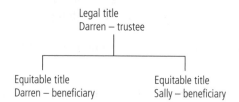

Normally you organise a mortgage in order to be able to buy a house. In the example that follows, Darren has created a mortgage over Greenacres with Bundy's Bank after Greenacres has been purchased. This is known as a post-acquisition mortgage. Darren may have decided that he wanted some money to build an extension to Greenacres, or to buy an expensive car, or to go to Rio without Sally. Bundy's Bank will have lent him this money on a mortgage using Greenacres as security for its loan. As Darren is the only person on the legal title, his signature alone would be required for the mortgage transaction. If Darren stopped paying the mortgage repayments, Bundy's Bank would want to realise its security. It can do this by taking possession of Greenacres and selling the property to recoup the outstanding money it lent to Darren. The problem here is Sally, as she played no part in the mortgage transaction. This means that she has an equitable interest under a trust of land which she has not mortgaged to the Bank as security for the loan. As a beneficiary under a trust of land she has rights under the Trusts of Land and Appointment of Trustees Act 1996, including the right to live in Greenacres under section 12. The result is that even though Bundy's Bank has the right to obtain possession of the land, it may be bound by Sally's right to live there. If this is the case, Bundy's Bank will be unable to sell Greenacres because Sally will still be living in the property. However, as in sale, Bundy's Bank can overreach her equitable interest in Greenacres by paying the money lent on the mortgage to a minimum of two trustees on the legal title, not just Darren.

Q: *So you're saying that when Bundy's Bank, or any other lender, lends money to Darren on a post-acquisition mortgage, the Bank must pay the mortgage money to Darren and a second person who is appointed as a trustee on the legal title?*

A: Yes. If Bundy's Bank does this, the rights of any beneficiary who has only an equitable interest under a trust of land, and so who is not on the legal title, will be overreached (deflected) from the land into the value of the house when it has to be sold by Bundy's Bank because Darren has stopped paying the mortgage repayments. Bundy's Bank must do the same if a house is remortgaged. Remortgaging means that there is already a mortgage and a further loan is agreed later using the same property as security.

The situation representing a post-acquisition mortgage is shown below.

Darren buys Greenacres. His name alone is on the legal title. Sally contributed 30% to the initial purchase price of the house and so has an interest under a constructive trust.	Darren creates a post-acquisition mortgage over Greenacres with Bundy's Bank. *A second trustee is appointed to the legal title of Greenacres to receive the mortgage money.*	Darren stops paying the mortgage repayments. Bundy's Bank wishes to possess Greenacres and sell the property to recoup the amount still payable on the mortgage loan.

Bundy's Bank has paid the mortgage money to a minimum of two trustees on the legal title of Greenacres and has therefore overreached (deflected) Sally's equitable interest from the land into the monetary value of the house. She no longer has a right of occupation in Greenacres under section 12 of the Trusts of Land and Appointment of Trustees Act 1996. By complying with the statutory provisions for overreaching, Bundy's Bank is able to take possession of the land free from any person with an equitable interest under a trust of land and so can sell an empty house.

Q: *How does paying the mortgage money to a minimum of two trustees help Sally?*

A: It may safeguard her interest a little, although not as much as when the house is sold. If Bundy's Bank pays the money lent on the mortgage to a minimum of two trustees on the legal title, there is less chance of Darren going straight off to Rio with the money. On the other hand, Darren and the second trustee simply have to give Bundy's Bank a receipt for the money. The second trustee can then discharge himself as trustee, still leaving Darren to go to Rio because his only function as second trustee was to allow overreaching to occur. The real aim of overreaching here is to protect Bundy's Bank if Darren stops paying the mortgage repayments. The bank will have overreached (deflected) Sally's equitable interest from the land, including her right of occupation, into the monetary value of the house and will be able to obtain vacant possession which it needs to sell the house. Sally will be entitled to her share of the money in the house once the outstanding mortgage money has been repaid.

Q: *In a post-acquisition mortgage, isn't it inconvenient for the Bank to ensure that there are two trustees on the legal title, and to have to appoint another if there's only one?*

A: Yes, especially as in normal circumstances lending money on a post-acquisition mortgage wouldn't be a problem. Darren and Sally would build their extension or buy the expensive car, the mortgage repayments would be met and that would be that. It's not in every situation that Darren is going to run off with the money and default on the mortgage repayments. However, banks and other lenders have been caught out by not complying with the provisions of overreaching and so, to avoid the expense and time of appointing two trustees to the legal title, they have come up with alternative solutions. These include:

- ensuring that all those living in the property have signed to say that their rights in the house are subservient to those of the Bank or other lender before the mortgage is created. (If the family home has been remortgaged and you are an occupier aged 17 or over, you should have been asked to sign over your rights in the property to the lender. This is why.)
- taking out insurance in case someone with an equitable interest under a trust of land in the property appears out of the blue;
- ensuring that people not on the legal title prove that they have an interest under a trust. After all, contributions years ago to the purchase price of the house can be imagined if necessary!

Q: *What should Peter and Bundy's Bank do if a request for the appointment of a second trustee is refused when Greenacres is sold, or when a post-acquisition mortgage is created using the property as security for the loan?*

A: Peter should not buy Greenacres and Bundy's Bank should not lend the money unless they have protected themselves in some other way.

Q: *Why?*

A: Because if Peter or Bundy's Bank pays to only one trustee, they will not have overreached the interest, and therefore the rights, of anyone with only an equitable interest under a trust of land.

Q: *Do you need overreaching when a mortgage is taken out by Darren when he first buys Greenacres?*

A: The situation here would look like this:

Darren buys Greenacres with the aid of a mortgage from Bundy's Bank amounting to 70% of the purchase price. Sally contributed 30% of the purchase price and so has an interest under a constructive trust. She was not a party to the mortgage transaction.	Darren stops paying the mortgage repayments and Bundy's Bank wishes to take possession of and sell Greenacres.

In this case, Sally does not have an equitable interest in Greenacres when Bundy's Bank pays the mortgage loan to Darren. This is because the purchase of Greenacres and the payment of the mortgage money are seen as simultaneous. It is deemed that there is no gap in time ('scintilla temporis' in Latin) between the conveyance of the property and the grant of the mortgage. When the mortgage money is paid by Bundy's Bank to Darren, Sally does not have an equitable interest in Greenacres that can be overreached: see *Abbey National Building Society v Cann* (1991) and *Cook v The Mortgage Business plc* (2012).

Furthermore, it's almost certain that Sally knows about the mortgage. In this case, she can't argue that her rights take precedence over those of Bundy's Bank when she knows that the only way she and Darren can afford to buy Greenacres is by means of a mortgage. Sally is estopped (prevented) from claiming that her equitable interest has priority. The authorities to support estoppel in this situation are *Bristol and West Building Society v Henning* (1985) in unregistered land and *Paddington Building Society v Mendelsohn* (1985) and *Bank of Scotland v Hussain* (2010) in registered land. In the latter case the defendant was aware that there was going to be a mortgage. She had also told the solicitors of the Bank of Scotland and others that the house would be sold with vacant possession and that she would not retain any rights in it. The Bank had created the mortgage based on this understanding. As the defendant had ratified the mortgage, she was estopped from claiming that her rights took precedence over those of the Bank.

A person will also be estopped from claiming that his interest has priority when he knows that a post-acquisition mortgage is to be created.

We have looked at overreaching and the need to ensure that there is a minimum of two trustees on the legal title when a post-acquisition mortgage is created in the context of a constructive trust. The same principles would apply if there were a post-acquisition mortgage created where there was beneficial co-ownership in land or where there were successive interests in land. Bundy's Bank must pay the mortgage money in a post-acquisition mortgage to two trustees on the legal title, even if it means appointing a second one. If it doesn't do so, it must protect itself by some other means.

State Bank of India v Sood (1997) is an unusual case. The property had been mortgaged to the Bank by two registered proprietors who were holding it on trust for five other members of the family who each had just an equitable interest under a trust of land. However, no actual money had been paid to the two registered proprietors. It was held that the equitable interests of the five other members of the family had been overreached even though there was no money into which to deflect their interests. Lord Justice Gibson said that section 2(1) did not require capital money to be paid, but, if it was, it had to be paid to two trustees.

Q: *Why had no money been paid to the two registered proprietors by the Bank?*

A: Because the mortgage was created to discharge existing debts and to cover future debts. This is like you having a £50 overdraft at the Bank. The Bank is concerned that you may not pay it back. You create a mortgage over your house for £100 with the Bank. This mortgage is the Bank's security for the overdraft of £50 should you not pay it off and it is also security if you wish to draw on your overdraft for a further £50. In these circumstances there is no actual transfer of money.

Summary of overreaching

Overreaching is the statutory mechanism by which a purchaser of land, or a lender on a post-acquisition mortgage, can take free from the rights of any person who is not on the legal title but who has only an equitable interest under a trust of land.

Q: *Can it be really disastrous if overreaching doesn't happen?*

A: Yes. This is the next subject for discussion.

The effect of not overreaching an equitable interest under a trust of land

> **Box C**
>
> THE EFFECT OF NOT OVERREACHING AN EQUITABLE INTEREST UNDER A TRUST OF LAND
>
> Look at either
>
> **1.** Unregistered land
>
> Or look at
>
> **2.** Registered land
>
> i) Dealings which must be completed by registration
>
> ii) Interests which override a registered disposition
>
> iii) Interests entered as a notice or protected by a restriction

This part of the chapter looks at what happens when land is sold, or when a post-acquisition mortgage is created, and the purchase money or the mortgage money is paid to only one trustee on the legal title of the land when there are beneficiaries who have only an equitable interest in the land. The purchaser or lender has also not protected himself in any other way. An example is when Peter has purchased land, let's say Greenacres, but has paid the purchase money to only one person on the legal title.

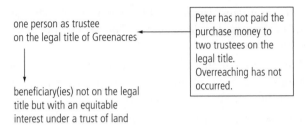

If this happens, the equitable interest in the land of any beneficiary not on the legal title will not have been overreached from the land into the money. This means that his equitable interest must still be in the land. One of the rights of a beneficiary under a trust of land is the right of occupation under section 12 of the Trusts of Land and Appointment of Trustees Act 1996. If the purchaser, Peter, is bound by this equitable interest, it will be a real problem because he will not be able to move into an empty house.

Another example is when Bundy's Bank has lent money on a post-acquisition mortgage but has paid the mortgage money to only one person on the legal title.

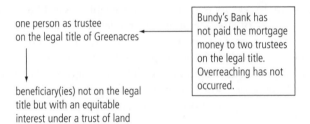

Again, the problem will be the same. Bundy's Bank may not be able to take vacant possession as a prelude to sale because of the continuing right of occupation by the beneficiary.

The conflict in both these cases is between the person with the continuing right of occupation in the land and the purchaser or lender who wants an empty property. You need to establish who has priority. This first depends on whether the land is unregistered or registered land.

Box C1   Unregistered land

Use the procedure given in Chapter 3 on page 44 to determine how interests are protected in unregistered land. This procedure is repeated below for your convenience.

Step 1. Establish whether it is a legal or equitable interest that is being claimed. If it is a legal interest, legal rights bind the world both before 1926, and, excluding a puisne mortgage, after then as well. If it is an equitable interest, you must see whether the equitable interest is capable of entry as a land charge under the Land Charges Act 1972.

Step 2. If the equitable interest is not capable of entry as a land charge, use the rule that governed equitable interests before 1926, known as the doctrine of notice.

If the equitable interest is capable of entry as a land charge, work out in whose interest it is to enter it as a land charge. This will be the person who benefits from the equitable interest.

Step 3. Check to see whether that person has entered his or her equitable interest as a land charge in the correct class on the Land Charges Register against the name of the owner of the land that the right is over.

▶ An equitable interest that has been entered as a land charge binds everyone who takes the land under section 198 of the Law of Property Act 1925.

▶ If the equitable interest has not been entered as a land charge, it will not be binding on some classes of purchaser.

You can apply the procedure above to Peter and Bundy's Bank.

Step 1. You are looking at an equitable interest under a trust of land. An equitable interest under a trust of land is not capable of being entered as a land charge under the Land Charges Act 1972.

Q: *Why isn't there a class of land charge dedicated to equitable interests under a trust of land?*

A: Because there was overreaching. Overreaching would automatically deflect the equitable interest of any person not on the legal title from the land into the money from the sale, so protection of the interest wasn't a worry. Whether you have £10,000 in land or £10,000 in your pocket doesn't matter. The value of the £10,000 is the same. Also, equitable interests under a trust of land can arise informally, and most people wouldn't know they had an equitable interest even if you did give them the opportunity of entering it as a land charge.

Step 2. An interest that cannot be entered as a land charge under the Land Charges Act of 1972 must be governed by the rule relating to equitable interests before 1926, which was the doctrine of notice. The doctrine of notice is as follows.

Equitable rights bind everyone except a *bona fide* purchaser of a legal estate for value without notice of the equitable interest.

The equitable interest here is the equitable interest under a trust of land. Notice, which means knowledge here, includes actual, constructive and imputed notice. Actual notice is what you actually know. Constructive notice is what you should know from an inspection of the documents relating to the property and by looking round the property. Imputed notice is knowledge that your solicitor has and should have passed on to you.

You can now apply this rule to the situation where Greenacres has been purchased by Peter, for example, but overreaching has not occurred.

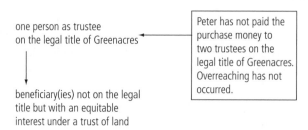

one person as trustee on the legal title of Greenacres

beneficiary(ies) not on the legal title but with an equitable interest under a trust of land

Peter has not paid the purchase money to two trustees on the legal title of Greenacres. Overreaching has not occurred.

Peter will be bound by the equitable interest of any beneficiary under a trust of land who is not on the legal title unless he is a *bona fide* purchaser of a legal estate for value without notice of the equitable interest.

You can assume Peter is *bona fide*. You know he has purchased the legal estate of Greenacres and has paid money for it. The answer then depends on whether he has actual, constructive or imputed notice of the equitable interest.

Q: *If he does have notice, will he be bound by the equitable interest and therefore by the beneficiary's right to live there?*

A: Yes. A beneficiary with an equitable interest under a trust of land will have a right of occupation under the Trusts of Land and Appointment of Trustees Act 1996. This means that Peter will be unable to move into an empty property.

The same principles apply to a post-acquisition mortgage:

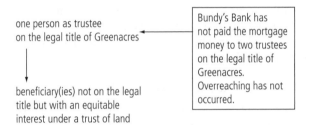

one person as trustee on the legal title of Greenacres

beneficiary(ies) not on the legal title but with an equitable interest under a trust of land

Bundy's Bank has not paid the mortgage money to two trustees on the legal title of Greenacres. Overreaching has not occurred.

If the mortgage repayments are not being met, Bundy's Bank will want to take possession of Greenacres and then sell to recoup its outstanding loan money. The question now is whether Bundy's Bank is bound by the equitable interest of any beneficiary under a trust of land, and therefore will not be able to obtain vacant possession of the property. Trying to sell a house with someone who already has a right to continue to live there is not exactly a good idea.

Q: *And the answer is that Bundy's Bank will be bound by the equitable interest under a trust of land of any beneficiary who is not on the legal title, including his right of occupation, unless Bundy's Bank is a bona fide purchaser of a legal estate for value without notice of the equitable interest when the mortgage was created?*

A: Correct.

Q: *How can Bundy's Bank be a purchaser for value of a legal estate?*

A: It is a purchaser of a legal estate because, when a mortgage is created, either the borrower grants a 3,000 year legal lease in the land to the lender or a charge is created over the land, which has the same effect. In this way, Bundy's Bank purchases a legal leasehold estate which is a legal estate and it gives value in the form of the loan money. This may not make much sense. There are some things in life that you just have to accept. This is one of them. Mortgages are discussed in full in Chapter 18, but all you need to know now is that a lender of money on a mortgage is a purchaser of a legal estate for value.

Q: *So if Bundy's Bank is deemed to have actual, constructive or imputed notice of the equitable interest, it will not be able to obtain an empty property when it tries to take possession?*

A: That's right. And of course, if it can't obtain an empty property it won't be able to sell it and so recoup the outstanding money lent on the mortgage.

Q: *How exactly do you obtain notice of a person's equitable interest in the property?*

A: If a person is in occupation of the land, a purchaser should ask what interests he or she has in the land. He will then have actual knowledge of these interests. A purchaser is also deemed to have constructive notice of the interests of a person who is in occupation. This means that even if the purchaser hasn't actually asked the person in occupation about his or her interests, the courts will take the view that he should have done so, and he will therefore be bound by them. After all, both Peter and Bundy's Bank, as purchasers, had the opportunity to overreach these equitable interests in the land by paying to at least two trustees on the legal title, but chose not to do so and chose not to protect themselves in any other way. Agents such as solicitors should also make inquiries and inform their clients. This is known as imputed notice.

Q: *How do you know whether someone is in occupation?*

A: Really just by inspection and inquiries. If there are children, there is likely to be a mother around who should be asked whether she has an interest in the house. Having said that, in *Caunce v Caunce* (1969), which wasn't so long ago, Mr Justice Stamp said that the woman was not in apparent occupation because 'ostensibly she was the husband's wife'. She was there as an adjunct to her husband, not as a human being in her own right. This decision was not effectively overruled until 1981 in *Williams & Glyn's Bank Ltd v Boland* (1981).

Kingsnorth Finance Co Ltd v Tizard (1986) is an illustration of constructive notice and occupation in unregistered land. Mrs Tizard was not on the legal title to the house but had acquired an equitable interest under a resulting trust. She didn't live in the house permanently because the marriage had broken down, but she returned there every day to look after the children. She also slept there when Mr Tizard was away. Mr Tizard wanted to create a post-acquisition mortgage over the house with Kingsnorth Finance Company, which arranged for a surveyor to go and look round the house on a Sunday afternoon. This should have been a productive move as Mr Tizard had actually lied to the Finance Company about his marital status and had told them he was single. Although Mrs Tizard wasn't living there permanently, her clothes were still there. There was also evidence of the children, probably on account of the state of the bedrooms. Mr Tizard also told the surveyor that he was married but separated from his wife. The court held that these were factors which should have put the surveyor on enquiry to find out more. As such, the surveyor was deemed to have constructive notice of Mrs Tizard's interest in the house. As the surveyor was the agent of Kingsnorth Finance, his knowledge was imputed to it, and so it was bound by her interest.

Q: *So that means that if either Peter or Bundy's Bank is deemed to know about a person's equitable interest under the trust of land, they can't obtain an empty* *property because they are bound by that person's interest and right of occupation. Is there anything they can do?*

A: Not a lot. You should comply with the provisions for overreaching. If you don't overreach, you won't be able to move into an empty house if you are deemed to know about the equitable interest.

The only possible hope for Peter is to argue the following. Look at the situation when Peter buys Greenacres and pays the purchase money to only one trustee when there is a beneficiary with just an equitable interest under a trust of land and Peter is deemed to know about his or her interest. Peter will acquire the legal and equitable title of the vendor of Greenacres and will now be a trustee holding the property on trust for himself and any beneficiary with an interest under a trust of land. Although he has the right as a beneficiary himself to live in the property, he'd have to share it with a total stranger. He could try applying to the court under section 14 of the Trusts of Land and Appointment of Trustees Act 1996 and ask for the property to be sold. Under section 15, he would have to argue that the original purpose of the trust was no longer achievable, not least because two total strangers would now have to share the house! This probably won't elicit a lot of sympathy from the court as it was entirely Peter's fault that he paid to only one trustee. Even if the court did order sale, any beneficiary with only an equitable interest under a trust of land would receive his monetary share of the proceeds from this sale before Peter. This is because his equitable interest was not overreached and remained in the land. As Peter was deemed to have notice of the equitable interest, it was binding on him and will still be binding on him if the court orders sale and the land is turned into money. He must therefore pay any beneficiary with an equitable interest in the land their share of the proceeds first.

Q: *Is there anything Bundy's Bank can do if it is deemed to have notice of the equitable interest and therefore can't obtain vacant possession?*

A: The answer for the Bank is to sue the person to whom it originally gave the mortgage loan for not paying the mortgage repayments, and force him into bankruptcy. A trustee in bankruptcy will be appointed to manage the affairs of the bankrupt. The trustee in bankruptcy can then apply under section 14 of the Trusts of Land and Appointment of Trustees Act 1996 for a sale of the property. Usually the factors in section 15 will be taken into account here. However, when there is a bankruptcy of a beneficiary under a trust of land, the Insolvency Act 1986 will be relevant and the courts will order sale after a year unless there are exceptional circumstances. When sale is ordered, any person with only an equitable interest under a trust of land will receive his or her share of the money from the sale before Bundy's Bank can claim any of its loan money back. As Bundy's Bank was deemed to have notice of the equitable interest, it was binding on it and will still be binding on it when the court orders sale and the land is turned into money. It must therefore pay any beneficiary with an equitable interest under a trust of land his or her share of the proceeds first.

Q: *And if either Peter or Bundy's Bank is deemed not to have notice of the equitable interest, he or it will not be bound by it?*

A: Correct. They can take possession of an empty property.

There is one exception to the usual rule that an equitable interest in the land will bind a purchaser with notice unless overreaching has taken place. It applies to unregistered land only. This is where the trustees and the beneficiaries are the same people, holding as joint tenants at law and as joint tenants in equity. This is where Greenacres is conveyed to Thomas and Lucy and they hold both the legal and the equitable title as joint tenants. Thomas and Lucy wear the labels of trustees and beneficiaries. If Lucy dies, the legal title simply vests in Thomas under the right of survivorship. On her death, the equitable title also vests in Thomas under the right of survivorship and so he owns Greenacres absolutely. A purchaser of Greenacres will know from the documentation to the land that there had been a trust. You could then argue that a purchaser should be able to buy Greenacres without having to appoint another trustee alongside Thomas because he owns the property outright. But, what would happen if Lucy had severed her interest and left it in her will to her sister, Fiona? If a purchaser did pay the purchase price to Thomas alone, he would not have overreached Fiona's inherited interest, and may be bound by Fiona's rights. To save a purchaser having to worry about whether there has been any severance, the Law of Property (Joint Tenants) Act 1964 allows a purchaser to buy Greenacres free of any undisclosed severed interests even if he pays to only one trustee on the legal title. The purchaser will be bound only if there is notice of severance attached to the conveyance (the document of sale) that transferred Greenacres to Thomas and Lucy. Also, there must be nothing on the Land Charges Register to indicate a bankruptcy, which would have automatically caused severance. This exception allows a purchaser to take free only from any undisclosed severed interests, not from any other equitable interests in the land arising under a constructive or resulting trust, for example. So you still can't afford not to overreach here.

A summary of the effect of not overreaching in unregistered land

An equitable interest arising under a trust of land cannot be entered on the Land Charges Register. The pre-1926 rule relating to equitable interests, known as the doctrine of notice, will determine whether the equitable interest binds a purchaser when the land is sold.

Box C2 ### Registered land

Q: *Has the idea of asking people whether they have an interest in the land disappeared in registered land as there's a register where people can put notification of their interests?*

A: Not really. The trouble is that interests under a trust of land can arise informally and people may not even know they have one, let alone that they should protect it even if you gave them the opportunity to do so. The Land Registration Act 2002 actually goes as far as preventing people from putting these types of interests on the Charges Register. Instead, people who can claim an interest under a trust of land are protected by actually being in occupation of the land. However, let's start at the beginning.

Registered land is governed by the Land Registration Act 2002. There are three categories which determine how interests in registered land are protected. They are:

- Dealings which must be completed by registration under section 27 of the Land Registration Act 2002 (Box C, point 2(i)).
- Interests in Schedule 3 to the Land Registration Act 2002 which override a registered disposition (Box C, point 2(ii)).
- Interests entered as a notice under section 34 of the Land Registration Act 2002 and interests protected by a restriction under section 43 of the Land Registration Act 2002 (Box C, point 2(iii)).

A purchaser for valuable consideration will take the land subject to the interests in these three categories. You must establish into which category equitable interests under a trust of land fall.

Box C2i   Dealings which must be completed by registration

Acquiring an equitable interest under a trust of land is not a dealing under section 27 of the Land Registration Act 2002 which must be completed by registration, so you must look at the other two categories.

Box C2ii   Interests which override a registered disposition

Box C2iii   Interest entered as a notice or protected by a restriction

There is a formal way of protecting an equitable interest under a trust of land in Box C point 2iii, and this method is discussed first. Most of the case law in this area has arisen because people have not protected their interests by this formal means and so rely on the category of interests that override a registered disposition (Box C, point 2ii) to safeguard their equitable interest.

Interests that are entered as a notice on the Charges Register of the land that the right is over under section 34 of the Land Registration Act 2002 are binding on a purchaser. However, section 33 of the Act expressly forbids the protection of equitable interests under a trust of land by means of a notice. The only way is to enter a restriction. If a person knows he has an interest under a trust of land, he can place a restriction on the Proprietorship Register of the land that is affected. A restriction gives the conditions under which any dealing with the land should take place. The restriction specified here would be that a second trustee is appointed to receive the money if the house is sold or to receive money lent on a post-acquisition mortgage. Such a restriction ensures that any equitable interest under a trust of land is thereby overreached.

Q: *As you say, though, would a person always know that he had an interest under a trust of land, let alone that he had to enter a restriction on the Proprietorship Register?*

A: If the interest has arisen through a constructive or resulting trust, it's highly unlikely. If there is express co-ownership, the Land Registrar is under a duty to place a restriction on the Proprietorship Register when ownership of the land is registered. This means that if the right of survivorship operates and there is only one trustee left on the legal title, a purchaser will know that a second trustee should be appointed to overreach the rights of any remaining beneficiary with just an equitable interest under a trust of land. If successive interests in land have been created, trustees will be appointed to the legal title. When their names are entered on the Proprietorship Register of the land, the Registrar will again enter a restriction to the same effect.

Assuming that an equitable interest under a trust of land has not been overreached, under paragraph 2 of Schedule 3 to the Land Registration Act 2002 the interests of a person in actual occupation are interests that override (take priority over) a registered disposition (sale or post-acquisition mortgage) if the following conditions are met:

1. The person claiming the right has a proprietary interest in the land

and

2. That person is in actual occupation at the time of the disposition.

However, the interest will not be an overriding interest if:

1. At the time the land was purchased, the fact that the person was in actual occupation was not obvious on a reasonably careful inspection of the land and the purchaser didn't know about the interest

or

2. The person in actual occupation claiming the interest did not tell the purchaser about his interest in the land if asked, and it would have been reasonable for him to have done so.

Paragraph 2 of Schedule 3 is essentially saying that a person who is relying on the fact that he is living in the property to claim priority over a purchaser must make it obvious that he lives in the property. If asked, he should tell any purchaser about his interest if it would be reasonable to do so. If the purchaser still chooses to buy the property, he deserves to be bound by the rights of anybody who lives there.

Apply this to the examples of Peter when he purchases Greenacres, or Bundy's Bank when it lends money on a post-acquisition mortgage:

1. An equitable interest under a trust of land is a proprietary interest in land.
2. If the person claiming this equitable interest is in actual occupation of the land at the time of the sale to Peter or when the post-acquisition mortgage is created, his equitable interest will bind Peter or Bundy's Bank.

However, his equitable interest under the trust of land will not bind Peter or Bundy's Bank if:

1. The fact that he was in actual occupation wasn't obvious if Peter or Bundy's Bank made a reasonably careful inspection of the land, and Peter or Bundy's Bank didn't know about his interest,

or

2. The person claiming the equitable interest under a trust of land didn't disclose his interest to Peter or Bundy's Bank if asked when it would have been reasonable for him to have done so.

You must note that it is the equitable interest under the trust of land that will bind either Peter or Bundy's Bank, not the fact that someone is occupying the property.

The rights of people who have an interest under a trust of land are found in the Trusts of Land and Appointment of Trustees Act 1996. One of these rights is a right of occupation under section 12. It is this right of occupation which prevents Peter or Bundy's Bank from obtaining vacant possession. If the conditions under paragraph 2 of Schedule 3 are not met, the equitable interest under the trust of land will not be one that overrides the sale or the post-acquisition mortgage, and so the right of occupation arising from the interest will not bind Peter or Bundy's Bank.

The most well-known case that illustrates a failure to overreach in registered land is *Williams & Glyn's Bank Ltd v Boland*. Although this case occurred under the Land Registration Act 1925, and not the Land Registration Act 2002, the principles are the same. The reference in the case to rights acquired under section 70(1)(g) of the Land Registration Act 1925 means the same as interests that override under the Land Registration Act 2002. In the 1925 Act this category of overriding rights was given a section, a number and a letter. As the Land Registration Act 1925 has now been repealed by the Land Registration Act 2002, this is not a section, number and letter you should cite without very careful thought about why you are doing so.

Mr and Mrs Boland had bought a house together, the title of which was conveyed (transferred) to Mr Boland alone. Mrs Boland had contributed to the purchase price, and so had an interest under a resulting trust. Mr Boland then arranged a post-acquisition mortgage with Williams and Glyn's Bank which paid the mortgage money to Mr Boland alone. Mr Boland defaulted on the mortgage repayments. As the Bank had paid to only one trustee on the legal title, Mr Boland, it had not overreached the equitable interest of Mrs Boland arising under the resulting trust from the land into the monetary value of the house. Her interest in the house was an equitable interest in the land under a trust. This is a proprietary right in land. She was in actual occupation. Her interest, and her right to live there which arose from it, therefore bound Williams & Glyn's Bank as an overriding interest. It was unable to obtain vacant possession of the house in order to sell it to recoup its mortgage loan.

Q: *What would have happened if Williams & Glyn's Bank had overreached Mrs Boland's equitable interest?*

A: If the mortgage money had been paid to Mr Boland and another person appointed to the legal title, the Bank would have been fully protected. It would have overreached the equitable interest of Mrs Boland and would have obtained vacant possession of the house, and so could have sold it. Mrs Boland would not have fared so well. The mortgage money would have been paid to Mr Boland and a second trustee, and they would have given a receipt to the Bank. Mrs Boland's interest would then have been in the value of the house. If the Bank had possessed the house and sold it, it would have taken what was owed to it on the mortgage loan. Mr Boland would have been entitled to anything that was left over, and Mrs Boland would have been entitled to a share proportionate to her contribution to that remaining money, if any.

HSBC Bank Plc v Dyche (2009) is a recent case here showing that banks still have lessons to learn. The defendant, Mr Collelldevall, had an equitable interest only under a trust of land by means of a constructive trust. HSBC had paid mortgage monies to one trustee only on the legal title and so had not overreached his equitable interest. Mr Collelldevall had a proprietary right in the land (his equitable interest under the trust of land) and had been in actual occupation throughout. Therefore his equitable interest under the trust of land was an overriding interest under the Land Registration Act 1925, now replaced by the Land Registration Act 2002. His interest overrode that of HSBC's.

There are further points to note here. The right that overrides takes effect over only the part of the land that is actually occupied: see paragraph 2 of Schedule 3 to the Land Registration Act 2002. It is also important to note the date when a post-acquisition mortgage is created. The person who is not on the legal title but has an equitable interest under a trust of land must be in actual occupation on the date when the post-acquisition mortgage is created.

Q: *Why is there so much importance attached to the date?*

A: A problem may arise in registered land when a post-acquisition mortgage is created if the date for determining the existence of an overriding interest is the date of registration of the mortgage. When a post-acquisition mortgage is created, there is a time gap between the date of the creation of the mortgage and its registration at the Land Registry. This means that, theoretically, someone could acquire an equitable interest under a trust of land and occupy the land between these two dates. His equitable interest in the land, plus the fact of actual occupation, would give him an overriding interest. This overriding interest would be in existence before the mortgage lender registered his mortgage and so would bind him, even though he couldn't have known that this would happen. Putting this in a diagram:

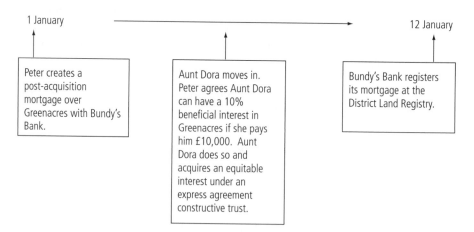

If Peter had failed to pay the mortgage repayments, Bundy's Bank would not have overreached Aunt Dora's equitable interest because it paid the mortgage money only to Peter, and so it could be bound by her interest and her right of occupation. This was clearly unacceptable, as Bundy's Bank couldn't have known that these later events concerning Aunt Dora were going to happen. In *Abbey National Building Society v Cann* it was held that the person claiming the right must be in actual occupation at the time the mortgage is created for his interest to be overriding. *Cook*

v The Mortgage Business plc confirms that this applies to paragraph 2 of Schedule 3 to the Land Registration Act 2002. In *Thompson v Foy* (2009) there is a discussion, albeit obiter and inconclusive, of whether a person has to be in actual occupation at the time of registration of the mortgage as well but this appears to add nothing in protecting the lender as the lender won't be inspecting the property at the date of registration of the mortgage. The reasoning that explains why a person must be in actual occupation at the date of the creation of the mortgage applies also when property is sold. The person claiming the right must be in actual occupation at the date of the sale so the purchaser is not bound by anyone who acquires an equitable interest in the property between the date of the sale and the date of registration of that sale.

There is another important case in the context of registered land. Although it was decided under the Land Registration Act 1925 again, the principles remain the same. The case is *City of London Building Society v Flegg* (1988) and it concerned Bleak House. Mr and Mrs Maxwell-Brown bought Bleak House and were both on the legal title. Mr and Mrs Flegg, the wife's parents who lived with them, had contributed to the purchase price but were not on the legal title. They had both therefore acquired an equitable interest under a resulting trust. Five years later, Mr and Mrs Maxwell-Brown mortgaged the house by means of a post-acquisition mortgage with the City of London Building Society. Mr and Mrs Flegg were not aware of this. The Maxwell-Browns then stopped paying the mortgage repayments. The Building Society demanded possession of the house in order to sell it to recoup the outstanding mortgage loan. Mr and Mrs Flegg argued that they had an interest in the house under a resulting trust; they were in occupation and therefore had an overriding interest that was binding on the Building Society. However, in this case, the Building Society *had overreached* the Fleggs' equitable interests under the resulting trust because it had paid the mortgage loan to Mr *and* Mrs Maxwell-Brown. This meant that it had paid the mortgage loan to two trustees on the legal title of Bleak House and overreaching had occurred. The court held that once an equitable interest under a trust in land had been overreached, the interest could no longer be overriding. The Fleggs no longer had an interest in the land itself and therefore had no rights of occupation. The Building Society could take possession and sell the house.

Q: *What could the Fleggs do here?*

A: As their equitable interest in Bleak House had been overreached into the value of the house, they would be entitled to claim their proportionate share of the money back from the Maxwell-Browns once the Building Society had taken the mortgage money it was owed.

Q: *And if the Maxwell-Browns had disappeared?*

A: Bad luck for the Fleggs.

There is a section covering recent cases that look at what is meant by actual occupation under paragraph 2 of Schedule 3 to the Land Registration Act 2002 on page 289. These cases are also useful to read because they show you how a post-acquisition mortgage arises and they illustrate overreaching, both when it has and when it hasn't taken place.

A summary of the effect of not overreaching in registered land

If the equitable interest under a trust of land of a beneficiary who is not on the legal title has not been overreached, and the beneficiary is in actual occupation, his or her interest can override the interests of a purchaser or of a lender of money on a post-acquisition mortgage. The rights of a person with an equitable interest under a trust of land are found in the Trusts of Land and Appointment of Trustees Act 1996 and include the right of occupation. This means that the right of occupation can bind the purchaser or the mortgage lender and vacant possession will not be obtained. If the equitable interest is one that is capable of overriding but has been overreached, the overreaching mechanism will take priority.

A question on overreaching when there are successive interests in land

This example is intended to illustrate how to use the Boxes in this chapter to analyse the legal position. If you are using this method in undergraduate law exam questions, you will need to include statutory and case authority and detailed discussion of the various points of law. This information is found both in the text and from other sources.

A question on successive interests was given at the end of Chapter 10 and is repeated below. It has now been extended to include sale of the land and a discussion of overreaching. land law is like a jigsaw puzzle and, by the end of this chapter, you should be able to understand the overall working of the chart 'The Use of Trusts in Land' in Chapter 6 on page 132.

> A year ago Den made a will in which he left Greenacres to his trustees, Tick and Tock, on trust for his nephew Samuel and his niece Edwina for their joint lifetimes, and then to Clarissa absolutely. Den has just died. Tick and Tock have decided that it is in the financial interests of the trust to sell Greenacres. Samuel and Clarissa do not wish Greenacres to be sold as they are emotionally attached to it. Samuel, Edwina and Clarissa are all over 18.
>
> Advise whether Tick and Tock are able to sell the property, whether they can delegate their powers to Samuel and Edwina and whether Samuel and Clarissa have the right to live there.

This is the conclusion to the question from Chapter 10, page 246.

Greenacres will be held under a trust of land governed by the Trusts of Land and Appointment of Trustees Act 1996. Tick and Tock, as trustees, have the powers of an absolute owner and so are able to sell Greenacres. Only Samuel and Edwina need to be consulted over this decision but, if it is in the general interest of the trust to sell Greenacres, their wishes may be ignored. Any dispute over sale can be taken to court, where the judge will look at the purposes of the trust and the wishes of Samuel and Edwina. Tick and Tock can delegate to Samuel and Edwina their tasks as trustees in relation to the land. They must exercise reasonable care and review the delegation. Only Samuel and Edwina can occupy Greenacres if the property is available and suitable, not Clarissa. Compensation may be payable to the non-occupying party if only one of them occupies Greenacres.

Now add the final part of the question.

> Tick recently died and Tock decided to sell Greenacres. Samuel and Edwina agreed with his decision. Greenacres was sold to Peter last week. Advise the parties of their respective positions.

As Greenacres has been sold, you need to discuss whether overreaching has taken place.

Box A   *Interests that can be overreached*

Successive interests in land; express co-ownership interests in land; implied co-ownership interests in land

This is an example of successive interests in land. Samuel, Edwina and Clarissa are not on the legal title to Greenacres. They are beneficiaries under a trust of land and hold only an equitable interest in the property. As Greenacres has been sold to Peter, you must establish whether their equitable interests have been overreached under sections 2 and 27(2) of the Law of Property Act 1925.

Box B   *Action which must be taken in order to overreach an equitable interest under a trust of land*

The payment of purchase money or money lent on a post-acquisition mortgage must be paid to two trustees on the legal title of the property and a valid receipt obtained

You are told that Tick has recently died. The legal title would have been held as a joint tenancy and so the right of survivorship would have operated, leaving Tock as the sole legal owner holding Greenacres on trust for Samuel, Edwina and Clarissa. This means that Peter paid the purchase money to one trustee only, Tock, and therefore the equitable interests of the beneficiaries under the trust of land have not been overreached.

Box C   *The effect of not overreaching an equitable interest under a trust of land*

You must now establish whether the beneficiaries' interests under the trust of land will bind Peter. On the facts of the question Greenacres must be registered land, either because it was registered before Den died, or because the property would have been the subject of compulsory registration when it was conveyed to Tick and Tock. You would therefore need to consider only the position in registered land. For the sake of completeness, though, both unregistered and registered land have been considered in this answer. When it is clear from the question that the land is either registered or unregistered, you must ensure that you only look at one or the other.

C1 Unregistered land

Interests under a trust of land are equitable. Equitable interests under a trust of land cannot be entered as a land charge on the Land Charges Register as there is no designated class. These equitable interests are therefore subject to the rule relating to equitable interests before 1926, known as the doctrine of notice.

Equitable interests bind everyone except a *bona fide* purchaser of a legal estate for value without notice of the equitable interest.

The equitable interests here are equitable interests under a trust of land. Notice includes actual, constructive and imputed notice. Peter will be bound by the equitable interest of any beneficiary under a trust of land unless he is a *bona fide* purchaser of a legal estate for value without notice of his or her equitable interest.

We can assume Peter is *bona fide*. He is a purchaser for value, as the word 'sold' implies he paid money, and he purchased the legal estate of Greenacres. The question is whether he has actual, constructive or imputed notice of the beneficiaries' interests.

Peter may have actual notice of the beneficiaries' interests. Even if he doesn't, it is highly likely that he will be deemed to have constructive notice of Samuel's and Edwina's interests if they are living in Greenacres. Failing that, he may well have imputed notice from his solicitor. If he is deemed to have notice by any of these ways, he will be bound by their equitable interests and therefore by the rights which arise from these equitable interests. These rights are found in the Trusts of Land and Appointment of Trustees Act 1996 and include a right of occupation under section 12. Samuel and Edwina can claim this right of occupation and so will prevent Peter from obtaining vacant possession of Greenacres.

Q: *What's Peter's position now then?*

A: Tock held only the legal title of Greenacres. The equitable or beneficial title was with Samuel, Edwina and Clarissa. All Tock could convey to Peter was the legal title. This means that Peter will now hold the legal title as trustee of Greenacres, and Samuel, Edwina and Clarissa will continue to hold the equitable title to Greenacres. Peter will take no benefit from Greenacres at all and, in his capacity as trustee, he will be governed by the Trusts of Land and Appointment of Trustees Act 1996. This is extremely serious for Peter, and some would say he receives his just desserts for not making sufficient enquiries about Greenacres in the first place. He must now hold the land on trust for Samuel and Edwina. When both Samuel and Edwina have died, Peter must convey the property to Clarissa if he purchased it with notice of her interest. She will then own Greenacres absolutely. If Peter purchased Greenacres without notice of Clarissa's interest, probably because she was not living there at the time of purchase, the trust will end and he will own Greenacres absolutely on the death of the survivor of Samuel and Edwina. If Peter himself has died at this point, Greenacres will pass under his will or under the rules of intestacy.

If Peter does not have notice of the equitable interests of Samuel, Edwina and Clarissa, he will take Greenacres free from them and can recover possession.

C2 Registered land

C2i Dealings which must be completed by registration
Acquiring an equitable interest under a trust of land is not a dealing which must be completed by registration under section 27 of the Land Registration Act 2002, so you must look at the other two categories.

C2ii Interests which override a registered disposition

C2iii Interests entered as a notice or protected by a restriction
When Den died and Greenacres was conveyed to Tick and Tock, it is highly likely that a restriction would have been placed on its Proprietorship Register. This restriction would have specified that if Greenacres were to be sold or mortgaged, the purchase or mortgage money should be paid to two trustees on the legal title to ensure overreaching.

Assuming, however, that this has not happened, you are looking at whether Samuel, Edwina and Clarissa's equitable interests under the trust of land are interests under paragraph 2 of Schedule 3 to the Land Registration Act 2002 that override a registered disposition, here the sale to Peter. Paragraph 2 states that the interests of a person in actual occupation are interests that override. Equitable interests under a trust of land are proprietary interests in land so, providing Samuel and Edwina are in actual occupation when Greenacres is sold, their interests will override and take priority over Peter's rights. Peter will be unable to move into an empty house as he will be bound by their right of occupation under section 12 of the Trusts of Land and Appointment of Trustees Act 1996.

If Samuel and Edwina are living there, but their occupation is not obvious on a reasonably careful inspection of the land and Peter didn't know about their interests, their interests will not be overriding and will not bind him. If Samuel and Edwina are living there but hadn't disclosed their interests to Peter if he'd asked them, and it would have been reasonable for them to do so, again Peter will not be bound by their interests.

If Samuel and Edwina are not living there, their interests will not be overriding and will not bind Peter.

If the equitable interests of Samuel and Edwina do not override, Peter can recover possession.

Clarissa's interest will not be binding on Peter as an overriding interest because she was not living there at the time of the sale.

Conclusion

Peter did not comply with the statutory requirements of overreaching. Whether he takes free from the interests of Samuel, Edwina and Clarissa depends on the doctrine of notice in unregistered land and actual occupation in registered land.

A question on overreaching when there is express co-ownership in land

This example is intended to illustrate how to use the Boxes in this chapter to analyse the legal position. If you are using this method in undergraduate law exam questions, you will need to include statutory and case authority and detailed discussion of the various points of law. This information is found both in the text and from other sources.

A question on express co-ownership was started at the end of Chapter 8 and was continued at the end of Chapter 10. It is repeated below. The question has now been extended to include sale of the land and a discussion of overreaching. Land law is like a jigsaw puzzle and, by the end of this chapter, you should be able to understand the overall working of the chart 'The Use of Trusts in Land' in Chapter 6 on page 132.

> Two years ago, four workmates, Donatello, Leonardo, Michelangelo and Raphael decided to purchase a house called Greenacres. They all contributed equally to the purchase price of the property and intended to live there together.
> Things soon started to go wrong when Donatello was killed in a skiing accident. He left nothing in his will for his estranged wife and three children. Then Leonardo, who had fallen out with the others, verbally agreed to sell his interest in the property to Frankie.

Leonardo did not tell his fellow co-owners of his intention. Leonardo then changed his mind about the sale, but shortly afterwards served written notice on Michelangelo and Raphael that he was holding his interest in Greenacres as a tenant in common. Finally Michelangelo and Raphael were involved in a serious road accident.

Michelangelo died immediately, having left his property in his will to his sister, Cassandra. Raphael died several days later in hospital, having left his property in his will to his sister, Eugenie.

Advise on the devolution of the legal and equitable title.

Advise on the duties of the trustees and the rights of the beneficiaries from the time of purchase to the present.

This is the conclusion to the question from Chapter 8, page 168, and Chapter 10, page 249:

When the four workmates purchased Greenacres, there was express beneficial co-ownership and a trust of land was created. The legal title had to be held as a joint tenancy. The four workmates also held the equitable title as a joint tenancy. Severance of the legal title is never possible. The right of survivorship operated on the legal title, leaving Leonardo as the sole legal owner. The right of survivorship and severance operated on the equitable title, with the result that Eugenie and Leonardo hold equitable interests in Greenacres as tenants in common. If Greenacres were to be sold, Eugenie would receive a 2/3 share of the proceeds and Leonardo a 1/3 share.

As the trust contained land, this would be a trust of land governed by the Trusts of Land and Appointment of Trustees Act 1996. The main rights of D, L, M and R were a right to sell Greenacres, a right of occupation and a right to apply to the court in the event of dispute. Leonardo is the sole surviving owner on the legal title, holding Greenacres on trust for himself and Eugenie. He must consult Eugenie and give effect to her wishes if they accord with the general interests of the trust. Both parties could live in Greenacres, although this is unlikely as Eugenie inherited her interest in the property. If Leonardo and Eugenie can't agree on what is to happen to Greenacres, an application could be made to the court. In view of the circumstances, the court would be likely to order sale or else compensation to the non-occupying party.

Now add on the final part of the question.

Leonardo has just sold Greenacres to Peter. Advise the parties of their respective positions.

As Greenacres has been sold, you need to discuss whether overreaching has taken place.

Box A   Interests that can be overreached

Successive interests in land; express co-ownership interests in land; implied co-ownership interests in land

This is an example of express co-ownership. Leonardo is the sole legal owner. Eugenie is not on the legal title but has only an equitable interest under a trust of land. Leonardo will have conveyed his legal and his equitable interests in Greenacres to Peter. Eugenie has not conveyed her equitable interest in Greenacres to Peter. You must now establish whether her equitable interest has been overreached under sections 2 and 27(2) of the Law of Property Act 1925.

Box B   Action which must be taken in order to overreach an equitable interest under a trust of land

The purchase money or money lent on a post acquisition mortgage must be paid to two trustees on the legal title of the property and a valid receipt obtained
The equitable interest of Eugenie has not been overreached as Peter has not paid the purchase money for Greenacres to two trustees on the legal title of Greenacres. He has paid only to Leonardo.

Box C   The effect of not overreaching an equitable interest under a trust of land
You must now establish whether Eugenie's equitable interest under the trust of land, and the rights that arise from it, bind Peter. On the facts of the question Greenacres must be registered land, either because it was registered before the four workmates purchased the property or because it would have been the subject of compulsory registration when they did so. You would therefore need to consider only the position in registered land. For the sake of completeness, though, both unregistered and registered land have been considered in this answer. When it is clear from the question that the land is either registered or unregistered, you must ensure that you look at only one or the other.

C1 Unregistered land
Interests under a trust of land are equitable. Equitable interests under a trust of land cannot be entered as a land charge on the Land Charges Register as there is no designated class. These equitable interests are therefore subject to the rule relating to equitable interests before 1926, known as the doctrine of notice.

Equitable interests bind everyone except a *bona fide* purchaser of a legal estate for value without notice of the equitable interest.

The equitable interest here is an equitable interest under a trust of land. Notice includes actual, constructive and imputed notice. Peter will be bound by the equitable interest of any beneficiary under a trust of land unless he is a *bona fide* purchaser of a legal estate for value without notice of this equitable interest.

We can assume Peter is *bona fide*. He is a purchaser for value as the word 'sold' implies he paid money. He purchased the legal estate of Greenacres. The question is whether he has actual, constructive or imputed notice of Eugenie's equitable interest.

Peter may have actual notice of her interest. If he doesn't, it is debatable whether he has constructive notice, as Eugenie is unlikely to be living there because she inherited her interest in the property from her brother. Failing that, he may well have imputed notice from his solicitor. If he is deemed to have notice by any of these ways, he will be bound by her equitable interest and therefore by the rights which arise from the equitable interest. These rights are found in the Trusts of Land and Appointment of Trustees Act 1996 and include a right of occupation under section 12. In this case he would be unable to obtain vacant possession of Greenacres. He would be a trustee of Greenacres, holding the land on trust for himself and Eugenie. He could apply to the court for sale under section 14 of the Trusts of Land and Appointment of Trustees Act 1996, but the court may well remind him of the statutory provision of overreaching instead. Even if the court did order sale, Eugenie would obtain her share of the money from the sale first, as Peter had notice of her interest when he purchased Greenacres, and so would still be bound by it when the land was turned into money.

If Peter did not have notice of Eugenie's equitable interest, he could recover possession.

C2 Registered land

C2i Dealings which must be completed by registration
Acquiring an equitable interest under a trust of land is not a dealing which must be completed by registration under section 27 of the Land Registration Act 2002, so you must look at the other two categories.

C2ii Interests which override a registered disposition

C2iii Interests entered as a notice or protected by a restriction
It is highly likely that a restriction will have been placed on the Proprietorship Register of Greenacres when it was first purchased because there was express beneficial co-ownership. A restriction stating that any purchaser should pay to two trustees on the legal title would have ensured that Peter overreached Eugenie's equitable interest.

Assuming there was no such restriction, you are looking at whether Eugenie's interest is an interest in paragraph 2 of Schedule 3 to the Land Registration Act 2002 that overrides Peter's registered disposition. The registered disposition here is the sale to Peter after it has been registered at the District Land Registry. Paragraph 2 states that the interests of a person in actual occupation are interests that override. An equitable interest under a trust of land is a proprietary interest in land, so, providing Eugenie is in actual occupation of the land when Greenacres is sold, her interest will bind Peter. Peter will then be a trustee of Greenacres, holding the land on trust for himself and Eugenie. He will be bound by Eugenie's right of occupation under section 12 of the Trusts of Land and Appointment of Trustees Act 1996, which means that he will not be able to obtain vacant possession. Peter could apply to the court for sale under section 14 of the Trusts of Land and Appointment of Trustees Act 1996, but the court may well remind him of the statutory provision of overreaching instead. Even if the court did order sale, Eugenie would obtain her share of the money from sale first, as her interest was binding on Peter when he purchased Greenacres, and remains binding on him when the land is turned into money.

If Eugenie's occupation was not obvious on a reasonably careful inspection of Greenacres and Peter didn't know about her interest, her interest will not be one that overrides and will not be binding on Peter. If Eugenie was living there and she hadn't disclosed her interest to Peter if he'd asked her, when it would have been reasonable for her to have done so, then again her interest will not override and will not bind Peter.

If, as is likely, Eugenie is not in actual occupation because she inherited her interest in the property, her interest is not one that overrides and Peter can move into an empty house. This emphasises the point that Eugenie must be in actual occupation for her interest to be classed as overriding.

Conclusion

Peter has not complied with the statutory requirements of overreaching. Whether he takes free from Eugenie's interest depends on the doctrine of notice in unregistered land and actual occupation in registered land.

A question on overreaching when there are interests arising under a constructive or resulting trust

This example is intended to illustrate how to use the Boxes in this chapter to analyse the legal position. If you are using this method in undergraduate law exam questions, you will need to include statutory and case authority and detailed discussion of the various points of law. This information is found both in the text and from other sources.

A question on constructive and resulting trusts was started at the end of Chapter 9 and continued at the end of Chapter 10. This question is repeated below. It has now been extended to include sale of the land and a discussion on overreaching. land law is like a jigsaw puzzle and, by the end of this chapter, you should be able to understand the overall working of the chart 'The Use of Trusts in Land' in Chapter 6 on page 132.

> Six years ago, John and Claire purchased Greenacres together for £200,000. The legal title to the house was put in John's name. John paid £70,000 of the purchase price in cash and Claire contributed £30,000 in cash. John raised the remainder of the purchase price by means of a mortgage in his name. Claire has contributed to the mortgage repayments. Six months after the couple moved in, John's mother, Lily, who had recently become infirm, came to live with them. She paid for the conversion of two rooms downstairs into rooms specially adapted for her needs at a cost of £10,000. Shortly afterwards John agreed with her that she would always have a 10% share in the house. Since they have been there, Claire has done the accounts of John's business in the evenings without payment and has decorated the house throughout. Both John and Claire suffered pay cuts at work six months ago and Lily has helped out with the household expenses since. The parties have now fallen out, and John has just told both Claire and Lily that they have no interest in the house at all.
>
> Advise Claire and Lily what interest, if any, they have in Greenacres.
> Advise the parties of their duties and rights.

This is the conclusion to the question from Chapter 9, page 218 and Chapter 10, page 251.

Claire and Lily are not on the legal title to the house. There is no express declaration of trust in their favour, so they must try to claim an equitable interest in the house under a constructive or resulting trust. This is a domestic situation so a constructive trust will almost certainly be pleaded. Claire has contributed to the purchase price and also to the mortgage repayments. There was no express agreement between her and John so she must claim under an implied agreement constructive trust where her contributions will form the basis of the implied agreement. The court will infer what shares were intended between herself and John by looking at their whole course of conduct. If the shares they intended cannot be inferred, the court will impute an intention to them and the allocation of shares will be decided on the basis of fairness. Lily must rely on the express agreement made to her by John and her contribution to the housekeeping expenses as the basis for an express agreement constructive trust. If her claim were successful, the court would award her the promised 10% share.

A trust of land has been created and will be governed by the Trusts of Land and Appointment of Trustees Act 1996. John has the powers of an absolute owner in his capacity as trustee, and could sell Greenacres. However, he should consult Claire and Lily. An application could be made to the court to determine any disputes.

Now add on the final part of the question.

> Claire and Lily have now discovered that John has sold Greenacres to Peter. Advise the parties.

As Greenacres has been sold, you need to discuss whether overreaching has taken place.

Box A   Interests that can be overreached

Successive interests in land; express co-ownership interests in land; implied co-ownership interests in land

This is an example of implied co-ownership. John is the sole legal owner. John will have conveyed his legal and equitable interest in Greenacres to Peter when the house was sold. Claire and Lily are not on the legal title, but both have only an equitable interest under a trust of land. These equitable interests have not been conveyed to Peter. You must establish whether their equitable interests have been overreached under sections 2 and 27(2) of the Law of Property Act 1925.

Box B   Action which must be taken in order to overreach an equitable interest under a trust of land

Purchase money or money lent on a post-acquisition mortgage must be paid to two trustees on the legal title of the property and a valid receipt obtained

The equitable interests of Claire and Lily have not been overreached, as Peter has not paid the purchase money for Greenacres to two trustees on the legal title of Greenacres. He has paid only John.

Box C   The effect of not overreaching an equitable interest under a trust of land

You must now establish whether the equitable interests of Claire and Lily and the rights that arise from these interests bind Peter. On the facts of the question Greenacres must be registered land, either because it was registered before John purchased the property or because it would have been the subject of compulsory registration when he did so. You would therefore need to consider only the position in registered land. For the sake of completeness, though, both unregistered and registered land have been considered in this answer. When it is clear from the question that the land is either registered or unregistered, you must ensure that you look at only one or the other.

C1 Unregistered land

Interests under a trust of land are equitable. Equitable interests under a trust of land cannot be entered as a land charge on the Land Charges Register as there is no designated class. These equitable interests are therefore subject to the rule relating to equitable interests before 1926, known as the doctrine of notice.

Equitable interests bind everyone except a *bona fide* purchaser of a legal estate for value without notice of the equitable interest.

The equitable interests here are those under a trust of land. Notice includes actual, constructive and imputed notice. Peter will be bound by the equitable interest of any beneficiary under a trust of land unless he is a *bona fide* purchaser of a legal estate for value without notice of this equitable interest.

We can assume Peter is *bona fide*. He is a purchaser for value as the word 'sold' implies he paid money and he purchased the legal estate of Greenacres. The question is whether he has actual, constructive or imputed notice of Claire's and Lily's interests. It is highly likely that he will be deemed to have actual or constructive notice of their interests as they are both living in Greenacres. This means that he will be bound by these interests and the rights arising from them, namely their right of occupation under section 12 of the Trusts of Land and Appointment of Trustees Act 1996. In this case he would be unable to obtain vacant possession of Greenacres. He could apply to the court for sale of Greenacres under section 14 of the Trusts of Land and Appointment of Trustees Act 1996, although the court could simply remind him of the mechanism of overreaching and refuse to order sale. Even if sale were ordered by the court, Claire and Lily would be paid first out of the money from sale, as their interests were binding on Peter when he purchased Greenacres and remain binding on him when the land is turned into money.

If Peter does not have notice of the equitable interests of Claire and Lily, he will not be bound by them and can move into an empty property.

C2 Registered land

C2i Dealings which must be completed by registration
Acquiring an equitable interest under a trust of land is not a dealing which must be completed by registration under section 27 of the Land Registration Act 2002, so you must look at the other two categories.

C2ii Interests which override a registered disposition

C2iii Interests entered as a notice or protected by a restriction
It is unlikely that a restriction will have been placed on the Proprietorship Register of Greenacres, not least because Claire and Lily will probably have no idea that they hold an equitable interest under a constructive trust. So you are looking at whether their equitable interests are interests in paragraph 2 of Schedule 3 to the Land Registration Act 2002 that override a registered disposition, the sale to Peter here. Paragraph 2 states that the interests of a person in actual occupation are interests that override. Lily and Claire have equitable interests under a trust of land. These are proprietary interests in land. Providing Lily and Claire are in actual occupation when Greenacres is sold, as is likely, their interests will override or take priority over Peter's rights. Their equitable interests give them a right of occupation under section 12 of the Trusts of Land and Appointment of Trustees Act 1996, and so Peter will be unable to move into an empty house. Peter will be a trustee of Greenacres holding the land on trust for himself, Claire and Lily. He can apply to the court for sale under section 14 of the Trusts of Land and Appointment of Trustees Act 1996, but the court may well remind him of the statutory provision

of overreaching instead. Even if the court did order sale of the house, Claire and Lily would obtain their proportionate share of the money from sale first, as their interests were binding on Peter when he purchased Greenacres and remain binding on him when the land is turned into money. If only Claire had been in occupation, her interest alone would be classed as overriding; likewise if only Lily had been in occupation.

If Claire's and Lily's actual occupation would not have been obvious on a reasonably careful inspection of the land and Peter didn't know about their interests, their interests will not override and will not bind Peter. If Peter had asked Claire and Lily about their interests in Greenacres and they hadn't disclosed this information to him when it would have been reasonable for them to have done so their interests will not override and will not take priority over Peter's rights.

Conclusion

Peter has not complied with the statutory requirements of overreaching. Whether he takes free from the interests of Claire and Lily depends on the doctrine of notice in unregistered land and actual occupation in registered land.

A variation on the question on overreaching and constructive and resulting trusts

The question we have just looked at concerned overreaching and the sale of the property. A popular variation of this concerns overreaching and the creation of a post-acquisition mortgage. Imagine the following.

> A year ago John decided to create a mortgage over Greenacres with Bundy's Bank. John has now disappeared to Rio with the money lent on the mortgage and Bundy's Bank is seeking possession of Greenacres with a view to selling the property to recoup the outstanding loan money. Advise the parties on their respective positions.

Remember that overreaching applies when a post-acquisition mortgage is created.

You are still faced with the problem that Bundy's Bank did not comply with the requirements of overreaching because they paid the post-acquisition mortgage money to John alone. You must establish whether the equitable interests under the trust of land of Claire and Lily are binding on Bundy's Bank.

Unregistered land

If Bundy's Bank had actual, constructive or imputed notice of the equitable interests of Claire and Lily at the time the mortgage was created, it would be bound by these interests and the rights that arise from them, namely the right of occupation under section 12 of the Trusts of Land and Appointment of Trustees Act 1996. In this case Bundy's Bank would not be able to obtain vacant possession of the house. The Bank would have to sue John for breach of contract for failing to pay the mortgage repayments. This would force him into bankruptcy. John's trustee in bankruptcy would apply for sale under section 14 of the 1996 Act. As there was a bankruptcy of one of the beneficiaries under the trust of land, John here, the Insolvency Act 1986 would come into play. This means that if a year had passed since the bankruptcy happened, the house would be sold to pay off John's debts unless there were exceptional circumstances. Claire and Lily would receive their proportionate monetary share in the house before Bundy's Bank as the Bank had notice of their interests when the mortgage was created.

If the Bank did not have notice of Claire's and Lily's equitable interests under the trust of land, it would not be bound by them and could obtain vacant possession.

Registered land

Again, there has been no overreaching. As Claire and Lily are likely to be in actual occupation, their equitable interests will be interests that override the rights of Bundy's Bank. As in unregistered land, Bundy's Bank must sue John for breach of contract for failing to pay the mortgage repayments, and the same result will ensue as in unregistered land.

Recent cases on the meaning of actual occupation

The following cases illustrate the meaning of actual occupation. They are also useful to read because they show you how a post-acquisition mortgage arises and they illustrate overreaching, both when it has and when it hasn't taken place.

In *Link Lending Limited v Bustard* (2010) Ms Bustard suffered from a mental disorder. In 2004 Mrs Hussain took advantage of Ms Bustard's vulnerability with the effect that Ms Bustard transferred the property in question to Mrs Hussain. Mrs Hussain took a mortgage from HSBC over the property. Note that this was a first mortgage. Ms Bustard didn't receive any money from the transfer or the mortgage. In 2007 Ms Bustard was sectioned under the Mental Health Act 1983 and taken into psychiatric care. She visited her own home on a supervised weekly basis to check the property and pick up the post. She was not allowed to live there although she kept furniture in the house and paid the outgoings. In 2008 Mrs Hussain took out a mortgage secured on the property from Link Lending (so this was a post-acquisition mortgage) and the mortgage from HSBC was paid off. Mrs Hussain defaulted on the repayments to Link Lending and Link Lending wanted to take possession of the property with a view to selling it to recoup the mortgage money it had lent Mrs Hussain. Ms Bustard claimed that the transfer to Mrs Hussain should be set aside as she, Ms Bustard, had not had the legal capacity to effect the transfer. This claim was successful which gave Ms Bustard an equity in the property. She claimed that she had an overriding interest under paragraph 2 of Schedule 3 to the Land Registration Act 2002 at the time the mortgage with Link Lending was created. Link Lending couldn't argue that it had overreached Ms Bustard's interest because it had paid the post-acquisition mortgage money to one trustee only on the legal title, Mrs Hussain. Link Lending therefore argued that Ms Bustard had not been in actual occupation on the date the charge was registered, so it could take possession. The court found in Ms Bustard's favour. The meaning of actual occupation was looked at in the case by the Court of Appeal. First, the court endorsed the obiter but accurate and helpful summary found in *Thompson v Foy* which highlighted the following:

> The words 'actual occupation' should be given their plain English meaning.
> The word 'actual' underlines the requirement for a physical presence.
> The person claiming actual occupation does not have to be present personally. A caretaker

or the representative of a company can occupy on behalf of his employer.

A licensor cannot count the occupation of his licensee as his own occupation.

The fact that a claimant's furniture is there does not usually count as actual occupation.

If the person who is claiming actual occupation isn't physically present on the land at the relevant time, his occupation has to be shown together with a continuing intention to occupy.

In Link Lending Ltd Lord Justice Mummery then gave the following summary which will give you some idea of what needs to be taken into account when deciding whether someone is in actual occupation. They are sentences taken from paragraphs 27 and 30 in the judgement.

The trend of the cases shows that the courts are reluctant to lay down, or even suggest, a single legal test for determining whether a person is in actual occupation.

The degree of permanence and continuity of presence of the person concerned, the intentions and wishes of that person, the length of absence from the property and the reason for it and the nature of the property and personal circumstances of the person are among the relevant factors.

In this case the new and special feature is in the psychiatric problems of the person claiming actual occupation. The judge was, in my view, justified in ruling, at the conclusion of a careful and detailed judgment, that Ms Bustard was a person in actual occupation of the Property. His conclusion was supported by evidence of a sufficient degree of continuity and permanence of occupation, of involuntary residence elsewhere, which was satisfactorily explained by objective reasons, and of a persistent intention to return home when possible, as manifested by her regular visits to the Property.

Q: *How can a purchaser or a bank lending money on a mortgage know about a person's intent?*

A: This is unclear, particularly as the idea behind land registration is to remove as far as possible any idea of who might have known what, where and when.

Bank of Scotland v Hussain is a case where the meaning of actual occupation was considered under section 70(1)(g) of the Land Registration Act 1925. Section 70(1) (g), now repealed, was similar to paragraph 2 of Schedule 3 of the Land Registration Act 2002. It was held that Mrs Qutb, one of the defendants in the case, was in actual occupation. The court held that whilst the defendant did not live in the property permanently, a person could still be in actual occupation of more than one property. It was likely that Mrs Qutb had spent some nights there in a four month period. Although the mere presence of furniture in property would not normally count as actual occupation, the fact that her furniture had been in the property right up until the time of sale and afterwards was of some relevance and, furthermore, she had not intended to vacate the property. Whilst Mrs Qutb was held to be in actual occupation, her interest was not deemed to be overriding for the reasons described on page 265.

Clearly a number of factors can come into play in determining whether someone is in actual occupation or not. This is further illustrated in *Thomas v Clydesdale Bank* (2010). Mr Burtenshaw had purchased property with the aid of a mortgage from the Bank of Scotland in March 2006 in his own name (so a first mortgage). The property needed renovation so he obtained a mortgage in July 2006 from Clydesdale Bank (this was the post-acquisition mortgage) to pay off the mortgage with the Bank of Scotland and to pay for the renovations being carried out by Batty Builders. This mortgage was registered in August 2006. Mr Burtenshaw and his partner, Ms Thomas, and their children moved into the property in September 2006 after the renovations had been completed over that summer. Mr Burtenshaw subsequently became bankrupt and Clydesdale Bank sought possession. Ms Thomas claimed an equitable interest in the house under a constructive trust which was binding on the Bank under paragraph 2 of Schedule 3 of the Land Registration Act 2002 as an overriding interest because she said she had been in actual occupation in July 2006. Remember that overreaching had not taken place because Clydesdale Bank had paid the post-acquisition mortgage money to one trustee only, Mr Burtenshaw. The question the court was asking (for various procedural reasons) was whether she would have a reasonable chance of success in proving that she had an overriding interest. Following a useful recap of the cases of what is meant by actual occupation, the Honourable Mr Justice Ramsey came to the following conclusions.

The fact that the property was being renovated had to be taken into account and there were reasonable prospects of establishing that the occupation of the premises by builders and interior designers was occupation on behalf of both Mr Burtenshaw and Ms Thomas.

Ms Thomas was present at the property almost daily and there was a degree of permanence and continuity in her presence.

Both Mr Burtenshawe and Ms Thomas intended that she should live there when the renovation was complete, which she did.

The physical presence of Ms Thomas, the builders and the interior designers was of the nature and extent that one would expect of an occupier given the property was being renovated.

As far as whether her occupation was obvious on a reasonably careful inspection, there had to be relevant and visible signs of occupation. In determining whether someone is in actual occupation though, it wasn't just the visible signs that mattered but enquiries also had to be made which would include asking about the permanence and continuity of the presence of the person concerned, their intentions and wishes and their personal circumstances.

And, even if it was decided that the claimed occupation wasn't obvious on a reasonably careful inspection of the land, the Bank would have actual knowledge. This was not knowledge of the actual interest but knowledge of the facts which could give rise to an interest. This was because the Bank knew that Mr Burtenshaw had a partner, that she was going to contribute to the purchase price of the property and that she was going to move into the property as the family home. Overall, Ms Thomas had a reasonable chance of proving she had an overriding interest based on actual occupation.

In *Chaudhary v Yavuz* (2011) the use of a stairway with a balcony alongside to enter a building was held to be 'actual use' but not 'actual occupation' of the stairway or balcony so no overriding interest under paragraph 2 of Schedule 3 could be claimed.

The cases show you the interesting ways the courts are deciding that someone is in actual occupation.

Further reading

C. Harpum, 'Overreaching, Trustees' Powers and the Reform of the 1925 Legislation', 49 *CLJ* (1990) 277

N. Jackson, 'Overreaching in Registered Land Law', 69 *MLR* (2006) 214

M. Oldham, 'Overreaching where No Capital Monies Arise', 56 *CLJ* (1997) 494

P. Omar, 'Equitable Interests and the Secured Creditor: Determining Priorities', *Conv and Prop Law*, Nov/Dec (2006) 509

M. Thompson, 'The Purchaser as Private Detective', *Conv and Prop Law*, Jul/Aug (1986) 283

M. Thompson, 'Overreaching without Payment', *Conv and Prop Law*, Mar/Apr (1997) 134

Chapter 12

Proprietary estoppel

www.palgrave.com/law/Stroud4e

Introduction

Proprietary estoppel is an equitable remedy which has developed considerably over recent years. It has provided a further avenue for claiming an informally created interest in land, particularly in the context of the family home.

Proprietary estoppel arises when person A has either actively encouraged person B to believe that he has present or future rights in person A's land or when person A has stood by knowing that person B is mistaken as to his present or future rights in A's land. Even though the formalities for the creation of an interest in land have not been followed, it is still possible for person B to claim an interest in the land. This is because person A is estopped, or stopped, from relying on the lack of formalities if he tries to deny person B an interest because it would be unfair for him to do so. There are four areas you need to consider in proprietary estoppel which are covered in the chart on page 294. Box A looks at the elements required for a claim based in proprietary estoppel. The remedies that the courts have awarded are considered in Box B, and Box C looks at the protection of estoppel rights.

The elements of proprietary estoppel

Box A

THE ELEMENTS OF PROPRIETARY ESTOPPEL

You must tick all boxes

☐ **1.** An assurance or representation

☐ **2.** Reliance on the assurance or representation

☐ **3.** Detriment

☐ **4.** Unconscionability

You must meet all the conditions here.

PROPRIETARY ESTOPPEL

Box A

THE ELEMENTS OF PROPRIETARY ESTOPPEL

You must tick all boxes

☐ **1.** An assurance or representation

☐ **2.** Reliance on the assurance or representation

☐ **3.** Detriment

☐ **4.** Unconscionability

Box B

THE RANGE OF REMEDIES AVAILABLE TO SATISFY A CLAIM

1. Grant of the freehold estate

2. Grant of a lease

3. Grant of a licence

4. Grant of an easement or right of access

5. Monetary compensation

6. Combined remedies

Box C

THE PROTECTION OF ESTOPPEL RIGHTS

Look at either:

1. Unregistered land

or look at

2. Registered land

i) Dealings which must be completed by registration

ii) Interests which override a registered disposition

iii) Interests entered as a notice or protected by a restriction

Traditionally, proprietary estoppel arose in three different ways:

▶ Person A assured person B that person B would have rights in A's land (the imperfect gift cases: see *Dillwyn v Llewelyn* (1862)).

or

▶ Person A and person B dealt with each other in such a way that B had a reasonable right to suppose that he had acquired rights in A's land (the common expectation cases: see *Ramsden v Dyson* (1866)).

or

▶ Person A did not encourage person B to do something on A's land, but stood by without saying anything to B knowing that B was mistaken as to his rights (the unilateral mistake cases: see *Ramsden v Dyson*).

Willmott v Barber (1880) was a case concerning unilateral mistake, the last ground outlined above. Five conditions, known as the 'five probanda' were set out, and these had to be met for a claim in proprietary estoppel to succeed. They were:

▶ The claimant must have made a mistake as to his legal rights.
▶ The claimant must have expended some money or done some act on the strength of his mistaken belief.
▶ The owner must have known of the existence of some right of his own which was inconsistent with the right claimed.
▶ The owner must have known of the claimant's mistaken belief in his rights.
▶ The owner must have encouraged the claimant in his expenditure of money or in the other acts which he had done, either directly or by abstaining from asserting his legal rights.

These probanda were subsequently applied to the 'common expectation' and the 'imperfect gift' cases, even though they relate only to the 'unilateral mistake' cases. As a result it became very difficult to prove proprietary estoppel, and so there was relief when *Taylor Fashions Ltd v Liverpool Victoria Trustees Co Ltd* (1982) took a broader approach, and the following elements must now be met to succeed in a claim:

▶ an assurance or representation;
▶ reliance on the assurance or representation;
▶ detriment; and
▶ unconscionablity.

There must be an assurance or a representation by the landowner, which is relied on by the claimant. The assurance or representation is subsequently withdrawn by the landowner, and the claimant suffers detriment as a result. These elements are interlinked, as the reliance must be linked to the assurance or representation, and the detriment must be linked to the reliance. You must then satisfy the overall requirement of unconscionablity.

Box A1   An assurance or representation

The first element required is an assurance or representation by the landowner that the claimant will have an interest in or over the land.

Q: Does the assurance or representation have to be express?

A: No. In *Thorner v Major* (2009), sometimes referred to as *Thorner v Curtis*, David Thorner was claiming entitlement to a farm through proprietary estoppel. For 30 years without payment David Thorner had devoted his life to helping Peter run his farm both physically and in its financial management. David had relied on implied 'understandings' that he would inherit the farm from Peter. Peter had revoked his will following a disagreement with one of the intended beneficiaries (not David) and had never made another will and so David had not inherited the farm.

Q: Surely the problem with implied understandings is exactly that – they are implied?

A: This was the conclusion of the Court of Appeal which had not recognised proprietary estoppel because there should be a clear promise by conduct or words. If it were otherwise, proprietary estoppel could be claimed if someone made a general statement about how he wanted his property distributed after his death. In the House of Lords, though, it was held that the assurance must be 'clear enough'. Whether the assurance is clear enough depends on context. Here, the deputy judge had found a continuing pattern of conduct by Peter that David should inherit the farm and it was not helpful to break that pattern down into discrete elements. Peter's assurances, objectively assessed, were intended to be relied on. The deputy judge was also sensitive to the unusual circumstances of the case (you'll need your hanky for this one) –

> The deputy judge heard a lot of evidence about two countrymen leading lives that it may be difficult for many city-dwellers to imagine – taciturn and undemonstrative men committed to a life of hard and unrelenting physical work, by day and sometimes by night, largely unrelieved by recreation or female company.

Proprietary estoppel was recognised and David Thorner was awarded the farm. *Thorner v Major* was followed in *Thompson v Foy* (2009).

Q: So a claimant can rely on an assurance that property will be left to him in a will?

A: Yes. In *Re Basham (decd)* (1986) an assurance by the stepfather that he would leave his property, including his house, in his will to his stepdaughter was a valid assurance even though he was promising a future interest. Interesting observations on this decision have been made in *Thorner v Major* and *MacDonald v Frost* (2009). In *Taylor v Dickens* (1998), Mrs Parker had promised her gardener that she would leave her property to him in her will. On the basis of this promise the gardener worked without payment. Mrs Parker made a will as promised, but subsequently changed it, leaving her property to her carer, Mrs Bosher, and Mrs Bosher's husband. She didn't inform the gardener of her actions. It was held that because Mrs Parker had not promised not to change her will, the gardener could not claim the property through proprietary estoppel.

Q: That's surely unconscionable, isn't it? You shouldn't be allowed to promise something and then withdraw the promise without informing the other party that you have done so.

A: I agree. Although it is always possible to revoke a will, it becomes unconscionable to do so once the claimant has acted in reliance on it and is disadvantaged by its revocation. This case was strongly criticised, and in *Gillett v Holt* (2001) it was held that you did not also have to promise not to revoke the will. In this case, Mr Gillett had been assured that he would inherit Mr Holt's farm. Although Mr Holt had made a will to this effect, he had subsequently revoked it. Mr Gillett still succeeded in his claim. In *Sutcliffe v Lloyd* (2007), following an agreement with Mr Lloyd, Mr Sutcliffe understood that he would receive half the profits from a business venture. It was held that:

> The law requires that the promisor should make clear not that the promise cannot be revoked but that it will not be revoked.

The crucial element was whether the landowner had encouraged the belief that he would not withdraw from the agreement. In the case the defendants had persistently given Mr Sutcliffe assurances by words and conduct that he was to enjoy a share in the profit from the development and 'so protractedly watched him act to his detriment in reliance upon them that they thereby made clear that their assurances would not be revoked'.

It also suffices if the landowner deliberately says or does nothing when the claimant behaves as though he has rights over the land: see *Ramsden v Dyson*.

Q: *Does it have to be an assurance of a definite and quantifiable interest in the land?*

A: The terms used can be imprecise as long as some type of interest in the land is promised and the land is identifiable although this identification does not have to be precise. In *Yeoman's Row Management Ltd v Cobbe* (2008) there was an oral agreement between Yeomans and Mr Cobbe that if Mr Cobbe obtained planning permission to develop a property owned by Yeomans, Yeomans would sell it to him. Mr Cobbe said he spent £197,000 obtaining planning permission, after which Yeomans refused to sell to him at the previously proposed price. In the House of Lords Lord Scott stated that Mr Cobbe had to have an expectation of 'a certain interest in land'. Mr Cobbe had only an expectation that, once he had got planning permission, the remaining terms of the contract would be negotiated, for example, the time for completion of development and financial arrangements. An expectation that depended on a successful negotiation was not a certain interest in land and proprietary estoppel was not found. *Yeoman's Row Management Ltd v Cobbe* is an important case and is discussed in full at the end of this chapter. In *Thorner v Major* assurances given to the claimant, David, had to relate to identified property owned or about to be owned by the defendant, Peter. In the case the extent of the farm under dispute had changed over time as developments took place and tenancies changed but both parties would have understood that the assurance related to the extent of the farm at Peter's death. This was no different to the position under the Wills Act 1837 if the farm had been left to David in Peter's will. Instances where the landowner has given general assurances that the claimant can stay in a house for as long as he or she wants will suffice: see *Greasley v Cooke* (1980). Very vague phrases such as a promise of 'financial security' may not be enough: see *Layton v Martin*.

Q: *What happens if the promised property has been sold, for example, when the claimant goes to court?*

A: In *Thorner v Major* it was confirmed that proprietary estoppel looks backward from the time when the promise falls to be met. The words of Hoffmann LJ in *Walton v Walton* (unreported 1994) were quoted:

> because it [equitable estoppel] does not look forward into the future and guess what might happen. It looks backwards from the moment when the promise falls due to be performed and asks whether, in the circumstances which have actually happened, it would be unconscionable for the promise not to be kept.

In *Thorner v Major*, if the farm had been sold in Peter's lifetime, Lord Neuberger said that the remedy would have been a matter for the court determined by looking at all the facts as had happened in *Gillett v Holt*.

Box A2 Reliance on the assurance or representation

Reliance means a change of position by the claimant induced by the assurance or representation.

Q: *What acts have been recognised as a change of position?*

A: Spending money on the land is the traditional way of proving a change of position. In *Inwards v Baker* (1965) the son had built a bungalow on his father's land in the expectation that he, the son, could live there for as long as he wanted. The expenditure, however, must relate to building on the land or to substantially improving it. Spending money on minor repairs and keeping the property in a useable state will not be seen as sufficient: see *Appleby v Cowley* (1982).

Q: *Do you always have to spend money to prove a change of position?*

A: No. Other acts that have shown a change of position include the following. In *Re Basham (decd)* a stepdaughter and her husband had moved in with her stepfather to care for him in the expectation that they would inherit his property. In *Gillett v Holt* working for lower wages had counted as a change of position. In this case Mr Gillett had also forgone career opportunities and the opportunity to buy his own home on the assurance that he would inherit Mr Holt's farm. In *Maharaj v Chand* (1986) giving up a flat was seen as a change of position.

Q: *Do the acts carried out in reliance on the assurance have to be detrimental to the claimant?*

A: Not as such. The actual detriment arises when the landowner withdraws the assurance. A change of position must be such that if the assurance was withdrawn the claimant would suffer detriment. Look at this in an example. In *Maharaj v Chand* a woman gave up her own flat to move in with her partner, who had previously assured her that she would always have a home with him. Moving in with her partner was a change of position, but it wasn't detrimental to the woman. However, the act of giving up her flat would be detrimental to her if the assurance were withdrawn, which it was.

Q: *Does the landowner have to know that the claimant is acting on his assurance or relying on the fact that the landowner is standing by and saying nothing?*

A: The landowner must be aware of the claimant's reliance, although he doesn't necessarily have to have actual knowledge of it. It's also sufficient that the landowner should have realised that the claimant might act on his representation or failure to do something. If the landowner has no idea a claimant is relying on his assurance, there is nothing unconscionable in his behaviour if he refuses to acknowledge the claimant's expectation.

Q: *Must there be a direct link between the assurance or the representation and the change of position?*

A: Yes. In *Stillwell v Simpson* (1983) the claimant had carried out repairs to the house because he was a jobbing builder and because the landowner could not afford to do so. He failed in his claim because he couldn't define what he had been led to believe he might receive. There was no causal link between an assurance and a change in position. In *MacDonald v Frost* there was no clear assurance of a share in the property and the claimed change in position was not linked to the alleged assurance. The claimant must believe that by changing his position he will acquire the promised interest in the land: see *Gillett v Holt*.

Q: *Isn't that belief difficult to prove?*

A: It is, but the courts take a common sense approach. The courts will presume that an act is in reliance on an assurance if a reasonable person would have acted likewise.

Q: *What happens if there are several reasons why a person has changed his or her position?*

A: In *Campbell v Griffin* (2001) Mr Campbell had looked after an elderly couple for a number of years in the house where he was a lodger. They had assured him that he would have a home for life. Although the husband had made a will leaving Mr Campbell a life interest in the house, the wife had been unable to change her will through mental illness. This meant that the house passed to others when she died. Mr Campbell made a claim based on proprietary estoppel. His claim failed in the County Court because it was decided that he had acted out of friendship and responsibility, not in reliance on the assurance from the couple. Mr Campbell appealed. The Court of Appeal held that he had done much more than would have been expected in the circumstances, and it was highly probable that the assurances of the couple had influenced his behaviour. The assurance did not have to be the sole factor that caused him to act and he was awarded a charge over the house.

Q: *If a woman leaves her husband or partner for another man based on an assurance that she'll always be able to live in his house, is this a recognised change of position?*

A: In *Maharaj v Chand* a woman had given up her flat to move in with her partner, having been assured that she would have a permanent home for herself and her children. She had also supported his application to the housing authority for the house they were living in. When he tried to evict her, she succeeded in a claim based on proprietary estoppel. Conversely, in *Coombes v Smith* (1986) a married woman had left her husband to live with a new partner. Although her new partner had assured her that she would always have accommodation, when the relationship broke down she was evicted. She failed in a claim based on proprietary estoppel.

Q: *What's the difference between the* Coombes *case and the* Maharaj *case?*

A: In the *Maharaj* case, the woman had given up a flat and supported her partner's application to the housing authority because she thought she was to have a permanent home. In the *Coombes* case, the woman had changed her position and left her husband because she wanted to live with her partner, not because of the expectation of any interest in the house.

Q: *Is it fair to differentiate like this when a woman will usually find herself homeless if a previous assurance by her partner that she would always have a home with him is withdrawn, whatever the reason for moving in with him?*

A: This is an intractable problem. You could argue that an informal promise uttered in the context of a new relationship is far removed from the usual degree of formality required to create an interest in land. You could also argue that relationship breakdowns are part of life and people should take precautions against such eventualities, preferably by visiting a solicitor. The difficulty is in determining to what extent, and in what circumstances, you should be able to rely on these informal promises to acquire an interest in property, if at all.

Box A3 Detriment

Detriment occurs when the assurance or representation is withdrawn, and the claimant who has changed his position in reliance on the assurance is disadvantaged. Until then the claimant has no reason to complain.

In *Henry v Henry* (2010), a Privy Council case, Sir Jonathan Parker said:

> ... the inquiry as to detriment falls to be made in the context of the nature and quality of the particular conduct or course of conduct adopted by the claimant in reliance on those assurances. Thus, notwithstanding that reliance and detriment may, in the abstract, be regarded as different concepts, in applying the principles of proprietary estoppel they are often intertwined.

Box A4 Unconscionability

Finally, the overall requirement for proprietary estoppel is unconscionability. It must be unconscionable for the landowner to be allowed to rely on his strict legal rights.

Q: *How do you prove unconscionability?*

A: You do this by looking at all the circumstances of the parties. Sometimes a claimant has benefited from his change of position more than he has been disadvantaged by it. The courts will balance the advantages and disadvantages of the case and decide whether it would be unconscionable to deny the claimant a remedy. In *Watts and Ready v Storey* (1984) the benefit of rent-free accommodation and additional benefits the claimant received under the will more than compensated for any disadvantage suffered by him in having to move from his own rent-protected flat.

Sledmore v Dalby (1996) is another case where the court took the view that the detriment suffered by the claimant had already been adequately compensated for, and refused to award a remedy.

Mr and Mrs Sledmore purchased a house in 1965. Mr Dalby and his wife, the daughter of the Sledmores, moved into the house and paid rent. The following events occurred.

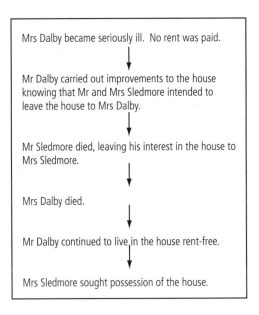

Mrs Dalby became seriously ill. No rent was paid.

↓

Mr Dalby carried out improvements to the house knowing that Mr and Mrs Sledmore intended to leave the house to Mrs Dalby.

↓

Mr Sledmore died, leaving his interest in the house to Mrs Sledmore.

↓

Mrs Dalby died.

↓

Mr Dalby continued to live in the house rent-free.

↓

Mrs Sledmore sought possession of the house.

Although he didn't live there permanently, Mr Dalby refused to move out and claimed proprietary estoppel on the basis that he had carried out work on the house and had expected to be able to live there for his lifetime. However, the court gave possession of the house to Mrs Sledmore.

Q: *Why was Mrs Sledmore awarded possession?*

A: It was decided that Mr Dalby had enjoyed rent-free accommodation for 20 years and this would compensate for the detriment that he had suffered. There had to be proportionality between the disadvantage suffered by the claimant and any interest awarded. Mr Dalby's improvement work on the house was balanced by the rent-free accommodation. The case was also decided in Mrs Sledmore's favour as her own house was in need of repair, she was in receipt of social security benefits and wanted the house to live in herself and sell. Mr Dalby, though, was in employment, and did not live in the house permanently.

Q: *Why should the circumstances of Mrs Sledmore have anything at all to do with the remedy the court decides to award?*

A: Because the underlying basis of proprietary estoppel is unconscionability, both the circumstances and the conduct of the landowner and the claimant can also be taken into account. In *Pascoe v Turner* (1979) the court took into account the relative wealth of the parties and the fact that the landowner might continue to harass the claimant. In *Brynowen Estates Ltd v Bourne* (1981) Mrs Bourne had disturbed and annoyed the occupants of Brynowen Estates Holiday Centre by driving around late at night hooting her car horn, and so she was denied a claim. Another case that shows the court's ability to take conduct into account is *Crabb v Arun District Council* (1976). Mr Crabb had sold off part of his land, relying on an assurance from the Council that he would be able to pay for a right of way over the Council's land to obtain access to the land that he still owned. The Council then refused to grant him the right of way and behaved very high-handedly towards him over the following four years. The court awarded him his right of way, technically called an easement. Because the Council had behaved high-handedly towards him, the court determined that he no longer had to pay for this right.

In *Jennings v Rice* (2002) Mrs Royle had promised Mr Jennings that she would leave him the house and furniture worth £435,000 in her will. She died without having made a will. Mr Jennings claimed the entire estate worth £1.3 million, but was actually awarded £200,000. The court emphasised the idea of proportionality, the need to take into account all the circumstances of the case and unconscionability. *Lester v Woodgate* (2010) concerned an easement of a right of way over a pathway which had been expressly granted in 1980. The predecessor in title to the defendant, Mr Mees, had removed the pathway and built a car parking space on it making the right of way unusable. The claimant's predecessor in title, Mr Chitty, had not complained about this interference with his right of way. The claimant in the case was now trying to enforce the right of way. The defendant claimed estoppel or laches. The court held that the lack of objection to the destruction of the pathway made it unconscionable for the previous owners of the dominant land, and therefore now the claimant, to try and enforce the right.

Q: *So this was a case where the defendant wasn't acquiring a right over the claimant's property but rather a case where the claimant's conduct meant he was estopped from enforcing his legal rights?*

A: Yes. This was estoppel by acquiescence.

The following are cases where unconscionability was not found.

In *Uglow v Uglow* (2004) Uncle Percy had promised the family farm 'Treludick' to Richard Uglow if Richard left his own family farming partnership and joined a new farming partnership with Uncle Percy. When Uncle Percy died, Richard received only a quarter share of the residuary estate and a legacy of £1,000 and so claimed the farmhouse under proprietary estoppel. (What is it about farmers and proprietary estoppel?) It was held that Uncle Percy's words meant that Richard would inherit the farmhouse if all went well with the partnership, but the court could take into account subsequent events. In the event the partnership had failed but Uncle Percy had made a tenancy agreement which allowed Richard to farm all but about 60 acres of Treludick on his own account. This became a protected tenancy transmissible when Richard died. Having 'looked at the entire matter broadly and in the round' it was not unconscionable for Uncle Percy to leave the farmhouse to someone other than Richard, given the tenancy agreement already made in favour of Richard. In *McGuane v Welch* (2008) Mr Welch had been encouraged by Mr McGuane that he, Mr Welch, would be the owner of a lease. The court did not award the lease to Mr Welch because Mr McGuane's refusal to transfer the lease was not unconscionable for the following reasons given by Lord Justice Mummery.

> Mr McGuane did not have the benefit of independent legal advice when he agreed to dispose of the Lease; the price paid for it was substantially less than its estimated market value; and the agreement was implemented in documents prepared by solicitors who, although acting as solicitors for him as vendor, received and acted on inaccurate instructions from Mr Welch as purchaser.

Mr Welch received financial compensation for his loss instead.

Q: *So can proprietary estoppel enter into a commercial transaction?*

A: Apparently so. In *Scottish & Newcastle plc v Lancashire Mortgage Corporation Ltd* (2007) Lancashire Mortgage Corporation (LMC) had taken a legal mortgage, called a legal charge, over property. It had registered this legal charge under the then Land Registration Act 1925. Scottish & Newcastle (S & N) had registered its own legal charge over the same property two days earlier. As priority of a legal charge depends on its date of first registration, not its date of creation, S & N claimed that its charge had priority. However, S & N had stood by (passive acquiescence), knowing that LMC thought there was an understanding between them that LMC would have priority regardless of the order of registration. LMC had acted to its detriment by lending money to the borrower, who paid off his debt to S & N with part of the money. S & N was estopped from claiming that its legal charge had priority.

Although the following case was an appeal against a summary judgment only, it illustrates many of the elements of proprietary estoppel. In *Clarke v Meadus* (2010) Mrs Clarke was claiming sole beneficial ownership of a house, 'Bonavista', under either proprietary estoppel or a constructive trust. Under an express declaration of trust she was joint owner of the property with her mother. She had been promised that she would inherit the house on her mother's death and based on the promise had moved in to help care for her mother. Her mother then changed her will leaving her 50% share to Mrs Clarke's sister instead. Mrs Clarke claimed detriment including moving her family and business, incurring a loss on the sale of her house, caring for her mother without payment, making improvements to the property, contributing to the lending secured on the property and using her own money to purchase adjoining land which would enhance the value of 'Bonavista'.

The result was a successful appeal against a summary judgment against Mrs Clarke and the following principles were stated:

> Even though there had been an express declaration of the beneficial interest in the house in the trust deed, the express trust could be overridden if events showed that the elements of proprietary estoppel were satisfied.
> When looking at reliance, rather than ask what Mrs Clarke would have done had the representation never been made, another question to ask was what she would have done if she had been told that the promise was not going to be kept. If Mrs Clarke had been told that she would not inherit the house, she would not have sold her own house to move in with her parents.

The court does not have to wait until the time when the promise falls due to give effect to proprietary estoppel. This can be when the promisor breaks his promise or indicates that he intends to do so, here by Mrs Clarke's mother changing her will.

A factor in a resolution of the case is the closeness of the facts to a 'bargain': *Jennings v Rice* and here there had been a 'bargain' made.

And let's end with *Suggitt v Suggitt* (2012) which is another of the cases you will come across about sons who have been promised the family farm in their father's will, who then work on the land during their lifetime only to discover that the promised farms have been left elsewhere in their father's will. This case was a father's repeated promises to his son that he would inherit the farm, the son going to college to study farming (albeit not completing the course), and then returning to work on the farm in reliance on the promise (although the farm was now being managed by others) and the promise not honoured. What was noteworthy about the case was the apparently weak nature of the evidence required to support the son's claim. This is shown by what was said by the first instance judge:

> John's own evidence as to the promises or assurances made by his father is opaque to say the least.

and

> But all in all it (the work done on the farm) was nothing like the sort of work done in *Thorner v Major*. John's problem is he wants the maximum for the minimum. The work he did was barely, vaguely and weakly particularised …

The Court of Appeal said it would only interfere with the first instance judgment if the decision was perverse or clearly wrong and repeated the following sentence from that judgment:

> John had positioned his whole life on the basis of the assurances given to him and which were reasonably believed by him.

So, son John received the farm land and a house to live in worth some £3.3 million. Such a decision must gladden the hearts of farmers' sons.

Summary of the elements of proprietary estoppel

The claimant must have relied on a representation or an assurance which has been subsequently withdrawn by the landowner, causing the claimant detriment. The overall requirement of unconscionability must then be satisfied. The elements of reliance, assurance, detriment and unconscionability are inextricably linked.

The nature of the interest

Q: *If you meet the requirements of assurance, reliance, detriment and unconscionabilty, what right do you have?*
A: You have an equity.

Q: *Is an equity the same as equitable interest?*
A: No. It falls halfway between a personal right and an equitable proprietary right. A personal right can be enforced only between the original parties. An equitable proprietary right gives a right in the land itself which is capable of binding a purchaser of the land that the equitable right is over. For some time the

status of an equity by estoppel was unclear, on the basis that it was unfair that a purchaser could be bound by a right that was not a full equitable right. *Inwards v Baker* suggested, obiter dicta, that an equity by estoppel could bind a purchaser with notice. In *E R Ives Investment Ltd v High* (1967) it was established that an equity by estoppel could bind a purchaser who took the land with express notice of the equity. The position in registered land has now been clarified by the Land Registration Act 2002. Section 116 of the Act states that an equity by estoppel is an interest that can bind third parties, confirmed in *Halifax Plc v Curry Popeck* (2008).

Q: *When does the equity arise?*

A: An equity arises as an interest in land when a landowner has made a representation or an assurance and the claimant has acted in reliance on it. The equity is sometimes referred to as an inchoate equity at this stage, which means that the nature of the interest that the claimant is ultimately awarded is not yet clear.

Q: *What right does this equity give to a claimant?*

A: The claimant is allowed to apply to the court to claim his promised right in the land and the landowner will be stopped from denying the claim.

The range of remedies available to satisfy a claim

> **Box B**
>
> THE RANGE OF REMEDIES AVAILABLE TO SATISFY A CLAIM
>
> **1.** Grant of the freehold estate
>
> **2.** Grant of a lease
>
> **3.** Grant of a licence
>
> **4.** Grant of an easement or right of access
>
> **5.** Monetary compensation
>
> **6.** Combined remedies

It has been held that the court must award the 'minimum equity to do justice to the plaintiff': see *Crabb v Arun District Council* and *McGuane v Welch*. In doing so, the court has a wide discretion in determining the remedy, taking into account proportionality and all the circumstances of the case. In *Henry v Henry* it was said by Sir Jonathan Parker that 'proportionality lies at the heart of the doctrine of proprietary estoppel and permeates its every application'. *Suggitt v Suggitt* (2012) confirmed *Jennings v Rice* when Lady Justice Arden said:

> But if the claimant's expectations are uncertain, or extravagant, or out of all proportion to the detriment which the claimant has suffered, the court can and should recognise that the claimant's equity should be satisfied in another (and generally more limited) way.

In some claims the expectation may be awarded in full. In other cases it may not be practical or possible to award the expected interest in the land. Compensation may also be seen as a satisfactory solution. The following are some of the most cited cases which illustrate this discretion.

Box B1 | ### Grant of the freehold estate

In *Dillwyn v Llewellyn* the son had built a house on land owned by his father in the expectation that the land would then be his. The court awarded the transfer of the land to the son. In *Pascoe v Turner* a woman was awarded ownership of her partner's house having spent a substantial amount of money on furnishing and decoration. This reflected her expectation, but the court also took into account her financial position and the possibility that her partner would continue to aggravate her unless there was a clean break. In *Thorner v Major* David Thorner was awarded the promised farm.

Box B2 | ### Grant of a lease

In *Griffiths v Williams* (1977) the court awarded the claimant a long lease. The claimant was forbidden to assign the lease to anyone else, and the rent was kept sufficiently low to ensure that the lease would not receive the protection of the Rent Acts. These measures ensured she would literally only have the lease for her lifetime, which was what she had been originally promised.

Box B3 | ### Grant of a licence

In *Inwards v Baker* a son had built a bungalow on his father's land in the expectation that he could live there for as long as he wanted. The court granted the son a licence, or permission, to live there for the rest of his life. A similar result was reached in *Greasley v Cooke,* where the maid had looked after the members of a family in the expectation that she would have a home with them for life.

Box B4 | ### Grant of an easement or right of access

In *Crabb v Arun District Council* Mr Crabb was granted a right of way over the Council's land after he had sold his own land, following the Council's assurance that it would grant him a right of way over its land to obtain access to the land he still retained. The remedy reflected the Council's assurance.

In *Bexley London BC v Maison Maurice Ltd* (2006) Maison Maurice was led by the Council to believe that it could construct a new safer right of access to Butler's Yard from the road to replace an existing right of access. It was led to believe that it could do this without additional payment other than the Council's costs, the costs of the works and consulting with the Works and Contracts Department. Some years later the Council stated that it owned the half metre strip of land between Butler's Yard and the road. It demanded over £1 million from Maison Maurice to cross the strip as a permanent access if planning permission for development of Butler's Yard was obtained.

Q: *Is that where using the phrase 'a ransom strip of land' is appropriate?*
A: Yes. The Bexley Chronicle had a field day with this case and ran a nice front page saying in relation to the ransom strip 'A million pounds won't get you much

in Bexleyheath!' Maison Maurice argued estoppel. The Council argued that it was carrying out its statutory duty and this could not be interfered with by a claim of estoppel. Furthermore, the Council claimed that it would be acting outside its powers if it granted Maison Maurice a right of way in the form of an easement over the strip of land. The court confirmed that estoppel cannot stop or hinder (fetter in legal terms) a public body carrying out its statutory duties, nor could it allow a public body to act outside its powers – ultra vires. However, the Council had acted unconscionably by letting Maison Maurice believe that it could have permanent access over the land. It was now estopped from denying Maison Maurice this access which it could legally grant either by a right of access under the Highways Act 1980 or by means of a licence.

Box B5 | Monetary compensation

In some cases it may be more appropriate to award monetary compensation. In *Dodsworth v Dodsworth* (1973) a couple had spent money improving a property in the expectation they would live there for as long as they wanted. When possession of the property was sought, the court awarded monetary compensation to the value of the cost of the improvements and their labour costs. This was because to grant them a right of occupation would lead to a greater interest than ever contemplated by the parties because of the effect of the Settled Land Act 1925. In *McGuane v Welch* it was held that there was a wide judicial discretion when determining how an equity by estoppel should be satisfied. The court did not have to give effect to the bargain between the parties (not least because Mr Welch had behaved unconscionably) but had to look for the minimum equity to do justice. Mr Welch's loss could be quantified in financial terms. Mr McGuane kept the property subject to paying back Mr Welch for his expenditure on the property.

Box B6 | Combined remedies

The courts have the option of combined remedies in order to achieve a just outcome. For instance, in *Gillett v Holt* Mr Gillett had worked for a low wage and had forgone career opportunities on the assurance that he would inherit property from Mr Holt. Even though Mr Holt was still alive, Mr Gillett was awarded ownership of a farm and compensation, as Mr Holt had changed his will to exclude Mr Gillett.

The protection of estoppel rights

> **Box C**
>
> THE PROTECTION OF ESTOPPEL RIGHTS
>
> Look at either:
>
> **1.** Unregistered land
>
> or look at
>
> **2.** Registered land
>
> i) Dealings which must be completed by registration
>
> ii) Interests which override a registered disposition
>
> iii) Inteests entered as a notice or protected by a restriction

The final aspect to consider is whether a purchaser is bound by an equity by estoppel that affects the land that he has bought. In the example that follows, Peter would want to know whether he was bound by an equity by estoppel acquired by Emma over Greenacres.

Sold to Peter ← Greenacres ← Emma has acquired an equity by estoppel over Greenacres

Box C1 Unregistered land

Q: *What happens in unregistered land if Emma has been successful in a claim based on proprietary estoppel and the court has already awarded her a remedy before Peter buys Greenacres?*

A: If necessary, the successful claimant, Emma, must protect whatever interest in the land she has been awarded in the usual way in unregistered land before Peter buys Greenacres.

Q: *What happens if Emma has acquired an equity by estoppel but has not asked the court to determine a remedy before Peter buys Greenacres?*

A: An equity by estoppel cannot be entered as a land charge on the Land Charges Register under the Land Charges Act 1972. However, an equity by estoppel has been held to be sufficiently similar to an equitable interest to be covered by the same pre-1926 rule that relates to equitable interests also not able to be entered as a land charge. This rule, known as the doctrine of notice, states that equitable interests bind everyone except a *bona fide* purchaser of a legal estate for value without notice of the equitable interest. In the example given, we can assume that Peter is *bona fide*. He purchased the legal estate of Greenacres and gave money, so he is a purchaser for value of the legal estate. Whether he is bound by the equity now depends on whether he has notice of it. Actual notice is notice that Peter actually has. Constructive notice is notice that he should have from a physical inspection of the land and from inspecting the documentation to the land. Imputed notice is what his solicitor or agent knew and should have told him. This means that there is every chance that Peter will have notice of Emma's equity by estoppel and will be bound by it when he buys Greenacres. He will therefore be bound by any remedy that the court awards Emma in satisfaction of her claim. If the court decides that Emma should own Greenacres, Peter will have to transfer the land back to her, regardless of the fact that he paid for it.

If Peter can prove he did not have notice of Emma's equity, he will not be bound by it.

Q: *If Peter doesn't know about Emma's equity and it is therefore not binding on him, is it still worth her going to court to plead that she has an equity by estoppel?*

A: Yes, but her remedy will be limited to a personal right of compensation from the former owner of Greenacres who made the assurance to her. Peter would still not be bound by her equity.

Box C2   Registered land

Q: *What happens in registered land if Emma has been successful in a claim based on proprietary estoppel and the court has already awarded her a remedy before Peter buys Greenacres?*

A: If necessary, the successful claimant, Emma, must protect whatever interest in the land she has been awarded in the usual way before Peter buys Greenacres.

Q: *What happens if Emma has acquired an equity by estoppel but has not asked the court to determine a remedy before Peter buys Greenacres?*

A: She will be governed by the Land Registration Act 2002. There are three categories which determine how interests are protected in registered land. They are:

▷ Dealings which must be completed by registration under section 27 of the Land Registration Act 2002 (Box C point 2i).
▷ Interests in Schedule 3 to the Land Registration Act 2002 which override a registered disposition (Box C point 2ii).
▷ Interests entered as a notice under section 34 of the Land Registration Act 2002 and interests protected by a restriction under section 43 of the Land Registration Act 2002 (Box C point 2iii).

A purchaser for valuable consideration will take the land subject to the interests in these three categories.

Emma must establish how her equity should be protected in registered land.

Box C2i   Dealings which must be completed by registration

Acquiring an equity by estoppel is not a dealing that must be completed by registration under section 27 of the Land Registration Act 2002.

Box C2ii   Interests which override a registered disposition

These are interests that are binding on everyone including a purchaser.
Paragraph 2 of Schedule 3 to the Land Registration Act 2002 states that an interest in this category will override (take priority over) a registered disposition if:

1. The person claiming the right has a proprietary interest in the land.

and

2. That person is in actual occupation at the time of the disposition.

However, the interest will not be an overriding interest if

1. When the land was purchased the fact that the person was in actual occupation was not obvious on a reasonably careful inspection of the land and the purchaser didn't know about the interest

or

2. The person in actual occupation claiming the interest did not tell the purchaser about his interest in the land if asked, and it would have been reasonable for them to have done so.

Paragraph 2 of Schedule 3 is essentially saying that a person who is relying on the fact that he or she is living in the property to claim priority over a purchaser must make it obvious that he or she lives in the property. If asked, he or she should tell any purchaser about his or her interest if it would be reasonable to do so. If the purchaser still chooses to buy the property, he deserves to be bound by the rights of anybody who lives there.

You can apply this to the example:

1. Emma has an equity by estoppel. This is a proprietary interest in land.
2. Providing Emma is in actual occupation of Greenacres when it is sold to Peter, her equity will bind Peter.

In this case, the remedy that the court awards Emma will be binding on Peter. If the court decides that Emma should own Greenacres, Peter will have to transfer the land back to her, regardless of the fact that he paid for it.

However, her equity will not bind Peter if:

1. Emma's actual occupation would not have been obvious to Peter if he had made a reasonably careful inspection of the land, and he didn't know about her interest;

or

2. If asked, Emma didn't disclose her interest to Peter when it would have been reasonable for her to have done so.

In this case, Peter can take Greenacres free from any claim by Emma.

Box C2iii Interests entered as a notice or protected by a restriction

These are interests which are entered as a notice on the Charges Register of the land or protected by a restriction on the Proprietorship Register of the land which the right is over in order to bind a purchaser.

An equity by estoppel should be entered as a notice on the Charges Register of the land which the equity is over under section 34 of the Land Registration Act 2002. In our example, Emma should enter her equity as a notice on the Charges Register of Greenacres.

Q: *How likely would she be to do this?*

A: Extremely unlikely. However, she will still be protected if her interest overrides by virtue of her occupation in Box C point 2ii.

Q: *What would happen if Emma were claiming a right by estoppel over Greenacres but wasn't living there, so her equity could not be protected by her actual occupation?*

A: If Emma were claiming only a right of way over Greenacres, for example, her interest would not be protected by her occupation. It would not be binding on Peter unless she had protected it by means of a notice under section 34, which would be unlikely.

Q: *Is that fair on Emma?*

A: Probably not but this is what happens when you allow interests in land to be created informally.

Q: *If her equity did not bind Peter because it was not entered as a notice, and she was not in actual occupation either, is it still worth her going to court to plead that she has an equity by estoppel?*

A: Yes, but her remedy will be limited to a personal right of compensation from the former owner of Greenacres who made the assurance to her. Peter will still not be bound by her equity.

Q: *Can you overreach an equity by estoppel?*

A: Although this point has never been decided, the view of the court appears to be that it can, provided the equity would have given rise to an interest that was capable of being overreached. This means the interest must be a beneficial interest in land: see *Birmingham Midshires Mortgage Services Ltd v Sabherwal* (2000).

The differences between a proprietary estoppel-based claim and a constructive trust-based claim

The requirements of a constructive trust are essentially an express or implied agreement followed by reliance on that agreement, followed by a refusal to honour the agreement. These requirements are certainly very similar to those for estoppel and, in many cases, you can plead both remedies. If you cannot meet the requirements for a constructive trust, you should always consider the remedy of proprietary estoppel in cases where ownership of the family home is in dispute. In *Grant v Edwards* (1986) Lord Browne-Wilkinson vc stated that the two principles rested on the same foundation. In *Yaxley v Gotts* (2000) Lord Justice Robert Walker stated that while there were differences, a constructive trust was closely akin to, if not indistinguishable from, proprietary estoppel. The same was stated in *Oxley v Hiscock* (2004), and in *Scottish & Newcastle plc v Lancashire Mortgage Corporation Ltd* it was held that whether you used the label constructive trust or proprietary estoppel the effect was the same. There are differences though, and these differences have been commented on in *Stack v Dowden* (2007), *Lalani v Crump Holdings Ltd* (2007) and *Yeoman's Row Management Ltd v Cobbe*. The main ones are given in the table that follows.

THE DIFFERENCES BETWEEN A PROPRIETARY ESTOPPEL-BASED CLAIM AND A CONSTRUCTIVE TRUST-BASED CLAIM	

CONSTRUCTIVE TRUST	PROPRIETARY ESTOPPEL
There is an express or implied agreement	There is an express or implied agreement or a mistaken belief as to the claimant's rights
The agreement is to share beneficial ownership in land	
An equitable interest arises and is subject to the normal rules relating to equitable interests in land	The agreement can relate to rights other than beneficial ownership of the family home, for example a right to live in a property for life, or a right of way
The equitable interest gives effect to the express or implied agreement	An equity arises which gives the claimant the right to ask the court for a remedy
The remedy is an equitable interest in land	The remedy may not fully reflect the nature or the extent of the assurance
	The remedy is not restricted to an interest in land but can include compensation

A question on proprietary estoppel

This example is intended to illustrate how to use the Boxes in this chapter to analyse the legal position. If you are using this method in undergraduate law exam questions, you will need to include statutory and case authority and detailed discussion of the various points of law. This information is found both in the text and from other sources.

> For many years Anneka had nursed her elderly uncle, Tom, having given up secure accommodation and her own work in order to do so. She had lived with him in his house, Redacres, as he had needed constant attention. Anneka had been rather worried about what would happen to her when Tom died, but he had always said that he had made a will leaving her the house, Redacres, and that she need not worry.
>
> Two years ago, the roof of Redacres was damaged in high winds and Anneka agreed to pay for the repairs using a small sum of money that she had inherited from her father. Tom died last month and Anneka has discovered that Tom had sold Redacres to Peter the day before he died. Advise Anneka and Peter.

You need to establish whether Anneka can claim an interest in Redacres and, if she can, whether it is binding on Peter. Although at first glance this appears to be a question about proprietary estoppel, you must eliminate any other avenues of discussion. Tom did not contract to sell Anneka any interest in Redacres. Any such contract must meet section 2 of the Law of Property (Miscellaneous Provisions) Act 1989 and must be in writing and signed by or on behalf of both Tom and Anneka. There is no evidence of any such contract here. There is no express declaration of trust by Tom in Anneka's favour, as this should have been in writing and signed by Tom in order to meet section 53(1)(b) of the Law of Property Act 1925. There is no resulting trust, as Anneka did not contribute either directly or indirectly to the purchase price of Redacres. There is no constructive trust as there was no express or implied agreement regarding the immediate beneficial ownership of Redacres. You now need to work through the requirements of proprietary estoppel.

Box A   The elements of proprietary estoppel
You must meet all the conditions here.

A1 An assurance or representation
Tom had always told Anneka that he would leave Redacres to her in his will. This is an assurance. It does not matter that this is a promise of future property in a will: see *Thorner v Major*. You can tick this box.

A2 Reliance on the assurance or representation
Anneka must prove reliance in the form of a change of position. She has given up secure accommodation and her own work and has looked after Tom for many years. Although these acts are recognised as a change of position, for example as in *Maharaj v Chand* and *Re Basham (decd)*, there has to be a causal link between the assurance and the change of position: see *Gillett v Holt* and *Stillwell v Simpson*. You do not know when Tom told Anneka that he would leave Redacres to her in his will, only that he had *always* said he would do so. If Anneka had moved in to look after Tom because he had assured her that she would inherit Redacres, her change of position is linked directly to Tom's assurance. If Anneka had moved in before Tom told her that she would inherit Redacres, there is no causal link, as Tom told her about the inheritance only after her change of position. In this case Anneka would have to rely on her expenditure on the roof to prove a change of position linked to Tom's assurance. This may not be possible, as expenditure on minor repairs is unlikely to constitute a sufficient change of position: see *Appleby v Cowley*. You could also argue that Anneka spent the money to keep the house watertight, or simply because Tom couldn't afford to repair the roof, not necessarily in anticipation of her expected inheritance: see *Stillwell v Simpson*. If there is no causal link, or her change of position is not recognised, this box will not be ticked and Anneka will have no claim based on proprietary estoppel. However, assuming Anneka moved in with Tom because he had assured her she would inherit Redacres, this box can be ticked.

A3 Detriment
Tom has withdrawn his assurance by selling Redacres to Peter and Anneka has been disadvantaged as she has not inherited Redacres.

A4 Unconscionability
When looking at unconscionability, the court will look at all the circumstances of the case and the conduct of the parties: see *Jennings v Rice* and *Lalani v Crump Holdings Ltd*. Any disadvantage that Anneka may have suffered by giving up her secure accommodation may well have been compensated for by her long-term free accommodation with Tom: see *Watts and Ready v Storey*. Even so, her position is strengthened by the fact that she also gave up her work. The withdrawal of the promise seems to be unconscionable, given Anneka's change of position and her long-term care of Tom.

Summary of Box A
Assuming the causal link is proved, Anneka appears to satisfy the requirements for a proprietary estoppel-based claim. Anneka will have an equity by estoppel.

Box B The range of remedies available to satisfy a claim
Clearly Anneka would ask the court to give effect to the assurance made by Tom that she would own Redacres following his death: see *Re Basham (decd)*. An

alternative remedy would be accommodation for life: see *Inwards v Baker*. This would not totally reflect Tom's assurance, as he promised the house to Anneka unconditionally, not just for her lifetime, but it may be more in proportion to her actions as she has benefited from long-term free accommodation.

Box C The protection of estoppel rights

Redacres was sold to Peter before Anneka had asked the court for quantification of her remedy. Peter is a third party, so you will need to establish whether he is bound by Anneka's equity by estoppel. You are not told whether Redacres is unregistered or registered land, so you must consider both.

C1 Unregistered land

An equity by estoppel cannot be entered as a land charge on the Land Charges Register under the Land Charges Act 1972. However, an equity by estoppel has been held to be sufficiently similar to an equitable interest to be covered by the same pre-1926 rule that relates to equitable interests also not able to be entered as a land charge. This rule, which is known as the doctrine of notice, states that equitable interests bind everyone except a *bona fide* purchaser of a legal estate for value without notice of the equitable interest. The position of Peter would depend on whether he could claim that he was a *bona fide* purchaser of a legal estate for value without notice of Anneka's equity. We can assume that Peter is *bona fide*. Peter purchased the legal estate of Redacres for money, as money is implicit in the word 'sold'. This means that he is a *bona fide* purchaser of a legal estate for value. As notice includes actual, constructive or imputed notice, it is highly likely that Peter will be deemed to have notice of Anneka's equity. He will therefore be bound by it and by any remedy the court chooses to award her. If the court chooses to award the fee simple of Redacres to Anneka, Peter must transfer the house to her. Remember that Peter is given every opportunity to inspect and make inquiries about Redacres before he purchases the land. If he chooses not to do so, he is very foolish.

Q: *What would happen if Peter did not have notice of Anneka's equity?*

A: Her equity would not bind him, and he could take Redacres free from any claim by her. Anneka's only claim would be a personal one against Tom's estate.

Q: *What would happen if Tom had left Redacres to the Home for Abandoned Dogs in his will instead of selling the property to Peter?*

A: Again, the position of the Home would depend on whether it could claim it was a *bona fide* purchaser of a legal estate for value without notice of Anneka's equity. In this case, the Home was not a purchaser for value as it inherited Redacres. It is therefore bound by the equity. Assuming the court honoured Tom's assurance, the court would transfer Redacres to Anneka and the Home would receive nothing under Tom's will.

C2 Registered land

Anneka's position is governed by the Land Registration Act 2002.

C2i Dealings which must be completed by registration

Acquiring an equity by estoppel is not a dealing that must be completed by registration under section 27 of the Land Registration Act 2002.

C2ii Interests which override a registered disposition

The position of Peter depends on whether Anneka was in actual occupation of Redacres. Assuming she was and that the conditions in paragraph 2 of Schedule 3 to the Land Registration Act 2002 were satisfied, her equity would be an interest that overrides a registered disposition, here the sale to Peter. Peter would be bound by her interest, and therefore by any remedy the court chose to award her. If the court chose to award the fee simple in Redacres to Anneka, Peter would have to transfer the house to her. Remember that Peter has had every opportunity to make inquiries about the rights of other people in Redacres.

C2iii Interests entered as a notice or protected by a restriction

There is no indication that Anneka has protected her equity by a notice on the Charges Register of Redacres under section 34 of the Land Registration Act 2002.

Q: *What would happen if Anneka's equity was not protected by the entry of a notice and she was not in actual occupation either?*

A: Her equity would not bind Peter, and he could take Redacres free from any claim by her. Anneka's only claim would be a personal one against Tom's estate.

Q: *What would happen if Tom had left Redacres to the Home for Abandoned Dogs in his will instead of selling the property to Peter?*

A: The Home would be bound by Anneka's equity whether or not she was in actual occupation. This is because the Home was not a purchaser of Redacres for valuable consideration and so would be bound by any proprietary interest over the land under section 29 of the Land Registration Act 2002.

The court would transfer Redacres to Anneka and the Home would receive nothing under Tom's will.

Conclusion

Assuming Anneka can prove a causal link between Tom's assurance of her inheritance and her own change of position, it is likely that a claim by her based on proprietary estoppel will be successful. Peter's position is dependent on the doctrine of notice in unregistered land and Anneka's actual occupation of registered land. It is highly likely that he will be bound by Anneka's equity by estoppel in either case. The court can award her the fee simple of Redacres, or indeed any other remedy it feels appropriate.

Constructive trusts, proprietary estoppel and the requirements of section 2 of the Law of Property (Miscellaneous Provisions) Act 1989

This section looks at whether the constructive trust and proprietary estoppel have been used to avoid the formal requirements of section 2 of the Law of Property (Miscellaneous Provisions) Act 1989. The discussion here shows that things are not as clear cut as they might appear at first sight. You may well find this area coming up either in an essay question ending in the word 'discuss' or else in a problem question where the parties have not met the required formalities of section 2, which is why there is a discussion on it.

Section 2(1) of the Law of Property (Miscellaneous Provisions) Act 1989 states that a contract for the sale or disposition of an interest in land must be in writing, contain all the express terms of the contract and be signed by both parties. This was discussed in Chapter 1. The problem was that before section 2 was enacted, an oral contract followed by part performance of that oral contract was capable of enforcement where it would be inequitable to do otherwise. This was known as the doctrine of part performance. Section 2 effectively put an end to this because a contract not satisfying its written requirements was void and you cannot have part performance of a void contract.

Q: *Why was section 2(1) enacted?*

A: To remove the uncertainty of the doctrine of part performance by ensuring that a contract for the sale or disposition of an interest in land was created in writing.

Section 2(5) of the Law of Property (Miscellaneous Provisions) Act 1989 expressly states that the creation of resulting, implied and constructive trusts does not have to meet the written requirements of section 2.

Q: *Does that mean that people have tried to use these exceptions to get over the fact that they haven't met the requirements of section 2?*

A: Yes, namely the constructive trust. The courts have also been able to recognise proprietary estoppel here because the requirements for a constructive trust and proprietary estoppel are very similar.

Q: *The exceptions in section 2(5) don't mention proprietary estoppel, do they?*

A: No, but the Law Commission report, Formalities for Contracts for Sale etc. of Land (No 164) referred to the possibility of using proprietary estoppel.

> We see no cause to fear that the recommended repeal and replacement of the present section as to the formalities for contracts for sale or other disposition of land will inhibit the courts in the exercise of the equitable discretion to do justice between parties in individual otherwise hard cases.

Proprietary estoppel is recognised in equity. The court aims to do justice between the parties in otherwise individual hard cases. The remedy is at the court's discretion and, so, on that basis, you should be able to include it. A hard case could be where one party has deliberately taken advantage of the fact that section 2 has not been complied with.

Q: *Even so, should you be relying on the views of the Law Commission when proprietary estoppel isn't specifically mentioned in section 2(5)?*

A: You should look at the Law Commission's views only when you are trying to identify the defect in the law that was being addressed. We know the defect in the law giving rise to section 2, so there is no need to look at the Law Commission's report. However, in *Yaxley v Gotts* Lord Justice Beldam laid out a pretty good argument for taking the Law Commission's views into account by quoting from Lord Simon of Glaisdale in *Black-Clawson International Ltd v Papierwerke Waldhof-Aschaffenburg AG* (1975):

that experts publicly expressed the view that a certain draft would have such-and-such an effect is one of the facts within the shared knowledge of Parliament and the citizenry. To refuse to consider such a commentary, when Parliament has legislated on the basis and faith of it, is for the interpreter to fail to put himself in the real position of the promulgator of the instrument before essaying its interpretation. It is refusing to follow what is perhaps the most important clue to meaning. It is perversely neglecting the reality, while chasing shadows. As Aneurin Bevin said: 'Why gaze in the crystal ball when you can read the book?' Here the book is already open; it is merely a matter of reading on. Certainly, a court of construction cannot be precluded from saying that what the committee thought as to the meaning of its draft was incorrect. But that is one thing: to dismiss, out of hand and for all purposes, an authoritive opinion in the light of which Parliament has legislated is quite another.

Q: *And in English, please?*

A: You can only interpret the law by understanding the basis on which the law was made.

Another way of justifying a claim in proprietary estoppel is to argue that the constructive trust and proprietary estoppel overlap so much that proprietary estoppel comes into the exception of section 2(5). Both claims are based on a promise or assurance, reliance on that promise or assurance, and detriment when the promise is withdrawn. If a constructive trust can be claimed under the exemption in section 2(5), you should also be able to claim proprietary estoppel.

Q: *If you can find a constructive trust, why would you want to argue proprietary estoppel?*

A: As we have already seen, in a constructive trust the claimant will be awarded an interest in the land. The legal owner holds property or the money from the proceeds of sale on trust for the beneficiary of the trust, the person who has been disadvantaged. This is fine if the oral agreement involves a sale of land, as it did in *Oates v Stimson* (2006) where Mr Oates refused to honour an informal agreement for the sale of land to Mr Stimson, but less fine if there is an agreement to create another interest over land, for example an easement. It is difficult to say that a landowner holds an easement on trust for a beneficiary for the following reason. I cannot hold the benefit of an easement on trust for you because I do not have the benefit. It is you as the neighbouring landowner who has the benefit. Also, I am not in a position to hold the benefit on trust for you because I cannot sue myself if I breach my position as a trustee. However, if the claim were in proprietary estoppel, a right having the same effect as an easement could simply be awarded as a remedy, or indeed compensation or anything else the court had in mind. In proprietary estoppel the range of remedies available is much wider, which makes life much easier for the courts to award what they think is fair in the circumstances.

Q: *If you use the constructive trust or proprietary estoppel, aren't you just getting round the written requirements of section 2(1)?*

A: Not necessarily. If you argue that an oral contract is void if section 2 requirements are not met, there is no contract. Section 2 is saying that whether you have a loose agreement that is largely uncertain or a contract with all terms agreed, if it's not in writing, it's as though it doesn't exist and is void. On that basis there is nothing to stop you using a constructive trust or proprietary estoppel instead to argue your case as a totally separate cause. You don't need to consider the exemptions in section 2(5) at all.

Q: *So let's say that you orally agree to sell me your house. If you change your mind after I've spent a lot of money on expensive solicitors, can I claim a remedy under a constructive trust or proprietary estoppel?*

A: No. It was held in *Kinane v Mackie-Conteh* (2005), which concerned an oral agreement to create a mortgage, that there must be something other than just a reliance on an invalid agreement. In a constructive trust, one party must have led the other to believe that he would have an interest in the land, and the other party must have relied on that promise to his detriment. Unconscionablity was the touchstone. This emphasis on unconscionablity had been examined in *Ravenocean Ltd v Gardner* (2001) where there was an oral agreement for the sale of land. The sale was dependant on the purchaser, a company, obtaining planning permission for the property, which it did. The defendant then refused to transfer the property. The court refused to award a constructive trust. This was because the amount spent on obtaining planning permission was very small and it was not inequitable or unconscionable to restrict the company to simply receiving the money it had spent on obtaining planning permission. In *Kinane v Mackie-Conteh* it was likewise held that if a person wanted to claim proprietary estoppel, he must prove that the defendant encouraged him or represented to him that there would be an enforceable agreement over and above the usual sorts of discussions. As Lord Justice Arden said:

> The cause of action in proprietary estoppel is thus not founded on the unenforceable agreement but upon the defendant's conduct which, when viewed in all relevant respects, is unconscionable.

Yeoman's Row Management v Cobbe is an important House of Lords case. There was an oral agreement between Yeomans and Mr Cobbe. Mr Cobbe was a very experienced property developer. The oral agreement was that if Mr Cobbe obtained planning permission to develop a property owned by Yeomans, Yeomans would sell it to him for £12 million subject to an arrangement over sharing the profits after development of the site. The parties knew that the 'in principle' agreement wasn't legally binding because it wasn't in writing and it lacked certainty. A legally binding contract would be signed when planning permission had been obtained and other terms discussed. Yeomans went back on their word the day after planning permission was granted and refused to sell unless Mr Cobbe paid Yeomans £20 million, rather than the previously agreed £12 million. We'll discuss the Court of Appeal decision first, then the House of Lords' decision. The Court of Appeal found proprietary estoppel and Mr Cobbe was awarded compensation.

Q: *Surely as this was an oral contract between Yeomans and Mr Cobbe for the sale of land, you could argue that it didn't meet the requirements of section 2 and was therefore void?*

A: In the Court of Appeal Lord Justice Mummery held that as there was no contract, section 2 of the Law of Property (Miscellaneous Provisions) Act 1989 was irrelevant. The cause of action was based on a representation and proprietary estoppel.

Q: *So a different cause of action, then, which is what we were saying before? The contract was void because it wasn't in writing so there was nothing to stop Mr Cobbe pleading a different cause of action?*

A: That's right. Yeomans had then argued that the promise of 'a contract' where the terms weren't defined couldn't form the basis for proprietary estoppel. Estoppel was based on the promise of an immediate or future interest in or over land. The promise of 'a contract' was meaningless if the terms of the contract weren't known and hadn't been fully discussed. In the Court of Appeal Lord Justice Mummery stated that the court was not trying to enforce an agreement. It was trying to establish whether Mr Cobbe had been led to believe he would have an interest in the property, whether through a contract or otherwise.

Q: *But if the terms of the oral agreement weren't certain how would Mr Cobbe know what interest to expect?*

A: The crucial element in proprietary estoppel is the unconscionable behaviour by the defendant in leading the claimant to believe that the claimant will obtain an interest in the defendant's property, and that the defendant will not go back on his word. In this case, Mr Cobbe spent money acquiring planning permission that increased the value of Yeomans' land based on the expectation that he would obtain an interest in the land, ultimately by buying and developing it. Yeomans' unconscionable action was to allow Mr Cobbe to proceed under that expectation and then refuse to honour the agreement Mr Cobbe had understood to be in place. The promises made by Yeomans didn't have to be the certain terms required in a contract. As long as the promises made to Mr Cobbe were sufficiently certain to form a realistic expectation of the promise being kept as far as Mr Cobbe was concerned, proprietary estoppel could be claimed. Yeomans appealed to the House of Lords. The House of Lords overturned the decision of the Court of Appeal and held that that Mr Cobbe had to repay Yeoman's Row Management the £2 million he had been awarded by the Court of Appeal, plus interest. Before you read the case, note that a 'second agreement' is referred to. This is the oral agreement that was in contention. It is referred to as the second agreement because there had been an earlier agreement in place which had been replaced by this second agreement and it was this second agreement upon which Mr Cobbe was basing his claim. Mrs Lisle-Mainwaring (Mrs L-M), a director of Yeoman's Row Management was the person with whom Mr Cobbe had been dealing. Lord Scott held that the nature of a proprietary estoppel was as follows: 'an "estoppel" bars the object of it from asserting some fact or facts, or, sometimes, something that is a mixture of fact and law, that stands in the way of some right claimed by the person entitled to the benefit of the estoppel'. This sentence is quoted in many of the discussions and commentaries on this case. Despite this, it still makes no more sense now than it did than when it was first uttered. You cannot define the nature of an object by referring to the object itself. For example, you cannot say the nature of a horse is that is has four legs, a mane and a tail and looks like a horse because it refers to itself. Lord Scott has attempted to define proprietary estoppel in the same way and it doesn't work. Rather clearer is his statement that proprietary estoppel requires 'clarity as to what it is [facts or a mixture of fact and law] that the object of the estoppel is to be estopped from denying, or asserting, and clarity as to the interest in the property in question that that denial, or assertion, would otherwise defeat'. So, whatever it was Mrs L-M was stopped from denying had to be clear and whatever interest Mr Cobbe was claiming had to be clear. Look at the second part of this quote first – was it clear what interest Mr Cobbe was claiming? Lord Scott stated that the principles of proprietary estoppel required Mr Cobbe to have an expectation of a 'certain interest in land'. The requirement of a 'certain interest in land' had been cited in *Taylor Fashions Ltd v Liverpool Victoria Trustees Co Ltd* and *Ramsden v Dyson*. Mr Cobbe had only an expectation that once he had got planning permission the remaining terms of the contract would be negotiated (for example for Mrs L-M it would be the length of time in which the development had to be completed and how and when she would be paid her share if the profits exceeded a certain amount, and for Mr Cobbe it would be how soon Yeoman's were going to move out of the building so that he could start his development). The already agreed terms together with the outstanding terms that would have to be negotiated following the grant of the planning permission would be concluded by means of a contract. An expectation which depended upon a successful negotiation was not a certain interest because 'the outcome of future negotiations has always an inherent uncertainty' and nor could the court infer what terms further negotiations might have produced. Now deal with the first part of Lord Scott's statement on the requirements of proprietary estoppel. What exactly was Mrs LM stopped from asserting or denying? She was not stopped from saying that the agreement should have been in writing and was therefore unenforceable because Mr Cobbe wasn't claiming otherwise. She was not stopped from denying that all the terms of the agreement hadn't been reached because Mr Cobbe agreed that all the terms hadn't been agreed. Even if she was stopped from denying that the price they had agreed should be the price Mr Cobbe should be allowed to buy the property for, it wouldn't help Mr Cobbe because he still didn't have the promise of a certain interest in land, i.e. a complete agreement. The requirements of proprietary estoppel were not met and Mrs L-M's unattractive conduct, as Lord Walker of Gestingthorpe put it, on its own was not enough.

Q: *So what happened then?*

A: Things were not looking good for Mr Cobbe and life got steadily worse when it was decided that he was not entitled to claim a constructive trust under the section 2(5) exception either. A constructive trust would be imposed if two or more people agreed that one of them would buy land and they would develop it jointly but, afterwards, the party who bought the land kept it for his own benefit. In the case the property had been bought by Yeomans long before any discussion with Mr Cobbe and so was it was not a joint property venture. Mr Cobbe only expected to acquire an interest in the property when a formal contact was negotiated. Imposing a constructive trust in such circumstances would be 'an indignant reaction to Mrs Lisle-Mainwaring's unconscionable behaviour rather than a principled answer to Mr Cobbe's claim for relief'. Mr Cobbe could, however, claim a remedy for unjust enrichment because Mrs L-M had obtained his services without paying for them. He could equally claim a quantum meruit payment (meaning 'the amount deserved') which would consist of his costs in obtaining the planning permission and a fee for his services. It could also be seen as an agreement where the consideration for Mr Cobbe providing money and services had totally failed because Mrs Lisle-Mainwaring had not carried out her promise. In the event the court held that Mr Cobbe was entitled to a quantum meruit. Mr Cobbe was not entitled to any increase in the value of the property due to the planning permission he had obtained. Obtaining the planning permission simply unlocked the development potential. Lord Scott likened his situation to that of a locksmith called out to mend the lock on a box. Mending the lock on the box enabled the money inside to be accessed but did not entitle the locksmith to any of that money. Lord Walker, concurring with Lord Scott, said that if the Court of Appeal's decision was allowed to stand, it would create too much uncertainty in commercial negotiations.

Q: *Was there any comment on section 2(5) of the Law of Property (Miscellaneous Provisions) Act 1989?*

A: It was held obiter that section 2(5) of the Law of Property (Miscellaneous Provisions) Act 1989 did not include proprietary estoppel as an exception. The court also didn't have to look at whether a complete agreement (i.e. where there was the promise of a certain interest in land) that didn't meet the section 2 requirements could be enforced by proprietary estoppel because Mr Cobbe didn't have a complete agreement. Lord Scott did state though that using proprietary estoppel to avoid the formalities of section 2 is unacceptable – 'equity can surely not contradict the statute' (although the Court of Appeal in *Yaxley v Gotts* said the opposite).

Q: *Have there been any more cases since which look at the formal requirements of section 2 of the Law of Property (Miscellaneous Provisions) Act 1989 and proprietary estoppel?*

A: In *Hutchison v B & DF Ltd* (2008) Mr Hutchinson was trying to enforce a five year lease on BD & F through estoppel. The lease had not been made in writing and so was void under section 2 of the Law of Property (Miscellaneous Provisions) Act 1989. Mr Hutchinson said that BD & F were estopped from denying the existence of a lease. Mr Hutchinson had relied on assurances by BD & F before he let them into possession; he had acted to his detriment because he didn't insist on the lease being executed; BD & F had paid and Mr Hutchinson had accepted rent as though the lease had been executed. In the House of Lords in *Yeoman's Row Management Ltd v Cobbe* it had been held obiter that proprietary estoppel could not be used to enforce an agreement that statute has declared to be void. Whilst acknowledging that the comment was obiter, the judge in *Hutchison v B & DF Ltd* followed 'the present view' in *Yeoman's Row Management Ltd v Cobbe* and held that Mr Hutchinson's claim to enforce the 5 year lease on estoppel grounds would fail. He also said:

> I do not believe for one minute that Claimants (including an experienced property lawyer and an experienced surveyor) believed that there was a enforceable agreement for a five year term made orally. They cannot say that they allowed the Defendant into possession in a mistaken belief that there was a binding agreement.

Herbert v Doyle (2010) was a case in which the parties had agreed to transfer parking spaces orally thereby not complying with section 2 of the Law of Property (Miscellaneous Provisions) Act 1989. Whilst Lady Justice Arden said that the issue was whether there was a constructive trust, she talked about proprietary estoppel as well. She said that whilst the distinction between proprietary estoppel and constructive trusts must be kept in mind, in some situations both doctrines need completeness of agreement with respect to an interest in property. One of those situations was where there was a commercial agreement as in the case. She talked about a common thread coming from the speeches of Lord Scott and Lord Walker in *Yeoman's Row Management Ltd v Cobbe* and said:

> that common thread is that, if the parties intend to make a formal agreement setting out the terms on which one or more of the parties is to acquire an interest in property, or, if further terms for that acquisition remain to be agreed between them so that the interest in property is not clearly identified, or if the parties did not expect their agreement to be immediately binding, neither party can rely on a constructive trust as a means of enforcing their original agreement. In other words, at least in those situations, if their agreement (which does not comply with section 2(1)) is incomplete, they cannot utilise the doctrine of proprietary estoppel or the doctrine of constructive trust to make their agreement binding on the other party by virtue of section 2(5) of the 1989 Act.

In the case between Mr Herbert and Mr Doyle the court found that there was sufficient certainty and completeness to impose a constructive trust, thereby coming under the exception in section 2(5), and Mr Doyle was held to be beneficially entitled to the disputed parking spaces. Pointing out that the litigation had been extremely costly, Lady Justice Arden said

> All this could have been saved if a written agreement had been made in the first place or at least if the parties had made their arrangements subject to contract.

Advice that should be noted well.

In *Whittaker v Kinnear* (2011), which involved a commercial transaction, Bean J considered that proprietary estoppel had survived the enactment of section 2 although this view is contrary to Lord Scott's obiter words in *Yeoman's Row Management Ltd v Cobbe*. Bean J based his opinion on the view of Beldam J who had been both a judge in *Yaxley v Gotts* and also chairman of the Law Commission that had produced the report on which the 1989 Act was based. In the report it had been expressed that proprietary estoppel would survive the enactment of section 2. Bean J also stressed the fact-sensitive nature of claims in proprietary estoppel. The case was remitted to the County Court to see whether estoppel had arisen on the facts.

Q: *Is it appropriate to argue proprietary estoppel and constructive trusts in such a business context? For example, Yeomans and Mr Cobbe would have had access to legal advice and should have known better when negotiating over the sale of land worth millions of pounds.*

A: You could argue that proprietary estoppel is best suited to dealing with informal agreements such as were found in *Oates v Stimson*, not in commercial dealings where both parties have access to legal advice and should be fully aware of the law. In *Thorner v Major* in the House of Lords Lord Neuberger distinguished between the situation in *Yeoman's Row Management Ltd v Cobbe* and that in *Thorner v Major*, the facts of which are on page 296. He said that Mr Cobbe's claim had failed because he was trying to use proprietary estoppel to enforce a contract that the parties had 'intentionally and consciously not entered into'. The whole arrangement had been a speculative one and all Mr Cobbe had been trying to do was to seek a remedy against Yeoman's because the company had behaved unconscionably. On the other hand, in *Thorner v Major* the relationship between Peter and David Thorner was a family one and they had never intended to enter into a contract. They were not business men and the idea of a contract had never crossed their minds. This reasoning appears to distinguish between a commercial case (*Yeoman's Row Management Ltd v Cobbe*) and a family case (*Thorner v Major*). In the commercial case (*Yeoman's Row Management Ltd v Cobbe*) it was very clear that first, no specific right in land was promised, and second, that the parties had not entered into a contract deliberately. In the family/domestic case (*Thorner v Major*) the representation was clear enough in the context of the situation and there was no contractual connection. Avoiding the formalities is unacceptable in the former business/commercial situation but there is leeway in the latter domestic/family situation. In this sense *Yeoman's Row Management Ltd v Cobbe* has not narrowed the scope of proprietary estoppel on the basis that the court takes context into account although there is still no clear line drawn in the sand distinguishing commercial situations and family situations. Whatever view you take, the use of proprietary estoppel, or indeed a constructive trust, in a commercial situation, is a question for discussion, probably on an exam paper.

Q: *Have the courts tended to favour the constructive trust or have they favoured proprietary estoppel when the requirements of section 2 haven't been met and there is a clear case of unconscionable behaviour?*

A: Start off with *Yaxley v Gotts* which was the first important case to be heard after the 1989 Act. There was an oral agreement that Brownie Gotts would buy property and, in return for carrying out work on it, Mr Yaxley would have the ground floor flats 'for ever'. The property was actually bought by Alan Gotts, Brownie Gott's son, and Alan Gotts refused to convey the flats to Mr Yaxley after he had done the work. The court awarded Mr Yaxley a 99-year lease of the flat rent-free under a constructive trust.

Q: *But there never was an oral contract with Alan Gotts, was there? It was with Brownie Gotts, so surely there was no need to discuss section 2 at all?*

A: This is quite true, so you could argue that *Yaxley v Gotts* is simply a case of proprietary estoppel where Alan Gotts stood by knowing of the promise his father had made, and watched Mr Yaxley carry out the work. However, the court awarded Mr Yaxley a 99-year lease of the flats under a constructive trust on the basis of an express agreement, reliance and detriment when the promise was withdrawn. The judges in the case expressed their views as to whether proprietary estoppel could have succeeded instead.

Lord Justice Walker found a constructive trust. He wasn't totally happy with the idea of finding the claim in proprietary estoppel on the basis that you shouldn't use the doctrine to circumvent a statute and so defeat the policy behind section 2, which was to make contracts more certain and to stop the difficulties associated with the doctrine of part performance. He did say, though, that there could be situations where a constructive trust and proprietary estoppel overlapped. Lord Justice Clarke also found a constructive trust and reiterated Lord Simon of Glaisdale's views in that it was appropriate and permissible to take the recommendations of the Law Commission regarding proprietary estoppel into account. Lord Justice Beldam gave considerable weight to the Law Commission report. He said that circumstances that gave rise to a constructive trust could also give rise to proprietary estoppel. Although section 2 made oral contracts void, the public policy notion that you shouldn't be able to avoid the formalities of a statute was not enough to exclude proprietary estoppel.

In *Kinane v Mackie-Conteh*, a case which was to do with an oral agreement for a mortgage, a constructive trust was found although the court talked about 'a finding of proprietary estoppel overlapping with constructive trust'.

In *Oates v Stimson* an oral agreement for the sale of land gave rise to a constructive trust where the seller had relied on the agreement to his detriment. The terminology of proprietary estoppel was used when discussing what remedy to award.

Yeoman's Row Management v Cobbe cast no further light on this because the court found neither proprietary estoppel nor a constructive trust.

In *Herbert v Doyle* a constructive trust was found and emphasis was placed on certainty and completeness in certain situations, such as commercial ones, whether proprietary estoppel or a constructive trust was argued.

This is a brief summary of what has been discussed in this section. In cases where there has been unconscionable behaviour by one party, the courts have awarded a constructive trust or proprietary estoppel when the requirements of section 2(1) of the Law of Property (Miscellaneous Provisions) Act 1989 have not been met. Proprietary estoppel is included either because it is seen as a separate cause of action, or because the Law Commission saw it as having a place, or because the requirements of a constructive trust and proprietary estoppel overlap. The courts have tended to award a constructive trust in the past. The highpoint of proprietary estoppel appears to be the Court of Appeal decision in *Yeoman's Row Management Ltd v Cobbe* although don't forget that this decision was overturned by the House of Lords. In *Thorner v Major* context was everything, which explained the decision in the commercial situation in *Yeoman's Row Management Ltd v Cobbe* compared to the decision in the family situation in *Thorner v Major*.

The words 'subject to contract' and proprietary estoppel

Q: *What do the words 'subject to contract' mean?*

A: Before 1989, an oral contract for the sale or disposition of an interest in land could be enforced if there had been part performance of that oral contract by one of the parties. Under section 40(1) of the Law of Property Act 1925 an oral contract could also be enforced if it was subsequently evidenced in writing.

The oral contract didn't have to be in writing: it just had to be evidenced in writing. To avoid anybody evidencing anything in writing inadvertently, the words 'subject to contract' were put at the top of any correspondence during negotiations for the sale of land before exchange of contracts. This meant that nothing said or done was binding on the other party. Either party could walk away from the negotiations until the contract was signed and everyone knew where they were. The enactment of section 2 meant that the words 'subject to contract' were no longer needed because it would be impossible for the parties to enter inadvertently into a written and signed contract containing all the express terms of that contract. Following *Yaxley v Gotts* though, people started to include these words again as a precaution in case a constructive trust or proprietary estoppel was argued. Proof that this precaution worked was seen in *James v Evans* (2000) where the main reason the purchaser couldn't rely on proprietary estoppel or a constructive trust to enforce a written agreement not satisfying section 2 was that the words 'subject to contract' had been used throughout the correspondence.

Q: *It seems quite sensible to protect yourself in this way. What has happened since?*

A: In *Edwin Shirley Productions Ltd v Workspace Management Ltd* (2001) in the High Court it was held that there could be no claim under a constructive trust or through proprietary estoppel where the parties had agreed terms 'subject to contract', particularly where the parties were commercial enterprises. In *Yeoman's Row Management Ltd v Cobbe* Lord Scott held obiter that where the words 'subject to contract' were used, proprietary estoppel would not normally arise. The purchaser's expectation of acquiring an interest in the property was subject to a contingency (the contract) that was under the control of the vendor. Any expectation was therefore speculative, i.e. not certain. Lord Scott accepted that such a reservation (the words 'subject to contract') could be withdrawn either expressly or implied from conduct but such debate was not relevant to the present case because the agreement was oral, not written. In *Haq v Island Homes Housing Association* (2011) the Council had negotiated 'subject to contract'. Any departure from 'subject to contract' had to have the agreement of both parties and that had not happened. The Council could rely therefore on its strict legal rights and this was one of the grounds on which the claim for proprietary estoppel failed.

Q: *How should commercial companies like Yeomans entering these sorts of business negotiations protect themselves so they don't end up in court?*

A: A company needs to make it very clear in written format in any dealing with a property developer that the developer meets all its own costs at its own risk. A company must ensure that it can withdraw any time before a legally binding contract is made. The developer of course should simply ensure that there is a written contract satisfying section 2, which states that if planning permission is granted, the developer will be able to buy the land on specified terms. All of which is what you could argue Yeomans and Mr Cobbe should have done in the first place.

Further reading

G. Battersby, 'Informal Transactions in Land, Estoppel and Registration', 58 *MLR* (1995) 637

S. Bright and B. McFarlane, 'Personal Liability in Proprietary Estoppel', *Conv and Prop Law*, Jan/Feb (2005) 14

C. Davis, 'Proprietary Estoppel: Future Interests and Future Property', *Conv and Prop Law*, May/Jun (1996) 193

T. Etherton, 'Constructive Trusts and Proprietary Estoppel: The Search for Clarity and Principle', *Conv and Prop Law*, 2 (2009) 104

S. Gardner, 'The Remedial Discretion in Proprietary Estoppel', 115 *LQR* (1999) 438

C. Harpum, 'Overreaching, Trusts of Land and Proprietary Estoppel', 116 *LQR* (2000) 341

M. Thompson, 'Estoppel: A Return to Principle', *Conv and Prop Law*, Jan/Feb (2001) 78

R. Wells, 'The Element of Detriment in Proprietary Estoppel', *Conv and Prop Law*, Jan/Feb (2001) 13

Proprietary estoppel and constructive trusts

P. Ferguson, 'Constructive Trusts – A Note of Caution', 109 *LQR* (1993) 114. A reply: D. Hayton, 'Constructive Trusts of Homes – A Bold Approach', 109 *LQR* (1993) 485

D. Hayton, 'Equitable Rights of Cohabitees', *Conv and Prop Law*, Sep/Oct (1990) 370

M. Thompson, 'Constructive Trusts, Estoppel and the Family Home', *Conv and Prop Law*, Nov/Dec (2004) 496

Section 2 of the Law of Property (Miscellaneous Provisions) Act 1989

G. Griffiths, 'Part Performance – Still Trying to Replace the Irreplaceable?' *Conv and Prop Law*, May/Jun (2002) 216

B. McFarlane, 'Proprietary Estoppel and Failed Contractual Negotiations', *Conv and Prop Law*, Nov/Dec (2005) 501

G. Owen and O. Rees, 'Section 2(5) of the Law of Property (Miscellaneous Provisions) Act 1989: A Misconceived Approach?' *Conv and Prop Law* (2011) 495

R. Smith, 'Oral Contracts for the Sale of Land: Estoppels and Constructive Trusts', 116 *LQR* (2000) 11

M. Thompson, 'Oral Agreements for the Sale of Land', *Conv and Prop Law*, May/Jun (2000) 245

Chapter 13

Licences

www.palgrave.com/law/Stroud4e

Introduction

This chapter is about licences. A licence is when one party gives another party permission to do something. In the context of land law, it is permission given to do something on someone else's land. Although licences are discussed in Chapter 15 on leases and in Chapter 17 on easements, they can arise in other circumstances. Licences by estoppel are covered in Chapter 12.

A licence can take the form of a bare licence, a contractual licence or a licence coupled with the grant of a property right. The person who grants the permission is called the licensor, and the person who receives the benefit is called the licensee. There are three aspects to any discussion on licences. The first is whether the person who granted the licence can revoke or withdraw it.

The question is whether Fred can subsequently revoke or withdraw the licence.

The second aspect is whether the person with the benefit of the licence can assign or pass that benefit on to another person. The question is whether Emma can assign or pass the benefit of the licence to Syed.

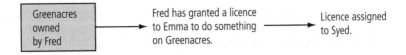

The third aspect is whether a purchaser who buys land that is affected by the licence is bound by it.

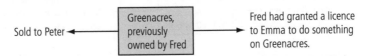

The question is whether Emma's licence is binding on a purchaser, here Peter.

You can now look at the different types of licence in the context of these scenarios.

Bare licences

A bare licence occurs when one party gives another permission to do something on his land and there is no consideration or payment between the parties. You are taken to have given the postman permission to walk up the drive to deliver mail: see *Robson v Hallett* (1967). This is a bare licence. Other examples range from asking people round to dinner to allowing your next-door neighbour to use your swimming pool while you are away.

Revocation of a bare licence

Q: *Presumably I can always revoke a bare licence if I don't want the postman to come up the drive, for example?*

A: Yes. You must allow a reasonable amount of time for the person to leave though: see *Minister of Health v Bellotti* (1944). If the person doesn't leave after this time, he will become a trespasser. The licence is also revoked automatically on the death of the licensor, the person who granted the licence.

Look at the example of Fred and Emma.

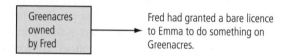

Fred can revoke the bare licence he granted to Emma, but he must allow her a reasonable time to leave.

Assigning the benefit of a bare licence

It is possible to assign the benefit of a bare licence.

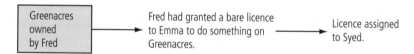

Although Emma can assign the benefit of the bare licence to Syed, this is unlikely to occur as the licence can be revoked by the licensor at any time. This means that Fred can immediately revoke the licence if he doesn't want Syed to benefit.

The effect of a bare licence on a third party

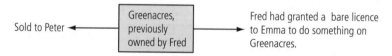

The question is whether Emma's bare licence is binding on a third party, Peter here.

Peter will not be bound because a bare licence is not a proprietary interest in land. A proprietary interest in land is one that has the capacity to bind people who take the land subsequently. The nature of a proprietary interest in land was discussed in Chapter 1, Box D. A bare licence is a personal right that is binding only between the original parties to the agreement. Emma's bare licence will not bind Peter.

Contractual licences

A contractual licence arises when consideration or value is given for it. Common examples include paying for a ticket to watch a film or paying to stay in a hotel. A person who occupies land but who cannot satisfy all the requirements for a lease will have a contractual licence, as discussed in Chapter 15.

Revocation of a contractual licence

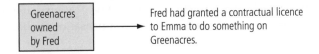

Greenacres owned by Fred → Fred had granted a contractual licence to Emma to do something on Greenacres.

The question is whether Fred can later revoke the contractual licence.

At common law a contractual licence could be revoked at any time: see *Wood v Leadbitter* (1845). The licensee had to leave whether or not he had completed what he was given permission to do on the land and could claim damages for breach of contact. If he failed to leave, he would be a trespasser.

Q: *How much time was he given to leave?*

A: Reasonable notice: see *Winter Garden Theatre (London) Ltd v Millennium Productions Ltd* (1948).

Q: *Wasn't that very unfair on the licensee?*

A: Yes. The reason it happened was that a contractual licence was not a proprietary interest in land. It was a normal contract and followed the normal contractual rules. If a contractual licence was revoked unlawfully, the licensee's remedy lay in damages. This was unsatisfactory, which was why equity intervened in the interests of justice: see *Hurst v Picture Theatres Ltd* (1915). If the terms of the contract indicated that the contractual licence would not be revoked prematurely, an injunction would be granted to prevent revocation. If revocation had already taken place, an order for specific performance would be granted to ensure that the contractual licence continued according to its terms.

Q: *How can you tell from the terms of the contract that it's not to be revoked prematurely?*

A: The terms can expressly prevent revocation of the contractual licence. Failing that, the courts will look at the construction of the contract and see whether they can infer a term that the contractual licence should not be revoked. If the contract has been granted for a certain time, there is an inference here that it should be allowed to run for that period of time. A term preventing revocation will also be implied where damages would not compensate for a breach of the contract. In *Verrall v Great Yarmouth BC* (1981) the Council tried to revoke a contractual licence that it had granted to the National Front to hold a conference. Had it been allowed to do so, no amount of damages for breach of contract would have compensated the National Front, as it would not have been able to find alternative premises in which to hold the conference. The court awarded specific performance of the contract.

Q: *Do the equitable rules apply to all contractual licences?*

A: Yes. There was even an attempt to incorporate the equitable rules preventing revocation of a contractual licence into family relationships. In *Tanner v Tanner* (1975) a married man bought a house for his mistress to live in. They had children together and she paid for some of the furnishings in the house. When the relationship broke down, he evicted her. Had she still been living there, the court would have awarded an injunction to prevent revocation of the contractual licence. As she had moved out, she was awarded compensation for breach of a contractual licence.

Q: *Where was the contract though? Surely she would have had children and paid for the furnishings because of the relationship, rather than consideration for a contract?*

A: Yes. It's difficult to find a contract in *Tanner v Tanner*, let alone to infer that the contract should not be revoked. Proprietary estoppel, which is discussed in Chapter 12, is now claimed in these types of family relationship instead of a contractual licence.

In our example, Fred can revoke Emma's contractual licence unless there is an express or implied term in the contract that it will not be revoked.

Assigning the benefit of a contractual licence

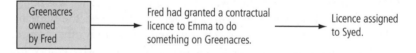

It is possible to assign the benefit of a contractual licence if this is permitted by the contract. If the contract expressly prohibits assignment of the benefit, then it cannot be assigned. If the nature of the contract is inherently personal, such as a contract to paint a portrait, then again the benefit cannot be assigned. In all other cases it can be assigned either under section 136 of the Law of Property Act 1925 or else in equity. Assigning the benefit of a contract in these ways is discussed in Chapter 14.

The effect of a contractual licence on a third party

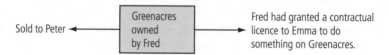

The question is whether Emma's contractual licence is binding on a third party, Peter in our example.

Traditionally, contractual licences were not seen as proprietary interests in land: see *King v David Allen & Sons, Billposting Ltd* (1916). The contract took effect only between the two parties who created it and could not bind a third party.

However, in *Errington v Errington and Woods* (1952) Lord Justice Denning claimed that a contractual licence was a proprietary interest in land, and so could bind a third party, Peter in our example.

Q: *Where did this idea come from?*

A: It came from the development of the equitable rules relating to the revocation of a contractual licence. If such a licence couldn't always be revoked, then it wasn't a huge leap of the imagination to claim that a contractual licence was a proprietary interest in land – a leap that was extremely convenient in the circumstances of the case. In *Errington v Errington and Woods* Mr Errington senior had bought a house with the aid of a mortgage. He had allowed his son and daughter-in-law to live in the house on the basis that they paid the mortgage repayments. When the mortgage had been paid off, Mr Errington senior would convey the house to them. Mr Errington senior then died. Mrs Errington senior, the son's mother, inherited the house. The son returned to live with his mother, who then tried to evict the daughter-in-law. Lord Justice Denning decided that the daughter-in-law's contractual licence was an equitable proprietary interest in the land and would bind Mrs Errington senior.

Q: *Why did the contractual licence bind Mrs Errington senior?*

A: The land in question was unregistered. There was no provision for protecting an equitable interest arising under a contractual licence under the Land Charges Act 1925. The status of the equitable interest was therefore determined by the pre-1926 rule relating to equitable interests, known as the doctrine of notice, which was as follows:

Equitable rights bind everyone except a *bona fide* purchaser of a legal estate for value without notice of the equitable interest.

The interest acquired under the contractual licence was equitable, so Mrs Errington senior would be bound by it unless she was a *bona fide* purchaser of a legal estate *for value*.

Q: *But she couldn't have been a purchaser for value because she inherited the property from her husband?*

A: Correct. This meant that the interest was binding on her because she was not a purchaser for value. Mrs Errington senior also, of course, had notice of her daughter in law's equitable interest. The decision in the *Errington* case was heavily criticised, for several reasons. First, it was contrary to the decision in *King v David Allen & Sons, Billposting Ltd*, which held that contractual licences were not proprietary interests in land, and so bound only the original parties to the contract. Secondly, although the wording of section 4 of the Law of Property Act 1925 is ambiguous, there is an argument that this section prevents the creation of new interests in land. Look at the number of contractual licences that exist over land in all sorts of different situations. If contractual licences became proprietary interests in land capable of binding third parties, nobody would know where they were when they bought land.

Q: *What happened then?*

A: *Ashburn Anstalt v Arnold & Co* (1989) reaffirmed the traditional view that contractual licences were not proprietary interests in land, and so would not bind anyone who was not party to the contract. It was stated that Lord Justice Denning's decision in *Errington v Errington and Woods* was *per incuriam*.

Q: *So that's the final word, then?*

A: Yes. A contractual licence is not a proprietary interest in land and cannot bind anyone who takes the land over which it is exercised. It would not bind Peter in our example. However, you can explain the decision in *Errington v Errington and Woods* in other ways. You can also use these other ways to achieve the same result in similar situations today. The first way is by arguing that there was an estate contract.

Q: *What's an estate contract?*

A: An estate contract is a contract to sell or transfer a legal estate in land. When you buy land, a house for example, there are two stages. There is a contract in which the vendor agrees to sell and the purchaser agrees to buy the land. The legal estate in the land is then conveyed to the purchaser by deed at a later date. The contract, which is known as an estate contract, must meet section 2 of the Law of Property (Miscellaneous Provisions) Act 1989, which essentially means that it must be in writing, signed by or on behalf of both parties and contain all its expressly agreed terms. In unregistered land it must then be entered as a class C(iv) land charge on the Land Charges Register against the name of the person who owns the land that is being sold. In registered land an estate contract must be entered as a notice on the Charges Register of the land that is being sold.

Q: *Could you have explained the decision in the* **Errington** *case on this basis?*

A: Yes, although the explanation is not without its critics. There was an estate contract between Mr Errington senior and his son and daughter-in-law. Mr Errington senior agreed to convey the house to them when the mortgage was paid off. The son's and daughter-in-law's consideration for this contract was the payment of the mortgage repayments. Although the requirements for the creation of the contract were not governed by section 2 of the Law of Property (Miscellaneous Provisions) Act 1989 at the time, it was still a valid estate contract under the existing law. The land was unregistered. As the son and daughter-in-law had the benefit of the estate contract, they should have entered it as a class C(iv) land charge against Mr Errington senior's name on the Land Charges Register. This hadn't happened. If a land charge in class C(iv) is not entered on the Land Charges Register, it is not binding on a purchaser of the legal estate for money or money's worth. Mrs Errington senior inherited the land and so was never a purchaser for money or money's worth. She would therefore have been bound by the estate contract. The contract for the transfer of the land was capable of specific performance, because land is unique and equity looks on that as done which ought to be done. This means that the court could have enforced the terms of the contract by the remedy of specific performance, and so Mrs Errington senior would have been forced to convey the house to the son and daughter-in-law.

Q: *Is there any other way of avoiding the rule that a contractual licence is not a proprietary interest in land and so will not bind a third party?*

A: A second way is to establish a constructive trust. The definition of a trust is covered in Chapter 6. The idea behind a constructive trust here is that when a person buys land knowing perfectly well that someone else has an interest in it and pays less for the land because of it, a trust will be imposed in the interests of fairness and equity. The classic example is *Binions v Evans* (1972), where a purchaser bought land expressly subject to person A's rights to live there, and at a reduced price because of person A's rights. Lord Denning MR argued that the purchaser held the property on constructive trust for person A and had to honour his interest in the property. In our example, if Peter had bought Greenacres expressly subject to Emma's contractual licence to live there for the rest of her life, and he had paid less for Greenacres because of it, you could argue that Peter held Greenacres on constructive trust for the benefit of Emma.

Q: *And a third way?*

A: The third way is to argue proprietary estoppel which is discussed in Chapter 12.

A licence coupled with the grant of a property right

This type of licence exists when a property right is granted by person A to person B which necessitates person B going onto person A's land to exercise the right. Such licences can arise in the context of sporting rights and are generally known as *profits à prendre*. A profit is a benefit and *'prendre'* means 'to take' in French. Examples of *profits à prendre* include the right to catch and take fish, known as a profit of piscary, and a right to take wood, known as a profit of estover. A right to hunt wild animals is also a *profit à prendre*.

Q: *So if you've been granted a profit, you must have also been granted permission to go on the land, unless you're going to fish from a helicopter?*

A: Yes. A licence must have automatically been granted over the land in order to exercise the right. This means that the licence has become part of the interest itself and cannot be revoked while the interest continues. The benefit of a profit can be assigned to another party. Profits must also be protected by the party enjoying the benefit of the right in unregistered and registered land in a similar way to easements, which are again a right over someone else's land and discussed in Chapter 17. Thus, whether a *profit à prendre* binds a subsequent purchaser of the land over which it's exercised depends on whether the requirements for registration have been met.

There is no dedicated question on licences. They are discussed within Chapter 15 on leases and within Chapter 17 on easements.

Further reading

G. Battersby, 'Contractual and Estoppel Licences as Proprietary Interests in Land', *Conv and Prop Law*, Jan/Feb (1991) 36

J. Hill, 'The Termination of Bare Licences', 60 *CLJ* (2001) 89

S. Moriarty, 'Licences and Land Law: Legal Principles and Public Policies', 100 *LQR* (1984) 376

Freehold covenants

Introduction

This chapter looks at freehold covenants. A covenant is a promise contained within a deed. Covenants arise in the context of land law because one party promises that he or she will do something, or that he or she will not do something, on land.

Covenants are probably more familiar to you in relation to leases. If land is leased to you, the agreement that you sign will inevitably contain a clause that you promise to pay rent, for example. The landlord could promise to keep the roof in good repair and to insure the property. These promises are called covenants and, because they are attached to a lease, they are called leasehold covenants. Leasehold covenants are discussed in Chapter 16 and must not be confused with the freehold covenants discussed here. The covenants discussed in this chapter are created between people who actually own the land outright, rather than holding it on a lease. They are called *freehold* covenants because they are created between *freehold owners*. The following is a classic example of how a freehold covenant is created.

Fred owns Greenacres.

```
Greenacres
owned by Fred
```

Like most people, he is rather short of money and decides that he will sell off that part of Greenacres called The Orchard, in order to raise some cash. Victor makes him an offer he can't refuse. However, Fred has been rather worried that whoever bought The Orchard might actually develop the land and build several houses there, which would have the effect of ruining his view and also devaluing

Greenacres. So when The Orchard is conveyed (sold) to Victor, Fred can insist that Victor promises in the deed of sale that he will not build more than one house on The Orchard. This promise by Victor within the deed of sale is called a covenant where the double-headed arrow represents the covenant between Fred and Victor.

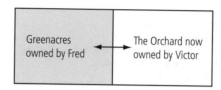

Victor may decide to sell The Orchard on to another person, Jack.

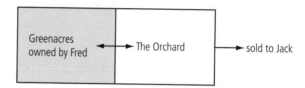

The question, then, is whether Fred can enforce against Jack the original promise Victor made with him.

Another problem will arise if Fred decides to sell Greenacres to Amy.

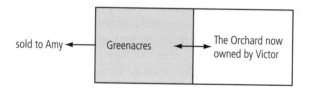

The question, then, is whether Amy has the right to enforce the promise Victor made to Fred.

In fact, the situation could eventually end up looking like this – or seems to in exam questions.

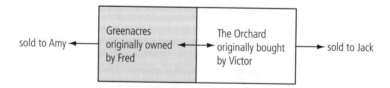

This chapter works through each of the different scenarios described above.

The nature of a freehold covenant

A covenant is a promise contained within a deed. One party promises the other that he will either do something or not do something in relation to a piece of land.

The person who makes the promise is called the covenantor and the person who has the benefit of the promise is the covenantee.

Q: *What sort of covenants are made between people who own land?*

A: Covenants usually arise in the context of the example at the start of this chapter when one party, Fred, wants to sell off part of his land, The Orchard, but doesn't want the person who buys it, Victor, to do anything that might devalue or be a nuisance to the piece of land that's retained – Greenacres in our example.

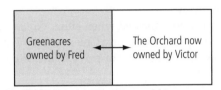

Fred could make it a condition of sale, for example, that Victor promises to build only one house on The Orchard or that Victor maintain the boundary fence between the properties, or that Victor promises not to use The Orchard for commercial purposes.

Q: *In these examples is Victor the covenantor because he is the person who has made the promise, and is Fred the covenantee because he has the benefit of the covenant?*

A: Yes.

Q: *What happens if Victor covenants not to build more than one house on The Orchard and then starts to build several blocks of flats there?*

A: A covenant is a promise or a contract between the parties Fred and Victor, so the remedy is for Fred to sue for breach of contract. The usual remedy for breach of contract is damages, but damages would be inadequate here. However much you compensated Fred with money, it wouldn't actually solve the problem of the several blocks of flats spoiling his view or devaluing Greenacres. Therefore, Fred should ask for an injunction against Victor to stop him building his blocks of flats.

An injunction is an order preventing someone from doing something, here building blocks of flats. If Victor had already built the flats, Fred would have to ask for a mandatory injunction. This type of injunction orders someone to undo something they shouldn't have done in the first place, so Victor would have to pull his flats down.

Q: *So there isn't a problem if the original party breaks the covenant?*

A: No. It's a breach of contract between two parties who were both privy to the contract and the party who broke the covenant can be sued by the other party. Remember: a covenant is a promise, a contract.

Q: *What happens if it's not clear whether the covenant has been breached?*

A: In the example we've been looking at between Fred and Victor, it's easy to see if there's been a breach of the covenant not to build more than one house if a block of flats goes up. In *Dennis v Davies* (2008) the question was whether an extension to a building which would partially or totally obscure the views of the river from properties on the estate was in breach of a covenant which said nothing could be done on the land which would be a nuisance or annoyance to the owners of properties on the estate. The test was an objective one, judged on common sense standards (there's a first) and asked whether ordinary sensible English inhabitants would see it as a nuisance or annoyance. On the facts the extension to the building constituted an annoyance.

Life becomes more complicated when either Greenacres or The Orchard or both are sold, because the parties who buy Greenacres or The Orchard, Amy and Jack in the example below, were not party or privy to the original covenant (contract).

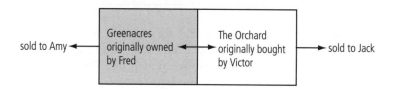

You will need to establish whether there is any way Amy can enforce the covenant against Jack.

Q: Surely you can't expect people who weren't party to the original covenant (contract) to be able to enforce it or to be bound by the promise in it?

A: Well, under certain circumstances you can. There are two viewpoints here. On the one hand, Amy and Jack weren't parties to the original covenant (contract) and shouldn't be able to take the benefit of it or be bound by it. On the other hand, the point of the original promise was to prevent the owner of The Orchard damaging the interests of Greenacres. If both properties are sold, is it fair that the new owner of The Orchard is allowed now to damage the interests of the new owner of Greenacres at will? Look at the following example. Victor buys The Orchard from Fred and covenants not to build more than one house on it. Victor is the covenantor. Fred is the covenantee.

The first scenario is where Fred sells Greenacres to Amy and looks like this.

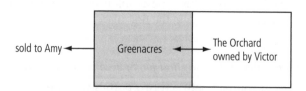

If Amy cannot enforce the covenant against Victor, then Victor can do what he wants. He can build a multi-story car park or a nuclear power station provided he obtains planning permission. The value of Greenacres will fall to almost nothing, Amy will go slowly mad with the nuisance and nobody in their right minds would buy Greenacres from her to live in.

The second scenario is when The Orchard is sold to Jack.

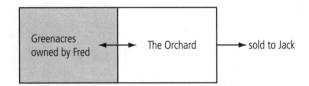

The question is whether Fred can enforce the original covenant against Jack. If he can't, then Jack can do what he wants. He can build a multi-storey car park or a space station, subject to planning permission. The value of Greenacres will fall to almost nothing, Fred will go slowly mad with the nuisance and nobody in their right minds would buy Greenacres from him to live in.

And of course this situation doesn't bear thinking about. Yet.

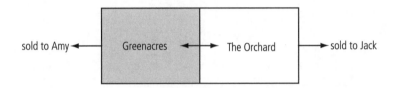

The question here is whether Amy can enforce the covenant against Jack.

Q: *So what happens now, on the basis that you've proved that it's not very socially acceptable if the covenant binds only the original parties?*

A: The answer depends on a number of rules.

The rules divide nicely into three parts:

- ▶ Including strangers in the contract.
- ▶ Assigning the covenant to future purchasers.
- ▶ Attaching the covenant to the land.

We will go through each of these via the chart on page 340 using the example of Fred, Greenacres, The Orchard, the covenant by Victor not to build more than one house on The Orchard, Amy and Jack.

Including strangers in the contract

> **Box A**
>
> INCLUDING STRANGERS IN THE CONTRACT
>
> **1.** Section 56 of the Law of Property Act 1925
>
> or
>
> **2.** The Contracts (Rights of Third Parties) Act 1999

The first aspect to consider is whether you can include anyone else in the covenant (contract) even though he wasn't party to it. If you could, then you could say that he was included in the covenant (contract) and was therefore bound by it.

FREEHOLD COVENANTS – All references to covenantor and covenantee refer to the original parties to the covenant

Box A

INCLUDING STRANGERS IN THE CONTRACT

1. Section 56 of the Law of Property Act 1925

or

2. The Contracts (Rights of Third Parties) Act 1999

Box B

ASSIGNING THE BENEFIT OF THE COVENANT TO FUTURE PURCHASERS

You must prove either

1. A legal assignment under section 136 of the Law of Property Act 1925

Or

2. Assignment in equity

Box C

THE RUNNING OF THE BENEFIT AT COMMON LAW

You must prove annexation of the benefit at common law

You must tick all boxes.

☐ **1.** The covenant must have touched and concerned the covenantee's land.

☐ **2.** When making the covenant, the original parties must have intended that the benefit should run with the land.

☐ **3.** The covenantee and his successors in title must own a legal estate in the land.

Box D

THE RUNNING OF THE BENEFIT IN EQUITY

You must prove either annexation of the benefit in equity

You must tick boxes 1 and 2.

☐ **1.** The covenant must have touched and concerned the covenantee's land.

☐ **2.** When making the covenant, the original parties must have intended that the benefit should run with the land.

Or

☐ **3.** You must prove that a scheme of development exists.

Box E

THE RUNNING OF THE BURDEN AT COMMON LAW

The burden does not run with the land at common law.

As an alternative you can use devices such as:

1. There must be a chain of indemnity covenants

Or

2. The covenant must be compulsorily renewable

Or

3. There must be mutual benefit and burden.

Box F

THE RUNNING OF THE BURDEN IN EQUITY

You must prove annexation of the burden in equity

You must tick all boxes.

☐ **1.** The covenant must have been negative.

☐ **2.** (i) The covenant undertaken by the covenantor on his land must have touched and concerned the covenantee's land,

(ii) The two plots of land must have been sufficiently proximate.

☐ **3.** When the covenant was created, the covenantee must have owned land that was benefited by the covenant.

☐ **4.** When making the covenant, the original parties must have intended that the burden should run with the land.

☐ **5.** The restrictive covenant must be protected.

Q: *Can you contract on someone else's behalf?*

A: You can only contract to give *the benefit* or *the advantage* of a contract to someone else, and you can do this under statute law. When Fred and Victor originally created the covenant, Fred had the benefit or the advantage of the covenant that Victor would not build more than one house on The Orchard. Victor had the burden of the covenant not to build more than one house on The Orchard. If Fred sold Greenacres to Amy, then we need to know whether she can also obtain the benefit of the covenant, even though she wasn't party to the original agreement.

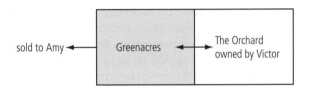

Q: *What's the answer for Amy?*

A: There are two ways she can do this. Both ways relate only to whether the benefit of the covenant is enforceable by Amy.

Box A1

Section 56 of the Law of Property Act 1925

The first way is under section 56 of the Law of Property Act 1925, which states:

> A person may take an immediate or other interest in land or other property, or the benefit of any condition, right of entry, covenant or agreement over or respecting land or other property, although he may not be named as a party to the conveyance or the instrument.

This section allows a stranger to the original contract to take the benefit of a covenant even though he was not a party to it: see *Re Ecclesiastical Commissioners for England's Conveyance* (1936). However, the original covenant must have been made *with him* rather than being merely expressed to be for *his benefit*: see *Amsprop Trading Ltd v Harris Distribution Ltd* (1997).

Q: *What do you mean by 'with him'?*

A: The original person who made the promise, the covenantor, would have to say in the covenant 'I covenant with X and *with person B*', rather than 'I covenant with X and for *the benefit of B*'. The stranger to the contract doesn't have to be actually named because it's sufficient that he comes within a general category. An example is 'I covenant with X and *with the owners for the time being of the lands adjoining*'. However, anyone in the general category must be existing and identifiable at the date of the covenant. This necessarily excludes future purchasers (successors in title) because the people X subsequently sells the land to are not in existence and not identifiable.

Q: *So section 56 is not much use to Amy then, in our example?*

A: Correct. She is a future purchaser and not existing and identifiable at the date of the original covenant.

Box A2   The Contracts (Rights of Third Parties) Act 1999

All is not lost, though. Section 1 of the Contracts (Rights of Third Parties) Act 1999 applies to all contracts made after May 2000. Under section 1(1) of the Act a stranger who is not privy to (party to) a contract can enforce a term of the contract if the contract expressly provides that he can, or the term of the contract purports to confer a benefit on him. Under section 1(3) a stranger can be expressly identified by name or he can come under a general category such as 'successors in title'. More importantly, the stranger to the contract needn't be in existence at the date of the original covenant provided he comes within the general category. So Victor would have to have made a covenant along the lines of 'I covenant with Fred and any successors in title of Greenacres [the people Fred subsequently sells Greenacres to] not to build more than one house on The Orchard'. Under the 1999 Act, successors in title to Fred do not have to be in existence and identifiable. They will be included within the general category, and can sue Victor if he breaches the covenant. Amy is a successor in title to Fred, and so could sue Victor.

Q: *That's a possibility then?*

A: Yes, but the trouble is that the Act is not retrospective and it applies only to contracts made after May 2000. And it doesn't deal with the problem if Victor sells The Orchard on to Jack, because it allows only *the benefit of* the covenant to pass to Amy when she buys Greenacres from Fred. When Victor sells The Orchard to Jack, Jack cannot be included under either of these Acts because he has the burden of the covenant, not the benefit.

Assigning the benefit of the covenant to future purchasers

> **Box B**
>
> ASSIGNING THE BENEFIT OF THE COVENANT TO FUTURE PURCHASERS
>
> You must prove either
>
> **1.** A legal assignment under section 136 of the Law of Property Act 1925
>
> Or
>
> **2.** Assignment in equity

Another method is to see whether the original party to the covenant can assign the benefit of the covenant to a purchaser. Assignment means 'passing on' to the next owner of the land. This is possible at common law or in equity, but again it is only the benefit that can be assigned and not the burden. This is the situation we are looking at, and the question is whether Fred, the original party to the covenant, can assign the benefit of the covenant to Amy.

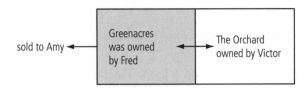

Box B1 A legal assignment under section 136 of the Law of Property Act 1925

Section 136 of the Law of Property Act 1925 governs assignment and states that the benefit of the covenant can be assigned to the next person who buys the benefited land. The conditions are as follows:

▷ The assignment must be in writing. Fred must therefore assign the benefit in writing to Amy.

and

▷ Written notice of this assignment is given to the original covenantor. In our example, written notice of the assignment would have to be given to Victor.

Q: *If Fred had assigned the benefit to Amy, and then Amy had sold Greenacres on to Jemima, would Amy have to assign the benefit to Jemima in writing and give written notice to Victor?*

A: Yes. Assignment is a means by which people can pass the benefit on, and each person must pass the benefit on to the next person personally. It is rather unrealistic to expect that people are going to do this.

Box B2 Assignment in equity

The benefit of the covenant can be assigned in equity to the next person who buys the benefited land. In our example, Fred would have personally to assign the benefit of the covenant to Amy. The following conditions given in *Re Union of London and Smith's Bank Ltd's Conveyance* (1933) must first be satisfied:

▷ The land benefited by the covenant must be identifiable using extrinsic (outside) evidence if necessary: see *Newton Abbott Cooperative Society Ltd v Williamson & Treadgold Ltd* (1952).

and

▷ The covenant must have been taken for the benefit of the land owned by the covenantee at the date of the covenant.

and

▷ The land that benefited from the covenant must be retained in whole or part by the person now claiming the benefit of the covenant.

and

▷ The land that benefited from the covenant must still be capable of benefiting from the covenant.

and

▶ The assignment must be at the same time as the transfer or sale of the land to which it relates.

In our example, Greenacres must be identifiable as the benefited land. The covenant with Fred must have been for the benefit of his land, Greenacres, and Amy must now own all or part of Greenacres. Greenacres must still be capable of benefiting from the covenant. And, most importantly, the assignment of the benefit of the covenant to Amy must be at the same time as the sale to her.

Q: *Why at the same time?*

A: Because the covenant relates to the land of Greenacres. If the covenant and the land become separated, first the covenant becomes meaningless because it's not attached to land. Secondly, if it is not attached to the land, Amy will not be able to claim the benefit of it for Greenacres.

Fred must then either expressly or impliedly assign or pass the benefit of the covenant to Amy. Usually this is done in writing, but there must be some representation by Fred to Amy that she is to have the benefit of the covenant.

If Amy were to sell Greenacres on, she would then have to assign the benefit of the covenant on to the purchaser in the same way: see *Re Pinewood Estate, Farnborough* (1958). As at common law, assignment simply passes the benefit to the next person down the line.

Summary of assignment

The effect of satisfying the assignment conditions is that the benefit of the covenant passes to the next person, so that person can sue Victor if he builds more than one house. The benefit of the covenant must be specifically assigned each time to the next person, which is unrealistic. It also does not deal with the problem which arises if Victor sells The Orchard to Jack, as Jack has the burden of the covenant, not the benefit.

Q: *How do you deal with these problems then?*

A: We have to try a different tack. When Victor covenants with Fred not to build more than one house on The Orchard, the land known as Greenacres has the benefit of the covenant and the land known as The Orchard has the burden. So, instead of looking at the people and asking whether they could possibly be included in the contract or whether the benefit has been assigned to them, you could start asking whether the benefit of the covenant stays with Greenacres regardless of who owns it, and whether the burden of the covenant stays with The Orchard regardless of who owns it. You are looking at the idea of stamping the original covenant on both pieces of land so that the benefit becomes attached to, or a part of, the land that was originally benefited, and the burden becomes attached to, or a part of, the land that was original burdened. The technical term in land law is, as usual, less than helpful. It asks whether the benefit and the burden of the covenant 'run with the land'. Had those who invented land law language used phrases like 'does the benefit of the covenant become attached to the land originally benefited' and 'does the burden of the covenant become attached to the land originally burdened', we might all be better off. But they didn't, so you are left with the words 'run with the land'. Use 'attached to', or try 'the covenant has become part of the land', if you prefer.

It may also be helpful here to look at benefit and burden in terms of the benefit giving the owner of the land the right to sue, and the burden meaning that the owner of the land runs the risk of being sued. If the benefit becomes attached to the land, it gives the current owner the right to sue if the covenant is breached, and if the burden is attached to the land, it means the current owner of the burdened land runs the risk of being sued if the covenant is breached.

Some of the textbooks refer to dominant and servient tenements here. Tenement simply means a piece of land in which you own a legal estate. The dominant tenement is the land that has the benefit of the covenant, which is the right to sue if there is a breach. The servient tenement has the burden of the covenant, which is the risk of being sued if there is a breach.

Q: *And do the benefit and burden actually become attached to, or a part of, the land?*

A: They can do. Under both section 56 of the Law of Property Act 1925 and section 1 of the Contracts (Rights of Third Parties) Act 1999, we were looking at whether the covenant was transferred to a person. We are now looking at the land itself, and it is simply a matter of applying a few straightforward rules. There are two sets of rules for determining whether the benefit and burden have become part of the land. They are the common law rules and the equitable rules.

Q: *Why are there two sets of rules?*

A: The common law rules are inflexible and not much help to anyone. As a result, the rules in equity were developed. They are far more flexible and generally give a just result, which, after all, is what equity is about.

As there are the common law rules and the equitable rules that govern whether the benefit and burden become attached to the land, rather than transferred to people, that makes four possible scenarios:

1. the rules relating to the benefit at common law;
2. the rules relating to the benefit in equity;
3. the rules relating to the burden at common law;
4. the rules relating to the burden in equity.

These rules are summarised in Boxes C to F in the chart on page 340. To establish whether the benefit and burden of a covenant become attached to the land, you need to see whether you can meet the rules either at common law or in equity.

You must note that all references to covenantor and covenantee in the chart relate to the original parties to the covenant. They are the only people who can be called covenantor and covenantee, because they were the only parties privy to the covenant. Other people may have bought the land, but they were not party to the covenant and so cannot be called covenantor and covenantee.

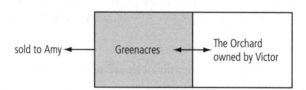 **The running of the benefit at common law**

Box C

THE RUNNING OF THE BENEFIT AT COMMON LAW

You must prove annexation of the benefit at common law

You must tick all boxes.

☐ **1.** The covenant must have touched and concerned the covenantee's land.

☐ **2.** When making the covenant, the original parties must have intended that the benefit should run with the land.

☐ **3.** The covenantee and his successors in title must own a legal estate in the land.

You must prove annexation of the benefit at common law.

Q: *What does annexation mean?*

A: Attachment.

This is the situation we're looking at.

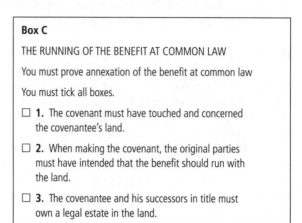

Fred has sold Greenacres to Amy, and she now wants to know whether she can enforce the benefit of the covenant against Victor and sue him if he builds more than one house. You will be looking at whether the benefit of the covenant (the right to sue if the covenant is broken) runs with or becomes attached to Greenacres, in which case Amy can claim the benefit and sue Victor. The burden of the covenant is still with Victor because he is the original party to the covenant and still owns The Orchard.

This is a brief summary of what we have established so far. Fred was the covenantee and Victor the covenantor. There is no privity of contract between Amy and Victor; section 56 of the Law of Property Act 1925 did not include future purchasers and the Contracts (Rights of Third Parties) Act 1999 applies only to contracts made after May 2000, which is fine if the contract was after then, but not if it wasn't. Having given up looking at the people front, we're now going to look at the set of rules that governs whether the benefit of the covenant became attached to Greenacres, and therefore stays with it, regardless of who buys the land, therefore giving him or her the right to sue.

The conditions for annexation of the benefit of the covenant at common law are as follows.

Box C1   The covenant must have touched and concerned the covenantee's land

Q: *What does 'touch and concern' mean?*

A: It means that the covenant must affect the land of the covenantee. It must affect the way in which the land is used or affect its value. In our example, the promise not to build more than one house on The Orchard touches and concerns Greenacres because it affects the value of Greenacres. If 20 houses were built on The Orchard, the value of Greenacres might fall. If the covenant has to affect the land, it can't be a personal covenant. If Victor covenanted to take Fred's dog for a walk every day, this would be a personal covenant as it wouldn't affect the value or use of Greenacres. Another way of looking at it is to ask whether the covenant is of any value to Fred if he doesn't own Greenacres. If it isn't, then the covenant is likely to touch and concern the land.

In *P&A Swift Investments v Combined English Stores Group plc* (1989) a test was devised for determining whether a covenant touched and concerned the land. The case was about leasehold covenants, but the principles are the same for freehold covenants:

- The benefit must be of benefit to the covenantee only when he owns the land.
- The covenant must affect the way his land is used, its nature, its quality or its value.
- The covenant must not be expressed to be personal in nature. This means that it wasn't expressed to be binding just between the two original parties.

In *Newton Abbott Cooperative Society Ltd v Williamson & Treadgold Ltd* a covenant not to carry on a business that competed with the business of the covenantee was a covenant that touched and concerned the covenantee's land.

Box C2   When making the covenant, the original parties must have intended that the benefit should run with the land

You have to show that it was the intention of the original parties that the benefit was to run with or become attached to the benefited land. This used to be shown by the wording in the covenant where the covenantor would covenant with 'the covenantee, his successors in title, and those deriving title under him'. Very conveniently you can now use section 78 of the Law of Property Act 1925 for all covenants made after 1925. Section 78 states:

> A covenant relating to any land of the covenantee shall be deemed to be made with the covenantee and his successors in title and the persons deriving title under him or them, and shall have effect as if such successors and other persons were expressed.

Under section 78 this intention is automatically implied when a covenant is made for the benefit of the covenantee's land, here Fred's land.

Box C3   The covenantee and his successors in title must own a legal estate in the land

The authority for this requirement is *Webb v Russell* (1789). The common law used to require any successor in title of the covenantee to have the same legal estate in the land as the covenantee. However, in *Smith and Snipes Hall Farm Ltd v River Douglas Catchment Board* (1949), section 78 of the Law of Property Act 1925 was held to mean that although a successor in title to the covenantee must hold a legal estate in the land, it does not have to be the same legal estate. There are two legal estates recognised by section 1 of the Law of Property Act 1925. They are the fee simple absolute in possession (ownership as we know it) and the term of years absolute (the lease). In our example, the covenantee, Fred, the person who had the benefit of the covenant, held the legal fee simple estate in Greenacres, and Amy, his successor in title, now holds the legal fee simple estate in Greenacres, so the condition is met. If Amy had taken a legal leasehold estate, a legal lease of Greenacres, she would also have met this condition.

In *Smith and Snipes Hall Farm Ltd v River Douglas Catchment Board* the River Douglas Catchment Board had covenanted with the owners of the surrounding land that they would keep the banks of a brook in repair. One of the original covenantees had sold his land expressly with the benefit of the covenant to the first claimant. The first claimant had then granted a legal lease over the benefited land to Smith and Snipes Hall Farm, the second claimant. The banks of the brook were not maintained and the brook burst its banks. Smith and Snipes Hall Farm held a legal lease of the benefited land, which is a legal estate in land, and so satisfied section 78. It was held that the first claimant could claim the benefit of the covenant because it had been expressly assigned to him. Smith and Snipes Hall Farm could claim the benefit of the covenant because the requirements for annexation had been met. Both could therefore claim damages.

Summary of annexation of the benefit at common law

The effect of ticking all the boxes in Box C for annexation at common law is that the benefit of the covenant is permanently annexed or attached to the land. This gives Amy the right to sue Victor. If Amy were to sell the land to Jemima, Jemima would be able to enforce the covenant against Victor and sue him if he built more than one house because the covenant is annexed or attached to Greenacres permanently. The same would apply if Jemima then sold Greenacres to Zeus and so on.

The running of the benefit in equity

Box D

THE RUNNING OF THE BENEFIT IN EQUITY

You must prove
either annexation of the benefit in equity

You must tick boxes 1 and 2.

☐ **1.** The covenant must have touched and concerned the covenantee's land.

☐ **2.** When making the covenant, the original parties must have intended that the benefit should run with the land.

Or

☐ **3.** You must prove that a scheme of development exists.

We will now look at the running of the benefit in equity in Box D.
The situation you're looking at is this.

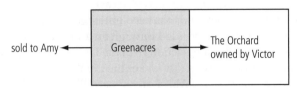

Q: *Why must you look at the benefit in equity? There wasn't a problem with the benefit at law; it all looked quite straightforward.*

A: Because you may not be able to meet the common law rules and, more importantly, because you cannot use the common law rules in every situation. This latter reason is important and is discussed in detail later in the chapter.

For the benefit to run with or become attached to the land in equity, you must prove either annexation of the benefit or that there is a scheme of development.

Annexed means attached to the land. The covenant is attached forever to the land regardless of who owns the land. You must tick Boxes D1 and D2 for this to happen.

Box D1 The covenant must have touched and concerned the covenantee's land

This is exactly the same as before and was discussed in Box C1.

Box D2 When making the covenant, the original parties must have intended that the benefit should run with the land

This intention was originally achieved by the wording in the covenant. Not only did the wording have to state that the benefit of the covenant was to pass to future successors of the covenantee, but it also had to be made clear that the benefit of the covenant was annexed to or attached to the land, not just to the person. The wording had to show that the covenant was attached to the land.

Here are two examples.

In *Rogers v Hosegood* (1900) there was an

> intent that the covenant may enure to the benefit of the vendors (who were the covenantees), their successors and assigns and others claiming under them to all or any of *their lands* adjoining.

'Enure to' means to serve. The *land* was specifically mentioned, and so the benefit was attached to it and could run with or become attached to the land.

In *Renals v Cowlishaw* (1879) the covenant was made with:

> the covenantees, their heirs, executors, administrators and assigns.

Because there was no mention of annexing or attaching the covenant to any land, the benefit did not run with and become attached to the land.

It is argued that annexation or attaching the covenant to the land can also be implied from the circumstances surrounding the grant of the covenant provided the benefited land can be identified: see the obiter dicta in *Newton Abbott Cooperative Society Ltd v Williamson and Treadgold Ltd* and *Marten v Flight Refuelling Ltd* (No. 1)

(1962). However, in *Marten v Flight Refuelling Ltd* (No. 1) the claimants were the covenantees so there was no need to look at whether the benefit ran with or became attached to the land by annexation, which casts some doubt over this decision. Also, the idea of implied annexation has been criticised because it creates uncertainty, in that the claim can only be decided through an application to the court.

Fortunately for everyone, section 78 of the Law of Property Act 1925 now implies an intention automatically so this makes life much easier for covenants created after 1925. *Federated Homes Ltd v Mill Lodge Properties Ltd* (1980) is the important case where Lord Justice Brightman established that section 78 implied this automatic intention. There was (and still is) a lot of academic debate on whether this decision was correct and the arguments for and against are discussed at the end of this chapter. After the *Federated Homes* case the courts went quiet for 26 years until *Crest Nicholson Residential (South) Ltd v McAllister* (2004). The Court of Appeal held that there was automatic annexation, but it also held that there had to be some reference in the covenant to the land intended to be benefited and that land had to be easily identified (for example from schedules or plans). In the case the benefited land could not be clearly identified and so the benefit was not annexed to the land. In *Small v Oliver and Saunders (Developments) Ltd* (2006) the benefited land could be identified so the covenant was annexed to the land. In contrast, in the recent case of *Re Hutchinson's Application* [2009] the reference to 'the retained land' as the land to be benefitted was not enough to be able to identify it so the benefit was not annexed to the land.

Q: *What happens if the parties want to exclude the effect of the section so the covenant remains personal between them?*

A: Section 78 does not say anything about excluding the effect of the section, which would indicate that the intention is implied regardless of what the parties wanted. However, in *Roake v Chadha* (1984) the covenant stated that the benefit of it could pass only if it had been expressly assigned. The effect of this wording was to exclude annexation under section 78. The fact that the benefit had to be expressly assigned in person meant a contrary intention to the implication of annexation under section 78. This decision was confirmed in *Crest Nicholson Residential (South) Ltd v McAllister* where, again, in a different covenant, the words indicated a contrary intention to automatic annexation. In *Sugarman v Porter* (2006) the covenant was expressed to be for the benefit of any part of the property remaining unsold. This meant that when the land, or any part of the land, was sold, the benefit would not pass by annexation. The wording 'expressed to be for the benefit of any part remaining unsold' excluded the automatic annexation of section 78. The benefit could only be assigned expressly. In *Norwich City College of Further and Higher Education v McQuillin* (2009) the wording again excluded automatic annexation under section 78.

Q: *What happens if the covenantor needed consent from the covenantee before the covenantor could make alterations to a building on the burdened land, for example, but the benefited land had been sold on by the covenantee?*

A: This very much depends on the wording of the covenant as it did in *Margerison v Bates* (2008). In 1966 Swaynes Jumps and Priors Knock (what lovely place names that could have come straight out of a Beatrix Potter story) were under the common ownership of Jennie Fisher Horn, 'Mrs Horn'. She had sold off Swaynes Jumps with permission to build a bungalow. Any alterations to the bungalow had to have written consent from 'the vendor'. The vendor was Mrs Horn. Following a dispute, the court held that the reference to 'vendor' did not include the successors in title to the vendor i.e. the people to whom Mrs Horn had sold Priors Knock. When looking at the conveyance as a whole, where the draftsman had meant to include the successors in title to the vendor, he had made this quite clear. So, only Mrs Horn could give consent. *Mahon v Sims* (2005) was distinguished because in that case the draftsman had not made any reference to successors in title in the covenant which would allow the court to find a distinction between 'transferor only' and 'transferor and successors in title'. Unfortunately, though, Mrs Horn had died. Following *Crest Nicholson Residential (South) Ltd v McAllister* the covenant was held to be discharged. In *City Inn (Jersey) Ltd v Ten Trinity Square Ltd* (2007) it was decided that the word 'transferor' did not include successors in title and a similar result ensued in *Churchill v Temple* (2010).

Q: *Does this mean that the right to give consent can be separated from the right to enforce the covenant if the right to give consent does not pass to successors in title?*

A: Yes, but in *Margerison v Bates* it was said that the covenant still touches and concerns the benefited land even if consent is needed from a third party and the third party can't act arbitrarily in refusing consent or refuse for reasons which have nothing to do with the benefited land.

Q: *If Greenacres were a huge plot of land covering hundreds of acres, how could a covenant not to build more than one house on The Orchard possibly benefit the part of Greenacres furthest away from The Orchard?*

A: It doesn't necessarily do so. In *Re Ballard's Conveyance* (1937) the covenantee had kept 1,700 acres of land. It was held that the covenant undertaken on the burdened land couldn't possibly benefit the whole of the 1,700 acres, and so it was not enforceable by a successor in title to the covenantee. The standard way of putting this is to say that the covenant couldn't benefit 'all and every part of the land'. These days it's more a matter of looking at the situation sensibly: see *Earl of Leicester v Wells-next-the-Sea Urban District Council* (1973).

Federated Homes Ltd v Mill Lodge Properties Ltd also established that the covenant became annexed to each and every part of the land. In equity you used to have to annex the benefit to each and every part of Greenacres in the wording of the covenant, because if Fred sold a part of Greenacres off to someone else, the benefit of the covenant wouldn't be attached to the part sold off: see *Re Ballard's Conveyance*. The *Federated Homes* case has now established that the covenant will be annexed automatically to each and every part of the benefited land under section 78 for covenants made after 1925.

Q: *Is this a good idea?*

A: Not necessarily. Imagine the following situation. Victor covenanted not to build more than one house on The Orchard. Fred then sold that part of Greenaces called

Greenacres Meadow to David. Under section 78 of the Law of Property Act 1925 the benefit of the covenant becomes annexed to the part of Greenacres sold off, Greenacres Meadow. David now has the ability to sue Victor if he tries to build more than one house on The Orchard. Fred subsequently finds he is short of money. Victor offers to give Fred a percentage of the proceeds of sale if he, Victor, builds 20 houses on The Orchard. This is on the basis that Fred will not enforce the covenant not to build more than one house on The Orchard against Victor. Fred wants to accept this offer. If the deal went ahead, David could still enforce the covenant against Victor and either prevent him building or seriously undermine his profit margin if damages were awarded. Fred is now the victim of his own covenant because section 78 annexed the benefit of the covenant automatically to each and every part of Greenacres.

Box D3   ## Or you must prove that a scheme of development exists

Schemes of development were devised to take into account the following problem.

Apollo builds a housing estate of 26 houses. He sells house '1' to Zeus. Zeus covenants with Apollo not to build another house on his, Zeus's, land. Apollo then sells house '2' to Pluto. Pluto covenants with Apollo not to build another house on his, Pluto's, land. This goes on until all 26 houses are sold with the last house going to Galaxy. Apollo does not have any land left at all to be benefited, so cannot enforce the benefit of the covenant against Galaxy.

Q: *Couldn't Apollo sue Galaxy because there was privity of contract between them?*

A: He could, but there isn't a lot of point. Apollo's loss is nil because he doesn't have any land which benefits from the contract, so his damages will be nominal and not worth pursuing. And why should he anyway? He's well out of it now. He's got no land that is affected by the covenant and is probably miles away building even more houses on housing estates.

The other problem in this situation is that Zeus cannot sue Pluto for the latter's breach unless he can be included in the covenant between Apollo and Pluto under section 56 of the Law of Property Act 1925 or under the Contracts (Rights of Third Parties) Act 1999 (Box A). Working out who can sue whom like this is not easy, and still may not allow Zeus to sue Pluto. It is therefore a popular scenario for exam questions.

To overcome these problems, equity developed a set of rules especially for schemes of development, of which a housing estate is one.

The original conditions were set out in *Elliston v Reacher* (1908) and were very restrictive. The result was that a scheme of development was found in only very few cases after 1908. In *Re Dolphin's Conveyance* (1970) these conditions were relaxed and are now as follows:

1. The area affected by the scheme of development must be clearly identified.

    In *Whitgift Homes Ltd v Stocks* (2001) it was held that there had to be a defined area where the scheme would operate, so that every purchaser would know which plots were within the scheme and which weren't. As there was no defined area there was no building scheme, although annexation was argued successfully instead.

2. There must be an intention that every plot is mutually bound by the covenants and can mutually enforce the benefits i.e. there is mutual reciprocity.

    In *Small v Oliver and Saunders (Developments) Ltd* the claimant had not shown that the purchasers of the properties were aware of the reciprocal nature of the covenants. However, as the covenants had been annexed to the land, the claimant relied on annexation instead.

3. All the purchasers must have been aware of the common restrictions and bought on the basis that the restrictions were for the benefit of all other plots: see *Jamaica Mutual Life Assurance Society v Hillsborough Ltd* (1989).

When establishing whether there is a building scheme emphasis is placed on the required common intention in point 2: see *Baxter v Four Oaks Properties Ltd* (1965). In *Emile Elias & Co Ltd v Pine Groves Ltd* (1993) there was no common intention because different covenants had been imposed on the different plots of land and there was no uniformity. *Clarke v Murphy* (2009) is a recent example where the requirements necessary for a building scheme were found. It is a useful case to read.

The effect of a scheme of development is that once the first plot is sold all the others must be sold subject to the same restrictions. All the plot owners are then able to sue all the other plot owners for breach of the covenants. There are two important limitations here. First, any covenant must be negative. It must be a promise not to do something. The nature of a negative covenant is discussed further in Box F1. Secondly, any covenant must be protected whether the land is unregistered or registered. This is discussed in detail in Box F5.

Summary of annexation of the benefit in equity

Annexation of the benefit in equity is achieved either by satisfying the rules for annexation or by proving that a scheme of development exists. The effect of annexing the benefit in equity is to attach the benefit of the covenant to the land.

The running of the burden at common law

> **Box E**
>
> THE RUNNING OF THE BURDEN AT COMMON LAW
>
> The burden does not run with the land at common law.
>
> As an alternative you can use devices such as:
>
> **1.** There must be a chain of indemnity covenants
>
> Or
>
> **2.** The covenant must be compulsorily renewable
>
> Or
>
> **3.** There must be mutual benefit and burden.

This is the situation we're looking at.

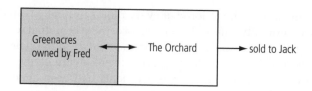

In the example above, Victor covenanted with Fred not to build more than one house on The Orchard. Victor has now sold the Orchard to Jack. Section 56 of the Law of Property Act 1925 does not cover the burden, nor does the Contracts (Rights of Third Parties) Act 1999. This is because you cannot force someone to do something if he or she was not a party to the original contract. So we need to look at the rules which establish whether the burden of the covenant runs with or becomes attached to The Orchard permanently, so that when Victor sells the land to Jack, Jack can be sued if he builds more than one house. Fred will still have the benefit of the covenant because he was the original party to it.

The burden does not run with the land at common law

At common law the burden of the covenant does not run with or become attached to the land. In our example the burden does not run with or become attached to The Orchard. It doesn't matter whether the covenant is to do something or not to do something.

Q: *What? That's it?*

A: That's it. The authority for the fact that the burden does not run with the land at common law is *Austerberry v Oldham Corporation* (1885), an authority you need to have at your fingertips. This authority was confirmed in *Rhone v Stephens* (1994).

Q: *That's rather easy for land law, isn't it?*

A: The reason is that it is not possible to saddle someone else with the burden of a contract. Let's say you were employed to build a wall. You have the burden of building the wall. You are not allowed to assign this burden to your best friend so that he gets sued if the wall isn't built. In our example, as the burden does not run with or become attached to the land, it must stay with the original covenantor, Victor. This means that Victor is going to remain permanently liable on the covenant, even if he doesn't own The Orchard any more. This is not a very enviable position to be in for Victor. It's not a very enviable position for Fred either, as he has the task of finding Victor to sue him if Jack buys The Orchard and breaches the covenant.

Q: *Are there ways out of this situation?*

A: Yes. The most common of the avoidance devices of the common law rules, as they are called, are discussed next. These are steps to be taken to avoid the common law rule when you create a covenant or sell on land. They are not steps to recover from a bad situation after it has occurred.

Box E1   There must be a chain of indemnity covenants

One answer is to ensure that when Victor sells The Orchard to Jack, Victor makes it a condition of sale that Jack promises that if he, Jack, builds more than one house and Victor is then sued by Fred, or by any of Fred's successors in title, for Jack's breach of the covenant, Jack has to pay back any damages that Victor has to pay. You can have a chain of indemnities like this as long as you like. So if Jack then sells The Orchard to Belinda and Belinda undertakes the same condition of sale, Jack can get his money back from Belinda when she breaches the covenant and he, Jack, is sued by Victor. The problem is that the chain falls apart very easily when Victor can't find Jack, or Jack can't find Belinda.

Box E2   The covenant must be compulsorily renewable

This is where the original covenant has to be renewed each time the burdened land is sold. When Fred sells The Orchard to Victor, he must make it a permanent condition of sale that if The Orchard is sold, any new owner must enter into a new covenant with Fred or his successors in title (anyone who buys Fred's land) that they will not build more than one house on The Orchard. So before Victor can sell to Jack, Jack must enter into a new covenant with Fred. Before Jack can sell to Belinda, she must enter into a new covenant with Fred or his successors, the people who subsequently purchase Greenacres. This tactic works best in registered land because, under section 43 of the Land Registration Act 2002, Fred can put a restriction on the Proprietorship Register relating to The Orchard. This means that The Orchard should not be sold unless the potential new owner has entered into a new covenant with Fred or his successors in title.

Box E3   There must be mutual benefit and burden

In *Halsall v Brizell* (1957) the original owners of land covenanted to pay for the upkeep of sewers and a road. It was held that a subsequent purchaser from the original owners couldn't benefit by using the sewer and the road if he didn't also take the burden and contribute to their upkeep.

Q: *So if there's a reciprocal arrangement, an interlinked benefit and burden, then you can't have the benefit without the burden?*

A: Correct. There are conditions attached here: see *Rhone v Stephens*. One is that the benefit and burden must be linked. In *Halsall v Brizell* the benefit of the use of the sewer and the road was linked to the burden of repairing them. Secondly, a successor in title to the person with the burden must be able to choose whether or not he decides to accept the whole arrangement. This must be a real choice: see *Thamesmead Town Ltd v Allotey* (1998). Thirdly, the benefit and burden must be conferred in or by the same transaction. If the transaction related to land, it would have to be by deed. In *Davies v Jones* (2009) the transaction related to land but there was no deed. Whilst there might have been a clear understanding between the parties in the case, an understanding wasn't sufficient. Also, the benefit and burden were not conditional on each other.

Q: *Could you use the* **Halsall v Brizell** *doctrine in the example that we've been looking at?*

A: Not really, because there was no mutual benefit and burden between Fred and Jack. You could have used either a chain of indemnity covenants or else a compulsorily renewable covenant, particularly if The Orchard was registered land, but neither of these is ideal because they require forethought.

Summary of the running of the burden at common law

The burden of a freehold covenant does not run with or become attached to the land at common law. There are alternative devices which can be used.

The running of the burden in equity

Box F

THE RUNNING OF THE BURDEN IN EQUITY

You must prove annexation of the burden in equity

You must tick all boxes.

☐ **1.** The covenant must have been negative.

☐ **2.** (i) The covenant undertaken by the covenantor on his land must have touched and concerned the covenantee's land,

(ii) The two plots of land must have been sufficiently proximate.

☐ **3.** When the covenant was created, the covenantee must have owned land that was benefited by the covenant.

☐ **4.** When making the covenant, the original parties must have intended that the burden should run with the land.

☐ **5.** The restrictive covenant must be protected.

You must prove annexation of the burden in equity.

The fact that the burden did not run with or become attached to the land at common law was very unsatisfactory. It meant that even if Victor entered into a covenant with Fred, that covenant was worthless if Victor sold his land on. This problem became serious as the industrial expansion of the early nineteenth century encroached on the amenity of land. If the burden of covenants did not run with or become attached to the land, landowners could do what they wanted with little redress. As a result, the courts of equity, which were based on fairness and justice, developed their own set of rules which were more flexible.

This is the situation we're looking at:

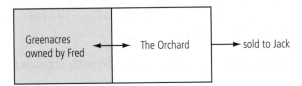

The very important case of *Tulk v Moxhay* (1848), which should be quoted in all answers concerned with the running of the burden in equity, established that the burden of a freehold covenant could run with or become attached to the land in equity if the purchaser knew of the covenant when he bought the land. The rules that follow have been developed subsequently.

Q: *Does the burden run only under the rules of equity?*

A: Yes.

Box F1 The covenant must have been negative

This means that the covenant must have been negative or restrictive in nature. A covenant not to build more than one house is negative, whereas a covenant to build a wall is positive. You can also have covenants that sound as though they are positive but are actually negative in nature. Often a covenant that says you can do something does so to stop you doing something unwanted. For example, a covenant to use land for residential purposes only is restrictive in nature, in that the land cannot be used for commercial purposes. Its effect is negative and therefore it is a negative covenant. A covenant to build a wall is clearly positive, and a covenant not to let property fall into disrepair is also positive because you are under an obligation to do something positive.

Q: *What's the best way of telling whether a covenant is positive or negative if you're not sure?*

A: You might use the test of 'can I meet the covenant by doing absolutely nothing?' If so, then it is likely to be negative. Also ask whether any money would have to be spent to conform with the covenant. If the answer is 'yes', it is likely to be positive. In *Haywood v Brunswick Permanent Benefit Building Society* (1881) the covenant under discussion was a covenant to repair. Lord Justice Cotton said, 'The covenant to repair can only be enforced by making the owner put his hand into his pocket, and there is nothing which would justify us in going that length'.

From now on, then, when looking at these rules, we can apply them only to restrictive or negative covenants because they are the only ones where the burden is allowed to run with or become attached to the land in equity. The burden of a positive covenant can never run in equity.

Box F2i The covenant undertaken by the covenantor on his land must have touched and concerned the covenantee's land

The restrictive covenant undertaken by the covenantor must have affected the use or value of the covenantee's land, or else have preserved his use of it. This means that personal covenants that don't affect the use of the covenantee's land do not run with or become attached to the burdened land. If Victor had entered into a covenant not to wear blue trousers, that would be a personal covenant and nothing to do with the land of Greenacres and its use.

Box F2ii   The two plots of land must have been sufficiently proximate

Q: *Why?*

A: Because if the two plots of land are too far apart, a burden on one can't possibly benefit the other. A covenant to build only one house on The Orchard is pointless if Greenacres is 60 miles away, because it won't affect the value or use of Greenacres. The two plots of land don't have to be next door to each other, but they must be reasonably close: see *Kelly v Barrett* (1924) where Pollock MR said that 'land at Clapham would be too remote and unable to carry a right to enforce the covenants in respect of ... land at Hampstead'. This condition reflects the fact that the covenant must be for the benefit of the covenantee's land (Box F2i).

Box F3   When the covenant was created, the covenantee must have owned land that was benefited by the covenant

Q: *Why must the covenantee have owned land which is benefited at the date of the covenant?*

A: When a covenantor undertakes not to do something on his land, it is for the benefit of other land. If Fred doesn't keep any land which can be benefited by the covenant, then the covenant is no longer attached to any land. It ceases to be proprietary in nature and cannot bind a successor in title to the covenantor.

In *London CC v Allen* (1914) the Council sold land to Mr Allen, a builder. He covenanted not to build on one part of the land. Mr Allen then sold this part of the land to his wife who promptly started to build on it. The Council applied for an injunction to stop her on the basis that the burden of the covenant ran with the land. The injunction was refused because the Council had sold the whole plot of land to Mr Allen and hadn't kept any land back to be benefited. (This would be like Fred selling both Greenacres and The Orchard to Victor. Fred wouldn't have any land left to benefit from the covenant not to build more than one house on the Orchard.) As a result, the Council had no land which could be benefited by the covenant. There was no point in worrying whether the burden of the covenant ran with the land Mr Allen sold to his wife because the Council hadn't kept any land to benefit in the first place. The covenant was only personal between Mr Allen and the Council, and therefore not binding on Mrs Allen.

To overcome this difficulty as far as local authorities are concerned, statute law can give them the right to enforce covenants whether or not they hold land to be benefited.

Box F4   When making the covenant, the original parties must have intended that the burden should run with the land

If the covenant was created before 1926, the intention to bind successors of the covenantor has to be shown by the wording used in the deed. Words such as 'I covenant for myself *and my successors in title'* will suffice. If the covenant was created after 1925 and there are no express words, this intention is presumed under section 79 of the Law of Property Act 1925, which states:

> A covenant relating to any land of a covenantor or capable of being bound by him, shall, unless a contrary intention is expressed, be deemed to be made by the covenantor on behalf of himself, his successors in title and the persons deriving title under him or them, and, subject as aforesaid, shall have effect as if such successors and other persons were expressed.

The intention will be presumed unless a contrary intention is expressed. Section 79 can be excluded by the parties expressly stating that section 79 is to be excluded or where a contrary intention is shown. In *Re Royal Victoria Pavilion (Ramsgate)* (1961) the wording in clause 5 itself showed that the covenant was intended to be personal to the covenantor, particularly when compared with the wording in other clauses.

Box F5   ## The restrictive covenant must be protected

You need to establish whether the restrictive covenant was made before or after 1925. A restrictive covenant made after 1925 must be protected in both unregistered and registered land.

Q: *Why has it got to be protected?*

A: The original basis of the burden of a restrictive covenant running with or becoming attached to the land was that the person who bought the burdened land had notice of the covenant and knew about it before he bought the land. As equity is based on fairness and justice, it wouldn't be very fair and just if Jack bought the burdened land, The Orchard, from Victor, and then discovered that he couldn't build more than one house on it and nobody had bothered to tell him. The idea of notice or knowing about the restrictive covenant is still relevant, and there are different ways of giving this notice in unregistered and registered land.

Q: *Is a restrictive covenant a legal or equitable proprietary interest?*

A: It is equitable.

Q: *Why is it equitable when it's created within a deed? Interests created in a deed are normally legal.*

A: Section 1(2) of the Law of Property Act 1925 does not include restrictive covenants in the list of interests capable of being legal proprietary interests, so a restrictive covenant can only ever be an equitable proprietary interest. Also, remember that the running of the burden of a restrictive covenant is only ever recognised in equity, and can therefore be only an equitable proprietary interest anyway.

Unregistered land
Use the procedure given in Chapter 3 on page 44 to determine how interests are protected in unregistered land.

Step 1. Establish whether it is a legal or equitable interest that is being claimed. If it is a legal interest, legal rights bind the world both before 1926, and, excluding a puisne mortgage, after then as well. If it is an equitable interest, you must see whether the interest is capable of entry as a land charge under the Land Charges Act 1972.

Step 2. If the equitable interest is not capable of entry as a land charge, use the rule that governed equitable interests before 1926, known as the doctrine of notice. If the equitable interest is capable of entry as a land charge, work out in whose interest it is to enter it as a land charge. This will be the person who benefits from the equitable interest.

Step 3. Check to see whether that person has entered his or her equitable interest as a land charge in the correct class on the Land Charges Register against the name of the owner of the land that the right is over:

▶ An equitable interest that has been entered as a land charge binds everyone who takes the land under section 198 of the Law of Property Act 1925.
▶ If the equitable interest has not been entered as a land charge, it will not be binding on some classes of purchaser.

You can apply the procedure above to the example of Fred, Victor and Jack. Assume the covenant was created after 1925.

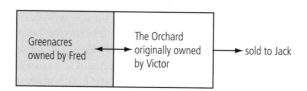

Step 1. A restrictive covenant is an equitable interest. An equitable restrictive covenant created after 1925 is capable of entry as a land charge under the Land Charges Act 1972.

Step 2. It is in Fred's interest to enter the equitable restrictive covenant as a land charge, as he receives the benefit from it.

Step 3. Fred should have entered the equitable restrictive covenant as a class D(ii) land charge against Victor's name.

▶ If Fred has entered his equitable restrictive covenant as a land charge against Victor's name, it will bind Jack under section 198 of the Law of Property Act 1925 and he will not be able to build more than one house on The Orchard.
▶ If Fred has not entered his equitable restrictive covenant as a land charge, it will not be binding on a purchaser of a legal estate for money or money's worth under section 4(6) of the Land Charges Act 1972. Jack paid money and purchased the legal estate of The Orchard. If Fred has not entered the restrictive covenant as a land charge, Jack will not be bound by it and he can build as many houses as he likes subject to planning permission.

Q: *When does Fred have to enter his restrictive covenant as a land charge?*

A: As soon as it has been created, or at least before The Orchard is sold on. Fred won't know if and when Victor may sell The Orchard. If Fred's restrictive covenant is not entered on the Land Charges Register before any sale of The Orchard, a purchaser, Jack here, will not have found out about it even though he inspected the Register, and he will therefore not be bound by it.

Restrictive covenants created before 1926

You must apply the procedure again.

Step 1. A restrictive covenant is an equitable interest. An equitable restrictive covenant created before 1926 cannot be entered as a land charge under the Land Charges Act 1972, because before 1926 there wasn't a Land Charges Act, and only post-1925 equitable restrictive covenants can be entered on the Land Charges Register.

Step 2. As an equitable restrictive covenant created before 1926 cannot be entered as a land charge, you must use the rule that governed equitable interests before 1926, known as the doctrine of notice. The doctrine of notice is as follows.

Equitable rights bind everyone except a *bona fide* purchaser of a legal estate for value without notice of the equitable interest.

Imagine that the restrictive covenant between Fred and Victor had been created in 1920. The restrictive covenant will bind Jack unless he is a *bona fide* purchaser of a legal estate for value without notice of the restrictive covenant. Jack has given money for the legal estate of The Orchard and we can assume he is *bona fide*. The answer then depends on whether Jack has actual, constructive or imputed notice (knowledge) of the restrictive covenant. Actual notice is notice he actually has. Constructive notice is notice he would have had if he had inspected the documentation to the land or the land itself. Imputed notice is notice that his solicitor had and should have passed on. Given the three different types of notice, one would conclude that the chances are that he probably does have notice of the restrictive covenant and so will be bound by it.

Registered land

Registered land is governed by the Land Registration Act 2002. There are three categories which determine how interests in registered land are protected. They are:

- Dealings which must be completed by registration under section 27 of the Land Registration Act 2002.
- Interests in Schedule 3 to the Land Registration Act 2002 which override a registered disposition.
- Interests entered as a notice under section 34 and interests protected by a restriction under section 43 of the Land Registration Act 2002.

A purchaser for valuable consideration will take the land subject to the interests in these three categories.

A restrictive covenant falls into the third category of an interest which must be entered as a notice under section 34 of the Land Registration Act 2002. These are interests which are entered as a notice on the Charges Register of the land which the right is over in order to bind a purchaser.

It is in Fred's interest to enter the restrictive covenant by means of a notice giving details of the covenant on the Charges Register of The Orchard under section 34 of the Land Registration Act 2002. When Jack is thinking of buying The Orchard he will look at the Charges Register and discover that there is a restrictive covenant on it which will bind him under section 29 of the same Act. He can then decide whether he really wants to buy The Orchard.

Q: *When does Fred have to enter his restrictive covenant as a notice on the Charges Register?*

A: As soon as it has been created, or at least before The Orchard is sold. He won't know if and when Victor may sell The Orchard. If the restrictive covenant is not entered by means of a notice on the Charges Register of The Orchard before any sale, a purchaser of The Orchard, Jack here, would not have found out about it even though he had inspected the Register, and he will therefore not be bound by it.

Summary of the running of the burden in equity

Provided the rules in Box F are met, the burden of a restrictive covenant will run with or become attached to the land. It will bind anyone who buys or takes the burdened land, so he or she can be sued if he or she breaches the covenant.

Summary of the running of the benefit and burden

It is possible to attach the benefit of a covenant and the burden of a restrictive covenant to land. This avoids the problems of trying to include people in the original contract or of assigning the benefit personally, particularly as neither of these methods allows for the burden of a covenant to pass.

The modification or discharge of a restrictive covenant

Sometimes covenants run for years and years before becoming obsolete. An example is where the original covenant not to build more than one house on The Orchard was made 100 years ago. Greenacres is now surrounded by housing estates and suburbia. The present owner of The Orchard may then ask the present owner of Greenacres for the discharge or release of the covenant. This is possible under section 84(1) of the Law of Property Act 1925. Until June 2009 this involved an application to the Lands Tribunal. The Lands Tribunal has now been abolished. Its functions have been transferred to the Lands Chamber of the Upper Tribunal established by the Tribunals, Courts and Enforcement Act 2007 as part of a reorganisation of tribunals to benefit those who use them. The circumstances under which a restrictive covenant can be modified or discharged are as follows.

- The covenant has become obsolete due to the changing nature of the neighbourhood (section 84(1)(a)); or
- The restrictive covenant is preventing public or private use of the land and any loss could be compensated by money (section 84(1)(aa)); or

▶ The people entitled to the benefit are over 18 and consent and wouldn't be harmed in any way (section 84(1)(b)); or
▶ There would be no injury to those benefited by the covenant (section 84(1)(c)).

Section 84(7) states that section 84 cannot be used where the burdened land has not been conveyed for consideration. In *Re Robin's Application* (2005) section 84 couldn't be used because the burdened land had been a gift.

If the covenant is being modified or discharged under section (1)(aa), under section 1A the Lands Chamber must be satisfied that either there are no practical benefits of substantial value or advantage to the person who has the benefit of the covenant or the covenant is contrary to the public interest and that money will be adequate compensation.

In *George Wimpey Bristol Ltd v Gloucestershire Housing Association Ltd* (2011) the Upper Chamber of the Lands Tribunal rejected an application by Wimpey for the modification of a covenant which prevented residential development. Wimpey argued that the continued existence of the covenant would impede its reasonable use of the land, and that there was no substantial benefit to other people. The objectors argued that the development would mean, amongst other issues, a risk of flooding, a loss of privacy and views and the proposed modification would set a precedent for further modification(s) of the restriction. The Court agreed with the objectors. Whilst Wimpey's proposed use was reasonable and the covenant impeded such use, there were continued substantial benefits for the objectors and the application for modification was refused. The Tribunal also pointed out that even if this had not been the case, it was unlikely they would have exercised their discretion and modified the covenant. This was because Wimpey had gone ahead with the development knowing about the objections in the hope that changing the appearance and character of the land would convince the Tribunal to discharge the covenant. As was said

> It is appropriate for the Tribunal to make it clear that it is not inclined to reward parties who deliberately flout their legal obligations in this way.

In *Re Perkins* (2011) it was held that there were still practical benefits of substantial advantage to the objector to the covenant because otherwise houses would be overlooked.

Winter v Traditional & Contemporary Contracts Ltd (2007) looked at the principles relating to compensation. Compensation under section 84 was based on the loss to the objectors of the use or value of their land although a hypothetically negotiated share of the profits argument could still be used where the loss in value was not a fair reflection of the objector's subjective loss.

Q: *If, later on, you've purchased adjoining land which benefits from the covenant but doesn't actually have the benefit of the restrictive covenant attached to it, can you oppose an application for the discharge of the covenant on the basis of the adjoining land benefits as well?*

A: No. It's not possible to take into account the benefits arising in respect of your whole land ownership, only those benefits which accrue to the land which has the benefit of the restrictive covenant attached to it: *Re Stanborough's Application* (2012).

Q: *What happens if you have already obtained planning permission and then discover that there is a restrictive covenant which says that you can't build what you propose?*

A: You will still be bound by the restrictive covenant. A grant of planning permission may be taken into account by the Lands Chamber of the Upper Tribunal if you apply for a discharge of a restrictive covenant, but it is under no duty to discharge a restrictive covenant because of it: see *Re Martin's Application* (1989).

Q: *What happens if words used in a restrictive covenant made years ago are no longer used today or don't have the same meaning?*

A: In *Dano Ltd v Earl Cadogan* (2003) a covenant made in 1889 restricted the use of the land for housing of the working classes. It was argued that the words 'working classes' were no longer capable of meaningful definition. The court reinterpreted the words to mean 'the use of the Property for the housing of those who, by virtue of their low incomes, might find it difficult to purchase or rent suitable and appropriate accommodation in the private sector'. The covenant was held unenforceable on other grounds on appeal though.

Q: *If someone obtains a discharge of a restrictive covenant so that he can build in his back garden, for example, isn't there an argument to say that this would open the door for everyone in the street burdened by a similar restrictive covenant to apply for a discharge so they could do the same?*

A: This is known as the 'thin end of the wedge' argument raised by people who don't want to lose the protection of restrictive covenants.

Q: *What is meant by the 'thin end of the wedge'?*

A: When you drive a wedge into something, you use the thin end first because it's easier than using the thick end. The argument is that if you allow the discharge of one covenant, for building development for example, any further applications for discharge to the Lands Chamber of the Upper Tribunal would be viewed in the light of that building development. The discharge of one covenant in the street would open the door just that little bit to allow other people to ask for a discharge and then the overall protection given by the covenants could be lost.

Re Snaith and Dolding's Application (1996) is a case heard by the then Lands Tribunal that considered this argument. It was held that when looking at the thin end of the wedge argument, the Lands Tribunal would look at the facts and merits of each application, the scheme of covenants as a whole and the importance of maintaining the integrity of the scheme. It was also clearly acknowledged that modifying the particular covenant in question could affect the context in which future applications were seen. In the case the substantial practical benefits of the scheme of covenants could not be compensated for in money and modification was refused. In *Shephard v Turner* (2006) an appeal against the Lands Tribunal decision to allow modification of a covenant raised the thin end of the wedge argument again. The objectors argued that if this modification, albeit relatively innocuous on its own, went through then it could pave the way for further developments which would undermine the effectiveness of the protection of the restrictive covenants. It was held that the decision to allow modification was based on the facts. The modification in this particular application was not the thin end of the wedge, because it was extremely unlikely that any further development would take place. The owners of the properties who had asked for modification had a special case within Orchard Close because of the size and position of their land. Out of interest, and on a different matter, in the same case it was held that construction works for the development were not in breach of the covenant not to cause nuisance and annoyance provided the works were carried out with reasonable care. The covenant not to cause nuisance and annoyance related to the ultimate use of the property, not to short-term construction works. In *Re Perkins*, though, the facts of the case were exceptional in terms of the potential disturbance during the construction works and this was taken into account.

Developers can also use section 610 of the Housing Act 1985 to apply for variation of a covenant. Where developers propose to convert a single dwelling into two or more separate dwellings, section 610 can be used to apply for variation of a restrictive covenant that would otherwise prevent such construction. The court can vary the covenant as it thinks fit taking into account all relevant considerations. Even so, there is no presumption of variation under this Act and the court's task is to exercise its own judgement regardless of any planning permission already given as in *Lawntown Ltd v Camenzuli* (2007).

A restrictive covenant will also be extinguished when the benefited and the burdened land come in the hands of the same person.

Q: Is that because if you own both the benefited and the burdened land you can't sue yourself?

A: Yes, it's called unity of seisin (possession) and the covenants can become effective again only if they are expressly recreated. This rule will not apply when a public body, a Council for example, holds both the benefited and burdened land for different statutory purposes, as in *University of East London Higher Education Corporation v London Borough of Barking and Dagenham* (2004). In this situation the covenant will not be extinguished. The rule will not apply either if there is a building scheme. If two plots of land in a building scheme come into common ownership, the covenant will not be extinguished. It can still be enforced by other parties in the scheme and will be revived if the land comes into separate ownership again: see *Texaco Antilles Ltd v Kernochan* (1973).

Remedies for the breach of a restrictive covenant

A restrictive covenant is an equitable proprietary interest, and the remedies are therefore equitable. The usual remedy is an injunction. If the covenant has not actually been broken then the claimant can ask for a quia timet injunction, which is an injunction that prevents someone from doing something, here from breaching the covenant. If the covenant has already been breached the claimant can ask for a mandatory injunction, which means that the defendant has to undo what he shouldn't have done in the first place. Instead of an injunction there is the alternative remedy of damages, which has been available since the Chancery

Amendment Act of 1858, and is now available under section 50 of the Supreme Court Act 1981. The guidelines for awarding damages are found in *Shelfer v City of London Electric Lighting Co* (1895). Damages can be awarded where:

> The injury to the claimant's right is small.

and

> The damages can be estimated in money.

and

> The damages would adequately compensate the claimant.

and

> It would be oppressive to the defendant to grant an injunction.

Q: *When would it be oppressive to the defendant to grant an injunction?*

A: If he had already constructed a building in breach of a restrictive covenant, as in *Wrotham Park Estate Co Ltd v Parkside Homes Ltd* (1974) where Mr Justice Brightman said:

> But I cannot close my eyes to the fact that the houses now exist. It would, in my opinion, be an unpardonable waste of much needed houses to direct that they now be pulled down and I have never had a moment's doubt during the hearing of this case that such an order ought to be refused. No damage of a financial nature has been done to the plaintiffs by the breach of the layout stipulation. The plaintiffs' use of the Wrotham Park estate has not been and will not be impeded. It is totally unnecessary to demolish the houses in order to preserve the integrity of the restrictive covenants imposed on the rest of area 14. Without hesitation I decline to grant a mandatory injunction. But the fact that these houses will remain does not spell out a charter entitling others to despoil adjacent areas of land in breach of valid restrictions imposed by the conveyances. A developer who tries that course may be in for a rude awakening.

The blatant contradiction in these words here is apparent to all except Mr Justice Brightman.

Q: *Doesn't an award of damages mean that the defendant gets away with it if you can just buy him off?*

A: Yes. Where it would be oppressive to award an injunction to the defendant, the damages awarded are assessed on the basis of a hypothetical negotiation of what could reasonably have been expected if the covenant had been released or discharged: see *Wrotham Park Estate Co Ltd v Parkside Homes Ltd*.

Q: *Does this mean that the profit of the defendant who is in breach of covenant is ignored?*

A: An account of profits will be awarded only in exceptional circumstances. However, the courts will take the future profit of the defendant who is breaching the covenant into account as part of the hypothetical negotiation: see *Lunn Poly Ltd v Liverpool & Lancashire Properties Ltd* (2006) and the principles in *Tamares (Vincent Square) Ltd v Fairpoint Properties (Vincent Square) Ltd* (2007), a case which is discussed in Chapter 17. This means that developers should start to worry rather more about breaching restrictive covenants because profits may not be quite as high as anticipated if they are sued.

On the bright side, *Wakeham v Wood* (1982) is a case where an injunction was granted. The *Wakeham* case was about a man who had constructed a building in breach of a restrictive covenant not to obscure the view of the sea and the beach. A loss of the view of the sea could not be estimated in monetary terms and so he had to pull the building down. How very English.

Also, don't forget that equitable remedies are discretionary, so any delay on the part of the claimant may defeat his claim. In *Harris v Williams-Wynne* (2006) Williams-Wynne had stood and watched building work that was in breach of a restrictive covenant for six years. His lack of action meant that the court refused to grant a mandatory injunction, but it didn't stop him from obtaining damages based on the sum that could reasonably have been agreed for release of the covenant. *Gafford v Graham* (1999) is another case illustrating the detrimental effect of delay to the claimant.

Reform

There are several arguments for reforming the law relating to covenants. The benefit of a covenant cannot be protected by means of registration. The covenantor remains liable on the covenant even if he has sold the burdened land. Applying to the Lands Chamber of the Upper Tribunal for discharge of a restrictive covenant is time-consuming and not always easy. This led the Law Commission to review positive and restrictive covenants. Its aim was to produce a coherent system of obligations over land that tied in with the commonhold system (described next) and the Land Registration Act 2002. A report, 'Making Land Work: Easements, Covenants and Profits à Prendre' (2011) Law Com No 327, was published in June 2011. The full report together with a draft Bill and an Executive Summary is on the Law Commission's website at www.justice.gov.uk/lawcommission/areas/easements.htm

The following summarises the main recommendations relating to freehold covenants.

- A new legal interest in land is proposed to be called a land obligation. The benefit and burden of the land obligation would be capable of registration at the Land Registry. Once the original parties had parted with the land, they would no longer have any further liability.
- A land obligation could either be negative or positive. This would remove the need for alternative devices such as a chain of indemnity covenants which are used now because the burden of a positive covenant does not run with the land at common law or in equity (Box E page 353). Positive obligations could also be 'reciprocal payment' obligations, for example contributing to the cost of a shared driveway.
- Existing restrictive covenants would not be affected by reform.
- The Lands Chamber of the Upper Tribunal should be able to make orders for the modification and discharge of land obligations.

Commonhold

The Commonhold and Leasehold Reform Act 2002 was passed to solve the problem that positive covenants do not run with freehold land (Boxes E and F), which means that it is impossible to enforce positive covenants against successors in title of people who own, rather than lease, a flat in a block of flats. This Act enables the complete block of flats, for example, to be registered as commonhold land. The owner of each individual flat or unit will own the freehold of his property, and will be known as a unit holder.

Q: *Can both residential and commercial property be held as commonhold land?*

A: Yes. An application for commonhold can be made either when a new development is created or else by people who currently hold long leases in an existing development. In this latter case, section 3 of the Act requires the consent of the registered proprietor of the freehold, of all registered proprietors of leases granted for more than 21 years and of all registered proprietors of charges (mortgages) over the leased units before an application can be made. It may be difficult to obtain all such consents.

Each unit holder will automatically be a member of the commonhold association. This will be a private company limited by guarantee and will be registered as the freehold proprietor of the common parts of the building, which could include the entrance hall, the lifts, the stairs, the rubbish areas and the grounds, for example. The commonhold association will manage the external structure and the common parts of the building. Under section 35 of the Act, day-to-day responsibility for this management will be given to its Directors.

Q: *Who appoints the Directors?*

A: The members of the commonhold association appoint the Directors, who can be appointed from within the membership or from professionals outside. Under section 35 of the Act, the Directors must exercise their powers so that each unit holder can exercise his rights and enjoy the freehold estate in his unit.

Under section 31 there must be a commonhold community statement in a form prescribed by the Act. The statement will make provision for the rights and duties of both the commonhold association and the unit holders. Section 31 defines such duties to include the duty to grant access and undertake works, for example, but most importantly it includes the duty of the unit holders to contribute towards the common expenses which will be used by the commonhold association to manage the property. Restrictions in the commonhold community statement can include requiring unit holders not to cause a nuisance and restrictions on the use of the property. Section 14 states that provisions must be made in respect of insurance, repair and maintenance of each commonhold unit. This responsibility can be given to either the unit holders or the commonhold association.

Q: *What happens if a unit holder fails to meet his obligations as stated in the commonhold community statement?*

A: Under section 35 of the Act, the Directors are responsible for ensuring that unit holders comply with their obligations and they must consider whether to use arbitration, mediation or conciliation to resolve any dispute, rather than legal proceedings. The Directors needn't take action if a unit holder doesn't comply with his obligations if they consider that such inaction is in the best interests of ensuring or maintaining a harmonious relationship between all the unit holders and the other unit holders won't suffer significant loss. Even if a unit holder doesn't comply, section 31 of the Act states that nothing in the commonhold community statement can require a unit holder to forfeit his interest in the land.

Q: *If you own a commonhold unit, can you then lease it to another party?*

A: This aspect is covered in section 17. There are prescribed restrictions on leasing a residential unit relating to the length of the lease, the circumstances in which it is granted or any other matter. One reason for imposing such restrictions is that any unit holder granting a lease will be out of touch with the property as he won't be living there, whilst the person who is living there, the lessee, will have no say in the management of the property. Non-residential commonhold units can be leased subject to any provisions in the community commonhold statement.

Q: *What happens when a unit holder sells his unit?*

A: A potential purchaser will be able to obtain details of the commonhold association and he will be able to inspect the community commonhold statement. If the sale goes ahead, the purchaser will take the property subject to the same rules and obligations as the previous unit holder by virtue of section 16 of the Act.

Q: *Can you bring a commonhold association to an end?*

A: Yes. The unit holders may want to do this when it is no longer financially viable to maintain the structure and repair of an old building and they want to sell the site to a property developer. Provided at least 80% of the members of the commonhold association agree, and a termination statement has been drawn up setting out the proposals and determining how the proceeds of sale are to be divided up, the commonhold association can be put into voluntary liquidation. In this case, the association will be registered as the freehold proprietor in each commonhold unit and therefore will be able to sell the site as a whole. The proceeds of sale will then be divided up between the unit holders in accordance with the termination statement. A commonhold association will also be brought to an end if it becomes insolvent.

How to use the Boxes in this chapter

Remember that the benefit of a covenant gives the ability to sue and the burden of a covenant means the liability to be sued.

If the benefited land has not been sold, you do not need to look at any Boxes relating to the running of the benefit. The benefit is still with the original owner. If the burdened land has not been sold, you do not need to look at any Boxes relating to the running of the burden. The burden is still with the original owner.

If only the benefited land has been sold, then you have to determine only whether the benefit runs with the land. If only the burdened land has been sold, you have to determine only whether the burden runs with the land. If both have been sold then you must evaluate both.

If the burdened land has been sold, you know from Box E that the burden does not run at common law unless there is an avoidance device. You will therefore have to rely on the rules relating to the running of the burden in equity in Box F. If the benefited land has also been sold, you should also have looked at the rules relating to the running of the benefit. For historical reasons that no longer make a lot of sense, you must use the rules in the same jurisdiction. This means that you cannot mix the common law rules and the equitable rules together. If you are using the rules for the burden in equity, you must use the rules for the benefit in equity. This need to use the rules in the same jurisdiction also relates to the fact that generally an injunction is required to prevent a breach of a restrictive covenant and an injunction is an equitable remedy. Remember: keep the common law rules and the equitable rules separate.

The process

If a person wishes to claim the benefit of a covenant but was not a party to it, you can use section 56 of the Law of Property Act 1925 or section 1 of the Contracts (Rights of Third Parties) Act 1999 (Box A).

Determine whether the benefited land has been sold. If it hasn't, then the benefit remains with the original owner who can still sue. If it has been sold, you have a choice. You can look at whether the benefit has been assigned to a future purchaser (Box B). If not, you must determine whether the benefit runs with the land either at common law (Box C) or in equity (Box D).

Establish whether the burdened land has been sold. If it hasn't, the burden remains with the original owner. If it has been sold, you have a choice. You must determine whether the burden runs at common law or in equity. Unless the avoidance devices have been used, the burden will not run at common law (Box E). This means that you must be looking at the rules in equity (Box F). If the burden does run with the land in equity, you must tie this finding with the benefited land because you must use the rules in the same jurisdiction. If the burden has run in equity you must use the rules relating to the running of the benefit in equity as well because you cannot mix the jurisdictions.

Q: *If the burden runs only in equity, is it quicker just to check whether the burden has run in equity first? If it has, then you know you have to use the rules in equity for the benefit as well, so you can miss out the rules at common law.*

A: Yes. This is quicker and you can do this. The purpose of this chapter is to ensure that you understand all the rules, although you can now be selective as to which ones you use first.

A question on freehold covenants

This example is intended to illustrate how to use the Boxes in this chapter to analyse the legal position. If you are using this method in undergraduate law exam questions, you will need to include statutory and case authority and detailed discussion of the various points of law. This information is found both in the text and from other sources.

Amble owned 30 acres of land. Fourteen years ago Amble split this land into two equal-sized plots called Redacres and Blueacres and built a small organic working farm on Redacres for himself. He agreed to sell Blueacres to Blunt, a local farmer. In the conveyance Blunt covenanted with Amble and with the current owners of all land adjoining Blueacres to keep the land as agricultural land. In the same conveyance Blunt made a second covenant with Amble to keep the boundary fence between Redacres and Blueacres in good repair. At that time Chadwick owned Yellowacres, a farm adjoining Blueacres.

Six years ago Amble sold Redacres to Dearing, and last year Blunt sold Blueacres to Edington. Neither conveyance mentioned the covenants cited above. Dearing and Chadwick have just discovered that Edington intends to build a factory on Blueacres. Dearing wants to prevent this development because it will impair his organic farming and cause the value of Redacres to fall. Chadwick wants to prevent this development as the value of Yellowacres will fall. The fence between Blueacres and Redacres has fallen into disrepair and Edington refuses to repair it.

Advise the parties.

There are two covenants in this question – the covenant to keep Blueacres as agricultural land and the covenant to keep the boundary fence in good repair. Draw a diagram of the situation. The parties are Amble, Blunt, Chadwick, Dearing and Edington.

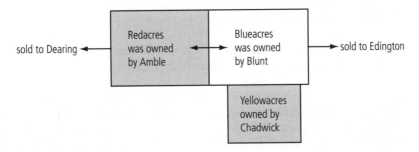

This is the information we have.

Amble was the covenantee who had the benefit of the covenant to keep Blueacres as agricultural land and the benefit of the repairing covenant. The benefited land, Redacres, has been sold. You must look at whether Dearing can claim the benefit of the covenants and can sue Edington.

Blunt was the covenantor who had the burden of the covenant to keep Blueacres as agricultural land and to keep the boundary fence in good repair. The burdened land, Blueacres, has been sold. You must look at whether the burden of the covenants has run with Blueacres so that Edington can be sued if he breaches the covenants.

Chadwick was not party to the original covenant so you must look to see whether there is any way that he can be included in the covenant between Amble and Blunt.

The covenant to keep Blueacres as agricultural land and the position between Dearing and Edington

Dearing's position

Box A Including strangers in the contract

A1 Section 56 of the Law of Property Act 1925 or A2 The Contracts (Rights of Third Parties) Act 1999

Amble and Blunt were the original parties to the contract (covenant). It is not possible to include Dearing in the contract as far as the benefit is concerned, as section 56 of the Law of Property Act 1925 does not apply to future purchasers. The Contracts (Rights of Third Parties) Act 1999 will not apply as the covenant was made before May 2000. These boxes cannot be ticked.

Summary of Box A

You cannot include Dearing in the contract between Amble and Blunt.

Box B   Assigning the benefit of the covenant to future purchasers

B1 A legal assignment under section 136 of the Law of Property Act 1925 or B2 Assignment in equity

You are told that the conveyance of Redacres to Dearing did not mention any of the covenants and there is no indication that the benefit of the covenant was assigned by Amble to Dearing personally either at common law or in equity. These boxes cannot be ticked.

Summary of Box B

There is no evidence of assignment of the benefit of the covenant.

Box C   The running of the benefit at common law

You must prove annexation of the benefit at common law.

C1 The covenant must have touched and concerned the covenantee's land

The covenant must meet the test determined in *P&A Swift Investments v Combined English Stores Group plc.* The covenant touched and concerned Amble's land as it affected the value and use of Redacres, which was run as an organic farm. The covenant would be of value to Amble only when he owned Redacres. You can tick this box.

C2 When making the covenant, the original parties must have intended that the benefit should run with the land

Amble and Blunt must have intended that the benefit should run with Redacres. Section 78 of the Law of Property Act 1925 implies this for all covenants made after 1925. You can tick this box.

C3 The covenantee and his successors in title must own a legal estate in the land

Dearing is a successor in title to Amble. Amble owned Redacres and therefore the legal estate, as Dearing does now. You can tick this box.

Summary of Box C

The benefit of the covenant will have run with or become attached to the land at common law. Dearing has the ability to sue for breach of the covenant by using the common law rules.

Box D   The running of the benefit in equity

From Box D you must prove annexation of the benefit in equity or that a scheme of development exists.

D1 The covenant must have touched and concerned the covenantee's land

The covenant touched and concerned Amble's land as it affected the value and use of Redacres, which was run as an organic farm. You can tick this box.

D2 When making the covenant, the original parties must have intended that the benefit should run with the land

Amble and Blunt must have intended that the benefit should run with Redacres. The covenant was made after 1925. Under section 78 of the Law of Property Act 1925 and following the *Federated Homes* case, this intention is now implied automatically provided the land to be benefited is referred to in the covenant and can be identified: see *Crest Nicholson Residential (South) Ltd v McAllister*. Assuming this was so, you can tick this box.

D3 Or you must prove that a scheme of development exists

This is not an area affected by a scheme of development: see *Re Dolphin's Conveyance*. This box cannot be ticked.

Summary of Box D

The benefit of the covenant has become attached to the land in equity so Dearing has the ability to sue for breach of the covenant by using the equitable rules.

Edington's position

Box E   The running of the burden at common law

The burden of a covenant does not run at common law: see *Austerberry v Oldham Corporation*. There is no evidence of any alternative mechanism in place. This box cannot be ticked.

Box F   The running of the burden in equity

You must prove annexation of the burden in equity by meeting the rules that were developed from the case of *Tulk v Moxhay*.

F1 The covenant must have been negative

Although the covenant to keep Blueacres as agricultural land is framed in a positive way, it is restrictive in nature. The land could not be developed for industrial or commercial use. The covenant did not require any expenditure by Blunt. You can tick this box.

F2i The covenant undertaken by the covenantor on his land must have touched and concerned the covenantee's land

The covenant undertaken by Blunt touched and concerned Amble's land as it affected the value and use of Redacres, which was run as an organic farm. You can tick this box.

F2ii The two plots of land must have been sufficiently proximate

Redacres and Blueacres were adjacent. You can tick this box.

F3 When the covenant was created, the covenantee must have owned land that was benefited by the covenant

The authority here is *London CC v Allen*. Amble was the covenantee. He owned Redacres, land which was benefited at the date of the covenant. You can tick this box.

F4 When making the covenant, the original parties must have intended that the burden should run with the land

Amble and Blunt must have intended that the burden should run with Blueacres. Although Blunt appears to have covenanted only on his own behalf, section 79 of the Law of Property Act 1925 implies an intention that the covenant was made on behalf of Blunt and his successors in title unless a contrary intention was expressed. There is no indication of a contrary intention. You can tick this box.

F5 The restrictive covenant must be protected

This is a covenant created after 1925. There is a problem as the question does not indicate whether the land is registered or unregistered, or whether the covenant has been protected in either case. We must bear this in mind when advising the parties and must find out the true situation from either the Land Charges Register for unregistered land or the Land Registry for registered land.

Unregistered land

Look at the procedure for protecting interests in unregistered land.

A restrictive covenant is an equitable interest that is capable of entry as a class D(ii) land charge on the Land Charges Register under the Land Charges Act 1972. It was in Amble's interest to enter the restrictive covenant as a class D(ii) land charge against Blunt's name on the Land Charges Register under the Land Charges Act 1972 when the covenant was created, or at least before Blueacres was sold to Edington. If the restrictive covenant was entered in this way, it binds everyone under section 198 of the Law of Property Act 1925. So, if the restrictive covenant has been entered as a class D(ii) land charge against Blunt's name, then, on the basis that all the other conditions have been met, the restrictive covenant is binding on Edington when he buys Blueacres. Edington is liable to be sued if he breaches the covenant.

If the restrictive covenant is not entered as a land charge, an interest in class D(ii) is not binding on a purchaser of the legal estate for money or money's worth under section 4(6) of the Land Charges Act 1972. Edington purchased the legal estate of The Orchard for money. If Amble did not enter the restrictive covenant as a class D(ii) land charge against Blunt's name when it was created, or at least before Blueacres was sold to Edington, it will not be binding on Edington, even if all the other conditions have been met. Subject to planning permission, Edington will be able to build a factory because you have not satisfied this final condition and Edington will not be liable to be sued for breach of the covenant.

Registered land

Amble must protect the restrictive covenant under section 34 of the Land Registration Act 2002 by entering a notice on the Charges Register of Blueacres when the restrictive covenant is created, or at least before Blueacres is sold to Edington. When Edington is thinking of buying Blueacres he will look at the

Register and discover that there is a restrictive covenant on it. Because the covenant is on the Register, it will bind him under section 29 of the Land Registration Act 2002. On the basis that all the other conditions have been met, Edington will be liable to be sued if he breaches the covenant.

If the restrictive covenant is not entered as a notice, it will not be binding on Edington. As you have not satisfied all the conditions in Box F, Edington will not be bound by the covenant and, subject to planning permission, he can build a factory as he has no liability to be sued.

Summary of Box F

You need to check to see whether the restrictive covenant has been protected in both unregistered and registered land. If it has, you satisfy all the conditions in Box F and the burden of the restrictive covenant to keep Blueacres as agricultural land will have run with the land. It will bind Edington, who is liable to be sued if he builds a factory. If it is not protected, you have not met all the conditions, and so the burden has not run with Blueacres. Edington cannot be sued if he breaches the covenant. If the burden has not run with the land to Edington, it must still be with Blunt. This is bad luck for Blunt, who remains liable to be sued.

The only area you haven't looked at now is whether it would be appropriate for Edington to ask for a discharge or release of the covenant under section 84(1) of the Law of Property Act 1925 if he is liable to be sued. There is no obvious indication that the covenant has become obsolete so any request for a release should be refused.

Conclusion concerning Dearing, Edington and the covenant to keep Blueacres as agricultural land

If you have proved that both the benefit and burden have run with the land, you now need to be more selective as to which rules you are going to rely on in court. You cannot mix the common law rules with the equitable ones. Assuming that the covenant has been protected, the burden has run only in equity (Box F), so you must rely on these rules to say that Edington can be sued. As you have used the rules for the burden in equity, this means that you must use the rules relating to the running of the benefit in equity as well (Box D). As these have been met, Dearing has the ability to sue. Dearing can therefore sue Edington if Edington breaches the covenant to keep the land as agricultural land. Dearing will ask for an injunction.

Q: *What would happen if, for example, the benefit ran with Redacres but the burden was held not to have run with Blueacres, perhaps because the restrictive covenant was not protected as a land charge in unregistered land or by a notice in registered land?*

A: Assuming the benefit went to Dearing he had the right to sue, but, as the burden didn't run with Blueacres, there is no point in suing Edington because he does not bear the liability of being sued. As the burden has not run with Blueacres, then the burden must have remained with the covenantor, who was Blunt. Dearing can sue Blunt, if he can find him. If Dearing finds Blunt, he will not be able to obtain an injunction against him because this is a personal remedy against the person in default. Blunt is not the person who is actually breaching the covenant in default.

This is Edington. If the factory was built, Blunt could be told only to pay damages, which wouldn't have achieved the objective of preventing the building of the factory.

Q: *What would happen if the burden had run to Edington but the benefit had stayed with Amble because annexation under section 78 had been expressly excluded and there had been no express assignment in person from Amble to Dearing?*

A: Theoretically, Amble can sue, but, as he has no land to benefit, his loss will be nil and any damages awarded will be nominal. There is no reason for him to do so anyway, as he has nothing to do with Redacres anymore. Edington could build a factory as Dearing cannot sue him and Amble would have no wish to.

The covenant to keep Blueacres as agricultural land and the position between Edington and Chadwick

Edington's position

Assuming that all the conditions in Box F are satisfied, the burden will run in equity with Blueacres to Edington.

Chadwick's position

Now you must determine whether Yellowacres can claim the benefit of the covenant and whether Chadwick can sue Edington. We must look at Boxes A, B, C and D.

Box A   Including strangers in the contract

A1 Section 56 of the Law of Property Act 1925 or A2 The Contracts (Rights of Third Parties) Act 1999

The owner of Yellowacres, Chadwick, was not an express party to the original covenant and was merely alluded to in the conveyance. Section 56 of the Law of Property Act 1925 allows a stranger to the original contract to take the benefit of it even though he was not a party to it. However, the original covenant must have been made with him rather than being merely expressed to be for his benefit and the stranger must be in existence and identifiable at the time of the covenant. The covenant was made with the current owners of all land adjoining Blueacres, so Chadwick can claim the benefit of it as he meets these conditions. This box can be ticked. The Contracts (Rights of Third Parties) Act 1999 cannot be used here as it applies only to contracts made after May 2000.

Box B   Assigning the benefit of the covenant to future purchasers

B1 A legal assignment under section 136 of the Law of Property Act 1925 or B2 Assignment in equity

Chadwick was not a purchaser of Redacres. This box cannot be ticked.

Box C   The running of the benefit at common law

You cannot use annexation at common law, as Chadwick was never a covenantee. This box cannot be ticked.

Box D   *The running of the benefit in equity*

You cannot use annexation in equity as Chadwick was never a covenantee. This box cannot be ticked.

Conclusion concerning Edington, Chadwick and the covenant to keep Blueacres as agricultural land

Assuming that the burden of the restrictive covenant has run with Blueacres, Chadwick can claim the benefit of the covenant under section 56 of the Law of Property Act 1925, and therefore is able to sue if there is a breach. Chadwick can seek an injunction to stop Edington building a factory.

The covenant to repair the fence and the position between Dearing and Edington

Dearing's position

You must see whether the benefit of the covenant to repair the fence can be claimed by Dearing. As Dearing could claim the benefit of the covenant to keep Blueacres as agricultural land, he will also be able to claim the benefit of the repairing covenant. This was proved by meeting the conditions for annexation at common law in Box C and annexation in equity in Box D. Dearing has the ability to sue either at common law or in equity.

Edington's position

The question is whether Edington bears the burden of the covenant to repair the fence.

Box E   *The running of the burden at common law or Box F The running of the burden in equity*

The burden of this covenant is positive and does not run with Blueacres in either Box E or Box F. The covenant will not run with Blueacres, so the burden stays with Blunt. As the benefit has run with Redacres, Dearing can sue only Blunt.

There are a very few cases, an example being *Crow v Wood* (1971), where an obligation to repair a fence was recognised as an easement. However, an easement of fencing has been held to be a spurious easement and is likely to be found only in specific situations. Easements are discussed in Chapter 17.

Conclusion concerning Dearing, Edington and the covenant to repair the fence

The burden of repairing the fence does not run with the land, so Blunt remains liable for maintaining the fence. The benefit runs with Redacres under both common law and in equity, so Dearing can sue Blunt. As Dearing wants the fence repaired, his best remedy is to use the common law rules and sue for damages. If he tried to sue for specific performance for Blunt to repair the fence, the courts would not wish to supervise this, and Edington could refuse permission for him to come onto Blueacres anyway. This is bad luck for Blunt, who should have got an indemnity from Edington (Box E1). Since he didn't, he will be out of pocket.

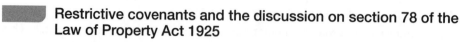

Restrictive covenants and the discussion on section 78 of the Law of Property Act 1925

This section looks at the reasons why some academics disagree with the interpretation of section 78 of the Law of Property Act 1925 in *Federated Homes Ltd v Mill Lodge Properties Ltd*. In that case Lord Justice Brightman established that section 78 implied an automatic annexation of the benefit of the covenant to the land so the benefit of the covenant ran with and became attached to the land.

Q: *Why was there a problem with the* Federated Homes *decision?*

A: There were concerns because annexation would be implied automatically rather than through the intentions of the parties. The reasoning behind Lord Justice Brightman's decision in *Federated Homes Ltd v Mill Lodge Properties Ltd* was as follows. He highlighted the following people who were covered in section 78: successors in title to the covenantee, people deriving title from the covenantee or his successors in title, and owners and occupiers of the land that was intended to be benefited by the covenant. Brightman couldn't think of anyone else who was able to enforce the benefit of a covenant. The covenant therefore had to run with the land, so it was seen as an automatic annexation. Concern was voiced because arguably it should be the parties who decide whether the benefit of the covenant should pass to people who become the new owners of the land or whether the benefit of the covenant remains personal to the covenantee. The problem is compounded because section 79 of the Law of Property Act 1925, which is the statutory counterpart of section 78 for the running of the burden, expressly states that the parties can exclude its effect if they want. There is nothing in section 78 which states that automatic annexation can be excluded.

Q: *Surely the parties should be able to exclude the automatic annexation of section 78 if they want?*

A: In *Roake v Chadha* the covenant stated that the benefit of the covenant could pass only if it had been expressly assigned. The effect of the wording in the case was to exclude annexation under section 78. The fact that the benefit had to be expressly assigned in person meant that the parties did not intend the land itself to be benefited. This was a contrary intention to the automatic implication of annexation to the land under section 78. This decision was confirmed in *Crest Nicholson Residential (South) Ltd v McAllister* by the following reasoning. Look at section 78 and at the last nine words in it.

> A covenant relating to any land of the covenantee shall be deemed to be made with the covenantee and his successors in title and the persons deriving title under him or them, and shall have effect as if such successors and other persons were expressed.
>
> For the purposes of this subsection in connection with covenants restrictive of the user of land 'successors in title' shall be deemed to include the owners and occupiers for the time being of *the land of the covenantee intended to be benefited* [emphasis added].

The words '… of the land of the covenantee intended to be benefited' are the answer because they allow the effect of the section to be excluded if the parties don't intend the land itself to be benefited. In the *Crest Nicholson Residential (South) Ltd v McAllister* case the words in one covenant 'For the benefit of the property at Claygate ... or the part thereof for the time being remaining unsold' meant that the benefit of the covenant existed only while the land was unsold. When a part of the land was sold, the words implied that the benefit of the covenant would not be attached to that part of the land. In *Sugarman v Porter* the covenant was expressed to be for the benefit of any part of the property remaining unsold. This meant that when the land, or any part of it, was sold, the benefit would not pass by annexation. The wording 'expressed to be for the benefit of any part remaining unsold' excluded the automatic annexation of section 78. The benefit could be assigned only expressly. Similar wording in *Norwich City College of Further and Higher Education v McQuillin* excluded annexation of the benefit. *City Inn (Jersey) Ltd v Ten Trinity Square Ltd* is another case where annexation under section 78 was excluded on the true construction of the wording as it was in *Margerison v Bates*.

The critics put forward a further argument against the decision in *Federated Homes Ltd v Mill Lodge Properties Ltd*, claiming that section 78 was a word-saving device, not a device for automatic annexation. The section that governed the running of the benefit before section 78 of the Law of Property Act 1925 was section 58(1) of the Conveyancing Act 1881. Section 58(1) named only the covenantee, his heirs and assigns (people he specifically assigned the covenant to) as people who would benefit from the covenant. If you wanted to annex the covenant to the land and include future purchasers, you had to spell this out expressly in the covenant. Because section 78 of the Law of Property Act 1925 now included future purchasers (successors in title) you didn't have to spell them out and so you saved words. However, the critics said that you still had to show that the benefit had been annexed to the land by express words in the covenant. Only if this had happened would all the people mentioned in section 78 be included. Lord Justice Brightman rejected this argument in the case, preferring an automatic annexation.

Q: *Can you also argue that if section 78 is just a word-saving provision and you still have to annex the benefit to the land expressly, this should have been stated far more clearly?*

A: If this was the case it should have been stated clearly. Equally though, if the intention was to achieve automatic annexation, this also should have been stated clearly.

Q: *Given that the Law of Property Act was passed in 1925 and Federated Homes was heard in 1979, why did it take so long to have a discussion about section 78?*

A: Automatic annexation had been suggested earlier in academic writing but it had been ignored. The discussion surfaced again just a mere 26 years after this in *Crest Nicholson Residential (South) Ltd v McAllister*. The Court of Appeal held that there was automatic annexation but it also held that there had to be some reference to the land that was to be benefited in the covenant and the land that was to be benefited had to be sufficiently defined (from schedules or plans if necessary) for section 78 to imply an automatic annexation confirming *Marquess of Zetland v Driver* (1939).

Q: *Had the benefited land been identified in the* **Federated Homes** *case?*

A: Yes, not from the covenant itself but from references made in the conveyance. Crest Nicholson has confirmed that the benefited land has to be referred to in the covenant, and it has to be easily identifiable using schedules or plans if necessary. This is because it would be unacceptable for the person with the burden of the covenant to have to find out this information by other means, especially as that person could be trying to identify the benefited land years later. In *Crest Nicholson Residential (South) Ltd v McAllister* the benefited land could not be clearly identified and so the claimant, Mrs McAllister, was unable to claim that the benefit of a covenant had been annexed to her land.

Q: *How could the benefit have been transferred to her then?*

A: By express assignment, according to Mr Justice Chadwick. In *Small v Oliver & Saunders (Developments) Ltd* (2006) the benefited land could be clearly identified and annexation was found. In contrast, in *Re Hutchinson's Application* the reference to the retained land to be benefitted was simply 'the retained land'. There was nothing to ascertain what 'the retained land' comprised and so the covenant was not annexed to the land.

Q: *Why is there so much emphasis on the benefited land being identified?*

A: There are practical reasons for identifying the benefited land. First, so you know who has the benefit of the covenant and the ability to sue. Secondly, so the person who has the burden of the covenant knows who he can be sued by. Thirdly, a person with the burden of the covenant can ask for release from the covenant from the person who has the benefit or he can ask for discharge of the restrictive covenant. Either way, the person with the burden will need to know who to ask for release or discharge.

Q: *Why can there be a problem identifying the benefited land?*

A: Look at it from this point of view. When Victor covenanted with Fred, the original owner of Greenacres, that he, Victor, would not build more than one house on The Orchard, the land that had the burden would be very clearly identified in the covenant. The covenant would say, 'I, Victor, covenant on behalf of my heirs, assigns and successors in title not to build more than one house on The Orchard'. The covenant would be meaningless if Victor simply said 'I covenant on behalf of my heirs, assigns and successors in title not to build more than one house', so by definition, you will know The Orchard is the land that bears the burden. On the other hand, Victor has to covenant with someone, Fred here, so the parties need to decide whether Victor is going to covenant with Fred only, or with Fred's successors in title as well. They must also decide whether the benefit is for Greenacres or whether it is for the benefit of other land that Fred owns, whether the benefit is for all or part of Fred's land, the effect of any statutory provision, and so on. It's far easier inadvertently to miss out or not explain clearly which land is intended to be benefited. Also, in the good old days when computers were a twinkle in a solicitor's eye, you couldn't just download a standard covenant and it was much easier to omit the exact land that was to be benefited.

Q: *If there is automatic annexation under section 78, does this mean that express assignment largely becomes redundant?*

A: Yes.

Q: *Do you discuss* **Federated Homes Ltd v Mill Lodge Properties Ltd** *only when you are looking at the running of the benefit in equity?*

A: Yes. Equity took a different view from the common law in its interpretation of section 78.

Q: *What happens to covenants made before 1925?*

A: They remain governed by the Conveyancing Act 1881 which still requires express words to annex the benefit to the covenantee's land because there is no automatic annexation.

Q: *What happened after section 78 of the Law of Property Act 1925 had been passed but before the decision in* **Federated Homes Ltd v Mill Lodge Properties Ltd***?*

A: Section 78 did not lead to an automatic annexation and the benefit had to be annexed expressly to the land.

As a summary of section 78 of the Law of Property Act 1925: *Crest Nicholson Residential (South) Ltd v McAllister* has confirmed the decision in *Federated Homes Ltd v Mill Lodge Properties Ltd* that there is automatic annexation under section 78. The effect of section 78 is excluded if the wording in the covenant indicates that the parties did not intend the land itself to be benefited, but rather that the benefit of the covenant remained personal to the covenantee. *Crest Nicholson Residential (South) Ltd v McAllister* has also clarified *Federated Homes Ltd v Mill Lodge Properties Ltd* by stating that reference must be made to the benefited land in the covenant and the benefited land must be clearly identified.

Further reading

P. Clark, 'The Benefit of Freehold Covenants', *Conv and Prop Law* (2012) 145

N. Gravells, 'Enforcement of Positive Covenants Affecting Freehold Land', 110 *LQR* (1994) 346

Law Commission, *Making Land Work: Easements, Covenants and Profits à Prendre* (Law Com No 327, 2011)

J. Martin, 'Remedies for Breach of Restrictive Covenants', *Conv and Prop Law*, Sep/Oct, (1996) 329

G. Newsom, 'Universal Annexation?' 97 *LQR* (1981) 32

G. Newsom, 'Universal Annexation? A Postscript', 98 *LQR* (1982) 202

P. O'Connor, 'Careful What You Wish For: Positive Freehold Covenants', *Conv and Prop Law* (2011) 191

P. Todd, 'Annexation after Federated Homes', *Conv and Prop Law*, May/Jun (1985) 177

Further reading cont'd

L. Turano, 'Intention, Interpretation and the "Mystery" of Section 79 of the Law of Property Act 1925', *Conv and Prop Law*, Sep/Oct (2000) 377

Commonhold

D. Clarke, 'The Enactment of Commonhold – Problems, Principles and Perspectives', *Conv and Prop Law*, Jul/Aug (2002) 349

L. Crabb, 'The Commonhold Association – As You Like It', *Conv and Prop Law*, Jul/Aug (1998) 283

P. Kenny, 'Commonhold – At Last?' *Conv and Prop Law*, Jan/Feb (2001) 1

P. Smith, 'The Purity of Commonholds', *Conv and Prop Law* (2004) 194

Chapter 15

Leases

www.palgrave.com/law/Stroud4e

Introduction

Essentially, a lease is a right made in a contract to occupy someone else's land for a set period of time.

For example, Mr Theirland owns Theirland in its entirety.

Mr Theirland wants to make some money. He makes an agreement with you, a contract, which allows you to occupy that part of Theirland called Yourland for a set period of time, four years for example, in return for monetary payment. This is commonly known as renting Yourland or leasing Yourland.

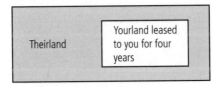

You have the right to use Yourland for four years, after which Yourland will return to form part of Theirland again.

There are three main areas to look at in leases.

First, what is a lease? What constitutes a lease? What do you have to show in order to be able to say that you have something that is capable of being a lease?

Secondly, has the lease been created in a recognised way? As elsewhere in land law, you need a certain degree of formality before you can create a valid lease.

Lastly, if the leased land is sold, is the lease binding on the new owner? In the example below, if Theirland, subject to the lease of Yourland, is sold to Peter, is the lease of Yourland binding on Peter? Peter will want to know whether he has to let you occupy Yourland for the full four years of the lease. You will also want to know whether you have the right to stay there for the full four years, even though Peter has purchased Theirland.

The chart on page 385 shows the three areas that will be looked at in this chapter. Box A looks at the essence of a lease. Box B looks at how a lease is created and Box C looks at how leases are protected when land is sold. You must meet the requirements in both Boxes A and B in order to have a valid lease. Box C is relevant if there is a purchaser who buys land subject to a lease.

LEASES

Box A

THE ESSENCE OF A LEASE

You must tick boxes 1, 2 and 3

A LEASE CAN EXIST IF THERE IS:

☐ **1.** Exclusive possession

and

☐ **2.** A certain term

and

☐ **3.** Rent or consideration

BUT A LEASE WILL NOT EXIST IF

4. There is no intention to create a legal relationship

or

5. There is an act of friendship or generosity

or

6. There is a service occupancy

or

7. There is a lodger

Box B

THE CREATION OF A LEASE

Tick as many boxes as possible but at least one:

A lease can be created by the following means. The type of lease that results is in brackets

☐ **1.** By deed (legal lease)

☐ **2.** Under section 54(2) of the Law of Property Act 1925 (legal lease)

  (i) A fixed term lease or

  (ii) An express periodic tenancy or

  (iii) An implied periodic tenancy

☐ **3.** Under section 2 of the Law of Property (Miscellaneous Provisions) Act 1989 (equitable lease)

☐ **4.** By proprietary estoppel

Box C

THE PROTECTION OF A LEASE

Look at either

UNREGISTERED LAND

1. Legal lease

2. Equitable lease

OR look at

REGISTERED LAND

3. Dealings which must be completed by registration

4. Interests which override a registered disposition

5. Interests entered as a notice or protected by a restriction

The essence of a lease

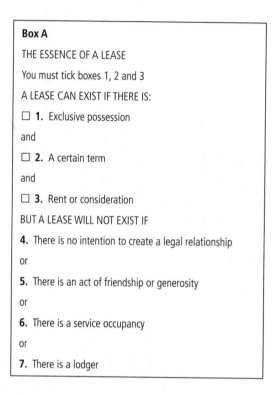

Box A

THE ESSENCE OF A LEASE

You must tick boxes 1, 2 and 3

A LEASE CAN EXIST IF THERE IS:

☐ **1.** Exclusive possession

and

☐ **2.** A certain term

and

☐ **3.** Rent or consideration

BUT A LEASE WILL NOT EXIST IF

4. There is no intention to create a legal relationship

or

5. There is an act of friendship or generosity

or

6. There is a service occupancy

or

7. There is a lodger

Box A gives the conditions you need to satisfy in order to claim a right that can be called a lease. We'll use the example of Theirland and Yourland as shown in the introduction when talking about Box A.

Q: *Is there a difference between a lease and a tenancy?*

A: Essentially, a lease and a tenancy are the same, and mean the occupation of someone else's land for a set period of time. The word 'lease' is usually used when the set period runs for a fixed term of over one year, for example three years or 99 years. A tenancy usually relates to a period of a year or less, for example, a year, a week or a month. In a lease, the term lessor is given to the person who grants the lease and the term lessee is the word given to the person who takes the lease and occupies the land. In a tenancy, the word landlord is used for the person who grants the tenancy and the word tenant for the person who takes the tenancy and occupies the land. Although this is a guide, the terms are used interchangeably.

Q: *Does this chapter apply as much to residential leases, as in the lease of a flat, as to leases of industrial or commercial property?*

A: Yes. Although you'll find that some of the cases discussed in this chapter relate to residential accommodation, while others relate to commercial property, the principles are the same. The main differences between a residential and a commercial lease are the terms agreed in the lease. Whereas a promise to pay rent is likely to be common to both, a promise to paint the outside of a house every year will not be relevant to a commercial property. Residential and commercial leases are also governed by different statutes.

Q: *What is meant by the term 'freehold reversion?'*

A: In the example at the beginning of the chapter, Theirland was owned by Mr Theirland. He owned the freehold estate of Theirland. When he granted you a lease, he carved a leasehold estate out of Theirland for four years. At the end of the four years, this leasehold estate ends. Yourland becomes part of Theirland again. Throughout the duration of the lease Mr Theirland owns what is called the *freehold reversion* of Yourland. He owns the right to Yourland when it reverts to being part of Theirland.

| Box A1 | Exclusive possession

Q: *What's exclusive possession?*

A: It's the hallmark of a lease. It means that you have the right to exclude or resist everyone coming onto Yourland during the period of your lease, including the landlord, Mr Theirland.

Q: *Including the landlord?*

A: Especially the landlord. If you have exclusive possession it means you can exclude everyone, and that means you must be able to exclude the landlord as well. If the landlord wishes to come and inspect the premises to make sure that you're keeping them in a presentable state, he should make an appointment to come and visit you. If he is able to enter at will, and come and go as he pleases, you do not have exclusive possession. Exclusive possession is a key element of a lease, and it means the right to resist anyone coming onto the land, including the landlord.

Shell-Mex and BP Ltd v Manchester Garages Ltd (1971) is an example of a situation in which there was no exclusive possession. An agreement allowed Manchester Garages to use Shell's garage for selling petrol. Manchester Garages had not been granted exclusive possession because Shell still had rights of possession and control. Shell could decide on the layout of the garage and could move the pumps and storage tanks.

Q: *What happens if the landlord has said in the lease agreement that he will come in and inspect the premises on the last Friday of every month?*

A: That doesn't mean you don't have exclusive possession. In fact, an agreement like this actually confirms that you *do* have exclusive possession because the landlord can't just wander in at will. He has had to make an appointment to enter the premises, thereby confirming your exclusive possession.

Q: *What happens if the landlord has kept a key to Yourland in case there is an emergency, for example, the taps freezing?*

A: Again, this will not deny you exclusive possession: see *Family Housing Association v Jones* (1990). Because the landlord has reserved the right to enter in an emergency, it confirms that he cannot just enter at will, emergency or no emergency, and so you have exclusive possession. In *Aslan v Murphy* (1990) Lord Donaldson MR stated that it didn't matter that the landlord kept a key. What really mattered was why he wanted to keep a key and what he used it for.

Note the difference between exclusive occupation, where you are the only one living there, and exclusive possession, which is the right to resist the entry of everyone including the landlord. You can have exclusive occupation of premises, but this may not also amount to exclusive possession.

Q: *What happens if you have your own room but share a bathroom or kitchen?*

A: You will have exclusive possession of your own room and a licence to use the bathroom or kitchen. It is possible to claim statutory security of tenure for the entirety. The land that you are claiming exclusive possession of must be clearly identified. In *Clear Channel UK Ltd v Manchester City Council* (2005), as the land over which Clear Channel claimed exclusive possession had not been identified precisely there was no intention to grant exclusive possession.

Box A2   A certain term

Q: *What's a certain term?*

A: A certain term is one where the duration of the lease is known to both parties when the lease is created. If you are given a lease of Yourland for four years, both you and the landlord, Mr Theirland, know at the beginning of the lease that you have the right to occupy Yourland for four years.

Q: *Why is it important to know how long a lease is going to last?*

A: So that both you and your landlord, Mr Theirland, know where you are. Life in rented property would be very uncertain if you couldn't ever be sure how long you were going to be there for. The landlord could give you notice to leave at any time, and vice versa. Remember that it wasn't so long ago that most people spent their entire lives in rented accommodation, and many still do. A large number of shops and business premises are leased and will also require certainty of term. Furthermore, if you don't put a time limit on a lease, it becomes difficult to distinguish between a freehold estate, ownership as we know it which goes on forever, and a leasehold estate, which is for only a set period.

Q: *What is an uncertain term?*

A: An uncertain term is one where you don't know how long the lease is going to last. In *Lace v Chantler* (1944) a lease was granted for the duration of the war. As nobody knew how long the war was going to last, the lease was not of a certain term and was therefore invalid.

Q: *Isn't having to decide a certain term inconvenient if the landlord doesn't know how long he wants to tie his land up for? What happens if he wants to develop his land sometime in the future, but isn't sure when?*

A: There were several attempts to get round the requirement of a certain term for this exact reason. In *Ashburn Anstalt v Arnold & Co* (1989) it was held that as long as both parties knew of the event which would bring the lease to an end, even if they didn't know when that event would be, then you could say that it was a certain term. A certain term for the parties at any rate. Imagine you were the tenant. You knew Yourland was going to be developed sometime in the future and you agreed with Mr Theirland that the lease would come to an end when he showed you a letter giving him planning permission for the development of Yourland. You also agreed with him that you could leave at any time. Both you and he would know the events that would bring the lease to an end. It's arguable that there is a certain term because you both know this, although you don't actually know when either of those events will occur. This example is similar to the facts in *Ashburn Anstalt v Arnold & Co*, where the court decided that a term defined in this way was certain. Such lateral thinking was overruled in *Prudential Assurance Co Ltd v London Residuary Body* (1992), which confirmed that *Lace v Chantler* remained good law. You had to know at the beginning of the lease how long it would go on for, and that was final. *Prudential Assurance Co Ltd v London Residuary Body* was followed in *Mexfield Housing Co-operative Limited v Berrisford* (2011) where a written agreement which said that the tenancy would continue until either the rent was in arrears or a condition of the agreement had been breached was held not to be a certain term. Mrs Berrisford's counsel proposed a clever solution here, though, by putting two pieces of information together. First, before 1926 at common law, an agreement for an uncertain term was construed as a lease for life. An example of an uncertain term here could be the condition that the agreement would end if the tenant stopped paying the rent. The resulting lease for life ended on either the death of the tenant or if any of the conditions that the parties had entered into in the agreement was met. This pre-1926 rule still applies today. Because a lease for life was itself an uncertain term, provided rent or a premium was being paid, section 149(6) of the Law of Property Act 1925 converted it into a 90-year term. So, an uncertain term was converted into a lease for life which itself was converted into a 90-year lease. On this basis, Mrs Berrisford could claim a 90-year lease. This was determinable only on Mrs Berrisford's death or if one of the conditions in the original agreement had been breached. As neither of these had happened, Mrs Berrisford was entitled to stay for whatever remained of the 90-year term.

Q: Does this mean that any agreement with an uncertain term will become a lease for a 90-year term under section 149(6) of the Law of Property Act 1925?

A: Yes, provided the other requirements for a lease are met, but this solution will work only for individuals, not for companies which do not have lives. This differentiation is unacceptable but will probably make a good exam scenario in the meantime. It also means that where an uncertain term is converted into a 90-year term, it may come as a surprise to either the landlord or the tenant, or both, and it may not necessarily be what they planned. Also in *Mexfield Housing Co-operative Limited v Berrisford*, the court reaffirmed the need for certainty of term as found in *Prudential Assurance Co Ltd v London Residuary Body* which had approved *Lace v Chantler* but considered that the requirement of certainty of term should be looked at by the courts or Parliament on the basis that if parties know where they stand in an agreement, that should be enough.

Q: *Does a lease have to start at the time when it's created, or can it be created to start at some time in the future?*

A: Either. If it starts in the future it can't start more than 21 years after the date of the grant of the lease. If it starts later than that, it will be void under section 149(3) of the Law of Property Act 1925.

Q: *Can you have a certain term for less than one full year?*

A: Yes. Section 205(1)(xxvii) of the Law of Property Act 1925 states that a term of years includes a term for a year or years, a term for less than a year, a term for a fraction of a year and a term from year to year. Short periods of time are still certain periods, or certain terms, because one week is a certain period of time, as is one month and so on.

Box A3   Rent or consideration

In the important case of *Street v Mountford* (1985) Lord Templeman held that 'the only intention which is relevant (to the creation of a lease) is the intention demonstrated by the agreement to grant exclusive possession for a term at a rent'. Although he appears to say that rent is necessary, this is not true. Section 205(1) (xxvii) of the Law of Property Act 1925 talks about a term of years whether or not at a rent. *Ashburn Anstalt v Arnold & Co* confirmed that rent was not an essential requirement of a lease, as did *Skipton Building Society v Clayton* (1993).

Q: *Why did Lord Templeman appear to make rent one of the requirements of a lease?*

A: Possibly because the case was to do with eligibility under the Rent Acts. For a tenant to be eligible for protection under the Rent Acts, rent has to be paid.

The other side of the argument is that if a lease is created in a written agreement, the agreement will not be enforceable unless there is some form of consideration. The rent is consideration for that agreement. Furthermore, you can create a short legal lease under section 54(2) of the Law of Property Act 1925 but the lease has to be at the market rent, and, again, you need rent here. If a lease is created in a deed, you do not require consideration because the deed itself makes the contract enforceable.

So a discussion of rent or consideration is included here because, for some types of leases, a lease cannot be created without it. On a more practical note, it's highly unlikely that anyone is going to let you occupy their property unless you pay them. In most leases or tenancies the lessee or the tenant pays rent money to the landlord. Payment does not necessarily have to take the form of money.

Boxes A4, A5 and A6 show a set of circumstances that were noted in *Facchini v Bryson* (1952) that exclude the finding of a lease if they occur. The circumstance in Box A7 was defined in *Street v Mountford*, and again excludes the finding of a lease. Although you may be able to tick the boxes for exclusive possession, A1, a certain term, A2, and rent, A3, there are some circumstances in which, even though you've ticked these boxes, you will still not have a lease.

Box A4   There is no intention to create a legal relationship

A lease is a contract, a legally binding relationship. A lease-type relationship could arise in a family situation. Take an example where Fred allows Auntie Dora to occupy his spare room for six months while her house is being redecorated. Auntie Dora may consider that she has exclusive possession of her room. It is presumed that Fred had no intention of entering into a legally binding contract to give Auntie Dora a lease, even if she did have exclusive possession of the spare room, and even if she paid Fred for the use of the room. This is common sense really. You don't want everyone who stays with you in this kind of situation to start claiming a lease and all associated rights. So the fact that there is no intention to create a legal relationship will exclude the finding of a lease.

In *Cobb v Lane* (1952) the owner allowed her brother to occupy a house rent-free. There was no intention to create a legal relationship, and accordingly the brother did not have a lease.

In *Heslop v Burns* (1974) Mr and Mrs Burns occupied rent-free accommodation in a house owned by a benefactor who had taken pity on their impoverished circumstances. It was held that there was no intention to create a legal relationship and therefore the couple did not have a lease.

Box A5   There is an act of friendship or generosity

This is similar to Box A4 where a person is allowed to occupy someone else's premises as a friend. For example, Jane allows her student friend, Janine, to stay in her spare room when Janine can't find a room of her own. Acts of friendship or generosity will exclude the finding of a lease because, again, there is no intention to create a legal relationship.

In *Marcroft Wagons Ltd v Smith* (1951) the tenant died and her daughter was allowed to remain in the house through the generosity of the landlord. Despite the fact that the landlord accepted rent from the daughter while he was considering the situation, the court decided that a lease did not exist because his conduct showed an act of kindness, not an intention to form a legally binding contract.

Box A6   There is a service occupancy

This is where someone occupies premises for the purpose of being better able to carry out his or her employment. Take an example where Fred is appointed as caretaker of a boarding school. He is given the use of a cottage in the school grounds for himself and his wife so that he is on the premises if anything goes wrong or needs repairing in an emergency. The reason he will not be seen to have a lease, despite the fact that he is likely to have exclusive possession, is that he is occupying the cottage as part of his employment. The relationship is one of employer and employee, not landlord and tenant.

Q: *Does the accommodation have to be absolutely necessary in order for a person to be able to carry out the job that goes with it?*

A: No. It's enough that the accommodation enables better performance of duties. However, the accommodation must not be just a perk or a fringe benefit. In *Norris v Checksfield* (1991) Lord Guest stated:

> The residence must be ancillary to the duties which the servant has to perform, or, put in another way, the requirements must be with a view to the more efficient performance of the servant's duties.

In *Norris v Checksfield* a coach mechanic had permission to use a bungalow which was close to where he worked. In return for the use of the bungalow, the mechanic had agreed to apply for a passenger service vehicle licence and to drive coaches for his employer. In fact he had been disqualified from driving! Not surprisingly, his employer brought an action for possession of the bungalow. It was held that the mechanic was occupying the bungalow for the better performance of his duties as a coach driver. As this was a service occupancy, he did not have a lease and his use of the bungalow came to an end when his employment ended. The relationship was one of employer and employee, not landlord and tenant.

Box A7 ### There is a lodger

This last category was defined in *Street v Mountford*. A lodger is defined as an occupier who receives services or attendance from the owner that are personal to the occupier. Services can include the provision of meals, laundry, internal window cleaning or the collection of rubbish from within the accommodation, for example. As the owner is able to enter when he wishes in order to carry out these services, the lodger can never claim exclusive possession and can therefore never claim a lease. People occupying bed-sits where personal services are provided, guests staying in hotel rooms and people living in residential homes are all classified as lodgers. They may well have exclusive occupation, but they do not have exclusive possession, and so they do not have a lease.

In *Abbeyfield (Harpenden) Society Ltd v Woods* (1968) the occupier of a room in an old people's home did not have a lease because meals were provided and there was a resident housekeeper.

In *Street v Mountford* Lord Templeman stated:

> An occupier of residential accommodation at a rent for a term is either a lodger or a tenant. The occupier is a lodger if the landlord provides attendance or services which require the landlord or his servants to exercise unrestricted access to and use of the premises. A lodger is entitled to live in the premises but cannot call the place his own.

Summary of the essence of a lease

The formula for a lease is exclusive possession plus a certain term plus rent. Although rent is not essential, it does support a contractual arrangement. Even if there is exclusive possession for a certain term at a rent, if the claimant falls into one of the exclusion categories, he will not have a lease.

The effect of not meeting the requirements for a lease

Q: *What do you have if you don't have exclusive possession?*

A: You have a licence to occupy the land, which is permission to be on the land. The person who grants the licence for the other party to occupy the land is called the licensor, and the person who takes the licence and occupies the land is called the licensee.

The licence is called a bare licence where no consideration is given for the permission to be on the land. The postman has a bare licence to walk up the drive to your door as he doesn't pay you for the privilege of doing so. A licence granted for consideration is called a contractual licence. When you go to the cinema, you pay for the privilege of being on the premises. You have a licence or permission to be there, and, as you have given consideration in the form of buying a ticket, you have a contractual licence. If you have permission to occupy another's land and you do not meet the requirements of a lease, you have a licence. Any money paid in return for permission to occupy the land will be called consideration for the licence, not rent, because you do not have a lease.

Q: *What happens if you don't have certainty of term?*

A: Where the person has gone into possession and is paying rent, a tenancy may be implied. This is discussed further in Box 2(iii). Alternatively, it was held obiter in *Mexfield Housing Co-operative Ltd v Berrisford* that there could be a contractual licence. This would be on the same terms as the void lease but would be a contractual licence instead.

Q: *What happens if no consideration is given for the use of the property?*

A: This does not deny a lease as such but it then depends on how the lease has been created as to whether consideration is needed. This was discussed in Box A3.

Q: *What happens if you have any of the special circumstances excluding the finding of a lease that were noted in* Facchini v Bryson (1952) *and* Street v Mountford (1985)?

A: You do not have a lease but you have a licence, either a bare licence or a contractual licence.

Q: *What's the difference between a lease and a contractual licence?*

A: The answer to this is conveniently in the next section.

The distinction between a lease and a licence

Q: *Is it important to distinguish between a lease and a licence?*

A: Yes. There are some very important differences between the two.

First, a lease is a proprietary right in the land and is capable of binding a person who buys the land that is subject to the lease. A contractual licence is not a right in the land. It is a personal claim binding only on the parties who made the original agreement.

This said, you need to be aware of the heavily criticised case of *Bruton v London & Quadrant Housing Trust* (2000). A leasehold estate is a proprietary right in the land. The *Bruton* case allowed a landlord and tenant relationship to arise even though the landlord did not own the freehold estate from which to carve out a leasehold estate. This means that you can have a landlord and tenant relationship which is purely personal between the parties and has no estate of land attached to it. Such a decision is contrary to all known theory and has provided hours of entertainment for the academic world. There is more discussion on the matter of non-proprietary leases at the end of this chapter.

Secondly, a lease cannot be revoked (withdrawn) by the landlord because it is a proprietary interest in land and this prevents unilateral revocation. However, both a bare and a contractual licence can be revoked (withdrawn) at any time by the licensor, as long as reasonable notice to leave is given. Although the occupier can claim damages for breach of contract or, in some cases, obtain an injunction to stop the contract being revoked, this is clearly a precarious position to be in. If you occupy residential premises under a licence and the licence is revoked (withdrawn), you are going to have to find somewhere else to live whatever damages are awarded. Licences are discussed in detail in Chapter 13.

Thirdly, and most importantly, if you have a lease you may be able to claim statutory protection from the demands of a landlord. You may well have heard of the Rent Acts or the Landlord and Tenant Acts. Statute can give a tenant protection against an unreasonable rent increase or protection from eviction before the lease has come to its end, for example. Whilst there is some protection for licensees under the Protection from Eviction Act 1977, protection is not at the same level as for tenants. Bare and contractual licences are simply permissions to occupy land.

Q: *So if you occupy land, you clearly need to make sure you have been granted a lease?*

A: Yes. Very definitely. If you are occupying land, the importance of being able to obtain the statutory protection available to a tenant is paramount. This means that you need to ensure you have a lease. Conversely, the owner of the land will try and ensure that you have only been granted a licence as it is not in his interests for you to have this statutory protection. As exclusive possession is the hallmark of a lease, whether you have a lease or a licence is mainly determined therefore by whether or not you have exclusive possession.

Q: *Presumably, landlords will try and avoid granting exclusive possession because, if there is no exclusive possession, there cannot be a lease or a tenancy?*

A: Yes. This is where conflict between the owner of the land and the occupier can arise. The owner would claim that he had not granted exclusive possession and the occupier would claim that he had. This conflict culminated in the important case of *Street v Mountford* but, before we look at this case, we need to backtrack to a case called *Somma v Hazelhurst* (1978). In this case the owner, Miss Somma, had given Mr Hazelhurst and his partner, Miss Savelli, the use of an upstairs room. The agreements that each party signed were called licences. In these licence agreements it was stated that Mr Hazelhurst could share the room with Miss Savelli and vice versa. Miss Somma also reserved the right to share the accommodation with Mr Hazelhurst and Miss Savelli herself, or to move total strangers in with them.

Q: *Was this specifically with the aim of ensuring that Mr Hazelhurst and Miss Savelli could not claim exclusive possession, and therefore statutory protection, because other people were entitled to share the room with them?*

A: Almost certainly, even though Miss Somma had probably no intention of sending anyone else to live with them, let alone moving in herself.

Q: *So the court just looked at what was stated in the agreement and, because it was called a licence, it was held actually to be a licence?*

A: Yes. The court looked at the parties' expressed intentions. The agreements stated that Mr Hazelhurst and Miss Savelli had been given licences, and the terms of the agreement also indicated that licences had been granted. While the court may have disapproved of the nature of the arrangement, disapproval was insufficient to classify the agreement as unreal or bogus.

Q: *Were landlords in a very powerful position here because they could ensure that they created a licence simply by putting in a clause similar to the one included by Miss Somma and calling the arrangement a licence?*

A: Yes, because the court looked at the parties' expressed intentions, not what was happening in reality. They were only in a powerful position though until *Street v Mountford*. In this case Mrs Mountford had been given the use of rooms belonging to Mr Street. The agreement they had signed was again called a licence. Mr Street was referred to in the agreement as the 'licensor' and Mrs Mountford as the 'licensee'. However, the House of Lords held that it didn't matter whether the parties had called the agreement a lease or a licence. What really mattered was what Mrs Mountford had been given as a matter of law. Looking at the objective reality of the situation, she had actually been given exclusive possession of the premises for a certain term at a rent. She had therefore been granted a lease, regardless of the label the parties had attached to the agreement. As Lord Templeman said:

> My Lords, the only intention which is relevant is the intention demonstrated by the agreement to grant exclusive possession for a term at a rent.

An often-quoted statement that highlights the fact that the agreement must be looked at objectively to decide whether a lease or a licence has been created again comes from Lord Templeman in this case:

> If the agreement satisfied all the requirements of a tenancy, then the agreement produced a tenancy, and the parties cannot alter the effect of the agreement by insisting that they only created a licence. The manufacture of a five-pronged implement for manual digging results in a fork even if the manufacturer, unfamiliar with the English language, insists that he intended to make and has made a spade.

Lord Templeman was saying that if, by looking at the situation objectively, you could determine that exclusive possession had been granted and the other requirements for a lease were met, there would be a lease even if the parties themselves had called the agreement a licence. In *Street v Mountford* the court found that Mrs Mountford had a lease, despite the fact that the word 'licence' was used throughout the agreement. In objective reality she had exclusive possession for a certain term at a rent. The case also overruled *Somma v Hazelhurst*.

Q: *What was the effect of* **Street v Mountford***?*

A: Cases that followed were decided on the objective reality of the situation, not on what the parties thought or said or wrote. This inevitably led to some creative thinking by owners of land as to how they could avoid granting exclusive possession, and thereby avoid granting a lease. Unfortunately they came up with some very disingenuous ways to achieve this. The first way was to put into the occupancy agreement a wide range of services, such as cleaning or the provision of meals. The occupier would be seen as a licensee because he couldn't resist the owner's unrestricted access in order to supply those services (Box A7) and so couldn't claim exclusive possession. Owners also tried to insert clauses into the occupancy agreement which stated that the occupier had to move out of the premises for a certain time each day, thereby excluding exclusive possession because the landlord could use the property in that time. The courts became wise to these pretence clauses as they were called, and awarded a lease where there was clearly exclusive possession for a certain term at a rent.

A classic example of a pretence clause occurred in *Aslan v Murphy*. The owner of the basement property, Aslan, granted a licence to the occupier, Murphy. Aslan retained a set of keys and stated that he could enter the property at any time. Although the basement measured only 4′3″ by 12′6″, Murphy was required to share the accommodation with another party and also to be out of the accommodation for an hour and a half each day. These clauses were held to be wholly unrealistic and clearly pretences. The agreement did not represent the actual situation, and the court found a lease, not a licence. Similarly, in *Crancour Ltd v Da Silvaesa* (1986) the occupiers could occupy the rooms in a house for 26 weeks but not between 10.30 am and midday on any day. The owner also retained an absolute right of entry for carrying out management and cleaning and providing attendance. The clauses were held to be pretences and the court again found a lease, not a licence. In both cases the objective reality was exclusive possession for a term at a rent

Q: What happens if these clauses for services and cleaning are in the occupancy agreement, but the services are never carried out?

A: The obvious implication is that they are pretence clauses put in to try and deny exclusive possession. If the services start but subsequently stop, you can argue that they are genuine. The occupier can always insist that they are resumed, otherwise it is a breach of the occupancy agreement. Even if the occupier chooses not to insist on their resumption, there will still be a licence because the owner continues to have unrestricted access. The occupier is simply not insisting that the services are resumed. Be careful though. Not all clauses put in occupancy agreements are pretences. *Westminster City Council v Clarke* (1992) concerned a hostel for homeless men. The licence agreement stated that the occupier could be asked to change rooms or share rooms with another occupier. These clauses were held to be genuinely required for the management of the hostel. They were not designed to avoid exclusive possession and statutory protection, and so a licence was created.

Q: What happens if two or more people share a flat? Can they still have a lease even though they're sharing?

A: The answer to this concerns the requirements for a joint tenancy which were discussed in Chapter 8. If two or more people take a legal lease and satisfy the four unities of possession, interest, time and title, they will hold the legal lease as joint tenants. As such, they 'own the whole' and can exclude anyone not in the joint tenancy. As they can exclude anyone else, they have exclusive possession and can therefore claim a lease. Again, it doesn't matter whether the agreement is called a licence or a lease, as the same approach is adopted here as in *Street v Mountford*. If the reality of the situation satisfies the four unities, which then gives exclusive possession, there will be a lease. Two cases illustrate these points. The first is *Antoniades v Villiers* (1990), where a couple entered into separate agreements called licences for a small one-bedroom flat. In these licence agreements the landlord had reserved to himself the right to introduce other parties, including himself, into the double bed with the couple! Not surprisingly this was considered to be a pretence clause which was ignored. In reality the couple actually had a joint tenancy with the right to be able to exclude anyone not in the joint tenancy. This gave them the exclusive possession necessary for a lease.

However, in *AG Securities v Vaughan* (1990) four different parties signed different licence agreements on different days. There was no joint tenancy because the agreements had been signed on different days, so the unities of time and title, which are both required for a joint tenancy to exist, were missing. As there was no joint tenancy, they could not collectively exclude anyone else and so did not have exclusive possession of the flat. Furthermore, although the parties had exclusive occupation of the property, the landlord could introduce new occupiers of his choice if any occupant left, which again meant that they did not have exclusive possession. Each party therefore had a licence. A similar result occurred in *Stribling v Wickham* (1989) where it was held that 'The three licences were in substance and reality just what they purported to be' and there were no pretence clauses. In *Mikeover Ltd v Brady* (1989) there was no unity of interest because each party was responsible for his agreed share of the money payable only and not for that of the other party and a licence was found.

The objective reality test came up recently in the context of a claim for a commercial lease in *Clear Channel UK Ltd v Manchester City Council*. Clear Channel put up advertising displays on sites owned by Manchester City Council and tried to argue that the agreement between them was a tenancy and not a licence. This was clause 14.1 of that agreement:

> This Agreement shall constitute a licence in respect of each Site and confers no tenancy on [Clear Channel] and possession of each Site is retained by [the Council] subject however to the rights and obligations created by this Agreement.

Again, the answer went back to the substantive nature of the agreement, whether there was exclusive possession for a certain term at a rent. Clear Channel never had exclusive possession of the sites and had also agreed to allow the Council access. It therefore had licence agreements. The case is important because Lord Justice Jonathan Parker said that although he didn't want to cast doubt on *Street v Mountford*, in a situation like this where both parties had equal bargaining power, both had full legal advice and the legal consequences of the agreement were spelt out – a licence and not a tenancy – he would take some persuading that what was said in the agreement was different from what they intended.

Q: *Does that mean that what parties put in a document starts to become more conclusive?*

A: His words were obiter but in cases where both parties have equal bargaining power, full legal advice and the effect of the agreement clearly spelt out are likely to be uncommon. Lord Justice Jonathan Parker also said he was surprised and unedified that a substantial organisation like Clear Channel, with the benefit of full legal advice, should enter into an agreement where the expressed intention in that agreement was not to create a tenancy, and then invite the court to say that it did.

In *Scottish Widows plc v Stewart* (2006) it was confirmed that the test for a lease was whether the agreement gave exclusive possession. Occupation was not the same as possession. In the case there was nothing in the agreement which entitled the occupier to exclude the owner, and so there was a licence. The court also said that whereas residential leases required different considerations, it agreed with the views of Lord Justice Jonathan Parker in Clear Channel in holding that where commercial undertakings had clearly spelt out what they intended, it would be hard for either party to argue otherwise.

Q: *Why do residential leases require different considerations?*

A: Because the parties don't necessarily obtain legal advice and the parties in a residential lease are unlikely to have equal bargaining power. So it looks as though, if parties to a commercial lease spell out what they intend in the agreement with full legal advice and equal bargaining power, they are unlikely to be able to wriggle out of what they call their agreement. In other cases and in residential leases, the objective reality test will continue to govern the situation.

Summary of the distinction between a lease and a licence

There are significant differences between a lease and a licence. As a lease may attract statutory protection for the tenant, owners of land have tried to avoid granting exclusive possession, and therefore a lease, by inserting pretence clauses into occupancy agreements. The courts will look beyond these pretence clauses at the objective reality of the situation in determining whether there is a lease or a licence.

The creation of a lease

Box B

THE CREATION OF A LEASE

Tick as many boxes as possible but at least one:

A lease can be created by the following means. The type of lease that results is in brackets

☐ **1.** By deed (legal lease)

☐ **2.** Under section 54(2) of the Law of Property Act 1925 (legal lease)

    (i)   A fixed term lease or

    (ii) An express periodic tenancy or

    (iii) An implied periodic tenancy

☐ **3.** Under section 2 of the Law of Property (Miscellaneous Provisions) Act 1989 (equitable lease)

☐ **4.** By proprietary estoppel

Assuming you have been able to tick all the boxes in Box A, you have something that is capable of being a lease. You haven't actually got a lease at this stage because you still have to prove that it has been created in a way that is recognised by the courts or by statute. If you can't prove that it's been created in a recognised way, you do not have a valid lease. You must tick as many boxes as possible in Box B, but at least one. We'll use an example where you have taken a lease of Yourland from Mr Theirland. When creating a lease, you must look at both the degree of formality required and also the length of the lease.

Box B1 ## By deed (legal lease)

A legal lease can be created by deed. The requirements of a deed are found in section 1 of the Law of Property (Miscellaneous Provisions) Act 1989.

In essence the deed must be:

▶ in writing

and

▶ clear on the face of it that it is intended to be a deed

and

▶ signed by the person making the deed in the presence of a witness who attests his signature

and

▶ delivered as a deed.

The process of witnessing a deed is called attestation and the witness has to sign and date the deed. A deed does not have to be delivered physically. It's sufficient that the person granting the interest in the deed makes it clear that he intends to be bound by it. This is usually inferred from the fact that he signs it.

Creating a lease by this method results in a legal lease for the following reason. First, section 1 of the Law of Property Act 1925 states that there are only two estates in land capable of subsisting or being created at law, i.e. of being legal. They are:

▶ the estate in fee simple absolute in possession, generally known as freehold ownership, and
▶ the term of years absolute, the lease.

Secondly, excluding the exception under section 54(2) of the Law of Property Act 1925 discussed in Box B2, section 52(1) of the Law of Property Act 1925 states that no legal estate or interest will be created in land unless a deed is used. Therefore, in order for a lease to be legal, it must be created by deed. Overall, then, these sections mean that a lease is capable of being legal under section 1 of the Law of Property Act 1925, but must be made by deed under section 52(1) of the same Act in order to be legal.

Q: *How long does a legal lease by deed go on for?*

A: A fixed term lease will go on for the term stated in the deed. So a legal lease for 50 years of Yourland created by deed will go on for 50 years. At the end of 50 years the lease comes to an end and you must leave. It is possible for a lease to contain terms that enable it to be brought to an end prematurely.

In Box A2 the case of *Mexfield Housing Co-operative Ltd v Berrisford* was discussed. If you have an uncertain term that you would like converted into a 90-year term under section 149(6) of the Law of Property Act 1925, the agreement creating the uncertain term must have been created by deed in order for there to be a valid 90-year legal lease created by this means.

Box B2 Under section 54(2) of the Law of Property Act 1925 (legal lease)

Q: *Do you always have to have a deed to create a legal lease?*

A: No. Section 54(2) of the Law of Property Act 1925 creates an exception to section 52(1) which requires a deed to create a legal interest. Section 54(2) is a quick and easy way to create a legal lease. There are four conditions which must all be met:

▶ The agreement can be oral (spoken) or in writing.

and

▶ The lease must be for a period of three years or less.

and

▶ The lease must take effect in possession: see *Long v Tower Hamlets London BC* (1998). This means the tenant must have the right to go into the property immediately.

and

▶ The lease must be at the best rent which can reasonably be obtained without taking a fine. The best rent is usually the market rent. In *Fitzkriston LLP v Panayi* (2008) £4,000 was not the best rent for the property because the best rent would have been somewhere between £12,000 and £20,000 and so no lease was created under section 54(2). A fine is a lump sum payable at the start of a lease in consideration of a reduction in rent.

Q: *Why are you allowed to create a legal lease without a deed?*

A: Practicality. Think of the number of short-term leases created in this country. It runs into millions. You wouldn't want this number of people queuing outside solicitors' offices trying to create all these short leases by deed, even if they knew they had to have a deed in the first place. Unless of course you were a solicitor.

There are three ways of using section 54(2) of the Law of Property Act 1925 to create a legal lease.

Box B2i A fixed term lease

If you have a fixed term lease, the lease will finish at the end of the given term. A fixed term lease for three years or less can be created under section 54(2).

Q: *So Mr Theirland could grant me a legal lease simply by agreeing orally that I can occupy Yourland for two years, for example?*

A: Yes, providing of course you also met the other conditions under section 54(2) of paying the market rent and you have the right to go into the property immediately. He could also grant a two-year lease to you in writing. The writing does not have to meet any statutory conditions or other formality, and this would again create a legal lease for two years.

Box B2ii An express periodic tenancy

When tenancies for one year or a part of a year are expressly granted for a period of time which is stated to recur, for example from week to week, they are express periodic tenancies. They are granted *expressly*, they are *tenancies* because there is a relationship of landlord and tenant, and they are for *periods of time*, whether for a week, a month, three months, six months, a year or any other part of a year. The main feature of these periodic tenancies is that, at the end of the period, the week, month, three months, six months or year, they can renew themselves automatically until either the landlord or the tenant gives notice that they want the tenancy to end.

Q: *When would they renew themselves automatically?*

A: They would renew themselves if the words used in the grant indicated that the parties saw the tenancy as continuing automatically. If you are granted a tenancy of Yourland 'from week to week' for example, the tenancy will continue 'from week to week' until either you or the landlord, Mr Theirland, gives notice. This saves you having to find Mr Theirland at the end of every week to renew your tenancy agreement. This automatic renewal applies only to periodic tenancies for a year or less, and it applies only if the wording indicates that the term is to be continuous. The words 'from week to week' indicate that the periodic tenancy will continue to run until brought to an end. However, if you are granted a tenancy for 'one week', this will be a fixed term of a week. It will not be renewed automatically and must be specifically granted again if this is what you and the landlord, Mr Theirland, want.

Q: *Are these periodic tenancies created under section 54(2)?*

A: Yes, provided of course you meet the conditions in section 54(2). Periodic tenancies come under this section because a year or less is a period of less than the three-year limit given under section 54(2). As section 54(2) gives you a *legal* lease, these express periodic tenancies are known as *legal* periodic tenancies. An express legal periodic tenancy granted from week to week will give you an express legal *weekly* periodic tenancy, one granted from month to month will give you an express legal *monthly* periodic tenancy.

Q: *If an express legal weekly periodic tenancy carries on for over 156 weeks (52 weeks for three years) because neither the landlord nor the tenant gives notice, then the period of time will be over the three years allowed in section 54(2). Does that matter?*

A: No. Each period of time in a periodic tenancy is seen as a separate period of time. Only a weekly periodic tenancy is being created each time, even though you may do this for as long as you like until one party gives notice and, overall, it is seen as one whole term. If notice is given, the periodic tenancy comes to an end. It's not an uncertain term because either party can give notice at the end of one of the periods. There is a problem if there is a restriction on either party to give notice (for example, notice can't be given to the tenant unless the rent is in arrears) because this means there is an uncertain term: see *Mexfield Housing Co-operative Ltd v Berrisford*.

Box B2iii   An implied periodic tenancy

A periodic tenancy can be created expressly between the parties, as in the parties talking expressly to one another about the terms and conditions. A periodic tenancy can also be implied by operation of law: see *Martin v Smith* (1874). Implied legal periodic tenancies are implied from the circumstances where a person is in occupation of land with the owner's permission, paying rent on a periodic basis with the intention to create a landlord and tenant relationship. In this case, a legal periodic tenancy will be implied. Again, if the circumstances indicate the continuation of an implied legal periodic tenancy, it will renew itself automatically.

Q: *If the tenancy is only implied between the parties, how do you know whether it's a weekly, monthly or yearly periodic tenancy?*

A: The tenancy is defined by reference to how frequently the rent is said to be paid. If rent is paid every week, this will create an implied legal weekly periodic tenancy, if monthly, then an implied legal monthly periodic tenancy, and, if yearly, an implied legal yearly periodic tenancy. If rent is said to be paid at £12,000 *per annum* with £1,000 paid every month, this will still give an implied legal yearly periodic tenancy because you determine the time by reference to the overall period of time.

Q: *How are these implied legal periodic tenancies created?*

A: They are created under section 54(2) again, and so must meet the conditions stipulated in that section.

   Look at an example where an implied legal periodic tenancy can arise. Imagine you have a fixed term legal lease of Yourland for 10 years which has been created by deed. You pay rent every month. If, at the end of your 10-year lease you pay a further month's rent, which is accepted by the landlord without any further express agreement, an implied legal monthly periodic tenancy will arise. It will be implied from the fact that you are occupying the land and paying rent. This will happen whether the occupation is of commercial or residential property. In *Mann Aviation Group (Engineering) Ltd v Longmint Aviation Ltd* (2011) there had been no documentation creating a lease. However, an implied periodic tenancy had arisen because Mann Aviation was in occupation of Longmint Aviation's land and there was an intention to create the relationship of landlord and tenant and rent was being paid: *Street v Mountford*. The one factor which might exclude an implied legal periodic tenancy arising is any lack of intention to create the legal relationship of a tenancy: see *Javad v Aqil* (1991).

Q: *Are there other examples where a periodic tenancy will be implied?*

A: If you try to create a lease with an uncertain term, the lease will be void unless it's converted into a 90-year term as happened in *Mexfield Housing Co-operative Limited v Berrisford*. If you have gone into possession, though, and are paying rent, you could argue that you have an implied legal periodic tenancy. This is what happened in *Prudential Assurance Co Ltd v London Residuary Body* where an agreement that was to last until the land was required for road widening was deemed to be an uncertain term. Instead, the court found an implied legal yearly periodic tenancy because the tenant had gone into possession and was paying rent by reference to a year.

Q: *Could you have had a contractual licence here instead of the implied legal yearly periodic tenancy?*

A: In *Mexfield Housing Co-operative Ltd v Berrisford*, the Supreme Court stated obiter that you could. After all, if the parties intended to create a licence in *Street v Mountford* but the court found a lease instead, you can't really argue about the logic of finding a licence even though the parties intended a lease.

Q: *Which would you have, an implied periodic tenancy or a contractual licence?*

A: In *Mexfield Housing Co-operative Ltd v Berrisford,* it was said that which you would have would depend on the circumstances.

Q: *How does a legal periodic tenancy end?*

A: If either the landlord or the tenant wants to bring an express or an implied legal periodic tenancy to an end, notice must be given. The notice period is usually that of a full period, and this is the same for both express and implied periodic tenancies.

A weekly periodic tenancy requires notice of one week expiring at the end of one of the weekly periods.

A monthly periodic tenancy requires notice of one month expiring at the end of one of the monthly periods.

A yearly periodic tenancy requires notice of half a year expiring at the end of a year of the tenancy.

These common law rules can be altered by statutory exceptions which prescribe different notice periods. You also need to be aware of the Protection from Eviction Act 1977 which creates some exceptions in favour of the tenant if the leased property is a dwelling house.

Q: *How do leases other than periodic tenancies end?*

A: They end when the term comes to an end. If you have a lease of Yourland for five years or 999 years, you will have the right to occupy Yourland for five years or 999 years. At the end of the period, the lease comes to an end.

Q: *So it's only periodic tenancies that carry on automatically until either the landlord or the tenant actually brings them to an end by notice?*

A: Yes, but only if this continuation is indicated by the wording in any express agreement, or from the circumstances in an implied agreement.

Q: *Can I end a five-year or 999-year lease early?*

A: This will depend on the terms specified in the lease.

Q: *If two people, A and B, rent a flat together, what happens if they have an argument and A gives notice to end the tenancy to the landlord?*

A: In *Hammersmith and Fulham LBC v Monk* (1992) it was held that this will bring the tenancy to an end.

Q: *So B's interest will come to an end even though he didn't actually give notice. Don't joint tenants have to act together on the legal title to bring the lease to an end?*

A: No. The reasoning behind this is that a joint tenancy of a periodic tenancy, let's say a weekly periodic tenancy, will carry on until either the landlord or the tenant brings it to an end by giving a week's notice. However, the 'tenancy will carry on' part of the sentence relies on the fact that both A and B agree to this, even if it's a tacit agreement that's not actually put into words. If one of them doesn't agree by giving notice, A here, the tenancy will come to an end.

Q: *Isn't this rather hard on the party left behind?*

A: Yes, and this happened in *Harrow London BC v Qazi* (2003). And, just to make matters worse, if one party stops paying the rent, you and anyone else in the tenancy with you is jointly and severally liable for paying it, which means the landlord can come after any or all of you in the joint tenancy to pay the absentee's share. Even if you find someone to take the absentee's place, that is called subletting and there is a fairly good chance that the agreement you have made with the landlord will not allow subletting so you risk losing the property. Under Law Commission proposals, only the party who gave notice would be able to bring his/her interest to an end: see Renting Homes: The Final Report (Law Com No 297).

Box B3

Under section 2 of the Law of Property (Miscellaneous Provisions) Act 1989 (equitable lease)

Section 2 of the Law of Property (Miscellaneous Provisions) Act 1989 governs contracts for the creation, sale or disposition of an interest in land. The contract must be

▷ in writing

  and

▷ signed by or on behalf of both the parties to the contract

  and

▷ it must contain all the express terms of the agreement.

A written agreement to create a lease satisfying section 2 of the Law of Property (Miscellaneous Provisions) Act 1989 will create an equitable lease.

This agreement can arise in one of two ways. The first is when you and Mr Theirland have some chats about the possibility of a lease of Yourland. He then

Q: *Are there any circumstances in which I would need to rely on the implied legal monthly periodic tenancy, rather than on the equitable lease?*

A: Yes. If your written agreement turned out to be defective because it didn't satisfy section 2 of the Law of Property (Miscellaneous Provisions) Act 1989, it would be void. You would then have to rely on the implied legal monthly periodic tenancy.

Q: *And could I continue to occupy Yourland under the implied legal monthly periodic tenancy?*

A: Yes. However, an implied legal periodic tenancy carries on until one party wants to bring it to an end, and gives notice. As the notice period for a monthly periodic tenancy is one month, Mr Theirland will have to give you only one month's notice expiring at the end of one of the monthly periods, after which time you must go. Your implied legal monthly periodic tenancy gives you some stay of execution, but only for the length of the notice period.

Another example when you may need to rely on the implied legal monthly periodic tenancy is in the following situation. Let's say that when you occupied Yourland under the equitable lease, you created so much trouble that Mr Theirland evicted you. You asked the court to insist that Mr Theirland allow you to remain in Yourland for the full four years granted to you. After all, you did have a written agreement, a contract that you could occupy Yourland for four years. A contract for the creation of an interest in land is a contract that is capable of specific performance because you would never be able to find an identical lease elsewhere, and so specific performance should be awarded. Specific performance is an equitable remedy and will be awarded only if you have behaved equitably yourself. You clearly haven't if you have caused trouble, and the courts have the discretion to refuse the remedy. In this case you will have to fall back on your implied legal monthly periodic tenancy.

Q: *And could I continue to occupy Yourland under the implied legal monthly periodic tenancy again?*

A: Yes. Again though, as the notice period for a monthly periodic tenancy is one month, Mr Theirland will have to give you only one month's notice expiring at the end of one of the monthly periods, after which time you must go. Again, your implied legal monthly periodic tenancy gives you some stay of execution, but only for the length of the notice period.

Q: *If I hadn't caused trouble, how long could I have stayed under the equitable lease?*

A: The full four years. You are much better off with your equitable lease because the landlord can always give notice in a periodic tenancy.

The effect of not creating a lease in a recognised way

If a lease has not been created in a recognised way, the occupier will have only a bare or a contractual licence. The distinction between a lease and a licence was discussed on page 393.

Summary of the creation of a lease

A deed must be used to create a legal lease. An exception to this requirement is found in section 54(2) of the Law of Property Act 1925, which allows for the creation of a legal lease for three years or less. An equitable lease will be created if the requirements of section 2 of the Law of Property (Miscellaneous Provisions) Act 1989 are met. A lease can also be created by estoppel. If a lease has not been created in a recognised way, the occupier will have only a bare or a contractual licence.

The protection of a lease

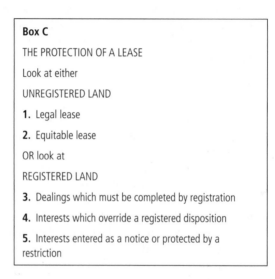

> **Box C**
>
> THE PROTECTION OF A LEASE
>
> Look at either
>
> UNREGISTERED LAND
>
> **1.** Legal lease
>
> **2.** Equitable lease
>
> OR look at
>
> REGISTERED LAND
>
> **3.** Dealings which must be completed by registration
>
> **4.** Interests which override a registered disposition
>
> **5.** Interests entered as a notice or protected by a restriction

In the example that follows, Mr Theirland, the owner of Theirland, granted you a lease of Yourland. Mr Theirland has now decided to sell Theirland to Peter. The question is whether your lease of Yourland is binding on Peter as Yourland forms part of Theirland, even though it is leased to you. There is no period of time given in this example, as the protection of a lease depends not only on how it was created, but also for how long it was granted.

sold to Peter ← Theirland | Yourland leased to you

Unregistered land

Use the procedure given in Chapter 3 on page 44 to determine how interests are protected in unregistered land. This procedure is repeated below for your convenience.

Step 1. Establish whether it is a legal or equitable interest that is being claimed. If it is a legal interest, legal rights bind the world both before 1926 and, excluding a puisne mortgage, after then as well. If it is an equitable interest you must see whether the equitable interest is capable of entry as a land charge under the Land Charges Act 1972.

Step 2. If the equitable interest is not capable of entry as a land charge, use the rule that governed equitable interests before 1926, known as the doctrine of notice. If the equitable interest is capable of entry as a land charge, work out in whose interest it is to enter it as a land charge. This will be the person who benefits from the equitable interest.

Step 3. Check to see whether that person has entered his equitable interest as a land charge in the correct class on the Land Charges Register against the name of the owner of the land that the right is over.

- An equitable interest that has been entered as a land charge binds everyone who takes the land under section 198 of the Law of Property Act 1925.
- If the equitable interest has not been entered as a land charge, it will not be binding on some classes of purchaser.

Now apply the procedure.

Box C1   Unregistered land – legal lease

Step 1. A legal lease is a legal interest. Legal rights bind the world.
   This means that if you have a legal lease, it will be binding on Peter.

Q: *So Peter must let me continue to stay in Theirland if I have a legal lease?*

A: Correct. That means that leases created in the following ways will be binding on Peter:

- a lease created by deed (Box B1); or
- a fixed term lease created under section 54(2) of the Law of Property Act 1925 (Box B2i); or
- an express periodic tenancy created under section 54(2) of the Law of Property Act 1925 (Box B2ii); or
- an implied periodic tenancy created under section 54(2) of the Law of Property Act 1925 (Box B2iii).

Q: *How does Peter find out about the legal lease?*

A: When unregistered land is sold, a purchaser must look back through the title deeds of that land. The chances are that any grant of a legal lease by deed will be attached to the title deeds, so Peter can find out that way. As far as any lease is concerned, though, it should be fairly obvious to Peter that someone else is living on that part of Theirland called Yourland. To have a lease in the first place you must have exclusive possession, which would imply some sort of privacy and separate occupation. In his capacity as purchaser, Peter should exercise reasonable care and look round the property himself. His solicitor should also ask questions. Therefore a legal right, here a legal lease, will bind anyone who takes Theirland, either as a purchaser or by gift or by inheritance.

Unregistered land – equitable lease

This will be an equitable lease of Yourland satisfying the requirements of section 2 of the Law of Property (Miscellaneous Provisions) Act 1989.

You can apply the same procedure as before if you have an equitable lease of Yourland:

Step 1. An equitable lease is an equitable interest. An equitable lease is capable of entry as a land charge under the Land Charges Act 1972.

Step 2. It is in your interest to enter the equitable lease as a land charge as you benefit from the interest.

Step 3. You should have entered your equitable lease as a class C(iv) land charge on the Land Charges Register against the name of Mr Theirland, who is the owner of the land that your lease is over:

▶ If you have entered your equitable lease as a class C(iv) land charge, it will bind Peter under section 198 of the Law of Property Act 1925 and he must let you remain in occupation according to the terms of the lease.

▶ If you have not entered your equitable lease as a land charge, it will not be binding on a purchaser of a legal estate for money or money's worth under section 4(6) of the Land Charges Act 1972. Peter paid money for the legal estate of Theirland, so, if you have not entered your equitable lease as a land charge, you will have to leave Yourland immediately.

Q: *When does my equitable lease have to be entered as a land charge?*

A: As soon as it has been created, or at least before Theirland is sold. You won't know if and when Mr Theirland may sell Theirland. If your equitable lease is not entered on the Land Charges Register before any sale of Theirland, a purchaser, Peter here, would not have found out about it even if he had inspected the Register and he will therefore not be bound by it.

Q: *And if I haven't entered my equitable lease as a land charge, then I have to leave immediately?*

A: Yes. The equitable lease is quite simply not binding on Peter and he does not have to give you any form of notice.

Q: *Do I have any redress if I don't protect my equitable lease?*

A: Not as far as your equitable lease is concerned. However, there is another avenue to pursue. If you look back to page 406 in this chapter, you will see that it is possible to have two different types of lease in the same piece of land. If you had gone into possession under your equitable lease and were paying the best rent every month, for example, an implied legal monthly periodic tenancy would also be created under section 54(2) of the Law of Property Act 1925. A lease created in this way is a legal lease. In unregistered land legal rights bind the world. You could therefore argue that even though you hadn't protected your equitable lease, your implied legal monthly periodic tenancy would still bind Peter.

Q: *But isn't the notice period for bringing a monthly periodic tenancy to an end by either party one month expiring at the end of one of the monthly periods?*

A: In the absence of any statutory provision to the contrary, yes. This means that Peter would only have to give you one month's notice to leave expiring at the end of one of the monthly periods. This is the disadvantage in having to rely on an implied legal periodic tenancy. It's better than nothing, as you would have a month to find a new home. Remember also that you are given the opportunity to protect your equitable lease on the Land Charges Register. If you have failed to do so, then perhaps you deserve the consequences.

Registered land

Registered land is governed by the Land Registration Act 2002. There are three categories which determine how interests are protected in registered land. They are:

▶ Dealings which must be completed by registration under section 27 of the Land Registration Act 2002 (Box C3).
▶ Interests in Schedule 3 to the Land Registration Act 2002 which override a registered disposition (Box C4).
▶ Interests entered as a notice under section 34 of the Land Registration Act 2002 and interests protected by a restriction under section 43 of the Land Registration Act 2002 (Box C5).

A purchaser for valuable consideration will take the land subject to the interests in these three categories.

Box C3 ### Dealings which must be completed by registration

Under section 27 of the Land Registration Act 2002, dealings which must be completed by registration include a legal lease granted for more than seven years.

This means that a legal lease created by deed for more than seven years taking effect in possession immediately (meaning it starts immediately) must be completed by registration. These leases must be registered with their own title number. If you have this type of lease over Yourland, you must register it with its own title number at the Land Registry for it to be binding on Peter.

Q: *And if I don't do this?*

A: You will be deemed to have only an equitable lease until such time as you do register it. In order to bind Peter, an equitable lease must be an interest that overrides in paragraph 2 of Schedule 3 to the Land Registration Act 2002 (discussed in Box C4), or it must be protected by a notice (discussed in Box C5). However, you won't be able to protect it by means of a notice because, if you try to do so, the Land Registrar will simply ensure that you complete the dealing by registration properly, thereby ensuring its legal status. Assuming you have not approached the Land Registry at all, you must therefore rely on the fact that your equitable lease is an interest that overrides (discussed in Box C4).

Interests which override a registered disposition

Interests that override are found in Schedule 3 to the Land Registration Act 2002, and they are interests that are binding on everyone including a purchaser.

First, a legal lease granted for seven years or less is an interest that overrides a registered disposition (sale) under paragraph 1 of Schedule 3 to the Land Registration Act 2002. The types of lease in this category are as follows:

▶ a legal lease granted by deed for seven years or less;
▶ a fixed term lease created under section 54(2) of the Law of Property Act 1925 (Box B2i);
▶ an express periodic tenancy created under section 54(2) of the Law of Property Act 1925 (Box B2ii); or
▶ an implied periodic tenancy created under section 54(2) of the Law of Property Act 1925 (Box B2iii).

A legal lease created in any of these ways will override Peter's rights and will be binding on him.

Secondly, paragraph 2 of Schedule 3 to the Land Registration Act 2002 states that an interest of a person in actual occupation will override (take priority over) a registered disposition (sale). An equitable lease which meets the requirements of section 2 of the Law of Property (Miscellaneous Provisions) Act 1989 will come into this category.

Paragraph 2 of Schedule 3 states that an interest in this category will override (take priority over) a registered disposition if:

1. The person claiming the right has a proprietary interest in the land

   and

2. That person is in actual occupation at the time of the disposition.

However, the interest will not be an overriding interest if:

1. When the land was purchased, the fact that the person was in actual occupation was not obvious on a reasonably careful inspection of the land and the purchaser didn't know about the interest

   or

2. The person in actual occupation claiming the interest did not tell the purchaser about his interest in the land if asked, and it would have been reasonable for him to have done so.

Paragraph 2 of Schedule 3 is essentially saying that a person who is relying on the fact that he is living in the property to claim priority over a purchaser must make it obvious that he lives in the property. If asked, he should tell any purchaser about his interest if it would be reasonable to do so. If the purchaser still chooses to buy the property, he deserves to be bound by the rights of anybody who lives there.

You can now apply this when you have an equitable lease of Yourland:

1. You have an equitable lease. This is a proprietary interest in land.

2. If you are in actual occupation of Yourland at the time of the sale, your equitable lease will bind Peter and he must let you remain in occupation for the full period of time given in the lease agreement.

However your equitable lease will not bind Peter if:

1. Your actual occupation would not have been obvious to Peter if he had inspected the land reasonably carefully and he didn't know about the equitable lease; or
2. You didn't disclose your equitable lease if Peter asked you when it would have been reasonable for you to have done so. In either of these cases you must leave immediately.

Box C5   Interests entered as a notice or protected by a restriction

These are interests which are entered as a notice on the Charges Register or protected by a restriction on the Proprietorship Register of the land which the right is over in order to bind a purchaser.

Under section 34 of the Land Registration Act 2002, an equitable lease can also be entered as a notice on the Charges Register of Theirland. If you had an equitable lease of Yourland and entered it as a notice on the Charges Register of Theirland, your equitable lease would bind Peter under section 29 of the same Act.

Q: *When does my equitable lease have to be entered as a notice on the Charges Register of Theirland?*

A: As soon as it has been created, or at least before Theirland is sold. You won't know if and when Mr Theirland may sell Theirland. If your equitable lease is not entered as a notice on the Charges Register of Theirland before any sale, a purchaser will not be given the opportunity to find out about it and he will therefore not be bound by it.

This means that an equitable lease has dual status. It can be an interest that overrides a registered disposition if the lessee is in actual occupation (Box C4), or it can be entered as a notice (Box C5). An equitable lease will lose its status as an interest that overrides if it has been entered as a notice. If you have failed to enter it as a notice, it will still have overriding status providing all the conditions are met. This is very convenient if you are forgetful.

Q: *Why would I want to enter an equitable lease by means of a notice if it has overriding status already?*

A: Because you must be in actual occupation for the lease to have overriding status. If you had gone abroad, for example, you would not be in actual occupation when a potential purchaser inspected the land.

You know already that it is possible to have two different types of lease in the same piece of land. This was discussed on page 406 in this chapter. Whether they are binding on a purchaser, Peter here, depends on whether either of them has been protected in registered land by the means described above.

The effect of a contractual licence on a third party

Now look at what happens if you are occupying Yourland but do not have a lease. If you haven't ticked Boxes A and B, you will have only a licence. Assuming you are paying some form of monetary consideration, this will be a contractual licence. You need to establish whether your contractual licence is binding on Peter when he buys Theirland as shown below.

Q: *And the answer?*

A: The answer is very short. Contractual licences do not bind third parties as they are not proprietary interests in land: see *Ashburn Anstalt v Arnold & Co.*

A contractual licence binds only the parties who created it. Peter will not be bound by your contractual licence.

Q: *So would I have to leave?*

A: Yes. Immediately.

Q: *Does Peter have to give me notice?*

A: No. Your contractual licence to occupy Yourland quite simply does not bind him. If you don't go when asked you are a trespasser. So this is yet another reason why it's better to have a lease than a licence. Your only remedy is to sue Mr Theirland for breach of contract. Imagine you were occupying Yourland under a contractual licence from Mr Theirland for consideration of £500 per month. There would be a breach of this contract if Peter told you to leave and you had already paid £500 to Mr Theirland for that particular month. Mr Theirland would be liable for breach of his contract to let you occupy Yourland. He would be liable for damages to the extent of your overpayment.

Q: *Does it matter whether the land is registered or unregistered if there is only a contractual licence?*

A: No. A contractual licence will not bind a third party.

A question on leases

This example is intended to illustrate how to use the Boxes in this chapter to analyse the legal position. If you are using this method in undergraduate law exam questions, you will need to include statutory and case authority and detailed discussion of the various points of law. This information is found both in the text and from other sources.

Dan is the frail and aged proprietor of Sandyacres, a large Victorian house.

Dan has employed Parker, a professional nurse, to care for him and particularly to be available in times of emergency because of Dan's poor health. Parker has been given the use of a small cottage on the estate so he is able to come to Dan's assistance speedily.

Dan's niece, Penelope, is occupying the attic rooms during her university course. She pays Dan £20.00 a week.

Dan also let the self-contained basement flat to Rory for five years in a written agreement called a licence agreement. Rory moved in and is paying the full market rent of £6,000 *per annum*. Although Dan agreed to clean the inside of the basement windows and remove the rubbish every month from the hall within the flat, this has never been done.

Two months ago Dan sold the freehold of Sandyacres to Peter, who has told Parker, Penelope and Rory to leave Sandyacres immediately.

Advise the parties.

This question concerns leases and licences and all three Boxes. You need to work out whether there is any interest capable of being a lease (Box A) and then look at whether it has been created in a recognised way (Box B). Sandyacres has been sold to Peter so you will also have to look at the protection of any interest to see if it is binding on Peter (Box C).

Box A   The essence of a lease

You are looking for exclusive possession, a certain term and rent: see *Street v Mountford*. Exclusive possession is the right to resist anyone, including the landlord, coming onto the property. The duration of the lease must be certain: see *Lace v Chantler*. Rent or consideration would support a contract, although it is not essential: see section 205(1)(xxvii) of the Law of Property Act 1925 and *Ashburn Anstalt v Arnold & Co*.

Look at each of the parties separately. You must tick Boxes A1, A2 and A3.

ParkerA1 Exclusive possession

Parker is likely to have exclusive possession of the cottage. There is no indication that Dan goes there or that Parker is not able to resist his entry if he did. You can tick this box.

A2 A certain term

There is no certain term of years known at the outset. The use of the cottage will last as long as Parker's employment, which is not a known term of years but, under the authority of *Mexfield Housing Co-operative Limited v Berrisford*, Parker could argue a 90-year lease under section 149(6) of the Law of Property Act 1925 determinable on his death or when his employment ends. The problem here is with meeting the requirements and formalities required by section 149(6). This is because there is no indication that Parker pays rent or a premium (Box A3) and there is no indication that the agreement has been created either in a deed (Box B1) or in a written contract (Box B3), conditions which must be met if a claim under section 149(6) of the Law of Property Act 1925 is to be successful. This Box cannot be ticked.

A3 Rent or consideration

You are not told whether Parker pays any rent but as Parker is employed by Dan as a nurse, his nursing services provide consideration. This would be fine if Parker had a certain term because rent is not essential for the finding of a lease and this consideration would support a contract between Parker and Dan. As discussed above, though, Parker does not have a certain term.

BUT A LEASE WILL NOT EXIST IF:

A4 There is no intention to create a legal relationship or
A5 There is an act of friendship or generosity or
A6 There is a service occupancy or
A7 There is a lodger

It is likely that Parker has the use of the cottage to enable him to carry out his job more efficiently. The accommodation does not have to be essential to the job, but there must be some connection: see *Norris v Checksfield*. This is met here, as Parker has been given the cottage specifically to be able to go to Dan's assistance speedily. This means that there is a service occupancy and the relationship is one of employer and employee, not of landlord and tenant. A service occupancy will exclude the finding of a lease.

In conclusion, Parker does not have a certain term of years. He also appears to have a service occupancy, which would exclude a lease. He therefore has a licence (permission) to be on the land, and it is a contractual licence because he gives consideration in the form of his services.

Penelope A1 Exclusive possession

It is unclear whether Penelope has exclusive possession of the attic rooms and the right to resist Dan's entry. This box cannot be ticked.

A2 A certain term

'While she is at university' is not a certain term of years known at the outset. Under the authority *Mexfield Housing Co-operative Limited v Berrisford* she could argue for a 90-year lease under section 149(6) of the Law of Property Act 1925 determinable on her death or when she finishes university. The problem here is with meeting the requirements and formalities required by section 149(6). This is because whilst Penelope pays rent, there is no indication that the agreement has been created in a deed (Box B1) or in a written contract (Box B3), a requirement which must be met if a claim under section 149(6) of the Law of Property Act 1925 is to be successful. This Box cannot be ticked.

A3 Rent or consideration

Although Penelope pays £20.00 a week in rent, this won't help her because she does not have a certain term as discussed above.

BUT A LEASE WILL NOT EXIST IF:

A4 There is no intention to create a legal relationship or
A5 There is an act of friendship or generosity or
A6 There is a service occupancy or
A7 There is a lodger

It is likely that Dan did not intend to create a legal relationship with his niece: see *Cobb v Lane*. It sounds more like a family agreement which would exclude the idea of a legally binding contract resulting in a lease. It could also be an act of friendship or generosity by Dan which would also exclude a lease: see *Marcroft Wagons Ltd v Smith*.

In conclusion, it is unclear whether Penelope has exclusive possession, there is no certain term and the likelihood is that there was no intention to create a legal relationship between her and Dan. This means she has a licence (permission) to be on the land, and it is a contractual licence because she pays consideration.

Rory A1 Exclusive possession

Rory is in a self-contained basement flat. This implies that he has exclusive possession. The fact that the agreement calls itself a licence will not stop the courts from looking at the objective reality of whether he has been given exclusive possession: see *Street v Mountford*. Assuming he has exclusive possession, you can tick this box.

A2 A certain term

Five years is a certain term. You can tick this box.

A3 Rent or consideration

Rory pays Dan £6,000 per annum. You can tick this box.

So far, it appears that Rory satisfies the requirements for a lease as you can tick all three Boxes.

BUT A LEASE WILL NOT EXIST IF:

A4 There is no intention to create a legal relationship or
A5 There is an act of friendship or generosity or
A6 There is a service occupancy or
A7 There is a lodger

The agreement envisaged that Dan would provide services to Rory, so the question is whether Rory is a lodger as defined in *Street v Mountford*. Normally, the provision of such services would deny exclusive possession on the basis that Dan needed unrestricted access in order to carry them out. However, the services have not been provided. In this case there is an argument that the clause for the provision of services is a pretence clause put in by Dan to deny exclusive possession and therefore a lease: see *Crancour Ltd v Da Silvaesa*. The fact that Dan is frail could also imply that the provision of the services was a pretence, as he would be unlikely to be fit enough to provide them. The court will look objectively at the actual arrangement and, if exclusive possession has been granted, the agreement is capable of being a lease. Taking all the circumstances into account, it is likely that Rory has exclusive possession.

In conclusion, Rory has an interest in the land that is capable of being a lease. He does not have a lease at this stage as you have not yet proved that it has been created in a recognised way.

Box B   *The creation of a lease*
As Rory is the only person with an interest capable of being a lease, he is the only person you have to deal with here.

B1 By deed
Although Rory and Dan had a written agreement, there is no indication that it meets the requirements of a deed as given in section 1 of the Law of Property

(Miscellaneous Provisions) Act 1989. There is no evidence of the agreement being witnessed. This box cannot be ticked.

B2 Under section 54(2) of the Law of Property Act 1925

B2i A fixed term lease

Rory was granted a lease for five years. This does not meet the requirement for a legal lease granted under section 54(2) of the Law of Property Act 1925 as leases created by this method must be for three years or less. This box cannot be ticked.

B2ii An express periodic tenancy

This was a fixed-term lease for five years, not an express periodic tenancy. Periodic tenancies cover periods for a year or less and the wording must indicate that the term is to continue until notice is given by either the landlord or the tenant. This box cannot be ticked.

B2iii An implied periodic tenancy

Rory went into possession of Sandyacres following the agreement and is paying rent by reference to a year with the intention to create a landlord and tenant relationship. A legal yearly periodic tenancy can therefore be implied: see *Martin v Smith*. Rory is paying the full market rent and there is no mention of a fine, so he will have an implied legal yearly periodic tenancy created under section 54(2) of the Law of Property Act 1925. You can tick this box.

B3 Under section 2 of the Law of Property (Miscellaneous Provisions) Act 1989

Providing the agreement meets the requirements of this section and is in writing, signed by or on behalf of both Dan and Rory, and contains all the terms of the lease, Rory has an equitable lease. On this assumption you can tick the box.

B4 By proprietary estoppel

Proprietary estoppel is covered in detail in Chapter 12. There is no indication that the requirements for proprietary estoppel have been met here. This box cannot be ticked.

Summary of Box B

Rory appears to have both a legal lease, an implied legal yearly periodic tenancy created under section 54(2) of the Law of Property Act 1925 (Box B2iii), and an equitable lease created under section 2 of the Law of Property (Miscellaneous Provisions) Act 1989 (Box B3).

Box C The protection of a lease

We are not told here whether Sandyacres is unregistered or registered property, so you need to examine both possibilities.

Unregistered land

Rory can claim two leases, an implied legal yearly periodic tenancy and an equitable lease.

C1 Unregistered land – legal lease

Rory's implied legal yearly periodic tenancy binds Peter as legal rights bind the world. The notice period for a yearly periodic tenancy is half a year expiring at the end of a year of the tenancy. Peter must give Rory half a year's notice expiring at the end of a year of the tenancy to end this tenancy.

C2 Unregistered land – equitable lease

It was in Rory's interest to enter his equitable lease as a class C(iv) land charge against Dan's name on the Land Charges Register under the Land Charges Act 1972 when the lease was created, or at least before Sandyacres was sold to Peter. If he had done so, his equitable lease would have bound everyone, including Peter, under section 198 of the Law of Property Act 1925. The equitable lease would also have prevailed over his legal lease: see *Walsh v Lonsdale*. If Peter were bound by the equitable lease, he could not evict Rory because the equitable lease gave Rory a term of five years. Peter was therefore bound by the full five-year term.

If Rory had not entered his equitable lease on the Land Charges Register, it would not be binding on a purchaser of the legal estate for money or money's worth under section 4(6) of the Land Charges Act 1972. Peter paid money for the legal estate of Sandyacres. If Rory's equitable lease has not been entered as a land charge, Peter will not be bound by it. Peter will still be bound by Rory's implied legal yearly periodic tenancy, though, and so must give him half a year's notice to leave expiring at the end of a year of the tenancy.

Summary of the protection of Rory's leases in unregistered land

If Rory has protected his equitable lease he is home and dry and can stay there for five years. If he hasn't done so, Peter is not bound by it. However, an implied legal yearly periodic tenancy also arises which binds Peter. Peter's solution here is to give notice of half a year expiring at the end of a year of the tenancy.

Registered land

C3 Dealings which must be completed by registration

Rory has not entered into a dealing which must be completed by registration under section 27 of the Land Registration Act 2002 as he does not have a legal lease granted for more than seven years.

C4 Interests which override a registered disposition

Under paragraph 1 of Schedule 3 to the Land Registration Act 2002, a legal lease granted for seven years or less is an interest that overrides a registered disposition. Rory's implied legal yearly periodic tenancy is a legal lease for seven years or less. It therefore overrides and takes priority over Peter's rights, even though Peter will have registered his purchase of Sandyacres at the District Land Registry. The disadvantage here is that Peter can give Rory half a year's notice expiring at the end of a year of the tenancy.

Under paragraph 2 of Schedule 3 to the Land Registration Act 2002, the interest of a person in actual occupation can be an interest that overrides. If Rory was in actual occupation of the basement flat at the time of sale to Peter, his equitable lease is binding on Peter. Peter is bound by the equitable lease and has to let Rory stay for the full five years. Rory's equitable lease is not binding on Peter if his occupation was not obvious and Peter does not know about his interest. Rory's equitable lease also does not bind Peter if Rory failed to disclose his interest to Peter if asked and it would have been reasonable for him to do so. If it is not binding on Peter, Rory must leave immediately.

C5 Interests entered as a notice or protected by a restriction

Rory could have entered his equitable lease as a notice on the Charges Register of Sandyacres under section 34 of the Land Registration Act 2002. If he had done so, his equitable lease would be binding on Peter. If he had not entered it as a notice, it would not be binding on Peter by this means under section 29 of the Land Registration Act 2002.

Even if Rory hadn't protected his equitable lease by a notice, if he is in actual occupation he will still be protected as his equitable lease will be an interest that overrides under paragraph 2 of Schedule 3 to the Land Registration Act 2002.

Summary of the protection of Rory's leases in registered land

Even if Rory hasn't entered his equitable lease as a notice, it is highly likely that the fact of his occupation will protect him. The equitable lease will prevail over the implied legal yearly periodic tenancy, and so Rory must be allowed to stay there for the full five years. If Rory has to rely on the implied legal yearly periodic tenancy as an interest that overrides, Peter can give him half a year's notice to leave expiring at the end of a year of the tenancy.

The effect of a contractual licence on a third party

The contractual licences of both Penelope and Parker will not bind a third party, here Peter: see *Ashburn Anstalt v Arnold & Co*. They will have to leave immediately. They can both sue Dan for any breach of their original contract and can claim damages, but they will still have to leave Sandyacres immediately.

Conclusion

Both Parker and Penelope fail to satisfy the requirements for a lease. They have contractual licences.

Rory appears to have both an equitable lease and an implied legal yearly periodic tenancy. If Rory was unable to claim that he had either of these leases, he also would have a contractual licence to be on the land.

If Rory's equitable lease is protected by registration in unregistered land or by registration or actual occupation in registered land, it will bind Peter and he must let Rory stay for the remainder of the five years.

If Rory has to rely on his implied periodic tenancy, it will bind Peter whether the land is unregistered or registered although Peter can give Rory notice of half a year.

The contractual licences of both Penelope and Parker will not bind a third party, Peter here. They will have to leave immediately. They can sue Dan for any breach of their original contract and can claim damages, but they will still have to leave Sandyacres.

A variation of the question

Given *Mexfield Housing Co-operative Limited v Berrisford* it is interesting to look at a variation of the question.

This is to ask what would have happened if Dan had allowed Startup Company to occupy a large converted barn that stood in the grounds of Sandyacres for 'as long as it wanted' where Startup Company paid the market rent by reference to a year. Startup Company could have claimed exclusive possession, the payment of rent and an intention to create a legal relationship but the term of 'as long as it wanted' is not a certain term and would not be converted into a 90-year lease under section 149(6) of the Law of Property Act 1925 because a company does not have a life to be converted. Provided section 54(2) of the Law of Property Act 1925 was met, Startup Company would have an implied legal yearly periodic tenancy which would be binding on Peter but subject to determination by notice of half a year. Alternatively, following obiter in *Mexfield Housing Co-operative Ltd v Berrisford* (2011), it could try to claim a contractual licence but contractual licences do not bind third parties and so Peter would not be bound by it. The contractual licence would have been enforceable only between Startup Company and Dan.

The mystery of the non-proprietary lease

We have already referred to the heavily criticised case of *Bruton v London & Quadrant Housing Trust*. This section looks at recent judicial decisions involving the non-proprietary lease in detail. It shows just how far people will go to try and argue the unarguable. Here are the facts of the case. Lambeth Council gave the London and Quadrant Housing Trust (LQHT) a licence to use houses owned by the Council for occupation by homeless people. It could only be a licence because statute law prevented Lambeth Council from granting LQHT a lease. Mr Bruton was a homeless person who went to live in one of the houses. His agreement with LQHT said that he had a licence, but he then claimed that he had a lease because he had exclusive possession. If he was able to claim a lease, LQHT would have to carry out repairs under the Landlord and Tenant Act 1985 but the Act would not apply if all Mr Bruton could claim a licence. The House of Lords held that Mr Bruton had exclusive possession, which meant that a lease existed and the relationship between LQHT and Mr Bruton was one of landlord and tenant.

Q: *But how could Mr Bruton have a lease from LQHT if LQHT had only a licence from Lambeth Council? LQHT had no leasehold estate in the land itself from which it could carve out another leasehold estate for Mr Bruton.*

A: You're right to ask this question. Lambeth Council held the freehold estate. If Lambeth Council had granted LQHT a lease, it would have carved a leasehold estate for LQHT out of its own freehold estate. If that had been the case, LQHT could have carved another leasehold estate for a shorter period out of its own leasehold estate for Mr Bruton and that would have been a sublease. The problem was that LQHT had only a licence from Lambeth Council and so didn't have a leasehold estate from which to carve anything for Mr Bruton. Despite this, Lord Hoffmann said that a lease describes a relationship between two people who are landlord and tenant. A lease usually creates a leasehold estate, but this depends on whether the person granting the lease has an estate from which to grant a leasehold estate. If he doesn't, you have a landlord and tenant relationship which is purely personal between the parties and has no estate of land attached to the relationship. This decision has been argued by some to be perverse.

Q: *So Mr Bruton's agreement with LQHT had the legal effect of creating a relationship of landlord and tenant between them but it could not give a leasehold estate to Mr Bruton because LQHT had no leasehold estate itself?*

A: Yes. Although the freehold owner of the property, Lambeth Council, was not included in the relationship between LQHT and Mr Bruton, the lease relationship could still exist between LQHT and Mr Bruton with rights and duties on both sides. This meant that LQHT had to carry out the repairs. As Mr Bruton had no estate in the land, we can call this a non-proprietary lease.

Q: *What is a non-proprietary lease?*

A: It means that the lease does not have the capacity to bind a third party. This is in comparison to a proprietary lease, which does have the capacity to bind a third party. The kinds of leases we have been talking about in this chapter so far are proprietary leases and have the capacity to bind a third party. If Jemima leases Greenacres from Fred for five years, she has a leasehold estate in Greenacres for five years. Because her leasehold estate is a proprietary right in the land, it has the capacity to bind Peter if Fred sells Greenacres to him. If it does bind Peter, he will have to let Jemima stay for five years. Mr Bruton, though, had a non-proprietary lease, also called a contractual lease or a 'Bruton' lease, which did not have the capacity to bind a third party.

Q: *As Mr Bruton's lease was a non-proprietary lease because he didn't have a leasehold estate in the land, presumably it could never be binding on Lambeth Council?*

A: The House of Lords left this open because Lambeth Council was never a party in the case, but you are quite right. It was argued in a later case that a non-proprietary lease could be binding on a third party, but we'll look at those arguments shortly.

In the judgment the words 'tenancy' and 'estoppel' were used. A tenancy by estoppel arises if Fred grants you a lease and then says that he didn't have a legal estate from which to grant it. In that case he is estopped from denying the lease, and both you and Fred are bound by it.

Q: *So it can't have been a tenancy by estoppel in the Bruton case, can it, because LQHT never said that it was granting Mr Bruton a lease?*

A: That's right. LQHT only ever gave Mr Bruton a licence so the words used in the case do not mean a tenancy by estoppel. Instead, it was the agreement between the parties that formed the tenancy. The parties were estopped from denying the tenancy and were (e)stopped from trying to avoid the contractual duties that came about because of that relationship.

The story continued in *Kay v Lambeth London BC* (2004) and *Leeds City Council v Price* (2005). Here there were two issues. The first was whether a Bruton-type lease could be binding on a third party, which is discussed next. The second issue was to do with human rights, which is discussed in the next section. In order to understand the arguments behind the claim that a Bruton-type lease could bind a third party you need to know more about a sublease. To create a lease, you carve a leasehold estate out of a freehold estate. To create a sublease, you carve another leasehold estate out of the existing one. This sublease must be shorter than the leasehold estate it is carved out of, even if only by a day. As example of a sublease is when Fred leases Greenacres to Jemima for 25 years. Jemima decides to live abroad for five years but wants to return to Greenacres after then so she subleases it to Hugo for five years. Now say that during this five years, Fred gives Jemima notice to leave.

Q: *Can Fred just do that?*

A: It depends on the terms of the lease. Fixed-term leases can have break clauses which give the parties the opportunity to bring the lease to an end earlier than the stated term if notice is given.

If this were the case and Fred brought Jemima's lease to an end following due process, Hugo's sublease would also come to an end. The same would happen if Jemima breached one of the terms in the lease, for example she didn't pay the rent. In this case Fred could forfeit the lease, which means bring it to an end, and this would bring Hugo's sublease to an end as well. The reason for this happening in both these cases is because Hugo's sublease is governed by the terms of Jemima's lease. If Jemima's lease comes to an end for either of these reasons, so does Hugo's. However, if Jemima buys Greenacres from Fred, so that her leasehold interest is merged with the freehold and she now owns the freehold of Greenacres, Hugo's sublease will carry on for the remainder of his five years. Jemima will be Hugo's landlord and Hugo will be her direct tenant. Hugo's sublease would also carry on if Jemima surrendered (voluntarily gave up) the lease to Fred and both Jemima and Fred agreed that their obligation as landlord and tenant was at an end. Jemima would disappear from the picture, Hugo's sublease would carry on for the remainder of his five years and he would become a direct tenant of Fred. The reason for the difference here when Hugo's sublease carries on is that the sublease belongs to the sublessee. Nobody else can give it up or surrender it on his behalf. To summarise: if the lessor takes possession either because he has given the lessee notice to quit or because he has forfeited the lease for breach of one of its terms, any sub-lease will be governed by the terms of the lease and will also have to be given up. In merger and surrender of a lease, any sublease will carry on for the remainder of its term. Now, to return to the case under discussion. In *Bruton v London & Quadrant Housing Trust* the original licence between Lambeth Council and LQHT was agreed in 1986. In 1995 Lambeth Council had replaced the licence agreement with a formal lease agreement. Following the *Bruton* case in 1999 Lambeth Council gave notice to LQHT that it was ending LQHT's formal lease and claimed possession. Mr Kay, an occupier of one of the houses in the same position as Mr Bruton had been, resisted possession on the basis that his Bruton-type lease was binding on Lambeth Council.

Q: *But it couldn't be, could it, because it was a non-proprietary lease and so couldn't bind third parties, here Lambeth Council?*

A: Mr Kay argued his case on two grounds. Just before Lambeth Council granted the formal lease to LQHT in 1995, LQHT must have surrendered its licence agreement. Now, use the analogy with a sublease whereby, if the lessee surrenders the lease to the lessor, the sublease will continue. In our example, when Jemima surrendered her lease to Fred Hugo's sublease carried on and he became a direct tenant of Fred. Mr Kay argued that he was in a similar position to Hugo when LQHT surrendered its licence to Lambeth Council. The second after LQHT surrendered its licence to Lambeth Council, Mr Kay became a direct tenant of Lambeth Council and his non-proprietary lease carried on against it. Lambeth Council therefore could not take possession.

Q: *Did it matter that LQHT was granted a lease by Lambeth Council immediately after the surrender of the licence?*

A: No. The rights Mr Kay had against Lambeth Council in that split second of time between the surrender of the licence and the grant of the lease continued to exist against Lambeth Council. This argument failed though because, unlike a sublessee, Mr Kay never had a leasehold estate in the land that was derived from Lambeth Council and so could never be in the same position as a sublessee. It would have been different if there had been a lease between Lambeth Council and LQHT and LQHT had granted a sublease to Mr Kay. Any surrender of the lease by LQHT to Lambeth Council would have had no effect on Mr Kay, who would have become the direct tenant of Lambeth Council and could have stayed there. In the case, though, Mr Kay's interest came from LQHT remember, not from Lambeth Council.

The alternative argument put forward was that when Lambeth Council gave notice to LQHT that it was ending LQHT's lease, this affected LQHT only and only LQHT was removed from the picture. Mr Kay's non-proprietary lease had been created before Lambeth Council granted the lease to LQHT and so Mr Kay was not affected by the terms for ending the lease between Lambeth Council and LQHT. Mr Kay therefore would continue to have the same rights he had before Lambeth Council granted the formal lease to LQHT, but those rights were now against Lambeth Council due to the removal of LQHT from the picture. This argument failed as well. When Lambeth Council granted the formal lease to LQHT, it meant that LQHT now held a leasehold estate in the land. LQHT could now give Mr Kay an estate in the land, turning Mr Kay's non-proprietary lease into a proprietary lease, a normal sublease in fact. This was a tenancy by estoppel in the true sense of the word that turned a non-proprietary lease into a proprietary lease when LQHT acquired a leasehold estate. Now use the analogy with a sublease when the lessee is given notice to leave and the sublease comes to an end. In our example, when Fred gave notice to Jemima to leave, Hugo's sublease came to an end. When Lambeth Council gave LQHT notice to leave, Mr Kay was in Hugo's position and his now proprietary sublease was automatically brought to an end as well, because his sublease was governed by the terms of the lease to LQHT. Mr Kay had to go.

Further confirmation (as if we needed it) came in the form of *London Borough of Islington v Green* (2005). In this case Islington Council allowed Patchwork Community Housing to use a property as temporary housing accommodation under a licence agreement, much as in the *Bruton* case. When the Council ended the agreement Mr O'Shea, the last remaining occupant, claimed a Bruton-type tenancy that he argued was binding on the Council. It was held that whether a lease creates a proprietary interest in land depends on whether the landlord has an estate out of which he granted the lease. Although Mr O'Shea had a Bruton-type tenancy he did not have an estate in land. To resist the Council's claim Mr O'Shea would have to show he had an estate binding on the Council. Patchwork had no estate and so could not give Mr O'Shea an estate, so possession was granted to Islington Borough Council. Mr O'Shea's counsel said he thought people would find it surprising that, as Islington had given Patchwork, a licensee, permission to create a Bruton-type tenancy, Islington could then turn round and say that Mr O'Shea was a trespasser. Lord Justice Gibson said that people would find it surprising if Islington was bound by a Bruton tenancy that went on beyond the licence agreement and contrary to the terms of the licence. So at least we can agree that we are all surprised whichever viewpoint you take.

To summarise: the courts have recognised a non-proprietary lease although the decision has been subject to criticism: see *Bruton v London & Quadrant Housing Trust*. A non-proprietary lease does not have the capacity to bind a third party: see *Kay v Lambeth London BC; Leeds City Council v Price* (2005).

Taking possession and human rights

The Annex at the end of this book contains a brief description of human rights legislation and how it works.

A number of recent cases have come before the courts challenging the right of a public authority to take possession, even though it has a right to do so, because such action is incompatible with human rights. The most important cases include *McCann v UK* (2008), *Kay v UK* (2010), *Manchester City Council v Pinnock* (2010) and *Hounslow LBC v Powell* (2011) and all have involved public authorities. The question that has yet to be answered is whether there is a human rights defence to taking possession in the private rented sector.

Further reading

S. Bright, 'Uncertainty in Leases – Is It a Vice?' 13 *Legal Studies* (1993) 38

C. Harpum, 'Leases, Licences, Sharing and Shams', 48 *CLJ* (1989) 19

K. Low, 'Certainty of Terms and Leases: Curiouser and Curiouser', 75 *MLR* (2012) 401

P. Smith, 'What is Wrong with Certainty in Leases?' *Conv and Prop Law*, Nov/Dec (1993) 461

P. Sparkes, 'Certainty of Leasehold Terms', 109 *LQR* (1993) 93

R. Street, 'Coach and Horses Trip Cancelled? Rent Act Avoidance after *Street v. Mountford*', *Conv and Prop Law*, Sep/Oct (1985) 328

The non-proprietary lease

S. Bright, 'Leases, Exclusive Possession and Estates', 116 *LQR* (2000) 7

M. Dixon, 'The Non-proprietary Lease: the Rise of the Feudal Phoenix', 59 *CLJ* (2000) 25

M. Lower, 'The Bruton Tenancy', *Conv and Prop Law* (2010) 38

J. Morgan, 'Exclusive Possession and the Tenancy by Estoppel: "a familiar problem in an unusual setting"', *Conv and Prop Law*, Nov/Dec (1999) 493

M. Pawlowski, 'Occupational Rights in Leasehold Law: Time for Rationalisation?' *Conv and Prop Law*, Nov/Dec (2002) 550. A reply: J-P. Hinojosa, 'On Property, Leases, Licences, Horses and Carts: Revisiting *Bruton v London & Quadrant Housing Trust*', *Conv and Prop Law*, Mar/Apr (2005) 114

N. Roberts, 'The Bruton Tenancy: A Matter of Relativity', *Conv and Prop Law* (2012) 87

P. Routley, 'Tenancies and Estoppel – After *Bruton v London & Quadrant Housing Trust*', 63 *MLR* (2000) 424

Chapter 16

Leasehold covenants

www.palgrave.com/law/Stroud4e

Introduction

Leasehold covenants are those terms agreed in a lease that relate to the parties' obligations in their capacities as landlord and tenant. This chapter looks at the types of covenant you can expect to find in a lease, then examines the rules governing the enforceability of these covenants when the leased land or the lease is sold. Probably the best way of looking at this area is to look at the individual covenants separately. This is because some of the covenants between the landlord and the tenant will be implied at common law, whilst many will be made expressly between them and others will be imposed by statute. We will look at some of the more common covenants in this same order. An express covenant will override an implied covenant, whilst a covenant that arises through statute will override both express and implied covenants if the statute states that the parties cannot contract out of the statutory provisions. At the end of the discussion on each covenant, we will look at the remedies available. The pronoun 'he' is used throughout for convenience. A summary of the covenants discussed in this chapter together with the remedies available for breach is on page 452.

A landlord's covenant that the leased premises are fit for habitation

Implied covenants imposing an obligation on the landlord that the premises are fit for habitation

There is no general implied covenant that the property that is being leased is fit for habitation.

Q: *Why not? If I am going to rent a property to live in, it seems reasonable that it should be habitable.*

A: This is simply because a landlord can lease a property in whatever state he likes. What you see is what you get, and you can then choose whether or not to lease the property. It's similar to 'buyer beware' when you purchase land. There is one exception though. There is an implied condition under *Smith v Marrable* (1843) that if the property is a furnished house or flat used for residential purposes, it will be fit for habitation at the start of the lease. Note that there is no implied condition that the landlord has to keep the property fit for habitation throughout the lease. This is a condition, not a covenant, and it arises from the contractual relationship between landlord and tenant.

Q: *What's the difference between a condition and a covenant?*

A: A *condition precedent* is one which must be met before the lease takes effect. A *condition subsequent* is one that is breached during the lease which will bring the lease to an end, and the landlord can then re-enter the premises. A *covenant* is an agreement between the parties as one of the terms of the lease. If a covenant is breached, the lease carries on and the aggrieved party can sue for damages or pursue another remedy. In *Smith v Marrable* there was an infestation of bugs, so the landlord was in breach of the implied condition that the house was fit for human habitation at the start of the lease. The tenant had given up the lease and the court held that the landlord could not sue for rent.

The landlord's express covenant that the premises are fit for habitation

There is unlikely to be an express covenant here.

Statute law imposing obligations on the landlord that the premises are fit for habitation

In tenancies with a low yearly rent, section 8 of the Landlord and Tenant Act 1985 imposes a covenant that a dwelling house will be fit for human habitation at the start of the tenancy and throughout. As the yearly rent is set at such a low level though, £80 in London and £52 elsewhere, it is unlikely that any lease would ever come under this section anyway.

Q: *Why isn't the amount of the yearly rent changed?*

A: This is for several reasons: the increase in the provision of local authority housing which usually provided better accommodation than the private rented sector; the decline in the private rented sector; the rise in the number of people owning their own houses and the introduction of the implied repairing obligation in 1961 in what is now section 11 of the Landlord and Tenant Act 1985. It is also because of the cost to local authorities of then having to get their housing stock up to standard. It has been held that judges cannot order councils in their capacity as landlords to spend money on housing because that is a function of Parliament. Parliament won't do anything because it would mean raising taxes, and that would be unpopular, so nothing happens. Another triumph for democracy.

Remedies available to the tenant if the landlord is in breach of the implied condition or any statutory obligation that the property is fit for habitation at the start of the lease

The tenant can repudiate (give up) the lease or he can keep it and claim damages. There is only one reported case of repudiation of a lease, *Hussein v Mehlman* (1992).

A landlord's covenant for quiet enjoyment

The landlord's implied covenant for quiet enjoyment

Every lease, however created, will contain an implied covenant for quiet enjoyment. Quiet enjoyment does not necessarily mean keeping the noise level down, although it can do. It means that the landlord must not directly or physically interfere with the way in which the tenant uses the premises. Examples showing the breach of an implied covenant for quiet enjoyment by the landlord include causing the land to subside by mining operations: see *Markham v Paget* (1908); cutting off the gas and electricity supply to the premises: see *Perera v Vandiyar* (1953); and intimidation: see *Kenny v Preen* (1963). In *Browne v Flower* (1911) it was argued that the construction of an outside staircase interfered with the tenant's privacy because anyone using the staircase could see into the tenant's rooms. It was held that there had to be some physical interference and that invasion of privacy was not enough to constitute breach of the covenant for quiet enjoyment. In *Scottish Widows & Life Assurance Society Plc v Stewart* (2006) the landlord had installed speed bumps which caused damage to the high performance cars brought in to the tenant for repair. This had led to a fall in trade and was a breach of the covenant for quiet enjoyment. In *Heronslea (Mill Hill) v Kwik-Fit Properties Ltd* (2009) the lease allowed the landlord to enter the premises to undertake a survey, which here entailed drilling boreholes. Although the case was about the legal interpretation of the word 'survey', it was also said that allowing such an activity would undermine the landlord's covenant for quiet enjoyment. If the landlord had intended such an activity, it should have been more clearly stated at the start of the lease.

Q: What happens if the landlord was already carrying out the activity when the tenant moved in?

A: In this case the landlord will not be in breach of the implied covenant. It's only if the landlord starts carrying out the activity after the tenant has moved in that he will be in breach. This is because there is no implied covenant as to the state of the property at the start of the lease. At the start of the lease the tenant takes the premises as he finds them. In *Southwark LBC v Tanner* (2001) excessive noise from the flats of other tenants was held not to be a breach of the landlord's covenant for quiet enjoyment as the noise was in existence before the lease was granted. The landlord had done nothing since the start of the lease to affect the previous position. Here it was also acknowledged that, while excessive noise could be a breach of the covenant for quiet enjoyment, normal use of the flats did not constitute such a breach.

Q: *Is the landlord responsible for other parties interfering with the tenant's quiet enjoyment?*

A: The landlord is not responsible for the acts of third parties, but he is responsible for those of his own agents and for those of other tenants he may have. Even so, he is responsible only for their lawful acts and not any unlawful acts they may commit, as in *Sanderson v Berwick on Tweed Corporation* (1884). The landlord Corporation had leased two farms, one of which caused flooding on the other. The flooding was caused partly because the tenant was using the drainage system excessively. This was an unlawful act and so the landlord was not liable. The flooding was also caused because the drains hadn't been properly built and so flooded even though the tenant was using them correctly. The landlord was liable for the damage caused here.

The landlord's express covenant for quiet enjoyment

In many leases the landlord will expressly covenant that he will allow the tenant quiet enjoyment. The meaning of quiet enjoyment is the same as for an implied covenant.

Statute law imposing obligations on the landlord for quiet enjoyment

There is no statutory provision for quiet enjoyment.

The tenant's remedies for breach of the landlord's covenant for quiet enjoyment

The tenant can claim damages either in contract or else in tort if he can claim nuisance or trespass. A claim in tort will allow the court to award exemplary or aggravated damages. An injunction is another remedy. In *Drane v Evangelou* (1978) removing the tenant's possessions into the backyard and installing the landlord's in-laws in the leased property constituted breach of the covenant for quiet enjoyment. The tenant obtained an injunction enabling him to move back in, and he was awarded exemplary damages for the landlord's tort of trespass to 'teach the landlord a lesson'. If the tenant has to leave the property he can claim removal costs. He may also be able to claim for unlawful eviction and harassment under section 1(3) of the Protection from Eviction Act 1977.

A landlord's covenant not to derogate from his grant

The landlord's implied covenant not to derogate from his grant

This means that the landlord cannot grant a lease and then do something on adjoining land which interferes with or prevents the purpose for which the lease was granted. Interference has a wider meaning here than in a covenant for quiet enjoyment because interference other than just direct or physical interference is taken into account. In *Aldin v Latimer, Clerk, Muirhead & Co* (1894) the premises had been let to a timber merchant. The landlord was prevented from erecting a building that would interfere with the flow of air to the sheds which were used for drying the timber. In *Harmer v Jumbil (Nigeria) Tin Areas Ltd* (1921) a tenant was using the leased land for storing explosives. He required a licence to do so, a condition of which was that there should be no buildings within a certain distance. When the landlord leased his adjoining land to a company that built on it, it was held that the landlord was in breach of the implied covenant not to derogate from his grant because he had allowed the building which would cause the tenant to lose his licence. In *Scottish Widows & Life Assurance Society Plc v Stewart* (2006) the fall in the tenant's trade following the installation of speed bumps was a breach of the covenant for quiet enjoyment and also of the covenant not to derogate from the landlord's grant.

The landlord's express covenant not to derogate from his grant

There is not usually an express covenant here. The tenant will rely on the implied covenant.

Statute law imposing obligations on the landlord not to derogate from his grant

There is no statutory provision here.

The tenant's remedies for breach of the landlord's covenant not to derogate from his grant

The tenant can claim damages or ask for an injunction.

A tenant's covenant to pay rent

The tenant's implied covenant to pay rent

A covenant that the tenant will pay rent is usually implied at common law into a lease.

Q: *Even though there is no requirement for rent in a lease under section 205(1)(xxvii) of the Law of Property Act 1925 as confirmed by* **Ashburn Anstalt v Arnold & Co** *(1989)?*

A: Because there is no requirement for rent under the Law of Property Act 1925, it is not an inevitable implication. However it's nearly always certain that the parties will intend rent to be paid. If no rent is intended, this must be said. Under section 4 of the Landlord and Tenant Act 1985 the landlord must give a rent book to a weekly residential tenant.

The tenant's express covenant to pay rent

It is extremely unlikely that a landlord is going to lease his property to a tenant without expressly reserving rent.

Q: *Will the covenant to pay rent state the date on which the rent must be paid?*

A: The rent will be paid periodically by reference to a week, or month, or quarter, or year. If the rent is not paid by midnight on the due day, it will be in arrears and interest will be charged on the amount owing. Fixed-term leases are also very likely to contain rent review clauses which state that the tenant must pay a revised rent, inevitably upwards, from specified rent review dates which are usually set at every five or seven years.

Q: *Why and how do you review a rent clause?*

A: A landlord will review the rent to ensure that the tenant is paying the going market rent rather than a rent that was fixed years ago. Also, landlords wouldn't grant longer term leases if they thought the rent had to remain the same all the way through. In terms of how you review the rent, some leases work on index-linked increases, for example the Retail Prices Index. Some rent reviews are linked to the turnover of the business run from the premises, but the most common one is the open market review. This is where the landlord looks at the current state of the market and the terms and conditions of the lease itself. He aims to establish the rent that he could ask for the property if it were let on the open market on the rent review date on the same terms as the existing lease. Rents can go up significantly at this point.

Q: *Is there any redress against a huge increase in rent following a rent review?*

A: You can go to arbitration, but if the landlord can prove that a similar nearby property would fetch the kind of rent he is asking, you would be unlikely to succeed. You might also find that the arbitration increased the rent still further. In the case of *Ideal View Ltd v Bello* (2009), a rent review which was due in 1994 was agreed finally after arbitration in 2007 when it then became payable. Mr Bello had purchased the leased premises in 2005 and claimed that because of the delay Ideal View was barred from recovery. It was held that time was not of the essence, the rent review did not have to be completed within any particular time, the claim was not statute barred and there was no evidence of estoppel because there had been no representation by the landlord that the review would not take place. If Mr Bello had wanted to raise the issue about delay, he should have done so in front of the arbitrator.

Statute law imposing obligations on the tenant to pay rent

There is no statutory obligation on the tenant to pay rent; in fact quite the contrary, as section 205(1)(xxvii) of the Law of Property Act 1925 states that you do not need rent to create a lease.

The landlord's remedies for breach of the tenant's covenant to pay rent

Sue on the contract

The landlord may sue for non-payment of rent. If the tenant is not paying rent anyway, this remedy is unlikely to further the landlord's cause.

Commercial Rent Arrears Recovery

Before the Tribunals, Courts and Enforcement Act 2007, the landlord could use the remedy of distress. This meant that he could take the tenant's goods on the property in order to sell them and recoup the arrears of rent. Other than in tenancies protected under the Rent Acts, the landlord did not have to give notice and no court order was needed. Unsurprisingly, the remedy of distress raised the question whether it was a breach of human rights by denying the right to a fair trial. In *Fuller v Happy Shopper Markets Ltd* (2001) the court stated per curiam that the remedy of distress involved a serious interference with human rights, in terms of the tenant's rights to respect for privacy and his home, and for peaceful enjoyment of his possessions. The remedy of distress will be abolished by the Tribunals, Courts and Enforcement Act 2007 and will be replaced by the Commercial Rent Arrears Recovery Scheme (CRAR) under the same Act. A consultation paper, 'Transforming bailiff action', was published in February 2012 which looked at the bringing into force of the Tribunals, Courts and Enforcement Act 2007 and it is likely that, following some changes, the CRAR scheme will be implemented. The essence of the CRAR is as follows. It can be used only when there is a lease of commercial premises, so not when the premises leased are residential. A certain minimum amount of rent must be owed, and this amount will be specified in regulations. The procedure allows an enforcement agent to take control of the tenant's goods. The tenant must first be given notice. Under section 78 of the Act, the tenant has the right to ask the court to put aside the notice if he meets grounds which will be specified in regulations. The enforcement agent can either secure the goods on the premises, or take them somewhere else, or enter into a controlled goods agreement. This is where the tenant keeps his goods but agrees that they are now under the control of the enforcement agent and that he, the tenant, will not remove them elsewhere. The enforcement agent must give the tenant an inventory of what he has taken. Following a prescribed minimum period, the enforcement agent can sell the goods, ensuring that he receives the best price that can reasonably be obtained. The sale must be by auction unless the court states otherwise.

Q: *What are the advantages of this new procedure?*

A: It is compliant with human rights; only the enforcement agent can enter the leased property and take the goods and he must be acting on the written instructions of the landlord; the tenant is given notice.

Forfeiture of the lease

Forfeiture of the lease means that the landlord can re-enter the property and the lease is brought to an end. The now ex-tenant becomes a trespasser.

Q: *Is forfeiture the most drastic remedy?*

A: Yes. There are two different procedures regarding forfeiture. The first is for non-payment of rent and the second is for breaches of covenant other than non-payment of rent.

Q: *Why are there two procedures?*

A: Because equity would grant relief only for breach of the covenant to pay rent, so statutory procedures were made for breaches of covenants other than to pay rent. The procedure for non-payment of rent is relevant here as we are talking about the breach of a covenant to pay rent. The landlord can forfeit the lease only if:

▶ the lease contains an express clause stating that the landlord has the right of re-entry if there is a breach of a covenant, here breach of the covenant to pay rent.

Assuming a clause to this effect is contained in the lease, the landlord must make the demand for payment of the rent on the day it is due. The process is hedged about with archaic tradition such as 'not on Sundays' and 'only between dawn and dusk' but it is essentially easy to do and is effective. All this can be avoided if the landlord has put a clause in the lease which states that there can be forfeiture for non-payment of rent 'whether formally demanded or not'. The process can also be excluded under section 210 of the Common Law Procedure Act 1852 (when amended by section 72 of the Tribunals, Courts and Enforcement Act 2007) if the rent is at least six months in arrears and either the landlord cannot use the Commercial Rent Arrears Recovery procedure or, if the procedure was used, there would not be enough goods on the premises to cover the arrears of rent if sold. As the Commercial Rent Arrears Recovery procedure applies to commercial leases only, this means that in a residential lease the landlord need not formally demand the rent provided it is at least six months in arrears.

A landlord may then re-enter the property physically or else obtain a court order for possession. Re-entering the property physically involves changing the locks, and this must be done peacefully as force may amount to a criminal offence under the Criminal Law Act 1977. Peaceable re-entry cannot be used for residential premises. Section 2 of the Protection from Eviction Act 1977 provides that, in relation to premises which are let as a dwelling and are lawfully occupied, a right of re-entry or forfeiture can be enforced only by proceedings in court. In *Patel v Pirabakaran* (2006) it was held that the phrase 'let as a dwelling' meant 'let wholly or partly as a dwelling', and so applied to premises which were let for mixed residential and business purposes. Peaceful re-entry is likely therefore only in business premises where the tenant has already left. If the court grants a possession order the tenant must leave.

Q: *Can the tenant do anything here to prevent possession?*

A: This is called relief from forfeiture. It means that the remedy of forfeiture will no longer be pursued. The tenant can ask for relief whether the landlord has re-entered the property physically or obtained a possession order from the court. Paying the rent arrears and the landlord's costs is a good start to obtaining relief from forfeiture. Failing that, the tenant can apply to the High Court if the Common Law Procedure Act 1852 has been used where, if the tenant pays the arrears and the landlord's costs before the hearing, he can automatically obtain relief under section 212 of the same Act. Alternatively, the tenant can apply to the County Court under section 138 of the County Courts Act 1984. In the county court relief from forfeiture will be granted automatically if arrears and costs are paid up to five days before, or within four weeks of, the hearing. Relief will be granted at the court's discretion in either court within six months of the landlord re-entering, but only if the landlord has not let the property to anyone else.

Q: *Why is the tenant allowed relief from forfeiture when it's clear that he's a bad payer?*

A: Because, if the tenant can pay, the landlord has nothing to complain about. The covenant to pay rent is seen as security for the property. If the rent is not paid the landlord is simply enforcing his security by forfeiting the lease. If the tenant pays the rent and all the landlord's expenses, there is no reason why the lease should be forfeited. Even if the tenant is in prison for his behaviour, the court will not refuse relief if the rent is paid up as in *Gill v Lewis* (1956), although the court could refuse relief if there were exceptional circumstances. Also, the act of forfeiting the lease may be totally disproportionate to the actual breach of the covenant, especially if the tenant is going through a short-term 'bad patch'. There is a lesson here, though, if you ever find yourself in the role of landlord. Choose your tenants carefully.

Covenants to repair

Before looking at implied repairing covenants, express repairing covenants and repairing covenants imposed by statute, we need to see what is meant by repair. The discussion on this applies whenever there is any form of covenant to repair, whether express, implied or imposed by statute. The discussion applies whether it is the landlord or the tenant undertaking the repair.

Q: *When there is a covenant to repair, how exactly do you define the word 'repair', as people must have different views on what is meant by repair? The property could be some crumbling mansion, in which case you would expect the windows to rattle and the cobblestones to be damaged.*

A: Repair should be given its normal meaning in the context of the lease. In *Holding & Management Ltd v Property Holding & Investment Trust plc* (1989) it was held that the following factors, although not exhaustive, could be taken into account:

> the nature of the building, the terms of the lease, the state of the building at the date of the lease, the nature and extent of the defect sought to be remedied, the nature, extent, and cost of the proposed remedial works, at whose expense the proposed remedial works are to be done, the value of the building and its expected lifespan, the effect of the works on such value and lifespan, current building practice, the likelihood of a recurrence if one remedy rather than another is adopted, the comparative cost of alternative remedial works and their impact on the use and enjoyment of the building by the occupants. The weight to be attached to these circumstances will vary from case to case.

The following principles were laid down in *Carmel Southend Ltd v Strachan and Henshaw Ltd* (2007). A covenant 'to keep in good and substantial repair' does not mean the tenant has to put the property into perfect repair or pristine condition; if there is more than one way of doing the repair satisfactorily, the tenant can choose which way; replacement is only necessary if repair is not reasonable or possible; the tenant can't rely on his own breaches of covenant to argue for a lower standard of repair; and the standard of repair is objective taking into account a reasonably-minded incoming tenant. There has to be disrepair, though. Something that wasn't broken must have broken for it to need repairing, and there must be a covenant in which either the landlord or the tenant has taken on the obligation to repair. If neither has taken on the obligation, nobody need repair anything. You must also distinguish between something which is actually broken, which is where something is no longer able to fulfil its intended function, and damage, where something is no longer in pristine condition. In *Quick v Taff Ely BC* (1986) there was a problem with condensation. It was argued that the Council was in breach of its covenant implied by what is now section 11 of the Landlord and Tenant Act 1985 to keep the structure and exterior of the house in repair. It was held that there had to be disrepair before anyone could start arguing breach of covenant. Here, the walls and structure of the house were not in disrepair as they still held up the building. Although the tenant's furnishings, bedding and clothes had rotted, there was no physical disrepair to the walls so the Council was not liable for breach of covenant. Not being able to use the building and inefficiency in how the building circulated the air didn't come into the definition of disrepair. This decision was confirmed both in *Southwark LBC v McIntosh* (2002), where the tenant could not prove that the damp came from breach of the landlord's covenant to repair, and in *Lee v Leeds City Council* (2002), where condensation was again not the landlord's problem. In *Post Office v Aquarius Properties Ltd* (1987) the basement of the leased building had been built defectively and flooded. As the flooding hadn't caused any damage and there had been no deterioration in the building, there was no disrepair, and so the tenants were not liable for breach of the covenant to repair. The next question is whether internal plasterwork forms part of the structure of a property. In *Quick* the landlord conceded that the plasterwork formed part of the structure as did the landlord in *Staves v Leeds City Council* (1991) so the point was not decided. In *Irvine v Moran* (1992) it was held that internal plasterwork was not part of the structure of the building but decorative only. This was disapproved in *Grand v Gill* (2011) which decided that the plaster finish to an internal wall was also part of the structure of the house because it gave a 'smooth constructional finish to walls and ceilings, to which the decoration can then be applied, rather than [being] a decorative finish in itself'. This decision expands a landlord's liability as damage to plasterwork now has be to repaired even if it comes from bad design or an inherent defect. It is arguable, though, whether mould on a wall would constitute disrepair and it is also arguable that it might be a better idea to deal with the inherent defect in the first place.

Q: What happens if there is something wrong in the design of the building that causes problems?

A: This is where you are looking at defects that are inherent in the building and asking whether the tenant is liable for repair when the disrepair is caused by the inherent defect or by a design fault.

Q: This would seem to be taking things a bit far, wouldn't it, making the tenant liable in such cases?

A: In *Ravenseft Properties Ltd v Davstone (Holdings) Ltd* (1980) the building had an inherent defect to do with a lack of expansion joints. This meant that the stone cladding was in danger of falling off. The tenant was liable for the cost of remedying the inherent defect and putting in the expansion joints.

Q: *Isn't that unfair?*

A: The court said that, regardless of whether or not there was a defect, it was a question of degree between the tenant being made liable for something that could reasonably come under the term 'repair' and being asked to do something which would give the landlord back a totally different building at the end of the lease. It didn't matter whether or not the defect was inherent; what mattered was whether the tenant was giving back the landlord something different. The expansion joints, which weren't seen as necessary at the time of building, now had to be included. They were such a trivial part of the whole building that they couldn't alter its nature, so the tenant wouldn't be giving back a building that was very different from the original. In *Lister v Lane & Nesham* (1893) a wall of a leased house was bulging out and, at the end of the term, the house had to be demolished. The house had been built on wooden timbers on top of mud, and time and nature had caused the house to collapse. The tenants were not liable for rebuilding the foundation in a totally different way. In *Brew Brothers Ltd v Snax (Ross) Ltd* (1970) the tenants were not liable for rebuilding walls because the landlord should have been aware of the state of the building and, looking at the case as a whole, the rebuilding could not be called a repair. In *Smedley v Chumley & Hawke* (1982) the landlord had covenanted to keep the walls and roof in good structural repair. Unfortunately the foundations were defective and caused damage to the walls. The landlord argued that he shouldn't be liable for the defective foundations as he would be either improving the premises or giving different premises to the tenant. The court held that under the covenant the landlord had to do whatever was required to ensure that the walls and roof were in good structural repair, even if it meant carrying out works on the foundations. He wasn't giving the tenant different premises but simply giving him premises in the condition envisaged at the start of the tenancy. You can link disrepair and inherent defect together in *Janet Reger International Ltd v Tiree Ltd* (2006), where the basement of leased premises became damp due to the defective installation of the damp proof course. The landlord was not liable on his covenant to repair the structure because the damp had not affected the brickwork or the structure. The damp proof course was part of the structure, but it had been installed defectively. Because it had been installed defectively, it was not in disrepair and the landlord was not liable. Instead, the tenant was liable on its own covenant to put and keep the premises in good repair and condition. It therefore had to put in a waterproof lining to protect the plasterwork and tiles.

Q: *Is there a solution for the tenant here so that he doesn't suddenly find himself landed with repairing damage resulting from a design fault or an inherent defect?*

A: The tenant should ask for an express covenant in the lease which puts the liability for repairing such defects on the landlord. Another solution is for the tenant to insure against the risk of an inherent defect. Alternatively, a developer of a new residential or commercial building can obtain a guarantee from the National House Builders' Council who will indemnify him for any inherent defects found in the first 10 years of the life of the property. The tenant may be able to claim the benefit of this indemnity directly under the Contracts (Rights of Third Parties) Act 1999.

Q: *At what point does repair become renewal because if you repair something you'll be replacing the broken parts with new parts?*

A: This depends on the facts in the individual cases and on the wording in the covenant. If the tenant has to do repairs that essentially mean he is giving a different property back to the landlord, this will count as renewal, not repair, and the tenant will not be liable. In *McDougall v Easington District Council* (1989) three tests were given. You had to look at:

- whether the alteration affected the whole building or only part of it;
- whether after the alterations the building had a wholly different character;
- the cost of the alterations in relation to the previous value of the building, their effect on its value and its lifespan.

The nature and age of the building, the condition it was in when first let and other express terms of the lease should also be considered. In the actual case the work done on the house was so extensive that it could not be called repair.

We can now look at repairing covenants – implied, express and those imposed by statute.

A landlord's covenant to repair

The landlord's implied covenant to repair

There is no implied covenant by the landlord to repair the leased property.

The landlord's express covenant to repair

Q: *Although we're talking about the landlord's express covenant to repair here, presumably express repairing covenants can be made by either the landlord or the tenant?*

A: Yes. In express covenants, either party can covenant to repair. In general the landlord will covenant to keep the property in repair when there is only a short lease. If there is a weekly periodic tenancy created orally under section 54(2) of the Law of Property Act 1925, for example, the parties are only likely to agree on the property, the length of the term and the rent. If there is a long lease, though, it's more likely that the tenant will have to covenant to repair the property. If a tenant takes a lease of the entire property, he is likely to be responsible for all repairs. If he takes a lease of part of the property, he and other tenants will usually be asked to pay service charges, which will be used by the landlord to pay for the repair of the common parts. Much of who does what depends on the bargaining position of the parties. There is an implied covenant on behalf of the tenant that he will allow the landlord a right of entry if the landlord is under an obligation to repair the property.

Statute law imposing obligations on the landlord to repair

Statutory liability comes under the Landlord and Tenant Act 1985 and the Defective Premises Act 1972.

The Landlord and Tenant Act 1985

Section 11(1) of the Landlord and Tenant Act 1985 states that where a dwelling house has been let since 24 October 1961 for a term of less than seven years, there is an implied covenant by the landlord:

▶ To keep the structure and exterior in repair;

and

▶ To keep in repair and proper working order the installations for the supply of water, gas and electricity, and for sanitation;

and

▶ To keep in repair and proper working order the installation for space heating and heating water.

The aim of this legislation was to ensure that the landlord repaired the premises when there was a short lease because it would be unfair to expect the tenant to do so. Keeping the structure and exterior in repair extends to any part of a building in which the landlord has an estate or interest. In *Niazi Services Ltd v Van der Loo* (2004) the landlord was not liable for a poor water supply as he had no estate or interest in that part of the building where the water supply was installed. Section 11(3) of the Landlord and Tenant Act 1985 states that the standard of repair should be determined by the age, character, prospective life and the locality of the property. If the repairing problem is in the tenant's premises, the landlord won't be responsible until the tenant has told him about it. A third party can tell the landlord on the tenant's behalf as in *Dinefwr BC v Jones* (1987).

For residential tenancies granted on or after 15 January 1989 there will be an implied term in the lease that the landlord will also keep the structure and exterior of the common parts of the building in repair under section 11(1) of the Landlord and Tenant Act 1985 as added to by section 116 of the Housing Act 1988. The common parts of the building in a block of flats are the stairs and the hall, for example. The landlord doesn't need notice here as he is expected to keep an eye on the place. If the tenancy was granted before 15 January 1989, a contractual duty of care instead is implied for the landlord to keep the common parts of the building in repair. Such an example arose in *Liverpool City Council v Irwin* (1977) which concerned a block of flats. The Council landlord was held responsible for the repair of the common parts of the flats, which included the staircases and the lifts, on the basis that the whole leasing arrangement wouldn't work unless such a contractual duty was implied into the contract. In the event the Council was not liable because repeated acts of vandalism had caused the state of disrepair and the Council had only a duty to take reasonable care, not an absolute duty, and it had done this. This contractual duty of care will continue to cover leases not coming under the provisions of the Landlord and Tenant Act 1985.

The Defective Premises Act 1972

Section 4 of the Defective Premises Act 1972 states that a landlord with either a duty to maintain or repair, or a right to enter and repair, must take reasonable care to ensure that defects in the property don't cause damage to anyone who might reasonably be expected to be there, or their property. This definition covers the tenant and his family. The provisions in the Act covered a defective gas fire in *Sykes v Harry* (2001). In *Alker v Collingwood Housing Association* (2007) it was held that the duty under section 4 of the Defective Premises Act 1972 did not extend to making the premises safe. Here, glass in the front door of the property, which would now be deemed hazardous but was acceptable at the time, was not in disrepair. As such, the landlord was under no duty to replace it with newer and safer glass and he was not responsible for the claimant's injury when she injured herself on it.

Tenant's remedies for breach of the landlord's covenant to repair

Damages
As a lease is a contract, the tenant is entitled to sue for damages for breach of the landlord's covenant to repair. The aim is to restore the tenant to the position he would have been in if the covenant had not been broken. He can also claim for inconvenience and loss of amenity.

Self-help
Provided the landlord has been given notice of the need to repair, the tenant may pay for the repairs himself and then deduct the cost from his rent, as in *Lee-Parker v Izzet* (1971). The tenant would be well advised first to send an estimate of the cost of the repairs to the landlord, allowing the landlord himself time to do the repairs, and also obtain a declaration from the court that the landlord is in breach.

Specific performance
It is possible for the tenant to obtain an order for specific performance for repairs under the equitable jurisdiction of the court. In *Jeune v Queens Cross Properties Ltd* (1974) the landlord was ordered to reinstate a partially collapsed stone balcony. You could argue that this type of order for specific performance would be difficult to supervise, but in that case there was no doubt what was to be done. It is now possible to obtain an order for specific performance for residential dwellings under section 17 of the Landlord and Tenant Act 1985, and such an order can apply to the repair of the common parts of the building as well.

Appointment of a receiver
A receiver can be appointed under the Supreme Court Act 1981 if the landlord has disappeared, for example. The receiver will try and ensure that the repairs are carried out.

Q: *Can the tenant just give up the lease and walk away?*

A: Yes, if the circumstances are sufficiently serious to warrant this kind of action – *Hussein v Mehlman* (1992). In the case there were severe breaches of the covenant to repair and the landlord had made it quite clear that he wasn't going to do anything about it. This amounted to repudiation (disclaimer) of the lease which the tenant accepted by giving back the keys and leaving.

A tenant's covenant to repair

The tenant's implied covenant to repair

There is no implied repairing covenant as such here. The closest you can get to it is the implied covenant that the tenant will not commit waste, and that he will use the premises in a tenant-like manner.

The tenant's covenant not to commit waste

This covenant relates to liability for damage, although it can cover repair. The tenant is said to be liable for waste, where waste is defined as an act or omission of the tenant which alters the state of the land. Waste can be one of two types:

1. Voluntary waste, which means doing something which shouldn't be done, for example, altering the premises without the landlord's consent with the consequence that the value of the leased premises is detrimentally affected.
2. Permissive waste, which means not doing something which ought to be done, for example not repairing a wall to prevent it falling down.

Tenants are liable for the different types of waste depending on the type of tenancy.

In weekly, monthly and quarterly tenancies, the tenant is liable only for voluntary waste. He is not liable for normal wear and tear. In a yearly tenancy, the tenant is liable for voluntary waste and must keep the property wind and watertight. This means closing gates and windows to prevent wind and rain damage. The yearly tenant is not liable for normal wear and tear. In a fixed term lease the lessee is liable for voluntary and permissive waste.

Q: *Does this mean that the lessee with a fixed term lease has to repair the property?*
A: Yes. He is liable for not doing something which ought to be done, so that means he has to keep the property in repair.

The tenant's implied covenant to use the premises in a tenant-like manner

Under the rule in *Warren v Keen* (1954) the tenant must use the premises in a tenant-like manner. This basically means keeping things working properly and doing small jobs around the place, such as cleaning the windows and unblocking the sink if necessary.

The tenant's express covenant to repair

Q: *How will a tenant's express covenant to repair be worded?*
A: Words like 'to keep in repair', for the tenant 'to deliver up in repair' or for the tenant to 'put in repair'.

Q: *Why would a tenant take a lease where he has to covenant to 'put the property in repair'?*

A: If a tenant takes over a shop that has just been built, for example, he may offer to fit it out in return for a rent-free period or a reduced rent for a number of months.

The following is the repairing covenant in *Ravenseft Properties Ltd v Davstone (Holdings) Ltd* (1980).

> When where and so often as occasion shall require well and sufficiently to repair renew rebuild uphold support sustain maintain pave purge scour cleanse glaze empty amend and keep the premises and every part thereof (including all fixtures and additions thereto) and all floors walls columns roofs canopies lifts and escalators (including all motors and machinery therefor) shafts stairways fences pavements forecourts drains sewers ducts flues conduits wires cables gutters soil and other pipes tanks cisterns pumps and other water and sanitary apparatus thereon with all needful and necessary amendments whatsoever ...

Q: *Are all covenants worded quite like that?*

A: Many are like this, simply because there is no definition of the word 'repair', so obligations have to be clearly defined. A tenant should make up a Schedule of Conditions at the start of the lease to protect himself. This is a document which describes the condition of the property in detail, often accompanied by photographs. Such a document can run to many pages but avoids arguments at the end of the lease when the landlord tries to argue that the premises are not in the same state of repair as they were at the start of the lease.

Q: *If the tenant covenants to repair the property, how do you determine the standard of repair? The tenant may think that something is repaired to a satisfactory standard and the landlord may disagree.*

A: In *Proudfoot v Hart* (1890) it was held that where the tenant was under an obligation to keep and return the house in 'good tenantable repair', he would have to leave it reasonably fit for occupation by a tenant of the class which would be likely next to take the lease, bearing in mind the age, character and locality of the house. If the property was a 200-year-old house it wouldn't be in the same condition as a modern house, for example. Repairs that you might do to a palace wouldn't be necessary to a cottage and the state of repair of a house in Grosvenor Square would be different from a house in Spitalfields.

Q: *Do you take into account the condition of the house at the start of the lease or at the end of it?*

A: At the start of the lease. If the area had become run down during the period of a long lease, it wouldn't be fair if the tenant could argue that his state of disrepair now matched the general disrepair in the area, therefore he didn't have to do any repairs. Similarly, if the area had gone upmarket, there is no reason why the tenant should be liable for improving the state of repair simply to keep up with the Joneses.

Statute law imposing obligations on the tenant to repair

There are no statutory provisions here.

Landlord's remedies for breach of the tenant's covenant to repair

Damages

As a lease is a contract, the landlord may sue for damages for breach of the covenant to repair. The amount awarded will aim to put the landlord back into his original position before the breach. Section 18(1) of the Landlord and Tenant Act 1927 limits the damages awarded for breach of a covenant to repair to the difference between the value of the property with the repairs done and the value of the property without the repairs done. This means that the landlord can't claim for the stress the tenant has caused him. The landlord can sue for the cost of the repairs subject to the provisions of section 18(1) so if these costs are greater than the loss in the value of the reversion, they will be capped. If he is going to sell the property without doing the repairs, he can ask for its loss in value. In *Latimer v Carney* (2006) the court determined by how much the property had been devalued due to breach of the covenant to repair by the tenant by looking at the estimated cost of the repairs. If the landlord is going to demolish the property he cannot claim any damages.

Injunction

An injunction can be awarded to prevent further breach of the tenant's covenant to repair.

Specific performance

Specific performance, which is an order forcing someone to do something, is unlikely to be obtained, as it would require the court to supervise the tenant and ensure that he had carried out his obligations. However, in *Rainbow Estates v Tokenhold* (1999) it was decided that an order of specific performance could be given where damages would be an inadequate remedy. In this case there was an unusual set of circumstances because the landlord had no right of access to carry out any repairs. Specific performance was granted to ensure that the tenant carried out the repairs.

Forfeiture

There are two different procedures regarding forfeiture. The first is for non-payment of rent and the second for breaches of covenant other than non-payment of rent. The second procedure is relevant here as we are talking about the breach of a covenant to repair.

The landlord can claim forfeiture only if:

▶ the lease contains an express clause stating that the landlord has the right of re-entry if there is a breach of a covenant, here breach of the covenant to repair.

Assuming a clause to this effect is contained in the lease, the landlord needs to serve a notice on the tenant under section 146 of the Law of Property Act 1925 which must:

▶ Specify the breach complained of; and
▶ Ask for the breach to be remedied if it is capable of remedy; and
▶ Ask for compensation if required.

Q: *Why would a breach not be capable of being remedied?*

A: You could argue that a negative covenant could never be remedied because the breach has happened and you can't undo it. A covenant to repair is likely to be a positive one, and therefore capable of remedy. Even if there is a negative covenant, though, a remedy is still possible. An example of this approach was found in *Savva v Hussein* (1997) where a negative covenant not to alter the premises without the landlord's consent could be remedied because the alterations could be changed back again. When serving a section 146 notice, the landlord must specify very clearly the breach that is to be remedied.

Q: *What happens if the landlord doesn't specify the breach that is to be remedied when he serves the notice?*

A: The notice is invalid. The notice will also be invalid if the landlord doesn't ask for the breach to be remedied. In *Expert Clothing Service and Sales v Hillgate House Ltd* (1986) the court held that a breach of a positive covenant could ordinarily be remedied by performance of the covenant and payment of compensation. Here, the landlord hadn't suffered any loss from the tenant's breach of the covenant to demolish and rebuild the premises. The breach could have been remedied by the work being carried out within a reasonable time. Unfortunately for the landlord, the section 146 notice was invalid because the landlord hadn't asked for the breach to be remedied. The landlord must give the tenant a reasonable time to remedy the breach if this is possible.

If the tenant doesn't carry out the repairs, the landlord can pursue his claim either by peaceful re-entry, which, given the provisions of the Protection from Eviction Act 1977 and the Criminal Law Act 1977, is not a good idea, or by applying for a possession order through the court process.

Q: *Has the tenant got any defence here?*

A: If the tenant doesn't want to lose his lease, he should carry out the repairs within the reasonable time given. Even after the landlord has re-entered the property or commenced court proceedings, the tenant can still claim relief from forfeiture if he carries out the repairs and also pays the landlord's costs as required under section 146(3) of the Law of Property Act 1925. The court can make an order giving a time frame in which the repairs must be completed. The Leasehold Property (Repairs) Act 1938 may also be of assistance. If the lease was for seven years or more and there are still at least three years left to run, the landlord must tell the tenant in the section 146 notice that the tenant can serve a counter-notice under section 1 of the 1938 Act. If the tenant serves a counter-notice within 28 days, the court will allow the landlord to forfeit only if either: the value of the leased property has or will fall if the repairs aren't done; or the repair is necessary by order of an authority or under a local bye-law; or, if the tenant doesn't occupy all the premises, other occupiers might be affected by the lack of repair; or it would be cheaper to repair at the time rather than wait for further deterioration when the cost of the repairs would have gone up; or it would be just and equitable for the landlord to forfeit.

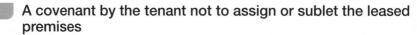

A covenant by the tenant not to assign or sublet the leased premises

An assignment occurs when the tenant sells the remainder of the lease term. Subletting occurs when the tenant sublets the leased property for a term shorter than his own lease, even if by only one day.

The tenant's implied covenant that he will not assign or sublet the leased premises

There is no implied covenant that the tenant will not assign or sublet the leased premises.

The tenant's express covenant that he will not assign or sublet the leased premises

An express covenant by the tenant not to assign or sublet can be absolute or qualified. An absolute covenant against assignment or subletting is definitive. This means that however irrational the landlord's decision that the lease should not be assigned or sublet, the tenant cannot argue.

Q: *Isn't that rather hard on the tenant who may have taken out a long lease and then discovered that his circumstances have changed and he wants to find someone else to take over the lease?*

A: A lease is a contractual arrangement. There is no obligation on a person to take a lease that includes this covenant. Also, look at it from the point of view of the landlord, who has probably chosen his tenant very carefully. It would be most unfair if the original tenant could immediately assign the lease to a substitute who was less than desirable. If the covenant is qualified, it means that the tenant cannot assign or sublet without the landlord's consent. The landlord cannot take a long time deciding whether he is going to give consent, as section 1(3) of the Landlord and Tenant Act 1988 states that if the tenant applies in writing asking to assign or sublet, the landlord must decide the issue within a reasonable time. In *NCR Ltd v Riverland Portfolio (No.1) Ltd* (2005) there were unusual and complicated issues to be considered and a period of less than three weeks was not considered unreasonable, particularly as it was in the summer holiday period.

Q: *What happens if consent is not given in a reasonable time?*

A: The tenant can sue for damages for breach of the statutory duty. In *Design Progressions Ltd v Thurloe Properties Ltd* (2004) the landlord had unreasonably delayed its decision. The Court wanted to mark its disapproval of the cynical way the landlord had operated which was designed to frustrate the tenant, and so awarded exemplary damages as well. Under section 19(1) of the Landlord and Tenant Act 1927 the landlord cannot withhold his consent unreasonably. The landlord can either give consent or, if he fails to do so, he must justify why his refusal is reasonable. Under section 1(6) of the Landlord and Tenant Act 1988 the landlord has the burden of proving that his decision was reasonable.

Q: *On what grounds can the landlord justify his refusal to give consent as being reasonable?*

A: The courts have gone on to lay down long lists of what constitutes a reason for refusing consent and what doesn't. The first of these lists is found in *International Drilling Fluids Ltd v Louisville Investments (Uxbridge) Ltd* (1986) and was added to in *Straudley Investments Ltd v Mount Eden Land Ltd (No 1)* (1997). As statute law has modified some of the points in these lists, it is worthwhile looking at *Ashworth Frazer Ltd v Gloucester City Council* (2001), which gave three overriding principles.

(1) A landlord cannot refuse consent to an assignment on grounds which have nothing to do with the relationship of landlord and tenant. Consent cannot be withheld because of personal factors that have nothing to do with the lease. In *Houlder Bros & Co Ltd v Gibbs* (1925) a landlord had refused consent to assignment because the assignment would have been to another of his tenants in Number 12 and Number 12 would be difficult to relet if the present tenant moved out. It was held that consent had been unreasonably refused as the reason was personal and was to do with the reletting of other property, not with the relationship of landlord and tenant.

(2) Whether the landlord's conduct was reasonable or unreasonable will be a question of fact to be decided by the tribunal of fact.

(3) A landlord does not have to prove that the conclusions which led him to refuse consent were justified if they were conclusions which could be reached by a reasonable man in the circumstances.

It was also stated that 'reasonable' should be given a common sense meaning.

In *Landlord Protect Ltd v St Anselm Development Co Ltd* (2009) two further propositions were added. First, the landlord could refuse consent if his rights under the lease would be prejudiced by the assignment. Secondly, the landlord is not allowed to impose a condition which increases or enhances his rights under the lease. In the case the landlord wanted the guarantor of the assignee to remain liable after any further assignment. This was rejected because it would enhance the landlord's rights. If the landlord didn't think a proposed assignee were suitable, he could always refuse consent to assign.

Q: *What happens if the landlord refused consent because he thought that the proposed assignee might breach a covenant in the lease?*

A: In *Killick v Second Covent Garden Property Co Ltd* (1973) the landlord's worry that there might be a breach of covenant by the proposed assignee was not seen as a reasonable refusal. In *Ashworth Frazer* the House of Lords overruled *Killick*. It was decided *per curiam* that it is possible for such a refusal to be reasonable, but it will always depend on the facts of the case.

Q: *Why was there this change? Even if the proposed assignee went on to breach the covenant, the landlord could always forfeit the lease.*

A: The landlord would have to do this via expensive legal proceedings.

One reason for refusal is that any breach of covenant has the potential to cause damage to the reversion.

Q: *How could the reversion be damaged?*

A: The proposed assignee might be able to claim a statutory right to remain after the end of the tenancy, for example, as argued in *Deverall v Wyndham* (1989), although on the facts of the case the tenants were allowed to assign. You could also argue that if, for example, the assignee ran a different business at the premises from the previous tenant, a change of use of the premises might cause a fall in the value of the property should the landlord ever wish to sell the reversion. The courts will treat this argument with caution, though, particularly if no evidence of the anticipated fall in value is produced, as in *Footwear Corporation Ltd v Amplight Properties Ltd* (1999). This case was to do with the inappropriateness or otherwise of the proposed use as a pet shop.

Q: *Why can't the landlord just rely on the assigning tenant if there is a breach of covenant?*

A: Because it's not the same as the occupying tenant carrying out the covenants in the first place. In *Royal Bank of Scotland v Victoria Street (No 3)* (2008) consent to assign was refused on the basis that the proposed assignee company was not 'respectable or responsible' as, amongst other things, it had only been incorporated as a company for two months. The tenant said that because it would remain liable on the covenants following assignment, the landlord could refuse consent only if the value of the reversion would be damaged. The court held that the landlord could refuse consent in circumstances other then where the value of the reversion would be damaged. Even though the assigning tenant would have continuing liability and could pay the rent or other damages if the proposed assignee company didn't pay or didn't comply with the leasehold covenants, this was not the same as the assignee company performing the covenants in the first place not least because the landlord would have to have to chase up the assigning tenant. Also, the assigning tenant would have responsibilities but no control of the premises and that could cause problems for both the landlord and the assigning tenant. A refusal to consent was justified here and was a question of fact in each individual case.

Q: *Does the landlord have to take into account any effect on the tenant if he refuses consent?*

A: In *International Drilling Fluids* it was held that the landlord need look only at his interests and not those of the tenant, except in unusual circumstances. In the actual case there would have been a disproportionate detriment to the tenant if consent had been refused.

Q: *Can the landlord take up references before giving consent?*

A: Yes, and he is allowed to ask for financial information regarding the standing of the proposed assignee. It is, of course, in the tenant's interests to give it if the proposed assignee is financially sound because there is more chance of consent being given.

Q: *What happens if the property is in a state of disrepair from the previous tenant and the proposed assignee isn't willing to commit to put things right?*

A: It's not usually considered a ground for refusing consent: see *Orlando Investments Ltd v Grosvenor Estate Belgravia* (1990). After all, the landlord can still sue the proposed assignee for any breach of a leasehold covenant to repair.

Q: *Can the tenant just go ahead anyway if he thinks the landlord doesn't have a valid reason for refusing consent?*

A: Yes, but the tenant would be advised to go to court to get a declaration that such an assignment would be reasonable. Alternatively he could ask for specific performance of the proposed assignment or sublease.

You must also note the following. Section 19 of the Landlord and Tenant Act 1927 has been amended by section 22 of the Landlord and Tenant (Covenants) Act 1995 for leases created after 1 January 1996. This amendment applies to commercial leases only. If the landlord and tenant have agreed any conditions on which the landlord can withhold consent, then, providing the conditions are met, the landlord cannot be challenged on withholding consent unreasonably. The same applies if there is a condition the tenant must meet before he can assign. If the condition is met, the landlord cannot refuse consent. This effectively means that parties in a commercial lease are free to make their own arrangements which cannot be challenged.

Statute law imposing obligations on the tenant not to assign or sublet

There is no statute law imposing such obligations.

Landlord's remedies for breach of the tenant's covenant not to assign or to sublet

Damages
The landlord can sue for damages.

Injunction
The landlord can ask for an injunction to prevent the assignment or subletting.

Forfeiture
There are two different procedures regarding forfeiture. The first is for non-payment of rent and the second for breaches of covenant other than non-payment of rent. The second procedure is relevant here as we are talking about the breach of a covenant not to assign or sublet.

The landlord can forfeit the lease only if:

- the lease contains a right of re-entry to the property if the tenant is in breach of a covenant, here breach of a covenant not to assign or sublet.

The landlord must serve a notice on the tenant under section 146 of the Law of Property Act 1925. The notice must:

- Specify the breach complained of; and
- Ask for the breach to be remedied if it is capable of remedy; and
- Ask for compensation if required.

The section 146 notice must specify very clearly the breach that is to be remedied. In *Akici v Butlin Ltd* (2005) Mr Akici was not allowed to part with possession or share possession without the landlord's consent. The landlord had served a notice on him stating that he was in breach of covenant for *parting* with possession of the premises without the landlord's consent. The Court held that he was *sharing* possession and, as the section 146 notice had not referred to sharing possession specifically, the landlord could not forfeit the lease.

Q: *Why do the courts look at this in such technical detail?*

A: The tenant must know the exact reason why he is in breach because only then can he know exactly the breach he has to remedy.

Q: *If the tenant has assigned or sublet in breach of covenant, can the landlord ask for the breach to be remedied?*

A: This raises the question again whether such a breach can be remedied. You might argue that if the tenant puts things right and compensates the landlord there is no reason why a negative covenant shouldn't be remedied. On the other hand, you might argue that things can never be put right simply because the breach has happened. The official answer is that when there is breach of a covenant not to assign or sublet without the landlord's consent, the breach is not remediable. As breach of the covenant not to assign or sublet without the landlord's consent is not remediable, this means that the landlord still has to serve the section 146 notice but does not have to ask for the breach to be remedied. Forfeiture will therefore follow immediately. In *Scala House & District Property Co Ltd v Forbes* (1974) there had been breach of a covenant not to assign without the landlord's consent. As the breach was incapable of remedy, the landlord did not have to ask for it to be remedied and could seek possession immediately. However, in *Akici v L R Butlin Ltd* (2005) it was held that if a breach falls short of creating a legal interest, like just sharing or parting with possession of the premises rather than assigning or subletting, it is capable of being remedied. You could do this because sharing or parting with possession doesn't create a legal interest which can't be 'uncreated', as in assigning or subletting. Lord Justice Neuberger did say, though, that if he wasn't bound by authority he would be attracted to the view that you could simply assign the property back if it had been assigned in breach of covenant to sublet. In *Patel v K&J Restaurants* (2010) a tenant had shared occupation of the premises in breach of covenant but it was a remediable breach. Relief from forfeiture was granted on the basis that the sharing occupier had gone and, if there was forfeiture, the tenant would suffer financially and the landlord would make a windfall profit out of all proportion to the breach or any resulting damage.

Q: *Can the tenant ever obtain relief from forfeiture even though the breach is not remediable?*

A: In *Scala House & District Property Co Ltd v Forbes* (1974) relief from forfeiture was obtained because the subtenant was no longer in possession, an error by the solicitor had led to the subletting in the first place, no harm had been done to the landlord and the landlord couldn't have reasonably refused consent if he'd been asked. Relief from forfeiture will not be granted where a stigma would attach to the landlord though. In *Dunraven Securities Ltd v Holloway* (1982) the premises were being used as a pornography shop in breach of covenant. There was no relief from forfeiture because the stigma of the pornography shop would still be associated with the property. There is a distinction, though, between immoral use by a tenant and immoral use by a sublessee. When the tenant is committing the immoral use, it is an irredeemable breach and there is no relief from forfeiture. When the sublessee is committing the immoral use, the breach can be remedied provided the tenant (who carved the sublease out of his own lease) acts quickly enough to stop the immoral use. In *Glass v Kencakes Ltd* (1966) the sublessee had been using the premises for immoral purposes but the tenant had served a section 146 notice the moment he knew and there had been no publicity. It was held that you had to take all the circumstances into account in making a decision and it could well be that in other cases with 'revolting circumstances ... the slate could not be wiped clean'. In comparison, in *Patel v K&J Restaurants* (2010) the lease contained a covenant against illegal or immoral user but one of the sublet flats was being used as a brothel. The tenant had delayed in stopping the sublessee's immoral use so the breach could not be remedied although relief from forfeiture still was granted. The relief was granted on the basis that 'The nature of Tottenham Court Road is well known. It is not a road where such a stigma could easily attach to particular premises.'Also, there was a new tenant and in addition, if the lease was forfeited, the landlord would make a large profit.

Other aspects of leases and leasehold covenants

Waiver

There is no obligation on the landlord to act if the tenant breaches a covenant. At the point when the landlord knows about the breach, if he does anything which is consistent with the existence of the tenancy despite the breach, then it will be seen as waiver of the breach and the landlord will not be allowed to pursue any remedy until there is another breach. Accepting future rent is the most common way in which the landlord waives his right to take action against the tenant. For example, if a tenant sublets in breach of covenant, once the landlord has then accepted rent, he can no longer forfeit the lease. This is known as a once and for all breach. Even though the sublease carries on after the landlord has accepted rent, the landlord cannot sue. This is in comparison to a continuing breach, such as breach of a covenant to repair. If the property is in disrepair and the landlord accepts rent, the disrepair continues the day after and so the landlord can still sue.

The effect of forfeiture on subleases

If the landlord forfeits the lease, any sublease the tenant has granted will automatically come to an end. The sublessee is able to ask for relief from forfeiture at the court's discretion under section 146(4) of the Law of Property Act 1925 and apply for a new tenancy. This new tenancy will have a maximum term consisting of the time that remained on the sublease, and the sublessee will become the direct tenant of the landlord.

Usual covenants in a lease

If there is a contract to grant a lease in the future, it is an implied term of the contract that the lease, when granted, will contain what are called the usual covenants. These are: the tenant will pay rent, rates and taxes and will keep the premises in repair; if the landlord covenants to repair the premises, the tenant will allow reasonable access; the landlord will covenant for quiet enjoyment and not to derogate from his grant; the landlord will have the right to re-enter the premises if the rent is not paid. This list can be added to depending on local custom and usual practice of the business to be conducted on the premises. If the lease does not contain these terms when granted then it will be amended to do so.

Modification or discharge of leasehold covenants

The Lands Tribunal of the Upper Chamber can modify or discharge a covenant contained in a lease under section 84(12) of the Law of Property Act 1925 provided that the lease has been granted for a term of more than 40 years and 25 years has expired already. Section 84 of the Law of Property Act 1925 is described in Chapter 14 on page 362 and the grounds for modification or discharge are the same for leasehold covenants as for freehold covenants. In *Re Phillips* (2011) a restriction on the use of holiday chalets by the lessees was not modified or discharged because the landlord would be disadvantaged by its removal. In *Lee v Courtenay Gate Lawns Ltd* (2012) a covenant preventing subletting was not modified or discharged as it was of benefit to the landlord to have owner occupied flats rather than flats that had been sublet by their owner occupiers.

Reform

The Landlord and Tenant (Termination of Tenancies) Bill, put forward by the Law Commission in 2006, aims to promote a level playing field between landlord and tenant. The doctrine of waiver would be abolished and forfeiture would also be abolished because it doesn't allow the tenant enough time to respond. Under the proposed statutory scheme, if a tenant was in breach of a covenant he would be given written notice explaining the breach, together with the remedial action he must take and the deadline for doing so. The landlord would not be able to do anything further until either seven days or the date in the default notice had passed, allowing negotiation time between landlord and tenant and hopefully avoiding court proceedings.

Q: *What would happen if the tenant didn't comply?*

A: The landlord would have six months in which to go to court where the court could give an order that aimed to reflect the particular circumstances of any case and ensure proportionality between landlord and tenant. Remedies could include ending the lease or ordering a sale of the lease. If there was a sale of the lease, the landlord could be paid anything that he was owed from the proceeds, any creditors of the tenant could be paid from the proceeds and the tenant would receive anything that was left. This would be a proportionate remedy, and any investment by the tenant in the property would be recognised because the sale price would reflect the investment.

Q: *What would happen if the tenant had left the premises or there was no hope of ever complying with a request to remedy the breach?*

A: There would be a summary procedure which could be followed, and the tenancy could be ended a month later if the tenant did nothing, but this could not be used for residential tenancies.

Q: *Why would these proposed procedures be better?*

A: Because it would satisfy those worried about human rights issues and it would lead to a fairer process as far as the tenant was concerned. A voluntary Code for Leasing Business Premises published in March 2007 aims to ensure fairness between landlord and tenant in new leases.

The Law Commission has also reviewed housing law in England and Wales with a report and draft Bill published in May 2006: *Renting Homes: The Final Report* (Law Com No 297). The aim is to simplify the law as far as the different types of tenancy are concerned, to ensure transparency and to give consumer protection to occupiers. A contract signed by a landlord and a tenant would be in a standard format and would be compulsory. The contract would contain fundamental terms including repairing obligations and would give the grounds for possession. The scheme talks about occupiers and would therefore remove the distinction between a lease and a licence. The recommendations were accepted in part by the Government.

In August 2008 the Law Commission published its report 'Housing: Encouraging Responsible Letting'. Reform is proposed in stages by promoting self regulation and building on existing voluntary initiatives. Proposals include the introduction of a housing monitor in the private rented sector, the provision of a stakeholder board where all the parties in the private residential rented market are represented, a single code of housing practice management for landlords, landlord accreditation schemes and a pilot programme for home condition certificates. Further incentives would be given to landlords. The overall effect, it is said, would be that the existing law would work better, a tenant's rented accommodation would improve, landlords would have a better reputation and investment in the sector would be encouraged. The recommendations were accepted in part.

Q: *Have human rights come into this area?*

A: In *Lee v Leeds City Council* (2002) it was argued that local authorities should have a duty to ensure that their leased premises were fit for human habitation under section 11 of the Landlord and Tenant Act 1985 so as to comply with the European Convention on Human Rights. It was held that there was no general duty to do so, as local authorities could determine the allocation of their resources.

A summary of the covenants discussed in this chapter together with the remedies available for breach follows.

EXAMPLES OF LANDLORD AND TENANT COVENANTS

Type of covenant	Implied Covenant	Likelihood of an Express Covenant	Statutory Obligations	Tenant's Main Remedies	Landlord's Main Remedies
Landlord's covenant that the leased premises are fit for habitation	Condition implied under *Smith v Marrable (1843)*	No	Landlord and Tenant Act 1985	Damages Repudiate the lease	
Landlord's covenant for quiet enjoyment	Yes	Very likely	No	Damages Injunction Protection from Eviction Act 1977	
Landlord's covenant not to derogate from his grant	Yes	Unlikely	No	Damages Injunction	
Tenant's covenant to pay rent	Yes	A virtual certainty	No		Sue on the contract Commercial Rent Arrears Recovery Forfeiture
Landlord's covenant to repair	No	Very likely depending on the type of lease	Landlord and Tenant Act 1985 Defective Premises Act 1972	Damages Self-help Specific performance Appointment of a receiver Repudiate the lease	
Tenant's covenant to repair	Implied covenant 'not to commit waste' and to 'use premises in tenant-like manner'	Very likely depending on the type of lease	No		Damages Injunction Specific performance Forfeiture
Tenant's covenant not to assign or sublet	No	Very likely	No		Damages Injunction Forfeiture

The enforceability of leasehold covenants

The first part of this chapter looked at the types of contractual obligations the landlord and tenant were likely to enter into throughout the term of the lease and the remedies for breach of a leasehold covenant. Now imagine a situation where Leonard (L) owns several properties. He leases one of them, Greenacres, to Timothy (T) for 20 years. In the lease, L, now the landlord, covenants to keep the roof of Greenacres in repair, while T, now the tenant, covenants to pay rent. This can be depicted as follows where ↔ represents the lease containing these leasehold covenants.

As a lease is a contract, there is always privity of contract between the original parties, L and T. If T refuses to pay the rent, L can sue T for breach of contract. If L refuses to repair the roof, T can sue L for breach of contract.

Tenant T lives happily in Greenacres for five years, but is then offered the opportunity to work in Australia. He no longer wishes to lease Greenacres.

Q: *Can he just tell L that he doesn't want the lease anymore?*

A: No, not unless there are specific terms in the lease agreement which allow T to relinquish the lease early. Remember that a lease is a contract between two parties, the landlord and the tenant. As it was for a fixed term of 20 years, both L and T remain liable for any obligations they undertook in the original contract for the full 20-year term. Tenant T promised to pay rent for 20 years, and L promised to keep the roof of Greenacres in good repair for 20 years.

However, T can sell the remaining 15 years of the lease to Tina, T1. This sale is called an assignment. Tenant T is called the assignor and T1 is called the assignee. In an assignment T sells the whole of the outstanding lease term, so Tina will purchase the remaining 15 years of the lease. The assignment of a lease is usually shown using a horizontal arrow.

The question is whether T1 is now liable to pay the rent, and whether T still has any remaining liability to pay the rent, even though he has assigned the lease.

You could also have the converse situation where L decides to move to America and so sells the freehold reversion of Greenacres to Leonora, L1. The freehold reversion is the freehold estate subject to the leasehold estate. Leonora will purchase the freehold estate of Greenacres subject to the leasehold estate over the land. At the end of the 20-year term, she will own the freehold estate of Greenacres unencumbered by the lease. The sale of the freehold reversion is usually shown by the use of a horizontal arrow again.

The question is whether L1 is now bound by the covenant to repair the roof, and whether L still has any outstanding liability on the covenant, even though he has sold the freehold reversion to L1.

And, of course, L1 could sell the freehold reversion to Liam, L2, who could sell it to Lucy, L3. Meanwhile, T1 could sell the remaining term of the lease to Tessa, T2, who could in turn sell it to Tabitha, T3, and the picture would look like this.

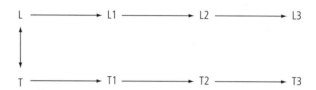

The question is whether L3 and T3 are bound by the covenants that L and T entered into at the start of the lease, and whether L and T, as the original parties to the lease agreement, still have any remaining liability.

Q: *Surely L3 and T3 would just become liable on the leasehold covenants?*

A: The problem here is that only L and T were party to the original contract in which these leasehold covenants were agreed. Landlords L1, L2 and L3 did not directly undertake to repair the roof, and tenants T1, T2 and T3 did not directly undertake to pay the rent. The answer to this dilemma is now governed by the Landlord and Tenant (Covenants) Act 1995. In general this Act was not retrospective, and so many leases are still governed by the preceding law. This means that you must look at the situation where a lease was created before 1 January 1996 and the situation where a lease was created after this date.

As with freehold covenants, it is easier to look at the position between the parties in terms of benefit and burden. The benefit of a leasehold covenant is the ability to sue for any breach of the covenant. The burden of a leasehold covenant is the liability to be sued for breach. If a landlord has the benefit of a leasehold covenant, he has the ability to sue for its breach. However, he can sue only if a tenant has the corresponding burden of the leasehold covenant, the liability to be sued. Conversely, if a landlord has the burden of a leasehold covenant, he bears the liability to be sued. However, he can be sued only if a tenant has the corresponding benefit of the leasehold covenant, the ability to sue. Thus:

Benefit	+	Burden	=	Enforceability of the leasehold covenant
(claimant)		(defendant)		

You can now look at the rules governing the enforceability of leasehold covenants both before and after 1996.

In the examples that follow, landlord L granted tenant T a legal lease of Greenacres for 20 years in which T covenanted to pay the rent and L covenanted to repair the roof.

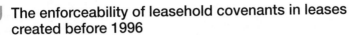

The enforceability of leasehold covenants in leases created before 1996

Look at the chart on page 456 which covers the situation where a lease was created before 1 January 1996.

The liability of a tenant to be sued

Box A

THE LIABILITY OF A TENANT TO BE SUED

1. THE LIABILITY OF A SUBSEQUENT ASSIGNEE OF THE LEASE TO BE SUED

Liable to be sued if conditions in Spencer's Case met:

- There must be a legal lease between the original parties L and T and
- Assignment of the lease must be by deed and
- There must be privity of estate between landlord and tenant and
- The covenant must touch and concern the land that is leased.

2. THE LIABILITY OF THE ORIGINAL TENANT TO BE SUED AFTER ASSIGNMENT OF THE LEASE

The original tenant remains liable to be sued on all covenants for the duration of the lease but can use an indemnity under

Statute or

Mode v Garrett (1872)

Box A1 The liability of a subsequent assignee of the lease to be sued

This is the situation we are looking at. Tenant T has assigned the lease by deed to T1.

Landlord L still has the benefit of the covenant relating to the rent and the ability to sue for payment as he has not sold the freehold reversion of Greenacres. The question is whether the burden of the covenant to pay the rent has passed to T1, which means he is liable to be sued if he doesn't pay. The problem here is that there was no privity of contract between L and T1.

THE ENFORCEABILITY OF LEASEHOLD COVENANTS IN LEASES CREATED BEFORE 1996

Box A

THE LIABILITY OF A TENANT TO BE SUED

1. THE LIABILITY OF A SUBSEQUENT ASSIGNEE OF THE LEASE TO BE SUED

Liable to be sued if conditions in Spencer's Case met:

- There must be a legal lease between the original parties L and T and
- Assignment of the lease must be by deed and
- There must be privity of estate between landlord and tenant and
- The covenant must touch and concern the land that is leased.

2. THE LIABILITY OF THE ORIGINAL TENANT TO BE SUED AFTER ASSIGNMENT OF THE LEASE

The original tenant remains liable to be sued on all covenants for the duration of the lease but can use an indemnity under

Statute or
Mode v Garrett (1872)

Box B

THE ABILITY OF A LANDLORD TO SUE

1. THE ABILITY OF A SUBSEQUENT PURCHASER OF THE FREEHOLD REVERSION TO SUE

Able to sue under section 141 of the Law of Property Act 1925 if the covenant has reference to the subject matter of the lease

2. THE ABILITY OF THE ORIGINAL LANDLORD TO SUE AFTER SALE OF THE FREEHOLD REVERSION

The original landlord retains the ability to sue the original tenant on personal covenants agreed in the original lease for the duration of the lease

Box C

THE ABILITY OF A TENANT TO SUE

1. THE ABILITY OF A SUBSEQUENT ASSIGNEE OF THE LEASE TO SUE

Able to sue if conditions in Spencer's Case met:

- There must be a legal lease between the original parties L and T and
- Assignment of the lease must be by deed and
- There must be privity of estate between landlord and tenant and
- The covenant must touch and concern the land that is leased.

2. THE ABILITY OF THE ORIGINAL TENANT TO SUE AFTER ASSIGNMENT OF THE LEASE

The original tenant retains the ability to sue the original landlord on all covenants for the duration of the lease

Box D

THE LIABILITY OF A LANDLORD TO BE SUED

1. THE LIABILITY OF A SUBSEQUENT PURCHASER OF THE FREEHOLD REVERSION TO BE SUED

Liable to be sued under section 142 of the Law of Property Act 1925 if the covenant has reference to the subject matter of the lease

2. THE LIABILITY OF THE ORIGINAL LANDLORD TO BE SUED AFTER SALE OF THE FREEHOLD REVERSION

The original landlord is liable to be sued by the original tenant for all covenants agreed in the original lease for the duration of the lease

At common law the burden of covenants in a lease can be annexed or attached to the leasehold estate of the tenant under *Spencer's Case* (1583). This means that the liability to be sued becomes attached to the lease itself and can therefore bind subsequent assignees. There are four requirements for this to happen:

▶ There must be a legal lease between the original parties L and T.

and

▶ Assignment of the lease must be by deed.

and

▶ There must be privity of estate between landlord and tenant.

and

▶ The covenant must touch and concern the land that is leased.

Take each of these points separately.

There must be a legal lease between the original parties L and T. The reason for this condition is that *Spencer's Case* passed only the burden of the covenant at common law so the original lease had to be legal, not equitable. A legal lease includes both one created by deed and one for three years or less in a written agreement created under section 54(2) of the Law of Property Act 1925: see *Boyer v Warbey* (1953). The status of an oral lease created for three years or less under section 54(2) has not yet been decided, but it would be very unusual for a short-term lease to be assigned anyway.

The assignment of the lease must be by deed. The reason for this condition is as follows. *Spencer's Case* states that an assignee of the lease must take a legal estate in the land. Section 52(1) of the Law of Property Act 1925 states that, in order to transfer a legal estate, a deed must be used. This means that the remainder of the term of the lease must be assigned by deed. A legal assignment by deed gives the assignee a legal lease, and therefore a legal estate in the land.

There must be privity of estate between landlord and tenant. Privity of estate means that there is a direct relationship of landlord and tenant in the same leasehold estate. When the lease was created in our example, L and T stood in the relationship of landlord and tenant and shared privity of estate in the leasehold estate of Greenacres, as well as privity of contract. Although both the landlord and the tenant of the leased property may change, the new landlord and tenant will still share the same leasehold estate, and so there is privity of estate between them. In our example, L and T1 now stand in the relationship of landlord and tenant and share privity of estate in the leasehold estate of Greenacres.

The covenant must touch and concern the land that is leased. This means that the covenant must affect the value or use of the land. The importance of finding that a leasehold covenant touches and concerns the land is that if a right is to bind subsequent assignees of the lease, it must be a proprietary right in the land. A right in land can be proprietary only if it is attached to the land and is not just personal. The test for whether a covenant touches and concerns the land was formulated in *P & A Swift Investments v Combined English Stores Group plc* (1989). A covenant undertaken by the tenant will touch and concern the land if:

▶ The covenant is of benefit to the landlord only while he holds the reversion. If the landlord sold the reversion, the covenant would no longer be of benefit to him.

▶ The covenant affects the nature, quality, mode of use or value of the leased land.

▶ The covenant is not expressed to be purely personal in nature.

If T had promised to service L's car in August every year, this would be an example of a personal covenant. It has nothing to do with the use of Greenacres. Whether or not L owned the freehold reversion of Greenacres, the covenant to service his car during August would still be valuable to him. As such, it is not a covenant that touches and concerns the land of Greenacres. Examples of covenants undertaken by the tenant that do touch and concern the land include the covenant to pay rent, to repair the property, to use the property as a domestic dwelling only and not to assign the lease without the landlord's consent.

Q: *How do you apply the conditions in* Spencer's Case *in our example?*

A: The burden of the covenant, the liability to pay the rent, will pass to T1 under *Spencer's Case* if the four conditions are met. It was stated in the facts of the scenario that the lease between L and T was legal. Tenant T assigned the lease by deed to T1, so T1 will have acquired a legal leasehold estate. Landlord L and T1 stand in the relationship of landlord and tenant and share privity of estate in the leasehold estate of Greenacres. A covenant to pay rent touches and concerns the land. As you have satisfied all the conditions, the burden of the covenant to pay rent has passed to T1 and he is liable to be sued if he doesn't pay the rent. As L still has the benefit of the covenant, L can sue T1 for the rent.

Q: *Would* Spencer's Case *apply if an equitable lease had been created between L and T?*

A: No, because the first condition that the lease must be legal would not be satisfied. *Spencer's Case* will also not apply if T had not assigned his legal lease to T1 by deed. This is because T1 would take an equitable estate in the land, not a legal estate.

A solution here is for L to use the rules that have developed from *Tulk v Moxhay* (1848) relating to the running of the burden of a freehold covenant in equity. This is discussed further in this chapter in the section on subleases. Alternatively, in some circumstances L can forfeit T1's lease for breach of the covenant.

Q: *What would happen if T had assigned the remainder of the lease by deed to T1, T1 had assigned it to T2 by deed, who had then assigned it to T3 by deed?*

A: The rules in *Spencer's Case* would apply. The lease between the original parties was legal. All the assignments have been made by deed and so T3 will take a legal leasehold estate. Landlord L and T3 stand in the relationship of landlord and tenant and so share privity of estate. The covenant to pay rent affects the value of Greenacres. As the conditions in *Spencer's Case* have been met, the burden of paying the rent has passed to T3 and he bears the liability to be sued by L if he does not pay the rent, as L still has the benefit of the covenant. This situation is represented in the following diagram where the dotted arrow shows that L can sue T3.

Box A2 The liability of the original tenant to be sued after assignment of the lease

You are now looking at whether T can still be sued even though he has assigned the lease to T1.

Landlord L still has the benefit of the covenant relating to the rent and the ability to sue for payment, as he has not sold the freehold reversion of Greenacres. As T was the original party to the lease agreement and has privity of contract with L, he will always be liable on the covenants in the lease for the whole of the 20-year lease term. This will apply to all covenants, whether they are personal or whether they touch and concern the land. This will give L an alternative person to sue if T1 is not paying the rent.

Q: *Isn't this unfair?*

A: No. Tenant T entered into a contract with L in which he undertook to pay the rent for 20 years, even though he may have subsequently decided to assign the lease. There was a legally binding contract between L and T.

Q: *What happens if T dies?*

A: His estate remains liable and provision must be made for any possible claims before his assets can be distributed.

Q: *Is there anything T can do if he is sued by L and he has to pay the rent that T1 owes?*

A: There are several ways out for T, although none of them is particularly satisfactory.

The first way is to use section 77 of the Law of Property Act 1925 if the leased land is unregistered. This section implies an automatic indemnity in favour of T against the person to whom he assigned the lease. This means that if T is sued by L for the rent that T1 owes, T is entitled to sue T1 for a refund under section 77. The equivalent section in registered land is paragraph 20 of Schedule 12 to the Land Registration Act 2002.

A right of indemnity also arises under *Moule v Garrett* (1872), which held that if one party pays the debts of another, the party who pays the debts can sue the defaulting party. As T has paid the debts of T1, T can sue T1 under *Moule v Garrett* (1872). Thus T has two choices. He can sue T1 using the implied indemnity either in section 77 of the Law of Property Act 1925 in unregistered land, or in paragraph 20 of Schedule 12 to the Land Registration Act 2002 in registered land, or else he can sue him under *Moule v Garrett* (1872).

Q: *Is there any point in T claiming a refund from T1? After all, T1 can't pay the rent in the first place.*

A: There is very little point here, which is why this is a very unsatisfactory position for T to be in. It means he can be sued by L for rent, or for the breach of any other covenant, long after he assigned the lease, with little hope of him claiming any money back from the subsequent assignees. If there was a rent review clause in the original lease, and the rent has gone up since he assigned the lease, he is also responsible for this increase, even though he had no say in it. Remember, though, that T did promise at the start of the lease that the rent would be paid for 20 years. Perhaps he should have been more careful when he assigned the lease because T1 was clearly not a good choice.

Q: *What would happen if T1 had paid the rent but had then decided to go to Australia and had assigned the remainder of the lease to T2 by deed, who then assigned the remainder of the lease by deed to T3, who stopped paying the rent?*

A: The obvious choice here is for L to sue T3. *Spencer's Case* will pass the burden to T3, the liability to be sued, if the four conditions are met. The original lease created between L and T was legal. All subsequent assignments have been made by deed. There is privity of estate between L and T3 because they stand in the relationship of landlord and tenant. The covenant to pay rent touches and concerns the land. This means that L can sue T3. In practice there is very little point in L doing this as T3 is not paying the rent and so is unlikely to have any money.

However, L can always sue T because of the privity of contract that exists between them. As T promised in the original lease agreement to pay the rent for the duration of the 20-year lease, he remains liable to be sued. If this happens, T can then sue T1 using the implied indemnity either in section 77 of the Law of Property Act 1925 or in paragraph 20 of Schedule 12 to the Land Registration Act 2002. Tenant T1 can then sue T2, again under the implied statutory indemnity. Tenant T2 can then sue T3, again under the implied statutory indemnity, although there wouldn't be a lot of point as T3 clearly hasn't got any money. There is some retribution here, though. As T2 assigned the remainder of the lease to T3, who was clearly unsuitable, T2 should face the consequences of the error of his ways. You might say that it serves T2 right for a poor choice in T3.

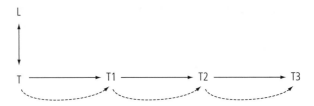

T can use the implied statutory indemnity, as can T1 and T2.

The alternative for T is to sue T3 directly under *Moule v Garrett* (1872) as T paid T3's debts, but this is less than helpful as T3 is unlikely to have any money.

T can use *Moule v Garrett* (1872).

Q: *So really there's not much hope for T, is there, because he either has to find T1 in order to claim an indemnity, which may be impossible, or he can sue T3, who we know has no money?*

A: There is not a lot of hope, and this makes T's position very unenviable. In *RPH Ltd v Mirror Group Newspapers and Mirror Group Holdings* (1992), the original tenant, T, was held liable for just over £1.5 million but was unable to recoup the money from the subsequent assignees of the lease.

The ability of a landlord to sue

> **Box B**
>
> THE ABILITY OF A LANDLORD TO SUE
>
> **1.** THE ABILITY OF A SUBSEQUENT PURCHASER OF THE FREEHOLD REVERSION TO SUE
>
> Able to sue under section 141 of the Law of Property Act 1925 if the covenant has reference to the subject matter of the lease
>
> **2.** THE ABILITY OF THE ORIGINAL LANDLORD TO SUE AFTER SALE OF THE FREEHOLD REVERSION
>
> The original landlord retains the ability to sue the original tenant on personal covenants agreed in the original lease for the duration of the lease

Box B1   The ability of a subsequent purchaser of the freehold reversion to sue

This is the situation we are looking at. Landlord L has sold the freehold reversion to L1. This means that L1 will own the freehold estate of Greenacres unencumbered by the lease when the lease comes to an end.

The burden of the covenant to pay the rent is still with T as he has not assigned the lease. The question is whether the benefit of the original leasehold covenant has passed to L1, so that L1 has the ability to sue if T does not pay the rent.

The position here is governed by section 141 of the Law of Property Act 1925. Section 141 attaches and passes the benefit, the ability to sue for breach of a leasehold covenant, if the covenant has 'reference to the subject matter of the lease'. This phrase has the same meaning as 'touch and concern'.

The covenant to pay rent affects the value of Greenacres and so has reference to the subject matter of the lease. This means that L1 can sue T under section 141 if T fails to pay the rent.

If L1 sold the freehold reversion to L2, L2 would have the ability to sue under section 141, and L1 would lose the ability to sue. If the freehold reversion was sold to L3, L3 likewise would have the ability to sue for the rent, and L2 would lose the ability to do so. This situation is shown below where the dotted arrow shows that L3 can sue T for the rent.

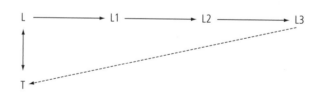

Q: *Does section 141 relate only to legal leases?*

A: No. Section 141 of the Law of Property Act 1925 applies when L and T create either an equitable lease, or else an oral lease under section 54(2) of the Law of Property Act 1925. The effect is to widen the circumstances in which the benefit of a covenant will pass to a landlord. This is bad news for tenants as more landlords are able to sue for the rent.

Box B2   The ability of the original landlord to sue after sale of the freehold reversion

You are looking at whether L is still able to sue once he has sold the freehold reversion to L1.

The burden of the covenant to pay the rent is still with T as he has not assigned the lease.

As discussed in Box B1, under section 141 of the Law of Property Act 1925 the ability to sue is passed to L1 if the covenant has reference to the subject matter of the lease, which means that it relates to the land. If this is so, L loses his right to sue on these types of covenant. Section 141 also appears to defeat L's right to sue based on his original privity of contract with T for covenants that have reference to the subject matter of the lease: see *Re King* (1963). Landlord L cannot sue T for the rent.

However, section 141 does not pass the benefit of personal covenants to L1. This means that L can always sue T for breach of a personal covenant at any time during the whole of the lease term of 20 years based on privity of contract. If T had entered into a covenant to service L's car in August each year, L could sue T if he failed to do so, even after L had sold the freehold reversion of Greenacres to L1. This is because a covenant to service a car is a personal covenant.

The ability of a tenant to sue

Box C

THE ABILITY OF A TENANT TO SUE

1. THE ABILITY OF A SUBSEQUENT ASSIGNEE OF THE LEASE TO SUE

Able to sue if conditions in Spencer's Case met:

- There must be a legal lease between the original parties L and T and

- Assignment of the lease must be by deed and

- There must be privity of estate between landlord and tenant and

- The covenant must touch and concern the land that is leased.

2. THE ABILITY OF THE ORIGINAL TENANT TO SUE AFTER ASSIGNMENT OF THE LEASE

The original tenant retains the ability to sue the original landlord on all covenants for the duration of the lease

Box C1   The ability of a subsequent assignee of the lease to sue

This is the situation we are looking at. Tenant T has assigned the lease by deed to T1.

In the original lease agreement L covenanted to keep the roof in repair. The burden of repairing the roof is still with L as he has not sold the freehold reversion of Greenacres. The question is whether the benefit of the leasehold covenant to have the roof repaired has passed to T1, and with it the ability to sue.

At common law, the benefit of covenants in a lease can be annexed or attached to the estate of the tenant under *Spencer's Case* (1583). This means that the ability to sue on the covenant becomes attached to the lease itself, and so later assignees can sue. There are four requirements for this to happen:

▶ There must be a legal lease between the original parties L and T

and

▶ Assignment of the lease must be by deed

and

▶ There must be privity of estate between landlord and tenant

and

▶ The covenant must touch and concern the land that is leased.

These are the same requirements which passed the burden of a leasehold covenant to T1, and you must go through exactly the same steps as in Box A1 when looking at the benefit. The lease between L and T was legal. Tenant T assigned the lease to T1 by deed. Landlord L and T1 stand in the relationship of landlord and tenant and share privity of estate in the leasehold estate of Greenacres. The covenant to repair the roof affects the use and value of Greenacres. Tenant T1 will then have the ability to sue L for breach of the covenant to repair the roof. If T1 assigned the lease by deed to T2, T2 would have the ability to sue L as the rules in *Spencer's Case* are met. If T2 then assigned the lease by deed to T3, T3 would have the ability to sue L if L failed to repair the roof as, again, the rules in *Spencer's Case* are met. This situation is represented in the following diagram where the dotted arrow shows that T3 can sue L.

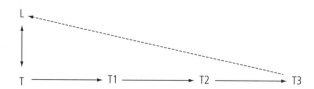

Box C2 The ability of the original tenant to sue after assignment of the lease

This is the situation we are looking at. Tenant T has assigned the lease by deed to T1.

The question is whether T retains any ability to sue L after he has assigned the lease to T1.

In the original lease agreement L covenanted to keep the roof in repair. The burden of repairing the roof is still with L as he has not sold the freehold reversion of Greenacres.

As T was an original party to the lease, he will be able to sue for the benefit of any of the leasehold covenants because he shares privity of contract with L for the whole of the lease term of 20 years. This continuing ability to sue will apply whether the covenants are personal or relate to the land.

Q: *Does this mean that T can always sue L for the repair of the roof?*

A: Yes, but as T no longer owns the lease, his loss will be nil and so damages will be nominal. There is one occasion on which the ability to sue L may be useful. If L had failed to repair the roof, and T had paid for the repair himself so that he could assign the lease of Greenacres to T1 with the property in a reasonable state, T could still sue L for damages. T would also succeed in any claim for breach of a personal covenant based on his privity of contract with L. This is because suing on a personal covenant is not dependant on owning the lease.

The liability of a landlord to be sued

> **Box D**
>
> THE LIABILITY OF A LANDLORD TO BE SUED
>
> **1.** THE LIABILITY OF A SUBSEQUENT PURCHASER OF THE FREEHOLD REVERSION TO BE SUED
>
> Liable to be sued under section 142 of the Law of Property Act 1925 if the covenant has reference to the subject matter of the lease
>
> **2.** THE LIABILITY OF THE ORIGINAL LANDLORD TO BE SUED AFTER SALE OF THE FREEHOLD REVERSION
>
> The original landlord is liable to be sued by the original tenant for all covenants agreed in the original lease for the duration of the lease

Box D1 The liability of a subsequent purchaser of the freehold reversion to be sued

Now let's look at what happens when L sells Greenacres subject to the lease to L1. This is known as the sale of the freehold reversion of Greenacres.

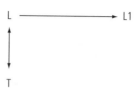

The benefit of the covenant to sue for repair of the roof is still with T as he has not assigned the lease. The question is whether the burden of the leasehold covenant has passed to L1, so that L1 bears the liability to be sued if he does not repair the roof during the term of the lease.

L1's liability is governed by section 142 of the Law of Property Act 1925. This section attaches and passes the burden of the liability to be sued for breach of a leasehold covenant to L1 provided the covenant has 'reference to the subject matter of the lease'. This phrase means the same as 'touch and concern'. Some examples of covenants undertaken by the landlord that have reference to the subject matter of the lease include the covenant to insure the leased premises, to renew the lease and to supply water to the let property.

A covenant to repair the roof affects the use and value of Greenacres and so relates to the land. Under section 142 L1 will bear the burden of the covenant and is liable to be sued if he does not repair the roof. As T still has the benefit of the repairing covenant because he has not assigned the lease, T can sue L1.

Q: *What happens if L1 then sells the freehold reversion of Greenacres to L2, who then sells it to L3?*

A: Section 142 of the Law of Property Act 1925 attaches and passes the burden of any leasehold covenants to L2 if they have reference to the subject matter of the lease. If L2 sells the freehold reversion to L3, L3 will in turn bear the burden of these covenants and is liable to be sued if he does not repair the roof. As the benefit of the covenant is still with T, T can sue L3 if L3 has let the roof fall into disrepair. This situation is represented in the following diagram where the dotted arrow shows that T can sue L3.

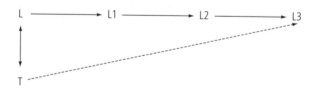

Q: *Does section 142 apply only to legal leases?*

A: No. Section 142 of the Law of Property Act 1925 applies when L and T create either an equitable lease or else an oral lease under section 54(2) of the Law of Property Act 1925. The effect is to widen the circumstances in which the burden of a covenant will pass to a landlord. This means that landlords are liable to be sued more often, which means more roofs will be repaired.

Box D2 The liability of the original landlord to be sued after sale of the freehold reversion

Landlord L has sold the freehold reversion of Greenacres to L1. The question is whether L still retains any liability to be sued.

There was always privity of contract between L and T for all the covenants. This means that L remains liable for the burden of any covenant throughout the whole of the term even though he has sold the freehold reversion. Tenant T could sue L if L1 had not repaired the roof.

The unsatisfactory position of the tenant before 1996

Before 1996 the position of the tenant was unsatisfactory for the following reasons:

- The original tenant, T, was liable for the whole of the term of the lease for the burden of the covenants he had agreed to in the original lease, even though he had subsequently assigned the lease (Box A2). These covenants would inevitably include the covenant to pay rent. This was particularly unjust as, although T could ensure that T1 was financially solvent before he assigned the lease to him, T had no say if T1 subsequently assigned the lease to T2.

- Although T remained liable for the whole of the term for all the covenants agreed in the original lease (Box A2) there was no time limit in which he had to be notified of the breaches committed by subsequent assignees, T1, T2 or T3. If T1, T2 or T3 didn't pay rent, arrears could build up and T could be liable for a considerable sum when sued by the landlord. These problems became particularly acute at the end of the 1980s when there was an economic recession. The number of bankruptcies rose and landlords looked more and more to the original tenant to pay if the covenant to pay the rent was broken by a subsequent assignee of the tenant.

- *Spencer's Case*, which allowed assignees of the original tenant to be sued and to sue, applied only if the lease was legal (Boxes A1 and C1). Sections 141 and 142 of the Law of Property Act 1925, which related to the landlord's ability to sue and liability to be sued (Boxes B1 and D1), applied to both legal and equitable leases. This meant that landlords had greater scope to sue, and there was also no parity between the enforcement of landlords' covenants compared to tenants' covenants.

- There was a lot of discussion over which covenants touched and concerned the land (Boxes A1 and C1) and which had reference to the subject matter of the lease (Boxes B1 and D1). This mattered, because if a covenant was deemed to be personal, it was not attached to the land. This meant that it could not be enforced by subsequent landlords who had purchased the freehold reversion, or by assignees of the original tenant.

These concerns led to the enactment of the Landlord and Tenant (Covenants) Act in 1995.

In general, the 1995 Act does not apply to leases created before 1 January 1996. This means that there is still an extremely large number of leases governed by the previous rules. Leases created after 1 January 1996 are called 'new tenancies' and are governed by the Landlord and Tenant (Covenants) Act 1995. Having used up 'new', if Parliament enacts a further Landlord and Tenant (Covenants) Act sometime in the future, one wonders what we will call leases after that.

We can now look again at each of the different situations concerning a landlord and tenant and see how they fare under the new legislation. Some sections of the 1995 Act also apply to pre-1996 leases, and these are denoted in the text in italics. The advantages of the Landlord and Tenant (Covenants) Act 1995 over the pre-1996 rules are also highlighted in italics.

The enforceability of leasehold covenants in leases created after 1995

Some general points can be made about the Landlord and Tenant (Covenants) Act 1995.

The main aim of the Act was to stop landlords trying to work matters to their own advantage at the expense of the tenant.

Q: *Can landlords opt out of the Act?*

A: Section 25 of the Landlord and Tenant (Covenants) Act 1995 prevents a landlord from contracting out of the Act and making his own arrangements with a tenant.

The first change is that, under section 28(1), both legal and equitable leases are covered by the 1995 Act.

The provisions of the Landlord and Tenant (Covenants) Act 1995 apply to both legal and equitable leases, thereby removing the restriction that Spencer's Case *applied only to legal leases.*

Section 2 of the Landlord and Tenant (Covenants) Act 1995 states that, unless an exception applies, the Act applies to a covenant whether or not it has reference to the subject matter of the tenancy.

Section 2 of the Landlord and Tenant (Covenants) Act 1995 removes the need to establish which covenants touch and concern the land or which covenants have reference to the subject matter of the lease.

You now need to look at the chart on page 469 to determine the position of subsequent assignees of the tenant and subsequent landlords who have purchased the freehold reversion in a lease created after 1 January 1996.

THE ENFORCEABILITY OF LEASEHOLD COVENANTS IN LEASES CREATED AFTER 1995

Box E

THE LIABILITY OF A TENANT TO BE SUED

1. THE LIABILITY OF A SUBSEQUENT AS-SIGNEE OF THE LEASE TO BE SUED

Liable to be sued under section 3 of the Landlord and Tenant (Covenants) Act 1995 unless the covenant is expressed to be personal

Liable for subsequent assignee if Authorised Guarantee Agreement in place and may be able to ask for an overriding lease

2. THE LIABILITY OF THE ORIGINAL TENANT TO BE SUED AFTER ASSIGNMENT OF THE LEASE

Liable for own assignee if Authorised Guarantee Agreement in place and may be able to ask for an overriding lease

Liable to be sued by the original landlord on covenants expressed to be personal for the duration of the lease Liable if the assignment was an excluded assignment

Box F

THE ABILITY OF A LANDLORD TO SUE

1. THE ABILITY OF A SUBSEQUENT PURCHASER OF THE FREEHOLD REVERSION TO SUE

Able to sue under section 3 of the Landlord and Tenant (Covenants) Act 1995 on a covenant not expressed to be personal

2. THE ABILITY OF THE ORIGINAL LANDLORD TO SUE AFTER SALE OF THE FREEHOLD REVERSION

Able to sue the original tenant on covenants expressed to be personal for the duration of the lease

Box G

THE ABILITY OF A TENANT TO SUE

1. THE ABILITY OF A SUBSEQUENT ASSIGNEE OF THE LEASE TO SUE

Able to sue under section 3 of the Landlord and Tenant (Covenants) Act 1995 on a covenant not expressed to be personal

2. THE ABILITY OF THE ORIGINAL TENANT TO SUE AFTER ASSIGNMENT OF THE LEASE

Able to sue the original landlord on covenants expressed to be personal for the duration of the lease

Box H

THE LIABILITY OF A LANDLORD TO BE SUED

1. THE LIABILITY OF A SUBSEQUENT PURCHASER OF THE FREEHOLD REVERSION TO BE SUED

Liable to be sued under section 3 of the Landlord and Tenant (Covenants) Act 1995 unless the covenant is expressed to be personal or unless he has been released

2. THE LIABILITY OF THE ORIGINAL LANDLORD TO BE SUED AFTER SALE OF THE FREEHOLD REVERSION

Liable to be sued by the original tenant on covenants expressed to be personal for the duration of the lease

Liable to be sued on covenants not expressed to be personal for the duration of the lease unless he has been released

The liability of a tenant to be sued

Box E

THE LIABILITY OF A TENANT TO BE SUED

1. THE LIABILITY OF A SUBSEQUENT ASSIGNEE OF THE
LEASE TO BE SUED

Liable to be sued under section 3 of the Landlord and
Tenant (Covenants) Act 1995 unless the covenant is
expressed to be personal

Liable for subsequent assignee if Authorised Guarantee
Agreement in place and may be able to ask for an
overriding lease

2. THE LIABILITY OF THE ORIGINAL TENANT TO BE SUED
AFTER ASSIGNMENT OF THE LEASE

Liable for own assignee if Authorised Guarantee
Agreement in place and may be able to ask for an
overriding lease

Liable to be sued by the original landlord on covenants
expressed to be personal for the duration of the lease
Liable if the assignment was an excluded assignment

Box E1   The liability of a subsequent assignee of the lease to be sued

This is the situation when T assigns the lease to T1.

Landlord L still has the benefit of the covenant, and so can sue for the rent as he has
not sold the freehold reversion of Greenacres. Section 3 of the Landlord and Tenant
(Covenants) Act 1995 annexes or attaches the burden of a covenant undertaken
by the tenant to the leased property and passes it to a subsequent assignee. This
means that T1 can be sued by L.

Q: Do all the covenants become attached to the leased property?

A: No. Section 3(6) states that those covenants expressed to be personal will not
become attached.

**Q: Does this avoid the problem of deciding which covenants touch and concern
the land?**

A: Yes. All covenants will become attached to the leased property unless they are *expressed to be personal*. If a covenant is expressed to be personal, it will always be binding on the original parties for the duration of the lease, but it will not be binding on anyone else. It's up to the parties to decide which covenants they want to be personal, and which they wish to become attached to the land. The danger here is that parties forget to identify any personal covenants. If L and T agree that servicing L's car in August is going to be a personal covenant undertaken by T, but forget to state that it is a purely personal covenant in the lease agreement, if T then assigns the lease to T1, T1 could find himself servicing L's car.

Authorised Guarantee Agreements

Section 16 allows an Authorised Guarantee Agreement (AGA) to be used when the tenant has to obtain the consent of the landlord before he is allowed to assign the lease. A condition of the landlord's consent will be that the tenant enters into an AGA with the landlord.

Q: *What does T guarantee in the agreement?*

A: That T1 will perform the covenants in the lease and that, if T1 doesn't do so, he, T, will be liable instead. Tenant T will therefore ensure that T1 is a 'decent sort of chap' who is likely to be able to comply with the leasehold covenants. If T is assigning to T1, a company, he should ensure that the company is financially viable.

Q: *If T1 assigns the lease to T2, is T still a guarantor if T2 breaches any of the covenants?*

A: No. A tenant is liable for only his own breaches and those of the tenant to whom he assigns the lease when he has entered into an AGA with the landlord before assignment. When T assigned the lease to T1 and entered into an AGA with L, he agreed to be a guarantor only for T1. When T1 assigns the lease to T2, T drops out of the picture as T1 no longer has the lease. Tenant T1 now becomes liable for T2's breaches if he himself has entered into an AGA with L. This is a much fairer way than under the pre-1996 rules.

Q: *Why?*

A: Because a tenant chooses the next tenant that he assigns the lease to. As he chooses the next tenant, he should be responsible for his actions. This kind of thinking is reflected in the Authorised Guarantee Agreement. It is not fair that a tenant should be responsible for further assignments, which is why he is allowed to drop out of the picture if the lease is assigned again.

Section 17 of the 1995 Act governs the procedure to be followed when T becomes liable to pay a fixed charge on T1's behalf under an AGA. A fixed charge is defined as:

Either:

▶ rent;

or

▶ a service charge;

or

▶ a charge where the sum to be paid is fixed and certain, otherwise known as liquidated damages. An example of where unliquidated damages might be awarded is where there was a breach of a covenant to repair because the amount of damages payable would not be fixed or certain at the time of the breach.

Under section 17(2) Landlord L must notify T of the breach of covenant by T1 giving rise to a fixed charge within six months of the breach. This notification is known as a problem notice, called a section 17(2) notice, and must state that L intends to recover the charge from T. If T is notified of the breach of a fixed charge by T1 within six months, he must pay for T1's fixed charge.

The requirement that notification of the breach relating to a fixed charge must take place within six months remedies one of the problems of the pre-1996 rules. Before 1996, there was no time limit within which a landlord had to notify the original tenant, T, of a breach of a covenant by a subsequent assignee, T1 or T2, for example. If the subsequent assignee, T1 or T2, was not paying rent, it meant that arrears could mount up without the original tenant knowing about the problem. This was clearly unsatisfactory, and this problem has now been remedied by the 1995 Act. Section 17 also applies the same period of notice when a fixed charge arises in a pre-1996 lease.

Q: *What happens if the fixed charge of rent has increased since T assigned the lease to T1? Will T be liable under the Authorised Guarantee Agreement to pay the increased rent on T1's behalf?*

A: Under section 18 of the 1995 Act, T will not necessarily be liable for any variations in the leasehold covenants that have been made since he assigned the lease to T1. T is not liable for any amount 'referable to any relevant variation' of any of the tenant's covenants following his assignment to T1. A 'relevant variation' is one which the landlord has an absolute right to refuse or allow. In plain English this means that the landlord must be able to choose whether or not to vary the covenant. Imagine that T entered into a covenant not to sublet the premises. A sublease occurs when a tenant grants another party a lease shorter than his own term. After T had assigned the lease to T1, L decided that T1 would be allowed to sublet the premises, but that in return he would increase the rent. As L could choose whether or not to vary this covenant, T will not be liable for the increase in rent. If L had to vary the rent because such a variation was imposed by statute, he would have had no choice in this, and so T would be liable for the increase.

Q: *What happens if there is a rent review clause in the lease and the rent has increased through rent reviews since T assigned the lease?*

A: T will be liable for the increase because it came about as a result of the covenant in the lease itself. The increase is not a 'relevant variation'.

Section 18 of the Landlord and Tenant (Covenants) Act 1995 extends this protection when a fixed charge arises in a lease created before 1 January 1996.

A lease agreement can specify dates on which the rent is to be reviewed. In case the parties don't agree the rent on the date specified, the landlord will put a clause in the lease saying that the extra backlog due to any increase must be paid once the amount has been determined under the rent review. Under section 17(4) of the Landlord and Tenant (Covenants) Act 1995 a former tenant (T in our example) is only liable for the backlog if the section 17(2) notice specifically states that he may be liable for this backlog at a later date. If a former tenant, T, does become liable for the backlog, the landlord must then serve a notice on him within three months, telling him that the landlord intends to recover this backlog. In *Scottish & Newcastle plc v Raguz* (2008) two pre-1996 leases had been assigned. Remember that sections 17 and 18 of the Landlord and Tenant (Covenants) Act 1995 apply to pre-1996 leases. Dates had been set for rent reviews in 1995 and 1996 although the exact amount following the reviews hadn't been settled until 2001.

Q: *Why does it take so long to agree a new rent?*

A: The landlord must serve a notice on the tenant to trigger the rent review. After that, there is no time limit so the parties spend a huge amount of time arguing. The landlord gets in a valuer, the tenant gets in a different valuer, they both get out a tape measure to measure the floor space again, and so it goes on. The tenant has to pay interest on the backlog so the landlord doesn't lose out, and the tenant holds on to his money for a bit longer which is cheaper than borrowing money from a bank, so no stress to either side really.

The problem was with the words 'becomes due' in section 17(2) because the section states that a former tenant is not liable unless the landlord has served a section 17(2) notice 'within the period of six months beginning with the date when the charge becomes due'.

The Court of Appeal decided that 'becomes due' meant the day the increase was due in theory (i.e. quarterly from 1995 and 1996), not the day it became demandable in practice (i.e. in 2001). The landlord should have served a section 17(2) notice on the assignee of the lease, S & N, on each of the quarterly rent days since 1995 and 1996, stating that any backdated rent resulting from the current rent review might be claimed. This would have been about 40 notices. Fortunately, the House of Lords decided that the Court of Appeal decision produced 'some remarkably silly consequences' and that if the rent is not in arrears, the landlord does not have to serve lots of section 17(2) notices when the rent review is outstanding. When the rent review is decided, the landlord must then, within 6 months, serve a section 17(2) notice on the former tenant telling him he is now liable for the increase. This is because when the increase is fixed, this is a new and separate fixed charge. This increase would become 'due' only when it had been decided. Until the increase in rent is decided, there is no increase to pay and so the tenant cannot be in default. Although this wasn't the literal interpretation of section 17, it was decided that Parliament could not have intended that the outcome was that of the decision of the Court of Appeal.

In our example L would have to serve a notice on T if T had entered into an AGA with L to guarantee T1's performance of the covenants in the lease.

Q: *Does section 17 apply to residential tenancies as well as business tenancies?*

A: Yes, and to agricultural ones as well.

Q: *What happens if an assignee of the lease becomes insolvent?*

A: If the assignee is a limited company, the liquidator can disclaim the lease under section 178(4) of the Insolvency Act 1986. This means that the company no longer has liabilities under the lease. Unfortunately, the assigning tenant will still remain liable. In *Shaw v Doleman* (2009) the tenant, Ms Shaw, had assigned the tenancy to the Ceramic Cafe Limited (CCL). At the same time she had entered into an AGA with the landlord. The AGA provided that the guarantee by the outgoing tenant, Ms Shaw, would apply 'throughout the period during which the assignee is bound by the tenant covenants of the lease'. CCL went into liquidation and the liquidator disclaimed the lease. Disclaiming the lease meant that CCL had no further obligations concerning covenants in the lease. The court, following *Hindcastle Ltd v Barbara Attenborough Associates Ltd* (1997) decided that Ms Shaw did have these continuing obligations despite the ending of the lease. Whilst section 178(4) of the Insolvency Act ended CCL's obligations under the lease, it also states that the liabilities of other parties are not affected. Under the terms of the AGA, Ms Shaw was liable for the arrears of rent and could also be required to take over the lease for the remainder of the term. If the parties had wanted anything different, they should have agreed it. Tenants should note carefully what they are signing up to in AGAs.

Overriding leases

Q: *Is there anything T can do if he's paid for T1's fixed charge?*

A: There is an added bonus here for T. He can insist on an overriding lease under section 19 of the Landlord and Tenant (Covenants) Act 1995.

Q: *Can't lawyers find a word other than over-something?*

A: Obviously not, although overwrought might have been a better choice. Just to confuse the issue even further, 'overriding' here has nothing to do with the overriding you have encountered in registered land. A tenant who has received a notice from a landlord under section 17 and who has paid the fixed charge can ask for an overriding lease at the time of payment of the fixed charge, or within 12 months of its payment.

Q: *What is an overriding lease?*

A: If T obtains an overriding lease, it means that he acquires an intermediate lease between L and T1 with an additional three days added on to the remainder of the term. Tenant T then becomes the landlord of T1 and can enforce the leasehold covenants directly against T1. This means that T can get his revenge on T1 as the covenants will be the same in the overriding lease as in the original lease, with the exception of covenants expressed to be personal. If T1 doesn't repay T the fixed charge that T paid to L on T1's behalf under the AGA, T can forfeit T1's lease and bring it to an end. He can then find another tenant who is more likely to comply with the covenants, or he can occupy the property himself.

The request for an overriding lease can be protected by a class C(iv) land charge in unregistered land under the Land Charges Act 1972 or by a notice under section 34 of the Land Registration Act 2002 in registered land. Protecting the request for an overriding lease in this way means that the request will be binding on any purchaser of the freehold reversion, if L decides to sell the freehold reversion to L1, for example. If the landlord fails to provide an overriding lease within a reasonable period, the tenant can claim damages.

Q: *Why doesn't the landlord just evict T1 for breaching the covenant?*

A: He can do but in the AGA, T guaranteed that T1 would comply with the covenants. Tenant T chose T1 as the next suitable tenant. If T1 turns out not to be quite as suitable as T thought, then L can turn to T to sort out the problem. Of course, L may not wish to grant an overriding lease to T if T showed himself to be an unsuitable tenant when he held the lease. In this case, it would be better for L not to serve a section 17 notice, which gives T the right to an overriding lease, but simply to forfeit T1's lease and find another tenant. This may be a more productive move, particularly if L can charge an increased rent to any new tenant.

Section 19 also applies to pre-1996 leases. Former tenants who remain liable under a lease created before 1996 can now claim an overriding lease if they have been sued by a landlord for the breach of a covenant by a subsequent assignee giving rise to a fixed charge which they have paid.

Authorised Guarantee Agreements and the position of guarantors

The reason for a landlord having a guarantor for a tenant is as follows. If you are a landlord and you want to lease premises to a company that is not particularly strong financially (this is called low covenant strength), and the company provides a strong guarantor who, for example, will be able to pay the rent if it doesn't, you are in a much stronger position. The decision in *K/S Victoria Street v House of Fraser (Stores Management) Ltd* (2011) revolved around guarantors and approved the decision in *Good Harvest Partnership LLP v Centaur Services Ltd* (2010). *K/S Victoria Street* held that the guarantor of a tenant cannot be required to guarantee the tenant's immediate assignee. This is because section 24 of the 1995 Act releases other parties such as guarantors from liability when a lease is assigned. Any agreement that frustrates this is void under section 25. The effect of these sections was to ensure that obligations assumed by a guarantor of a tenant came to an end when the tenant's obligations came to an end on assignment of the lease. If a guarantor had to enter into another agreement to guarantee an immediate assignee, this would frustrate the operation of the Act and the operation of section 24 which was designed to release the guarantor of a tenant, not impose further liability. This is so even though the guarantor would have given this guarantee willingly because it would be difficult to determine what was given willingly or unwillingly in any given case.

Q: *And what about the situation where a guarantor is asked to act as a guarantee that the outgoing tenant will perform any requirements under the AGA?*

A: This is called a sub-guarantee. It was held obiter in *K/S Victoria Street* that the landlord can make it a requirement that the guarantor guarantees any liability that may arise for the outgoing tenant under the AGA under a sub-guarantee. There appeared to be nothing inconsistent with section 24 if the outgoing tenant's guarantor was required to guarantee the outgoing tenant's liability under the AGA. The guarantor is released to precisely the same extent as the assigning tenant. Remember that entering into an AGA is entering into a new agreement which is not a leasehold covenant. As such, another company, for example, could act as guarantor of the outgoing tenant's obligations under the AGA.

The decision in *K/S Victoria Street v House of Fraser (Stores Management) Ltd* means that landlords should check their lease agreements carefully and ensure that new ones take account of the decisions in this case. They should make sure that if a tenant wants to assign the lease, a condition is that any guarantor will then guarantee the outgoing tenant's obligations under the AGA. Better still, landlords should choose reliable tenants so they don't have to rely on guarantors. Landlords should also try to obtain further security from an assignee of the lease if they are in any doubt about the assignee's strength.

| Box E2 | **The liability of the original tenant to be sued after assignment of the lease** |

You are now looking at whether T can still be sued once he has assigned the lease.

Landlord L still has the benefit of the covenant relating to the rent and the ability to sue for payment, as he has not sold the freehold reversion of Greenacres.

Before 1996, T was liable throughout the whole of the term even if he assigned the lease to T1, who then assigned the lease to T2, who then assigned the lease to T3. This was because of the privity of contract between T and L. Section 5 of the 1995 Act removed this enduring privity of contract, which meant that T was no longer liable to be sued on the leasehold covenants unless:

Either:

▶ An AGA was in place

or

▶ The covenant was expressed to be personal

or

▶ The assignment was an excluded assignment under section 11 of the 1995 Act. Take each of these points separately.

An AGA was in place
If T had entered into an AGA with L, he would remain liable for any breaches of covenant by T1. He may be able to insist on an overriding lease to sort out T1's wayward behaviour.

Or the covenant was expressed to be personal

Covenants that are expressed to be personal do not pass to a subsequent assignee but remain binding on the original parties to the lease. If there had been a covenant expressed to be personal between L and T, T would remain liable on it for the duration of the 20-year lease.

Or the assignment was an excluded assignment under section 11 of the 1995 Act

Excluded assignments are defined as those assignments in breach of covenant not to assign and those assignments that arise by operation of law, rather than voluntarily. An example of an excluded assignment by operation of law would be if T died and the leasehold estate vested in his executors. Another example would be if T became bankrupt, in which case his property would vest in his trustee in bankruptcy.

The overall effect here is that T will not be liable unless one of the exceptions applies.

Section 5 removes T's continuing liability after he has assigned the lease to T1 and retired to his bungalow on the South Coast unless T has entered into an AGA guaranteeing T1's performance or the covenant is expressed to be personal or the assignment is an excluded assignment.

The ability of a landlord to sue

> **Box F**
>
> THE ABILITY OF A LANDLORD TO SUE
>
> **1.** THE ABILITY OF A SUBSEQUENT PURCHASER OF THE FREEHOLD REVERSION TO SUE
>
> Able to sue under section 3 of the Landlord and Tenant (Covenants) Act 1995 on a covenant not expressed to be personal
>
> **2.** THE ABILITY OF THE ORIGINAL LANDLORD TO SUE AFTER SALE OF THE FREEHOLD REVERSION
>
> Able to sue the original tenant on covenants expressed to be personal for the duration of the lease

Box F1 The ability of a subsequent purchaser of the freehold reversion to sue

This is where L has sold the freehold reversion to L1. The question is whether the benefit of the original leasehold covenant has passed to L1, so that L1 has the ability to sue for payment of the rent.

As T has not assigned the lease, he remains liable to be sued for payment of the rent. Section 3 of the Landlord and Tenant (Covenants) Act 1995 annexes the benefit of leasehold covenants to the landlord's property and passes the benefit to a subsequent purchaser. Again, all covenants will be attached unless they are expressed to be personal, so L1 can sue T if T fails to pay the rent. If L1 sold the freehold reversion to L2, L2 would have the ability to sue.

Box F2 The ability of the original landlord to sue after sale of the freehold reversion

You are looking at whether L is still able to sue once he has sold the freehold reversion to L1.

The burden of the covenant to pay the rent is still with T as he has not assigned the lease.

Under section 6 of the Act, once L has sold the freehold reversion to L1, he retains no ability to sue on covenants that are not expressed to be personal if he has been released from the covenants in accordance with the procedure in section 8. Release under section 8 is discussed in Box H1. However, he does retain the ability to sue the original tenant on covenants that are expressed to be personal for the duration of the lease.

The ability of a tenant to sue

Box G

THE ABILITY OF A TENANT TO SUE

1. THE ABILITY OF A SUBSEQUENT ASSIGNEE OF THE LEASE TO SUE

Able to sue under section 3 of the Landlord and Tenant (Covenants) Act 1995 on a covenant not expressed to be personal

2. THE ABILITY OF THE ORIGINAL TENANT TO SUE AFTER ASSIGNMENT OF THE LEASE

Able to sue the original landlord on covenants expressed to be personal for the duration of the lease

---

Box G1 The ability of a subsequent assignee of the lease to sue

This is the situation we are looking at. T has assigned the lease to T1. The question is whether the benefit of the leasehold covenant to have the roof repaired has passed to T1, and with it the ability to sue if the roof is not repaired.

Landlord L retains the burden of the covenant to be sued for the repair of the roof as he has not sold the freehold reversion of Greenacres. Section 3 of the Landlord and Tenant (Covenants) Act 1995 attaches the benefit of the tenant's covenants to the leased property and passes the benefit to a subsequent assignee. This means that T1 can sue L if he does not repair the roof provided the covenant was not expressed to be personal and the assignment was not an excluded assignment. Covenants expressed to be personal and excluded assignments were discussed in Box E2. If T1 assigned the lease to T2, who then assigned it to T3, T3 would then have the ability to sue on the repairing covenant, again assuming that the covenant was not expressed to be personal or the assignment was not an excluded assignment.

Box G2 | The ability of the original tenant to sue after assignment of the lease

The question is whether T has any ability to sue after he has assigned the lease.

The burden of repairing the roof is still with L as he has not sold the freehold reversion of Greenacres.

Once he has assigned the lease, the original tenant loses the ability to sue under section 5 of the 1995 Act and can sue only on covenants that he entered into with L that were expressed to be personal for the duration of the lease.

The liability of a landlord to be sued

Box H

THE LIABILITY OF A LANDLORD TO BE SUED

1. THE LIABILITY OF A SUBSEQUENT PURCHASER OF THE FREEHOLD REVERSION TO BE SUED

Liable to be sued under section 3 of the Landlord and Tenant (Covenants) Act 1995 unless the covenant is expressed to be personal or unless he has been released

2. THE LIABILITY OF THE ORIGINAL LANDLORD TO BE SUED AFTER SALE OF THE FREEHOLD REVERSION

Liable to be sued by the original tenant on covenants expressed to be personal for the duration of the lease Liable to be sued on covenants not expressed to be personal for the duration of the lease unless he has been released

---

The liability of a subsequent purchaser of the freehold reversion to be sued

Now let's look at what happens when L sells the freehold reversion of Greenacres to L1.

Tenant T still retains the ability to sue for the repair of the roof as he has not assigned the lease. Section 3 of the Landlord and Tenant (Covenants) Act 1995 attaches the burden of leasehold covenants to the freehold reversion and passes the burden to a subsequent purchaser unless the covenant is expressed to be personal. This means that L1 bears the burden of being sued by T if he does not repair the roof. If L1 sold the freehold reversion to L2, L2 would bear the burden of being sued.

There is another solution here for T. On the sale of the freehold reversion, section 6 of the Act allows L to ask to be released from his liabilities on the leasehold covenants. If he has not been released, he will remain liable on the covenants and can be sued by T. In *BHP Petroleum Great Britain Ltd v Chesterfield Properties Ltd* (2002) it was held that a landlord cannot release himself from a covenant expressed to be personal. A covenant expressed to be personal was not a landlord's covenant as defined by the Act. Liability on a personal covenant continued after assignment of the reversion. If L wishes to be released from a covenant that is not expressed to be personal, he must follow the procedure given in section 8 of the Act. Under this section, L must serve a notice on T either before the sale of the freehold reversion to L1 or within four weeks of the sale, asking for a release from his covenants.

Q: *Why does a landlord have to ask to be released?*

A: Because a tenant has no control when a landlord sells the freehold reversion. The aim is to give some protection to a tenant when the freehold reversion is sold.

The notice asking for a release must be given in the prescribed form otherwise it is invalid.

Landlord L will be released if:

▶ T does not serve a notice of objection within four weeks of receiving the request for release.

or

▶ T serves a notice on L consenting to the release.

Tenant T can also serve a notice of objection to the release. L can then apply to the county court where it will be determined whether it is reasonable for L to be released from his covenants.

Q: *Why would either T or the County Court refuse to release L?*

A: This could happen if L were in breach of one of his covenants, for example the covenant to repair the roof. The court can order that the breach is remedied before L is released. Consent could also be refused if the proposed new landlord, L1, had previously shown himself unsuitable to be a landlord.

If L has not been released and L1 won't repair the roof, T can still sue L.

If L didn't ask for a release when he sold the freehold reversion to L1, he is given another opportunity to do so under section 7 of the Act if L1 sells the freehold reversion to L2.

Q: *How is L supposed to know if and when L1 sells the freehold reversion to L2?*

A: This is unclear. A possible solution for L is to ensure that L1 enters into a covenant with him that L1 will notify L if and when L1 sells the freehold reversion.

If L1 sells the freehold reversion to L2, L1 must also obtain a release. If he does not do so, he remains liable on the leasehold covenants until such time as he does. The same would apply if L2 sold the freehold reversion to L3. L2 must apply to be released and will again remain liable until such time as he does so. A request for release can take place only when the freehold reversion is next sold.

London Diocesan Fund v Avonridge Property Company Ltd (2005), sometimes referred to as to *London Diocesan Fund v Phithwa* (2005), is a warning to tenants. Avonridge held a lease and paid rent to the landlord (L). Avonridge then granted subleases out of its own lease, making a lot of money in the process.

Q: *Why did it make a lot of money?*

A: Because Avonridge asked the sublessees for a fine (a lump sum at the start of the lease) in consideration for a lower rent paid for the remainder of the lease.

Avonridge had covenanted with the sublessees that it would pay the rent to L. Avonridge then assigned its lease to P, a man with no money, who not surprisingly disappeared and didn't pay the rent to L as Avonridge had done. The sublessees obtained relief from forfeiture of the lease. They then made a claim for damages against Avonridge because they'd had to pay the arrears of rent to avoid forfeiture of the lease and so had lost money. The sublessees also had to pay the market rent for the new tenancies they were granted as a condition of the relief from forfeiture. Given that they'd already paid a lump sum in consideration of a low rent at the start of the original lease, this had made things very expensive for them. The sublessees' claim was on the basis that Avonridge hadn't used the provisions of section 8 of the Landlord and Tenant (Covenants) Act 1995 to release itself from the covenant with the sublessees to pay rent to L. Avonridge therefore still remained liable for paying the rent to L. Avonridge defended itself by relying on a covenant in the lease which stated that it was liable on the covenants only whilst it held the lease. It was therefore not liable after assignment. The Court of Appeal held that under the anti-avoidance provisions of section 25 of the Act, Avonridge couldn't limit its liability in this way. However, the House of Lords held that the provisions for release were not intended to impose a liability when there wasn't one. The provisions for release were seen as an exit route for landlords from existing liabilities which would carry on unless they did something about ending them. There was nothing in the Act that prevented parties limiting their liability in a leasehold covenant. Here, there was no continuing liability because Avonridge had specifically covenanted that its liability would cease on assignment.

Q: *But didn't Avonridge make a large profit at the expense of the sublessees?*

A: Yes, and it was held that the transaction had the appearance of a scam. Having made its profit, Avonridge was free to assign the lease, here to P, and end its liability. This left the fate of the sublessees in the hands of any unscrupulous third party (P) who might or might not have paid rent to the landlord.

Q: *Was there any remedy for the sublessees?*

A: Sue their solicitor for negligence for allowing such a clause to go undetected.

Q: *Presumably landlords will put release clauses like this in leases because it's to their benefit?*

A: Of course, but if you were a prospective tenant, would you accept this kind of clause in a lease? Your solicitor certainly shouldn't accept it. Such a clause would not look good for the landlord when it came round to rent review either, because it would lower the rent that could be charged compared to a lease without such a clause in it. If you really had no choice other than to accept such a clause, you could retaliate by asking for a leasehold covenant that gave you some control over whom the landlord could sell the reversion to.

Box H2 | The liability of the original landlord to be sued after sale of the freehold reversion

Landlord L has sold the freehold reversion of Greenacres to L1. The question is whether L retains any liability to be sued.

The original landlord L can be sued by T on all covenants that were expressed to be personal for the duration of the 20-year lease. He can also be sued on all covenants that were not expressed to be personal if he has not been released from them by following the procedure in section 8 of the 1995 Act.

The enforceability of leasehold covenants in a sublease

Q: *What is a sublease?*

A: Look at an example where T takes a lease of Greenacres from L for 20 years. T then decides to live in America for 10 years, after which he will return to live in Greenacres. In order to keep the money coming in, T leases Greenacres to Samantha (S) for nine years. The lease to S is called a sublease. A sublease is usually represented by a vertical arrow rather than a horizontal arrow.

Q: *Why would a tenant want to create a sublease?*

A: T will effectively become the landlord of S and can charge her rent. It also means that Greenacres will be lived in and looked after. T can sublease Greenacres to S for a period which is at least one day shorter than the length of time remaining on his own lease.

Q: *Why must the period be shorter?*

A: This is because T took out the lease for a set period. At the end of that period, the lease will come to an end. T cannot give S any time that will go beyond this original period. He can give her a shorter period though, even if it's only one day shorter. If T had lived in Greenacres for five years before he went to America, the maximum amount of time the sublease could be for would be 14 years and 364 days. If T transferred the remaining 15-year term to S, this would be an outright assignment of the lease, not a sublease. A sublease must always revert to the tenant.

Q: *Is it just the original tenant who can grant a sublease?*

A: No. Any subsequent assignee of the original tenant is able to do this.

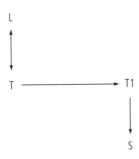

Remember, though, that the length of the sublease must be at least one day shorter than the term of the subsequent assignee.

Q: *If S has taken a sublease from T1, for example, will S enter into leasehold covenants with T1?*

A: Yes, and they are usually the same covenants that were entered into by L and T for the following reason. Imagine that in the original lease agreement T had covenanted not to use Greenacres for commercial purposes. It is in T1's interests to ensure that the same covenant is agreed between him and S. This is because if S takes the sublease and then uses Greenacres for commercial purposes, T1 can be sued by L for breach of his own leasehold covenant during the term of his lease, either because the conditions in *Spencer's Case* are met if the lease was created before 1996, or because section 3 of the Landlord and Tenant (Covenants) Act 1995 applies if the lease was created after 1 January 1996. If T1 is sued by L, he can either make sure that S does something about the breach by suing her on the same covenant agreed between them, or else he can bring the sublease to a premature end, again for breach of the covenant agreed between them. If T1 is unable to prevent S breaching the covenant, L can forfeit T1's lease altogether for breach of his own covenant. This will have the effect of automatically forfeiting the sublease.

Q: *What's the position if L wants to sue S directly for breach of a leasehold covenant contained in the original lease if the original lease was created before 1996?*

A: There was a problem if L wanted to enforce a leasehold covenant directly against S. In a lease created before 1996, either there must be privity of contract between a landlord and a tenant, or else the conditions in *Spencer's Case* must be met in order for a covenant to be enforceable against subsequent assignees of the lease. Subtenant S is not an assignee of the lease; she is only a sublessee. In a sublease there is no privity of contract between L and S, so L cannot sue S this way. L cannot sue S directly using *Spencer's Case* either. This is because there is no privity of estate between L and S because they are not in the relationship of landlord and tenant. Tenant T1 is the landlord of S, not L.

There is another way though. It comes from the law relating to freehold covenants which is covered in Chapter 14. The same rules that have developed from *Tulk v Moxhay* (1848) relating to the running of the burden of a freehold covenant in equity can be used by a head landlord, L here, to enforce a leasehold covenant against a sublessee: see *Regent Oil v J.A. Gregory* (1966). The dominant tenement in the context of leasehold covenants is the landlord's legal leasehold estate in the land. The main rule is that the covenant is restrictive or negative in nature. In unregistered land, a restrictive covenant in a lease cannot be protected as a land charge, so whether S is bound by it is determined by the doctrine of notice. This means that if the rules that have developed from *Tulk v Moxhay* (1848) have been satisfied and the lease is unregistered title, L can enforce any restrictive or negative covenants against S directly, unless S can claim that she did not know about them. Sublessee S, as an original sublessee, will always be deemed to have notice of the leasehold covenants as she is entitled to look at the original covenants entered into by L and T before she takes the sublease. In *Hemingway Securities Ltd v Dunraven Ltd* (1996) a covenant not to assign or sublet without the landlord's consent came within the rules of *Tulk v Moxhay*. If the title to the lease is registered and the rules that have developed from *Tulk v Moxhay* (1848) relating to the running of the burden of a freehold covenant in equity have been met, restrictive or negative covenants are enforceable against S under section 29(2)(b) of the Land Registration Act 2002. This alternative means is helpful to L as far as S is concerned, but only in so far as he can enforce a negative covenant. If L were to sell the freehold reversion to L1, L1 would have to prove that he had the ability to sue by meeting the relevant rules relating to the running of the benefit of a freehold covenant in equity (discussed in Chapter 14) before he could enforce a restrictive covenant directly against a sublessee.

Q: What's the position if L wants to sue S directly for breach of a leasehold covenant contained in the original lease if the original lease was created after 1995?

A: As in leases created before 1996, there is a way that L can deal with S directly. Section 3(5) of the 1995 Act states that restrictive or negative leasehold covenants in leases created after 1 January 1996 are enforceable against any occupier of the leased land. This will include a sublessee, S in our example, so L can sue S directly for breach of a restrictive or negative covenant.

There is also a possibility that L and S could use the Contracts (Rights of Third Parties) Act 1999 to enforce the benefit of a leasehold covenant. Providing the conditions in the Act were met, L could claim the benefit of a covenant entered into by T1 and S, and S the benefit of a leasehold covenant in the original lease. The Contracts (Rights of Third Parties) Act 1999 was discussed in Chapter 14.

Two questions on the enforceability of leasehold covenants

This example is intended to illustrate how to use the Boxes in this chapter to analyse the legal position. If you are using this method in undergraduate law exam questions, you will need to include statutory and case authority and detailed discussion of the various points of law. This information is found both in the text and from other sources.

Question 1

In 1990, landlord L granted tenant T a legal lease of Greenacres by deed for 50 years. T covenanted not to run Greenacres as a caravan park and to cook Christmas lunch for L and his family every year. L covenanted to insure Greenacres.

In 1993 L sold the freehold reversion by deed to L1. In 1994, L1 sold the freehold reversion by deed to L2 and in 1996 L2 sold it by deed to L3. In 1998, T assigned the lease by deed to T1, who in 2000 assigned it by deed to T2, who assigned it by deed to T3 in 2003. T3 has recently sublet Greenacres to Samantha, S, by deed.

Samantha is now running Greenacres as a caravan park. T did not cook lunch for L last Christmas. Greenacres has not been insured by L3. Advise the parties whether the covenants in the lease can be enforced against them.

This is a lease created before 1996, and so you will be looking at the pre-1996 rules found in the chart on page 456. The situation can be represented as follows.

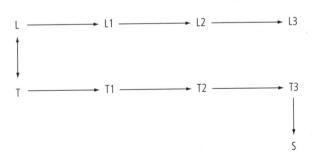

You now need to take each of the covenants separately and establish whether they can be enforced.

The covenant not to run Greenacres as a caravan park

A1 The liability of a subsequent assignee of the lease to be sued
T3 is a subsequent assignee of the lease. You are looking at whether T3 can be sued because the covenant not to run Greenacres as a caravan park has been breached. First, establish whether the burden, the liability not to run Greenacres as a caravan park, has passed to T3. *Spencer's Case* will pass the burden if the four conditions laid down in it are met. There was a legal lease between L and T. The assignments of the lease were made by deed. L3 and T3 stand in the relationship of landlord and tenant and share privity of estate in the leasehold estate of Greenacres. The covenant not to run Greenacres as a caravan park touches and concerns the land. T3 bears the liability to be sued.

A2 The liability of the original tenant to be sued after assignment of the lease
You are looking at the position of the original tenant, T. T remains liable on the leasehold covenants for the entire 50-year period because he was privy to the contract for the original lease agreement. T remains liable for breach of the covenant not to run Greenacres as a caravan park for 50 years, and this is something he should have thought of before he took a lease of Greenacres for this period. However, if sued for damages, T can claim an indemnity from T1 by using either section 77 of the Law of Property Act 1925 if the title to the lease is unregistered, or paragraph 20 of Schedule 12 to the Land Registration Act 2002 if title to the lease is registered. Alternatively, he can claim an indemnity from T3 using *Moule v Garrett* (1872). The breach need not be notified to T within the six-month period under section 17 of the Landlord and Tenant (Covenants) Act 1995 as any award of damages for breach of the covenant would not be fixed at the date of the breach. T bears the liability to be sued.

B1 The ability of a subsequent purchaser of the freehold reversion to sue
Now establish that the benefit, the ability to sue for the breach of the covenant, has passed to L3. Section 141 of the Law of Property Act 1925 attaches and passes the benefit of a leasehold covenant to L3 if the covenant has reference to the subject matter of the lease. The covenant not to run Greenacres as a caravan park relates to the land. L3 has the ability to sue.

B2 The ability of the original landlord to sue after sale of the freehold reversion
You are looking to see whether L, the original landlord, retains any ability to sue. Once L has sold the freehold reversion to L1, he can no longer sue on covenants that have reference to the subject matter of the lease. The covenant not to run Greenacres as a caravan park is one that has reference to the subject matter of the lease, and so L is unable to sue.

The position of a sublessee, Samantha
You must establish whether the burden of the covenant runs to Samantha under *Spencer's Case*. Samantha is not an assignee of the lease but a sublessee. There is no privity of estate between L3 and S because they are not in the relationship of

landlord and tenant. T3 is the landlord of S, not L3. Therefore, the condition of privity of estate as required by *Spencer's Case* has not been met, and Samantha will not be bound by the leasehold covenant. If the lease is unregistered title and the rules that have developed from *Tulk v Moxhay* (1848) can be satisfied, any restrictive or negative covenant can be enforced against S unless she can claim that she does not have notice of the covenant. A covenant not to run Greenacres as a caravan park is restrictive or negative. Samantha, as an original sublessee, will always be deemed to have notice of this covenant as she is entitled to look at the original covenants entered into by L and T before she takes the sublease. If the title to the lease is registered, assuming that the rules that have developed from *Tulk v Moxhay* (1848) have been satisfied, restrictive covenants are enforceable against S under section 29(2)(b) of the Land Registration Act 2002. In both cases Samantha bears the liability to be sued. If L3 wishes to sue her directly, he must meet the rules relating to freehold covenants concerning the running of the benefit in equity to prove that the benefit has run to him.

Conclusion relating to the covenant not to run Greenacres as a caravan park

L3 can sue T3 for damages, although it wouldn't stop the problem of the caravan park, or he could ask for an injunction or forfeit the lease for breach of the covenant not to run Greenacres as a caravan park. If T3 had entered into an identical covenant with Samantha when he granted her the sublease, T3 could sue Samantha based on privity of contract and ask for an injunction to prevent further breach of the covenant. Alternatively, T3 could forfeit her sublease for breach of the covenant. If T3 was unable to prevent Samantha's breach and Greenacres continued to be run as a caravan park, and then L3 forfeited T3's lease, this would automatically bring the sublease to an end.

A second possibility is for L3 to sue the original tenant T for damages. If T were sued, he could claim an indemnity from either T1 or T3. However, even if L3 sued T for damages, this would not solve the problem of the caravan park.

A third possibility is for L3 to sue S directly. The rules relating to freehold covenants discussed in Chapter 14 regarding the running of both the benefit and burden in equity must be satisfied. In this case, L3 can ask for an injunction, as either Samantha will be deemed to have notice of the restrictive covenant if the lease is unregistered title, or else the restrictive covenant will be enforceable against her under section 29(2)(b) of the Land Registration Act 2002 if the lease is registered title.

The covenant to insure Greenacres

C1 The ability of a subsequent assignee of the lease to sue

The question is whether the ability to sue for the breach of the obligation to insure Greenacres has passed to T3. The benefit of the covenant and the right to sue will pass to T3 if the four conditions in *Spencer's Case* are met. The lease between L and T was legal. The assignments of the lease were by deed. L3 and T3 stand in the relationship of landlord and tenant and share privity of estate in the leasehold estate of Greenacres. The covenant to insure Greenacres touches and concerns the land. T3 has the ability to sue for breach of the obligation to insure.

C2 The ability of the original tenant to sue after assignment of the lease

You are looking at the position of the original tenant, T. He retains the ability to sue on all covenants for the whole of the term based on his enduring privity of contract with L. However, as T no longer owns the lease, he has no interest in suing. Even if he did sue, his loss would be nil and so damages would be nominal.

D1 The liability of a subsequent purchaser of the freehold reversion to be sued

The question is whether L3 can be sued for not insuring Greenacres. Section 142 of the Law of Property Act 1925 attaches and passes the burden of the liability to be sued to L3 provided the covenant has reference to the subject matter of the lease. The covenant to insure Greenacres relates to the land. L3 bears the liability to be sued.

D2 The liability of the original landlord to be sued after sale of the freehold reversion

L remains liable to be sued by the original tenant for all covenants agreed in the original lease. However, as T no longer holds the lease, he would have no interest in doing so. Even if he did sue, his loss would be nil and so damages would be nominal.

The position of a sublessee, Samantha

As Samantha is only a sublessee, the ability to sue will not pass to her under *Spencer's Case* as there is no privity of estate between her and L3. However, if she entered into an identical covenant with T3 when she took the sublease, she has privity of contract with T3 and can sue him directly for failing to insure Greenacres.

Conclusion relating to the covenant to insure Greenacres

Samantha can sue T3 based on privity of contract assuming that the covenant to insure is repeated in the lease agreement between her and T3. T3 has the ability to sue L3, while L3 bears the burden of being sued. T3 can sue L3 for failing to insure Greenacres and can claim damages.

The covenant to cook Christmas lunch for L

A1 The liability of a subsequent assignee of the lease to be sued

The question is whether T3 has any liability to be sued for not cooking Christmas lunch for L and his family. The covenant is a personal one. It does not meet the touch and concern condition in *Spencer's Case*, and so the liability to be sued will not pass to T3.

A2 The liability of the original tenant to be sued after assignment of the lease

You are looking at whether the original tenant, T, retains the liability to be sued. T remains liable to be sued for all covenants in the lease for the full 50 years based on his enduring privity of contract with L.

B1 The ability of a subsequent purchaser of the freehold reversion to sue

The ability to sue for breach of the covenant will not pass to L3 under section 141 of the Law of Property Act 1925 as the covenant does not have reference to the subject matter of the lease and does not relate to the land.

B2 The ability of the original landlord to sue after sale of the freehold reversion
The original landlord, L, retains the ability to sue the original tenant on personal covenants agreed in the original lease for the duration of the 50-year lease. This is based on the enduring privity of contract between them. Landlord L retains the ability to sue as this is a personal covenant.

The position of a sublessee, Samantha
The liability to cook did not pass to Samantha under *Spencer's Case* as the covenant does not touch and concern the land. The conditions in *Spencer's Case* are not satisfied.

Conclusion relating to the covenant to cook Christmas lunch for L
Landlord L can sue T for damages for breach of the covenant to cook Christmas lunch for himself and his family.

Question 2

In 1997, landlord L granted tenant T a legal lease of Greenacres by deed for 50 years. T covenanted not to run Greenacres as a caravan park and to cook Christmas lunch for L and his family every year. L covenanted to insure Greenacres.

In 1998 L sold the freehold reversion by deed to L1. In 1999 L1 sold the freehold reversion by deed to L2, and in 2000 L2 sold the freehold reversion by deed to L3. In 2001 T assigned the lease by deed to T1, who in 2002 assigned it by deed to T2, who assigned it by deed to T3 in 2003. T3 has recently sublet Greenacres to Samantha, S, by deed.

Samantha is now running Greenacres as a caravan park. T did not cook lunch for L last Christmas. Greenacres has not been insured by L3.

Advise the parties whether the covenants in the lease can be enforced against them.

The scenario is the same as in the first question, but this time the lease was created after 1 January 1996 and so the Landlord and Tenant (Covenants) Act 1995 will be relevant. The situation is as follows.

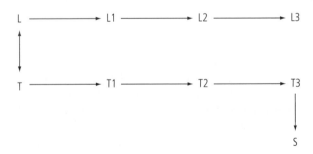

You now need to take each of the covenants separately and establish whether they can be enforced by looking at the chart on page 469.

The covenant not to run Greenacres as a caravan park

E1 The liability of a subsequent assignee of the lease to be sued
You are looking at whether T3 can be sued for breach of the covenant not to run Greenacres as a caravan park. The liability to be sued passes to T3 under section 3 of

the Landlord and Tenant (Covenants) Act 1995 as the covenant was not expressed to be personal. If T2 had entered into an AGA under section 16 of the 1995 Act with L3, T2 would also be liable to be sued. T3 bears the liability to be sued.

E2 The liability of the original tenant to be sued after assignment of the lease

You are looking at the position of the original tenant, T. Section 5 of the 1995 Act removes T's enduring liability unless the covenant was expressed to be personal or unless the assignment was an excluded one. As the covenant was not expressed to be personal, and the assignment was not an excluded one, T cannot be sued by L3. Even if T had entered into an AGA with L3 when he assigned the lease to T1, he would only have guaranteed T1's performance of the covenants and would have dropped out of the picture when the lease was assigned to T2. T bears no liability to be sued.

F1 The ability of a subsequent purchaser of the freehold reversion to sue

Now establish that the benefit, the ability to sue for breach of the covenant not to run Greenacres as a caravan park, has run to L3. As the covenant was not expressed to be personal, L3 has the ability to sue as the benefit has passed to him under section 3 of the Landlord and Tenant (Covenants) Act 1995.

F2 The ability of the original landlord to sue after sale of the freehold reversion

Under section 6 of the Act, once L has sold the freehold reversion to L1, he retains no ability to sue on covenants that are not expressed to be personal if he has been released from the covenants in accordance with the procedure in section 8. The covenant was not expressed to be personal and so, assuming L was released from the covenants, he has no ability to sue.

The position of a sublessee, Samantha

Samantha is not an assignee of the lease; she is only a sublessee. However, section 3(5) of the Landlord and Tenant (Covenants) Act 1995 allows restrictive or negative covenants to be enforced against her as an occupier of the land. As the covenant not to run Greenacres as a caravan park is a restrictive or negative covenant, it can be enforced against her.

Conclusion relating to the covenant not to run Greenacres as a caravan park

Landlord L3 has the ability to sue and has two choices here.

Landlord L3 can sue T3 for damages, although it wouldn't stop the problem of the caravan park, or he could ask for an injunction or forfeit the lease for breach of the covenant not to run Greenacres as a caravan park. If T3 entered into an identical covenant with Samantha when he granted her the sublease, T3 could sue Samantha as there is privity of contract, between them and ask for an injunction to prevent further breach of the covenant. Alternatively, T3 could forfeit the sublease for breach of the covenant. If T3 was unable to prevent Samantha's breach and Greenacres continued to be run as a caravan park, and then L3 forfeited T3's lease, this would automatically bring the sublease to an end. If there is an AGA between L3 and T2, L3 can sue T2 although this action could only be for damages which would not solve the problem of the caravan park.

The second way is for L3 to sue S directly under section 3(5) of the Landlord and Tenant (Covenants) Act 1995 as the covenant is restrictive or negative, and ask for an injunction.

The covenant to insure the premises

G1 The ability of a subsequent assignee of the lease to sue

The question is whether the ability to sue has passed to T3. T3 has the ability to sue under section 3 of the 1995 Act as the covenant was not expressed to be personal.

G2 The ability of the original tenant to sue after assignment of the lease

You are looking at the position of the original tenant, T. Under section 5, having assigned the lease, T can sue L only for covenants expressed to be personal. This is not the case here.

H1 The liability of a subsequent purchaser of the freehold reversion to be sued

The question is whether L3 can be sued. The liability to be sued has passed to L3 under section 3 of the 1995 Act as the covenant was not expressed to be personal. Section 6 of the Act allows a landlord to ask to be released from his liability on the covenants when the freehold reversion is sold by following the procedure in section 8. Thus the liability to be sued will also remain with L1 and L2 if they have not been released from the covenant by following the procedure in section 8.

H2 The liability of the original landlord to be sued after sale of the freehold reversion

The original landlord can be sued by the original tenant on covenants expressed to be personal. This is not a personal covenant. However, the original landlord is liable to be sued on all other covenants unless he has been released from them by following the procedure in section 8 of the 1995 Act. If L had not been released, he would still be liable to be sued.

The position of a sublessee, Samantha

If the covenant to insure Greenacres were repeated in the lease agreement between T3 and S, S could sue T3 based on privity of contract and ask for damages. The ability to sue L3 directly does not pass to Samantha under section 3 of the Landlord and Tenant (Covenants) Act 1995 as the section applies only when there has been an assignment of a lease. Samantha is a sublessee, not an assignee.

Conclusion relating to the covenant to insure Greenacres

Samantha can sue T3 as there is privity of contract between them, assuming that the covenant to insure is repeated in the lease agreement between her and T3. T3 can sue L3 for damages for breach of the covenant to insure Greenacres. He also has the ability to sue L2, L1 and L for damages if they have not been released from the leasehold covenants.

The covenant to cook a Christmas lunch for L

E1 The liability of a subsequent assignee of the lease to be sued

You are looking at whether T3 can be sued for breach of the covenant to cook Christmas lunch for L. The liability to be sued passes to T3 under section 3 of the Landlord and Tenant (Covenants) Act 1995 as the covenant was not expressed to be personal. If T2 had entered into an AGA with L3, T2 would also be liable to be sued.

E2 The liability of the original tenant to be sued after assignment of the lease

You are looking at the position of the original tenant, T. Section 5 of the 1995 Act removes the enduring liability of T unless the covenant was expressed to be personal or unless the assignment was an excluded assignment. As the covenant was not expressed to be personal and the assignment was not an excluded assignment, T cannot be sued by L3. Even if T had entered into an AGA under section 16 of the Act with L3 when he assigned the lease to T1, he would have guaranteed only T1's performance of the covenants and would have dropped out of the picture when the lease was assigned to T2. Tenant T bears no liability to be sued.

F1 The ability of a subsequent purchaser of the freehold reversion to sue

Now establish whether the benefit, the ability to sue for breach of the covenant to cook Christmas lunch, has run to L3. As the covenant was not expressed to be personal, L3 has the ability to sue as the benefit has passed to him under section 3 of the 1995 Act.

F2 The ability of the original landlord to sue after sale of the freehold reversion

Under section 6 of the Act, once L has sold the freehold reversion to L1, he retains no ability to sue on covenants that are not expressed to be personal if he has been released from them in accordance with the procedure in section 8. The covenant was not expressed to be personal and so, assuming L was released from the covenants, he has no ability to sue.

The position of a sublessee, Samantha

Samantha is not an assignee of the lease; she is only a sublessee. Section 3(5) of the Landlord and Tenant (Covenants) Act 1995 allows restrictive or negative covenants to be enforced against her as an occupier of the land. As the covenant to cook Christmas lunch is a positive one, it cannot be enforced against her. Tenant T3 could sue S for breach of the covenant to cook Christmas lunch only if he had entered into an identical covenant with S directly. T3's ability to sue here would be based on privity of contract.

Conclusion relating to the covenant to cook Christmas lunch for L

As the covenant was not expressed to be personal, the ability to sue and to be sued has passed to T3 and L3 under section 3 of the Landlord and Tenant (Covenants) Act 1995, should L3 choose to enforce this covenant against T3. Landlord L will have no redress against T. This is one of the dangers of the 1995 Act if parties omit to state that covenants are personal between the original landlord and the original tenant.

Further reading

S. Bridge, 'Former Tenants, Future Liabilities and the Privity of Contract Principle: the Landlord and Tenant (Covenants) Act 1995', 55 *CLJ* (1996) 313

M. Davey, 'Privity of Contract and Leases – Reform at Last', 59 *MLR* (1996) 78

T. Fancourt, 'Licences to Assign: Another Turn of the Screw?' *Conv and Prop Law*, Jan/Feb (2006) 37

P. Walter, 'The Landlord and Tenant (Covenants) Act 1995: A Legislative Folly', *Conv and Prop Law*, Nov/Dec (1996) 432

Chapter 17

Easements

www.palgrave.com/law/Stroud4e

Introduction

An easement is a right to use a person's land for the benefit of another piece of land.

For example, this could be a right granted to you to walk over Theirland, called a right of way, or your right to lay a drainage pipe over Theirland to stop Yourland flooding, as shown below.

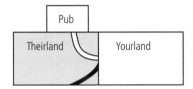

Before you can claim a valid easement, there are conditions you have to meet.

First, you have to establish that you have a right that is capable of being called an easement in the first place. Secondly, you must prove that the easement has been created in a recognised way. You may then need to look at the situation where Theirland has been sold to Peter. In this case, you will need to know whether the right that has been granted to you over Theirland is binding on Peter, or whether he can stop you using your right.

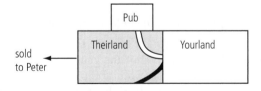

This chapter works through the conditions for the creation of an easement and the effect on a third party if the land which the easement is over is sold. In any problem scenario, draw a diagram similar to the one at the start of the chapter, label the different plots of land and draw in any rights that could be claimed as an easement. The example that will be referred to in this chapter is as follows. You own Yourland and are claiming an easement of a right of way over Theirland.

You now need to look at the chart on page 495.

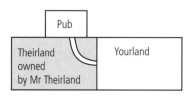

The essence of an easement

Box A

THE ESSENCE OF AN EASEMENT – RE ELLENBOROUGH PARK (1956)

Tick all boxes

☐ **1.** There must be a dominant and servient tenement

☐ **2.** The dominant and servient tenements must not be owned and occupied by the same person

☐ **3.** The right must accommodate or benefit the dominant tenement

☐ **4.** The right must be capable of forming the subject matter of a grant

☐ (i) There must be a capable grantor and a capable grantee

☐ (ii) The right must be sufficiently definite

☐ (iii) The right must be analogous to existing easements

☐ (iv) The right must not totally exclude the servient owner

Q: *What's an easement?*

A: A right over someone else's land.

Q: *What sort of rights are capable of being easements?*

A: A few common ones are a right of way: see *Borman v Griffith* (1930), where the court also asked Mr Borman to shut the gate behind him because of the sheep; a right to lay and maintain drains, sewers and pipes: see *Simmons v Midford* (1969) and *Attwood v Bovis Homes Ltd* (2001); the right to storage: see *Wright v Macadam* (1949); a right to the support of a connecting wall: see *Richards v Rose* (1853); and even the right to use a toilet: see *Miller v Emcer Products Ltd* (1956). You can also have an easement of a right to sufficient light to enable reasonable use of a building: see *Colls v Home and Colonial Stores Ltd* (1904). An easement of a right to light is not a right over another's land, but it is a right that restricts another person in the use of his land.

EASEMENTS

Box A

THE ESSENCE OF AN EASEMENT – RE ELLENBOROUGH PARK (1956)

Tick all boxes

☐ **1.** There must be a dominant and servient tenement

☐ **2.** The dominant and servient tenements must not be owned and occupied by the same person

☐ **3.** The right must accommodate or benefit the dominant tenement

☐ **4.** The right must be capable of forming the subject matter of a grant

☐ (i) There must be a capable grantor and a capable grantee

☐ (ii) The right must be sufficiently definite

☐ (iii) The right must be analogous to existing easements

☐ (iv) The right must not totally exclude the servient owner

Box B

THE CREATION OF AN EASEMENT

Application of section 1 of the Law of Property Act 1925

Tick at least one box. The type of easement that results is in brackets

The grant of an easement

☐ **1.** Express grant in a deed (legal easement)

☐ **2.** Express grant in a written contract (equitable easement)

☐ **3.** Implied grant of necessity (legal easement)

☐ **4.** Implied grant of mutual intention (legal easement)

☐ **5.** Implied grant under the rule in *Wheeldon v Burrows* (legal or equitable easement)

☐ **6.** Implied grant under section 62 of the Law of Property Act 1925 (legal easement)

☐ **7.** Prescription (legal easement)

The reservation of an easement

☐ **8.** Express reservation by deed (legal easement)

☐ **9.** Implied reservation through necessity (legal easement)

☐ **10.** Implied reservation through intention (legal easement)

Box C

THE PROTECTION OF AN EASEMENT

Look at either

Unregistered land

1. Legal easement or

2. Equitable easement

or look at

Registered land

3. Dealings which must be completed by registration

4. Interests which override a registered disposition

5. Interests entered as a notice or protected by a restriction

Q: *If there was an easement of a right of way, who would create and maintain it?*

A: This was confirmed in *Carter v Cole* (2006). The person who benefits from the right of way can go onto the land to create it. The person who granted the right of way is not under any obligation to construct it. There is no obligation on either party to maintain or repair the right of way although either party can do so if he wants. If the person with the benefit of using the right of way maintains or repairs it, he must pay the costs and is only allowed on the land to do the necessary work in a reasonable manner.

Q: *Can any sort of right over someone else's land be classed as an easement?*

A: No. It's generally only those that have been recognised by the courts before. That's not to say that the list is exhaustive, but you can't invent your own right. The reason for this is that if you're claiming a right to do something on someone else's land, you're effectively denying them the full use of their land. Any such restriction on the use of land has to be recognised by the courts.

Q: *So, if I just walk over Theirland, do I have an easement of a right of way?*

A: No. This is because you have to meet certain conditions to claim a right capable of being called an easement. These conditions were laid down in a case called *Re Ellenborough Park* (1956), which concerned a right to take air and exercise in a park. In order for a right to be capable of being an easement you have to tick all the conditions stipulated in *Re Ellenborough Park*, as follows.

Box A1 There must be a dominant and servient tenement

Q: *What's a tenement?*

A: A tenement is the old name for a piece of land in which the owner has a legal estate. The dominant tenement is the land which has the benefit of the right claimed. This is Yourland in the example we're using because Yourland benefits from the right of way. The servient tenement is the land that the right is exercised over, which has therefore to bear the brunt of that right. This is Theirland in the example.

Box A2 The dominant and servient tenements must not be owned and occupied by the same person

Q: *Why not?*

A: Because you cannot have an easement over your own land. If you own and occupy both Theirland and Yourland and walk over both each day to get to the pub, you are walking over your land because you are the owner of it. You cannot have a right against yourself: see *Roe v Siddons* (1888).

Box A3 The right must accommodate or benefit the dominant tenement

Q: *What does accommodate mean?*

A: It means that the right claimed must be of benefit to the dominant land, and not just a right that benefits the owner of the dominant land in his personal capacity. A right to lay drains across Theirland clearly benefits Yourland, in that Yourland doesn't flood when it rains. However, a right to play tennis on Theirland doesn't benefit Yourland; only you, your fitness and your personal enjoyment. It's a personal benefit only. This doesn't mean to say that a right to play tennis wouldn't be seen to accommodate the dominant land in future, but it has not been recognised yet. Another way of establishing whether a right is only a personal benefit is to ask whether the right would still be of benefit if the dominant tenement were sold to another party. If the new owner could still enjoy the right, the right could be said to benefit or accommodate the dominant tenement.

Hill v Tupper (1863) is an example of a right that was held to be of only personal benefit to the claimant. A canal owner leased land on the bank of the canal to Mr Hill and gave him the sole and exclusive right to put his pleasure boats on the canal. Mr Hill's business was to hire out the pleasure boats. Mr Tupper, who was the landlord of a neighbouring pub situated on the canal bank, then put his rival pleasure boats on the canal for hire. Mr Hill claimed that he had an easement to put his boats on the canal and that Mr Tupper should not interfere with this right. The courts held that the right did not benefit Mr Hill's land, but gave him only a personal business advantage. All he had was personal permission to put boats on the canal, which was not an easement. If Mr Hill had needed to get from one side of the canal bank to the other, he could well have claimed an easement of a right of way even though it would have been a right of way across water. In this case it would clearly have benefited the dominant land for Mr Hill to be able to cross from one side of the canal bank to the other and back again.

Q: *Could anyone have sued Mr Tupper?*

A: The canal owner could have sued in trespass. Still on the topic of boats, in *P&S Platt Ltd v Crouch* (2003) a right to use river moorings was recognised as an easement. Here the dominant land was a hotel and the use of the moorings on the servient land was part of the hotel's business and was enjoyed by its guests.

Q: *Are there other cases where an easement benefited a business?*

A: In *Moody v Steggles* (1879) placing a sign advertising a pub on the wall of the house on the servient land was capable of being an easement because the easement was connected with the business on the dominant land, which was the pub. Conversely, in *Re Webb's Lease* (1951) a sign advertising boxes of matches was held not to benefit the dominant tenement, which was a shop selling meat, groceries and provisions. Had the sign advertised the shop, rather than just the matches, an easement might have been found.

Q: *What happens if the dominant owner wants to use the easement to benefit other land that he owns, but that land wasn't identified as benefited land?*

A: This will not be permitted because you have to keep within the terms of what was agreed. The same will apply if the dominant owner buys more land and asks for the benefit of the easement to be extended to this land as well. Cases that illustrate this point are *Peacock v Custins* (2002) and *Das v Linden Mews Ltd* (2002). If the enhanced use of the easement is minor, or secondary to the primary use, this secondary use may be allowed: see *Massey v Boulden* (2002).

The condition that the right must accommodate the dominant tenement also means that the dominant and servient tenements must be sufficiently close for the dominant land to be able to claim the benefit from the right: see *Bailey v Stephens* (1862), where it was held that it was impossible for a right of way over land in Kent to benefit land in Northumberland. The dominant and servient lands do not have to be right next to each other though: see *Pugh v Savage* (1970).

Q: *What happens if the right means that the servient owner has to take positive action or to spend money to enable the dominant owner to carry out his right?*

A: If this is the case, the right will not be recognised as an easement: see *Regis Property Co Ltd v Redman* (1956). In *Duke of Westminster v Guild* (1985) a tenant had the right to use drains which ran through his landlord's land. There was no obligation on a landlord to keep drains in repair, although the tenant himself could go onto the landlord's land to clear a blocked drain. A recognised exception here is the requirement of the servient owner to maintain and repair fencing on the servient land: see *Crow v Wood* (1971).

Box A4 ## The right must be capable of forming the subject matter of a grant

This means that all easements must be capable of being granted expressly in a deed. The satisfaction of the following four requirements will meet this condition.

Box A4i ### There must be a capable grantor and a capable grantee

'Capable' means of sound mind and of full age. You are of full age when you are 18. The grantor is the person who gives you the right and the grantee is the person to whom the right is given. Think of the word *grantor* as equivalent to donor, the person who gives the permission or right, and the *grantee*, with the 'ee' on the end of the word, as the person to whom the permission is given.

If you had an express agreement with Mr Theirland, he would be the grantor of the easement of a right of way and you, as the owner of Yourland, would be the grantee. If the right of way was already there when you moved into Yourland, it's presumed somewhere along the line that previous owners of Yourland came to an agreement made in a deed with previous owners of Theirland for a right of way over Theirland. At that time there must have been two people who were legally capable of making this agreement in a deed.

Box A4ii ### The right must be sufficiently definite

You must be able to define the right you wish to claim as an easement. For example, you can define where a footpath goes or where a drain is placed. If you can't define what your right is, you won't be able to prove that someone has prevented you from using it. A right to privacy, *Browne v Flower* (1911), and a right to a view, *Aldred's Case* (1610), are not capable of definition. It's impossible to define what a view and privacy actually are, and how far they extend. Having said that, a right to a view was protected by means of a restrictive covenant in *Dennis v Davies* (2008), a case discussed on page 337. As a postscript to this section, if you can't have a right to privacy, does this mean no easement of a right to privacy in the toilet in *Miller v Emcer Products Ltd*? (see page 494).

Box Aiii   The right must be analogous to existing easements

Q: *What does 'analogous' mean?*

A: Similar to. The easement must already have been recognised in the courts or it must be similar to the one that you are claiming. A right of way is capable of being an easement, as a right of way as an easement has been recognised already by the courts: see *Borman v Griffith*. A right to play tennis on Theirland would fail. First, you could not meet the condition in Box A3 that the right must accommodate the dominant tenement and, even if you could, a right to play tennis has never been recognised as an easement.

Q: *Does this mean you can't create a new type of easement?*

A: Not necessarily. You can extend the rights recognised as easements by analogy with existing easements. As Lord St Leonards remarked in *Dyce v Lady Hay* (1852):

> The category of servitudes (obligations) and easements must alter and expand with the changes that take place in the circumstances of mankind.

If there is sufficient similarity to an existing easement, you can argue that the right you want to claim is an easement. For example what about claiming a right to keep a bicycle in a hallway as an easement? A claim to a right to store coal in a coal shed was accepted in *Wright v Macadam* and a right to park a car was recognised in *London & Blenheim Estates Ltd v Ladbroke Retail Parks Ltd* (1992). You are storing a bicycle that is a wheeled vehicle so you would have to argue that your right to store a bicycle was sufficiently similar to the right of storage and the right to park a car combined together.

Even so, the courts are reluctant to create new negative easements. A negative easement is one where the right exercised by the dominant owner prevents the servient owner from doing something on his land. This is in comparison to a positive easement which is where the dominant owner carries out a positive act over the servient owner's land, the use of a right of way for example. An example of a negative easement is a right to light where the servient owner is prevented from building on his land to protect the dominant owner's right to light. In *Phipps v Pears* (1965) the court refused to recognise the right to an easement of protection against the weather for a building when the adjoining house was demolished. If this negative easement had been recognised, the servient owner would have been prevented from having full use of his land to do what he wanted with it. The reason for refusing to extend negative easements is that they restrict the servient owner's use of his land too much. The servient owner could also have been forced to spend money on his house to keep it standing if such an easement was recognised.

Q: *A negative easement sounds very much like a restrictive covenant, doesn't it?*

A: Yes, but there are differences. An easement can be either legal or equitable, whereas the burden of a restrictive covenant can only ever be equitable. An easement can be acquired by long use but a restrictive covenant cannot be acquired by such means.

Box A4iv   The right must not totally exclude the servient owner

This means you must ensure that the right does not prevent the servient owner from using his land altogether. Exclusive possession of premises is more indicative of an estate in land. An easement is only a right over the land, not possession of it. Such exclusive possession could also form the basis for a claim in adverse possession. In the example of the bicycle and the hallway, you might run into difficulties if the hallway was very small and the bicycle was very large, so you prevented the servient owner from using the hallway at all. Cases that illustrate this point are *Wright v Macadam, Copeland v Greenhalf* (1952) and *Grigsby v Melville* (1974). In *Wright v Macadam* an easement to store coal in a coal shed was recognised although it could have excluded the servient owner's use completely. The facts were not clear on this and the decision seems to have been taken on the basis that the court felt sorry for Mrs Wright who wanted to store coal and not sorry for Mr Macadam who had already removed the shed following the decision in the County Court where the claim had been dismissed. In *Copeland v Greenhalf* leaving vehicles on a narrow strip of land amounted to claiming the whole beneficial use of the strip, and so could not amount to an easement. If anything, it was adverse possession. Claiming the whole use of someone else's land and preventing him from being able to use it is known as the 'ouster principle' and is a phrase you will come across in the cases.

Q: Why wasn't an easement recognised in Copeland v Greenhalf when you can argue that the right of storage in Wright v Macadam could just as easily have excluded the servient owner's use completely?

A: Because *Wright v Macadam* was not cited in *Copeland v Greenhalf*. In *Grigsby v Melville* the easement of a right to storage in a confined space wasn't recognised for different reasons but Mr Justice Brightman said whether there was exclusive use or not was a question of degree. He also said that had there been an easement, it would have amounted to exclusive use and he would have felt able to follow *Copeland v Greenhalf*. An attempt to reconcile *Wright v Macadam* with *Copeland v Greenhalf* was made by Paul Baker QC in *London & Blenheim Estates Ltd v Ladbroke Retail Parks Ltd* where he stated that whether the use amounted to exclusive use or not depended on the size of the servient tenement:

> A small coal shed in a large property is one thing. The exclusive use of a large part of the alleged servient tenement is another.

The test used here is whether the right granted would leave the servient owner without any reasonable use of his land. If so, it wouldn't be an easement.

The courts seem to spend an inordinate amount of time discussing the easement of car parking in this context. In *Newman v Jones* (unreported) (1982) a right to park a car anywhere in a defined area such as a car park was recognised. In *London & Blenheim Estates Ltd v Ladbroke Retail Parks Ltd* it was possible to claim the right to park a car as an easement provided the servient owner would still have reasonable use of his land. In *Batchelor v Marlow* (2001) the Court of Appeal followed *London & Blenheim Estates Ltd v Ladbroke Retail Parks Ltd*. The claimant wanted to park up to six cars between 8.30 am and 6.00 pm on the defendant's land. It was held that the right could not be an easement as the defendant would have no reasonable use of his land. *Moncrieff v Jamieson* (2007) is a Scottish case and it concerned an ancillary (incidental) right to park arising from a right of way so it was not a case where the claim to park was in one particular parking space. However, it was heard by the House of Lords and was therefore likely to be followed in England and Wales. Mr Moncrieff had a right of access by car to his house over Mr Jamieson's land but he had also parked his car in a turning circle at the end of this access road, again on Mr Jamieson's land, because there was nowhere to park on his own property. There was no other vehicular access to Mr Moncrieff's house. When the parties fell out, Mr Jamieson denied him the right to park in the turning circle (by unhelpfully constructing a wall), which meant that Mr Moncrieff would have had to park his car on the public highway, some considerable distance away, and walk down the access road to his house. It was held that an incidental right (to park) would be implied if it was reasonably necessary for the enjoyment of the main right (the right of access). In the circumstances of the case it was reasonably necessary for Mr Moncrieff to be able to park to enjoy his right of access. (In comparison, in *Waterman v Boyle* (2009) the fact that the incidental right to park was desirable did not make it reasonably necessary and *Moncrieff v Jamieson* was distinguished on its facts.) So, although different opinions were given in the case, the House of Lords paved the way for the recognition of a free standing easement of a right to park a car. This was on the basis that it wasn't so much whether the servient owner had reasonable use of his land but whether he kept possession and control of the land.

In *Moncrieff v Jamieson* Lord Scott put forward some criticisms of the reasoning behind the decisions of the English courts. Although his views were obiter, here are some of them. See if you agree.

▶ It didn't matter whether the dominant owner in *Wright v Macadam* was allowed to use the coal shed specifically and only to store coal because the servient owner could still have used the shed for other purposes provided those purposes didn't interfere with the storage of the coal. This was not the same as exclusive possession and the servient owner still had possession and control of the land.

Q: *In what way could you have used the coal shed if you were the servient owner?*

A: Arguably very little.

▶ Paul Baker QC's test in *London & Blenheim Estates Ltd v Ladbroke Retail Parks Ltd* was incorrect. Whether a right excludes the servient owner from his land doesn't depend on how much other land the servient owner owns. The servient land is the land over which the right is exercised, not the rest of the servient owner's other land which could be small or large.

Q: *But that could mean a very small piece of servient land for a right of way or drain, couldn't it?*

A: Yes, but it is still a matter of degree.

▶ The 'no reasonable use' test was wrong. What is reasonable is hard to define. Even if a car is parked in one space, for example, you could put advertising hoardings on the wall of the parking area. This lack of definition wasn't the issue though. The test itself was wrong. The test should be whether the servient owner retains possession and, subject to the reasonable exercise of the right, control of the servient land. On that basis the decision in *Batchelor v Marlow* was doubtful because the servient owner still had control and possession of his land.

Q: *Again, though, how do you define possession and control?*

A: That's a difficult question to answer.

What is important from *Moncrieff v Jamieson* is that the House of Lords paved the way for the recognition of a free standing easement of a right to park a car. It wasn't so much whether the servient owner had reasonable use of his land but whether he kept possession and control of the land. *Virdi v Chana* (2008), a case concerning a right to park a car in one space, was decided using *Batchelor v Marlow*. This was because the House of Lords in *Moncrieff v Jamieson* had not overruled *Batchelor v Marlow*. An easement was recognised because the servient owner still had reasonable use of the land that the car was parked on. The servient owner could still put up a fence, gravel the area, plant shrubs, erect signs, place decorative flower pots on the land, alter the surface or put a bicycle there provided this didn't obstruct the right to park.

Kettel v Bloomfold (2012) is a recent case where a developer landlord wanted to build over parking spaces designated to his tenants. Having established that the parking spaces were not included within the lease, the question was whether each tenant had an easement of a right to park a car in his designated space.

Q: *Presumably if the parking space had been included in the lease, the tenant would have had exclusive possession and the landlord could not have used the space at all, whereas if there was an easement of a right to park only, the landlord could still theoretically use the land?*

A: Yes. This difference is an important one. The court held that *Batchelor v Marlow* had not been overruled. A right to park a car could be an easement. The test still was whether the servient owner was left with any 'reasonable use' to which he could put his land whether for parking or anything else. Here, whilst the servient owner clearly couldn't park a car when the dominant owner had his car parked, the servient owner could do the following. He could pass by foot or vehicle over the space when there wasn't a car there; he could allow others to do the same; he could choose, change and repair the surface, clean it and remove obstructions. He could lay pipes, build above or put up overhead wires. These rights were not illusory and were important and even necessary. He still had reasonable use of the land and the claim of the tenants to an easement would be recognised.

And one more case on the car parking theme … in *Montrose Court Holdings Ltd v Shamash* (2006) the claimant had imposed parking regulations on the defendants, who claimed that having to pay for a parking permit, being limited to parking one car and being able to park for only 72 hours at a time was an unlawful interference with the easement to park cars. It was held that the restrictions did not reduce the right to compete for a car parking space (117 places for 100 households, some with more than one car) but simply ensured that everyone who had the right to park had an opportunity to compete to do so.

In June 2011 the Law Commission published its report 'Making Land Work: Easements, Covenants and Profits à Prendre' (2011) Law Com No 327, in which it recommended that whilst an easement should not grant exclusive possession, the ouster principle should be abolished thereby reversing *Copeland v Greenhalf*. An easement would be recognised even if it deprived the owner of much or of all reasonable use of his land. This would reverse *Batchelor v Marlow* and easements that gave an exclusive right to park a car would be recognised provided the servient owner could access his land, however limited that access was. This recommendation appears in Clause 24 of the draft Bill.

Q: *Do arguments arise over the wording when easements are granted?*

A: Yes. In *Brooks v Young* (2008) a grant allowing the dominant owners to exercise 'a right of way at all times ... for all proper purposes connected with the reasonable enjoyment of the property' allowed the dominant owner unlimited access provided the purpose was not improper, i.e. illegal or immoral. The words of the grant were to be given their natural meaning and the court would not take into account the opinion of the parties as to what they thought the words meant. Any claimed restriction on the use of the right of way could, and should, have been clearly stated in the grant. In *Risegold Ltd v Escala Ltd* (2008) the words restricting the easement of access to 'renewal and rebuilding' on the land included redevelopment of the land. Taking everything into account, the probable intention of the parties when the easement was granted and the need for flexibility meant that the words could be given a wider meaning than when used in planning law.

In *Davill v Pull* (2009) the words in the grant of easements of rights of way 'for all reasonable and usual purposes' were looked at. When the easements had been created in 1919 and 1920 the plots of land to be benefited had been described as 'garden ground'. The current owner of three of the benefited plots of land wanted to build a house on each and use the right of way for access. The court held that the right of way was not limited to the reasonable and usual use of the land at the time in 1920 which was as 'garden ground'. If the benefited land was built on, the right of way could be used as access because building and living in a dwelling house was a reasonable and usual use of the land. Again, the language of the grant and context was everything. If the parties had intended that the right of way could only ever be used in connection with the use of the dominant plot as garden land, the drafting of the document should have reflected that intention. It is interesting to note the view of Lord Justice Rimer on the use of the land belonging to those who were objecting to the use as a right of access:

> As the other plots are all used for stabling horses, also not a use as 'garden ground', the respondents' attitude might (if I may borrow from Russell LJ, as he then was) perhaps appear to be 'somewhat curmudgeonly' (*Keefe v Amor* [1965] 1 QB 334, at 343G/344A). But, as in that case, we are here concerned with rights, not attitudes.

'Curmudgeonly' means short tempered or grouchy.

In *Greatorex v Newman* (2008), though, the grant restricted a right of access to use 'as now used'. 'Now' was 1921 and access was by tradesmen, not customers. The right did not extend to the customers of a pub in the 'now' of 2008. In *Dewan v Lewis* (2010) a right of way by foot or by horse did not impliedly include the right to drive cattle and in *Alford v Hannaford* (2011) a right of way 'at all times and for all purposes with or without vehicles' did not extend to driving animals along a track.

Q: *What happens if you acquire an easement for a right of way by foot, and then you want to increase the use or change the use? You might want to drive a car over the right of way rather than go on foot, for example.*

A: If there's too much of a burden on the servient land, you won't be allowed to do so. In *Jelbert v Davis* (1968) the claimant used a right of way over a driveway to gain access to the highway from his agricultural land. He then got planning permission to turn the agricultural land into a caravan site for up to 200 caravans which would have to use the right of way. It was held that although the terms of the grant would allow the claimant to use the driveway for a different purpose, here the caravan site, he couldn't use it over and beyond what was contemplated at the time of the grant and so interfere unreasonably with the enjoyment of other people using the driveway. The proposed use was deemed to be excessive. The issue in *McAdams Homes Ltd v Robinson* (2004) was whether an easement of a right to drainage from the dominant land when the dominant land was used as a bakery could still be claimed when the bakery had been demolished and two residential houses had been built instead. Lord Justice Neuberger held that there were two tests:

(i) whether the development of the dominant land was a 'radical change in the character' or a 'change in identity' of the site as opposed to a mere change or intensification in the use of the site
(ii) whether the use of the site as redeveloped would result in a substantial increase or alteration in the burden on the servient land.

When both these tests are met, the use is deemed excessive and the dominant owner will no longer be able to use the easement while the tests are met. In the case the change from one building to two, and from an industrial use to residential use, satisfied the first test. The increased flow of water from the houses had substantially increased the burden on the servient land, and so the second test was satisfied. The right of drainage could no longer be claimed as an easement to benefit the houses.

Q: *It must be a very subjective decision here as to what radical and substantial mean?*

A: It is, and it was held that each case would turn on its facts. It was also admitted that different judges may still come to differing conclusions. No consistency there then.

In the case of *Thompson v Bee* (2009) a right of way expressed to be for 'at all times and for all purposes connected with the said Garth' (the dominant land) was to be interpreted literally and was not restricted to the agricultural use that it was used for at the time the easement was created. However, its proposed use as access for a new development of three houses on the dominant land was excessive. The reference to 'all purposes' did not allow usage which would interfere unreasonably with the servient owner's use of the track and the use of their property.

The effect of not meeting the conditions for the essence of an easement

Q: *What's the effect of not meeting all the conditions stipulated in* **Re Ellenborough Park***?*

A: You do not have a right that is capable of being an easement. You do not need to go on and look at how an easement is created, or the effect of an easement on a third party, because, quite simply, it will never be an easement.

Q: *What right do I have then?*

A: You have a licence to be on the land. A licence is permission. When the postman brings your post up the front drive you are taken to have given him permission, or a licence, to do so. If you didn't give this permission, he is a trespasser. Licences can be bare or contractual. A bare licence is when permission is given and there is no consideration or payment between the parties. A contractual licence arises when there is consideration, usually monetary payment, between the parties. Licences are discussed in Chapter 13.

Summary of the essence of an easement

A right can be claimed as an easement only if all the requirements in *Re Ellenborough Park* are met. If they are not all met, the claimant will have only a licence. A licence can be bare (no payment) or contractual (payment).

However, you can't yet say you've acquired an easement even if you have met all the conditions in Box A, because you have to look at how it was created. This means ticking a few more boxes in Box B. Easements can be created by more than one means. You need to prove that you have met only one of them.

The creation of an easement

Box B

THE CREATION OF AN EASEMENT

Application of section 1 of the Law of Property Act 1925

Tick at least one box. The type of easement that results is in brackets

The grant of an easement

- ☐ **1.** Express grant in a deed (legal easement)
- ☐ **2.** Express grant in a written contract (equitable easement)
- ☐ **3.** Implied grant of necessity (legal easement)
- ☐ **4.** Implied grant of mutual intention (legal easement)
- ☐ **5.** Implied grant under the rule in *Wheeldon v Burrows* (legal or equitable easement)
- ☐ **6.** Implied grant under section 62 of the Law of Property Act 1925 (legal easement)
- ☐ **7.** Prescription (legal easement)

The reservation of an easement

- ☐ **8.** Express reservation by deed (legal easement)
- ☐ **9.** Implied reservation through necessity (legal easement)
- ☐ **10.** Implied reservation through intention (legal easement)

Section 1 of the Law of Property Act 1925 must be considered before we look at the creation of an easement.

Application of section 1 of the Law of Property Act 1925

Section 1(2) of the Law of Property Act 1925 defines the interests in land that are capable of being legal. Section 1(2)(a) applies to the creation of easements in both unregistered and registered land. An easement that is granted for a period of time *equivalent to* a fee simple absolute in possession or a term of years absolute is capable of being a legal easement. *Equivalent to* in section 1(2)(a) means equivalent in terms of time. A fee simple absolute in possession is ownership as we know it and effectively goes on forever. A term of years absolute is otherwise known as a lease which has a set period of time to run. The length of time an easement is granted for must be *equivalent to* either of these terms and therefore must be granted indefinitely or for a set period of time to be capable of being legal. So if Mr Theirland grants you an easement of a right of way over Theirland without putting any time limit on it, it is capable of being a legal easement. The right is not yet recognised as a legal easement as it has not been created in a recognised way. It merely has the capability of being legal. Similarly, if the right of way is granted for a set period, 10 years for example, again it has the capability of being legal for its duration of 10 years. After the 10-year period, the right of way will end. Now imagine Mr Theirland grants you an easement of a right of way over Theirland for your lifetime. Your lifetime is not for ever, and so the time the easement is granted for is *not equivalent to* a fee simple absolute in possession. Your lifetime is not a set period so the time the easement is granted for is *not equivalent to* a term of years either. The easement, however created, is never capable of being legal. It has only the capability of being equitable. Even if the easement is capable of being legal it must then meet the requirements in section 52(1) of the Law of Property Act 1925, which states that you must use a deed in order to create a legal interest in land. If you want to create a legal easement you must first satisfy section 1(2)(a) of the Law of Property Act 1925 and, secondly, the right must be created in a deed.

Q: *So if Mr Theirland grants me an easement to walk over Theirland for my lifetime, this can never result in a legal easement, even if it has been created by a deed, because it doesn't satisfy section 1(2)(a) of the Law of Property Act 1925?*

A: Correct. You really just need to watch out for easements granted for life. If nothing is said on the matter, you can assume that the easement has been granted for ever and so is capable of being legal provided it has been created in a deed.

Q: *Are many people granted easements for life?*

A: Only in the eyes of examiners of land law.

First establish whether you can meet the requirements for the creation of an easement as described below, and then apply section 1(2)(a).

| Box B1 | Express grant in a deed (legal easement) |

Q: *What's an express grant by deed?*

A: An agreement made knowingly and deliberately between two people in a deed. A deed is not something you create accidentally and the requirements for a valid deed are found in section 1 of the Law of Property (Miscellaneous Provisions) Act 1989. In essence the deed must be:

▷ in writing

and

▷ clear on the face of it that it is intended to be a deed

and

▷ signed by the person making the deed in the presence of a witness who attests his signature

and

▷ delivered as a deed.

The witnessing of a deed is called attestation and the witness must sign and date the deed. You do not have to deliver a deed physically. It's sufficient that the person granting the interest in the deed makes it clear that he intends to be bound by it. This is usually inferred from the fact that he signs it.

If Mr Theirland expressly grants you a right of way over his land in a deed, a legal easement will be created.

Box B2 Express grant in a written contract (equitable easement)

You can also create an easement in a written contract which does not satisfy the requirements for a deed.

The requirements for a valid written contract for the creation of an interest in land are found in section 2 of the Law of Property (Miscellaneous Provisions) Act 1989. The contract must be:

▷ in writing

and

▷ signed by or on behalf of both parties to the contract

and

▷ must contain all the express terms of the agreement.

A contract that does not meet these requirements is void, which means it is as though it never existed.

If you agree with Mr Theirland that you can use the track over Theirland in a written agreement, and the written agreement satisfies section 2 of the Law of Property (Miscellaneous Provisions) Act 1989, you will have an equitable easement. It cannot be legal because it has not been created by a deed. Remember that contracts for the creation of an interest in land will create an equitable interest, here an equitable easement, because they are capable of specific performance, and because equity views that as done which ought to be done.

Box B3 Implied grant of necessity (legal easement)

Q: *What's an implied grant of necessity?*

A: Imagine a different example where Mr Theirland had owned both Theirland and Yourland as a whole plot and had then sold that part of it called Yourland to you. If Mr Theirland still owned all the land surrounding Yourland, you would have had difficulty getting to Yourland without trespassing on Theirland.

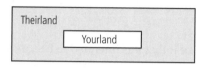

In this situation the courts will *imply* an easement of necessity of a right of way into the conveyance, which is the deed of sale between you and Mr Theirland. Although the easement of a right of way was not spelt out in the deed, either because it was not considered necessary or because it was too obvious, the court will still imply the right into the terms of the deed. Because the easement is implied into a deed, it acquires legal status. At the risk of repetition here, when Yourland was sold to you, this would have been in a conveyance by deed. The court will imply an easement of necessity of a right of way into that deed. If the court didn't do so, Yourland would be what is called landlocked land.

Q: *How do you define necessity if you are trying to claim an easement of necessity?*

A: Necessity means absolute necessity: see *Titchmarsh v Royston Water Co Ltd* (1899). In *Menzies v Breadalbane* (1901) there was an alternative route which prevented the creation of an easement of necessity. In *Nickerson v Barraclough* (1981) Lord Justice Brightman in the Court of Appeal stated that easements of necessity would not be created simply because it was public policy that land should not be landlocked. You had to look at all the circumstances of the case and decide whether an easement was actually implied between the parties but hadn't been spelt out in the deed of sale. If you weren't able to do this, or the right was expressly excluded in the deed of sale, an easement of necessity would not be created.

Q: *Does there always have to be a deed to claim an easement of necessity?*

A: Yes. Be careful here. A conveyance in the form of a deed is the means by which land is sold. Any easement of necessity is implied into this deed. This means that you must always be able to find a deed between the party claiming the easement and the party over whose land the right is exercised. If there is no deed between the parties, you cannot imply an easement of necessity because there is nothing to imply it into. You cannot imply an easement into thin air. In the example at the start of Box B3, Mr Theirland would have sold Yourland to you by a conveyance, a deed of sale. Any easement of necessity is implied into this deed of sale and will therefore be legal. Now look at an example where there is no deed and therefore no implied easement of necessity. In this example you purchased Yourland and Hayfield from Joe three years ago. Just consider the position between you and Mr Theirland.

Mr Theirland has allowed you to drive your tractors along a track which crosses his land to obtain access to Hayfield. Last month you had an argument with Mr Theirland and he has told you never to drive your tractors across his land again. This means that you cannot access Hayfield and it becomes landlocked. You cannot claim an easement of necessity, however necessary it is. This is because there has never been a conveyance, a deed of sale, between you and Mr Theirland into which you can imply an easement because you didn't buy Hayfield from him.

Q: *Won't that make Hayfield unusable?*

A: Yes. You could try using the Access to Neighbouring Land Act 1992. This is where the court can give you a temporary 'one-off' right to go on to someone else's land to carry out work on your own land. However, the right is limited to carrying out basic preservation works like tree clearing and repairing drains, so it won't really help you here.

Q: *Is there any way an easement of necessity could have been created in this example between me and Mr Theirland?*

A: Imagine Mr Theirland owned Theirland and Yourland together as one plot. He then sold that part of the plot called Yourland and that part of the plot called Hayfield to you. There was no access to Hayfield at all other than over Theirland. The sale would be made by deed and you could imply an easement of necessity into this deed.

Q: *Do easements of necessity always concern landlocked land?*

A: No. *Wong v Beaumont Property Trust Ltd* (1965) is a good illustration here. Mr Wong bought the remaining time running on the lease of a property which was designated to be a restaurant. When he bought the lease, he had agreed in the conveyance, the document of sale made by deed, that no noxious smells would be emitted from the restaurant and that he would comply with any necessary health and safety regulations. Although the parties didn't know it at the time of the sale, Mr Wong could satisfy the terms he had agreed to only by building a ventilation duct. The ventilation duct would go through the upstairs premises, which were still owned by Beaumont Property Trust. The courts implied an easement of necessity into the deed of sale. A ventilation duct was necessary for the premises to be run as a restaurant in accordance with the terms of the lease and the claimant was entitled to an easement of necessity.

Box B4 ## Implied grant of mutual intention (legal easement)

This is when the courts give effect to what they think the intention was between the parties when land is sold. The easement of mutual intention is again implied into the conveyance, the deed of sale. The courts are giving effect to terms that they think the parties would have put in had they thought about it a bit more. Sometimes things seem so obvious between the parties that no one thinks to mention things specifically. There are problems afterwards when one of the parties wants to carry out 'the obvious' and the other party refuses to co-operate. Because the easement is implied into a deed, it acquires legal status. An example of an easement by mutual intention is *Stafford v Lee* (1993) and, more recently, *Davies v*

Bramwell (2007). In *Davies v Bramwell*, the common intention of the parties was that servicing and repair of cars would take place in the garage on the land that had been conveyed. This included using a ramp in the garage to do so. To use the ramp safely, vehicles would have to be driven across the land which had been retained by the vendor, called the blue land. The common intention of the parties had been that the land would be used as a garage, which included the use of a ramp. To give effect to that common intention, a right of way over the blue land had been granted by implication. *Wong v Beaumont Property Trust Ltd* could also have been decided on the basis of an easement of mutual intention. In *J & O Operations Ltd v Kingston & Saint Andrew Corp (Privy Council) (Jamaica)* (2012) the local authority had created a public right of way. This meant there was no mutual intention of a private right of way rather than, or in addition to, the public right between the authority and the claimants. The public right of way also excluded a claim to an easement of necessity as the appellants were entitled as members of the public to use the existing right.

Q: *In the example concerning Hayfield in Box B3, could I claim an easement by mutual intention to reach Hayfield?*

A: No, because you still don't have a deed. An easement of mutual intention has to be implied into a deed. There was no conveyance, deed of sale, between you and Mr Theirland as he didn't sell the land to you.

Q: *So if there is no deed between the person claiming the easement and the person whose land the right is over, there can be no implied easement of mutual intention?*

A: Correct.

Q: *Can there be overlap between an easement of necessity and an easement of intention?*

A: Yes, because if the right was necessary for the use of land, the parties would generally have intended it.

Box B5   **Implied grant under the rule in Wheeldon v Burrows (legal or equitable easement)**

Now imagine that Mr Theirland owns Theirland in its entirety and that Yourland doesn't even begin to exist. There is a track that runs across Theirland from The Lane to the house.

Mr Theirland is starting to run out of money. He decides to sell a part of Theirland to raise some money, but to keep the remaining part of the land as an investment and perhaps build on it in the future. You purchase the part he is selling and call it Yourland.

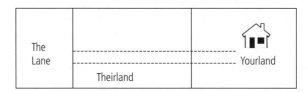

You would expect to be able to use the track to reach Yourland from The Lane. However, there was no easement of a right of way in existence before you bought Yourland because Mr Theirland owned the entire plot. He cannot have an easement over his own land. You cannot claim an implied easement of necessity as there is no indication that Yourland is landlocked. There is unlikely to be an implied easement of mutual intention because there is no reason why Mr Theirland should want you to cross the part of the land he has retained.

Q: *Couldn't you argue that it was obvious that the track would be used to reach Yourland?*

A: Yes. The right to use the track is called a quasi-easement. It's a 'sort of' easement, which literally translates from the Latin as an 'as if' easement. This simply means that when Mr Theirland owns the whole plot, he is using a right that would be capable of being an easement if the part of the land that benefited by the right, the dominant land, was sold off. The right tends to relate to something the owner habitually did, using a track for example to obtain access. It's not an easement in its true sense because Mr Theirland owns all the land and he cannot have a right against himself. It's only an easement in the sense that it could become one if the benefited land, the dominant land, were sold, in which case it would become a full-blown easement. The rules for determining this type of easement came from a case called *Wheeldon v Burrows* (1879).

Q: *Are there any conditions you must meet to be able to use the rule in* **Wheeldon v Burrows?**

A: Yes.

The right must be

(i) Continuous and apparent

　　and

(ii) Necessary to the reasonable enjoyment of the land sold

　　and

(iii) In use both previously and at the time of the sale for the benefit of the part of the land sold.

Continuous means that the right must be used on a regular basis. Apparent means that it must be visible. The right needs only to be necessary for the reasonable enjoyment of the land sold. This is unlike an implied easement of necessity where the right must be strictly necessary for the use of the land. There is some discussion whether conditions (i) and (ii) are alternative or whether both must be met but a right is unlikely to be used on a regular basis if it isn't also necessary to the reasonable enjoyment of the land. In *Wheeler v JJ Saunders Ltd* (1996) there were two ways of access to the house. It was held that the south entrance was not necessary for the reasonable enjoyment of the house because the east entrance would 'do just as well'. This was particularly so as the gate to the south entrance was usually shut and probably used only rarely. A right of way would not be implied through the south entrance.

Q: *So in our example here Mr Theirland must have been using the track regularly, the track must have been visible and reasonably necessary to the enjoyment of Yourland?*

A: Yes. The reason for allowing a quasi-easement to become an easement in its own right is as follows. If Mr Theirland sells you a plot of land which clearly benefits from a visible and regularly used right over the land he keeps, he is not allowed to deny you that right when he sells the benefited land to you. This is called non-derogation from grant, which means that Mr Theirland is not allowed to sell land to you that clearly benefits from a right, on one hand, then deny that right on the other.

Q: *How do you know whether a legal or an equitable easement has been created here?*

A: When the benefited land, the dominant land, is sold, the easement is implied into the conveyance, the deed of sale. It will acquire its legal status because it is implied into the deed. An easement can also be created under the rule in *Wheeldon v Burrows* if there is a written contract between the parties for the sale of the benefited land. Provided this contract satisfies section 2 of the Law of Property (Miscellaneous Provisions) Act 1989, an easement will be implied into the written contract, and it will be an equitable easement.

Q: *So you must have a deed or a written contract between the person who bought the benefited land, the dominant land, and the person who kept the remaining part of the land which the right is exercised over?*

A: Yes. An easement can also be created using *Wheeldon v Burrows* on the grant of a legal or equitable lease in the same circumstances: see *Borman v Griffith*.

Box B6 Implied grant under section 62 of the Law of Property Act 1925 (legal easement)

Section 62 lists the benefits that pass in a conveyance of land without being explicitly included. For the purposes of section 62, a conveyance is defined as a sale or lease of land. The benefits that pass include buildings, fences, hedges and existing easements. When a buyer purchases land, all the buildings, fences, hedges and existing easements on the land will be included in the conveyance. This means that if you own Yourland and have an easement of a right of way over Theirland, if you sell Yourland to Peter, he will be able to carry on using the right of way, as section 62 transfers the benefit of the easement to him unless there are contrary words. Section 62 also states that *rights, privileges and advantages* pass with the conveyance, which is what you need to know about in the context of creating easements.

A right, privilege (permission) or advantage will be converted into an easement (a proprietary right) under section 62 of the Law of Property Act 1925 if the following conditions are met:

- Section 62 must not be expressly excluded; and
- The right that is being claimed must be capable of being an easement by meeting the conditions stated in *Re Ellenborough Park*; and
- The dominant and servient tenements are owned by one person but there is separate occupation of the dominant and servient tenements; and
- The owner of the servient tenement uses a deed to sell or transfer the dominant tenement to the occupier; or
- The owner of the servient tenement uses a deed to grant or renew a lease of the dominant tenement to the occupier; or
- The owner of the servient tenement uses a written agreement to grant or renew a lease of the dominant tenement for three years or less to the occupier.

The effect is to convert any right, privilege or advantage enjoyed by the occupier of the dominant tenement before the sale or the lease into a legal easement.

It's easier to explain the operation of section 62 using an example.
This is Theirland.

Mr Theirland needed some more money and decided to rent out a part of Theirland. You took a four-year lease of that part of the land and called it Yourland. Soon after you moved in, Mr Theirland gave you verbal permission to use the track across Theirland to get to the pub. He also allowed you to play tennis on his newly refurbished tennis courts.

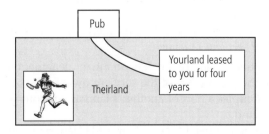

Everyone was very happy with the arrangement; so much so that, after two years, Mr Theirland agreed that you could purchase the freehold of Yourland. Yourland was conveyed to you by deed of sale. Section 62 states that a conveyance of land will include all the privileges and advantages that were enjoyed with the land at the time of the sale. At that time, you enjoyed the privilege of using the track across Theirland and playing tennis on it. Section 62 will have included these privileges in the conveyance when Yourland was sold to you. As the conveyance was by deed of sale, these privileges are included in the deed. The effect of including them in the deed is to give them legal status and to turn them into legal easements, with one proviso. The privilege must be capable of being an easement and must therefore satisfy the conditions in *Re Ellenborough Park*. This means that a privilege to play tennis can never become an easement under section 62. A right to play tennis does not benefit the dominant tenement and cannot satisfy Box A3. A right of way, however, is capable of being an easement. The privilege of using the track across Theirland will be included in the conveyance, the deed of sale, and will become a legal easement of a right of way.

Q: *Would Mr Theirland have necessarily intended this to happen?*

A: No. He should have withdrawn the permission before selling the land to you. The operation of section 62 can also be expressly excluded from the conveyance, but this does not always happen. A good reason for Mr Theirland to sue his solicitor.

Let's look at the conditions again.

Section 62 must not be expressly excluded
Section 62 should be expressly excluded to avoid the operation of this section. The alternative is to ensure that any privilege is withdrawn before dealing with the land.

The right that is being claimed must be capable of being an easement by meeting the conditions stated in Re Ellenborough Park (1956)

Q: *Is every right or privilege converted into an easement under section 62?*

A: No. Only those that are capable of being easements in the first place, which means that the right must meet the conditions in *Re Ellenborough Park*. The privilege of playing tennis in the example we've been using would not meet the conditions in Box A3, so you wouldn't even be discussing it here.

The dominant and servient tenements are owned by one person but there is separate occupation of the dominant and servient tenements

Q: *When would you find a situation where there is separate occupation of the dominant and servient tenements?*

A: This situation arises when the dominant tenement is occupied by another person with the permission of the servient owner. The obvious situation is where one person occupies a part of another's land as a favour or under a lease, as in the lease of Yourland.

Not everyone is agreed that there must be separate occupation of the dominant and servient tenements. There is an argument that section 62 will also operate when there is no diversity of occupation. Cases that look at this argument include *Broomfield v Williams* (1897), *Long v Gowlett* (1923), *Sovmots Investments Ltd v*

Secretary of State for the Environment (1979), *Payne v Inwood* (1997) and *P&S Platt Ltd v Crouch* and they are discussed at the end of this chapter.

The owner of the servient tenement uses a deed to sell or transfer the dominant tenement to the occupier
In the example we've been using, Yourland, the dominant tenement enjoying a privilege, was sold by deed to you, the person occupying Yourland under the lease.

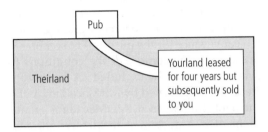

The privilege of walking over Theirland was included in the conveyance, the deed of sale, and a legal easement of a right of way was created.

Section 62 would have also operated if you had been living on Yourland with the permission of Mr Theirland where the permission didn't amount to a lease. If you had used the track and Mr Theirland had then sold Yourland to you, a legal easement would have again been created under section 62 in your favour.

Or the owner of the servient tenement uses a deed to grant or renew a lease of the dominant tenement to the occupier. Or the owner of the servient tenement uses a written agreement to grant or renew a lease of the dominant tenement for three years or less to the occupier.

Q: *In these last conditions, why is only a lease by deed or a lease for three years or less in a written agreement included in the ambit of section 62?*

A: This is because section 62 talks about the conveyance of a legal estate. A conveyance here, following the reasoning in *Rye v Rye* (1962), means there has to be a document. A legal estate includes a legal lease. This means a legal lease must have been granted in a document. The most obvious way of granting a legal lease in a document is by deed, which is why a lease created in a deed is included here. A lease created in a written document satisfying section 2 of the Law of Property (Miscellaneous Provisions) Act 1989 is equitable, not legal, and so is not included here: see *Borman v Griffith*. A legal lease for three years or less created orally under section 54(2) of the Law of Property Act 1925 is not included either because there is no document. However, you can create a legal lease for three years or less in writing under section 54(2) of the Law of Property Act 1925, which is why it *is* included here. Section 54(2) of the Law of Property Act 1925 was discussed in Chapter 15.

Q: *So would section 62 operate if the four-year lease in our example had been renewed for a further four years by deed?*

A: Yes. You were occupying Yourland. You enjoyed the privilege of walking over Theirland. If the renewal of the lease for a further four years was by deed, the privilege of walking over Theirland would be included in the grant of the renewed lease by deed, and therefore would become a legal easement of a right of way. The same would apply if you had been granted a lease for three years or less in a written document.

Wright v Macadam is an illustration of the operation of section 62 in the context of a lease. Mrs Wright was a weekly tenant in a flat in Mr Macadam's house. He gave her permission to store coal in his coal shed. She was granted a new tenancy of the flat. It was held that the right to store the coal was a recognised easement of storage. The privilege of storing the coal had been converted into a legal easement as it had been implied into the document granting the new tenancy, which was deemed to be a conveyance for the purposes of section 62.

Look at this case in the context of the conditions for section 62 to operate. Section 62 was not expressly excluded. A right to storage is a recognised easement. The house was owned by Mr Macadam, but Mrs Wright occupied the dominant tenement, the flat in it. Mr Macadam granted a new tenancy of the dominant tenement in a document to Mrs Wright and the effect of section 62 was to convert her privilege of storage into a legal easement of a right of storage. Other cases that show the remarkable effect of section 62 are *International Tea Stores Company v Hobbs* (1903), *Goldberg v Edwards* (1950) and *Hair v Gillman* (2000).

A summary of the situations in which you may be able to use section 62 is given on page 517.

Q: What are the differences between easements acquired under section 62 and those acquired under the rule in Wheeldon v Burrows?

A: The main differences are as follows.

▷ For section 62 to operate, the land is owned by one person but there is separate occupation of the dominant and servient tenements, although this is subject to debate. Under the rule in *Wheeldon v Burrows* the land is owned and occupied by the same person and the benefited part of the land, the dominant part, is sold off.

Section 62	**Wheeldon v Burrows**
Land owned by one person	Land owned and occupied by the same person
Occupied by another person	And .... Benefited (dominant) part of the land sold off and burdened land retained

THE POSSIBLE OPERATION OF SECTION 62 OF THE LAW OF PROPERTY ACT 1925

Status of person X enjoying the privilege on the dominant tenement	Followed by	A sale or lease of the dominant tenement
Person X is occupying the dominant tenement by virtue of a bare licence (permission to be there but no consideration)	followed by	The sale of the dominant tenement by deed to person X *or* A grant of a lease of the dominant tenement by deed to person X *or* A grant of a lease of the dominant tenement for three years or less in a written agreement to person X
Person X is occupying the dominant tenement by virtue of a contractual licence (permission to be there in return for consideration)	followed by	The sale of the dominant tenement by deed to person X *or* A grant of a lease of the dominant tenement by deed to person X *or* A grant of a lease of the dominant tenement for three years or less in a written agreement to person X
Person X is occupying the dominant tenement by virtue of a lease, however created	followed by	The sale of the dominant tenement by deed to person X *or* A grant of a new lease of the dominant tenement by deed to person X *or* A grant of a new lease of the dominant tenement for three years or less in a written agreement to person X *or* The renewal of the existing lease of the dominant tenement by deed to person X *or* The renewal of the existing lease of the dominant tenement for three years or less in a written agreement to person X

▶ The rights under section 62 do not have to be continuous and apparent and reasonably necessary for the enjoyment of the land.

▶ For section 62 to operate, the land enjoying the privilege must be sold by deed to the person enjoying the privilege. In the rule in *Wheeldon v Burrows*, an easement can be created if the sale of the land is by a written contract satisfying section 2 of the Law of Property (Miscellaneous Provisions) Act 1989. Because a written contract is not a deed, and section 52 of the Law of Property Act 1925 states that all legal interests must be made by deed, you can claim only an equitable easement here, not a legal one.

Box B7 ### Prescription (legal easement)

Before we start, you should note that easements of a right to light acquired by prescription differ in some respects from other easements acquired by prescription. These differences are discussed on page 525.

Q: *What does 'prescription' mean?*

A: The basis of a claim in prescription is that you have used the right for a sufficiently long period of time. The idea here is that if you do something long enough it becomes legal. Adverse possession works along the same kind of thinking, but whereas a claim in adverse possession bars the paper owner from seeking a remedy, a claim in prescription presumes that the right was yours in the first place and awards you a remedy.

Q: *How long is a long period of time?*

A: The ballpark figure is now 20 years.

Q: *How do you prove 20 years' use?*

A: You have to give a statutory declaration giving details about the right you are claiming. If you need to add in the time periods of successive owners, you need to provide statutory declarations for those periods as well from people who know about the use of the right claimed.

A claim in prescription presumes that the right was formally granted to you or your predecessors in the dim and distant past by means of a deed. If this wasn't the case, both you and your predecessors would have been thrown off the land as trespassers. This presumption that the right was originally granted by deed gives the easement by prescription its legal status. It also means that three other requirements must be met. These are *nec vi*, *nec clam* and *nec precario*, which means the right must be used without force, without secrecy and without permission.

The right must be used without force – nec vi
If you had to use force to exercise your right, it would imply that the right hadn't been formally granted in a deed and therefore you had now to be using the right unlawfully.

The right must be used without secrecy – nec clam
If you had to use the right secretly rather than openly, it would again negate any idea that the right had been granted lawfully by deed, and therefore you had now to be using the right unlawfully.

Union Lighterage Co v London Graving Dock Co (1902) decided there was no easement of a right to run rods under a wharf for ships because the rods were underground and hadn't been detected for over 20 years. You could also argue that the right to lay drains falls into the same category, so clearly there must be some evidence of the drains, or use of the drains, if you are claiming an easement of drainage by prescription.

The right must be used without permission – nec precario

If you actually had to ask for permission to use the right, again it would negate any idea that the right had been granted lawfully by deed and therefore you had now to be using the right unlawfully. Any express permission will clearly put an end to a claim by prescription because the use won't be 'as of right'. It will be because permission was granted. *London Tara Hotel Ltd v Kensington Close Hotel Ltd* (2011) looked at permission. In 1973 a personal permission (licence) had been granted to the owner of Kensington Close Hotel (KCT) to use a right of access over the servient land. Payment of £1 per annum could be demanded by the owners of the servient land although no such payment was ever asked for. KCT changed hands in 1978 and there had been several owners since. London Tara Hotel (TH), the current owners of the servient land, wanted to stop the use of access. The current owners of KCT claimed an easement acquired by prescription. The argument was over permission. The court held that the original permission had been personal to the owner of KCT. When that ownership of KCT changed, the permission ended. Therefore, any use after was not with permission. TH hadn't realised that the permission had ended but that was its lookout. It should have behaved as a reasonably alert owner diligent in protecting its interests but had not done so. TH couldn't argue that there was an implied licence either because, for TH to have implied a licence, there must have been a positive and open act on its behalf. Inactivity didn't count. There was no such positive and open act here, so the condition of *nec precario* was met. TH couldn't claim the use was secret either because the changes of ownership of KCT had not been concealed or misrepresented to them. The owners of KCT could claim an easement.

Q: *If TH had actually asked for the payment of £1 per annum, would that have been evidence of permission?*

A: Yes, and so an easement could not have been claimed.

In *Odey v Barber* (2006) it was held that it didn't matter whether permission was given voluntarily or in response to a request, i.e. whether permission was unsolicited or not. Either form of permission would defeat a claim by prescription. If you used the right in the mistaken belief that you had been granted it, this is still user as of right: see *Bridle v Ruby* (1989).

Q: *What happens if the landowner simply says nothing but just lets you go ahead and use a track as a right of way, for example?*

A: This is known as acquiescing in, or going along with, the use. This won't defeat a claim by prescription because the owner of the land is simply going along with the fact that you're using the track 'as of right', which is what prescription is all about. To go along with the use, the owner of the land: (1) has to have knowledge of the use, here your use of the track, (2) has to have the power to stop you using the track and (3) can't have used that power to stop you using the track. Knowledge includes actual knowledge – so he sees you from his bedroom window – or imputed knowledge, which is knowledge his solicitor or agent should have passed on to him.

Q: *So although actual permission will defeat a claim by prescription, going along with the use won't defeat a claim provided the owner of the land knows about the use and could put a stop to it if he wanted?*

A: Yes. After all, if the owner of the land doesn't know about something and can't put a stop to it, he can hardly be said to be acquiescing in your use and going along with it. Remember you've got to have 20 years' of use still.

Q: *What's the position here if a landlord has leased land to a tenant for a long period and then Fred, a third party, claims prescription because he's walked over the leased land for 20 years?*

A: This is a good question and one that was discussed in *Williams v Sandy Lane (Chester) Ltd* (2006). If there is no lease and the landowner knows of the use and doesn't stop it, you can claim prescription because the landowner is going along with your use as of right. The problem here in the question above is that Fred could acquire a right of way through prescription, yet the landlord wouldn't necessarily have known about him walking over the leased land. Neither would the tenant necessarily have told the landlord so that the landlord could take action. Either way, you can't say that the landlord has gone along with the use because he hasn't known about it. So the question now is at what point, if at all, can you say that the landlord knew about the use and therefore went along with it? The leading authority of *Pugh v Savage* was reviewed in *Williams v Sandy Lane (Chester) Ltd.*

Q: *If a landlord has leased land to a tenant, surely he can't be expected to know if some total stranger starts walking over the leased land as a right of way for example?*

A: This depends on when the lease was granted. Use an example where L is the landlord, the freehold owner, but has leased the land to a tenant, T. Fred is the person claiming the right of way over a track. If the lease was granted before Fred started to use the track, the question is whether L would have been able to stop Fred using the track in the first place. Remember that T is in possession of the land as a tenant. The answer to this will depend on the terms of the lease. If they do not allow L to obtain a possession order and stop Fred using the track, Fred cannot acquire a right by prescription against L. If the terms of the lease would allow L to stop Fred using the track, the question is at what point, if at all, L knew about Fred's use. This knowledge includes actual and imputed knowledge. There is an argument here for saying that there is no reason why L should begin to know about Fred's use because the land is leased to T. However, if L did know about Fred's use and didn't stop him, even though he could have done, L would have acquiesced in Fred's use of the track. Now look at another scenario. If Fred had used the track over L's land before the lease was granted to T, then you have to ask whether L knew about the use of the track before he granted the lease. This knowledge again includes actual and imputed knowledge. If L had either actual or imputed knowledge of Fred's use of the track before he granted the lease to T, L can't use the argument that he wasn't able to stop Fred doing so simply because he'd since leased the land. In other words, because L had chosen to do nothing about stopping Fred's use of the track before he leased the land, he had acquiesced in (gone along with) Fred's use. If L didn't know about Fred's use of the track before he leased the land, you'd have to ask whether L could have done anything to stop Fred's use of the track in the first place once he'd leased the land. If L could have stopped Fred, then you have to ask when, if at all, L knew about the use. The reason is that this was when the prescription countdown would start in Fred's favour if L were able to stop Fred's use, knew about it, and yet did nothing to stop him. If you read this through enough times, it does actually make sense. Eventually. In the *Williams* case the freehold owner, the Council, knew about the claimed right of way before granting the lease. As the Council knew about the right of way being used before it granted the lease and had done nothing to stop it, there was acquiescence. Prescription could be claimed for a right of way over land owned by it even though that land had been leased out by it.

Q: *What was the Council's defence in the case?*

A: It tried to argue that because it had put a covenant in the lease which required the tenant to try and prevent anyone acquiring rights such as easements over the land and to notify it if anyone did try and acquire such rights, it hadn't acquiesced in or gone along with the use of the right of way. This argument was of no avail because the Council knew about the use of the right of way before it granted the lease, therefore it couldn't put the responsibility of stopping it on the tenant once it had this knowledge. The Council could also have ended the lease because the tenant was in breach of the covenant to prevent anyone acquiring rights over the land and it could then have evicted the person using the right of way as a trespasser.

There was a different outcome in *Llewellyn (Deceased) v Lorey* (2011). The servient land had been subject to a tenancy. There was no evidence that the freehold owner knew or was taken to have known of the claimed use of an easement of a right of way for commercial purposes. Furthermore, under the terms of the tenancy, the freehold owner could not have objected to the claimed use. He could not be said to have acquiesced in the claimed right and so the claim for prescription failed. It might have been different if the use had started before the tenancy began because, assuming the freehold owner knew or could have found out about the use, he would have been in a position to stop it.

Q: *This all seems very complicated, doesn't it?*

A: So tempting for an exam question then? It is also a warning that if you ever decide to become a landlord, you should not rely on a covenant in the lease that requires the tenant to take steps to prevent people acquiring rights over the leased land. You must go and inspect the land yourself and do something about it if there is anyone doing so.

To summarise the three Latin phrases following this rather lengthy discussion on the meaning of *nec precario*, the right must be used *nec vi* (without force), *nec clam* (without secrecy) and *nec precario* (without permission). The phrase you need when you've proved these three conditions is 'user as of right'. It is as if your predecessors had the right granted to them lawfully in a deed and you are therefore entitled to continue to use it. The right must also have been used by or on behalf of one fee simple owner against another fee simple owner.

Once the conditions of *nec vi*, *nec clam* and *nec precario* have been met and the right has been used by or on behalf of one fee simple owner against another, there are three ways to claim prescription. These are under the common law, the lost modern grant or the Prescription Act 1832. All these ways of acquiring an easement are based on the assumption that there has been a deed in the past granting the right. The common law allows an easement to be claimed if the person claiming it could show that the right had been used since 3 September 1189.

Q: *3 September 1189?*

A: Yes. It's known as 'time immemorial'. This wasn't very practical so 'time immemorial' became 'within living memory', which in turn became 'for at least 20 years'. However, if the owner of Theirland can prove that the easement couldn't have been used since 1189, then you can't establish your claim.

Q: *That's not very difficult for him to prove, is it?*

A: No, not least because both plots were probably still in common ownership then. And it also means you can't start claiming an easement of a right of storage, for example, if the building you are using for storage was built after 1189. So that's why the courts invented the fiction of the lost modern grant: see *Dalton v Angus & Co* (1881). If you can prove that the right has been used for the last 20 years, the courts will presume that there was a grant by deed between the sometime owners of Theirland and the sometime owners of Yourland, but that the deed has been lost.

Q: *Lost?*

A: Yes. Presumed lost. The whole idea of the lost modern grant is based on the fact that some careless person has lost the paperwork. The claim can be defeated if it can be proved that the supposed grantor, the person who owned the servient land at the time of the supposed grant, was mentally incapable.

Q: *Do you have to have used the right continuously for 20 years for claims under the common law and the lost modern grant?*

A: No, although you must be careful that the right has been used sufficiently. In *Hollins v Verney* (1884) it was held that two uses in the preceding 20 years did not amount to sufficient usage.

Such fiction under the lost modern grant led to some raised eyebrows, so the Prescription Act 1832 was passed. The Act differentiates between easements of light and other easements, so we'll talk about easements other than a right to light first. Section 2 of the Act states that you must have at least 20 years' use and section 4 states that this must be a continuous use up to the time you claim your right to an easement in court. This means that if you have used the right for 30 years, but then have not used it for three years, you will not have a claim, as the right is not in use continuously immediately before the court action. A claim cannot be defeated by showing that the right couldn't have been used since 1189, although it is defeated by any form of oral or written permission given either at the start of the period or during it.

There is an alternative period of time under section 2 of the Prescription Act 1832. If you can show 40 years' uninterrupted use, there is an absolute right to the easement. A right claimed under the 40-year period still has to be used without force and without secrecy, although the requirements for permission are modified. A claim is defeated by written permission given at the start of the 40-year period. It is also defeated by oral or written permission given during the period. Oral permission at the start of the 40-year period though will not defeat a claim.

Q: *Should you use the common law, the lost modern grant or the Prescription Act 1832 to claim a right by prescription?*

A: The best way is to use the 40-year period under the Prescription Act 1832. Failing that, the lost modern grant could well be the most successful. This is simply because the right has to be used more or less continuously for any period of 20 years before a claim, whereas under the Prescription Act the right has to have been used continuously before any claim in court.

Q: *Is a legal or equitable easement created by prescription?*

A: Prescription creates a legal easement. The courts presume an express grant by deed sometime in the past which would have created a legal easement, as it would do today.

Q: *What happens when someone is prevented from acquiring the required 20 years?*

A: If 20 years' use under the common law or the lost modern grant cannot be proved, there is no claim to an easement. Section 4 of the Prescription Act 1832 allows for marginal leeway here. Imagine you are using a path over Theirland from Yourland. If Mr Theirland obstructs and blocks the path, time will not stop running in your favour unless you stop using the path for at least one year, i.e. 365 days or more. Not using the path is referred to as 'acquiescing in the obstruction' in section 4 of the Act. So let's say that you have been using the path for 19 years exactly. The path is then blocked off. You cannot claim an easement by prescription as you have only 19 years' use, not the required 20 years' use for the Prescription Act, or indeed for the common law or the lost modern grant. If you continue to use the path you will undoubtedly find yourself evicted as a trespasser, and that will be the end of any claim of an easement.

Now let's say that you have 19 years' plus one day's use when the path is blocked, like this:

| 19 years | one day | path blocked |

If the path is blocked at the end of the 19 years and the one day, you can still claim under the Prescription Act 1832. Although the path is blocked, time still runs in your favour unless you have stopped using the path because of the blockage for at least one year. The Act also states that in order to claim under the Act, you must have been using the path for a continuous 20-year period immediately before the date you claim the right of way in court. Now put these two clauses together. If you have 19 years plus one day, after which the path is blocked and you stop using it for the next 364 days, you can still claim 20 years' use. This is because time continues to run in your favour until you have stopped using the path for one year. 364 days' non-use is not a year. So 19 years plus one day plus 364 days' non-use which does not count against you equals 19 years plus 365 days, which equals 20 years' use.

19 years	one day	path blocked for 364 days	court action

This would be quite a coup, except that if the court action takes place after you have stopped using the path for 365 days, you will lose the claim, as the blockage of one year will now count against you and you will not have 20 years' use. The impractical effect of this is that you must claim on the 365th day and that day alone. The same reasoning applies if there are 39 years and one day's use if the 40-year period is being claimed.

If you want to show that you object to the obstruction you must communicate this clearly to the owner of the servient land. Just being discontented and failing to tell the owner of the servient land for two and a half years that you object to the obstruction shows submission, as in *Dance v Triplow* (1992).

Q: What happens if you try and claim an easement by prescription but the activity you're doing is illegal?

A: This happened in *Hanning v Top Deck Travel Group Ltd* (1994) where it was held that you can't acquire an easement which has been based on an illegal act even though you've carried out the activity for over 20 years. Driving across common land, Horsell Common, was illegal under section 193 of the Law of Property Act 1925 unless you had lawful authority. This lawful authority could be permission from the landowner, but in the case permission had not been granted. Since driving over the common was illegal, there could be no claim to a right of way by prescription.

In 2004 the House of Lords overruled *Hanning* in *Bakewell Management Ltd v Brandwood* (2004). The court held that you could acquire an easement of a right of way by prescription or by the lost modern grant by driving across land even though it was illegal to do so.

Q: So you didn't have to ask for permission?

A: No. It was held that where an easement could have been granted lawfully, it could be acquired by prescription or by the lost modern grant. The use of the land being claimed as an easement could have been made legal by an express grant from the owner, even if he hadn't actually done so, and this was what mattered. Remember that you still need 20 years' use.

Q: What happens if the activity can't be made legal by permission from the land owner?

A: It can't be acquired as an easement. The example the Land Registry gives is the claim to pollute a river contrary to statute. The right could not be lawfully granted by deed by a landowner and so there is no easement.

Q: *What happens if there never was anyone who could have lawfully granted the right?*

A: In *Housden v Conservators of Wimbledon and Putney Commons* (2008) Mr and Mrs Housden wanted to register the benefit of a private right of way from a public road to their house. The right of way went across a strip of land which formed part of Wimbledon Common. Their claim was based on section 2 of the Prescription Act 1832 and 40 years' use. The respondents were the Conservators of Wimbledon and Putney Commons who claimed that under the Wimbledon and Putney Commons Act 1871 the Conservators had no right, and had never had a right, to grant a right of way. If there was no capable grantor, there could be no easement of a right of way. The question then was could the Housdens still acquire a prescriptive right based on 40 years' use? Under section 2 of the Prescription Act 1832, 40 years' use gives an absolute and indefeasible right to the use.

Q: *Surely the answer has to be 'no'? If prescription is based on a presumed lawful grant, there must be someone who could lawfully have granted the right.*

A: On a true interpretation of the Wimbledon and Putney Commons Act 1871 the Conservators were able to grant an easement. It was held obiter that where it would have been unlawful for the grantor to grant such an easement, no right could be acquired under section 2 of the Prescription Act 1832.

So, to summarise prescription. The use must be *nec vi*, *nec clam* and *nec precario* and it must be by or on behalf of one fee simple owner against another. There must be 20 years' use claimed either under the common law or the lost modern grant or under the Prescription Act 1832.

Q: *How does an easement of a right to light differ?*

A: There is one fixed period under the Act. You can claim an absolute right to an easement of light after 20 years' actual enjoyment under section 3 of the Prescription Act 1832. Because it's 20 years' actual enjoyment, you do not have to show user as of right so *nec vi* and *nec clam* do not have to be shown. Again, because it's an absolute right granted based on actual enjoyment, you do not have to presume a grant and so you do not have to show enjoyment of the right by one fee simple user against another. This means that a tenant can acquire an easement against his landlord or against another tenant of the same landlord.

Q: *Does section 4 which states that it must be a continuous use up to the time you claim your right to an easement in court still apply?*

A: Yes. The claim, though, is defeated under section 3 by written permission at the beginning or during the 20-year period. In *RHJ Ltd v FT Patten (Holdings) Ltd* (2008) the lease reserved to the landlord a 'full and free right' to build on the land retained 'as they may think fit'. The tenant claimed that it had acquired a right to light through prescription because it had enjoyed continuous light for 20 years. Part of section 3 of the Prescription Act 1832 relating to written permission became relevant. The tenant argued that the reservation made in the lease did not refer to 'light' expressly and so it could still claim a right to light. The Court of Appeal held that the clause in the lease constituted written agreement and said that the agreement did not have to refer expressly to 'light' for it to exclude a claim to a right to light by prescription. The wording in the lease was important in this decision. In contrast, in *Salvage Wharf Ltd v G&S Brough Ltd* (2009) the wording in the agreement did not trigger section 3 and the claimant did not lose his right to light. The result in *Patten* will apply not only in the landlord/tenant situation but also where a developer sells off part of his land and retains the rest for future development. So, developers selling off plots of land may wish to take care with the wording in any conveyance to ensure that it comes within section 3, thereby ensuring that a purchaser cannot claim a right to light if the developer starts to build on the adjoining land. Potential purchasers need to make sure that their enjoyment of light on the land will not be lost if the adjoining property is developed. They will need to check this out before they even think about exchanging contracts.

Q: *If you want to obstruct someone's right of way, then clearly you block the path, but how do you obstruct a right to light if you want to prevent someone acquiring an easement of a right to light by prescription?*

A: If the owner of the servient tenement wants to prevent the owner of the dominant tenement acquiring a right to light by prescription, he has to put up a hoarding on his own land so as to obstruct the right to light to the dominant tenement. This is not a very sensible solution, so the same effect can be achieved by registering a notice on the Local Land Charges Register. This is a register held by local councils which records specific local rights. The notice must specify the size and position of the obstruction that the owner of the servient tenement would have put up. The owner of the dominant tenement must be notified, which gives him the chance to object. If the notice remains on the Register for a year without challenge, it counts as an obstruction under the Prescription Act 1832.

The reservation of an easement

Reservation of an easement occurs when a landowner sells off part of his land and retains a right over the land he has sold.

Box B8 Express reservation by deed (legal easement)

This is when Mr Theirland sells off part of his land, Yourland, to you, but expressly reserves a right for himself over the land in the deed of sale, for example, a right of way.

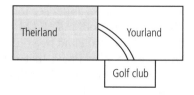

This creates a legal easement as the right will be created as one of the terms in the conveyance, the deed of sale.

Box B9 Implied reservation through necessity (legal easement) or implied reservation through intention (legal easement)

These easements arise for the same reasons as they did for an implied grant through necessity or intention. Reservation is when Yourland is sold to you and the courts imply an easement of necessity or intention in Mr Theirland's favour into the conveyance, the deed of sale, of Yourland to you. This could be that Mr Theirland should still, for example, have a right of way over Yourland based on necessity or intention, even though he has actually sold Yourland to you.

Q: *Is this kind of easement found a lot?*

A: No, it's not favoured by the courts because the balance of power in any sale lies with the seller. The seller has the power to sell and he also has the power to reserve any rights for himself that he wants to retain over the land he sells. If he doesn't do this expressly at the time of sale, he shouldn't then be allowed to claim an implied easement of necessity or intention: see *Re Webb's Lease*.

The technical way of putting this is to say that the grantor is not allowed to derogate from his grant. You can't sell land and then say 'by the way, I meant to say that I wanted to keep a right over the land I've just sold you' unless you have made this intention very clear. In *Peckham v Ellison* (1999) there was no reasonable explanation other than that an implied reservation of a right of way through mutual intention had been intended. In *Sweet v Sommer* (2005) an implied reservation of an easement through necessity was found. There was a different outcome in *Adealon International Proprietary Ltd v London Borough of Merton* (2007). Adealon claimed it was landlocked because access from its land to the highway to the south was denied on safety grounds. It argued that the benefit of an easement of a right of way over Merton Council's land to the north had been implied by reservation in a previous conveyance. It now wanted to claim the benefit of this implied easement of a right of way to cross Merton Council's land to get out of its own land. The court held that where land was completely surrounded by the land of the other party, an easement of necessity would be implied, in favour of either the seller or the buyer of the land. The problem was that Adealon's land was not completely surrounded by the land of one other party. It was bordered on the east and west by third parties. It was held that when landlocked land was surrounded by land belonging to third parties, so not surrounded completely by the land of one other person, the case for implying an easement by reservation was less clear because there was the possibility of access over the land of the third parties.

Q: *That sounds like an expensive negotiation, doesn't it?*

A: Doesn't it just. The law would look sympathetically on a buyer in a situation like this on the basis that a seller was not allowed to derogate from his grant. Conversely, it would be presumed that a seller would have had the intelligence to reserve any rights he wished to retain over the land he sold and the seller would have to justify any exception. Unfortunately the predecessors to Adealon had not reserved any right of way over the land when it was sold. The court also confirmed that easements of necessity were to be implied from the intentions of the parties, not as a matter of public policy, thereby confirming *Nickerson v Barraclough*. In the *Adealon* case there had never been any intention that an easement would be implied into the previous conveyance. There had always been a potential right of access onto a highway to the south from the land Adealon now owned. The fact that planning permission hadn't been granted to use it was just bad luck for Adealon and would not be taken into account. Because it had previously been assumed that planning permission would be granted for access from the land Adealon now owned onto the highway, there had never been any intention of a right over the land now owned by Merton Council. If there had never been any intention, there could be no reservation of a right of way through intention.

Q: *Did that leave Adealon with no way out of its land other than to try and negotiate with the owners of the surrounding land to the east and the west?*

A: Yes, and, as we said, that sounds expensive.

Q: *So if you sell part of your land off, should you be careful to reserve expressly any rights you think you may want over the land you are selling?*

A: Most certainly, because a claim for an easement of necessity by reservation will not be implied where there is no intention that there should be one.

The effect of not creating an easement in a recognised way

Q: *What happens if the easement has not been created in a recognised way?*

A: The claimant will only ever have a licence. A licence has already been discussed on page 505 and the same details apply here.

Summary of the creation of an easement

An easement can be created expressly or it can arise through implication. Depending on the way it has been created, an easement can be either legal or equitable. If an easement has not been created in a recognised way, the claimant will have only a licence.

The protection of an easement

Box C

THE PROTECTION OF AN EASEMENT

Look at either

Unregistered land

1. Legal easement or

2. Equitable easement

or look at

Registered land

3. Dealings which must be completed by registration

4. Interests which override a registered disposition

5. Interests entered as a notice or protected by a restriction

---

This part of the chapter looks at how an easement is protected if the land that the right is over is sold to another person. In the example that follows, you own Yourland and Mr Theirland grants you an easement of a right of way over Theirland. Mr Theirland then sells Theirland to Peter.

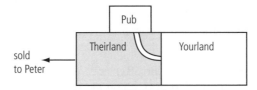

You will want to know whether you can still walk over Theirland. Peter will want to know whether he can tell you to get off Theirland when he wakes up the day after he moved in and discovers you walking across his land. The answer to this depends on whether the easement has been protected either in unregistered or in registered land.

Unregistered land

You will have realised from Box B that, depending on their method of creation, some easements are legal and some are equitable.

Use the procedure given in Chapter 3 on page 44 to determine how interests are protected in unregistered land. This procedure is repeated below for your convenience.

Step 1. Establish whether it is a legal or equitable interest that is being claimed. If it is a legal interest, legal rights bind the world both before 1926, and, excluding a puisne mortgage, after then as well. If it is an equitable interest you must see whether the equitable interest is capable of entry as a land charge under the Land Charges Act 1972.

Step 2. If the equitable interest is not capable of entry as a land charge, use the rule that governed equitable interests before 1926, known as the doctrine of notice. If the equitable interest is capable of entry as a land charge, work out in whose interest it is to enter it as a land charge. This will be the person who benefits from the equitable interest.

Step 3. Check to see whether that person has entered his equitable interest as a land charge in the correct class on the Land Charges Register against the name of the owner of the land that the right is over.

- An equitable interest that has been entered as a land charge binds everyone who takes the land under section 198 of the Law of Property Act 1925.
- If the equitable interest has not been entered as a land charge, it will not be binding on some classes of purchaser.

Box C1 ### Unregistered land – legal easement

You can now apply the procedure to see what happens if you have a legal easement of a right of way over Theirland.

Step 1. A legal easement is a legal interest. Legal rights bind the world.

If you have a legal easement of a right of way over Theirland, it will be binding on Peter, no argument.

Q: *So Peter must let me continue to use the right of way across Theirland if I have a legal easement?*

A: Correct. These are legal easements which will be binding on Peter provided they are:

- created expressly by deed (Box B1); or
- a legal easement implied through necessity (Box B3); or
- a legal easement implied through mutual intention (Box B4); or
- a legal easement under *Wheeldon v Burrows* when there is a deed (Box B5); or
- a legal easement under section 62 of the Law of Property Act 1925 (Box B6), or a legal easement acquired by prescription (Box B7).

Legal easements acquired through reservation (Boxes B8 to B10) also bind the world.

Q: *Why are legal easements binding on Peter although they cannot be entered on the Land Charges Register?*

A: In his capacity as purchaser, Peter should exercise a little care and look round the property himself. It is likely that the right of way is visible. His solicitor should also make inquiries. A legal right, here a legal easement, will bind anyone who takes Theirland, either as a purchaser or by gift or by inheritance.

Box C2	Unregistered land – equitable easement

This will be an equitable easement satisfying the requirements of section 2 of the Law of Property (Miscellaneous Provisions) Act 1989 (Box B2), or an equitable easement created under the rule in *Wheeldon v Burrows* where there is a written agreement but not a deed (Box B5).

You can apply the same procedure as before if you have an equitable easement of a right of way over Theirland. Assume that the equitable easement was created after 1925:

Step 1. An equitable easement is an equitable interest. An equitable easement created after 1925 is capable of entry as a land charge under the Land Charges Act 1972.

Step 2. It is in your interest to enter the equitable easement as a land charge as you benefit from the right.

Step 3. You should have entered your equitable easement of a right of way as a class D(iii) land charge against the name of Mr Theirland, who is the owner of the land that the right is over.

- If you have entered your equitable easement as a land charge, it will bind Peter under section 198 of the Law of Property Act 1925 and he must let you continue to use the right of way.

▶ If you have not entered your equitable easement as a land charge, it will not be binding on a purchaser of a legal estate for money or money's worth under section 4(6) of the Land Charges Act 1972. Peter paid money for the legal estate of Theirland, so, if you have not entered your equitable easement as a land charge, you will have to stop using the right of way over Theirland immediately.

Q: *When does my equitable easement have to be entered on the Land Charges Register?*

A: As soon as it has been created, or at least before Theirland is sold on. You won't know if and when Mr Theirland may sell Theirland. If your equitable easement is not entered on the Land Charges Register before any sale of Theirland, a purchaser, Peter here, will not have the opportunity to find out about it and he will therefore not be bound by it.

Equitable easements created before 1926

You must apply the procedure again.

Step 1. An equitable easement is an equitable interest. An equitable easement created before 1926 cannot be entered as a land charge under the Land Charges Act 1972.

Q: *Why not?*

A: Because before 1926 there wasn't a Land Charges Act, and only post-1925 equitable easements can be entered on the Land Charges Register.
Step 2. As an equitable easement created before 1926 cannot be entered as a land charge, you must use the rule that governed equitable interests before 1926, known as the doctrine of notice. The doctrine of notice is as follows.

Equitable rights bind everyone except a *bona fide* purchaser of a legal estate for value without notice of the equitable interest, here the equitable easement.

Imagine that the easement of the right of way had been granted by Mr Theirland to you in 1920. The equitable easement will bind Peter unless he is a *bona fide* purchaser of a legal estate for value without notice of the equitable easement. Peter has given money for the legal estate of Theirland and we can assume he is *bona fide*. The answer therefore depends on whether Peter has actual, constructive or imputed notice (knowledge) of the equitable easement. Actual notice is notice he actually has. Constructive notice is notice he would have had if he had inspected the documentation to the land or had inspected the land. Imputed notice is notice that his solicitor had and should have passed on. Given the three different types of notice, one concludes that the chances are that he probably does have notice of the equitable easement and will be bound by it.

Registered land

Registered land is governed by the Land Registration Act 2002. There are three categories which determine how interests are protected in registered land. They are:

▶ Dealings which must be completed by registration under section 27 of the Land Registration Act 2002 (Box C3).

▶ Interests in Schedule 3 to the Land Registration Act 2002 which override a registered disposition (Box C4).

▶ Interests entered as a notice under section 34 of the Land Registration Act 2002 and interests protected by a restriction under section 43 of the Land Registration Act 2002 (Box C5).

A purchaser for valuable consideration will take the land subject to the interests in these three categories.

Box C3 **Dealings which must be completed by registration**

This category includes an express grant or reservation of a legal easement.

Under section 27 of the Land Registration Act 2002, an express grant (Box B1) or express reservation (Box B8) of a legal easement must be completed by registration. The registration of an express grant or reservation of a legal easement is carried out as follows. The person who has the benefit of the legal easement is entered as owner of the legal easement on the Property Register of his own land. A notification of the legal easement is put on the Charges Register of the land over which the right is exercised. This notification takes the form of a notice. So you would have to be registered as owner of the legal easement on the Property Register of Yourland, and a notice of the legal easement would have to be put on the Charges Register of Theirland.

Q: *And if I don't do this?*

A: Your easement will not be recognised at law and will only be equitable. An equitable easement must itself be entered as a notice on the Charges Register to bind a purchaser of the land that the right is over. However, you won't be able to protect it by means of a notice in this case because, if you try to do so, the Land Registrar will simply ensure that you complete the dealing by registration properly, thereby ensuring its legal status. Assuming you have not approached the Land Registry at all, your easement will not be binding on Peter under section 29 of the Land Registration Act 2002.

Box C4 **Interests which override a registered disposition**

These are interests that are binding on everyone including a purchaser.

Under paragraph 3 of Schedule 3 to the Land Registration Act 2002 a legal easement acquired:

▶ By an implied grant of necessity (Box B3); or
▶ By an implied grant of mutual intention (Box B4); or
▶ Under the rule in *Wheeldon v Burrows* when there is a deed (Box B5); or
▶ Under section 62 of the Law of Property Act 1925 (Box B6); or
▶ By prescription (Box B7); or
▶ Under implied reservation through necessity (Box B9); or
▶ Under implied reservation through mutual intention (Box B10) will be an overriding interest if any of the following conditions is met.
▶ The person who bought the land that had the easement over it knew about the easement,

or

▶ The easement would have been obvious to the person who bought the land on a reasonably careful inspection of the land,

▶ *or*

▶ The easement had been used in the last year before the land was sold.

This last condition doesn't really fit in, does it? The first two conditions relate to the possibility of knowing about or noticing the easement, whereas the third condition just states that if it's been used in the last year then it's binding whether you've noticed it or not. Not much logic there then.

Q: *And don't the first two conditions sound like the doctrine of notice?*

A: Worryingly so.

The overall effect of this section means that if Peter doesn't know about your easement of a right of way and couldn't have found out about it by a reasonable inspection of the land, he will still be bound by it if you have used the right of way in the last year. The burden of proof is on you to show you have used the right of way in the last year. Only if he doesn't know about it and couldn't have found out about it on a reasonable inspection of the land, and you haven't used it in the last year, will he not be bound.

Box C5 Interests entered as a notice or protected by a restriction

These are interests which are entered as a notice on the Charges Register of the land or protected by a restriction on the Proprietorship Register of the land which the right is over in order to bind a purchaser.

An equitable easement must be entered as a notice on the Charges Register under section 34 of the Land Registration Act 2002. This is the Charges Register of Theirland in our example. Equitable easements here would be those satisfying the requirements of section 2 of the Law of Property (Miscellaneous Provisions) Act 1989 (Box B2) or those equitable easements created under the rule in *Wheeldon v Burrows* when there is a written contract but not a deed (Box B5). The notice will give the details of the easement. If you have entered the equitable easement as a notice, it will bind Peter and he must let you continue to use the right of way across Theirland.

Q: *When does my equitable easement have to be entered on the Charges Register?*

A: As soon as it has been created, or at least before Theirland is sold. You won't know if and when Mr Theirland may sell Theirland. If your equitable easement is not entered as a notice on the Charges Register of Theirland before any sale, a purchaser will not have the opportunity to find out about it and he will therefore not be bound by it.

Q: *What happens if I haven't entered my equitable easement as a notice?*

A: It will not be binding on Peter under section 29 of the Land Registration Act 2002 and he will not have to let you use the right of way across Theirland.

Summary of the protection of an easement

The method of protection of an easement depends on whether the land is registered or unregistered, and then whether the easement is legal or equitable.

Q: *What happens as far as Peter is concerned here if I haven't been able to meet the conditions in Boxes A and B?*

A: If you haven't ticked Boxes A and B, you have only a licence or permission to use the right, not an easement. The licence can be bare or contractual depending on whether there was consideration, usually payment, given for the use of the right. You need to establish whether your licence is binding on Peter when he buys Theirland if this is all you can claim.

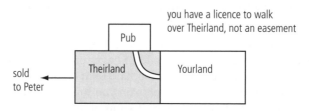

Q: *And will a licence bind Peter?*

A: The answer is very short. Licences do not bind third parties as they are not proprietary interests in land. They take effect only between the parties that created them. Peter would not be bound by your licence. The case authority for this is *Ashburn Anstalt v Arnold & Co* (1989).

Q: *So would I have to stop walking over Theirland immediately?*

A: Yes. Immediately. The licence is not binding on Peter.

Remedies for unlawful interference with an easement and how easements come to an end

Q: *What happens if someone stops me using my easement?*

A: There are a number of remedies. The first is called abatement, where the owner of the easement removes the obstruction to his use of the easement. This is not really seen as a good idea because the owner of the easement can't use unreasonable force to do this. You can also sue the person interfering with your easement in nuisance.

Q: *Can you ask for an injunction to stop the servient owner interfering with your easement?*

A: You can, although in some cases damages are awarded instead under section 50 of the Supreme Court Act 1981 following the guidelines in *Shelfer v City of London Electric Lighting Co* (1895) given on page 366. These guidelines are talked about in the context of restrictive covenants but are equally applicable to easements. An injunction was granted in *Owers v Bailey* (2006) where Mr Bailey had blocked a right of way by putting up chicken wire, erecting gates (supposedly to keep his livestock – one whole goat – in), and claiming that his tractor had broken down across the track. A mandatory injunction was granted ordering the removal of the gates and aggravated damages were awarded for Mr Bailey's persistent intimidatory and unpleasant conduct.

In *Kettel v Bloomfold* the servient owner landlord had tried to unilaterally change the site of parking spaces over which there were easements for alternative ones because he wanted to build over the spaces. It was held that, following *Shelfer v City of London Electric Lighting Co*, prima facie the dominant owners, the tenants, were entitled to an injunction. The injury to the tenants was not trivial, but rather the opposite, because no alternative parking spaces had actually been offered. The right to a parking space was valuable and was not of small financial loss. The landlord wanted to build on the site for his own profit not for the wider public benefit and had behaved highhandedly. The tenants hadn't waited to complain until after the development had started and an injunction preventing the landlord developing the land would not be oppressive.

Q: What happens if the servient owner obstructs a right of way but does provide an alternative route?

A: This had happened in *Heslop v Bishton* (2009). It was held that the servient owner, Mr Heslop, couldn't unilaterally change the route of Mr Bishton's right of way.

Q: Why not, if the alternative is just as good?

A: Because it would be a derogation from grant. Also, Mr Bishton might have negotiated a nice sum of money here in return for Mr Heslop changing the route. The court stated that the existence of an alternative route did not extinguish the existing right and the dominant owner could still bring an action for obstruction. The provision of an alternative route could affect the remedy though. Although an injunction to remove the obstruction wasn't necessarily appropriate because of this alternative route, the court could still award damages. Furthermore, Mr Bishton's right to deviate was an equitable right and it would be unfair for the existing legal right of way to be extinguished and replaced by a more precarious equitable right. Interestingly, Mr Heslop had resisted the District Judge's order in declaring the existence of the equitable right of deviation and instead had offered Mr Bishton a ten year licence only over a different part of his land as an alternative route.

Q: Wouldn't that have made Mr Bishton's position even more precarious because a licence is not a legal right and it can also be revoked?

A: Yes, and so the court's suspicions were aroused. Fortunately the judge recognised the other undermining activities of Mr Heslop, finding it 'entirely appropriate' to find in favour of Mr Bishton and allowing him to continue to use the deviation whilst the obstruction was in place.

Remedies have been discussed in cases concerning rights to light. In *Regan v Paul Properties* (2006) it was confirmed that the standard remedy for the claimant should be an injunction and a claimant should not have to convince the court that damages were insufficient. In the case Mr Regan's level of light in his living room had fallen from 67% to approximately 42% because of the development of two new properties across the road. This meant that he didn't have enough natural light for reading, painting, modelling, dressmaking and writing in his living room and, if he moved to the window to do these activities, he would be spied on by the people in the two new properties being developed across the road. A mandatory injunction was granted to pull down part of the new development because Mr Regan would suffer substantial interference with the amount of light that came into his living room. Although the developer's losses would be substantial, this would not determine what remedy was granted. Furthermore, the developers had taken the risk of continuing to build after Mr Regan had complained to them about the development. The *Regan* case does serve as a warning to developers because it shows the willingness of the courts to grant an injunction as the norm to prevent infringement of a right to light, even if it does cost the developer heavily in modifying any development. Developers beware.

In contrast, though, in *Tamares (Vincent Square) Ltd v Fairpoint Properties (Vincent Square) Ltd* (2006), a case involving commercial properties, the construction of a new building had interfered with a right to light. The right to light was claimed for four windows. Two of the windows had been blocked throughout the prescriptive period by panelling put behind the glass so no light had been let through. The court held that no right to light had been acquired by prescription.

Q: *Even though the light actually went through the window before it was stopped by the panelling? And couldn't you argue that pulling a curtain across permanently would have the same effect?*

A: Once a right to light has been acquired, altering the furniture or how the room is set up won't take away that right. Here, though, the set-up of the room had meant that no light had been let through in the 20-year period, so there was no enjoyment of light and therefore no right to light could be claimed as in *Smith v Baxter* (1900). As regards the other two basement windows which provided the light for a staircase and two landings, the stairs were now less safe and the right to light had been infringed. Damages were awarded as a mandatory injunction to pull the new building down would be disproportionate to the loss of light suffered by the claimant and wholly out of proportion to the injury claimed.

Q: *How were the damages assessed in the* **Tamares** *case?*

A: The case came back to court in *Tamares (Vincent Square) Ltd v Fairpoint Properties (Vincent Square) Ltd* (2007) because the parties were unable to agree on a sum. The sum claimed was the greater of either damages for the loss of the amenity or use of the land, or damages that reflected the fact that an injunction hadn't been granted, as here. It was held that damages would be based on a hypothetical negotiation between the parties at the date of the infringement of the right to light. The right to prevent a development or part of a development gives the dominant owner a significant bargaining position, meaning that he would normally expect to receive a fair percentage of the likely profit from the development: see *Wrotham Park Estate Co Ltd v Parkside Homes Ltd* (1974) and *Carr-Saunders v Dick McNeil Associates Ltd* (1986). The court must find a fair result bearing in mind the nature and seriousness of the breach.

Q: *So a buy-out?*

A: Yes, and with the negotiations centring round experts' reports from both sides on the likely profits there is a guarantee that one side will say the likely profit forecast is 'too much' and the other will say 'not enough'.

Q: *What happens if the likely profit can't be quantified?*

A: The court will award a multiple of the damages for the loss of use. Whichever way it's decided, the amount mustn't be so much that the development wouldn't have happened if such a sum had been payable at the start by the developer to the person who had his right disrupted. Before deciding finally on the amount, the court should consider whether the deal 'feels right'.

Q: *'Feels right'?*

A: Yes. A highly specified legal term it is not. In the *Tamares* case the court took into account the limited nature of the infringement and the need to find a sum which wouldn't put the developers off continuing that part of the development. £50,000 was awarded on the basis that £50,000 felt right but anything over £50,000 didn't feel right. An awful lot of feeling was put into this case.

Q: *In* **Regan v Paul Properties** *an injunction was granted. In* **Tamares (Vincent Square) Ltd v Fairpoint Properties (Vincent Square) Ltd** *damages were awarded. Does the fact that* **Regan** *involved a residential property and* **Tamares (Vincent Square) Ltd v Fairpoint Properties (Vincent Square) Ltd** *involved commercial property account for the difference in remedy?*

A: Almost certainly, especially as it was stairs and landings in *Tamares (Vincent Square) Ltd v Fairpoint Properties (Vincent Square) Ltd* that were affected, rather than an occupied room. It's easy to light a commercial building using artificial light, but this is not an appropriate solution in residential properties. In *Midtown Ltd v City of London Real Property Co Ltd* (2005), a case which involved commercial properties, the developer tried to argue that as the offices were lit by artificial light the loss of natural light would be irrelevant. This argument was dismissed, because otherwise it would mean that nobody could ever claim that a right to light had been infringed because the defendant could always say 'use artificial light then'. As the owner of the dominant land enjoying the right to light held the property as a financial investment and had plans for development of the dominant land, rather than actually using it, damages were awarded.

Q: *Have any recent cases made the outcome clearer for developers?*

A: In *HKRUK II (CHC) Limited v Marcus Alexander Heaney* (2010) HKRUK had added two floors to a commercial building aware that there would be an infringement of a right to light of the neighbouring commercial building belonging to Mr Heaney. After HKRUK had finished the building works it sought a declaration from the court that it had no liability to Mr Heaney. Mr Heaney counterclaimed for a mandatory injunction and HKRUK argued that it should pay damages so the question was one of remedy. The court identified *Shelfer v City of London Electric Lighting Co* as the leading case which had been approved in *Regan v Paul Properties*. Prima facie the injured party was entitled to an injunction although damages could be awarded where the four conditions in *Shelfer v City of London Electric Lighting Co* were met. The first condition is that the injury to the claimant's right is small. Although close to the margin, the injury to Mr Heaney was not small so HKRUK couldn't meet the first condition thereby allowing Mr Heaney the award of an injunction. Even so, the judge went on to consider the other conditions in case his conclusion was wrong and the case went to appeal. Although the injury was capable of being estimated in money, it could not be compensated for by a small monetary payment and the granting of an injunction would not be oppressive. HKRUK argued that an injunction requiring demolition of part of its building would be oppressive because the cost of doing so would be £1–2.5 million and Mr Heaney had not taken any action when he first became aware of the building going up. The court offset these factors against the fact that HKRUK had built for a profit knowing that there was an infringement of a right to light. It awarded a mandatory injunction requiring HKRUK to remove part of the top two floors. As was said

> In my judgment, it would be wholly wrong for the court effectively to sanction what has been done by compelling the defendant to take monetary compensation which he does not want.

The judge also answered the theoretical question of what damages he would have awarded had an injunction not been granted by following *Tamares (Vincent Square) Ltd v Fairpoint Properties (Vincent Square) Ltd*. This would have been £225,000, a figure which would have survived the final test of 'feeling right'. The case was due to go to the Court of Appeal but was settled out of court. Therefore, the decision stands. This means a developer needs to make sure that any issues relating to rights to light of neighbouring properties are sorted out before building; otherwise, instead of being able to buy a way out of trouble, buildings might have to be pulled down.

Q: *How do easements come to an end?*

A: By statute, by express release in a deed, by informal release in writing under section 2 of the Law of Property (Miscellaneous Provisions) Act 1989, through proprietary estoppel as in *Lester v Woodgate* (2010) dicussed in Chapter 12, or by implied release. Implied release is shown by conduct. In *Moore v Rawson* (1824) the claimant's predecessor rebuilt on the land, putting a blank wall where there had been a window 17 years before. The claimant could not claim an easement of a right to light when putting the window back again because his predecessor had ceased to enjoy the light, and had showed an intention never to make use of it again. In *Benn v Hardinge* (1992) nobody had used a right of way for 175 years because an alternative access was being used. The court did not feel able to presume that a right of way had been abandoned because there had to be an intention to abandon.

Q: *So exactly what does constitute an intention to abandon?*

A: In *Odey v Barber* Silber J used the principles of abandonment drawn from case law in the book *Gale on Easements* which state that whether a person intends an abandonment is not a subjective question; abandonment depends on the intention of the person alleged to be abandoning the right of way as perceived by the reasonable owner of the servient tenement. This means that the dominant owner must show a clear intention that neither he nor any successors in title have any further use for the easement. Whether an act is intended as abandonment is a question of fact. Abandonment is not to be lightly inferred. And non-use is not by itself conclusive evidence of abandonment. This is because there might be other reasons for the non-use. In the case a right of way had not been abandoned where the claimants had to construct an alternative track because the original track had been blocked by the owner. The claimants had also complained about the blockage from 1995 and so had never shown an intention to abandon the use of the original track.

Q: *That seems fairly straightforward, doesn't it?*

A: It does until you read some of the other cases. *CDC2020 plc v Ferreira* (2005) concerned an easement which had allowed access to garages and had been granted to the claimant's predecessor in title. The garages had been demolished and had been replaced by a two-storey car park. After 30 years the garages were rebuilt and the defendant argued that the easement had been abandoned because of the demolition of the garages and the construction of the car park. It was held that despite the substantial building works, the court would not infer abandonment lightly and the claimant could use the right of access again. In *Williams v Sandy Lane (Chester) Ltd* the following factors were put forward by the defendant as evidence of abandonment. The claimants had used an alternative path to the one being claimed as a right of way; they had moved the back door so they didn't need to use the path being claimed as a right of way; they had allowed vegetation to grow up so the path being claimed as a right of way couldn't be seen. It was held that these factors simply explained why the path hadn't been used. They didn't show an intention to abandon its use altogether. Furthermore, fencing off the access to the path and piling earth round it still didn't count as an intention to abandon, as the fence was insubstantial and the earthworks made the use of the path only difficult rather than impossible. The claimant, Mrs Hibbitt, had also written to the Council in 1984 to object to an application for planning permission because she was claiming the right of way by prescription. Clearly abandoning a use and having the intention to abandon a use is a subtlety beyond all except the finest legal minds.

If the servient owner has to comply with a statutory requirement, then you can lose the right to use the easement and you do not have any remedy for interference with it: see *Jones v Cleanthi* (2006).

Finally, when the same person owns and possesses both the dominant and servient tenements, the easement will be extinguished because you cannot have an easement against yourself.

Q: *Is the easement automatically resurrected again if one of the plots of land is sold on?*

A: No, but note the decision in *Wall v Collins* (2007) where it was held that the merger of a lease (which had the benefit of an easement of a right of way attached to it) with the freehold did not extinguish the easement which had been attached to the lease. An easement had to be attached to and benefit a dominant tenement, but it did not have to be attached to any particular interest in the dominant tenement. This was so if the person claiming the easement held an interest in the dominant tenement that was as least as long in time as the lease. This meant the right of way could be used by the freeholder for as long as the lease had been granted for originally, even though the lease was now merged in the freehold.

Reform

The Law Commission has been looking at the reform of easements with a view to coming up with a scheme that is compatible with the commonhold system and the system of registration under the Land Registration Act 2002. The reasons for reform are as follows. You can argue that the law relating to easements acquired by prescription is outdated and difficult, not least when the year 1189 comes into it. Implied easements, as you have discovered, are numerous and confusing. There is no definition of the words 'continuous' and 'apparent' in *Wheeldon v Burrows*, and section 62 of the Law of Property Act 1925 forms a trap for the unwary. There is also no counterpart for easements of section 84 of the Law of Property Act 1925 which looks at the discharge of a restrictive covenant when it serves little useful purpose. You could argue that it would be useful for an owner of land burdened by an easement to be able to apply for discharge in the same way. In June 2011 the Law Commission published its report 'Making Land Work: Easements, Covenants and Profits à Prendre' (2011) Law Com No 327. The full report together with a draft Bill and an Executive Summary is on the Law Commission's website at www.justice.gov.uk/lawcommission/areas/easements.htm

These are the main recommendations in relation to easements.

- A single statutory scheme to simplify the law relating to prescription.
- The current ways of acquiring an implied easement to be replaced by a single statutory principle that easements will be implied where they are necessary for the reasonable use of the land at the time of the transaction (unless the statutory provision has been expressly excluded). What is necessary for the reasonable use of the land will be determined by the following five factors: (1) the use of the land at the time of the grant; (2) the presence on the servient land of any relevant physical features; (3) any intention for the future use of the land, known to both parties at the time of the grant; (4) so far as relevant, the available routes for the easement sought; and (5) the potential interference with the servient land or inconvenience to the servient owner.
- Section 62 of the Law of Property Act 1925 should no longer transform precarious advantages such as licences into new easements.
- Profits à prendre should not be created by implication or by prescription as they are commercial in nature and should be created expressly.
- The means of creating rights to park vehicles and other similar easements should be facilitated but this should not enable the grant of an easement that gives a right to exclusive possession.
- A presumption of an intention to abandon an easement or profit following 20 years' non-use.
- Section 84 of the Law of Property Act 1925 (dealing with modification and discharge of restrictive covenants) should be extended to include easements and profits created after the proposed reform.

The Law Commission is also looking at whether the law relating to acquiring and enforcing rights to light provides a balance between landowners and developers. It will examine the relationship between the planning system and rights to light and whether the remedies available to the court are 'reasonable, sufficient and proportionate'. A consultation paper is expected in 2013.

A question on easements

This example is intended to illustrate how to use the Boxes in this chapter to analyse the legal position. If you are using this method in undergraduate law exam questions, you will need to include statutory and case authority and detailed discussion of the various points of law. This information is found both in the text and from other sources.

> Gordon was the freehold proprietor of a large plot of land called Highacres. A public highway abuts the southern boundary and a large detached house, Glebe Mansion, stands on the plot 100 metres back from the highway. The house is connected to the highway by a driveway that runs just within the western boundary of Highacres. A large garden stretches north from the house for 200 metres. At the end of the garden is a small cottage, Cosy Nook, which was let four years ago on a five-year lease granted to Hyacinth. The northern boundary of Highacres abuts a narrow country lane with access to Cosy Nook through a wide swing gate. However, Hyacinth finds it more convenient to drive her car from the highway along a dirt track within the eastern boundary of Highacres. Gordon gave Hyacinth oral permission to do this shortly after she took the lease. Gordon subsequently became financially embarrassed and decided to cash in on the value of his property by carving it up into three equal portions, the boundaries between them running west to east. He agreed to sell the freehold of the middle plot, containing Glebe Mansion, to Ian. Gordon decided to retain the southern plot for himself, intending to build a house on it. Last month, Gordon conveyed the freehold of Cosy Nook to Hyacinth and, a week later, the middle plot was conveyed to Ian, but neither conveyance mentioned rights of way over the land retained by Gordon, who has just sold the southern plot to Janice. Janice now refuses to let Hyacinth use the dirt track to gain access to Cosy Nook and refuses to let Ian use the driveway to gain access to Glebe Mansion.
>
> Advise Hyacinth and Ian.

This is a question on easements. First draw a diagram.

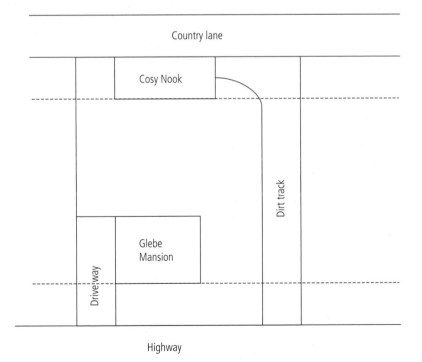

There are two rights in question here: Hyacinth's to continue to use the dirt track and Ian's to use the driveway up to Glebe Mansion. You must establish whether either Hyacinth or Ian can claim an easement of a right of way. This will be important to them, as an easement is a proprietary right in land and is capable of binding a third party, here Janice.

The claim to use the dirt track

First, look at the position between Gordon and Hyacinth and the permission to use the dirt track over Highacres. You must establish whether this is a right capable of being an easement by meeting the conditions laid down in *Re Ellenborough Park* in Box A.

Box A   The essence of an easement: Re Ellenborough Park (1956)
You must tick all boxes here.

A1 There must be a dominant and servient tenement
Cosy Nook is the dominant tenement and Highacres is the servient tenement. You can tick this box.

A2 The dominant and servient tenements must not be owned and occupied by the same person
Cosy Nook and Highacres were not owned and occupied by the same person. You can tick this box.

A3 The right must accommodate or benefit the dominant tenement
The right to use the dirt track benefited the land of Cosy Nook and was not just a personal advantage to Hyacinth. The case authority here is *Hill v Tupper*. You can tick this box.

A4 The right must be capable of forming the subject matter of a grant

A4i There must be a capable grantor and a capable grantee
Gordon is the grantor of the easement and Hyacinth is the grantee. There is no indication that either Hyacinth or Gordon was incapable in any way. You can tick this box.

A4ii The right must be sufficiently definite
A right of way is sufficiently definite. It is not like a right to a view: see *Aldred's Case*. You can tick this box.

A4iii The right must be analogous to existing easements
A right of way has been recognised as a valid easement by the courts: see *Borman v Griffith*. You can tick this box.

A4iv The right must not totally exclude the servient owner
The right of way did not totally exclude Gordon from Highacres. You can tick this box.

Summary of Box A
Hyacinth has a right that is capable of being an easement.
 You must now establish that the easement has been created in a recognised way.

Box B *The creation of an easement*

Application of section 1 of the Law of Property Act 1925
In order for an easement to be legal under section 1(2)(a) of the Law of Property Act 1925, it must be granted for a period equivalent to a fee simple absolute in possession or a term of years absolute. It must also be created within a deed to satisfy section 52(1) of the Law of Property Act 1925. Look at the different ways of creating an easement and then establish whether these conditions have been met.

B1 Express grant in a deed (legal easement)
Although Gordon sold Cosy Nook to Hyacinth, you are told that no mention was made of the right of way in the conveyance, the deed of sale. There was therefore no express grant in the deed of sale. You cannot tick this box.

B2 Express grant in a written contract (equitable easement)
There is no evidence of an express grant in a written contract between Gordon and Hyacinth sufficient to satisfy section 2 of the Law of Property (Miscellaneous Provisions) Act 1989. You cannot tick this box.

B3 Implied grant of necessity (legal easement)
Hyacinth's right of way is not absolutely necessary for the use of Cosy Nook: see *Titchmarsh v Royston Water Co Ltd*. You cannot imply an easement of necessity of a right of way over Highacres into the deed of sale when Gordon sold Cosy Nook to Hyacinth. You cannot tick this box.

B4 Implied grant of mutual intention (legal easement)
There is no indication that Gordon and Hyacinth intended that Hyacinth should continue to have a right of way over Highacres when Gordon sold Cosy Nook to her: see *Wong v Beaumont Property Trust Ltd*. You cannot tick this box.

B5 Implied grant under the rule in Wheeldon v Burrows (legal or equitable easement)
For the rule in *Wheeldon v Burrows* to operate, Highacres must have been owned and occupied by one person and the benefited part of the land sold off. Gordon owned Highacres but Hyacinth occupied that part of Gordon's land called Cosy Nook. This means that you cannot tick this box as the land was not owned and occupied by one person.

B6 Implied grant under section 62 of the Law of Property Act 1925 (legal easement)
Section 62 can have the effect of converting privileges into legal easements. Hyacinth has the privilege of using the dirt track. The conditions for section 62 to operate are as follows:

- Section 62 must not be expressly excluded; and
- The right that is being claimed must be capable of being an easement by meeting the conditions stated in *Re Ellenborough Park*; and
- The dominant and servient tenements are owned by one person but there is separate occupation of the dominant and servient tenements; and
- The owner of the servient tenement uses a deed to sell or transfer the dominant tenement to the occupier; or

▶ The owner of the servient tenement uses a deed to grant or renew a lease of the dominant tenement to the occupier; or

▶ The owner of the servient tenement uses a written agreement to grant or renew a lease of the dominant tenement for three years or less to the occupier.

You can now apply these conditions.

Gordon did not expressly exclude the operation of section 62 (and should probably sue his solicitor). The right of way claimed by Hyacinth is capable of being an easement. Highacres was owned by Gordon. Gordon occupied the servient tenement but Hyacinth occupied the dominant tenement called Cosy Nook. The owner of the servient tenement, Gordon, sold the dominant tenement, Cosy Nook, to the occupier, Hyacinth, by deed. The effect of section 62 is to convert Hyacinth's privilege of driving over Gordon's land into an easement of a right of way: see *Wright v Macadam*.

The easement is capable of being legal under section 1(2)(a) of the Law of Property Act 1925 for the following reason. Hyacinth was granted the fee simple absolute in possession in Cosy Nook. This is an estate which effectively goes on forever. The implied grant of the easement is attached to this estate and so has also effectively been granted forever. The grant was implied into the conveyance, the deed of sale, under section 62, thereby satisfying section 52(1) of the Law of Property Act 1925. You can tick this box.

B7 Prescription (legal easement)

Hyacinth has not used the right for 20 years. Gordon also gave her permission to use the right. Both these factors mean that Hyacinth will not have a claim based on prescription. You cannot tick this box.

B8, B9, B10 The reservation of an easement

This is not relevant here as Gordon is not claiming an easement over the land he has sold.

Summary of Box B

Hyacinth will be able to claim that she has a legal easement of a right of way over Highacres by virtue of section 62 of the Law of Property Act 1925.

Q: *Could you argue that an easement had been created between Hyacinth and Janice?*

A: You would have to argue here that when Janice bought the southern plot an easement was created between Janice and Hyacinth. However, Janice did not expressly grant Hyacinth a right of way by deed or in a written contract. You cannot argue an implied easement of necessity or of mutual intention or an easement under the rule in *Wheeldon v Burrows* or an easement implied under section 62 of the Law of Property Act 1925 because Janice did not sell Cosy Nook to Hyacinth. This means that there was no conveyance, deed of sale, into which to imply an easement. You cannot use prescription as Hyacinth had not used the right of way for 20 years. So no.

You must now establish whether Janice is bound by the legal easement that was created between Gordon and Hyacinth. You are not told whether Highacres is unregistered or registered land, so you must consider both situations.

Box C The protection of an easement

Unregistered land

C1 Legal easement
Hyacinth acquired a legal easement over Highacres. Legal rights bind the world in unregistered land. Her legal easement will be binding on Janice, no argument.

Q: *Does it matter that Hyacinth has to drive across the middle plot, which is now owned by Ian?*
A: No. Hyacinth acquired her legal easement to use the dirt track over Highacres before Ian bought the middle plot. As legal rights bind the world, Hyacinth's legal easement would bind Ian when he purchased the middle plot.

C2 Equitable easement
This is not relevant as we are talking about a legal easement.

Registered land

C3 Dealings which must be completed by registration
This was not an express grant of a legal easement and so is not a dealing that must be completed by registration under section 27 of the Land Registration Act 2002.

C4 Interests which override a registered disposition
A legal easement acquired under section 62 of the Law of Property Act 1925 will be an overriding interest under paragraph 3 of Schedule 3 to the Land Registration Act 2002 if any of the following conditions is met:

- The person who bought the southern plot that had the right of way over it, Janice, knew about the right of way; or
- The right of way would have been obvious to the person who bought the southern plot, Janice, on a reasonably careful inspection of the southern plot, or
- The right of way had been used in the last year before the southern plot was sold, here to Janice.

Both the last two conditions are satisfied. The first condition would be satisfied if Janice knew of the right of way.

As the easement is one that overrides, Janice will be bound by Hyacinth's right of way over the southern plot and must allow her to use the dirt track. The legal easement also overrides Ian's rights when he purchased the middle plot as he would also meet the last two conditions in paragraph 3 of Schedule 3.

C5 Interests entered as a notice or protected by a restriction
This is not relevant here, as this category relates to equitable easements.

Q: *What would happen if Janice refused to let Hyacinth use the dirt track?*
A: Hyacinth could sue Janice in nuisance for interfering with her lawful use of the land.

Q: *If you couldn't prove that Hyacinth had acquired a legal easement, could she still use the dirt track?*

A: Hyacinth would have a licence or permission to use the dirt track. As she had given no consideration for the use of the track, this would be a bare licence. A bare licence is not a proprietary interest in land and is purely personal between the original parties: see *Ashburn Anstalt v Arnold & Co.* It is therefore not capable of binding a third party, and so both Janice and Ian could have stopped Hyacinth from using the dirt track.

The claim to use the driveway

You now need to consider whether Ian can claim that an easement to use the driveway which runs over the southern plot to reach Glebe Mansion was created between him and Gordon.

Box A The essence of an easement

A1 There must be a dominant and servient tenement
Glebe Mansion is the dominant tenement and Highacres is the servient tenement. You can tick this box.

A2 The dominant and servient tenements must not be owned and occupied by the same person
Glebe Mansion and Highacres are not owned and occupied by the same person. You can tick this box.

A3 The right must accommodate or benefit the dominant tenement
The right to use the driveway would benefit Glebe Mansion and would not be just a personal advantage to Ian. The case authority here is *Hill v Tupper*. You can tick this box.

A4 The right must be capable of forming the subject matter of a grant

A4i There must be a capable grantor and a capable grantee
Gordon is the grantor of the easement and Ian the grantee. There is no indication that either Ian or Gordon was incapable in any way. You can tick this box.

A4ii The right must be sufficiently definite
A right over a driveway is sufficiently definite. It is not like a right to a view: see *Aldred's Case.* You can tick this box.

A4iii The right must be analogous to existing easements
A right of way has been recognised as a valid easement by the courts: see *Borman v Griffith.* You can tick this box.

A4iv The right must not totally exclude the servient owner
The right of way did not totally exclude Gordon from the southern plot. You can tick this box.

Summary of Box A
Ian has a right that is capable of being an easement.

Box B *The creation of an easement*

Application of section 1 of the Law of Property Act 1925

In order to be legal an easement must be granted for a period equivalent to a fee simple absolute in possession or a term of years absolute under section 1(2)(a) of the Law of Property Act 1925. It must also be created within a deed to satisfy section 52(1) of the Law of Property Act 1925. Look at the different ways of creating an easement and then establish whether these conditions have been met.

B1 Express grant in a deed (legal easement)

Although Gordon sold Glebe Mansion to Ian, you are told that no mention was made of the right of way in the conveyance, the deed of sale. There was therefore no express grant. You cannot tick this box.

B2 Express grant in a written contract (equitable easement)

There is no indication of an express grant between Gordon and Ian in a written contract sufficient to satisfy section 2 of the Law of Property (Miscellaneous Provisions) Act 1989.

B3 Implied grant of necessity (legal easement) and B4 Implied grant of mutual intention (legal easement)

You do not have enough information here to know whether the driveway was the only access to Glebe Mansion. If it was, you could argue a grant of an easement of necessity implied into the deed of sale of Glebe Mansion to Ian. You could also argue that there was a grant of mutual intention implied again into the deed of sale. In both these cases, the easement will acquire legal status by virtue of the fact that the grant is implied into the deed of sale. You cannot definitely tick these boxes without further information.

B5 Implied grant under the rule in Wheeldon v Burrows (legal or equitable easement)

For the rule in *Wheeldon v Burrows* to operate, Highacres must have been owned and occupied by one person and the benefited or dominant part of the land must have been sold off. This condition is met here. Gordon owned Highacres and sold Glebe Mansion, the benefited land, to Ian. The question now is whether the other conditions under the rule in *Wheeldon v Burrows* have also been met. The conditions are that the right claimed must have been:

- continuous and apparent;

  and

- necessary to the reasonable enjoyment of the land sold;

  and

- in use both previously and at the time of the sale for the benefit of the part of the land sold.

The right over the driveway would have been clearly visible, necessary for the reasonable enjoyment of the middle plot and in use at the time of the sale to Ian for the benefit of Glebe Mansion. The conditions in the rule in *Wheeldon v Burrows* are satisfied.

The easement is capable of being legal under section 1(2)(a) of the Law of Property Act 1925 for the following reason. Ian was granted the fee simple absolute in possession in the middle plot. This is an estate which effectively goes on forever. The implied grant of the easement is attached to this estate and so has also effectively been granted forever. The grant was implied into the conveyance, the deed of sale, thereby satisfying section 52(1) of the Law of Property Act 1925. You can tick this box.

B6 Implied grant under section 62 of the Law of Property Act 1925 (legal easement)
For section 62 to operate, Highacres must have been owned by Gordon but the dominant tenement occupied by another person. You cannot use section 62 as Ian did not occupy the middle plot before Gordon sold it to him. You cannot tick this box.

B7 Prescription (legal easement)
Ian has not used the driveway for 20 years. You cannot tick this box.

B8, B9, B10 The reservation of an easement
This is not relevant here as Gordon is not claiming an easement over the land he has sold.

Summary of Box B
Ian will be able to claim that a legal easement of a right of way was created over the driveway by virtue of the rule in *Wheeldon v Burrows*.

Q: *Could you argue that an easement had been created between Ian and Janice?*

A: You would have to argue here that, following Janice's ownership of the southern plot, an easement had been created between Ian and Janice. However, Janice did not expressly grant Ian a right of way by deed or in a written contract. You cannot argue an implied easement of necessity or of mutual intention or an easement under the rule in *Wheeldon v Burrows* or one implied under section 62 of the Law of Property Act 1925 because Janice did not sell the middle plot to Ian. This means that there was no deed of sale into which to imply an easement. You cannot use prescription as Ian had not used the right of way for 20 years. So no.

You must now establish whether Janice is bound by the legal easement of the right over the driveway that was created between Gordon and Ian. You are not told whether Highacres was unregistered or registered land so you must consider both situations.

Unregistered land

C1 Legal easement
Ian acquired a legal easement over Highacres. Legal rights bind the world in unregistered land. His legal easement will be binding on Janice, no argument.

C2 Equitable easement
This is not relevant as we are talking about a legal easement.

Registered land

C3 Dealings which must be completed by registration
This was not an express grant of a legal easement which must be completed by registration under section 27 of the Land Registration Act 2002.

C4 Interests which override a registered disposition
A legal easement acquired under the rule in *Wheeldon v Burrows* where a deed has been used will be an overriding interest in paragraph 3 of Schedule 3 to the Land Registration Act 2002 if any of the following conditions is met:

- The person who bought the southern plot that had the right of way over it, Janice, knew about the right of way; or
- The right of way would have been obvious to the person who bought the southern plot, Janice, on a reasonably careful inspection of the southern plot, or
- The right of way had been used in the last year before the southern plot was sold, here to Janice.

Both the last two conditions would be satisfied. The first condition would be satisfied if Janice knew of the right over the driveway.

As it is an easement that overrides, Janice will be bound by Ian's right of way over the southern plot and must let him use the driveway.

C5 Interests which must be protected by a notice or a restriction
This is not relevant here as this category relates to equitable easements.

Q: *What would happen if Janice refused to let Ian use the driveway?*
A: Ian could sue Janice in nuisance for interfering with his lawful use of the land.

Q: *If you couldn't prove that Ian had acquired an easement, could he still use the driveway to get to Glebe Mansion?*
A: No.

Conclusion

Both legal easements will bind Janice and she must continue to let Hyacinth and Ian use their respective easements of a right of way over her land.

Easements – the interpretation of section 62 of the Law of Property Act 1925

This is a discussion on section 62 of the Law of Property Act 1925. A right, liberty, privilege (permission) or advantage will be converted into a legal easement (a proprietary right) under section 62 of the Law of Property Act 1925 if certain conditions are met. These conditions were discussed in full earlier in the chapter. We said that not everyone agrees that there needs to be diversity of occupation in order for section 62 to convert existing rights, liberties and privileges into full blown legal easements. This section sets out some of those arguments using many ifs, buts and maybes. What would be really helpful is a case that determines the matter once and for all. There is plenty of reading matter on this area and references are included at the end of this chapter.

Q: *What is the problem here?*

A: Section 62 states that all easements, rights, liberties and privileges over the land pass in the conveyance to a purchaser. The words 'rights, liberties and privileges' are the words that concern us here because they imply that rights less than easements can pass to a purchaser in the conveyance under section 62, thereby becoming legal easements. One group of academics, let us call them the 'Diversity-of-Occupationists', believe that there must be diversity of occupation before any rights, liberties or privileges can become legal easements in favour of the purchaser under section 62. Other academics, the 'Continuous-and-Apparentists', believe that you do not need diversity of occupation before any rights, liberties or privileges become legal easements under section 62 in favour of a purchaser. Instead, any rights, privileges or liberties must meet the requirement of being continuous and apparent in order to do so. The true situation seems to be a combination of these two opposing views.

Start off by looking at the requirement that there must be diversity of occupation before section 62 can operate to convert a right, liberty or privilege that is capable of being an easement into a legal easement. Remember throughout this entire section that only rights, liberties or privileges capable of becoming easements by meeting the requirements in *Re Ellenborough Park* can become so.

The reasoning for the requirement of diversity of occupation is that you cannot have a right, liberty or privilege over your own land. If you own and occupy land, you cannot have rights against yourself because you are using the land in your capacity as owner of the entirety of the land. For example, you cannot sue yourself and you cannot give yourself a gift of the land. Look at a classic example of section 62 operating when there has been diversity of occupation. Landlord L owns the land but has leased part of it to T. L has given T permission to store coal in L's coal shed. If L subsequently sells that part of the land that T was leasing to him, the permission to store coal in L's coal shed becomes a legal easement through the conveyance of sale from L to T under section 62. Diversity of occupation here enabled T to have a right, liberty or privilege over L's land that became a legal easement when the dominant land was sold to T. If T didn't have that right, liberty or privilege, he would be a trespasser when he stored coal in the shed. T must have some form of right, even if it's only in the form of permission, to store coal in L's coal shed, which allows that right to become a legal easement upon sale.

Now look at the practicalities of the situation. If T had stored coal in L's coal shed during the time he leased land from L, T would expect that right to store coal in L's coal shed to continue when he bought the land.

BUT would L really have intended that any right, liberty or privilege he had given to T while T leased the land would become a legal easement when L sold the land to T?

HOWEVER section 62 can be excluded from the conveyance so L can easily avoid this happening. L can also avoid it by withdrawing all rights, liberties or privileges from T before L sells the land to T.

Diversity of occupation was stated to be a requirement for the operation of section 62 in *Long v Gowlett, Payne v Inwood* and also *Sovmots Investments Ltd v Secretary of State for the Environment*, albeit obiter.

The other camp of academics argues that you do not need diversity of occupation provided the right, liberty or privilege claimed is continuous and apparent.

Q: *How do these academics refute the argument that you cannot have a right over your own land?*

A: It's true to say that you cannot have an easement over your own land, because an easement is a right over someone else's land. Now imagine you own Watermill, land with a watermill and reed beds. You go onto the reed beds to clear them so that the water flows down to the mill. You could argue that you had made the use of one bit of your land (the watermill) dependant on the other (the clearing of the reed beds). You could then argue that you have created a use over one bit of land (the reed beds) in favour of the other bit of land (the watermill). In this case you don't need diversity of occupation.

Another way of looking at it is to say that there are certain things you are not allowed to do on Watermill. You do not have the right to excavate down so deep that the neighbouring houses collapse. You do not have the right to build an international airport unless you have planning permission. These are rights you haven't got. That means that the things you are allowed to do on your land are rights that you do have, whether you call them rights, privileges or liberties. You have the right to clear the reed beds, you have the right to have afternoon tea on the lawn and you have the right to feed the local hedgehog, for example. These are 'rights' you do have on the land in comparison to the rights you haven't got.

Q: *So the arguments of academics here is that you don't need diversity of occupation, just a continuous and apparent use?*

A: Correct.

Q: *Isn't this the same as* **Wheeldon v Burrows (1879)?**

A: No. This is because the right, permission or liberty that you are enjoying over your own land only has to be continuous and apparent. It does not have to be reasonably necessary for the enjoyment of the land, as in *Wheeldon v Burrows*.

Q: *Do you have to meet all the other rules as well for section 62 if there is no diversity of occupation but the right is continuous and apparent?*

A: Yes.

Q: *What does continuous and apparent mean?*

A: One presumes the same definition as in *Wheeldon v Burrows*, which is 'used on a regular basis' and 'visible on a reasonably careful inspection of the land'.

Q: *Why does the right, liberty or privilege have to be used on a regular basis?*

A: If the seller has been using a right, liberty or privilege for the benefit of that part of the land he has sold off, it might be considered unfair if he turned round after the sale and said to the purchaser 'you can't continue to use the right, liberty or privilege over the land I have kept, even though I was using that right, privilege or liberty on a regular basis'. The seller is not allowed to derogate from his grant here. This means that the seller can't convey part of his land which clearly benefits from a right, liberty or privilege over the part retained by him and then say to the purchaser, 'you can't use that same right, liberty or privilege'.

Q: *Why does the right, liberty or privilege have to be visible?*

A: Again, it goes back to non-derogation from grant. The seller can't turn round after the sale and tell the purchaser that he is not allowed to use a right that was clearly visible over the part of the land retained by the seller. Furthermore, if the purchaser didn't know about the right, liberty or privilege at the time he bought the land because it wasn't visible, he can hardly say the seller has derogated from his grant if he, the purchaser, didn't know about the right, liberty or privilege.

Q: *Where does it say 'continuous and apparent' in section 62?*

A: It doesn't.

Q: *So really all rights, privileges and liberties enjoyed by the seller over his land could pass under section 62, not just those that are continuous and apparent?*

A: Yes. It is argued, though, that section 62 is a word-saving device. Before section 62 and its predecessor, the Conveyancing Act of 1881, it took a long time in a conveyance actually to spell out the different rights and privileges that would pass to a purchaser. Section 62 meant all these rights didn't have to be spelt out because it was a word-saving device. When you interpret what is meant by the words rights, privileges and liberties in section 62, you should be looking at what the parties intended should pass in the conveyance – the normal contractual intentions of the parties. This would not be a wide interpretation of section 62. Only those rights, liberties or privileges that were continuous and apparent would pass, because that is what the parties would intend. If you didn't narrow section 62 down in this way, then any seller of part of his land would risk all potential rights, liberties and privileges that were capable of becoming easements over his remaining land actually becoming so under section 62. Section 62 would be excluded from a conveyance every time and the seller would have to write out his own list. This would totally defeat the purpose of section 62 as a word-saving device. An own goal in fact.

In *Broomfield v Williams* it was held that the benefit of a right to light passed under section 62 to a purchaser because a right to light is continuous and apparent, i.e. always present and visible. In *Watts v Kelson* (1871), which was decided under the 1881 Conveyancing Act, the predecessor to section 62 of the Law of Property Act 1925, a watercourse through clearly visible pipes became an easement in this way. In *P&S Platt Ltd v Crouch*, the right to moor boats on the retained part of the vendor's land passed to the purchaser under section 62 because the right to moor boats was held to be continuous and apparent.

A third camp of academics argues that the only right that is continuous and apparent that is capable of becoming an easement is the right to light under the authority of *Broomfield v Williams*. This is because a right to light is considered to be an exception to other easements.

Q: *Why is the right to light considered to be an exception?*

A: If you claim a right to light, you do not have to prove user as of right, i.e. without force, without secrecy and without permission. You are not likely to grant a right to light as you would a right of way. Easements of a right to light are generally recognised because someone has interfered with them, rather than because someone has granted someone else the right to them. If easements of a right to light are the only exceptions and pass under section 62 because they are also continuous and apparent, there is no justification for saying that other rights, privileges, permissions become easements under section 62 simply because they are continuous and apparent. The courts do not agree with this reasoning because the continuous and apparent right to moor boats was recognised as creating an easement under section 62 in *P&S Platt Ltd v Crouch* (2003).

Q: *Is this as confusing as it sounds?*

A: Probably. To summarise, section 62 will operate when there is diversity of occupation, as in *Wright v Macadam*. If there is no diversity of occupation, section 62 will also operate when the right being claimed is continuous and apparent. The obvious example here is a right to light as in *Broomfield v Williams*, but other rights have also been recognised as in *P&S Platt Ltd v Crouch*. In an exam, look for the landlord/tenant or the licensor/licensee situation where there is diversity of occupation for the classic question on section 62. If there is no diversity of occupation use *Wheeldon v Burrows* if the right is continuous and apparent and reasonably necessary for the enjoyment of the land. You can also consider section 62 if the right claimed is simply continuous and apparent. Remember, though, through all of this discussion, that only rights, privileges or liberties that are capable of being easements by meeting the requirement in *Re Ellenborough Park* can become easements under section 62.

Further reading

A. Baker, 'Recreational Privileges as Easements: Law and Policy', *Conv and Prop Law*, (2012) 37

D. Barnsley, 'Equitable Easements – Sixty Years On', 115 *LQR* (1999) 89

F. Burns, 'Prescriptive Easements in England and Legal "Climate Change"', *Conv and Prop Law*, Mar/Apr (2007) 133

P. Davis, 'Abandonment of an Easement: Is It a Question of Intention Only?' *Conv and Prop Law*, Jul/Aug (1995) 291

A. Dunn and I. Dawson, 'Negative Easements – A Crumb of Analysis', 18 *Legal Studies* (1998) 510

C. J. Gale, J. Gaunt and P. Morgan, *Gale on Easements*, 19th edn (London: Sweet and Maxwell)

M. Haley, 'Easements, Exclusionary Use and Elusive Principles – The Right to Park', *Conv and Prop Law*, 3 (2008) 244

C. Harpum, 'Easements and Centre Point: Old Problems Resolved in a Novel Setting', *Conv and Prop Law*, Nov/Dec (1977) 415. In reply: P. Smith, 'Centre Point: Faulty Towers with Shaky Foundations', *Conv and Prop Law*, Nov/Dec (1978) 449. In reply: C. Harpum, '*Long v. Gowlett*: A Strong Fortress', *Conv and Prop Law* Mar/Apr (1979) 113

C. Harpum, 'Acquisition of Easements', 51 *CLJ* (1992) 220

Further reading cont'd

A. Hill-Smith, 'Rights of Parking and the Ouster Principle after *Batchelor v Marlow*', *Conv and Prop Law*, May/Jun (2007) 223

Law Commission, Making Land Work: Easements, Covenants and Profits à Prendre (Law Com No 327, 2011)

M. Litman and B. Ziff, 'Easements and Possession: An Elusive Limitation', *Conv and Prop Law*, Jul/Aug (1989) 296

P. Luther, 'Easements and Exclusive Possession', 16 *Legal Studies* (1996) 51

C. Sara, 'Prescription – What is it For?' *Conv and Prop Law*, Jan/Feb (2004) 13

G. Spark, 'Easements of Parking and Storage: Are Easements Non-Possessory Interests in Land?' *Conv and Prop Law* (2012) 6

L. Tee, 'Metamorphoses and section 62 of the Law of Property Act 1925', *Conv and Prop Law*, Mar/Apr (1998) 115

J. West, '*Wheeldon v Burrows* Revisited', *Conv and Prop Law*, Jul/Aug (1995) 346

L. Xu, 'Easement of Car Parking: The Ouster Principle Is Out But Problems May Aggravate', *Conv and Prop Law* (2012) 291

Chapter 18

Mortgages

www.palgrave.com/law/Stroud4e

Introduction

Most people have heard about mortgages in the context of the family home. Greenacres is purchased partly or wholly using a loan from a bank or building society, and the property is used as security for the loan. The loan is paid back with interest over a set period of time. If the borrower is unable to pay the mortgage repayments, the bank can take possession of and sell the property in order to recoup the outstanding loan money it is owed. Mortgages can exist over property other than houses, and people other than banks and building societies can lend money on a mortgage. The borrower is known as the mortgagor. The lender is known as the mortgagee. This is not the way most people use the terms 'mortgagor' and 'mortgagee', but it is the correct way. We have used the terms 'borrower' and 'lender' in this chapter for simplicity, but note that you will have to use the terms 'mortgagor' and 'mortgagee' elsewhere.

This chapter looks at the creation of a mortgage, the rights of the parties in a mortgage situation and the priority of mortgages, where land is concerned.

The creation of a mortgage

A mortgage agreement is essentially a contract. It is a promise whereby the lender lends money to the borrower, who contracts to pay back the loan with interest on a specified date. When a mortgage was created before 1926, the land was conveyed (transferred) to the lender in return for the loan of money, on condition that when the loan and the interest on the loan had been paid back, the lender would reconvey (transfer) the land back to the borrower. If the money was not paid back in full on the date specified in the contract, the lender was entitled to take the land in its entirety.

Q: *If the loan hadn't been paid back and the lender took the land, who took any increase in the value of the land?*

A: If the value of the land was greater than the money owed on the mortgage, the lender took all the increase, and that was just bad luck for the borrower.

Q: *If the lender owned the land, did he have a right to occupy it?*

A: Yes, but the lender's main objective was to hold the land as security, not to use it. As the lender was also accountable for the state of the land and for any income from it if he went into occupation, the borrower was usually allowed to stay in residence.

Since 1925 the creation of a mortgage has been governed by sections 85–87 of the Law of Property Act 1925. A legal mortgage over land must now be made by:

either

(i) a demise for a term of years absolute, subject to a provision for cesser on redemption;

or

(ii) a charge by deed expressed to be by way of legal mortgage.

Q: *What does this mean in plain English?*

A: In (i), a demise for a term of years absolute is a lease for a set number of years. This term is set in the Act as 3,000 years. The provision for a cesser on redemption means that the lease is subject to a provision that it will end when the mortgage loan and the interest are paid back in full.

In (ii), a charge is a burden attached by deed to the borrower's land in favour of the lender. It gives the lender the same rights and powers as if he had been granted a lease of 3,000 years.

You should also note that, because the lender takes a lease or a charge over the property for which he gives money as consideration, he is a purchaser of a legal estate, the leasehold estate, for value.

Q: *Why does it matter whether the lender is a purchaser for value?*

A: Because as a general rule, if interests are not protected in unregistered or registered land, they are not binding on a purchaser for value, here the lender. This emphasises the importance of protecting any interest you have over another's land.

The way a mortgage is created accounts for the terminology used in the words *mortgagor* and *mortgagee*. The borrower actually creates a mortgage over his land in favour of the lender. He is the creator, or the grantor, of the lease or its charge equivalent, hence mortgagor. The mortgagee is the lender in whose favour the lease or charge equivalent is granted.

Q: *Does this mean that I grant a mortgage to the bank, not that it grants one to me?*

A: Yes.

Q: *Why was a lease for 3,000 years chosen? If Bundy's Bank, for example, had lent money to build the Pyramids, it would still be leasing them from the Egyptians if the loan hadn't been repaid.*

A: A lease for 3,000 years gives the lender the right to take rent-free possession for 3,000 years if the loan is not repaid. Although a lease is a wasting asset, this is very close to absolute ownership.

Q: *Why is a lease a wasting asset?*

A: Because as the amount of time remaining on a lease falls, so its value will also fall. If you take a lease for 50 years and pay rent, at the end of the 50 years you no longer have an interest in the property, nobody refunds you any money and you have nothing to show for your efforts. All leases come to an end sometime, even one of 3,000 years, but a lease of 3,000 years must be fairly close to absolute ownership as far as any lender is concerned.

Q: *Which way should you use to create a mortgage?*

A: A charge by deed is the most common way of creating a legal mortgage today, not least because of the difficulties in trying to explain to Mr and Mrs Brown that when they create a mortgage they are actually leasing their house to the bank. Hopefully, more people understand the concept of the word 'charge'. A charge by deed is also short and easy to create. Furthermore, section 23(1) of the Land Registration Act 2002 states that you cannot create a mortgage of registered land using method (i) above.

Q: *How do you create an equitable mortgage?*

A: If the borrower agrees to grant a legal mortgage to the lender in a contract that satisfies section 2 of the Law of Property (Miscellaneous Provisions) Act 1989, an equitable mortgage will be created. Under section 2 the contract must be in writing, signed by both parties and contain all the terms of the mortgage. Because such a contract is capable of specific performance and equity looks on that as done which ought to be done, the contract creates an equitable interest in favour of the lender, here an equitable mortgage. An equitable mortgage can also be created when the parties have not met the requirements for a deed but the document satisfies section 2 of the Law of Property (Miscellaneous Provisions) Act 1989. Before 1989 an equitable mortgage could be created by depositing the title deeds of the property with the lender with an intention that such title deeds were to be held as security for the loan: see *Russel v Russel* (1783).

Q: *Why would the title deeds be security for the loan?*

A: Because the borrower would find it extremely difficult to sell the land and disappear to Brazil with the proceeds if he didn't have the title deeds to prove his title to the property. A purchaser would be very foolish to go ahead with such a purchase without having first investigated the title deeds. It was possible to create an equitable mortgage in this way because an oral contract could be enforced if the party relying on the oral agreement had started to carry out his part of the contract, known as the doctrine of part performance. Here the act of part performance would be the borrower depositing the title deeds. In *United Bank of Kuwait v Sahib* (1997), though, it was decided that you could no longer create an equitable mortgage like this. Section 2 had abolished the doctrine of part performance because you cannot have part performance of a void contract. The parties now had to satisfy the requirement of section 2 of the Law of Property (Miscellaneous Provisions) Act 1989.

Finally, in registered land, a legal mortgage attains its legal status only when it is entered at the District Land Registry on the Charges Register of the land that is the security for the loan. Until then it remains equitable.

The right to redeem a mortgage

The right to redeem a mortgage is the right to pay off the debt and the interest, and to take back the property free of the mortgage and the lender's rights.

Q: *What date is usually set in the contract for repaying the loan?*

A: The date is called the legal date of redemption, and it is usually set at six months after the date of the contract. At common law the borrower has to pay the loan and the interest back on that specified date, and that date alone. If he misses the date, for whatever reason, the lender is entitled to take the property, including any increase in value.

Q: *What would happen if the borrower were just a couple of days late?*

A: The lender would still take the property. This is why equity stepped in, in the name of fairness, and granted the borrower the equitable right to redeem. From the 1600s equity allowed the borrower the equitable right to redeem the mortgage provided the contractual date that had been set between the parties had passed. The borrower would be entitled to his property if he paid the capital sum plus interest, even though the payment was after the date specified.

Q: *Why was this postponement allowed?*

A: The courts of equity saw no reason for the lender to obtain the entirety of the property just because the borrower was late in payment. The property was still valid security, and its value could be realised if the borrower never paid off the loan. The borrower no longer had to concern himself with the legal date of redemption because the equitable right to redeem meant that he was protected by equity. Provided he eventually paid off the mortgage, he could rely on the equitable right to redeem, and so could ignore the contractual date. However, the legal date of redemption remained important to the lender for the following reason. If the borrower couldn't keep up with the mortgage repayments, the lender would clearly want to sell the property to recoup the outstanding loan. The Law of Property Act 1925 will allow sale only if certain conditions are met, and one of these is that the legal (contractual) date of redemption has passed. The lender will want this date to arise early on in the mortgage so it can sell quickly if the borrower defaults on the mortgage repayments.

Q: *Does the equitable right to redeem a mortgage still exist today?*

A: Yes. It is a very important right for a borrower which arises the day after the legal date of redemption.

Q: *What ends the equitable right to redeem?*

A: If the statutory conditions allowing the lender to sell the house are met, the borrower will lose his equitable right to redeem when the lender sells the property.

Q: *What do people mean when they talk about the equity in a house? They talk about negative equity and positive equity.*

A: Imagine you buy a house for £100,000. You pay £20,000 in cash and raise £80,000 by means of a mortgage with Bundy's Bank. If the value of the house goes up to £200,000, the equity in the house exceeds the mortgage loan by £120,000. There is positive equity of £120,000 in the house. If the house falls in value to £60,000, there is not enough equity in the house to pay off the mortgage loan. There is negative equity in the house. Negative equity was a frequent occurrence in the 1990s. Because interest rates were low, people had large mortgages. This was followed by an economic recession, which, in turn, led to a drop in house prices. This meant that in many cases the value of the house didn't cover the mortgage loan. This was worrying for the lender because his security for his loan, the house, didn't cover the debt. It was also worrying for the borrower because the money from any sale wouldn't cover the cost of paying the lender the outstanding mortgage loan.

The equity of redemption

The phrase 'equity of redemption' is an overall name for the borrower's equitable rights. The equity of redemption includes the equitable right to redeem the mortgage after the legal date of redemption has passed (this is the right to pay off the debt and interest), plus the equity in the property, which is the value of the property minus the mortgage loan still owed to the lender. The equity of redemption is an interest in land and can be bought, sold or left in a will.

Restrictions on the right to redeem

There has always been a tension between the borrower and the lender. A lender can be in an extremely powerful position when asked to lend money, and he may take advantage of this. On the other hand, a mortgage is a commercial transaction, and the borrower has free choice whether to enter into that transaction. However, having given the borrower the equitable right to redeem, the courts of equity have always been concerned to see that the borrower's right to redeem the property is not taken away from him. Subject to paying off the mortgage loan and the interest, he should always be able to get his property back in its original condition. Equity has therefore tried to ensure that there are no clogs or fetters on the right to redeem.

Q: *Clogs and fetters?*

A: Despite the image this conjures up, it actually means that the lender must not hinder or prevent the borrower from being able to redeem the mortgage. Remember that the right to redeem the mortgage is the right to pay off the mortgage loan and interest. At this point, the lender's interest in the land will end. There are different ways in which the lender can try and stop the borrower from redeeming the mortgage. The first way is by postponing the right to redeem the mortgage. In *Fairclough v Swan Brewery Co Ltd* (1912) the mortgaged property was on a 171/2-year lease. The mortgage contract provided that the legal date of redemption, the first and only date at common law on which the mortgage debt could be wholly paid off, arose six weeks before the end of the lease. Despite the fact that the borrower could rely on the equitable right to redeem, this right was of no use to him. The value of the lease with six weeks to run was virtually zero. He couldn't have sold the lease of six weeks and raised enough money to pay back the mortgage loan. He claimed that the postponement of his right to redeem was effectively to make the mortgage irredeemable. The court held that the term in the mortgage postponing the right to redeem was void.

As Lord MacNaughten asked in the case:

> Is there any difference between forbidding redemption and permitting it, if the permission be a mere pretence?

To which the answer is 'No'.

However, in *Knightsbridge Estates Trust Ltd v Byrne* (1940) one of the terms of the mortgage stated that the borrower could not redeem the mortgage until after the end of a 40-year period. Interests rates then fell, and the borrower asked for an earlier redemption of the mortgage in order to obtain a lower interest rate elsewhere. The request was refused on the basis that the borrower had bargained hard for a long-term loan, there was nothing oppressive or unconscionable in the terms of the mortgage, and the borrower had entered freely into the contract. Unlike in the *Swan* case, the right of redemption was not a pretence as the property was not leased, and the borrower would still get his property back at the end of the 40 years. If the court had intervened, it would have meant that any borrower could get out of a mortgage if he could obtain a lower interest rate elsewhere, but that the lender couldn't get out of a mortgage if he wanted to invest his money at a higher rate of interest elsewhere. This would not be seen as fair in equity.

Q: *Although the terms in the Knightsbridge case were not seen as oppressive or unconscionable, what terms would be considered oppressive or unconscionable?*

A: Very high interest rates, for example. In *Cityland and Property (Holdings) Ltd v Dabrah* (1968) the effective rate of interest on the mortgage was 19% compared to a bank rate of 7%. If the borrower defaulted on a single repayment, the agreed terms of the mortgage meant that the effective interest rate would have been 57%. These agreed terms of interest were seen to be unfair and unconscionable, so the interest rate was reduced to 7%.

Q: *Wasn't this transaction entered into freely, though?*

A: Yes, but the balance of power lies with the lender, so the courts will intervene where the terms are oppressive.

However, in *Multiservice Bookbinding Ltd v Marden* (1979) the mortgage contract stated that the mortgage couldn't be redeemed for 10 years, nor could the lender call the mortgage in during that time. The rate of interest was linked to the Swiss franc. Changes in the exchange rate meant that interest repayments became very high. The agreement was not considered unfair or unconscionable, and 'unreasonableness' was deemed to be insufficient. The parties had equal bargaining power, and they had both received legal advice.

In *Paragon Finance plc v Nash* (2001) it was held that terms would be implied into agreements where there were variable interest rates. The implied terms would be that rates of interest would not be set dishonestly, for improper purposes, capriciously or arbitrarily.

Q: *Why do you have to imply such a term?*

A: To meet the reasonable expectations of the parties. Even so, a lender can still impose rates that the lender considers commercially necessary, even though the borrower would see such rates as unreasonable when compared to other lenders. In *Paragon Finance plc v Pender* (2005) it was held that a lender could raise interest rates above those of other commercial lenders where it was for a genuine commercial reason.

Another way to stop the borrower from redeeming the mortgage is to grant an option to purchase the mortgaged property to the lender. An option to purchase is where the lender pays for the option to buy the mortgaged property at a time of his choosing for a particular sum within a particular time frame. If the lender chooses not to exercise his option then he simply loses the sum he had to pay to acquire the option. In *Samuel v Jarrah Timber and Wood Paving Corporation Ltd* (1902) an option given to the lender to purchase the mortgaged stock at any time within 12 months of the date of the mortgage was struck out.

Q: *Why?*

A: Because the borrower would not be given the opportunity to redeem the mortgage if the lender exercised his option to purchase regardless of how fair the bargain was between the parties. The striking out of such clauses has been subject to criticism as indeed it was in the case itself. Lord Macnaghten asked if the rule could be changed to stop it being used to get out of a fair bargain where parties had negotiated on equal terms and dealt at arm's length. In the event he felt he couldn't interfere in a rule that had been around for so long.

Q: *What's the length of time a rule has been around got to do with it?*

A: Nothing. Don't forget, though, that the borrower is at the mercy of the lender. There is pressure on the borrower to agree to everything the lender asks for, here the option to purchase the mortgaged property, otherwise the borrower may not get his loan from the lender. In *Jones v Morgan* (2001) three years after a mortgage had been created a second agreement gave the lender the option to purchase a part of the mortgaged property. On the facts this second agreement was not seen as independent of the first mortgage. It was a variation of it so the option to purchase was seen as void. Lord Phillips MR likened the doctrine of a clog on the equity of redemption to the appendix in the human body that needs to be removed as it serves no useful purpose.

Q: *Does the doctrine apply to all options to purchase?*

A: In *Reeve v Lisle* (1902) an option to purchase was granted 12 days after the mortgage had been created. The option was valid because it was seen as a separate transaction outside the mortgage.

Q: Presumably having arranged the mortgage the borrower wasn't under any pressure to grant the option to purchase?

A: That's right. In *Warnborough Ltd v Garmite Ltd* (2006) it was held that a clog or fetter would be void only if it was seen as 'an objectionable restriction on the rights of a borrower who has mortgaged his property as security for the debt'. In the case though, the equally important question was whether the transaction was actually a mortgage or something else.

Q: What else could it be?

A: In *Warnborough Ltd v Garmite Ltd* it was held that, as always, the court had to look at all the circumstances and substance of the transaction and the true nature of the bargain to decide whether the transaction was a mortgage. Here the court decided that the option to purchase was a term of a contract of sale and purchase, not a term of the original mortgage. This meant that the rule on clogs and fetters did not apply because it was not a mortgage agreement. A similar result ensued in *Brighton and Hove City Council v Audus* (2009).

Q: Does the phrase 'once a mortgage, always a mortgage' come in here?

A: Yes. The phrase comes from *Santley v Wilde* (1899) and means that you can't create a mortgage and then call it or pretend it is something else. If what has been created is in substance a mortgage, it will be seen as such regardless of what it is called.

Unfair collateral advantages imposed by the lender

Given that the lender was usually in the position of greater power, equity also leant against any additional condition that the lender tried to incorporate in his own favour into the mortgage contract if it clogged the equity of redemption. *Clogging the equity of redemption* means that the borrower can't get his property back free from these conditions when the mortgage loan is paid off, and, as a result, the value of his property could fall. These additional conditions inserted into mortgage contracts are known as collateral advantages.

Until 1914, the courts leant heavily on those lenders who imposed any sort of collateral advantage in their own favour. The turning point came in *G & C Kreglinger v New Patagonia Meat and Cold Storage Co Ltd* (1914). The terms of the mortgage stated that the borrower would sell his sheepskins only to the lender provided the lender matched the best price of any third party. This is known as a right of first refusal. This arrangement was to endure for five years. The mortgage had been redeemed before the five years were up, and it was argued that the right of first refusal also had to come to an end. The House of Lords decided that there was no rule which prevented a lender from inserting a collateral advantage clause in its favour into the mortgage. Any such clause would be struck out only if it was either:

- unfair and unreasonable; or
- in the nature of a penalty clogging the equity of redemption; or
- inconsistent with, or repugnant to, the contractual and equitable right to redeem.

The clause in the *Kreglinger* case did not come into any of the above.

It was also held that even though a collateral advantage clause could be in the same document as the mortgage, if it was seen as a separate transaction outside the mortgage agreement it would be upheld.

Q: *A separate transaction but in the same document?*

A: Quite. A use of the word 'separate' of which we were previously unaware. *Warnborough Ltd v Garmite Ltd* is a useful case to read here.

Q: *Do you find collateral advantage clauses in mortgages when people buy houses?*

A: Not quite like this. These types of advantages are found in mortgages created between business parties. However, if you arrange a personal mortgage to buy a house, you may find that the lender insists that you insure the house with a specific company nominated by him. 'Specific' here has the same meaning as expensive. This could be seen to be a collateral advantage.

Clauses are also found where the borrower has to buy products from the lender for the duration of the mortgage. These are called solus agreements and are struck out if they continue after the redemption of the mortgage.

In *Noakes & Co Ltd v Rice* (1902) the borrower leased a pub with the aid of a mortgage loan and agreed with the lender that he would buy all his beer from the lender for the duration of the lease, even if the mortgage was redeemed before the end of the lease. This was held to be a clog on the equity of redemption because the pub would still be a tied house after the lender had redeemed the mortgage. In *Bradley v Carritt* (1903) there was a similar result, but this time it was to do with selling tea.

In *Biggs v Hoddinott* (1898) the length of time for which the borrower was required to buy the lender's products was limited to a period of five years. However, it was not possible to redeem the mortgage before this time. Consequently, this condition was not a clog on the equity of redemption.

There is also a doctrine in contract law which states that contracts in restraint of trade are against public policy. Mortgages are caught by this doctrine. In general, this means that short solus agreements will be upheld, and any long ones will be struck out. In *Esso Petroleum Co Ltd v Harper's Garage (Stourport) Ltd* (1968) there were two mortgages and two solus agreements. One solus agreement was for five years and the other was for 21 years. The case was decided on the ground of restraint of trade, and, whilst the solus agreement for five years was allowed, the one for 21 years was struck out.

Undue influence

This part of the chapter looks at undue influence. This occurs when one party exerts pressure on the other to enter into a transaction, here a mortgage. In *Allcard v Skinner* (1887) undue influence was described as 'some unfair and improper conduct, some coercion from outside … some form of cheating and generally, though not always, some personal advantage gained'.

There are two situations where you might find undue influence in a mortgage scenario. The first is where Peter, for example, deals directly with the Bank and then claims that the bank manager exerted undue influence over him and forced him into taking out the mortgage. This kind of situation is unlikely to arise because banks and mortgage lenders don't put themselves in positions where they can be accused of this. Banks and building societies have to follow codes of conduct. The second scenario where undue influence can arise is where Alan and his wife or partner, Sophie, are both on the legal title to Greenacres. Alan, who runs his own company, decides that he wants to invest further in it and so persuades Sophie to enter with him into a mortgage agreement over Greenacres with Bundy's Bank, or into a further mortgage agreement if a mortgage already exists. Both Alan and Sophie have to sign the paperwork for the new mortgage, although Sophie is very unhappy about it as she feels that they will not be able to meet the mortgage repayments. However, she loves Alan very much and believes that one day he will be very rich and all their financial problems will go away. When Alan's company goes bankrupt and Bundy's Bank wants to repossess and sell the house to recoup the money lent on the mortgage, Sophie realises that that day will never come. She may allege undue influence against Alan, claiming that he coerced her into entering into the mortgage agreement against her free will.

Q: *If she did prove undue influence, what would be her remedy?*

A: She would have to argue that because of his undue influence she didn't enter into the mortgage agreement voluntarily, so the mortgage is not enforceable against her share of the house as far as Alan is concerned. The bigger question though is the position in which Bundy's Bank finds itself. Alan and Sophie haven't met the mortgage repayments and Bundy's Bank now wishes to take possession of Greenacres with a view to sale to recoup the outstanding mortgage money. If Bundy's Bank is aware that Alan coerced Sophie into entering the mortgage agreement, there is an argument that it could enforce the mortgage against Alan's share of the house only.

Q: *But how would Bundy's Bank know about any coercion that might have gone on between Alan and Sophie?*

A: This is a question that has occupied the courts for a long time and it is what this part of the chapter is about. There are two areas to look at here. First, you need to ask what constitutes undue influence. If Alan hasn't exercised undue influence over Sophie, Bundy's Bank won't be affected at all and so it can take possession and sell Greenacres. Secondly, if there has been undue influence between Alan and Sophie, you need to look at the circumstances in which Bundy's Bank ought to have known that Alan might have exercised undue influence. *Barclays Bank plc v O'Brien* (1994) and *Royal Bank of Scotland v Etridge (No 2)* (2001) are the two important cases here. These are the facts.

In *Barclays Bank plc v O'Brien* the husband, Mr O'Brien, owned a company. He created a second mortgage using the family home as security for overdraft facilities. He falsely told Mrs O'Brien, who wasn't involved in his company at all, that the level of debt was limited to £60,000 and would be repaid within three weeks. Mrs O' Brien had simply signed the documents at Barclays Bank without reading them and the Bank hadn't bothered to explain them to her. When the overdraft went over £154,000 the Bank wanted to realise its security in the house.

It sought possession with the aim of selling the house to recoup the money lent on the mortgage. It was held that because Mrs O'Brien had been induced to enter into the mortgage by Mr O'Brien's misrepresentation, she had an equity against him to set the transaction aside. The Bank had constructive notice of this equity because it had not taken reasonable steps to ensure that her agreement had been properly obtained. This meant that it could not enforce the mortgage against her share of the house, and so could not take possession. Although the case was decided on the basis of misrepresentation, the principles laid out are just as applicable to undue influence.

Royal Bank of Scotland v Etridge (No 2) concerned eight appeals being heard at the same time (conjoined). In each case the wife claimed that she had signed the mortgage agreement because of the undue influence of her husband.

The first area to consider is what circumstances give rise to undue influence? The different forms of undue influence had been established in *Bank of Credit and Commerce International SA v Aboody* (1990) and were restated in *Barclays Bank plc v O'Brien*. There were three categories.

Class 1 was actual undue influence. This was where the claimant, Sophie in our example, could prove actual undue influence. In this case the mortgage transaction would be put aside whether or not Sophie was disadvantaged by it either at the time or later, although she probably wouldn't be going to court at all if everything had gone to plan and she and Alan were millionaires.

Class 2(A) was where the relationship between the parties itself would give rise to the presumption of undue influence. Examples of such relationships include doctor and patient and solicitor and client. The claimant would also have to show that he/she was disadvantaged by the transaction. If Sophie's doctor convinced her to transfer all her money to him, undue influence would be presumed if Sophie could show that she had been disadvantaged by the transaction. This disadvantage is called a manifest disadvantage.

Q: *Presumably giving all her money to her doctor without reason would be to her disadvantage?*

A: Yes. When there is a relationship giving rise to the presumption of undue influence together with manifest disadvantage, the burden of proof changes. The burden of proof is now on the wrongdoer, here Sophie's doctor. To rebut the presumption, the wrongdoer, Sophie's doctor, has to prove that he did not use undue influence and that Sophie gave him her money of her own free will.

Q: *What exactly is manifest disadvantage?*

A: It was stated in *National Westminster Bank v Morgan* (1985) that it's where someone is so disadvantaged by a transaction that the other party would have to show that there was no undue influence.

Class 2(B) was where the claimant had to prove that trust and confidence were placed in the wrongdoer. The relationship between husband and wife fell into this category: see *Barclays Bank v Rivett* (1999), as did other family relationships. Once this sort of relationship had been proved and the claimant again could show a manifest disadvantage, it was up to the wrongdoer to prove that there was no undue influence. If Sophie could show that she had placed trust and confidence in Alan as her husband in relation to her financial affairs, and if she had been manifestly disadvantaged by entering into the mortgage agreement, undue influence would be presumed. Alan would then have to prove that Sophie signed the mortgage agreement voluntarily to rebut this presumption.

Q: *Why did the claimant, Sophie, need to show a manifest disadvantage in classes 2(A) and 2(B)?*

A: Because otherwise every time Sophie gave Alan a Christmas present there would be a presumption that he had exerted undue influence over her to do so. To overcome this practicality, Sophie has to show that she has been manifestly disadvantaged: she has been disadvantaged by the transaction so much that Alan would have to prove that there had been no undue influence and that she had entered into the transaction of her own free will. Although the court in *Aboody* had said that Sophie had to show that she had been disadvantaged by the transaction where actual undue influence was proved in Class1, *CIBC Mortgages plc v Pitt* (1994) overruled this requirement.

Q: *Given the independence of women these days, why do husband and wife relationships come into this 2B category?*

A: Because it's felt that the risk of undue influence is greater in relationships where there are sexual and emotional ties. A lot of money is wrapped up in the matrimonial home which is usually owned jointly, and some women still follow the advice of their husbands regarding financial matters. In the *O'Brien* case Mrs O'Brien had put trust and confidence into her husband regarding her financial affairs. The relationship between a husband and wife used to fall into the 2A category but the courts have recognised that changing economic and social circumstances mean that wives should not automatically be assumed to be dependent on their husbands: see *Bank of Montreal v Stuart* (1911).

Q: *Is Class 2(B) restricted to husband and wife?*

A: No. In *Barclays Bank plc v O'Brien* Lord Browne-Wilkinson said that the same principles would apply whenever there was an emotional relationship between cohabitees, whether heterosexual or homosexual. Other relationships came into the category, for example, the relationship between a son and his elderly parents as in *Avon Finance Co Ltd v Bridger* (1985). A relationship between an unmarried couple fell into this category in *Massey v Midland Bank plc* (1995).

Q: *You said that these categories of undue influence were restated in* **Barclays Bank plc v O'Brien.** *Did the later case of* **Royal Bank of Scotland v Etridge (No 2)** *agree with this classification of undue influence?*

A: In *Royal Bank of Scotland v Etridge (No 2)* Lord Clyde decided that dividing undue influence into classes was unhelpful, mystifying rather than illuminating.

Q: *Why was dividing undue influence into classes unhelpful?*

A: In classes 2(A) and 2(B) providing Sophie meets the relationship requirements and can show a manifest disadvantage, undue influence is presumed. This has the effect of simply transferring the burden of proof either to Sophie's doctor or to Alan to prove that there was no undue influence. If neither Sophie's doctor nor Alan can talk his way out of it to rebut this presumption, then Sophie will win her claim. There is therefore no need to distinguish between Class 2(A) and Class 2(B), as in both cases all that happens is that the burden of proof is moved to the wrongdoer once the relationship and manifest disadvantage are proved.

Instead, Lord Nicholls of Birkenhead in *Royal Bank of Scotland v Etridge (No 2)* stated that the question was whether one person had trusted the other, rather than whether a relationship fell into a particular type. The position of trust could also be expanded to include vulnerable people, for example. He held that there was no single touchstone for determining whether undue influence was applicable. The claimant must prove that she (we'll use 'she' although in some cases it will be 'he') put trust and confidence in the other party in relation to the management of her financial affairs. There must also be a transaction that is not explicable by the relationship of the parties i.e. a transaction which called for an explanation. This is a situation where the transaction would raise eyebrows and couldn't be accounted for in the everyday way of life, the relationship between the parties and all the circumstances of the case. When both of these are proved the claimant has discharged the evidential burden. This allows the court to infer undue influence and the burden of proof is shifted to the wrongdoer. To summarise: there must be a relationship of trust and a transaction that calls for an explanation. If this is the case, the burden of proof shifts to the wrongdoer and the wrongdoer must prove that the claimant entered freely into the transaction.

Q: *Has manifest disadvantage been replaced by 'a transaction that calls for an explanation?'*

A: Yes. The label 'manifest disadvantage' had caused problems. If a wife guarantees her husband's overdraft, as in *Barclays Bank plc v O'Brien*, then technically the transaction is disadvantageous to her as she gets nothing out of the deal and undertakes a serious financial transaction. The husband's company could go bankrupt and the wife would lose the house to the Bank.

Q: *But she wouldn't have been disadvantaged if the money had been invested and the company had made a profit?*

A: This was the point raised in *Royal Bank of Scotland v Etridge (No 2)*. If the husband's company brings in the money for the family to live on, the wife has an inherent interest in supporting the husband. It's in her interests to sign the mortgage deed so that her husband gets the money for his company. You could argue that in the wider sense the transaction is not disadvantageous to her. It was for this reason that Lord Nicholls preferred not to use the term 'manifest disadvantage'. He preferred instead to return to the test in *Allcard v Skinner*. This said that where the gift or transaction is so large that it can't be accounted for on the grounds of friendship, relationship, charity or any other ordinary motive – a transaction that calls for an explanation in Lord Nicholls' words – then the burden of proof will shift to the wrongdoer. The wrongdoer must prove then that the transaction was fully understood and that the claimant fully intended to enter into it. If the gift or transaction is only small, then the claimant must give some proof that undue influence has been exercised.

Q: *So it's like a sliding scale then, the larger the gift or transaction where there is no obvious explanation for it, the more the burden of proof falls on the wrongdoer to rebut the presumption of undue influence?*

A: Yes. Lord Nicholls did add a cautionary note concerning the general approach of the courts when looking at whether there was undue influence. He said that 'undue influence has a connotation of impropriety. In the eyes of the law, undue influence means that influence has been misused'. Reasonable statements made by a husband to his wife within normal boundaries wouldn't give rise to undue influence. He also held that 'when a husband is forecasting the future of his business to his wife when encouraging her to sign the mortgage agreement, and expressing his hopes or fears, a degree of hyperbole may be only natural. Courts should not too readily treat such exaggerations as misstatements'.

Q: *A degree of hyperbole by the husband is natural?*

A: Perhaps *understandable* would have been a better word. The court then held that 'inaccurate explanations of a proposed transaction are a different matter' from hyperbole, so a good sliding scale there then as well.

Now let's look at the role of the mortgage lender, the Bank, for example, if undue influence is proved.

Q: *How can a bank or mortgage lender know about any undue influence that arises between parties, between husband and wife, cohabitees etc?*

A: It can't, so there has to be a different way. As was held in both *Barclays Bank plc v O'Brien* and *Royal Bank of Scotland v Etridge (No 2)*, this is a balancing act between protecting wives on the one hand and allowing banks to enter into financial transactions with confidence that they won't be sued later.

In *Barclays Bank plc v O'Brien* it was held that the Bank would be 'put on inquiry' (i.e. warned) that there could be undue influence if

a) the transaction was not of financial advantage to the wife and
b) there was a substantial risk that the husband had committed a legal or equitable wrong when getting the wife to enter the transaction which would enable her to have it set aside.

Once the bank knew this information, it had to prove that it had taken sufficient steps to protect itself.

Q: *What has the Bank got to do once it's been put on inquiry (warned)?*

A: According to *Barclays Bank plc v O'Brien*, a representative of the Bank should hold a private meeting with the wife without the husband being there. The representative of the Bank should tell the wife of the liability she is undertaking, the risk involved and then advise her to seek independent legal advice. If this had been done, the Bank would be protected against a claim from the wife that her husband exercised undue influence over her.

Q: *What happened if the Bank didn't do this?*

A: In *Barclays Bank plc v O'Brien* it was held that once the Bank is put on inquiry (warned) it is deemed to have either actual or constructive notice of the wife's rights to set the mortgage aside. This right of the wife is called an equity against her husband. So what you're saying is that the Bank will be deemed to have either actual or constructive notice of this equity (the right to set the mortgage aside) if it doesn't advise the wife to take independent legal advice. Once the Bank is deemed to have acquired actual or constructive notice of the equity, it can't enforce the mortgage against the wife.

Your own recollection of constructive notice should come from Chapter 3 on unregistered land in this book where a *bona fide* purchaser of a legal estate for value without notice, either actual, constructive or imputed, of an equitable interest over the land would take the land free from that equitable interest. Constructive notice is the knowledge that the purchaser would be deemed to have if he had investigated the documents relating to the land or inspected the land, whether or not he had done so in practice.

Q: *But if you apply this meaning of constructive notice in a mortgage situation, aren't you saying that the Bank ought to have known or ought to have found out about the undue influence going on between husband and wife or indeed any other parties?*

A: Yes, and that is, of course, impossible. How is the Bank going to find out what the husband said to the wife and, indeed, why should it? In the law of mortgages the traditional view of notice had been to refer to actual notice, here actual notice of the undue influence. If the Bank knew of actual undue influence it could not enforce the mortgage against the wife. Notice did not include constructive notice. Furthermore, the steps the Bank takes to avoid constructive notice, having a meeting with the wife, telling her to seek independent legal advice, don't involve making inquiries. The Bank is instead taking steps to make sure the wife understands what she is doing.

Q: *Did the court in* **Royal Bank of Scotland v Etridge (No 2)** *agree with the constructive notice explanation in* **Barclays Bank plc v O'Brien?**

A: Lord Nicholls said that it wasn't a conventional use of the concept of constructive notice. However, the law had needed to develop to protect wives, and these kinds of mortgage situations had special features of their own. He would continue to use the accepted term 'put on inquiry' (warned) though, and held that a creditor is put on enquiry when a wife offers to stand as surety for her husband's debts.

Q: *What's a surety?*

A: Surety means security given for the fulfilment of an undertaking.

Q: *What happened to the two tests in Barclays Bank plc v O'Brien which said that a bank is put on inquiry (warned) that there might be undue influence if*
a) *the transaction was not of financial advantage to the wife and*
b) *there was a substantial risk that the husband had committed a legal or equitable wrong when getting the wife to enter the transaction which would enable her to have it set aside?*

A: In *Royal Bank of Scotland v Etridge (No 2)* Lord Nicholls interpreted *Barclays Bank plc v O'Brien* to mean that parts (a) and (b) were the reasons *why* a creditor is put on inquiry when the wife offers to stand as surety. The type of transaction *when* a creditor is put on inquiry is where a wife offers to stand as surety for her husband's debts. As Lord Nicholls said:

> In my view, this passage (giving the two tests), read in context, is to be taken to mean, quite simply, that a bank is put on inquiry whenever a wife offers to stand surety for her husband's debts.

This means that Lord Nicholls greatly widened the test beyond the two circumstances in *Barclays Bank plc v O'Brien*. He said that a bank is put on inquiry (warned) that there may be undue influence whenever a wife offers to stand as surety. In *Royal Bank of Scotland v Etridge (No 2)* the Bank should have been put on inquiry (warned) simply because the wife was offering her share of the house as security for her husband's debts.

Q: *So if a wife signs the mortgage deed that means that the Bank is automatically put on notice and must take further steps?*

A: Yes, but if the mortgage is for joint purposes the Bank will not be put on inquiry. This was illustrated in *CIBC Mortgages plc v Pitt* where the reason for the mortgage was to purchase a holiday home. This was clearly for the benefit of both the husband and wife, and so the Bank was not put on inquiry.

Q: *What happens if a wife owns shares in her husband's company and the husband has asked for the loan to save the company?*

A: It was held that the bank would still be put on inquiry even when the wife was the director or secretary of the husband's company. Just because a wife was a shareholder or director didn't mean that she knew about the running of the business.

Q: *Is it just between husband and wife or is the Bank put on inquiry in other relationships?*

A: In *Barclays Bank plc v O'Brien* it was held that the Bank would be put on inquiry whenever there was an emotional relationship between cohabitees, whoever was doing the cohabiting. In *Royal Bank of Scotland (No 2) v Etridge* it was held that you couldn't produce a definitive list of relationships where there was a possibility of undue influence, so a bank would be put on inquiry in every transaction where someone stood as surety for someone else. An exception would be made where the relationship between the bank and the borrower was a commercial one or where the transaction was for the parties' joint purpose such as buying a holiday home.

Q: *That sounds like an onerous position for the Bank to be in, doesn't it?*

A: Yes, but it was held that it was a reasonable requirement in today's society and that it would impose only a modest burden on banks and other lenders, though I expect the banks and other lenders don't see it quite like that.

So, to recap. According to *Royal Bank of Scotland (No 2) v Etridge*, undue influence will be presumed where a claimant puts trust and confidence in the other party in relation to the management of his/her financial affairs together with a transaction that is not explicable by the relationship of the parties. This shifts the burden of proof to the person who allegedly exerted the undue influence. That person must now prove that there was no undue influence and the claimant entered into the transaction of his/her own free will. A bank or other lender will be put on inquiry as to the possibility of undue influence in any transaction where someone acts as a surety for someone else, except where the relationship between the bank and borrower is a commercial one, or where the transaction is for a mutual purpose.

Q: *The court in* **Barclays Bank plc v O'Brien** *had said the Bank had to take certain steps to absolve itself from responsibility for any undue influence that was going on. Did the court in* **Royal Bank of Scotland (No 2) v Etridge** *agree with those steps?*

A: Not exactly. In *Barclays Bank plc v O'Brien* it was held that to avoid landing itself with constructive notice, a representative of the Bank had to hold a private meeting with the wife without the husband being there. The Bank's representative had to tell the wife of the liability she was undertaking, the risks involved and then advise her to seek independent legal advice. In *Royal Bank of Scotland (No 2) v Etridge* Lord Nicholls had some things to say about the way banks had been behaving since *Barclays Bank plc v O'Brien*. He said that banks weren't holding meetings with wives because they had more to lose than to gain by doing so.

Q: *Was this because, if the Bank advised the wife of the risk, then she might just pull out of signing the mortgage deed with the knock-on effect that the mortgage wouldn't go ahead, so then the Bank wouldn't be able to charge a high rate of interest on the loan and make a handsome profit?*

A: Absolutely. Instead, the banks were advising the wife to seek legal advice and then they would ask the solicitor giving the legal advice for written confirmation that he had explained the nature and effect of the documents to the wife.

Q: *Was there a problem with this?*

A: The problem according to Lord Nicholls was the perfunctory nature of the legal advice, the fact that 'independent legal advice is a fiction' and that such advice provided little protection for the wife.

Q: *A damning indictment for the legal profession, then? What were banks and solicitors supposed to do?*

A: In *Royal Bank of Scotland (No 2) v Etridge* Lord Nicholls said that you can't expect the bank to ask the wife whether her husband has exercised undue influence over her, nor can you expect the solicitor to make such enquires on the basis that the wife would probably not be amused by such impertinent questioning, let alone the cost of all this legal questioning.

Q: *Since when has someone else footing the bill bothered the legal profession?*

A: Never. It was held that the best way was to ensure that the bank, or any other lender, took reasonable steps to ensure that the wife knew what the transaction was about. Having a private meeting with the wife wasn't the only way of doing this, and it was acceptable that this task should be undertaken by a legal adviser. The court then went on to give a detailed account of what the bank and the legal adviser had to do to avoid liability for any undue influence which might have gone on. We'll use the example of the wife, as in the *Barclays Bank plc v O'Brien* case to show this.

The lender must tell the wife that it requires written confirmation from a solicitor that the nature and implications of the mortgage transaction have been explained to her, and that this explanation will prevent any claim by her in the future. The wife must nominate the solicitor, and can nominate her own solicitor or the one used by her husband. The lender shouldn't proceed any further with the mortgage loan until the wife has informed it of her nominated solicitor.

Q: *Doesn't choosing the same solicitor as her husband mean a possible conflict of interest and duty for the solicitor?*

A: Lord Nicholls talked about balancing the extra cost of a separate solicitor against inhibiting the wife where she knows the solicitor is acting for her husband as well. He came to the conclusion that a solicitor owes responsibilities to the wife both professionally and legally. When advising the wife he is acting for her alone. He is not acting for her husband or for the bank. Such professional responsibilities should ensure that advice is given carefully and conscientiously.

The lender must then send all the relevant information concerning the mortgage to the nominated solicitor, having first obtained consent from the husband to do so. If the lender has any suspicions about undue influence, it must also notify this to the solicitor.

The solicitor must explain the documents, the practical consequences of the mortgage and the seriousness of the risk including the amount of money involved. He must also stress that it is the wife's choice whether or not to sign the paperwork. This meeting must be face-to-face, without the husband being present and in everyday language that can be understood.

Q: *How does the lender know all this has happened?*

A: The solicitor must send written confirmation to the lender who is not allowed to proceed until it has received it.

Q: *So you're protecting anyone who stands as a guarantor in a mortgage transaction because the lender, the bank for example, has to ensure that any such people have had legal advice?*

A: Yes. You're also protecting the bank from any claim that undue influence might have gone on by saying that it must ensure that everyone has had legal advice unless it's a commercial transaction or one for the joint purposes of the borrower and the guarantor. Even so, you will never stop undue influence occurring altogether. It's always a balance between protecting a vulnerable party on the one hand and the lender being able to rely on its security on the other.

Q: *Is there anything to stop the bank suing the husband on the personal covenant to repay the mortgage even if it can't enforce the mortgage against the wife?*

A: No. If this happens, the borrower will go bankrupt. The bank can go to court under sections 14 and 15 of the Trusts of Land and Appointment of Trustees Act 1996 as a party with an interest in a trust of land. The Insolvency Act 1986 will come into play and the court will order sale of the house. The bank can then recover whatever money it can from the husband's monetary share in the property. The wife's equitable interest in the house will be translated into money. This action won't be an abuse of process by the bank because it has a number of remedies available which it can choose to exercise. The authorities for this are *Alliance and Leicester plc v Slayford* (2001) and *First National Bank plc v Achampong* (2003).

Turkey v Awadh (2005) and *Hughes v Hughes* (2005) are recent cases looking at undue influence, although the transaction in question was not a mortgage. In *Turkey v Awadh* there was a relationship of trust and confidence. However, the transaction between the parties, although curious, could be explained by the relationship. There was no undue influence. In *Hughes v Hughes*, although there was a loving relationship between Mrs Hughes and her son, she had not entrusted him with the management of her financial affairs. Furthermore, she had not been as financially disadvantaged by the transaction as she had made out. The burden of proof did not shift to Mrs Hughes' son. *Thompson v Foy* (2009) is a further example where undue influence was not found. *Abbey National v Stringer* (2006) did concern undue influence in a mortgage situation. Mrs Stringer and her son purchased a property in joint names, the son being on the legal title to enable the mother to borrow money on a mortgage, as the building society would not lend to her because of her age. A second mortgage was taken out to fund the son's business. Mrs Stringer signed the documents although she was illiterate, had a limited understanding of English and was unaware of what she was signing. She had relied on her son to manage her financial affairs for her. When the building society wanted to take possession of the house because her son hadn't paid the mortgage, she alleged undue influence. The court held that Mrs Stringer had placed trust and confidence in her son and depended on him to deal with her affairs. In *Royal Bank of Scotland (No 2) v Etridge* Lord Nicholls had also said that undue influence wasn't limited to cases where trust and confidence had been abused. It also included vulnerable people. Mrs Stringer was one such vulnerable person, open to exploitation by her son because of her difficulties with the English language.

Q: *What did the defence argue back?*

A: Miss Smith acting for the defence claimed that even if there was a relationship of trust and confidence, which she denied, it was natural that a mother would want to help her son in supporting his business. It was a transaction that was perfectly explicable in a parent–child relationship. Lord Justice Longmore was not of the same view. Mrs Stringer's house was her only asset and she had put it at risk not only for her son but also for two of his business associates whom she didn't know. The only benefit would be if her son could better support her in her old age if his business was successful. She had no idea that she was risking her house as security and had been taken advantage of by her son in a transaction that was totally disadvantageous to her. It was a transaction that she wouldn't have entered into had she known what was going on, and it called for an explanation. In *Royal Bank of Scotland (No 2) v Etridge* Lord Nicholls had said that there had to be some degree of impropriety over and above the usual statements and conduct you would expect when such transactions are being discussed. Mrs Stringer's son had certainly satisfied these requirements of impropriety and undue influence was found. The Building Society had admitted notice of the undue influence if it were proved. This meant that the Building Society could not enforce the mortgage against the mother.

Q: *Could the Building Society claim against the son as he had to sign the mortgage deed as well?*

A: It was held that there must have been an agreement between the mother and son that the son was on the legal title as a nominee only. He was on the title simply to aid his mother obtain a mortgage and had no beneficial interest in the house. This was an implied agreement constructive trust, as in *Lloyd's Bank v Rosset*. As the son had no beneficial interest in the house, the Building Society could not claim against this either. All the Building Society could do was to sue the son on his personal covenant to repay the mortgage. Given that the son had defaulted on the mortgage payments anyway, this was a pointless exercise.

A recent case here is *Hewett v First Plus Financial Group* (2010). Mr and Mrs Hewett purchased a house in their joint names and lived there together with their children and Mrs Hewett's mother. Mr Hewett had credit card debts which he couldn't pay and so had to arrange refinancing in order to reduce the interest repayments. He persuaded Mrs Hewett to agree to a mortgage over the house from First Plus Financial Group. He told her that arranging the finances this way was the only way that they could stay in the family home and he also promised that he would make the repayments to First Plus Financial Group. Mrs Hewett's mother occupied the property and Mr Hewett forged her signature giving consent for the mortgage. Unknown to Mrs Hewett, Mr Hewett was having an affair. Mr Hewett left the marriage some time later and a divorce followed. This was then followed by Mr Hewett's bankruptcy. Mrs Hewett couldn't afford the mortgage repayments. First Plus Financial Group brought possession proceedings which Mrs Hewett challenged on the basis that her agreement to the mortgage had been obtained by undue influence. This was because Mrs Hewett had placed trust and confidence in her husband but he had failed to inform her that he was having an affair at the time the mortgage was created. This was an abuse of such trust and confidence.

It was held that Mrs Hewett put a sufficient degree of trust and confidence in her husband. Whilst she had participated in the financial decision making with Mr Hewett, putting trust and confidence in another wasn't confined to cases where the wife simply followed the advice of the husband or where her will was overridden. It covered cases where although the wife did participate in financial decisions, she still had to know the facts in order to make an informed decision. Mrs Hewett had agreed to the mortgage on the basis that Mr Hewett was committed to 'the marriage, to the family and to the preservation of their home life' whereas his affair carried the risk that he might leave the marriage taking with him emotional and financial support. The affair was a material fact and should have been disclosed. The test for disclosure wasn't whether disclosure of this material fact would have affected Mrs Hewett's decision in practice but was an objective one. It was met

> '… by asking whether a solicitor, consulted by Mrs Hewett for advice about the wisdom of the transaction, would have thought it relevant to know that her husband was, while asking for her unqualified trust, at the same time conducting a clandestine affair'.

To which the answer was yes. Mrs Hewett had also taken on trust Mr Hewett's promise to pay the mortgage repayments. First Plus knew that the money was going to be used to pay off Mr Hewett's debts but did not follow the guidelines in *Royal Bank of Scotland (No 2) v Etridge* in advising Mrs Hewett and so was fixed with constructive notice of the undue influence and the mortgage was set aside as far as Mrs Hewett's liability was concerned.

Or, as the *Daily Mail* succinctly put it:

> 'Mortgage written off over husband's affair'.

Summary of undue influence

The *Royal Bank of Scotland (No 2) v Etridge* case redefined the definition of undue influence in relation to mortgages, and laid down guidelines for lenders to protect themselves against such claims. Any second party to a mortgage likely to be disadvantaged by the transaction should receive independent, informed advice before the lender is allowed to proceed with the mortgage.

The next part of this chapter looks at the remedies of the lender and the rights of the borrower, both of which will be used if the borrower has defaulted on the mortgage repayments. These remedies and rights are summarised in the chart on page 576.

The remedies of the mortgagee (the lender) on default of the mortgage repayments

---

Box A

THE REMEDIES OF THE MORTGAGEE (THE LENDER) ON DEFAULT OF THE MORTGAGE REPAYMENTS

1. The right to sue on the contract

2. The right to take possession

3. Sale

(i) The right of sale

(ii) Duties on sale

4. The right to appoint a receiver

5. The right to foreclosure

THE REMEDIES OF THE MORTGAGEE (THE LENDER) AND THE RIGHTS OF THE MORTGAGOR (THE BORROWER)

Box A

THE REMEDIES OF THE MORTGAGEE (THE LENDER) ON DEFAULT OF THE MORTGAGE REPAYMENTS

1. The right to sue on the contract

2. The right to take possession

3. Sale

(i) The right of sale

(ii) Duties on sale

4. The right to appoint a receiver

5. The right to foreclosure

Box B

THE RIGHTS OF THE MORTGAGOR (THE BORROWER) ON DEFAULT OF THE MORTGAGE REPAYMENTS

1. The Administration of Justice Act 1970

(i) Postponement of possession

(ii) The period for postponing possession

2. The Financial Services and Markets Act 2000 and the Consumer Credit Act 2006

3. Social Security benefits

4. The position of the borrower's spouse who was not a party to the mortgage agreement

5. The Protocol

This section looks at the remedies of the lender when the borrower has not paid the mortgage repayments. These remedies are cumulative.

Box A1

The right to sue on the contract

A mortgage is a contract where one party, the lender, agrees to lend money at an agreed rate of interest. The second party agrees to pay back the amount borrowed at this agreed rate of interest. If the borrower defaults on the mortgage repayments, the lender can sue for breach of contract. The time limit for suing for payment of capital is a maximum of 12 years under section 20 of the Limitation Act 1980.

Q: *If the lender has the property as security, why would it choose to sue on the contract?*

A: There are two situations in which this may happen. If the borrower does not keep up with the mortgage repayments, the lender can take possession of the property, sell it, and use the proceeds from the sale to recoup the outstanding loan. If the proceeds do not cover the outstanding loan, the lender can sue for the difference.

Q: *Is there any point in this because the borrower clearly hasn't got any money?*

A: Not a lot of point. If the borrower has defaulted on the mortgage repayments leading to sale in the first place, then, unless he has other fixed assets, he is unlikely to be sitting on a sum of money which can be produced when he's sued for breach of contract. Had he had this sum of money, he would presumably have paid the mortgage repayments. As a result, you must be careful when arguing the right to sue on the contract as a possible remedy. It's more likely you'll be eliminating it as a lost cause, rather than discussing it as a sensible solution.

The second situation is where the house cannot be sold because someone else has an interest in it which is binding on the bank. Look at this in an example. Darren purchased Greenacres and he alone is on the legal title. Sally contributed to the original purchase price of the house and therefore acquired an equitable interest under a resulting trust. Darren subsequently created a post-acquisition mortgage over Greenacres with Bundy's Bank. Darren has not kept up with the mortgage repayments and Bundy's Bank wishes to take possession with the aim of selling the house to recoup the outstanding loan money. The Bank did not overreach Sally's interest when it paid the mortgage money to Darren alone. Sally's equitable interest will be binding on Bundy's Bank if it has notice of her interest in unregistered land, or she is in actual occupation in registered land. Assuming Sally's equitable interest in Greenacres is binding on the Bank, this gives her a right of occupation under section 12 of the Trusts of Land and Appointment of Trustees Act 1996. This right will be binding on the bank, so it will be unable to obtain vacant possession of Greenacres in order to sell.

Q: *What happens then?*

A: Bundy's Bank will *sue Darren for breach of contract* because he has not paid the mortgage repayments. The court will declare that Darren is bankrupt, and a trustee in bankruptcy will be appointed to manage his affairs. Under section 14 of the

Trusts of Land and Appointment of Trustees Act 1996, the trustee in bankruptcy can apply to the court for the sale of Greenacres in order to pay off Darren's debts. Where there is an application for sale because of the bankruptcy of a beneficiary under a trust of land, the Insolvency Act of 1986 will govern proceedings. When a trustee in bankruptcy applies for sale more than a year after the bankruptcy happened, the court will order a sale of the house unless there are exceptional circumstances. Sally will have to move out and the trustee in bankruptcy will sell Greenacres. Because Sally's equitable interest was binding on the Bank, she will receive her share of the proceeds before the remainder goes to pay off the mortgage debt. This situation was discussed in detail in Chapter 11.

Box A2 ## The right to take possession

As a mortgage takes the form of a long lease by virtue of section 87 of the Law of Property Act 1925 , the lender has an automatic right to possession.

Q: *Why?*

A: Because if you have a lease, you are entitled to immediate possession. This means the lender has a right to possession, and you should note that this is a right, not a remedy. In *Four-Maids Ltd v Dudley Marshall (Properties) Ltd* (1957) Mr Justice Harman said that the lender:

> may go into possession before the ink is dry on the mortgage unless there is something in the contract, express or by implication, whereby he has contracted himself out of that right.

This statement of law is often misinterpreted by students so I make no apologies for repeating it … The lender has a right to go into possession the moment the mortgage has been created because the mortgage takes the form of a long lease. This right to go into possession is not dependent on a default on the mortgage repayments or on the legal date of redemption having passed or on anything else. This is so unless the lender has actually contracted out of the right to go into immediate possession. An example of a lender contracting out of the right to go into immediate possession can be seen in residential dwellings where it is usual for the lender to give the borrower the right to possession until there is a default on the mortgage repayments: see *Birmingham Citizens Permanent Building Society v Caunt* (1962). This prevents the bank manager from wandering in during 'Eastenders'.

Q: *Why would the lender want to take possession?*

A: Because it's the prelude to sale. If the lender exercises his right to possession, the borrower will have to leave and the lender can sell the house with vacant possession. Vacant possession means you will get an empty house.

Q: *If possession is a right, can the bank literally just take possession?*

A: It is not wise to do so. Although technically lenders can use reasonable force to enter, they will usually obtain a court order for possession; otherwise they risk committing an offence under the Criminal Law Act 1977. Under this Act it is an offence to threaten or use violence when entering a property without lawful authority if the person entering knows there is someone there who is opposed to his entry.

Q: *Is the lender under any duty to look after the property after he's taken possession?*

A: Yes, he must take reasonable care of the property: see *Silven Properties Ltd v Royal Bank of Scotland plc* (2003). If it is a residential property and the lender intends to possess it rather than sell, he must pay the best market rent to the borrower. If it is a commercial property, the lender must account to the borrower for any income received. He is therefore accountable for any profits that would have accrued from the business. When the lender let a pub as a tied house in *White v City of London Brewery Co* (1889), he was held liable for the increase in rent he would have received had he let it as a free house. Because of this liability, a lender is more likely to appoint a receiver to run the business on his behalf when commercial property is possessed. The appointment of a receiver is discussed in Box A4.

Q: *Presumably a lender will always try and take possession as soon as possible once the borrower stops making payments?*

A: You'd have thought so but then look at *National Westminster Bank Plc v Ashe* (2008). The Bank had a right of possession immediately the mortgage was signed. Mr and Mrs Babai had stopped making the mortgage repayments some 13 years earlier so the Bank was out of time to sue on the contract (Box A1). The Bank hadn't taken possession either. Mr Babai was bankrupt and his trustee in bankruptcy claimed adverse possession of the land under the Limitation Act 1980. It doesn't matter that it was a claim by a trustee in bankruptcy – the principles would apply to any lender who does not take steps to possess the property. Adverse possession was discussed in Chapter 5 and this case is a good example of how, eventually, all the jigsaw bits of land law fit together. Possession was to be given its normal meaning (see *JA Pye (Oxford) Ltd v Graham* (2002) and the Babais were in ordinary possession of the land. Whilst the Bank had a right of possession, it was not actually in possession. The Bank argued it had given the Babais permission to remain in the property which would defeat their claim (Chapter 5 Box A2(iv)). The court held that the Babais were occupying the property because they were the registered proprietors of the land, not because the Bank had given them permission, so the Bank's charge was extinguished under sections 15 and 17 of the Limitation Act 1980. Mummery LJ used the words 'it may come as an unpleasant surprise to the Bank and other mortgagees that their mortgagors are in adverse possession of the mortgaged property', which is probably the understatement of the year.

Q: *Presumably if borrowers could never be said to be in adverse possession of their property, time would never be able to start running against a lender?*

A: That's right, and, as Mummery lj said, 'That would be a surprising state of affairs'.

Q: *Is the situation in this case likely to happen a lot?*

A: Not really. In many cases the right of possession is made dependent on default of the mortgage payments as an exception to the right of immediate possession that a lender acquires from his estate in the land (see *Four-Maids Ltd v Dudley Marshall*

(*Properties*) *Ltd*) so time will not start to run when the mortgage is created. Also, in many cases there is part payment of the mortgage payments which will prevent the running of time. As Mummery lj observed, lending institutions have access to expert legal advice and are well able to take steps promptly to prevent such a situation happening.

Box A3   Sale

Once possession has been obtained, the lender will want to sell the house in order to recoup the outstanding mortgage loan.

Box A3i   The right of sale

The power of sale is governed either by express terms in the mortgage contract or by the Law of Property Act 1925 if there are no other arrangements. It is a self-help remedy and the lender does not need a court order to sell. When sale is under the Law of Property Act 1925, you must distinguish between the power of sale arising and the power of sale becoming exercisable.

Q: *When does the power of sale arise?*
A: It arises under section 101 of the Law of Property Act 1925 and *both* the following conditions must be satisfied:

- the mortgage must have been created by deed; and
- the mortgage money has become due.

Q: *When does mortgage money become due?*
A: When the legal date of redemption has passed. This is usually six months after the creation of the mortgage.

Q: *What happens if the lender sells before this date has arisen?*
A: All the lender can sell is his own interest in the property, which is the mortgage. If there is a mortgage of £50,000 on a house, and the house is sold by the lender to a purchaser, Peter, before the power of sale has arisen, then all Peter receives is the right to receive the £50,000 due on the mortgage. Once the borrower has paid off this £50,000, the property will belong to him again, and Peter will own nothing except the £50,000.

Q: *Does this mean that the purchaser must ensure that the power of sale has arisen before he buys the property?*
A: Definitely.

Q: *How does he do this?*
A: He must inspect the mortgage deed in unregistered land or he must inspect the Charges Register of the mortgaged property in registered land to find out this information.

Section 103 determines when the power of sale becomes exercisable. One of the following conditions in this section must be met:

Either

▶ notice has been served on the borrower requiring payment and three months have gone by without the borrower doing so (section 103(i));
or

▶ some of the interest on the mortgage loan is at least two months in arrears (section 103(ii));
or

▶ there has been a breach of the term of the mortgage other than one relating to the payment of capital or interest (section 103(iii)).

Q: What could be a term of the mortgage that doesn't relate to the payment of capital or interest?

A: A term that the borrower will not lease the mortgaged property without the lender's consent, for instance, as in *Bishop v Blake* (2006).

Q: What happens if section 103 is not satisfied?

A: The purchaser's entitlement to the property is not in question. However, the sale can be put aside if the purchaser actually knew that the power of sale had not become exercisable: see *Bailey v Barnes* (1894). This is unlikely to happen, as the purchaser is not under any duty to check that section 103 has been complied with before he buys the property.

Q: What happens to the lender if the power of sale had not become exercisable?

A: The lender must pay damages to the borrower because he had no power to sell his property.

Box A3ii Duties on sale

Q: Can the lender sell at any time he wants, or does he have to wait for a good time to sell when property prices are high?

A: This raises the question of what duty, if any, the lender owes to the borrower when selling the property. On the one hand, all the lender wants to do is to raise enough money to be able to recoup the outstanding loan. On the other hand, if you were the borrower, you would not be best pleased if the lender sold your home at less than it was worth, not least because you will be entitled to any money left over once the lender has taken his outstanding money.

The Court of Appeal case of *Silven Properties Ltd v Royal Bank of Scotland plc* has confirmed and clarified these duties. Silven Properties was arguing that the bank and the receivers appointed by it should have taken pre-marketing steps to obtain the best price for the properties by pursuing planning permission for development and granting leases of vacant premises. Its argument failed. Mr Justice Lightman stated that if the borrower requires the lender to carry out these types of duties, it must be specified in the mortgage agreement. His alternative solution was for the borrower to redeem the mortgage instead. This last suggestion will be less than helpful to anyone in a situation where the lender is selling their property because they cannot afford the mortgage repayments in the first place. In the case Mr Justice Lightman identified the main duties of both a lender and a receiver. The duties of a lender are as follows.

> The lender is under no duty to exercise his powers of sale or possession, nor does he have to appoint a receiver or preserve the value of the property.
> The lender is free to investigate whether he could obtain a higher price for a property by obtaining planning permission. However, he is under no obligation to do so and, even if he has applied for planning permission, can change his mind and sell. You should also note that the lender cannot exploit this by selling to an associate who then immediately obtains planning permission. The lender is also under no obligation to increase the potential value of a property by granting a lease.
> The lender has an unfettered discretion to sell when he likes. This means that he doesn't have to wait for a good market. In *China and South Sea Bank Ltd v Tan Soon Gin* (1991) the lender was held not liable for failing to sell at a favourable time when conditions become less favourable later. The fact that the value of the property dropped from good to worthless was just unfortunate for the borrower.

Q: Why should the borrower be disadvantaged in this way?

A: Because of the arguments that would ensue about when was the best time to sell. We're all knowledgeable with the benefit of hindsight.

When the lender sells the property he is under a duty in equity to obtain the true market or proper price at the date of sale. Following *Cuckmere Brick Co Ltd v Mutual Finance Ltd* (1971) there had been some discussion whether the liability of the lender lay in tort or in equity. Following the *Silven* case, it is now clear that this liability lies in equity. The lender will be liable for what he should have received if he fails to take proper care to obtain the best price reasonably possible on the date of sale.

Q: How do you ensure you obtain the best market price for the property when the price can depend on the time of year you're selling, or on conditions in the housing market?

A: In the *Silven* case, Mr Justice Lightman stated that the lender must:
> take proper care whether by fairly and properly exposing the property to the market or otherwise to obtain the best price reasonably obtainable at the date of sale.

In *Bishop v Blake* the court held that the proper approach was to ask what steps the lender had taken when selling the property and whether those steps would give the best price possible. The approach was not to ask what price the property should have sold for, and such an approach had been criticised in *Michael v Miller* (2004). In *Bishop v Blake* a review by the court of the steps the lender had taken included the following phrases: 'The Inn was never marketed in any realistic sense. The advertisement in The Publican was pathetic. It was inserted at the last minute, it failed to include elementary contact details … no marketing had been undertaken … the Inn should have been exposed to the market in order to obtain the best price'. The words 'idleness', 'incompetence' and 'solicitor' were also used in the same sentence.

Q: This surely can't be the best approach?

A: It wasn't, and that's not even mentioning the collusion between the lender and the purchaser that went on. The lender was liable to the borrower for the difference in price between what was obtained and what should have been obtained.

In *Dean v Barclays Bank plc* (2007) there were three issues to be addressed: (i) whether Barclays Bank had properly assessed the condition of the properties; (ii) whether the marketing of the property had been sufficient; and (iii) what had been the market value of the property when sold. Barclays Bank had met its obligation to take reasonable care to obtain the best price possible.

Q: *What happens if the lender sells the property out of spite?*

A: This question arose in *Meretz Investments NV v ACP Ltd* (2006) where it was held that the court did not have to examine the lender's purity of purpose. Provided one of the motives of the lender was to recover the amount owed on the mortgage loan, the lender's power of sale would not be invalidated.

The duty to take proper care also means that the lender cannot sell the property to himself, for example.

Q: *Why not?*

A: Because of the conflict of interest. In his capacity as lender he should be looking for the best possible price for the borrower. In his capacity as purchaser, he would want the lowest price. If the lender sells to a friend or associate, he must prove that there has been no shady dealing. In *Tse Kwong Lam v Wong Chit Sen* (1983) the lender had sold at auction where, coincidentally, the one person bidding was his wife in the capacity of director of the company they owned. The price obtained was the reserve price which was known to the lender and, coincidentally, his wife. The lender, coincidentally, provided the funds for the purchase.

Q: *A lot of coincidence then?*

A: That's what the Privy Council thought, although for various reasons the sale was not put aside and the borrower received damages instead.

Q: *Why is it acceptable to sell at auction rather than putting the property on the open market?*

A: An auction is the best way of ensuring that you obtain the best market price because, by definition, there is nobody prepared to pay any more for the property. If the sale is by auction, the lender must advertise the property sufficiently, giving enough notice of the day and time. He must obtain a valuation of the property, choose a reasonable day, set a reserve price and let parties bid against each other if there is more than one purchaser.

In *Cuckmere Brick Co Ltd v Mutual Finance Ltd* the lender was held liable because he had failed to advertise the planning permission that had been granted for the property, which would have increased the selling price.

Q: *Is there anything the borrower can do to influence the date when the house is sold?*

A: Not generally, although borrowers have tried to hasten sale when there has been negative equity in the property by using section 91 of the Law of Property Act 1925. Negative equity is when the value of the property is not enough to cover the amount owed on the mortgage. Section 91 allows the borrower or the lender to apply for sale of the property at the court's discretion. The borrower can apply for sale under section 91 when the value of the property isn't enough to cover the mortgage loan, house prices are falling and the lender is delaying or wants to possess rather than sell. However, a request of this nature under section 91 is not usually favoured unless the value of the house is enough to pay off the mortgage loan or there are exceptional circumstances, as in *Palk v Mortgage Services Funding plc* (1993). In this case there was negative equity in the house. The lender wanted to possess the house, not with a view to selling it but with a view to renting it out. The lender had nothing to lose here as house prices could rise and he could always sue on the contract to repay the loan. The borrower was against this as, first, she would lose her home, secondly, the rental income wouldn't cover the monthly mortgage repayments, and, thirdly, house prices might not rise. The court ordered a sale of the property because it was just and equitable to do so in the circumstances.

Q: *Who can claim the money when the property is sold?*

A: Section 105 of the Law of Property Act 1925 states that the money from the sale of the property must be paid in the following order:

- First, to any lenders who gave mortgage loans before the lender who has just sold the property.
- Secondly, any expenses from the sale.
- Thirdly, the money owed to the lender selling the property.
- Fourthly, payment to any lenders who gave mortgage loans on the property after the lender who has just sold the property.
- Finally, anything left over to the borrower.

Q: *How do you know if there are any other mortgages over the property?*

A: By looking on the Land Charges Register in unregistered land and on the Charges Register in registered land.

Box A4 The right to appoint a receiver

A receiver can be appointed under section 109 of the Law of Property Act 1925. He is usually appointed in commercial situations when the lender does not wish to go into possession of the mortgaged property himself. The receiver's main duty is to use the profits from the land to pay the mortgage arrears of interest and capital until such time as they are paid off, as in *Medforth v Blake* (2000), or until the lender wishes to take possession himself and sell the property. The receiver can also sell the property. A lender can appoint a receiver when the power of sale has become exercisable under section 103 of the Law of Property Act 1925. Such an appointment must be in writing.

Under section 109 of the Law of Property Act 1925, the receiver is deemed to be the agent of the borrower, not the lender. This means that the lender will not be responsible for the receiver's actions. The receiver's duty of care was very clearly laid out in *Silven Properties Ltd v Royal Bank of Scotland plc*.

Box A5 The right to foreclosure

If you remember, the borrower has the equitable right to redeem the mortgage. Foreclosure involves taking away this right, leaving the whole value of the property with the lender, who is then entitled to the property subject only to any prior mortgages. It is very rare for foreclosure to be used, and you should be careful about putting it forward as a realistic remedy. Foreclosure can be applied for in court after the legal date of redemption has passed. Foreclosure nisi gives the borrower a specified amount of time to pay back the mortgage money. If this doesn't happen, there is foreclosure absolute. However, between foreclosure nisi and foreclosure absolute, the borrower can apply for sale under section 91 of the Law of Property Act 1925. He can also apply for a postponement of the foreclosure order under the Administration of Justice Act 1970 which is discussed in Box B1. Even after foreclosure absolute, the court has the discretion to reopen the order and transfer the property from the lender back to the borrower again: see *Campbell v Holyland* (1877). This makes an application for foreclosure time-consuming, expensive and unlikely to succeed.

Q: *Why would a lender apply for foreclosure?*

A: If there is no hope of the borrower paying off the loan and the value of the house doesn't cover the debt, the lender can take the property absolutely under a foreclosure order, then simply wait until house prices go up before selling. This gives the lender the whole value of the property, which could be worth far more than the actual mortgage money owed. Because it is such a draconian order, it is very rare, and the Law Commission has recommended its abolition. So beware. This is not a practical or even used remedy, so you should mention it largely to dismiss it.

Q: *Are the remedies available to the lender the same when the mortgage is equitable rather than legal?*

A: The lender can still sue on the contract. Whether he has the right to take possession is not so clear cut. One argument is that the right to take possession comes from the lender holding a legal leasehold estate in the land or its equivalent under a charge. A lender with only an equitable interest in the land cannot take possession unless there is a court order in place: see *Barclays Bank Ltd v Bird* (1954), or unless the right has been expressly reserved. On the other hand, academics have argued that the lender is able to take possession here. As far as sale is concerned, section 101 of the Law of Property Act 1925 states that the mortgage must have been created by deed for the power of sale to arise. Unless the equitable mortgage has been created in a deed, the power of sale will not arise. One way of getting round this is for the lender to hold an irrevocable power to convey the legal estate held by the borrower to a purchaser on the borrower's behalf. This is known as a power of attorney. The lender can also apply for sale under section 91 of the Law of Property Act 1925 here. As far as the right to appoint a receiver is concerned, the same reasoning applies in that, unless the equitable mortgage has been created by deed, the power to appoint a receiver will not arise under section 101 of the Law of Property Act 1925. Instead the lender can apply to the court under section 37 of the Supreme Court Act 1981 for such an appointment. The lender can also apply for foreclosure when an equitable mortgage has been created and the court will order the borrower to convey the legal title to the lender.

The rights of the mortgagor (the borrower) on default of the mortgage repayments

---

Box B

THE RIGHTS OF THE MORTGAGOR (THE BORROWER) ON DEFAULT OF THE MORTGAGE REPAYMENTS

1. The Administration of Justice Act 1970

(i) Postponement of possession

(ii) The period for postponing possession

2. The Financial Services and Markets Act 2000 and the Consumer Credit Act 2006

3. Social Security benefits

4. The position of the borrower's spouse who was not a party to the mortgage agreement

5. The Protocol

The borrower has a number of rights if he has defaulted on the mortgage repayments and the lender is threatening possession.

Box B1 The Administration of Justice Act 1970

The borrower's main rights come from the Administration of Justice Act 1970, which allows the borrower to ask that the lender's right to possession be postponed. The reasons behind the Act tie in with the living habits of the population. In the early 1900s it was common to rent rather than own property. In the mid-1900s the government encouraged people to buy their own houses with the aid of a mortgage. This was a good idea in theory, but there was no legislation to protect borrowers from possession when they were unable to meet the mortgage repayments because of temporary setbacks like redundancy and illness. The only remedy was to use the inherent jurisdiction of the court, which allowed possession to be postponed for 28 days. This situation was in contrast to that of those renting property who were protected by statute. In 1969 the Payne Committee reported these differences and the result was the Administration of Justice Act 1970.

Box B1i Postponement of possession

When a lender seeks possession of a dwelling house, if it appears that a borrower may be able to pay any sums due, section 36 of the Administration of Justice Act 1970 allows the court to postpone possession for a period of time which the court thinks is reasonable. A property has to be a dwelling house at the time the action for possession is brought, not when the mortgage was created.

There are several problems with this Act.

Section 36 can be used only where the lender *brings an action* in which he claims possession of the mortgaged property.

The problem occurs with the words *brings an action*. Although a lender can take possession by right, he will usually obtain a court order to do so because of the risk of being found liable under the Criminal Law Act 1977. If he doesn't obtain a court order, though, the borrower can't use section 36. This is what happened in *Ropaigealach v Barclays Bank plc* (2000). The husband and wife had fallen into arrears with the mortgage repayments on their home. Barclay's Bank sent them a letter telling them that the house was going to be auctioned in three weeks' time. The Ropaigealachs were not living there at the time and didn't receive the letter. The bank auctioned the house in their absence. The court confirmed that the 1970 Act hadn't removed the right of a lender to take possession without a court order. However, as there had been no such order, the Ropaigealachs could not have used section 36 of the Administration of Justice Act 1970 to ask the court to postpone possession. This is totally ridiculous. The case of *Horsham Properties Group Ltd v Clark* (2008) has also caused consternation. Whilst the case focused on the human rights aspect, it was confirmed that a lender can sell a property when the mortgage money becomes due under section 101 of the Law of Property Act 1925 without vacant possession and without a court order: *Ropaigealach v Barclays Bank plc*. The media coverage focusing on the fact that a lender could sell a house without first obtaining a possession order, thereby ensuring the borrower couldn't use the Administration of Justice Act 1970, led to the Council of Mortgage Lenders stating that where there is an owner-occupied residential property, its members will not sell when the borrower is in default without first obtaining a court order for possession nor will its members appoint a receiver to sell a residential property without first obtaining a court order for possession. This was followed by a consultation paper in 2009 entitled 'Mortgages: Power of Sale and Residential Property' (CP55/09) where it was proposed that in relation to residential owner-occupied properties, the lender should be able to sell only by agreement with the borrower or with a court order. Sale would only be ordered by the court where a possession order already existed or where the court made an order for sale having taking into account the same criteria as it does when making an order for possession. To date, there has been no further progress on this proposal.

Q: *What were the other problems with the Act?*

A: The next problem related to the actual wording of the Act. The court is able to exercise its discretion to postpone possession when:

> it appears to the court that in the event of its exercising the power the mortgagor is likely to be able within a reasonable period to pay *any sums due* under the mortgage or to remedy a default consisting of a breach of any other obligation arising under or by virtue of the mortgage.

The words any sums due caused problems. In *Halifax Building Society v Clark* (1973) the mortgage repayments were in arrears. Under the terms of the mortgage agreement, if the repayments weren't met the whole sum owed on the mortgage became due. This was over £1,420, which was a lot of money in those days. As the repayments weren't met, and any sums due now amounted to over £1,420, the court couldn't exercise its jurisdiction to postpone possession because the borrower couldn't afford to pay the usual mortgage repayments, let alone nearly £1,500.

Q: *Didn't that defeat the whole object of the Act?*

A: It did, until an amendment by section 8(1) of the Administration of Justice Act 1973. This stated that any sums due meant only the arrears that were owed, not the whole amount owed to the lender.

Q: *Are there any conditions that a borrower has to meet to be able to resist possession?*

A: The borrower must not only be able to pay off the outstanding arrears but also to keep up with the normal expected repayments: see *First National Bank v Syed* (1991). The borrower must provide evidence to the court that this will be possible. If there is no realistic way of the borrower paying off the loan and the arrears over the period allowed, possession will not be postponed. Pleas that the borrower is going to win the lottery or take the Managing Director's job in the near future will go unheeded.

Box B1ii

The period for postponing possession

Q: *What is a reasonable period for postponement of possession?*

A: Before 1996 it was in the region of two years. In 1996 the important case of *Cheltenham & Gloucester Building Society v Norgan* (1996) defined a reasonable period as capable of being the whole length of the remaining mortgage term. So it was possible that if a mortgage was to be paid over 25 years and the arrears occurred after five years, the borrower could be given the remaining 20 years to pay off the arrears, whilst also keeping up with the current repayments.

Q: *This sounds very advantageous for the borrower, doesn't it?*

A: It was. The Act has been called a piece of 'social legislation'. Not only that, but it put an end to repeated applications to court. If postponement was for only two years, and the borrower hadn't managed to keep up with the repayment plan, the lender had to apply to the court again for possession. The borrower could then ask for yet another two years' postponement. However, if the borrower has been given the remainder of the mortgage term to repay the arrears and keep up with the usual repayments, and still can't do so, he is deemed to have been given all possible help and possession will usually be granted.

Q: *Can the borrower ask for postponement of possession because he would rather sell the property himself?*

A: The argument the borrower will put forward here is that he could obtain a better price if he was actually living in the house, could put flowers on the table and exude the smell of coffee and fresh bread – all tactics known to impress a potential purchaser. Generally, though, the answer is no. Even the borrower saying that the house is already with an estate agent won't help.

Q: *Why not?*

A: Because estate agents always think the house will sell the next day for thousands over the asking price. Also, there's no guarantee that the borrower will genuinely attempt to sell the house, especially as it is not his decision to leave. Possession is likely to be delayed so the borrower can sell the property himself only when the proceeds of sale will easily cover the mortgage loan: see *Cheltenham and Gloucester plc v Krausz* (1997). In *Target Homes Ltd v Clothier* (1994) possession was delayed by three months as the prospect of an early sale could be best served by allowing Mr and Mrs Clothier to stay in the house to sell it, and the money received from the sale would pay off the mortgage. If the mortgage loan wasn't paid back within three months, the lender would obtain possession. In *National and Provincial Building Society v Lloyd* (1996) it was held that the borrower's estimate of what he could sell the property for to pay off the amount owed was 'a mere expression of hope', and so possession was granted.

There was some lateral thinking in *Bristol and West Building Society v Ellis* (1997). Mrs Ellis owed arrears on the mortgage repayments. She put forward a plan whereby she would pay a significant lump sum and then a token payment every month towards the arrears of interest. The estimated time for achieving payment was 98 years! Her argument was that her debt wouldn't increase and, in three to five years' time, when her children had finished university, she would sell the house and pay back everything she owed.

Q: *Some plan. What would have happened if house prices had fallen in those five years?*

A: The court's concerns exactly, which is why possession was ordered.

Box B2 The Financial Services and Markets Act 2000 and
The Consumer Credit Act 2006

Mortgage lenders who enter into a regulated mortgage contract come under the Financial Services and Markets Act 2000. A regulated mortgage contract is a contract where the lender provides the loan to an individual borrower, the security for the loan is secured by a first legal mortgage on land in the United Kingdom and at least 40 per cent of that land will be used as a dwelling by the borrower. Essentially this means it is a first legal mortgage on a residential property. From October 2004 such mortgage lenders need authorisation from the Financial Services Authority. Failure to obtain authorisation means that the lender cannot enforce the mortgage against the borrower and the lender also runs the risk of criminal liability. There is also a code of conduct which lenders must follow.

The Consumer Credit Act 2006 has amended the Consumer Credit Act 1974 to protect consumers and to create a credit market that is fair. Under the Consumer Credit Act 1974 the court could consider whether a credit agreement was extortionate and alter or delete any terms of a mortgage agreement, but only if the loan was for less than £25,000. From April 2008 this cap has been removed. The provisions relating to extortionate credit have been replaced by an unfair relationship test under the new section 140A–C. From April 2007 borrowers can challenge unfair treatment by lenders in court for new agreements and from April 2008 all existing agreements can be subject to challenge. Factors the court could look at would be the circumstances and age of the borrower and the level of interest charged. The court could alter the terms of the mortgage agreement, lower the amount payable or impose requirements on the lender. From April 2007 the Financial Ombudsman Service will provide a free and independent dispute resolution scheme for borrowers where the aim is mediation and conciliation. From October 2008 the Consumer Credit Act 2006 requires lenders to give borrowers clearer and more regular information on their mortgages, and there will be a tightening up on licensing agreements to give credit to cut down on the number of loan sharks. Only individuals, sole traders and partnerships of two or three persons can claim protection under the Act, therefore not companies. Mortgages for less than £25,000 for business purposes are subject to the Act. First mortgages for residential purposes created after October 2004 regulated under the Financial Services and Markets Act 2000 are not subject to the 2006 Act's provisions. All other mortgages whenever created and for whatever purpose are subject to the unfair credit relationship test. People who are of 'high net worth' can remove themselves from protection under the Consumer Credit Act but will still remain subject to the new unfair credit relationship test.

Q: *Why are people of a net high worth exempt apart from the unfair relationship test?*

A: Because they are unlikely to default on the mortgage repayments and they can negotiate a better interest rate if the lender does not have to comply with the Consumer Credit Act 2006.

| Box B3 | **Social security benefits** |

People who are claiming certain income related benefits can get help towards mortgage interest repayments as part of their benefits. This help is called Support for Mortgage Interest and is limited to interest repayments only at a rate linked to that of the Bank of England's published Average Mortgage Rate. It does not include help towards paying off any arrears and is normally paid direct to the lender. There is also a government backed mortgage rescue scheme which supports vulnerable owner-occupiers at risk of repossession.

| Box B4 | **The position of the borrower's spouse who was not a party to the mortgage agreement** |

Q: *If the borrower defaults on the mortgage repayments, is it possible for the borrower's husband or wife to offer to pay the mortgage arrears and instalments instead?*

A: Under section 30 of the Family Law Act 1996 this right is given to a spouse with a statutory right of occupation in a dwelling house. The problem here is that you immediately run up against the difficulty that not every wife or husband knows that her or his spouse is having difficulties meeting the mortgage repayments.

Q: *Isn't it possible for the lender to notify her or him?*

A: Not in general. How is a bank expected to find the wife or husband? Nor can you expect a bank to act as a go-between, or even marriage counsellor, if the spouses aren't talking to each other. There is statutory provision in the Family Law Act 1996, though, which may help a wife or husband here. The Family Law Act 1996 gives a right to a spouse not to be evicted from a dwelling house by the other spouse without a court order. If the spouse is not in occupation, the Act allows the non-occupying spouse to enter with leave of the court. The relevance of this is that under section 56 of the Family Law Act 1996 a lender who wishes to take possession of a dwelling house must notify any spouse who has protected his or her right of occupation under this Act, and the lender must serve notice of his or her action for possession on that spouse. The spouse then has a right to be heard in the action for possession, and can offer to pay the outstanding money and any future repayments.

Q: *Is this useful?*

A: Only in so far as happily married couples think about protecting their statutory right of occupation in case things go wrong. Knowing about the Family Law Act 1996 probably doesn't figure very highly on the 'to do' list. If it does, the right of occupation must be entered as a class F land charge in unregistered land, or it must be entered as a notice on the Charges Register of the mortgaged land in registered land.

`Box B5`   ## The Protocol

Further help has been provided for borrowers who find themselves in difficulty during the current recession. The Civil Justice Council has published the "Pre-action Protocol for Possession Claims based on Mortgage or Home Purchase Plan Arrears in Respect of Residential Property". The aim is to ensure that repossession is the last resort. The Protocol has effect from 19th November 2008 and applies to residential mortgages. It does not alter the parties' rights and obligations so the power of sale and the power to appoint a receiver are not affected. The lender must provide information about the arrears including the amount in arrears and the amount outstanding on the mortgage. It should take all reasonable steps to try and sort out a new payment plan with the borrower taking into account the borrower's circumstances, for example whether the cause of the arrears is short or long term. The borrower must be able to understand any payment plan and its implications and must be given time to consider the proposal. The Protocol also states that a lender should consider postponing possession proceedings where a borrower has already started to sell the property. If the lender does decide to postpone possession, the borrower must authorise communication between the lender and the estate agent and the conveyancer. This is so they can look at the progress of the sale and the buyer's conduct in such sale. Overall, the aim is to ensure that all other avenues have been looked at before repossession takes place and a lender must be prepared to stand up in court and say how it has complied with the Protocol. The downside is that there are no effective penalties for not complying with the Protocol and no indication that the court could stop the claim for repossession because the Protocol has not been complied with.

Summary of the remedies of the mortgagee (lender) and the rights of the mortgagor (borrower)

The most important rights of the lender are possession and sale. The borrower can claim postponement of possession under the Administration of Justice Act 1970, but must prove that both arrears and future repayments will be paid.

The priority of mortgages

This part of the chapter looks at what happens when two or more lenders lend money on a mortgage using the same property as security. We'll confine ourselves to a discussion of legal mortgages here.

Q: *How would this situation arise?*

A: Imagine that Fred owns Greenacres, a large mansion house. He originally purchased it for £400,000 with the aid of a £200,000 mortgage from Bundy's Bank. Four years ago, he created a second mortgage over it with Ransome Bank for £100,000 in order to finance the restoration of the west wing. Two years ago, he created a third mortgage of £50,000 over it with Sharp Loan Company to finance the crumbling clock tower. The property market then collapsed and Greenacres fell in value to £200,000. Fred stopped paying the repayments on all the mortgages, and Bundy's Bank has taken possession and sold Greenacres. The question is how the proceeds from the sale are shared between Bundy's Bank, Ransome Bank, Sharp Loan Company and Fred. The answer depends not necessarily on the order of creation of the mortgages, but on whether Greenacres is unregistered or registered land.

The priority of mortgages in unregistered land

Before 1926, Greenacres would have been conveyed (transferred) to Bundy's Bank. When the loan was repaid, Bundy's Bank would reconvey (transfer) Greenacres to Fred. Bundy's Bank would take the title deeds as it owned the property for the duration of the loan, and it would need the title deeds to sell the property if Fred failed to keep up with the mortgage repayments. Title deeds are the historical documentation to the property and are proof of ownership. If Fred wanted to create a second legal mortgage over the property with Ransome Bank, he couldn't do so as he would be unable to produce the title deeds. If Ransome Bank didn't have the title deeds, it would have no proof of its security in the property, and no means by which to sell it. After 1925, Fred no longer had to convey the property to Bundy's Bank and he would retain title. It was therefore possible for him to create a second legal mortgage with Ransome Bank. However, even after 1925, Bundy's Bank has a statutory right to the title deeds in unregistered land. If Fred couldn't produce the title deeds, Ransome Bank would be put on alert that probably Fred had already taken out a mortgage with someone else, and it might change its mind about lending him any more money on the property. Assuming it still decided to grant Fred a second mortgage, Fred didn't have any title deeds to give it. Ransome Bank had no way of protecting its interest and keeping its priority if Fred then obtained a third mortgage. Ransome Bank was therefore allowed to enter its legal mortgage in unregistered land as a class C(i) land charge on the Land Charges Register as a puisne (pronounced 'puny') mortgage. A puisne mortgage is a legal mortgage where the bank does not hold the title deeds to the land, and it is the only legal interest capable of entry on the Land Charges Register. This entry would ensure that its mortgage was binding on any lender Fred might arrange a third mortgage with.

Q: *If you have a legal mortgage where the lender has taken the title deeds, and a second mortgage that was entered as a class C(i) land charge, does the first legal mortgage take priority?*

A: Look back to the example of Fred. Assuming that Bundy's Bank took possession of the title deeds, it would rank first. If Ransome Bank had entered its legal mortgage as a class C(i) land charge, it would rank second. Similarly, Sharp Loan Company would rank third if it had entered its legal mortgage as a class C(i) land charge. Section 97 of the Law of Property Act 1925 is the statutory authority for this order of priority. It states that a mortgage not protected by a deposit of the title deeds will rank according to its date of registration as a land charge. There is a problem here, though, because section 4(5) of the Land Charges Act 1972 states that if a legal mortgage without the deposit of the title deeds is not entered as a land charge, it loses its priority. Look at the situation when Fred cannot produce the title deeds at all for anybody because he has lost them:

> 1 June: Fred created a first legal mortgage over Greenacres with Bundy's Bank. Bundy's Bank did not take the title deeds. This is a puisne mortgage. Bundy's Bank did not protect it by a class C(i) land charge.

> 10 June: Fred created a second legal mortgage over Greenacres with Ransome Bank. Ransome Bank did not take the title deeds. This is a puisne mortgage.

If you use section 4(5) of the Land Charges Act 1972 here, Ransome Bank's mortgage will take priority over that of Bundy's Bank as Bundy's Bank had not entered its mortgage on the Register when Ransome Bank granted its mortgage. This is because, under section 4(5) of the Land Charges Act 1972, any interest not entered on the Land Charges Register will lose its priority. If Bundy's Bank had any sense it would have entered its mortgage on the Land Charges Register before the second mortgage was granted. However, assume that it didn't, and the following happens:

> 15 June: Bundy's Bank decides to enter its puisne mortgage as a class C(i) land charge against Fred's name on the Land Charges Register.

> 20 June: Ransome Bank enters its puisne mortgage as a class C(i) land charge against Fred's name on the Land Charges Register.

If you now apply section 97 of the Law of Property Act 1925, it states that the first mortgage to be registered will take priority. This is the mortgage with Bundy's Bank.

Q: *What is the answer to this conflict?*

A: There is no answer. The question has never been decided. Since 1997 the creation of a first legal mortgage in unregistered land has been a trigger event for the registration of the freehold. This means that any mortgages created since 1997 will be governed by the rules in registered land, which have been rather more thought through than these.

Q: *If you had to decide which of the sections to use, which would it be?*

A: Section 4(5) of the Land Charges Act 1972. The whole purpose of entering an interest on the Land Charges Register is so that other people know about it. If the mortgage arranged with Bundy's Bank is not entered on the Register when Ransome Bank grants a second mortgage to Fred, Ransome Bank should not be bound by it. If Ransome Bank can find out about a prior mortgage, it can make a considered decision whether there's enough value in Greenacres to lend more money to Fred. If there's no such entry, it cannot make a considered decision.

The priority of mortgages in registered land

Under section 48 of the Land Registration Act 2002 priority is governed by when the mortgage was registered on the Charges Register at the District Land Registry. The mortgage registered first will take priority.

The tacking of mortgages

Tacking occurs when a mortgage has already been granted over property and a further loan is advanced, or added on, by the same lender. We will confine ourselves to a discussion of a legal mortgage again here. Fred could have taken out a mortgage over Greenacres with Bundy's Bank for £100,000. Some years later Bundy's Bank tacks or adds another loan in favour of Fred onto the original mortgage, still using Greenacres as security. This is all very well unless Fred has created a mortgage over Greenacres with Ransome Bank in the interim. If Fred does not pay the mortgage repayments, Bundy's Bank can sell Greenacres. It could then claim both its loans back from the proceeds of sale before Ransome Bank on the basis that they had been tacked together.

Q: *That wouldn't be very fair on Ransome Bank would it, or does it have to give permission for this to happen?*

A: Again, the answer to this depends on whether Greenacres is unregistered or registered land.

The tacking of mortgages in unregistered land

The situation is governed by section 94 of the Law of Property Act 1925. Tacking is allowed by Bundy's Bank if Ransome Bank consents to the arrangement.

The following is a summary of the position if there is no consent by Ransome Bank. It is as confusing as it looks:

▶ If Bundy's Bank has not put anything at all in the mortgage agreement about tacking, and if it has actual, constructive or imputed notice of the mortgage created with Ransome Bank, then it is not allowed to tack.

▶ If Bundy's Bank has not put anything at all in the mortgage agreement about tacking, and Ransome Bank has entered its mortgage as a class C(i) land charge, then Bundy's Bank is not allowed to tack.

▶ If Bundy's Bank is allowed to, but is not obliged to, make further advances under the mortgage agreement still using Greenacres as security, then it cannot tack if it has actual, constructive or imputed notice of Ransome Bank's mortgage.

▶ If Bundy's Bank is allowed to, but is not obliged to, make further advances under the mortgage agreement still using Greenacres as security, and if Ransome Bank has entered its mortgage as a class C(i) land charge, then Bundy's Bank can still tack as it can ignore the class C(i) land charge. Bundy's Bank is allowed to ignore the land charge because otherwise it would have to search the Land Charges Register every time it made a further advance.

▶ If Bundy's Bank is allowed to, but is not obliged to, make further advances under the mortgage agreement still using Greenacres as security, even if Ransome Bank has entered its mortgage as a class C(i) land charge, Ransome Bank should specifically tell Bundy's Bank about its mortgage. If it has specifically told Bundy's Bank about its mortgage, Bundy's Bank cannot tack. Don't forget that lenders are going to be very careful before they lend out any money using land as security, just in case they are not first in line in the queue, so Ransome Bank should make a point of telling Bundy's Bank.

▶ Bundy's Bank is expressly obliged to make a further advance up to the limit of the advance. It can tack even if it knows about Ransome Bank's mortgage or Ransome Bank has entered its mortgage by a class C(i) land charge.

Confused?

The tacking of mortgages in registered land

Tacking in registered land is governed by section 49 of the Land Registration Act 2002. Bundy's Bank can tack in the same situations as in unregistered land. However, because this is registered land, you must substitute 'a notice on the Charges Register of Greenacres' for a class C(i) land charge, and Bundy's Bank will receive notification of further mortgages from the Land Registrar. There is also one further way under the Land Registration Act 2002. Imagine Fred negotiated a maximum loan of £100,000 as he wasn't sure how much it would cost to restore the west wing of Greenacres. He managed to do the restoration work for £80,000. Should more work be required in the future, Bundy's Bank can tack the remaining £20,000 onto the original loan provided details of the negotiated maximum loan appear on the Charges Register of Greenacres.

Summary of the priority of legal mortgages and tacking

The priority of a legal mortgage depends on whether the land is unregistered or registered. There are conflicting statutory provisions in unregistered land which have not yet been addressed in litigation. Tacking of a legal mortgage is similar in unregistered and registered land, although the Land Registration Act 2002 has created an additional situation where tacking may occur.

A question on mortgages

This example is intended to illustrate how to use the Boxes in this chapter to analyse the legal position. If you are using this method in undergraduate law exam questions, you will need to include statutory and case authority and detailed discussion of the various points of law. This information is found both in the text and from other sources.

> Six years ago, Mr and Mrs Brown purchased Greenacres with the aid of a 15-year legal mortgage from Shark Loan Mortgage Company. Two years ago, they took out a second legal mortgage for 12 years, again with Shark Loan Mortgage Company, in order to finance an expansion in Mr Brown's business of leather goods. Shark Loan Mortgage Company included a term in the second mortgage that prevented the redemption of that mortgage for 10 years. Shark Loan Mortgage Company also stipulated that it would have the right of first refusal on all the leather goods produced by Mr Brown at a discount of 10% on Mr Brown's usual selling price, for a period of 25 years. Mr Brown deliberately did not tell Mrs Brown of the terms of the second mortgage. Mrs Brown signed the second mortgage agreement in the presence of a trainee cashier at Shark Loan Mortgage Company because the manager had forgotten to keep his appointment with her to discuss the mortgage application. Mr Brown's leather goods business is now in financial difficulty due to the discounted price he has to sell at to Shark Loan Mortgage Company. The mortgage repayments on both mortgages have not been met for the last nine months. Mrs Brown has recently forgiven Mr Brown for not telling her about the terms of the second mortgage, and has just taken up a full-time job in order to start paying off the arrears on both mortgages.

> Advise Mr and Mrs Brown on the issues of undue influence and collateral advantage, and advise Shark Loan Mortgage Company and Mr and Mrs Brown of their respective rights as mortgagee and mortgagors.

This question covers undue influence, collateral advantages and the remedies and rights of the mortgagee and mortgagor respectively when the mortgagor has defaulted on the mortgage repayments. The second mortgage has been tacked onto the first mortgage but, as there are no other mortgages, this is not a discussion on tacking.

First, advise Mr and Mrs Brown on the issues of undue influence and collateral advantage.

The 15-year mortgage taken out six years ago

There is no evidence of undue influence or collateral advantage by Shark Loan Mortgage Company. The courts would have no reason to intervene in this mortgage transaction.

The 12-year mortgage taken out two years ago

A discussion on undue influence in relation to Mrs Brown will revolve around *Royal Bank of Scotland v Etridge (No 2)* (2001). The *Etridge* case gave clear guidelines for lenders when faced with a situation where a second party to the mortgage was clearly not going to benefit from it. Shark Loan Mortgage Company should have ensured that Mrs Brown received independent advice from a solicitor. It should have sent written details of the mortgage agreement to her nominated solicitor, and not proceeded with the payment of the mortgage money until the solicitor had confirmed that Mrs Brown had received such advice. As there is no indication that this happened, Mrs Brown could ask to set the second mortgage aside as against Shark Loan Mortgage Company.

The terms of the second mortgage agreement stated that the mortgage could not be redeemed before the end of 10 years. This is not in itself unconscionable or oppressive. It is unlikely that Mr Brown will be able to ask the court to vary the term or set the mortgage aside because of this clause: see *Knightsbridge Estates Trust Ltd v Byrne*. The term requiring Mr Brown to sell his leather goods to Shark Loan Mortgage Company at a 10% discount is likely to be seen as a collateral advantage that is unfair and unconscionable. This is because the requirement to sell at a discount goes on beyond the length of the mortgage term: see *Noakes & Co Ltd v Rice*. Mr Brown could also plead that such a clause is in restraint of trade under the common law doctrine, and ask for it to be deleted: see *Esso Petroleum Co Ltd v Harper's Garage (Stourport) Ltd*. If the term were deleted, the court could award compensation or allow Mr Brown to move the mortgage to another lender.

Now advise Shark Loan Mortgage Company and Mr and Mrs Brown of their respective rights as mortgagee and mortgagors.

Box A   The remedies of the mortgagee (the lender) on default of the mortgage repayments

A1 The right to sue on the contract

As a mortgage is a contract, Shark Loan Mortgage Company could sue for the outstanding repayments. However, there is little value in doing this as Mr and

Mrs Brown clearly have no money or they would not be behind with the mortgage repayments.

A2 The right to take possession

Shark Loan Mortgage Company has an automatic right to possession: see *Four-Maids Ltd v Dudley Marshall (Properties) Ltd*. Vacant possession will be an essential prerequisite to sale. Shark Loan Mortgage Company would be well advised to obtain a court order for possession to avoid any liability under the Criminal Law Act 1977.

A3 Sale

Having obtained possession, Shark Loan Mortgage Company will want to sell Greenacres to recoup the outstanding loan money.

A3i The right of sale

Under sections 101 and 103 of the Law of Property Act 1925 the power of sale must have arisen and must have become exercisable. Both mortgages are legal and therefore must have been created by deed. We can assume that the legal date of redemption has passed, as this date is normally set six months after the creation of the mortgage. This means that section 101 is satisfied. As Mr and Mrs Brown are more than two months in arrears with the mortgage repayments, section 103 is also satisfied. Shark Loan Mortgage Company, therefore, has a right to sell Greenacres.

A3ii Duties on sale

Shark Loan Mortgage Company must take proper care to obtain the best price that is reasonably obtainable: see *Silven Properties v Royal Bank of Scotland plc*. When it chooses to sell Greenacres is ultimately its decision: see *China and South Sea Bank Ltd v Tan Soon Gin*. If the property were to be sold by auction, Shark Loan Mortgage Company would have to give notice of the auction and ensure that any planning approvals were notified to potential bidders: see *Cuckmere Brick Co Ltd v Mutual Finance Ltd*.

A4 The right to appoint a receiver

As Greenacres is not run as a commercial business, the appointment of a receiver need not be considered.

A5 The right to foreclosure

This is a drastic remedy which is rarely used. Even if the bank proceeds with an application for foreclosure, Mr and Mrs Brown can apply to the court for an order for sale under section 91 of the Law of Property Act 1925.

Box B The rights of the mortgagor (the borrower) on default of the mortgage repayments

B1 The Administration of Justice Act 1970

B1i Postponement of possession

Greenacres is a dwelling house. Mr and Mrs Brown can apply for the postponement of possession under the Administration of Justice Act 1970 provided Shark Loan Mortgage Company obtains a court order for possession: see *Ropaigealach v Barclays Bank plc*.

B1ii The period for postponing possession

The court will postpone possession if Mr and Mrs Brown can provide a financial plan which shows that they can pay both the arrears and the current repayments within a reasonable period. The reasonable period can be the whole of the remainder of the mortgage term: see *Cheltenham and Gloucester Building Society* (1996). As Mrs Brown has taken up full-time employment, it is possible that the court will postpone possession of Greenacres. This postponement will be relevant to both the mortgages, assuming Mrs Brown's ability to pay.

B2 The Financial Services and Markets Act 2000 and The Consumer Credit Act 2006

Whether the second mortgage was for more or less than £25,000, it will still be subject to the unfair credit relationship test under the Consumer Credit Act. The court could look at the terms of the mortgage and the way in which Shark Loan Mortgage Company had behaved. It could alter the terms of the mortgage, set it aside or order repayments to Mr and Mrs Brown.

B3 Social security benefits

Mr and Mrs Brown may be eligible for social security benefits.

B4 The position of the borrower's spouse who was not a party to the mortgage agreement

This is not relevant here.

B5 The Protocol

Shark Loan Mortgage Company should have followed the Protocol.

Conclusion

The first legal mortgage appears to be valid. There is no evidence of undue influence. However, Mrs Brown may be able to set the second legal mortgage aside as against Shark Loan Mortgage Company as it has not followed the guidelines in the *Etridge* case. Mr Brown could ask for deletion of the term requiring him to sell at a discount to Shark Loan Mortgage Company, as this is a collateral advantage. Although Shark Loan Mortgage Company has the right to possess and sell Greenacres, the court could postpone possession under the Administration of Justice Act 1970 in view of Mrs Brown's improved financial circumstances.

Mortgages and human rights

The annex at the end of this book contains a brief description of human rights legislation and how it works.

The question of whether taking possession in the context of a mortgage is in breach of human rights has reached the courts. In *Horsham Properties Group Ltd v Clark* Mr Clark and Ms Beech purchased a property together with the aid of a mortgage. They fell into arrears with the repayments and the lender appointed a receiver under the terms of the mortgage deed. The receivers were allowed to sell the property under the terms of the mortgage deed, and they did so. This purchaser then sold the property on to Horsham Property Group. The entire proceedings had avoided the Administration of Justice Act 1970, which was lawful following *Ropaigealach v Barclays Bank plc*. Horsham Property Group issued possession proceedings against

Mr Clark and Ms Beech who were still living in the house on the basis they were trespassers. Ms Beech claimed that there was a breach of human rights under Article 1 of the First Protocol to the Convention. The argument was on the basis that there was an unlawful deprivation of possessions because the lender hadn't first obtained an order for possession or made an application for sale through a court.

Article 1 of the First Protocol states:

Every natural or legal person is entitled to the peaceful enjoyment of his possessions. No one shall be deprived of his possessions except in the public interest and subject to the conditions provided for by law and by the general principles of international law.

The preceding provisions shall not, however, in any way impair the right of a State to enforce such laws as it deems necessary to control the use of property in accordance with the general interest or to secure the payment of taxes or other contributions or penalties.

It was held that the equity of redemption was a possession but the appointment of the receiver and the sale had arisen because of the terms in the mortgage agreement. It was not due to State intervention but due to the agreement between the borrower and the lender. As such, the question as to whether there was a deprivation of possessions didn't arise. The judge went on to consider what would have happened if the appointment of the receiver and the sale had been brought about by the legislation i.e. section 101 of the Law of Property Act 1925. Even if the property had been sold under section 101, and even though the 'equity of redemption' is a possession, this again would not be a deprivation of possessions. The statutory power of sale saved people having to write out the power to do so in every mortgage agreement. It also gave effect to the agreement between the parties that the property could be sold if the borrower was in default. Section 101 implemented rather than overrode the private bargain between the borrower and the lender. The powers in section 101 were also subject to a contrary intention (see section 101(4) of the Law of Property Act 1925) and so you couldn't argue that the power of the State here was rigid or arbitrary or discriminatory which you would have to do to prove a deprivation of possessions within the meaning of Article 1 of Protocol 1. It was also stated obiter that even if it was a deprivation of possessions, the fact that a lender could sell the property it held as security without having to go to court was justified in the public interest because the ability to do so meant lending could be secured on property at affordable rates of interest. The court did not have to look at the proportionality of the action on a case by case basis.

Q: *So there was no mileage in the human rights argument?*

A: No. The Administration of Justice Act 1970 could be argued only when the lender had gone to court: *Ropaigealach v Barclays Bank plc*. The court was bound by that decision and any change extending the circumstances in which the Administration of Justice Act 1970 could be pleaded would have to be through Parliament. As Mr Justice Briggs said, 'It would be quite wrong for the courts in a vigorous and imaginative interpretation of the Human Rights Convention to make that policy, as it were, on the hoof'.

So, if a lender sells a residential property without first obtaining vacant possession or obtaining a court order, which it is entitled to do, the borrower will not be allowed to plead extra time under the Administration of Justice Act 1970. This is good news for lenders but not such good news for borrowers. In response, the Council of Mortgage Lenders has voluntarily said that its members will not sell a mortgaged property when the borrower has defaulted on the mortgage payments without first obtaining a court order, nor will they appoint a receiver to sell a residential property without obtaining a court order. This does not apply to commercial mortgages where borrowers should read the terms of their mortgage agreement very carefully.

Interestingly, Ms Beech also thought she should be able to use the Administration of Justice Act 1970 and ask for postponement of possession against the person who had bought the property from the lender. She failed to convince the court.

Q: But surely there is no mortgage at this point because it has been paid off out of the proceeds of sale?

A: Yes, that's right. Section 36 of the Administration Act 1970 couldn't be used against purchasers from a lender not least because by that time the mortgage money had been paid off out of the sale. There was, therefore, no mortgage which would attract the provisions of section 36 of the Administration of Justice Act anyway. Mr Justice Briggs said:

> In my judgment, although the definition of mortgagee in section 36 includes successors in title to an original mortgagee, it necessarily refers only to successors in title to the mortgage, claiming under the mortgage, rather than to successors in title to the mortgaged property, taking free of the mortgage.

As an overall conclusion, to quote Mr Justice Briggs again,

> In conclusion therefore, it follows that the claimant is entitled to possession of the property as against Miss Beech, the Human Rights Act defence having entirely failed.

Further reading

G. Andrews, 'Undue Influence – Where's the Disadvantage?' *Conv and Prop Law*, Sep/Oct (2002) 456

L. Bently, 'Mortgagee's Duties on Sale – No Place for Tort?' *Conv and Prop Law*, Nov/Dec (1990) 431

S. Brown, 'The Consumer Credit Act 2006; Real Additional Mortgagor Protection?' *Conv and Prop Law*, Jul/Aug (2007) 316

D. Capper, 'Banks, Borrowers, Sureties and Undue Influence – A Half Baked Solution to a Thoroughly Cooked Problem', 10 *RLR* (2002) 100

M. Dixon, 'Combating the Mortgagees's Right to Possession: New Hope for the Mortgagor in Chains?' 18 *Legal Studies* (1998) 279

M. Haley, 'Mortgage Default: Possession, Relief and Judicial Discretion', 17 *Legal Studies* (1997) 483

P. Omar, 'Equitable Interests and the Secured Creditor: Determining Priorities', *Conv and Prop Law*, Nov/Dec (2006) 509

M. Thompson, 'Wives, Sureties and Banks', *Conv and Prop Law*, Mar/Apr (2002) 174

L. Whitehouse, 'The Mortgage Arrears Pre-Action Protocol: An Opportunity Lost', 72 *MLR* (2009) 793

A brief explanation of human rights law

This is a short outline of the law relating to human rights. It should enable you to understand the terms used and the context of the cases.

The Council of Europe was formed in 1949 to aid reconstruction and reconciliation within Europe after the Second World War. There were ten founder members, including the UK. In 1950, the Council of Europe adopted the European Convention for the Protection of Human Rights and Fundamental Freedoms, i.e. the Convention. The Convention was a human rights charter agreed between sovereign states designed to address some of the atrocities arising from the Second World War. It was also designed to protect individuals from the power of the State. In land law this means local authorities and other public authorities.

Q: *Was the Convention part of the UK legal system?*

A: No. The UK ratified approved) the Convention in 1951. Legislation had to be enacted to incorporate the Convention into domestic law, and this happened when the Human Rights Act 1998 came into force on 2nd October 2000.

Q: *What happened before the Human Rights Act 1998 came into force?*

A: Either you had to hope that the common law or statute law protected your human rights or from 1965 you were allowed to petition the European Court of Human Rights (ECtHR) in Strasbourg individually. The enactment of the Human Rights Act 1998 meant that human rights could be enforced in the UK courts. It meant also that a public authority could not behave in a way that is incompatible with Convention rights and freedoms. Today, an aggrieved person who thinks that his/her human rights have been breached must resolve the issue in the UK courts before going to the ECtHR. An aggrieved person is known as a victim. Note that the Convention protects rights and it can also enforce negative and positive obligations. A person can bring a claim for breach of a human right or he can rely on Convention rights as a defence.

Q: *What's the difference between an Article and a Protocol?*

A: An Article defines a right or freedom and any restrictions on that right or freedom. Article 1 requires all signatories to the Convention to secure the rights and freedoms identified to everyone within their jurisdiction, Articles 2 to 12 set out the different human rights and freedoms and Article 14 states that the enjoyment of rights and freedoms contained in the Convention are to be enjoyed without discrimination. The remaining Articles are generally procedural. A Protocol is an amendment or addition to the original Convention and is also divided into Articles. This can be confusing but is said to lead to consistency. States have the choice whether they sign up to the Protocols. The UK has signed up to most but not all the Protocols because, for example, there are inconsistencies that need to be sorted before the UK signs up.

Human rights were protected in three different ways under the Convention: human rights that could not be restricted, so absolute rights; human rights that could be restricted on clear legal authority which is proportionate to the legitimate aims of the Convention, so limited rights; and protection of property rights that were subject to limitations, so qualified rights.

Let's start off with what the Human Rights Act 1998 states before we look at the Articles most relevant to land law.

Section 3 – Primary and subordinate legislation must be interpreted in a way that is compatible with Convention rights.

Section 4 – If UK legislation is not compatible with certain Convention rights, a higher court may make a declaration of incompatibility. Only the Supreme Court, the Privy Council, the Court of Appeal and the High Court may make a declaration of incompatibility. If you are bringing a case in a lower court and the court concludes that the legislation concerned is incompatible with Convention rights, your case must be referred to one of the higher courts for a declaration of incompatibility. Parliament may then change the law so it is compatible with the Convention. There is now a constitutional convention that this will happen.

Q: *Doesn't it take a long time to change the law – in which case people could be disadvantaged?*

A: There is a fast track procedure under section 10 of the Human Rights Act 1998 which allows a minister of the Crown to make a remedial order, in the form of delegated legislation, amending legislation to remove any incompatibility with the Convention.

Q: *So what happens in the meantime before the law is changed?*

A: Section 6(1) states that it is unlawful for a public authority to act in a way which is incompatible with a Convention right.

Section 6(2) says section 6(1) does not apply if the public authority was only obeying incompatible legislation. In this case, you have the option of asking for judicial review. Judicial review is a procedure in administrative law which enables applicants with 'sufficient interest' to challenge the legality, rationality or fairness of an action or decision of a public authority.

Q: *How does judicial review fit in with human rights?*

A: Judicial review provides access to pursue alleged breaches of human rights by public bodies. The court will use the ground of proportionality (as to whether the interference with the applicant's human rights was proportionate to the objective sought by the public body) to determine the claim. A difference between judicial review and a claim under the Human Rights Act 1998 is that if you are claiming under the Act, you must be a victim of an alleged breach of your human rights. Claims under judicial review otherwise are wider and can include pressure groups as claimants.

Q: *Is proposed new legislation subject to scrutiny as far as human rights are concerned?*

A: If Parliament proposes new legislation today, the Minister concerned must state that the bill is compatible with Convention rights or else state that it isn't. This does not stop the bill going ahead but although a bill which breaches human rights may be enacted, this raises the future possibility of a challenge to actions and decisions based on its substance.

Section 8 allows the court to grant remedies or relief. The court can make any order within its powers that it considers just and appropriate.

In addition to all this, there is the margin of appreciation given to the different States. States have different cultures, different histories and different customs. Because of this no one rule fits all and so the governments and courts in each country are given some discretion in how they deal with national issues.

Protocol 1 Article 1

Protocol 1 Article 1 is looked at in the discussion sections in Chapter 5 on adverse possession and in Chapter 18 on mortgages. It states:

(1) Every natural or legal person is entitled to the peaceful enjoyment of his possessions. No one shall be deprived of his possessions except in the public interest and subject to the conditions provided for by law and by the general principles of international law.

(2) The preceding provisions shall not, however, in any way impair the right of a state to enforce such laws as it deems necessary to control the use of property in accordance with the general interest or to secure the payment of taxes or other contributions or penalties.

Possessions include land and buildings although the definition is not restricted to realty but includes pensions and shares, for example. Where a person is deprived of his property, the deprivation must come about through the law of the country and the law must be clear and accessible. When looking at whether the peaceful enjoyment of a person's possessions has been violated, the court will look for a balance between the fundamental rights and freedoms of the individual and the requirements of the public interest. There must be proportionality between the aim to be achieved and the means to achieve that aim. Governments and courts are given a wide margin of appreciation here in assessing this balance. One factor which comes into the balance is the availability of compensation if there is interference with a person's property rights. If reasonable compensation is paid, this is generally a fair balance between the rights of the individual and the public interest. Note that you cannot avoid paying taxes by claiming a breach of your human rights.

Article 8

The following is Article 8, an Article which is contained in the original Convention as opposed to a protocol. You will find it in land law in relation to taking possession of property by a public body in the discussion section at the end of Chapter 15.

1. Everyone has the right to respect for his private and family life, his home and his correspondence.

2. There shall be no interference by a public authority with the exercise of this right except such as is in accordance with the law and is necessary in a democratic society

in the interests of national security, public safety or the economic well-being of the country, for the prevention of disorder or crime, for the protection of health or morals, or for the protection of the rights and freedoms of others.

So, let's pick this apart. Article 8(1) defines the right. Article 8(2) gives the legitimate exceptions when a public authority can interfere with the right such as national security, public safety and so on. Article 8 is an example of a qualified right. The right is defined in Article 8(1) but interference with the right is justified if the requirements of Article 8(2) are met *so restrictions or interference may be legitimate if:*

- in accordance with the law and
- necessary in democratic society and
- within the substantive grounds specified, i.e. a 'legitimate aim'.

A *public authority* includes central government, local government, the courts, the police, statutory and regulatory bodies and residential social landlords following *Weaver v London & Quadrant Housing Trust* (2009).

This means that a public authority can interfere with the right in Article 8(1) providing that the interference has a proper legal basis in one of the grounds given in the text of the Article so in accordance with the law necessary in a democratic society i.e. proportionate to a legitimate aim within Article 8(2). The definition of a public authority does not include the Westminster Parliament.

In accordance with the law means that the interference must come about through the law of the country and the law must be clear and accessible. If the action of the public authority was not lawful in the first place, the Court will find a violation.

Assuming the action was lawful, the interference then has to be '*necessary in a democratic society*'. This means that first there must be a pressing social need for the interference as stated in Article 8(2). Secondly, the interference must not be any more than that which is necessary so it must be proportionate. There must be proportionality between the aim pursued and the means employed to pursue that aim. The means can't be unfair, over the top or take into account irrelevant considerations. You 'can't use a sledgehammer to crack a nut' is the colloquial phrase here.

Q: *So would religious issues come in here?*

A: Yes, also something like euthanasia and moral issues generally. In the context of land law, local authorities are given some discretion when making a decision over housing because they are best placed to make that decision.